The Elder Scrolls®

ONLINE

MORROWIND®

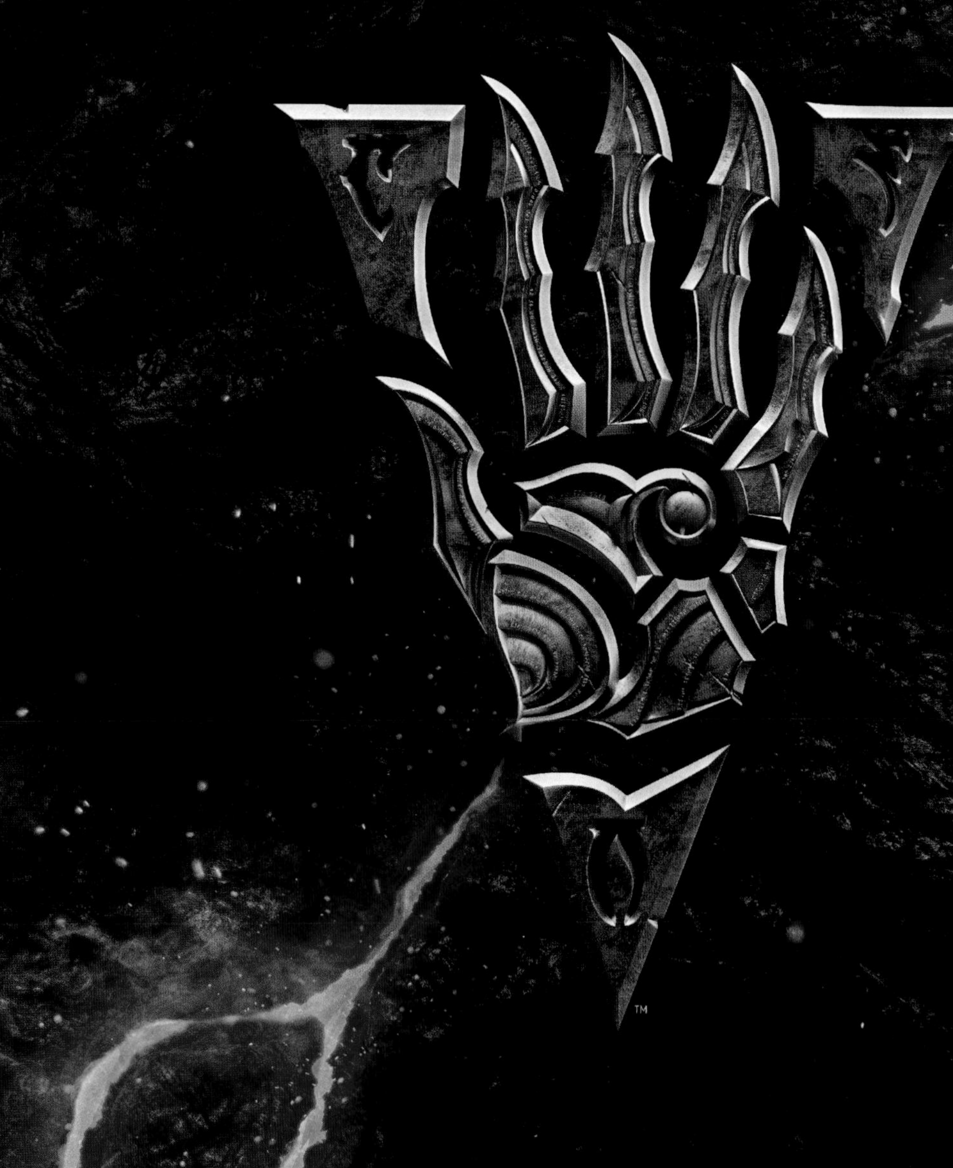

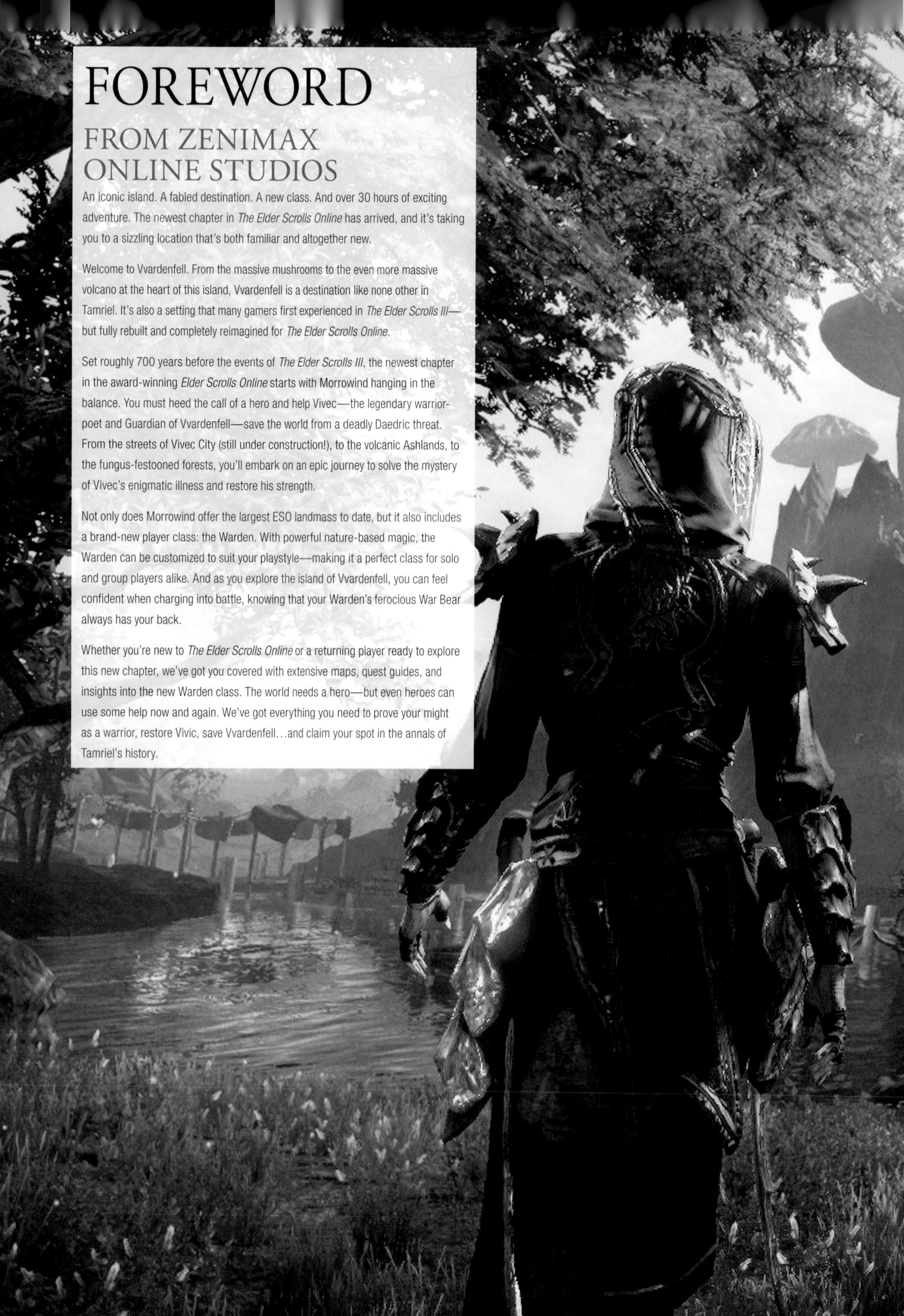

FOREWORD

FROM ZENIMAX ONLINE STUDIOS

An iconic island. A fabled destination. A new class. And over 30 hours of exciting adventure. The newest chapter in *The Elder Scrolls Online* has arrived, and it's taking you to a sizzling location that's both familiar and altogether new.

Welcome to Vvardenfell. From the massive mushrooms to the even more massive volcano at the heart of this island, Vvardenfell is a destination like none other in Tamriel. It's also a setting that many gamers first experienced in *The Elder Scrolls III*—but fully rebuilt and completely reimagined for *The Elder Scrolls Online*.

Set roughly 700 years before the events of *The Elder Scrolls III*, the newest chapter in the award-winning *Elder Scrolls Online* starts with Morrowind hanging in the balance. You must heed the call of a hero and help Vivec—the legendary warrior-poet and Guardian of Vvardenfell—save the world from a deadly Daedric threat. From the streets of Vivec City (still under construction!), to the volcanic Ashlands, to the fungus-festooned forests, you'll embark on an epic journey to solve the mystery of Vivec's enigmatic illness and restore his strength.

Not only does Morrowind offer the largest ESO landmass to date, but it also includes a brand-new player class: the Warden. With powerful nature-based magic, the Warden can be customized to suit your playstyle—making it a perfect class for solo and group players alike. And as you explore the island of Vvardenfell, you can feel confident when charging into battle, knowing that your Warden's ferocious War Bear always has your back.

Whether you're new to *The Elder Scrolls Online* or a returning player ready to explore this new chapter, we've got you covered with extensive maps, quest guides, and insights into the new Warden class. The world needs a hero—but even heroes can use some help now and again. We've got everything you need to prove your might as a warrior, restore Vivic, save Vvardenfell...and claim your spot in the annals of Tamriel's history.

TABLE OF CONTENTS

TRAINING

ADVICE FOR NEW ADVENTURERS

The Elder Scrolls Online (TESO) brings the world and lore of *Elder Scrolls* into a persistent, massively multiplayer game. Players assume the role of the Vestige as they're broken out of a Coldharbour prison by the Prophet. This leads players into the continent of Tamriel. Here, a long, tireless adventure offers hundreds of hours of gameplay, which ultimately leads the player back to an attack on Coldharbour.

A new chapter called *Morrowind* offers a new story that takes place on the island of Vvardenfell, located in the northeast corner of Tamriel. Create a character in *The Elder Scrolls Online: Morrowind* to begin a new tutorial, Broken Bonds, aboard a ship off the western coast of the zone.

Instead of a selection of servers to pick from, TESO offers one megaserver located in North America and another in Europe for each platform: PC, Xbox One, and PS4. Either megaserver can be selected, but characters cannot be transferred between them. This allows all local players to reside on the same server, which means you won't get stuck having to select a server separate from your friends.

In order to facilitate having everyone on the megaserver, players are split into shards, or copies, of the same world. This means you may never see your buddies, but forming a group guarantees that everyone remains together. As populations increase, more copies are made; as people log off, players are migrated onto more populated worlds. Because of this migration, the world always appears populated.

PTS SERVER

On PC and Mac, players have the option to choose the PTS Server, by activating it in the launcher settings and installing. This is where ZeniMax Online tests upcoming features and changes. Your characters may be available on PTS, but any progress made on PTS does not transfer to the regular game.

TAMRIEL STORY

Next, select from three alliances: the Aldmeri Dominion, Daggerfall Covenant, and Ebonheart Pact. While the Morrowind story is unaffected by your choice, the main Tamriel story line is different for each faction. This story line is found by travelling from Vvardenfell to a distant land, which is based on alliance.

The Aldmeri Dominion play through zones in the southwest, including Auridon, Grahtwood, and Reaper's March. The Daggerfall Covenant are found in the northwest as they work their way from Glenumbra to Bangkorai. The Ebonheart Pact are located in the northeast, questing from Stonefalls to The Rift. All three end up in Coldharbour in an attack against Molag Bal.

CADWELL'S SILVER AND THE ADVENTURER PACK

After completing the alliance quest line, players can talk to Cadwell to begin Cadwell's Silver, allowing a second alliance to be completed. With two alliances complete, Cadwell's Gold becomes available, unlocking the third and final alliance quests. By purchasing the Adventurer Pack from the Crown Store, players can create any race in the alliance of their choosing.

MORROWIND

Creating a new character in the new chapter of TESO, Morrowind, starts the player out in a new tutorial at Firemoth Island. The chosen alliance has no effect on where the player begins, though, when adventuring out to the rest of Tamriel, quests must be completed in the alliance's zones.

RACE

There are nine available races, with a tenth unlocked if you own the Imperial race upgrade. The race you choose affects the way your character looks and the racial skill line you receive at Level 5. Each skill line comes with an Experience boost for using a specific weapon or armor type, enhancements to specific abilities, and stat bonuses. These bonuses work well with particular classes, so consider your choices carefully.

Choice of alliance is restricted to the following races. However, if you own the Any Race, Any Alliance upgrade, you can choose any race, regardless of alliance.

Aldmeri Dominion	Daggerfall Covenant	Ebonheart Pact	Any Alliance
High Elf	Breton	Argonian	
Khajiit	Orc	Dark Elf	Imperial
Wood Elf	Redguard	Nord	

CLASS

Select from five classes—Dragonknight, Nightblade, Sorcerer, Templar, and Warden. Each comes with three unique skill lines, with any weapon and armor available to all. Refer to our **Classes** and **Skills** sections for details on each.

Class Skill Lines

Class	Skill Line 1	Skill Line 2	Skill Line 3
Dragonknight	Ardent Flame	Draconic Power	Earthen Heart
Nightblade	Assassination	Shadow	Siphoning
Sorcerer	Dark Magic	Daedric Summoning	Storm Calling
Templar	Aedric Spear	Dawn's Wrath	Restoring Light
Warden	Animal Companions	Green Balance	Winter's Embrace

CONTROLS

Getting comfortable with the controls is important in *Elder Scrolls Online*, which gives the player the choice to play in first or third person. Simply zoom in and out to switch between the two views. If playing on the computer, you also have the choice to play with a controller or keyboard. How you play is completely dependent on your comfort level. Note that the UI changes significantly between the two devices.

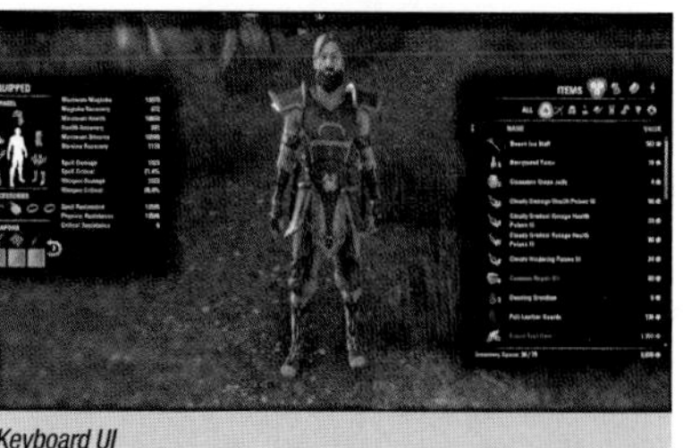
Keyboard UI

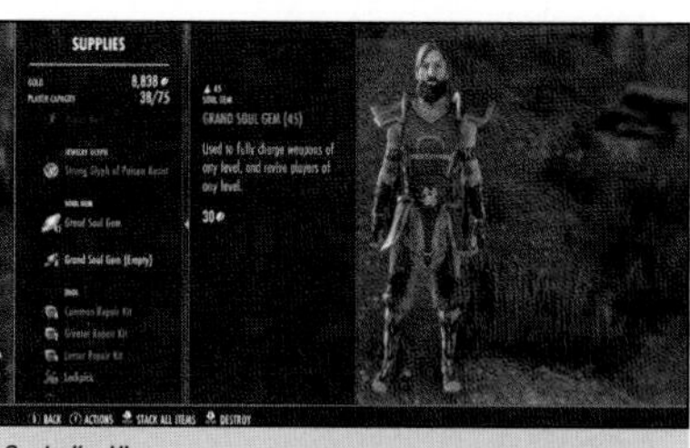

Controller UI

Controlling your character is similar to the methods of most action-and-adventure games. Use the two analog sticks, or W/A/S/D and the mouse, for movement and looking around. Important actions and attacks are mapped around the movement keys on the keyboard, giving the player quick access to most everything they need. This is also true for the controller, where these actions are placed on easily accessible buttons.

With keyboard and mouse, a dodge roll is performed by double tapping in the desired direction. This can be changed to a single key press in the settings. On a controller, you must hold block and press the jump button.

Play around with the various options to find your comfort level.

LEVELING AND ATTRIBUTES

Once in the game, you need to start thinking about leveling your character, which requires earning Experience (XP). There are several ways to earn XP in TESO—complete quests, defeat enemies, participate in world events, and even pick locks and discover new locations. Increasing your level allows you to use more powerful gear, consume more effective items, and unlock better skills.

At each level, Attribute Points are awarded, which can be allocated to Maximum Magicka, Health, and/or Stamina. Which stat gets the upgrade depends on the type of character you wish to build and is very dependent on the skills you select. If your skills are widely Magicka- or Stamina-based, put more points into that stat. To build the ultimate Tank, increase Maximum Health as much as possible.

Refer to our **Attributes** and **Archetypes** sections for more information.

SKILLS

Skill Points are rewarded at each level, for completing certain quests and events, from ranking up in the Alliance War, and by collecting skyshards. These points are used to unlock new Active, Passive, and Ultimate Abilities. There are 379 total Skill Points in the game, but it will take a long time to earn and find them all. Choosing which skills to spend your well-earned points on is a difficult decision. Examining a bookshelf has a slight chance of unlocking/upgrading a weapon, armor, or crafting skill line. Refer to our **Skills** section for help with understanding your options.

Unlocking and Leveling Skill Lines

Category	Skill Line	How to Unlock	How to Level
Class	Dragonknight (Ardent Flame, Draconic Power, Earthen Heart)	Create a Dragonknight	Gain XP with a skill from that skill line on the Action Bar
	Nightblade (Assassination, Shadow, Siphoning)	Create a Nightblade	Gain XP with a skill from that skill line on the Action Bar
	Sorcerer (Dark Magic, Daedric Summoning, Storm Calling)	Create a Sorcerer	Gain XP with a skill from that skill line on the Action Bar
	Templar (Aedric Spear, Dawn's Wrath, Restoring Light)	Create a Templar	Gain XP with a skill from that skill line on the Action Bar
	Warden (Animal Companions, Green Balance, Winter's Embrace)	Create a Warden	Gain XP with a skill from that skill line on the Action Bar
Weapon	Two-Handed, One Hand and Shield, Dual Wield, Bow, Destruction Staff, Restoration Staff	Land a killing blow with a weapon of that type	Gain XP with a skill from that skill line on the Action Bar or while wielding weapons of that type
Armor	Light, Medium, Heavy	Equip three armor pieces of that armor type	Gain XP while wearing armor of that type
World	Legerdemain	Pickpocket an NPC, pick a lock, or launder/fence a stolen item	Successfully pickpocket an NPC, pick a lock, and launder/ fence stolen items
	Soul Magic	Complete a tutorial (skipping the tutorial on subsequent characters unlocks the skill line)	Complete the base game story line quests
	Vampire	Become infected by a Vampire or bitten by a player	Gain XP with a Vampire skill on the Action Bar
	Werewolf	Become infected by a Werewolf or bitten by a player	Kill monsters in Werewolf form
Guild	Dark Brotherhood (requires DLC)	Complete the first quest of the Gold Coast story	Complete Gold Coast story quests, perform contracts, and fulfill Sacraments
	Fighters Guild	Complete the first Fighters Guild quest, or talk to a member of the Fighters Guild in Morrowind	Complete Fighters Guild quests, daily quests, and kill Undead and Daedra
	Mages Guild	Complete the first Mages Guild story quest, or talk to a member of the Mages Guild in Morrowind	Complete Mages Guild quests, daily quests, and read Lorebooks
	Thieves Guild (requires DLC)	Open a Thieves Trove or enter Hew's Bane	Complete criminal requests from the Tip Board, complete heists, and complete Thieves Guild quests
	Undaunted	Talk to members of the Undaunted in a tavern in Glenumbra, Stonefalls, or Auridon	Complete Dungeon Achievements and daily quests found at Undaunted Enclaves and do daily Undaunted Pledges unlocked at Level 45
Alliance War	Assault, Support	Gain an Alliance Point by killing an enemy player, finishing a Battleground, or doing a Cyrodiil quest	Gain Alliance Points from Battlegrounds and Cyrodiil
Racial	Each of the 10 races has its own skill line	Unlocked at Level 5	Gain XP
Craft	Alchemy, Blacksmithing, Clothing, Enchanting, Provisioning, Woodworking	Complete certification in that trade skill	Craft/deconstruct items and complete crafting writs

CHAMPION

Upon reaching the maximum level of 50, it's still possible to improve your character. The Champion System takes over at this point, with points rewarded immediately and by increasing your Champion Rank, which maxes out at Rank 630. Based on the type of points, they can be assigned to constellations, each with a unique selection of stat and ability bonuses. Refer to our **Champions** section for details on how the system functions.

PLAYER VERSUS PLAYER

When you reach Level 10, player-versus-player (PvP) combat unlocks in two locations: Cyrodiil and the Battlegrounds of Vvardenfell. Use the Activity Finder to enter either area.

The Alliance War constantly wages in Cyrodiil, located in the center of Tamriel. Lead your alliance to victory by taking over keeps and resources, stealing the opposition's Elder Scrolls, and, ultimately, becoming the Emperor. More PvP is found in the Imperial City at the center of Cyrodiil, though the Imperial City DLC or ESO Plus membership is required. Find quests, delves, Dark Anchors, and more of the usual activities within Cyrodiil.

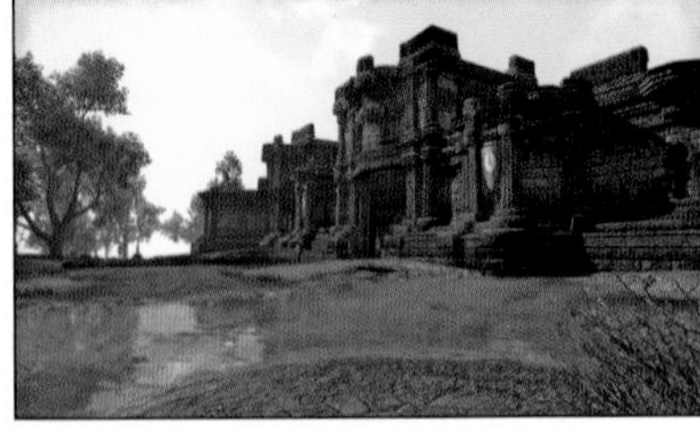

Also unlocked at Level 10, the Battlegrounds in Vvardenfell offers four-on-four-on-four gameplay in three different game modes: Team Deathmatch, Capture the Flag, and Domination. Enter the fast-paced matches for high-intensity team play.

EXPLORE TAMRIEL

There's much to experience in Tamriel—new lands to discover, quests to complete, group bosses to take part in, and much more. NPCs provide valuable services in the cities and towns of Tamriel, so feel free to seek help from them. Join a player guild and experience TESO with a group, or remain on your own—the choice is yours.

FLUCTUATING PRICES

Please note that prices listed throughout the guide are accurate as of printing. Prices may fluctuate up and down as the game is updated.

RACES AND FACTIONS

OVERVIEW

By default, each of the game's playable races belongs to one of three factions: the Daggerfall Covenant, the Aldmeri Dominion, or the Ebonheart Pact. Depending on your priorities, your choice of race determines your faction, or your choice of faction determines the races available to you. In either case, faction selection determines your allegiance in the Alliance War, certain quest locations, and your character's starting area. If playing Morrowind, the player begins off the western coast of Vvardenfell, no matter the alliance chosen.

CROWN STORE OPTIONS

Players interested in a more flexible approach will find additional options in the Crown Store. The Imperial race can belong to any faction, and the "Any Race, Any Alliance" collection item removes all race restrictions during character creation.

Each race offers a unique selection of Passive Abilities. The first racial Passive is active as soon as you reach Level 5; remaining racial Passives can be unlocked as the character progresses.

The nature of racial Passives means that each race has its own specific strengths. For example, High Elf Passives increase Maximum Magicka, Magicka Recovery, and various elemental damage types, while Redguard Passive Abilities increase Maximum Stamina and Stamina Recovery. All things being equal (build, equipped gear, playstyle, etc.), a High Elf's Magicka abilities will always be more effective than those cast by a Redguard—of course, the Redguard will always have the advantage in Stamina abilities, sprinting, blocking, and so on.

PLAY WHAT YOU LIKE

Race selection is an important part of character optimization, but it won't make or break your build. Gear, abilities, and playstyle have a much larger impact on your character's performance than racial Passives ever will. When in doubt, choose the race you find most appealing.

FACTIONS

THE DAGGERFALL COVENANT

Member Races:

- Breton
- Orc (Orsimer)
- Redguard

Controlled Zones:

- Stros M'Kai
- Betnikh
- Glenumbra
- Stormhaven
- Rivenspire
- Alik'r Desert
- Bankorai

Originally established to repel an invading Reachmen army, the Daggerfall Covenant aims to secure trade routes disrupted by years of war and turmoil—a goal that High King Emeric believes can only be achieved by claiming the Ruby Throne and uniting Tamriel under one banner.

Consisting of three previously warring races, the Covenant began as a somewhat precarious union. However, aligned self-interests and a shared respect for military might have allowed the Bretons, Redguards, and Orcs to work together, making the Daggerfall Covenant a serious contender in the war for the Imperial City.

THE ALDMERI DOMINION

Member Races:

- High Elf
- Khajiit
- Wood Elf

Controlled Zones:

- Khenarthi's Roost
- Auridon
- Grahtwood
- Greenshade
- Malabal Tor
- Reaper's March

When the Imperial City fell to Molag Bal's worshippers, the High Elves called upon their neighbors and frequent allies: the Wood Elves and Khajiit. The Aldmeri Dominon claims no interest in power for power's sake, but its members are determined to prevent younger and more reckless races from deciding Tamriel's fate.

With a shared appreciation for intelligence and logic, the races of the Aldmeri Dominion believe it falls on them to restore peace and order to a chaotic and war-torn land.

THE EBONHEART PACT

Member Races:

- Argonian
- Dark Elf
- Nord

Controlled Zones:

- Bleakrock Isle
- Bal Foyen
- Stonefalls
- Deshaan
- Shadowfen
- Eastmarch
- The Rift

Forged when the Dark Elves, Nords, and Argonians united against Akaviri invaders, the Ebonheart Pact is a fragile alliance between three disparate peoples. These unlikely allies share little in regards to culture and customs, but the value of the Pact consistently outweighs any old hatreds its member races harbor toward each other.

Due to internal politics, the Ebonheart Pact is considered the least stable of Tamriel's alliances. Still, its military might is undeniable. Together, its member races intend to defend their homelands against all potential threats—even if that means taking control of the Imperial City.

CHARACTER RACES

ARGONIAN

Faction: The Ebonheart Pact
Recommended Focus: Magicka

▲ Sample males. ▲ Sample females.

With origins that trace directly to the Hist, Argonians are completely unrelated to the races of men. This accounts not only for their reptilian appearance, but also for their deep connection with the unforgiving wilds of Black Marsh. They're known to be a resilient people—and uniquely skilled Healers—but the Argonians are considered something of an enigma by the other races of Tamriel.

RACIAL PASSIVES

Amphibian
(Default Passive) Increases your Experience gain with the Restoration Staff skill line by 15%. Increases your swimming speed by 50%.

Resourceful
(Rank I/II/III) Increases your Maximum Magicka by 1%/2%/3%. Whenever you drink a potion, you restore 1524/3049/4620 Health, Magicka, and Stamina.

Argonian Resistance
(Rank I/II/III) Increases your Maximum Health by 3%/6%/9% and Poison and Disease Resistance by 495/990/1485.

Quick to Mend
(Rank I/II/III) Increases your healing done and healing received by 1%/3%/5%.

CLASS/BUILD RECOMMENDATIONS

As a whole, Argonian Passives support Magicka builds. The Quick to Mend Passive makes this race a natural choice for a designated Healer, but it also serves to make the Argonian an excellent Tank. In any case, Argonians work particularly well as Templars, Wardens, and siphoning-focused Nightblades.

BRETON

Faction: The Daggerfall Covenant
Recommended Focus: Magicka

▲ Sample males. ▲ Sample females.

Due in part to their blood ties with the Altmer, Bretons have a natural affinity for the arcane. They're gifted spellcasters by any measure, but they're easily the Daggerfall Covenant's most talented Magicka users. Bretons are considered intelligent and resourceful, but they also have a reputation as an emotional and quarrelsome people.

RACIAL PASSIVES

Opportunist
(Default Passive) Increases your Experience gain with the Light Armor skill line by 15%. Increases your Alliance Points gained by 1%.

Gift of Magnus
(Rank I/II/III) Increases your Maximum Magicka by 4%/7%/10%.

Spell Resistance
(Rank I/II/III) Increases your Spell Resistance by 1320/2640/3960.

Magicka Mastery
(Rank I/II/III) Reduces the Magicka cost of your abilities by 1%/2%/3%.

CLASS/BUILD RECOMMENDATIONS

The Gift of Magnus makes this race a fine choice for any Magicka build, but the mix of power, efficiency, and survivability is what sets the Breton apart from other Magicka-proficient races. Magicka DPS is always an option, but a large Magicka pool combined with reduced Magicka use makes the Breton a reliable Healer, and the Spell Resistance Passive is a boon for Magicka Tanks or PvP builds.

DARK ELF

Faction: The Ebonheart Pact

Recommended Focus: Magicka

Dark Elves, or "Dunmer," are renowned for their intelligence and physical prowess—qualities that have allowed them to produce some of Tamriel's most formidable warriors and spellcasters. They also have a well-deserved reputation as a grim and prideful race. Dark Elves are slow to trust and quick to judge, but their prowess in battle is undeniable.

RACIAL PASSIVES

Ashlander

(Default Passive) Increases your Experience gain with the Dual Wield skill line by 15%. Reduces your damage taken from environmental lava by 50%.

Dynamic

(Rank I/II/III) Increases your Maximum Magicka and Maximum Stamina by 2%/4%/6%.

Resist Flame

(Rank I/II/III) Increases your Maximum Magicka by 1%/2%/3% and Flame Resistance by 693/1386/2080.

Destructive Ancestry

(Rank I/II/III) Increases your Flame Damage by 3%/5%/7%. Increases your Frost and Shock Damage by 0%/1%/2%.

CLASS/BUILD RECOMMENDATIONS

The Dark Elf is a solid choice for any Magicka build—and the boost to Maximum Stamina presents some intriguing options—but the bonus to Flame Damage makes this race a top pick for Dragonknight casters. It's also worth noting that the available Flame Resistance helps offset Vampirism's biggest drawback, making the Dark Elf a particularly good option for builds that include the Vampire skill line.

▲ *Sample males.* ▲ *Sample females.*

HIGH ELF

Faction: The Aldmeri Dominion

Recommended Focus: Magicka

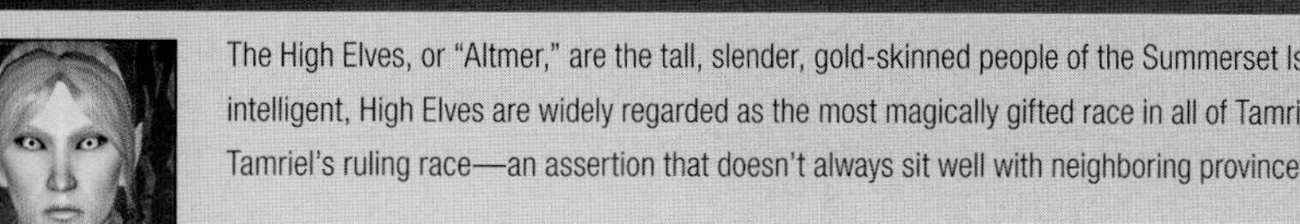

The High Elves, or "Altmer," are the tall, slender, gold-skinned people of the Summerset Isles. Sophisticated and intelligent, High Elves are widely regarded as the most magically gifted race in all of Tamriel. They also see themselves as Tamriel's ruling race—an assertion that doesn't always sit well with neighboring provinces.

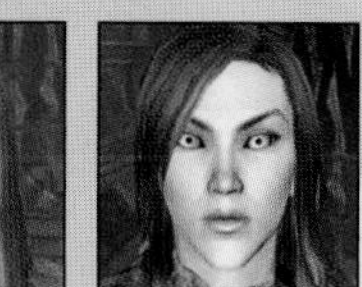

RACIAL PASSIVES

Highborn

(Default Passive) Increases your Experience gain with the Destruction Staff skill line by 15%. Increases your Experience gained by 1%.

Spellcharge

(Rank I/II/III) Increases your Magicka Recovery by 3%/6%/9%.

Gift of Magnus

(Rank I/II/III) Increases your Maximum Magicka by 4%/7%/10%.

Elemental Talent

(Rank I/II/III) Increases your Flame, Frost, and Shock Damage by 2%/3%/4%.

CLASS/BUILD RECOMMENDATIONS

The High Elf's combination of Maximum Magicka and Magicka Recovery makes this race one of the best options for any Magicka build. Dark Elves have the edge in Flame Damage, but no race can match the High Elf's potential for Frost Damage and Shock Damage. This advantage makes the High Elf a particularly good choice for Sorcerers and Wardens focusing on Magicka DPS.

▲ *Sample males.* ▲ *Sample females.*

IMPERIAL

Faction: None
Recommended Focus: Stamina

▲ Sample males. ▲ Sample females.

The natives of Cyrodiil are known to be well-educated and very diplomatic. They may not be as physically imposing as Nords or Orcs, but a focus on discipline and training has allowed the Imperials to produce some of Tamriel's finest soldiers—many of whom now find themselves outcasts in their home province. These days, rogue Imperials tend to align themselves with any faction that might drive Molag Bal's followers from the Ruby Throne.

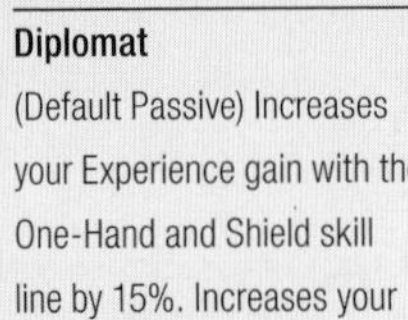

RACIAL PASSIVES

Diplomat
(Default Passive) Increases your Experience gain with the One-Hand and Shield skill line by 15%. Increases your gold gained by 1%.

Tough
(Rank I/II/III) Increases your Maximum Health by 4%/8%/12%.

Conditioning
(Rank I/II/III) Increases your Maximum Stamina by 4%/7%/10%.

Red Diamond
(Rank I/II/III) Your melee attacks have a 10% chance to restore 2%/4%/6% of your Maximum Health.

CLASS/BUILD RECOMMENDATIONS

With the largest available bonuses to Maximum Health and Maximum Stamina, the Imperial is a natural choice for a Stamina Tank—especially when one considers the potential healing effects of the Red Diamond Passive. Of course, this race isn't limited to a single role; the combination of Health and Stamina makes the Imperial an excellent choice for any Stamina-heavy build.

KHAJIIT

Faction: The Aldmeri Dominion
Recommended Focus: Stamina

▲ Sample males. ▲ Sample females.

Hailing from the deserts of Elsweyr, the Khajiit are generally counted among Tamriel's original inhabitants. This feline race is known for cleverness, agility, and a natural talent for stealth. These traits make the Khajiit excellent combatants, but they've also earned the cat-folk an unsavory reputation as a race of swindlers and thieves.

RACIAL PASSIVES

Cutpurse
(Default Passive) Increases your Experience gain with the Medium Armor skill line by 15%. Increases your chance to successfully pickpocket by 5%.

Nimble
(Rank I/II/III) Increases your Health Recovery by 6%/13%/20% and Stamina Recovery by 3%/6%/10%.

Stealthy
(Rank I/II/III) Reduces your detection radius in stealth by 1/2/3 meters. Increases your damage done while in stealth by 3%/6%/10%.

Carnage
(Rank I/II/III) Increases your Weapon Critical by 2%/5%/8%.

CLASS/BUILD RECOMMENDATIONS

Khakiit Passives offer an excellent mix of damage and sustainability, and players prioritizing Stamina DPS would be hard-pressed to find a more suitable race for any class. While other Stamina-focused races have their advantages, the Khajiit's bonus to Weapon Critical makes it the clear winner for burst damage.

NORD

Faction: The Ebonheart Pact

Recommended Focus: Stamina

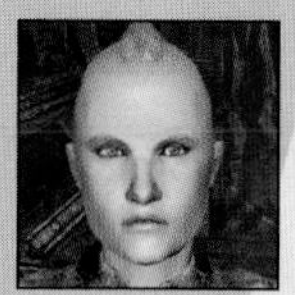

▲ Sample males. ▲ Sample females.

As a people, Nords are hardy, brave, and quick to violence, and Nord culture values strength and simplicity over cleverness or diplomacy. Outsiders typically see them as a dull, brutish, and uncivilized people—an image that most Nords are proud to embrace.

RACIAL PASSIVES

Reveler

(Default Passive) Increases your Experience gain with the Two-Handed skill line by 15%. Increases the duration of any consumed drink by 15 minutes.

Stalwart

(Rank I/II/III) Increases your Maximum Stamina by 2%/4%/6% and Health Recovery by 6%/13%/20%.

Resist Frost

(Rank I/II/III) Increases your Maximum Health by 3%/6%/9% and Frost Resistance by 639/1386/2080.

Rugged

(Rank I/II/III) Reduces your damage taken by 2%/4%/6%.

CLASS/BUILD RECOMMENDATIONS

The Nords' celebrated hardiness comes from its combination of Maximum Health, Health Recovery, and straightforward damage mitigation. These qualities make the Nord one of the best possible options for a designated Tank. The Nord's survivability is also great for PvP builds—especially now that a new frost-wielding class has joined the fray.

ORC

Faction: The Daggerfall Covenant

Recommended Focus: Stamina

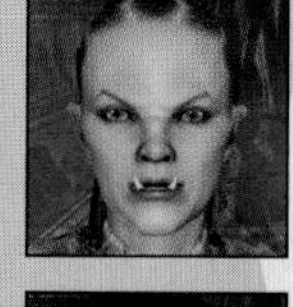

▲ Sample males. ▲ Sample females.

Long considered savages, the Orcs, or "Orsimer," have slowly gained acceptance among neighboring races. Powerfully built and fearless in battle, these hardy mountain dwellers live under a simple code by which only the strong survive—a pragmatic creed that has helped the Orcs endure countless hardships.

RACIAL PASSIVES

Craftsman

(Default Passive) Increases your Experience gain with the Heavy Armor skill line by 15%. Increases your crafting Inspiration gained by 10%.

Brawny

(Rank I/II/III) Increases your Maximum Health and Maximum Stamina by 2%/4%/6%.

Unflinching

(Rank I/II/III) Increases your healing received by 1%/3%/5% and Health Recovery by 6%/13%/20%.

Swift Warrior

(Rank I/II/III) Increases your damage done with melee attacks by 2%/3%/4%. Reduces the cost of Sprint by 4%/8%/12% and increases the movement speed bonus of Sprint by 3%/6%/10%.

CLASS/BUILD RECOMMENDATIONS

With an impressive mix of power and durability, the Orc is a strong option for virtually any Stamina build. Bonuses to Maximum Health, Health Recovery, and healing received make them well-suited to Tanking roles, but boosts in Maximum Stamina and melee damage make the Orc a solid option for DPS builds as well. However, this race's Sprint-related bonuses arguably provide the largest benefit—this outstanding mobility makes a well-built Orc shine in PvP.

REDGUARD

Faction: The Daggerfall Covenant
Recommended Focus: Stamina

▲ *Sample males.* ▲ *Sample females.*

With a culture built on preserving ancient traditions, the Redguards of Hammerfell prize honor and dignity above all else. Redguards are often suspicious of the arcane, but their natural athleticism and rigid training have made them a race of tireless warriors.

RACIAL PASSIVES

Wayfarer
(Default Passive) Increases your Experience gain with the One-Hand and Shield skill line by 15%. Increases the duration of any eaten food by 15 minutes.

Exhilaration
(Rank I/II/III) Increases your Stamina Recovery by 3%/6%/9%.

Conditioning
(Rank I/II/III) Increases your Maximum Stamina by 4%/7%/10%.

Adrenaline Rush
(Rank I/II/III) Your melee attacks restore 261/522/792 Stamina. This effect can occur once every five seconds.

CLASS/BUILD RECOMMENDATIONS

When it comes to Stamina use, few races can match the Redguards' sustainability. The Adrenaline Passive means they're best suited to melee combat, but the Conditioning Passive means the Redguard works well in any Stamina-focused build.

WOOD ELF

Faction: The Aldmeri Dominion
Recommended Focus: Stamina

▲ *Sample males.* ▲ *Sample females.*

Wood Elves, or "Bosmer," are quick and nimble combatants. On the field of battle, Wood Elves often serve as scouts and archers; in the criminal world, they're renowned thieves and assassins. Because the typical Wood Elf is rather small, they tend to favor wit and agility over brute force.

RACIAL PASSIVES

Acrobat
(Default Passive) Increases XP gained with the Bow skill line by 15% and reduces fall damage by 10%.

Y'ffre's Endurance
(Rank I/II/III) Increases your Stamina Recovery by 7%/14%/21%.

Resist Affliction
(Rank I/II/III) Increases your Maximum Stamina by 2%/4%/6% and Poison and Disease Resistance by 495/990/1485.

Stealthy
(Rank I/II/III) Reduces your detection radius in stealth by 1/2/3 meters. Increases your damage done while in stealth by 3%/6%/10%.

CLASS/BUILD RECOMMENDATIONS

Wood Elves feature the highest possible Stamina Recovery, making them a great choice for sustained Stamina DPS, or for builds that rely on mobility for survival. Players looking to invest in the Werewolf skill line would also do well to consider the Wood Elf—the focus on Stamina supports the Werewolf's greatest strength, while the Wood Elf's natural Poison Resistance helps offset Lycanthropy's primary drawback.

CLASSES

The Elder Scrolls Online: Morrowind contains five player classes, and choosing one ranks among your most important decisions during character creation. Every class features three exclusive skill lines, each of which offers its own selection of abilities and morphs.

While it's fair to say that each class has its own unique strengths, it's important to note that your choice of class doesn't limit your character's potential role. Any character can be used to tank, heal, or deal damage, and every class has access to support abilities that make them valued allies during group content.

The game contains no class-exclusive gear or quests, and the vast majority of skill lines are available to every character. If your class skills don't support your desired role, you're sure to find suitable abilities elsewhere.

New players should note that most class abilities are Magicka-based; while dedicated spellcasters have plenty of viable options, Stamina-focused characters often rely on other skill lines for damage, utility, and healing effects. Still, every character in the game is essentially a hybrid. Even the most Stamina-heavy characters have some amount of Magicka, and putting it to good use helps ensure that you get the most out of your character.

If you're determined to avoid Magicka use, you're bound to find value in class abilities. Most Ultimate Abilities scale off your highest resource pool, and many Passive Abilities grant bonuses that benefit all playstyles. Most importantly, some class abilities offer Stamina morphs—class-specific options that clearly favor Stamina builds.

DRAGONKNIGHT

Dragonknights use the power of fire and earth to scorch and pummel their enemies into submission. They make great Tanks, but these fierce warriors can also serve as devastating Damage-Dealers.

When it comes to DPS, the Dragonknight has access to some of the game's best single-target damage-over-time effects. Magicka-focused Dragonknights would do well to focus on Burning effects, but this class also features some great options for Poison Damage.

With a variety of short-range attacks, armor effects, and one of the game's only Pull abilities, Dragonknight skills tend to complement more aggressive playstyles. Those looking for long-range attacks or enhanced mobility should plan for heavy investment in outside skill lines.

CLASS SKILL LINES

ARDENT FLAME

With options for direct damage, area-of-effect damage, and damage over time, the Ardent Flame skill line contains several of the Dragonknight's signature attacks.

True to its name, this skill line heavily favors Flame Damage. However, select morphs make Poison Damage a viable option for Stamina builds. Many of the available Passive Abilities affect both of these damage types, making Ardent Flame a priority skill line for any Dragonknight Damage-Dealer.

STAMINA OPTIONS

The Ardent Flame skill line offers two Stamina morphs:

Venomous Claw: This Searing Strike morph offers a bit of direct damage with a great damage-over-time effect.

Noxious Breath: This Fiery Breath morph combines a limited area of effect with a moderate damage-over-time effect. It also applies Major Fracture to affected targets.

DRACONIC POWER

The Draconic Power skill line features self-heals, armor effects, and one of the best multi-target roots available to any class. In short, this skill line has a heavy focus on survivability.

Aspiring Tanks should consider deep investment, but virtually any Dragonknight build can benefit from Draconic Power abilities. **Spiked Armor**, **Dark Talons**, and **Dragon Blood** are particularly popular, and **Inhale** offers a great mix of healing and area-of-effect damage.

STAMINA OPTIONS

The Draconic Power skill line doesn't offer any Stamina morphs, but **Green Blood** (morphed from Dragon Blood) adds Stamina Recovery to an already useful self-heal.

EARTHEN HEART

Earthen Heart abilities tend to focus on utility and group support. **Stone Fist** and **Petrify** are both great crowd-control tools; **Molten Weapons** and **Obsidian Shield** grant powerful effects to an entire group. **Ash Cloud** combines AoE/DOT damage with a multi-target snare, and the **Magma Armor Ultimate** is an AoE/DOT attack that also mitigates incoming damage.

Whether you're looking to boost damage output or reduce damage taken, even a small investment can boost any Dragonknight's combat efficiency.

STAMINA OPTIONS

The Earthen Heart skill line doesn't offer any Stamina morphs, but **Igneous Weapons** (morphed from Molten Weapons) is a great way to boost Weapon Damage—particularly if you invest in the **Mountain's Blessing** Passive. It's also an exceptionally popular group buff, making this Magicka ability a worthy addition to any Dragonknight build.

NIGHTBLADE

With abilities that grant invisibility, teleportation, and high-damage attacks, the Nightblade is a natural fit for those who favor stealth and deception. Of course, that's just one way to play a Nightblade.

While popular builds often focus on burst damage and mobility, Nightblade skill lines also offer exceptional utility. With plenty of options for crowd control, self-healing, and resource generation, Nightblade abilities can support virtually any playstyle.

CLASS SKILL LINES

ASSASSINATION

The Assassination skill line leans heavily toward direct damage, but it offers a variety of useful effects. **Assassin's Blade** is a powerful execute, and **Teleport Strike** serves as a class-exclusive gap closer. **Mark Target** applies useful debuffs, and **Grim Focus** is a go-to ability for a variety of Nightblade builds.

While all of this skill line's Passive Abilities are worth consideration, **Hemorrhage** deserves special mention. This powerful Passive not only increases Critical Damage; it also procs Minor Savagery for you and nearby allies. This Passive requires a slotted Assassination ability, but the skill line features viable options for any build.

STAMINA OPTIONS

The Assassination skill line offers three Stamina morphs:

Killer's Blade: This Assassin's Blade morph acts as a Stamina-based execute with a potential self-heal.

Ambush: This Teleport Strike morph improves the Nightblade's gap closer by increasing the damage of any follow-up attack.

Relentless Focus: This Grim Focus morph deals Disease Damage. It also grants Minor Endurance, increasing Stamina Recovery by 10% for 20 seconds

SHADOW

The Shadow skill line largely focuses on mobility. With options for snares, stuns, fears, speed boosts, and invisibility, players hoping to outmaneuver their enemies would do well to consider each of the available abilities. However, most Shadow abilities feature multiple effects; you're sure to find buffs, debuffs, and damage abilities to complement any playstyle.

Nightblades often rely on **Veiled Strike** for single-target damage, and the available Stamina morph makes this ability a viable option for any melee build. It's also worth noting that Shadow Passive Abilities all serve to enhance survivability, making the skill line an important part of most Nightblade Tank builds.

STAMINA OPTIONS

The Shadow skill line offers one Stamina morph:

Surprise Attack: This Veiled Strike morph adds the Major Fracture debuff to a versatile direct-damage attack.

SIPHONING

True to its name, the Siphoning skill features abilities that simultaneously harm enemies and benefit the caster. The simplest example is **Strife**, which combines direct damage with a healing effect, but the skill line includes options for buffs, resource generation, and crowd control.

Siphoning is largely a support skill line, making it the focus of most healing builds. However, any Nightblade concerned with survivability and/or sustainability would do well to invest in one or two key abilities.

STAMINA OPTIONS

The Siphoning skill line offers one Stamina morph:

Power Extraction: This Drain Power morph serves as a Disease Damage area-of-effect attack. As with the base ability, a successful hit grants the caster Major Brutality.

This skill line also features another ability:

Leeching Strikes: This Siphoning Strikes morph costs a small amount of Stamina, but returns Stamina on each strike—restoring a larger amount of Stamina when the effect ends.

Of course, both morphs retain the Magicka and/or Stamina generation offered by **Siphoning Strikes**. A Stamina-based Nightblade might consider any version of this ability to be a viable option.

SORCERER

As a celebrated spellcaster, the Sorcerer is an obvious choice for those who favor powerful area-of-effect attacks and long-range Magicka attacks. Popular Sorcerer builds tend to focus on burst damage—and their mastery of lightning makes them well-suited to DPS roles—but this class also offers some of the game's best crowd-control abilities.

Of course, Sorcerer skill lines support far more than classic robe-and-staff damage builds. With access to summoned minions, resource conversion, and an on-demand damage shield, an appropriately built Sorcerer can perform any number of roles on the battlefield.

CLASS SKILL LINES

DARK MAGIC

With multiple options for crowd control, the Dark Magic skill line accounts for much of the Sorcerer's utility. **Crystal Shard** combines direct damage with a Knockdown effect, and the **Negate Magic** Ultimate is the only ability capable of inflicting the Silenced effect. **Encase** and **Daedric Mines** both offer area-of-effect crowd control, and **Rune Prison** features a lengthy Disorient.

This skill line is also an important part of a Sorcerer's resource management. **Dark Exchange**, which converts Stamina into Health and Magicka, is a key component of many Sorcerer builds.

STAMINA OPTIONS

The nature of Dark Exchange means that its Magicka morph, **Dark Deal**, is well-suited to Stamina-based builds. This ability converts Magicka to Health and Stamina, making it a useful tool for resource management and one of the Sorcerer's most reliable self-heals.

DAEDRIC SUMMONING

The Daedric Summoning skill line largely focuses on minions. **Unstable Familiar** and **Winged Twilight** both conjure long-lasting companions that fight by your side, and the **Summon Storm Atronach** Ultimate Ability conjures a short-lived but very powerful ally. Of course, available morphs can dramatically alter the nature of summoned companions. The **Unstable Clannfear** morph, for example, features a popular on-demand heal.

For those who don't care for summoned minions, the powers of Oblivion can be put to other uses. **Daedric Curse** acts as a delayed direct-damage attack; **Conjured Ward** and **Bound Armor** both serve to improve a Sorcerer's survivability.

STAMINA OPTIONS

The Daedric Summoning skill line offers one Stamina morph:

Bound Armaments: This Bound Armor morph features the same protective effects offered by the base ability. However, instead of increasing Maximum Magicka, Bound Armaments increases the damage of your light and heavy attacks, as well as Maximum Stamina

STORM CALLING

Storm Calling is primarily about Shock Damage, making it a priority skill line for most damage-focused Sorcerers. **Mage's Fury** is the Sorcerer's class-specific execute ability, and **Overload** is an exceptional offensive Ultimate Ability. **Lightning Storm** and **Lightning Splash** both combine area-of-effect damage with useful effects.

However, not all Storm Calling abilities deal damage. **Surge** combines the Major Brutality buff with a potential self-heal, and **Bolt Escape** is one of the Sorcerer's most popular defensive abilities. Virtually every effective Sorcerer build includes some investment in the Storm Calling skill line.

STAMINA OPTIONS

The Storm Calling skill line offers one Stamina morph:

Hurricane: This Lightning Form morph serves as an area-of-effect attack that grows in size and strength over time. It also adds Minor Expedition to the list of buffs granted by the base ability.

TEMPLAR

Renowned for their versatility, Templars use the power of the light and the burning sun to damage their enemies while supporting their allies. They're capable of outstanding group support and remarkable survivability, but an appropriately built Templar can deal considerable damage.

The Templar once stood as the only class with a healing-focused skill line—while that's no longer the case, they still rank among the game's most popular Healers; their celebrated durability also makes them excellent Tanks.

CLASS SKILL LINES

AEDRIC SPEAR

Most Aedric Spear abilities offer a good mix of damage and utility, making this a priority skill line for Templars who favor close combat. **Radial Sweep** is a low-cost Ultimate Ability that combines an area-of-effect attack with a brief damage-over-time effect. **Puncturing Strikes** is a popular short-range attack with a limited area-of-effect component, and **Sun Shield** pairs an area-of-effect attack with a powerful damage shield.

Aedric Spear is also an important source for Templar crowd control and mobility. **Piercing Javelin** is a long-range attack that stuns its target, and **Focused Charge** is a class-specific gap closer. **Spear Shards** combines area-of-effect damage, a popular Synergy, and a brief Disorient effect.

STAMINA OPTIONS

The Aedric Spear skill line offers two Stamina morphs:

Biting Jabs: This Puncturing Strikes morph not only makes this signature attack viable for Stamina builds, it also grants Major Savagery with each use.

Binding Javelin: This Piercing Javelin morph also extends the duration of the attack's Stun effect.

DAWN'S WRATH

Dawn's Wrath features some of the Templar's most powerful attacks, making it an important skill line for damage-focused Templars. **Sun Fire** not only combines direct damage with damage over time and buff effects; it also serves as the Templar's only class-specific source of Flame Damage. **Solar Flare** is a direct-damage attack that features the Empower buff, and **Radiant Destruction** is a powerful damage-over-time execute.

This skill line also contains two abilities that work particularly well during group content. **Backlash** is an intriguing ability that gains strength as the target takes damage—a steady stream of ally damage helps ensure this ability always reaches its full potential. **Eclipse** is often used to hinder troublesome spellcasters in PvP.

STAMINA OPTIONS

The Dawn's Wrath skill line offers one Stamina morph:

Power of Light: This Backlash morph features the same damage potential as its Magicka variants while inflicting the target with Minor Fracture and Minor Breach.

RESTORING LIGHT

Most Restoring Light abilities feature some sort of healing effect. **Rushed Ceremony** is an instant single-target heal; **Healing Ritual** is a group heal with a brief cast time. The **Right of Passage** Ultimate Ability is a channeled group heal that grants the caster immunity from all crowd-control effects.

Some of this skill line's abilities also offer valuable utility. **Purifying Ritual** not only heals nearby allies; it cleanses the caster of negative effects. Simply slotting **Restoring Aura** grants the Templar enhanced resource regeneration—activating this ability inflicts nearby enemies with Minor Magickasteal. **Rune Focus** grants the caster Major Resolve and Major Ward, greatly increasing survivability.

STAMINA OPTIONS

Although Restoring Light doesn't feature any Stamina morphs, **Repentance** (morphed from Restoring Aura) is a viable option for Stamina Templars.

While slotted, Repentance grants the same buffs offered by the base ability, but activation yields wildly different results: instead of consuming Magicka to inflict nearby enemies with Minor Maim, Repentance draws power from nearby corpses to restore Health and Stamina to the caster. This unique ability isn't widely used in PvP, but it's a popular part of many leveling builds.

WARDEN (NEW CLASS)

Exclusive to *The Elder Scrolls Online: Morrowind*, the Warden is the first new class to be added since the game's launch.

Wardens are masters of nature-based magic, and class skill lines reflect the deep connection they share with the land. Wardens can enlist the help of animal allies, summon regenerative plants, and conjure icy storms for powerful frost-based effects.

As one of only two classes with a healing-focused skill line, the Warden is an excellent option for a dedicated Healer. Wardens also have access to powerful defensive abilities that allow for some intriguing Tank builds. Of course, damage is always an option, and all Warden skill lines offer valuable utility effects.

ANIMAL COMPANIONS

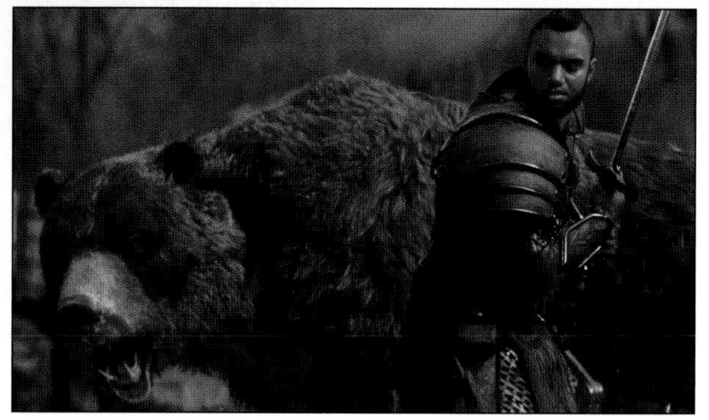

With Animal Companions, a Warden can summon powerful creatures to attack their enemies or provide valuable support. This skill line contains options for direct damage, area-of-effect damage, and damage over time—but it also features some outstanding utility skills.

Betty Netch is a great way to improve sustainability, and **Falcon's Swiftness** stands as one of the game's best mobility buffs. Animal Companions also contains two Stamina morphs, making this a viable skill line for any Warden.

ULTIMATE ABILITY

FERAL GUARDIAN

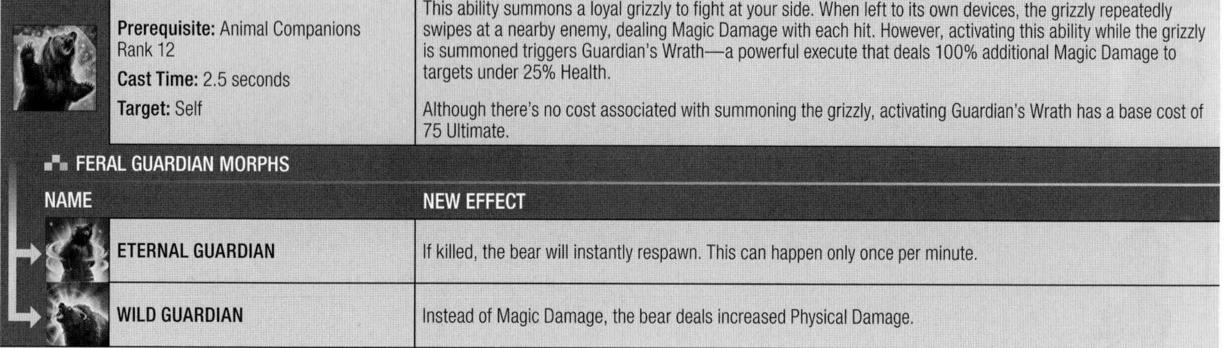

Prerequisite: Animal Companions Rank 12 **Cast Time:** 2.5 seconds **Target:** Self	This ability summons a loyal grizzly to fight at your side. When left to its own devices, the grizzly repeatedly swipes at a nearby enemy, dealing Magic Damage with each hit. However, activating this ability while the grizzly is summoned triggers Guardian's Wrath—a powerful execute that deals 100% additional Magic Damage to targets under 25% Health. Although there's no cost associated with summoning the grizzly, activating Guardian's Wrath has a base cost of 75 Ultimate.
FERAL GUARDIAN MORPHS	
NAME	**NEW EFFECT**
ETERNAL GUARDIAN	If killed, the bear will instantly respawn. This can happen only once per minute.
WILD GUARDIAN	Instead of Magic Damage, the bear deals increased Physical Damage.

ACTIVE ABILITIES

DIVE

Prerequisite: Animal Companions Rank 1 **Cast Time:** Instant **Target:** Enemy **Range:** 28 meters **Cost:** 2431 Magicka	This ability sends a Cliff Racer diving into the targeted enemy. With good range and no cast time, Dive stands as one of the Warden's best options for single-target damage. Dive is a solid choice for any caster, but melee-focused Wardens should note the available Stamina morph. **Cutting Dive** can add a bit of ranged damage to Stamina builds that lack Bow abilities.
FERAL GUARDIAN MORPHS	
NAME	**NEW EFFECT**
CUTTING DIVE	(Stamina morph) Costs Stamina and scales off of Weapon Damage and Maximum Stamina.
SCREAMING CLIFF RACER	Deals more damage against distant targets.

SCORCH

Prerequisite: Animal Companions Rank 4 **Cast Time:** Instant **Target:** Area **Area:** 20 x 7 meters **Duration:** 3 seconds **Cost:** 3240 Magicka	This ability summons a group of Shalks. After three seconds, the Shalks emerge in front of you, dealing Magic Damage to all enemies hit. Scorch has a moderate area of effect, and the delayed cast does present some interesting tactical options—just make sure you're facing your intended target(s) by the time the Shalks emerge.
FERAL GUARDIAN MORPHS	
NAME	**NEW EFFECT**
SUBTERRANEAN ASSAULT	(Stamina morph) The Shalks now deal Poison Damage. Affected enemies are afflicted with Major Breach and Major Fracture.
DEEP FISSURE	An eruption stuns one affected enemy for three seconds.

SWARM

	Prerequisite: Animal Companions Rank 20 **Cast Time:** Instant **Target:** Enemy **Range:** 28 meters **Duration:** 10 seconds **Cost:** 1891 Magicka	This ability calls a swarm of Fetcherflies to attack the targeted enemy, dealing Magic Damage over 10 seconds. As a long-range damage-over-time attack, Swarm is a great option for damage-focused Magicka Wardens.
FERAL GUARDIAN MORPHS		
NAME		**NEW EFFECT**
	FETCHER INFECTION	Every second cast of this ability deals 75% more damage.
	GROWING SWARM	When the ability ends, Fetcherflies infect up to six new targets.

BETTY NETCH

	Prerequisite: Animal Companions Rank 30 **Cast Time:** Instant **Target:** Self **Duration:** 24 seconds	This ability calls a Betty Netch that helps replenish the caster's Magicka for 25 seconds. The caster also gains Major Sorcery, temporarily increasing Spell Damage. Put simply, Betty Netch is a great resource-management tool. It costs nothing to cast, and the available morphs make it a viable option for any Warden build.
FERAL GUARDIAN MORPHS		
NAME		**NEW EFFECT**
	BLUE BETTY	Casting this ability also removes one negative effect from the caster.
	BULL NETCH	(Stamina morph) The ability now replenishes Stamina instead of Magicka and Major Brutality instead of Major Sorcery.

FALCON'S SWIFTNESS

	Prerequisite: Animal Companions Rank 42 **Cast Time:** Instant **Target:** Self **Duration:** 10 seconds **Cost:** 3512 Magicka	This ability grants the caster Major Expedition, increasing movement speed by 30% for 10 seconds. It also grants Major Endurance, increasing Stamina Recovery by 20% for the duration of the ability. Falcon's Swiftness is particularly well-suited to PvP builds, but it's an excellent option for any Warden who values mobility.
FERAL GUARDIAN MORPHS		
NAME		**NEW EFFECT**
	DECEPTIVE PREDATOR	The caster also gains Minor Evasion, increasing Dodge Chance by 5% for 10 seconds.
	BIRD OF PREY	The caster also gains Minor Berserk, increasing damage done by 8% for 10 seconds.

PASSIVE ABILITIES

The Flourish Passive grants bonuses to Magicka/Stamina Recovery, making it a useful option for all Warden builds. However, those hoping to benefit from any of this skill line's Passives should plan to slot at least one Animal Companions ability.

NAME	DESCRIPTION	PREREQUISITE
BOND WITH NATURE	Rank 1: When one of your animal companions is killed or unsummoned, you're restored 630 Health.	Animal Companions Rank 8
	Rank 2: When one of your animal companions is killed or unsummoned, you're restored 1260 Health.	Animal Companions Rank 18
SAVAGE BEAST	Rank 1: Damaging an enemy with an Animal Companions ability grants 2 Ultimate. This effect has a cooldown of eight seconds.	Animal Companions Rank 14
	Rank 2: Damaging an enemy with an Animal Companions ability grants 4 Ultimate. This effect has a cooldown of eight seconds.	Animal Companions Rank 27
FLOURISH	Rank 1: Increases your Magicka and Stamina Recovery by 6% if an Animal Companions ability is slotted.	Animal Companions Rank 22
	Rank 2: Increases your Magicka and Stamina Recovery by 12% if an Animal Companions ability is slotted.	Animal Companions Rank 36
ADVANCED SPECIES	Rank 1: Increases the damage of your Animal Companions abilities by 1% for each Animal Companions ability slotted.	Animal Companions Rank 39
	Rank 2: Increases the damage of your Animal Companions abilities by 2% for each Animal Companions ability slotted.	Animal Companions Rank 50

GREEN BALANCE

Through Green Balance, a Warden calls on the regenerative properties of nature itself. Every Green Balance ability features some sort of healing effect, making the Warden one of just two classes with a skill line dedicated to healing.

Aspiring Healers will find plenty of options for instant heals, area-of-effect heals, and healing over time, but there are two abilities that any Warden would do well to consider. **Fungal Growth** offers a Stamina morph, making it one of the most effective heals a Stamina-focused player could place on their Action Bar; **Living Vines** is a great way to boost survivability during difficult battles.

ULTIMATE ABILITY

SECLUDED GROVE

Prerequisite: Green Balance Rank 12 **Cast Time:** Instant **Target:** Ground **Range:** 28 meters **Radius:** 8 meters **Duration:** 6 seconds **Cost:** 75 Ultimate	This ability conjures a healing forest at a location of your choosing, instantly restoring Health to you and/or any allies within its area of effect. The forest continues to heal you and all allies in the area for the next six seconds. Offering a combination of instant healing and healing over time, Secluded Grove is a great group-support ability. It's also a very inexpensive Ultimate Ability, making it an excellent option for dedicated Healers.

SECLUDED GROVE MORPHS

NAME	NEW EFFECT
ENCHANTED FOREST	The caster gains 20 Ultimate if the ability heals an ally under 50% Health.
HEALING THICKET	Healing continues for four seconds after the ability ends.

ACTIVE ABILITIES

FUNGAL GROWTH

Prerequisite: Green Balance Rank 1 **Cast Time:** Instant **Target:** Cone **Radius:** 20 meters **Cost:** 4591 Magicka	This ability conjures a large patch of mushrooms that heals you and all allies in your frontal cone. As an instant heal with a moderate area of effect, Fungal Growth is an excellent ability for those concerned with survivability—and because it's one of the game's few on-demand heals that offers a Stamina morph, this ability is a viable option for any Warden build.

FUNGAL GROWTH MORPHS

NAME	NEW EFFECT
ENCHANTED GROWTH	Affected targets also gain Minor Intellect and Minor Endurance, increasing Magicka/Stamina Recovery by 10% for 20 seconds.
SOOTHING SPORES	(Stamina morph) The ability now costs Stamina; when healing an ally less than eight meters away, the heal is 15% stronger.

HEALING SEED

Prerequisite: Green Balance Rank 4 **Cast Time:** Instant **Target:** Ground **Range:** 28 meters **Radius:** 8 meters **Duration:** 6 seconds **Cost:** 3240 Magicka	This ability summons a field of flowers that blooms after six seconds, healing you and all allies in the area. The field also allows allies to activate the Healing Seed Synergy, granting them an additional five-second healing effect. Healing Seed is another solid group heal, and the featured Synergy makes it an excellent support ability. The effect's six-second delay means that positioning and proper timing are vital, but it also allows for powerful healing combinations. Note that only one field may be active at a time—activating a second Healing Seed will remove an existing field before it has a chance to bloom.

HEALING SEED MORPHS

NAME	NEW EFFECT
BUDDING SEEDS	Activating this ability at any time during the effect causes a field to bloom instantly.
CORRUPTING POLLEN	Enemies who enter the field are afflicted with Major Defile, reducing their healing received by 30% for four seconds.

LIVING VINES

Prerequisite: Green Balance Rank 20 **Cast Time:** Instant **Target:** Area **Area:** 28 x 12 meters **Duration:** 10 seconds **Cost:** 2700 Magicka	This ability conjures tangling vines around you or the lowest-Health ally in front of you for 10 seconds. While the ability lasts, the vines restore a bit of the target's Health each time they take damage; this effect can occur once per second. Its 10-second duration makes Living Vines a useful pre-pull cast for melee characters and area-of-effect specialists, and it's a great way for dedicated Healers to support their Tanks between larger heals.

LIVING VINES MORPHS

NAME	NEW EFFECT
LEECHING VINES	All enemies that attack the target are afflicted with Minor Lifesteal for 10 seconds.
LIVING TRELLIS	When the ability ends, the vines grant their target an additional heal.

LOTUS FLOWER

Prerequisite: Green Balance Rank 30 **Cast Time:** Instant **Target:** Area **Radius:** 12 meters **Duration:** 20 seconds **Cost:** 2971 Magicka	This ability invokes a lotus blessing that heals you or an ally each time you use a light or heavy attack. The amount healed is determined by the damage done by these attacks. The nature of Lotus Flower means it's most beneficial to players who weave frequent weapon strikes into their attack rotations. However, the powerful buffs offered by the available morphs make Lotus Flower a useful ability for a wide variety of Warden builds.

LOTUS FLOWER MORPHS

NAME	NEW EFFECT
GREEN LOTUS	The blessing also grants the caster Major Savagery, increasing Weapon Critical by 2191 for 20 seconds.
LOTUS BLOSSOM	The blessing also grants the caster Major Prophecy, increasing Spell Critical by 2191 for 20 seconds.

NATURE'S GRASP

Prerequisite: Green Balance Rank 42 **Cast Time:** Instant **Target:** Ally **Range:** 22 meters **Duration:** 10 seconds **Cost:** 4051 Magicka	This ability allows you to swing to the targeted ally, granting them a 10-second healing effect upon your arrival. Nature's Grasp serves as both a support heal and an escape ability, making it a great option for builds intended for Trials or PvP content. However, because it requires a targeted ally, this ability isn't a particularly good fit for those who prefer to adventure alone.

NATURE'S GRASP MORPHS

NAME	NEW EFFECT
BURSTING VINES	Swinging to an ally grants them an instant heal rather than a 10-second healing effect.
NATURE'S EMBRACE	Using this ability also heals the caster.

PASSIVE ABILITIES

Green Balance Passives have no effect outside of Green Balance abilities; those planning to slot at least one of this skill line's abilities should consider investing in all available Passives. Wardens relying on other healing sources would do well to spend their Skill Points elsewhere.

NAME	DESCRIPTION	PREREQUISITE
ACCELERATED GROWTH	Rank 1: When healing yourself or an ally under 40% Health with a Green Balance ability, you gain Major Mending, increasing your healing done by 25% for 1.5 seconds.	Green Balance Rank 8
	Rank 2: When healing yourself or an ally under 40% Health with a Green Balance ability, you gain Major Mending, increasing your healing done by 25% for three seconds.	Green Balance Rank 18
NATURE'S GIFT	Rank 1: When healing an ally with a Green Balance ability, gain 125 Magicka or 125 Stamina. (Restores your lowest resource pool.)	Green Balance Rank 14
	Rank 2: When Healing an ally with a Green Balance ability, gain 250 Magicka or 250 Stamina. (Restores your lowest resource pool.)	Green Balance Rank 27
EMERALD MOSS	Rank 1: Increases healing done for Green Balance abilities by 1% for each Green Balance ability slotted.	Green Balance Rank 22
	Rank 2: Increases healing done for Green Balance abilities by 2% for each Green Balance ability slotted.	Green Balance Rank 36
MATURATION	Rank 1: Healing yourself or an ally grants the target Minor Toughness, increasing Maximum Health by 10% for 10 seconds.	Green Balance Rank 39
	Rank 2: Healing yourself or an ally grants the target Minor Toughness, increasing Maximum Health by 10% for 20 seconds.	Green Balance Rank 50

WINTER'S EMBRACE

Winter's Embrace allows a Warden to summon icy winds to form defensive shields, replenish lost Health, deal damage, and more. With an impressive mix of defense and utility, this skill line has a heavy focus on survivability.

Winter's Embrace is a particularly good skill line for dedicated Tanks. **Frost Cloak** and **Crystallized Shield** are great defensive abilities, **Arctic Wind** is a reliable self-heal, and **Impaling Shards** is an area-of-effect snare with damage that scales based on Maximum Health. Of course, these abilities can benefit any Warden interested in survivability or group support.

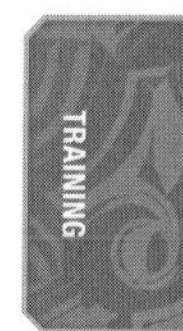

ULTIMATE ABILITY

SLEET STORM

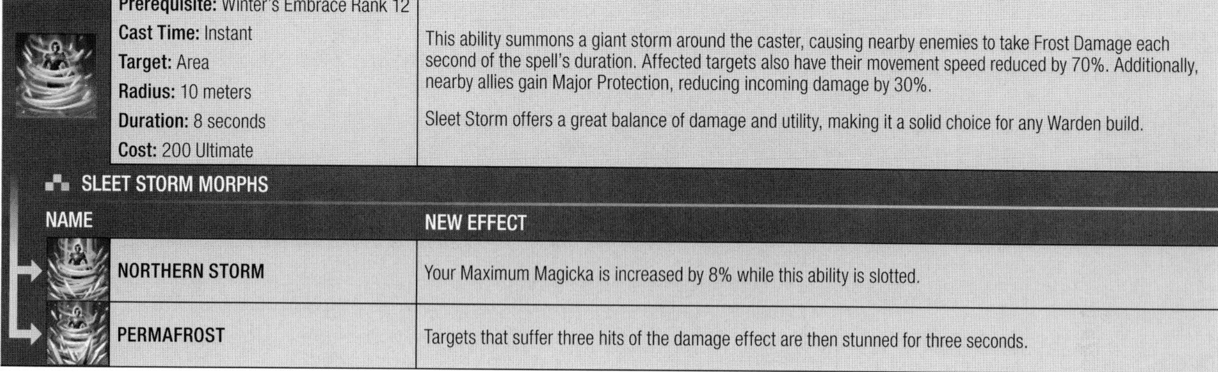

Prerequisite: Winter's Embrace Rank 12 Cast Time: Instant Target: Area Radius: 10 meters Duration: 8 seconds Cost: 200 Ultimate	This ability summons a giant storm around the caster, causing nearby enemies to take Frost Damage each second of the spell's duration. Affected targets also have their movement speed reduced by 70%. Additionally, nearby allies gain Major Protection, reducing incoming damage by 30%. Sleet Storm offers a great balance of damage and utility, making it a solid choice for any Warden build.

SLEET STORM MORPHS

NAME	NEW EFFECT
NORTHERN STORM	Your Maximum Magicka is increased by 8% while this ability is slotted.
PERMAFROST	Targets that suffer three hits of the damage effect are then stunned for three seconds.

ACTIVE ABILITIES

FROST CLOAK

Prerequisite: Winter's Embrace Rank 1 Cast Time: Instant Target: Area Radius: 8 meters Duration: 21 seconds Cost: 4050 Magicka	This ability wraps a thick cloak of ice around the caster and nearby allies. Affected targets gain Major Resolve, increasing Physical Resistance by 5280, and Major Ward, increasing Spell Resistance by 5280. Frost Cloak is an excellent defensive ability, making it a great option for Healers, Tanks, and anyone looking for increased survivability. While the Magicka cost might deter some Stamina Wardens, the featured buffs ensure that your chosen build has no effect on Frost Cloak's usefulness.

FROST CLOAK MORPHS

NAME	NEW EFFECT
EXPANSIVE FROST CLOAK	This ability features a larger radius and a reduced casting cost.
ICE FORTRESS	The caster also gains Minor Protection, reducing incoming damage by 8% for the duration of the ability.

IMPALING SHARDS

Prerequisite: Winter's Embrace Rank 4 Cast Time: Instant Target: Area Radius: 6 meters Duration: 12 seconds Cost: 3511 Magicka	This ability calls forth icy shards, dealing Frost Damage to all nearby enemies for 12 seconds; the damage done is based on the caster's Maximum Health. Affected targets also suffer a 30% decrease to movement speed for three seconds. Because the damage done by Impaling Shards scales off the caster's Maximum Health, it's an excellent area-of-effect attack for dedicated Tanks, and the brief Snare effect makes it a useful tool in PvP situations. It's also worth noting that one of the available morphs causes damage done to scale based on Maximum Magicka and Spell Damage.

IMPALING SHARDS MORPHS

NAME	NEW EFFECT
GRIPPING SHARDS	Casting this ability also immobilizes nearby enemies for three seconds.
WINTER'S REVENGE	The ability can now target any location within 28 meters. Damage is now based on the caster's Maximum Magicka and Spell Damage.

ARCTIC WIND

	Prerequisite: Winter's Embrace Rank 20 **Cast Time:** Instant **Target:** Area **Radius:** 8 meters **Duration:** 10 seconds **Cost:** 4321 Magicka	This ability envelops the caster in winter winds, healing 10% of Maximum Health instantly and an additional 2% of Maximum Health every two seconds for 10 seconds. Because Arctic Wind's effects scale off the caster's Maximum Health, this self-heal is an efficient option for heartier builds. It may not match the burst healing offered by other Warden abilities, but it's a solid choice for overall survivability.

ARCTIC WIND MORPHS

NAME	NEW EFFECT
POLAR WIND	Casting this ability also heals a nearby ally for 10% of your Maximum Health.
ARCTIC BLAST	The ability also deals Frost Damage to nearby enemies.

CRYSTALLIZED SHIELD

	Prerequisite: Winder's Embrace Rank 30 **Cast Time:** Instant **Target:** Self **Duration:** 6 seconds **Cost:** 2701 Magicka	This ability spins a shield of ice around the caster that can absorb up to three incoming projectiles. Each projectile absorbed restores some of the caster's Magicka. Crystalized Shield offers a mix of defense and resource generation that works particularly well in PvP situations, but it's a good option for any Warden with a focus on survivability.

CRYSTALLIZED SHIELD MORPHS

NAME	NEW EFFECT
CRYSTALLIZED SLAB	The shield also returns absorbed projectiles, dealing Frost Damage to the source of the attack.
SHIMMERING SHIELD	A successful absorption also provides Major Heroism, granting the caster 3 Ultimate every 1.5 seconds for six seconds.

FROZEN GATE

	Prerequisite: Winter's Embrace Rank 42 **Cast Time:** Instant **Target:** Ground **Range:** 28 meters **Radius:** 5 meters **Duration:** 30 seconds **Cost:** 2701 Magicka	This ability summons a portal at the target location. The first enemy to run over the portal is teleported to the caster and rooted for three seconds. The caster can only have one portal at a time, and an active portal vanishes once it's triggered. While Frozen Gate can be used as a trap, it can also be placed directly under a target enemy. It's particularly useful for Tanks who need to keep enemies away from vulnerable allies, but the Snare effect makes it a good crowd-control/support option for any Warden. It's also worth noting that one of the available morphs features the Frozen Retreat Synergy, allowing allies to teleport directly to the caster.

FROZEN GATE MORPHS

NAME	NEW EFFECT
FROZEN DEVICE	The teleported enemy is also afflicted with Major Maim, decreasing damage done by 30% for four seconds.
FROZEN RETREAT	The gate also grants nearby allies the Frozen Retreat Synergy, allowing them to teleport directly to the caster.

PASSIVE ABILITIES

Winter's Embrace offers a variety of Passive Abilities, two of which can benefit almost any Warden build. Even if you have no intention of using this skill line's Active Effects, consider investing in **Icy Aura** and **Piercing Cold**—the bonuses they grant should make progressing the skill line a worthy endeavor.

NAME	DESCRIPTION	PREREQUISITE
GLACIAL PRESENCE	Rank 1: Increases the chance of applying Chilled to enemies with Winter's Embrace abilities by 100%.	Winter's Embrace Rank 8
	Rank 2: Increases the chance of applying Chilled to enemies with Winter's Embrace abilities by 200%.	Winter's Embrace Rank 18
FROZEN ARMOR	Rank 1: Increases your Physical and Spell Resistance by 250 for each Winter's Embrace ability slotted.	Winter's Embrace Rank 14
	Rank 2: Increases your Physical and Spell Resistance by 500 for each Winter's Embrace ability slotted.	Winter's Embrace Rank 27
ICY AURA	Rank 1: Reduces the effectiveness of snares applied to you by 7%.	Winter's Embrace Rank 22
	Rank 2: Reduces the effectiveness of snares applied to you by 15%.	Winter's Embrace Rank 36
PIERCING COLD	Rank 1: Increases your Physical and Frost Damage by 3%.	Winter's Embrace Rank 39
	Rank 2: Increases your Physical and Frost Damage by 6%.	Winter's Embrace Rank 50

LEVELING

Earn Experience for every kill.

In order to improve your character's skill set and equipment and become more powerful, you must increase your level by earning Experience (XP). Completing quests, discovering new locations, killing enemies, picking locks, finishing a location's objective, running dungeons, and taking part in world events earn XP. You do not necessarily need to make the killing blow to get Experience. Assist in battles, even with friendly heals, to earn Experience.

RACIAL SKILLS

Your player level determines the abilities available from your racial skills. The first Passive Ability is unlocked at Level 5, with more unlocked and upgraded every five levels.

The following table shows the amounts of XP a player must accumulate to reach the next level, up to the maximum level of 50. Each increase in level earns the player a Skill Point as well as an Attribute Point that can be used to increase Maximum Magicka, Health, or Stamina. Every level that ends in five grants two Attribute Points, while multiples of 10 give three. Skill points are also awarded by collecting Skyshards, completing certain quests, and gaining alliance ranks in the Alliance War.

Level Progression

Level	XP to Next Level	Total XP	Standard Quest Completion	Normal Enemy Kill
1	—	—	—	—
2	70	70	508	37
3	500	570	508	40
4	1,324	1,894	741	41
5	2,726	4,620	796	44
6	3,859	8,479	832	46
7	3,871	12,350	886	49
8	4,047	16,397	904	50
9	4,728	21,125	958	53
10	6,033	27,158	1,012	56
11	6,583	33,741	1,067	59
12	7,659	41,400	1,103	61
13	9,338	50,738	1,193	66
14	10,865	61,603	1,248	69
15	12,733	74,336	1,284	71
16	13,489	87,825	1,374	76
17	15,131	102,956	1,446	80
18	18,444	121,400	1,501	83
19	21,274	142,674	1,573	87
20	24,368	167,042	1,681	93
21	25,672	192,714	1,754	97
22	29,186	221,900	1,826	101
23	32,950	254,850	1,935	107
24	34,618	289,468	2,043	113
25	39,322	328,790	2,152	119
26	42,744	371,534	2,242	124
27	44,457	415,991	2,368	131
28	49,845	465,836	2,477	137
29	53,983	519,819	2,604	144
30	60,171	579,990	2,766	153
31	59,625	639,615	2,893	160
32	66,890	706,505	3,056	169
33	75,065	781,570	3,200	177
34	79,594	861,164	3,363	186
35	80,655	941,819	3,544	196
36	84,104	1,025,923	3,724	206
37	85,323	1,111,246	3,905	216
38	90,945	1,202,191	4,104	227
39	96,014	1,298,205	4,321	239
40	101,897	1,400,102	4,538	251
41	100,817	1,500,919	4,773	264
42	110,146	1,611,065	5,008	277
43	118,131	1,729,196	5,261	291
44	121,894	1,851,090	5,551	307
45	131,212	1,982,302	5,840	323
46	141,280	2,123,582	6,129	339
47	149,516	2,273,098	6,436	356
48	166,516	2,439,614	6,762	374
49	178,557	2,618,171	7,124	394
50	187,494	2,805,665	7,485	414

This table also gives the approximate amount of XP gained from completing a standard quest. Most quests fall under this classification, but there are easy quests that reward less and tougher challenges, such as dungeons, that give even more Experience. There is a maximum amount of XP that can be gained at once, based on the XP required to reach the next level, so it is possible not to receive the full reward.

Apparel and weapons received and found are scaled to the player's level. A weapon rewarded for completing a quest has the same enchantment, trait, and name no matter who collects it, but level—and therefore the item's stats—are modified to match the player's level. Consumables are also collected with a level near your current level. In order to equip a piece of gear or use a consumable, your level must be equal to or greater than the level of the item.

INSPIRATION, REPUTATION, AND ALLIANCE POINTS

Instead of XP, creating and deconstructing items at crafting stations earns Inspiration, which goes directly toward that trade skill's rank.

Completing quests and other activities for the NPC guilds earns reputation toward that faction—advancing the appropriate skill line.

Earning Alliance Points in Cyrodiil and the Battlegrounds advances the Alliance War skill line.

EXPERIENCE BUFFS

There are several ways to obtain an Experience buff in *Elder Scrolls Online.* Note that most can be stacked.

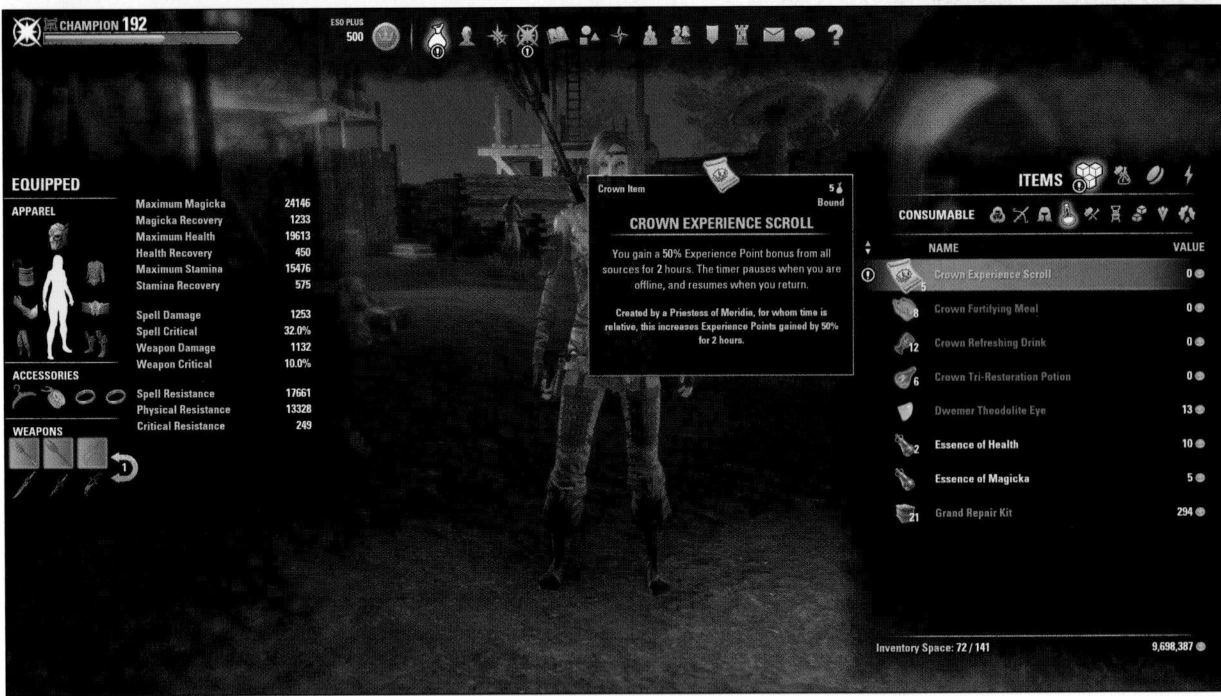

- Purchase a Crown Experience Scroll from the Crown Store for 300 crowns. This gives a 50% boost in XP for two hours. Cannot be stacked with the Psijic Ambrosia consumable.
- Craft a Psijic Ambrosia consumable for a 50% Experience boost for 30 minutes. Cannot be stacked with an Experience Scroll.
- Participate in a Ritual of Mara with a partner. This gives a 10% XP boost as long you fight with the same player and you both wear your Rings of Mara.
- ESO Plus members receive a 10% increase in Experience for as long as they are members.
- The Training trait, which can be placed on armor and weapons, gives an added XP buff. The amount of the boost is dependent upon how many and which items have the trait.
- Group with other players for a 10% XP buff.
- In the Alliance War, keeps owned by your Alliance give an Experience boost of 5-15%, based on the number of keeps captured. This buff only applies to monster and player kills.

VETERAN

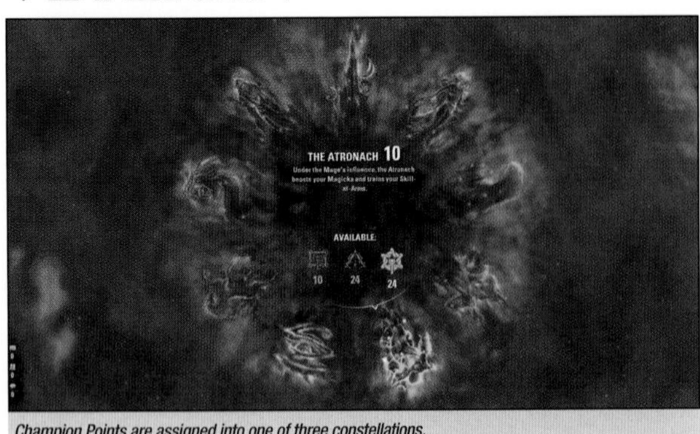

Champion Points are assigned into one of three constellations.

Once the maximum level of 50 is attained, XP no longer accrues toward your player level, as veteran content is unlocked. The Champion System takes over, with 10 points given right away. Champion Points continue to be rewarded as you keep making kills and completing objectives. Champion Points can be assigned to one of three constellations, each with a unique selection of stat and ability bonuses.

Attribute and Skill Points are no longer rewarded, but Maximum Magicka, Health, and Stamina are increased slightly. Refer to our **Champions** section for details on how the Champion System functions.

ATTRIBUTES

OVERVIEW

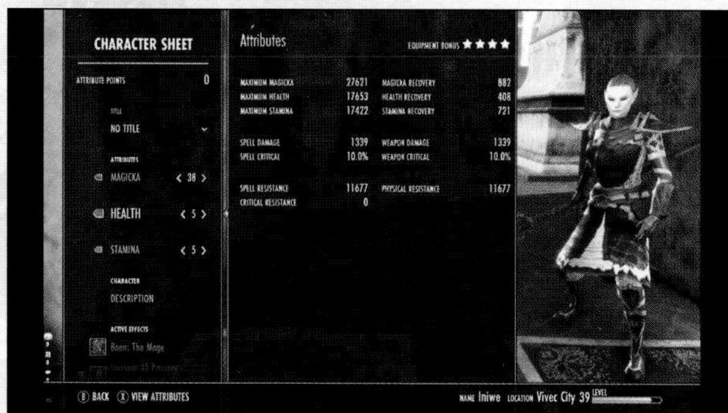

Attributes are qualities that determine your character's effectiveness in combat. Virtually every action a character takes is affected by one or more of these values, making proper Attribute management an essential part of character development.

PRIMARY ATTRIBUTES

Leveling up always grants at least one Attribute Point that can be spent in one of three primary Attributes:

Magicka: Each point invested raises Maximum Magicka by 111.

Health: Each point invested raises Maximum Health by 121.

Stamina: Each point invested raises Maximum Stamina by 111.

How you choose to invest Attribute Points goes a long way toward determining how well your character performs its intended role.

It's common for players to invest all 64 Attribute Points into a single resource, relying on the bonuses granted by equipment, consumables, and Mundus Stones to boost neglected Attributes. This allows for a highly specialized character, but it also supports experimentation and flexibility; it's easier to swap out gear and Active Effects than it is to redistribute spent Attribute Points.

Of course, some players prefer a more balanced approach. Don't hesitate to invest in any Attribute that might improve your character's performance. Reclaiming spent Attribute Points can be costly, but finding your most effective playstyle often takes a good deal of trial and error.

SECONDARY ATTRIBUTES

Secondary Attributes, or "stats," affect various aspects of a character's offensive and defensive capabilities:

Maximum Magicka: Affects how many Magicka abilities you can cast and how effective those abilities will be. It also determines damage done by staff weapons.

Maximum Health: Affects the amount of damage you can take before dying.

Maximum Stamina: Affects how many Stamina abilities you can use and how effective those abilities will be. It also determines damage done by bows and melee weapons.

Magicka Recovery: The amount of Magicka you recover every two seconds while in combat.

Health Recovery: The amount of Health you recover every two seconds while in combat.

Stamina Recovery: The amount of Stamina you recover every two seconds while in combat.

Spell Damage: Affects how much damage or healing your Magicka-based abilities and weapons cause.

Weapon Damage: Affects how much damage or healing your Stamina-based abilities and weapons cause.

Spell Critical: Gives your Magicka-based abilities and weapons a chance to do Critical Damage.

Weapon Critical: Gives your Physical Attacks a chance to do Critical Damage.

Spell Resistance: Decreases the amount of damage you take from Magical Attacks.

Physical Resistance: Decreases the amount of damage you take from Physical Attacks.

Critical Resistance: Decreases the damage you take when you are the victim of a Critical Strike.

AUGMENTING ATTRIBUTES

Aside from primary Attributes, which are only affected by Attribute Points, all character stats can be augmented by some combination of equipped gear, enchantments, Passive Abilities, consumable items, and Active Effects.

Depending on your preferred playstyle, finding the right balance of Attributes can be a challenge. In the end, it's all about building a character that suits your particular needs. While there's no "best" way to develop a character, new players looking for a bit of advice might consider the following:

Your character's listed stats include any boosts granted by the game's Battle Leveling mechanic. Because this bonus decreases as your character levels, rapid progression can actually hinder your combat effectiveness. To counter this, it's important to use level-appropriate gear, enchantments, and consumables.

The Character menu includes an Equipment Bonus rating that approximates the overall bonus granted by currently equipped gear. Try to maintain a minimum three-star rating during character progression. It's possible to achieve a five-star rating by filling every available slot with Legendary equipment (applied enchantments must also be of Legendary quality).

Enchantments are 60% less potent when applied to pieces that cover the waist, hands, feet, or shoulders. Only legs, headgear, and chest pieces receive the full benefits of an Armor Glyph.

Don't underestimate the importance of Active Effects. It's well worth seeking out a useful Mundus Stone boon as early as possible, and an appropriate food/drink effect makes a big difference in any combat situation.

Remember to invest in Passive Abilities. A few well-spent Skill Points can make a big difference in your character's Attributes and overall performance. In fact, it's often worth progressing an otherwise unused skill line to gain access to its Passive Abilities.

Attributes like Spell Resistance and Physical Resistance can prevent a maximum of 50% damage from a single attack. When and if your character reaches this threshold, additional mitigation will require ability use. Improving survivability doesn't always mean focusing on Maximum Health or donning heavy armor. All characters can sprint, block, bash, and dodge roll; the game also contains a wide variety of damage shields, healing effects, and crowd-control abilities. Determine if your character is best suited to absorbing damage, avoiding damage, or repairing damage, and then invest in Attributes that support the appropriate abilities.

Don't be afraid to experiment. Seek out Mundus Stones to try different boons, sample a variety of Provisioning recipes, and note changes in your performance each time you equip a new piece of gear. During group events, pay attention to the effects of group buffs and Synergies. Before long, you should have a good idea of which Attributes most benefit your character.

ACTIVE EFFECTS

The game includes a variety of Active Effects that can help or hinder a character's performance. Obviously, you should strive to maximize the benefits of positive effects while afflicting your enemies with negative effects. Of course, your enemies are sure to have similar goals in mind; knowing how to overcome a negative effect is just as important as knowing how to inflict it.

IMMOVABILITY

Disabling Effects are commonly referred to as "crowd control" or "CC" tactics. Disabling Effects that prevent a target from taking basic actions are commonly categorized as "hard CC." These effects include:

- Stunned
- Disoriented
- Knocked Back
- Knocked Down
- Pulled
- Feared

The moment one of these abilities ends, the afflicted target gains six seconds of Immovability, granting them temporary immunity from all hard CC effects.

Immovability can also be gained by performing the Break Free action, or by using abilities or potions that feature the Immovable effect.

SOFT CC

Disabling Effects that prevent some (but not all) basic actions are commonly categorized as "soft CC." These effects include Immobile, Snared, and Silenced.

Soft CC effects don't grant Immovability, making repeated application a viable Crowd Control tactic.

FOOD AND DRINK EFFECTS

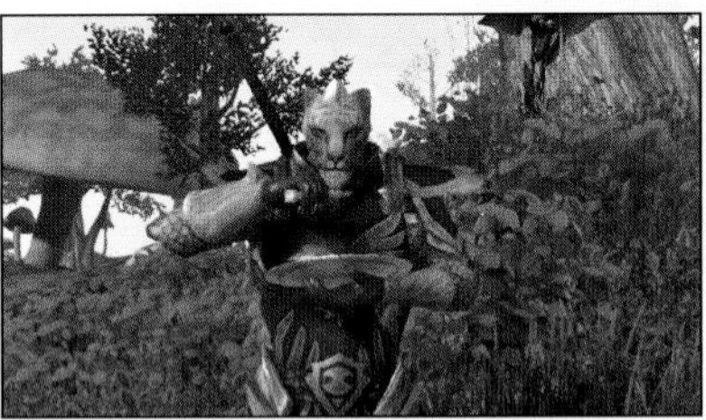

Your character can gain long-lasting effects by consuming food or drink. You'll find various consumables scattered throughout Tamriel, but they can also be crafted from raw materials, purchased from Merchants, or acquired from the Crown Store.

A basic food bonus increases Maximum Magicka, Maximum Stamina, or Maximum Health; a basic drink bonus increases Magicka Recovery, Stamina Recovery, or Health Recovery.

Higher-quality food and drink items affect multiple Attributes:

- White (normal) and green (Standard Recipe) items affect one Attribute
- Blue (Superior Recipe) items affect two Attributes
- Purple (Complex Recipe) items affect all three Attributes
- Yellow (Legendary Recipe) items feature special, recipe-specific bonuses

Food and drink effects don't stack—your character can only benefit from one food effect or one drink effect at any given time.

BUFFS AND DEBUFFS

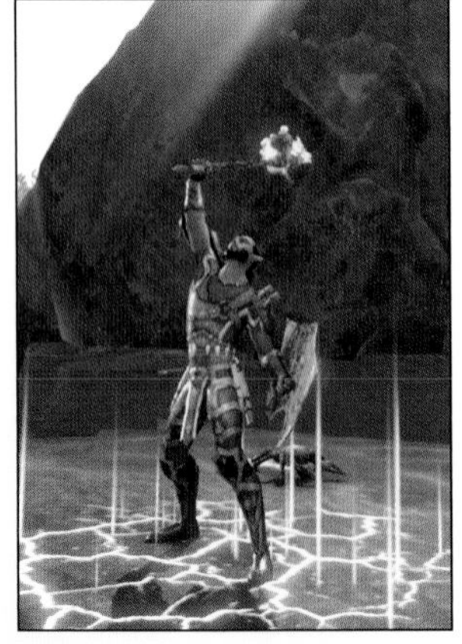

Buffs are temporary effects that boost a character's combat effectiveness. Conversely, debuffs are effects that compromise a character's performance in battle. Whether you're slaying creatures out in the wilderness or battling players in Cyrodiil, understanding the game's buff/debuff system is an important part of combat mastery.

A few basics on buff/debuff effects:

Depending on the effect, a buff/debuff might be granted by abilities, potions, poisons, or gear set bonuses. Most (but not all) buffs/debuffs can be acquired from more than one source.

Basic effects related to buffs and debuffs are standardized, meaning that they remain consistent regardless of the source. However, effect durations, potential targets, and the conditions that trigger an effect can vary from source to source.

Receiving the same buff/debuff from two sources doesn't double its power—it simply refreshes the effect's duration.

Most buff/debuff effects feature a "minor" variant and a "major" variant. Minor/major variants are treated as separate effects, meaning that you can utilize both variants simultaneously. For example, Minor Brutality and Major Brutality can be active at the same time.

ACQUIRING BUFFS

While it's often easy to identify buffs that support your playstyle, finding an appropriate source for that buff can be considerably more difficult.

Buff Sources

Base Buff	Effect	Sources	
		Minor	Major
Aegis	Decreases damage taken in dungeons and Trials	Set bonus	Set bonus
Berserk	Increases damage done	Ability, set bonus	Ability, set bonus
Brutality	Increases Weapon Damage	Ability, Alchemy	Ability, Alchemy, set bonus
Empower	Increases the damage of your next attack	Ability (this effect does not feature minor/major variants)	
Endurance	Increases Stamina Recovery	Ability	Ability, Alchemy
Evasion	Increases chance to dodge	Ability	Ability, set bonus
Expedition	Increases movement speed	Ability, set bonus	Ability, Alchemy, set bonus
Force	Increases Critical Damage	Ability, set bonus	Ability
Fortitude	Increases Health Recovery	Ability	Ability, Alchemy
Gallop	Increases mounted speed	—	Ability
Heroism	Grants Ultimate over time	Ability	Champion System, set bonus
Intellect	Increases Magicka Recovery	Ability	Ability, Alchemy
Mending	Increases healing done	Set bonus	Ability, set bonus
Prophecy	Increases Spell Critical	Ability, Alchemy	Ability, Alchemy, set bonus
Protection	Reduces damage taken	Ability, Alchemy, set bonus	Ability, set bonus
Resolve	Increases Physical Resistance	Ability, Alchemy	Ability, Alchemy, set bonus
Savagery	Increases Weapon Critical	Ability, Alchemy	Ability, Alchemy, set bonus
Slayer	Increases damage done in dungeons and Trials	Set bonus	Set bonus
Sorcery	Increases Spell Damage	Ability, Alchemy	Ability, Alchemy, set bonus
Toughness	Increases Maximum Health	Ability	—
Vitality	Increases healing received	Ability, set bonus	Ability, Alchemy, set bonus
Ward	Increases Spell Resistance	Ability, Alchemy	Ability, Alchemy, set bonus

All characters can make use of the same equipment and potions, but not all classes have access to the same abilities. It's recommended that new players review their skill lines to assess any buff-related abilities that might be of use.

BE INDISPENSABLE

While it's appropriate to prioritize buffs that benefit your character, consider investing in abilities that might benefit allies. Potential teammates tend to be more welcoming of players who are willing and able to provide some amount of group support.

AEGIS

Minor Aegis: Decreases damage taken in dungeons and Trials by 5%

Major Aegis: Decreases damage taken in dungeons and Trials by 15%

AEGIS

Minor Aegis and Major Aegis are only available as gear set bonuses.

BERSERK

Minor Berserk: Increases damage done by 8%

Major Berserk: Increases damage done by 25%

Abilities with Minor Berserk

Class	Skill Line	Ability	Ability Type	Buff Target
Any	Restoration Staff	Combat Prayer (Blessing of Protection morph)	Active	Group
Any	Fighters Guild	Camouflaged Hunter (Expert Hunter morph)	Active	Self
Nightblade	Assassination	Grim Focus	Active	Self
Nightblade	Assassination	Merciless Resolve (Grim Focus morph)	Active	Self
Nightblade	Assassination	Relentless Focus (Grim Focus morph)	Active	Self
Warden	Animal Companions	Bird of Prey (Falcon's Swiftness morph)	Active	Self

Abilities with Major Berserk

Class	Skill Line	Ability	Ability Type	Buff Target
Nightblade	Assassination	Reaper's Mark (Mark Target morph)	Active	Self
Sorcerer	Deadric Summoning	Summon Storm Atronach	Ultimate	Allies (Synergy)
Sorcerer	Deadric Summoning	Greater Storm Atronach (Summon Storm Atronach morph)	Ultimate	Allies (Synergy)
Sorcerer	Deadric Summoning	Summon Charged Atronach (Summon Storm Atronach morph)	Ultimate	Allies (Synergy)

BRUTALITY

Minor Brutality: Increases Weapon Damage by 5%

Major Brutality: Increases Weapon Damage by 20%

Abilities with Minor Brutality

Class	Skill Line	Ability	Ability Type	Buff Target
Dragonknight	Earthen Heart	Mountain's Blessing	Passive	Group

Abilities with Major Brutality

Class	Skill Line	Ability	Ability Type	Buff Target
Any	Dual Wield	Hidden Blade	Active	Self
Any	Dual Wield	Shrouded Daggers (Hidden Blade morph)	Active	Self
Any	Dual Wield	Flying Blade (Hidden Blade morph)	Active	Self
Any	Two-Handed	Momentum	Active	Self
Any	Two-Handed	Forward Momentum (Momentum morph)	Active	Self
Any	Two-Handed	Rally (Momentum morph)	Active	Self
Any	Werewolf	Rousing Roar (Roar morph)	Active	Allies
Dragonknight	Earthen Heart	Igneous Weapons (Molten Weapons morph)	Active	Group
Nightblade	Siphoning	Drain Power	Active	Self
Nightblade	Siphoning	Power Extraction (Drain Power morph)	Active	Self
Nightblade	Siphoning	Sap Essence (Drain Power morph)	Active	Self
Sorcerer	Storm Calling	Surge	Active	Self
Sorcerer	Storm Calling	Critical Surge (Surge morph)	Active	Self
Sorcerer	Storm Calling	Power Surge (Surge morph)	Active	Self

EMPOWER

Empower: Increases damage of next attack by 20%

EMPOWER

The Empower Active Effect doesn't feature minor/major variations.

Abilities with Empower

Class	Skill Line	Ability	Ability Type	Buff Target
Any	Mages Guild	Might of the Guild	Passive	Self
Any	Two-Handed	Wrecking Blow (Uppercut morph)	Active	Self
Dragonknight	Ardent Flame	Empowering Chains (Fiery Grip morph)	Active	Self
Nightblade	Assassination	Ambush (Teleport Strike morph)	Active	Self
Templar	Dawn's Wrath	Solar Flare	Active	Self
Templar	Dawn's Wrath	Dark Flare (Solar Flare morph)	Active	Self
Templar	Dawn's Wrath	Solar Barrage (Solar Flare morph)	Active	Self

ENDURANCE

Minor Endurance: Increases Stamina Recovery by 10%

Major Endurance: Increases Stamina Recovery by 20%

Abilities with Minor Endurance

Class	Skill Line	Ability	Ability Type	Buff Target
Any	Fighters Guild	Circle of Protection	Active	Area
Any	Fighters Guild	Turn Undead (Circle of Protection morph)	Active	Area
Any	Fighters Guild	Ring of Preservation (Circle of Protection morph)	Active	Area
Nightblade	Assassination	Relentless Focus (Grim Focus morph)	Active	Self
Templar	Restoring Light	Restoring Aura	Active	Self
Templar	Restoring Light	Radiant Aura (Restoring Aura morph)	Active	Self
Templar	Restoring Light	Repentance (Restoring Aura morph)	Active	Self
Warden	Green Balance	Enchanted Growth (Fungal Growth morph)	Active	Area

Abilities with Major Endurance

Class	Skill Line	Ability	Ability Type	Buff Target
Any	Dual Wield	Whirling Blades (Whirlwind morph)	Active	Self
Dragonknight	Draconic Power	Green Dragon Blood (Dragon Blood morph)	Active	Self
Templar	Restoring Light	Restoring Aura	Active	Group
Templar	Restoring Light	Radiant Aura (Restoring Aura morph)	Active	Group
Warden	Animal Companions	Falcon's Swiftness	Active	Self
Warden	Animal Companions	Deceptive Predator (Falcon's Swiftness morph)	Active	Self
Warden	Animal Companions	Bird of Prey (Falcon's Swiftness morph)	Active	Self

EVASION

Minor Evasion: Increases dodge chance by 5%

Major Evasion: Increases dodge chance by 15%

Abilities with Minor Evasion

Class	Skill Line	Ability	Ability Type	Buff Target
Warden	Animal Companions	Bird of Prey (Falcon's Swiftness morph)	Active	Self

Abilities with Major Evasion

Class	Skill Line	Ability	Ability Type	Buff Target
Any	Medium Armor	Evasion	Active	Self
Any	Medium Armor	Shuffle (Evasion morph)	Active	Self
Any	Medium Armor	Elude (Evasion morph)	Active	Self
Nightblade	Assassination	Blur	Active	Self
Nightblade	Assassination	Mirage (Blur morph)	Active	Self
Nightblade	Assassination	Double Take (Blur morph)	Active	Self

EXPEDITION

Minor Expedition: Increases movement speed by 10%

Major Expedition: Increases movement speed by 30%

Abilities with Minor Expedition

Class	Skill Line	Ability	Ability Type	Buff Target
Any	Vampire	Accelerating Drain (Drain Essence morph)	Active	Self
Any	Assault	Charging Maneuver (Rapid Maneuver morph)	Active	Self
Sorcerer	Storm Calling	Hurricane (Lightning Form morph)	Active	Self

Abilities with Major Expedition

Class	Skill Line	Ability	Ability Type	Buff Target
Any	Dual Wield	Quick Cloak (Blade Cloak morph)	Active	Self
Any	Dark Brotherhood	Padomaic Sprint	Passive	Self
Any	Bow	Hasty Retreat	Passive	Self
Any	Vampire	Elusive Mist (Mist Form morph)	Active	Self
Any	Assault	Rapid Maneuver	Active	Self
Any	Assault	Retreating Maneuver (Rapid Maneuver morph)	Active	Self
Any	Assault	Charging Maneuver (Rapid Maneuver morph)	Active	Self
Dragonknight	Ardent Flame	Fiery Grip	Active	Self
Dragonknight	Ardent Flame	Empowering Chains (Fiery Grip morph)	Active	Self
Dragonknight	Ardent Flame	Unrelenting Grip (Fiery Grip morph)	Active	Self
Nightblade	Assassination	Double Take (Blur morph)	Active	Self
Nightblade	Shadow	Path of Darkness	Active	Self
Nightblade	Shadow	Twisting Path (Path of Darkness morph)	Active	Self
Nightblade	Shadow	Refreshing Path (Path of Darkness morph)	Active	Self
Nightblade	Siphoning	Cripple	Active	Self
Nightblade	Siphoning	Debilitate (Cripple morph)	Active	Self
Nightblade	Siphoning	Crippling Grasp (Cripple morph)	Active	Self
Sorcerer	Storm Calling	Boundless Storm (Lightning Form morph)	Active	Self
Warden	Animal Companions	Falcon's Swiftness	Active	Self
Warden	Animal Companions	Deceptive Predator (Falcon's Swiftness morph)	Active	Self
Warden	Animal Companions	Bird of Prey (Falcon's Swiftness morph)	Active	Self

FORCE

Minor Force: Increases Critical Damage by 10%

Major Force: Increases Critical Damage by 15%

Abilities with Minor Force

Class	Skill Line	Ability	Ability Type	Buff Target
Any	Fighters Guild	Trap Beast	Active	Self
Any	Fighters Guild	Rearming Trap (Trap Beast morph)	Active	Self
Any	Fighters Guild	Lightweight Beast Trap (Trap Beast morph)	Active	Self
Any	Support	Stalwart Guard (Guard morph)	Active	Self and Ally

Abilities with Major Force

Class	Skill Line	Ability	Ability Type	Buff Target
Any	Assault	Aggressive Horn (War Horn morph)	Ultimate	Group
Any	Restoration Staff	Light's Champion (Panacea morph)	Ultimate	Self or Ally

FORTITUDE

Minor Fortitude: Increases Health Recovery by 10%

Major Fortitude: Increases Health Recovery by 20%

Abilities with Minor Fortitude

Class	Skill Line	Ability	Ability Type	Buff Target
Templar	Restoring Light	Restoring Aura	Active	Self
Templar	Restoring Light	Radiant Aura (Restoring Aura morph)	Active	Self
Templar	Restoring Light	Repentance (Restoring Aura morph)	Active	Self

Abilities with Major Fortitude

Class	Skill Line	Ability	Ability Type	Buff Target
Dragonknight	Draconic Power	Dragon Blood	Active	Self
Dragonknight	Draconic Power	Green Dragon Blood (Dragon Blood morph)	Active	Self
Dragonknight	Draconic Power	Coagulating Blood (Dragon Blood morph)	Active	Self
Templar	Restoring Light	Restoring Aura	Active	Group
Templar	Restoring Light	Radiant Aura (Restoring Aura morph)	Active	Group

GALLOP

Minor Gallop: (Unavailable)

Major Gallop: Increases mounted speed by 30%

Abilities with Major Gallop

Class	Skill Line	Ability	Ability Type	Buff Target
Any	Assault	Rapid Maneuver	Active	Self
Any	Assault	Retreating Maneuver (Rapid Maneuver morph)	Active	Self
Any	Assault	Charging Maneuver (Rapid Maneuver morph)	Active	Self

HEROISM

Minor Heroism: Grants 1 Ultimate every 1.5 seconds for nine seconds

Major Heroism: Grants 3 Ultimate every 1.5 seconds for eight seconds

Abilities with Minor Heroism

Class	Skill Line	Ability	Ability Type	Buff Target
Any	One Hand and Shield	Heroic Slash (Low Slash morph)	Active	Self
Any	Two-Handed	Carve (Cleave morph)	Active	Self

Abilities with Major Heroism

Class	Skill Line	Ability	Ability Type	Buff Target
Warden	Winter's Embrace	Shimmering Shield	Active	Self

INTELLECT

Minor Intellect: Increases Magicka Recovery by 10%

Major Intellect: Increases Magicka Recovery by 20%

Abilities with Minor Intellect

Class	Skill Line	Ability	Ability Type	Buff Target
Sorcerer	Deadric Summoning	Empowered Ward (Conjured Ward morph)	Active	Group
Templar	Restoring Light	Restoring Aura	Active	Self
Templar	Restoring Light	Radiant Aura (Restoring Aura morph)	Active	Self
Templar	Restoring Light	Repentance (Restoring Aura morph)	Active	Self
Warden	Green Balance	Enchanted Growth (Fungal Growth morph)	Active	Area

Abilities with Major Intellect

Class	Skill Line	Ability	Ability Type	Buff Target
Templar	Restoring Light	Radiant Aura (Restoring Aura morph)	Active	Group

MENDING

Minor Mending: Increases healing done by 8%

Major Mending: Increases healing done by 25%

Abilities with Minor Mending

Class	Skill Line	Ability	Ability Type	Buff Target
Templar	Restoring Light	Sacred Ground	Active	Self

Abilities with Major Mending

Class	Skill Line	Ability	Ability Type	Buff Target
Any	Restoration Staff	Essence Drain	Passive	Self
Dragonknight	Earthen Heart	Igneous Shield (Obsidian Shield morph)	Active	Self
Templar	Restoring Light	Sacred Ground	Passive	Self
Warden	Green Balance	Accelerated Growth	Passive	Self

PROPHECY

Minor Prophecy: Increases Spell Critical by 657

Major Prophecy: Increases Spell Critical by 2191

Abilities with Minor Prophecy

Class	Skill Line	Ability	Ability Type	Buff Target
Sorcerer	Dark Magic	Exploitation	Passive	Group

Abilities with Major Prophecy

Class	Skill Line	Ability	Ability Type	Buff Target
Any	Mages Guild	Magelight	Active	Self
Any	Mages Guild	Inner Light (Magelight morph)	Active	Self
Any	Mages Guild	Radiant Magelight (Magelight morph)	Active	Self
Dragonknight	Ardent Flame	Inferno	Active	Self
Dragonknight	Ardent Flame	Flames of Oblivion (Inferno morph)	Active	Self
Dragonknight	Ardent Flame	Cauterize (Inferno morph)	Active	Self
Templar	Dawn's Wrath	Sun Fire	Active	Self
Templar	Dawn's Wrath	Vampire's Bane (Sun Fire morph)	Active	Self
Templar	Dawn's Wrath	Reflective Light (Sun Fire morph)	Active	Self
Warden	Green Balance	Lotus Blossom (Lotus Flower morph)	Active	Self

PROTECTION

Minor Protection: Reduces damage taken by 8%

Major Protection: Reduces damage taken by 30%

Abilities with Minor Protection

Class	Skill Line	Ability	Ability Type	Buff Target
Any	Fighters Guild	Circle of Protection	Active	Area
Any	Fighters Guild	Turn Undead (Circle of Protection morph)	Active	Area
Any	Fighters Guild	Ring of Preservation (Circle of Protection morph)	Active	Area
Nightblade	Shadow	Dark Cloak (Shadow Cloak morph)	Active	Self
Templar	Restoring Light	Restoring Focus (Rune Focus morph)	Active	Self
Warden	Winter's Embrace	Ice Fortress (Frost Cloak morph)	Active	Self

Abilities with Major Protection

Class	Skill Line	Ability	Ability Type	Buff Target
Any	Restoration Staff	Light's Champion (Panacea morph)	Ultimate	Self or Ally
Nightblade	Shadow	Consuming Darkness	Ultimate	Group
Nightblade	Shadow	Bolstering Darkness (Consuming Darkness morph)	Ultimate	Group
Nightblade	Shadow	Veil of Blades (Consuming Darkness morph)	Ultimate	Group
Warden	Winter's Embrace	Sleet Storm	Ultimate	Group
Warden	Winter's Embrace	Northern Storm (Sleet Storm morph)	Ultimate	Group
Warden	Winter's Embrace	Permafrost (Sleet Storm morph)	Ultimate	Group

RESOLVE

Minor Resolve: Increases Physical Resistance by 1320

Major Resolve: Increases Physical Resistance by 5280

Abilities with Minor Resolve

Class	Skill Line	Ability	Ability Type	Buff Target
Any	Assault	Sturdy Horn (War Horn morph)	Ultimate	Group
Any	One Hand and Shield	Ransack (Puncture morph)	Active	Self
Any	Restoration Staff	Life Giver (Panacea morph)	Ultimate	Group
Any	Restoration Staff	Blessing of Protection	Active	Group
Any	Restoration Staff	Blessing of Restoration (Blessing of Protection morph)	Active	Group
Any	Restoration Staff	Combat Prayer (Blessing of Protection morph)	Active	Group
Dragonknight	Earthen Heart	Stone Giant (Stone Fist morph)	Active	Self
Nightblade	Assassination	Mirage (Blur morph)	Active	Self
Sorcerer	Daedric Summoning	Bound Armor	Active	Self
Sorcerer	Daedric Summoning	Bound Armaments (Bound Armor morph)	Active	Self
Sorcerer	Daedric Summoning	Bound Aegis (Bound Armor morph)	Active	Self

Abilities with Major Resolve

Class	Skill Line	Ability	Ability Type	Buff Target
Any	Heavy Armor	Immovable	Active	Self
Any	Heavy Armor	Immovable Brute (Immovable morph)	Active	Self
Any	Heavy Armor	Unstoppable (Immovable morph)	Active	Self
Any	Mages Guild	Balance (Equilibrium morph)	Active	Self
Dragonknight	Draconic Power	Spiked Armor	Active	Self
Dragonknight	Draconic Power	Hardened Armor (Spiked Armor morph)	Active	Self
Dragonknight	Draconic Power	Volatile Armor (Spiked Armor morph)	Active	Self
Nightblade	Shadow	Shadow Barrier	Passive	Self

Class	Skill Line	Ability	Ability Type	Buff Target
Sorcerer	Storm Calling	Lightning Form	Active	Self
Sorcerer	Storm Calling	Hurricane (Lightning Form morph)	Active	Self
Sorcerer	Storm Calling	Boundless Storm (Lightning Form morph)	Active	Self
Templar	Restoring Light	Rune Focus	Active	Self
Templar	Restoring Light	Channeled Focus (Rune Focus morph)	Active	Self
Templar	Restoring Light	Restoring Focus (Rune Focus morph)	Active	Self
Warden	Winter's Embrace	Frost Cloak	Active	Group
Warden	Winter's Embrace	Expansive Frost Cloak (Frost Cloak morph)	Active	Group
Warden	Winter's Embrace	Ice Fortress (Frost Cloak morph)	Active	Group

SAVAGERY

Minor Savagery: Increases Weapon Critical by 657

Major Savagery: Increases Weapon Critical by 2191

Abilities with Minor Savagery

Class	Skill Line	Ability	Ability Type	Buff Target
Nightblade	Assassination	Hemorrhage	Passive	Group

Abilities with Major Savagery

Class	Skill Line	Ability	Ability Type	Buff Target
Any	Fighters Guild	Expert Hunter	Active	Self
Any	Fighters Guild	Evil Hunter (Expert Hunter morph)	Active	Self
Any	Fighters Guild	Camouflaged Hunter (Expert Hunter morph)	Active	Self
Dragonknight	Ardent Flame	Flames of Oblivion (Inferno morph)	Active	Self
Templar	Aedric Spear	Biting Jabs (Puncturing Strikes morph)	Active	Self
Warden	Green Balance	Green Lotus (Lotus Flower morph)	Active	Self

SLAYER

Minor Slayer: Increases damage done in dungeons and Trials by 5%

Major Slayer: Increases damage done in dungeons and Trials by 15%

SLAYER

Minor Slayer and Major Slayer are only available as gear set bonuses.

SORCERY

Minor Sorcery: Increases Spell Damage by 5%

Major Sorcery: Increases Spell Damage by 20%

Abilities with Minor Sorcery

Class	Skill Line	Ability	Ability Type	Buff Target
Templar	Dawn's Wrath	Illuminate	Passive	Group

Abilities with Major Sorcery

Class	Skill Line	Ability	Ability Type	Buff Target
Any	Mages Guild	Entropy	Active	Self
Any	Mages Guild	Degeneration (Entropy morph)	Active	Self
Any	Mages Guild	Structured Entropy (Entropy morph)	Active	Self
Dragonknight	Earthen Heart	Molten Weapons	Active	Group
Dragonknight	Earthen Heart	Igneous Weapons (Molten Weapons morph)	Active	Group
Dragonknight	Earthen Heart	Molten Armaments (Molten Weapons morph)	Active	Group
Nightblade	Siphoning	Sap Essence (Drain Power morph)	Active	Self
Sorcerer	Storm Calling	Power Surge (Surge morph)	Active	Self
Warden	Animal Companions	Betty Netch	Active	Self
Warden	Animal Companions	Blue Betty (Betty Netch morph)	Active	Self

TOUGHNESS

Minor Toughness: Increases Maximum Health by 10%

Major Toughness: (Unavailable)

Abilities with Minor Toughness

Class	Skill Line	Ability	Ability Type	Buff Target
Any	Alliance War Assault	War Horn	Active	Self and Allies in Area
Warden	Green Balance	Maturation	Passive	Self or Ally

VITALITY

Minor Vitality: Increases healing received by 8%

Major Vitality: Increases healing received by 30%

Abilities with Minor Vitality

Class	Skill Line	Ability	Ability Type	Buff Target
Any	Undaunted	Bone Surge (Bone Shield morph)	Active	Allies (Synergy)
Any	Support	Mystic Guard (Guard morph)	Active	Self and Ally
Dragonknight	Draconic Power	Green Dragon Blood (Dragon Blood morph)	Active	Self
Nightblade	Siphoning	Swallow Soul (Strife morph)	Active	Self
Templar	Restoring Light	Restoring Focus (Rune Focus morph)	Active	Self

Abilities with Major Vitality

Class	Skill Line	Ability	Ability Type	Buff Target
Nightblade	Siphoning	Soul Siphon (Soul Shred morph)	Ultimate	Group

WARD

Minor Ward: Increases Spell Resistance by 1320

Major Ward: Increases Spell Resistance by 5280

Abilities with Minor Ward

Class	Skill Line	Ability	Ability Type	Buff Target
Any	Assault	Sturdy Horn (War Horn morph)	Ultimate	Group
Any	Restoration Staff	Life Giver (Panacea morph)	Ultimate	Ally
Any	Restoration Staff	Blessing of Protection	Active	Group
Any	Restoration Staff	Blessing of Restoration (Blessing of Protection morph)	Active	Group
Any	Restoration Staff	Combat Prayer (Blessing of Protection morph)	Active	Group
Dragonknight	Draconic Power	Reflective Plate (Reflective Scales morph)	Active	Self
Nightblade	Assassination	Mirage (Blur morph)	Active	Self
Sorcerer	Daedric Summoning	Bound Aegis (Bound Armor morph)	Active	Self

Abilities with Major Ward

Class	Skill Line	Ability	Ability Type	Buff Target
Any	Heavy Armor	Immovable	Active	Self
Any	Heavy Armor	Immovable Brute (Immovable morph)	Active	Self
Any	Heavy Armor	Unstoppable (Immovable morph)	Active	Self
Any	Mages Guild	Balance (Equilibrium morph)	Active	Self
Dragonknight	Draconic Power	Spiked Armor	Active	Self
Dragonknight	Draconic Power	Hardened Armor (Spiked Armor morph)	Active	Self
Dragonknight	Draconic Power	Volatile Armor (Spiked Armor morph)	Active	Self
Nightblade	Shadow	Shadow Barrier	Passive	Self
Sorcerer	Storm Calling	Lightning Form	Active	Self
Sorcerer	Storm Calling	Hurricane (Lightning Form morph)	Active	Self
Sorcerer	Storm Calling	Boundless Storm (Lightning Form morph)	Active	Self
Templar	Restoring Light	Rune Focus	Active	Self
Templar	Restoring Light	Channeled Focus (Rune Focus morph)	Active	Self
Templar	Restoring Light	Restoring Focus (Rune Focus morph)	Active	Self
Warden	Winter's Embrace	Frost Cloak	Active	Group
Warden	Winter's Embrace	Expansive Frost Cloak (Frost Cloak morph)	Active	Group
Warden	Winter's Embrace	Ice Fortress (Frost Cloak morph)	Active	Group

APPLYING DEBUFFS

Debuffs can be applied to targets by equipping certain armor sets, utilizing various poisons, or activating related abilities. As with buffs, selecting the best debuff source is just as important as identifying desired effects.

Debuff Sources

Base Debuff	Effect	Sources	
		Minor	Major
Breach	Decreases Spell Resistance	Ability, Alchemy	Ability
Cowardice	Increases Ultimate cost	Alchemy	—
Defile	Decreases healing received	Alchemy, set bonus	Ability, Disease Damage, set bonus
Enervation	Reduces Critical Damage	Alchemy	—
Fracture	Decreases Physical Resistance	Ability, Alchemy, set bonus	Ability
Lifesteal	Taking damage heals attackers	Ability	—
Magickasteal	Taking damage grants Magicka to attackers	Ability, set bonus	—
Maim	Decreases damage done	Ability, Alchemy, Shock Damage, set bonus	Ability
Mangle	Reduces Maximum Health	Ability	—
Uncertainty	Reduces Critical Chance	Alchemy	—
Vulnerability	Increases damage taken	Alchemy, set bonus	—

Again, it's recommended that new players review their character's skill lines to identify debuff-related abilities that might prove useful.Because a debuff is (ideally) applied to an enemy target, all debuff effects serve to benefit your allies in one way or another. During group content, coordinate with your teammates to ensure that priority enemies are continuously afflicted with negative effects.

BREACH

Minor Breach: Decreases Spell Resistance by 1320

Major Breach: Decreases Spell Resistance by 5280

Abilities with Minor Breach

Class	Skill Line	Ability	Ability Type	Buff Target
Templar	Dawn's Wrath	Power of the Light (Backlash morph)	Active	Enemy

Abilities with Major Breach

Class	Skill Line	Ability	Ability Type	Buff Target
Any	One Hand and Shield	Pierce Armor (Puncture morph)	Active	Enemy
Any	Destruction Staff	Weakness to Elements	Active	Enemy
Any	Destruction Staff	Elemental Susceptibility (Weakness to Elements morph)	Active	Enemy
Any	Destruction Staff	Elemental Drain (Weakness to Elements morph)	Active	Enemy
Nightblade	Assassination	Mark Target	Active	Enemy
Nightblade	Assassination	Piercing Mark (Mark Target morph)	Active	Enemy
Nightblade	Assassination	Reaper's Mark (Mark Target morph)	Active	Enemy
Warden	Animal Companions	Subterranean Assault (Scorch morph)	Active	Enemies

COWARDICE

Minor Cowardice: Increases Ultimate cost by 60%

Major Cowardice: (Unavailable)

COWARDICE

Currently, Minor Cowardice is only available through Alchemy recipes; there are no available sources of Major Cowardice.

DEFILE

Minor Defile: Decreases healing received by 15%

Major Defile: Decreases healing received by 30%

MINOR DEFILE

Currently, Minor Defile is only available through Alchemy recipes and gear set bonuses.

Abilities with Major Defile

Class	Skill Line	Ability	Ability Type	Buff Target
Any	One Hand and Shield	Reverberating Bash (Power Bash morph)	Active	Enemy
Any	Bow	Lethal Arrow (Snipe Morph)	Active	Enemy
Any	Werewolf	Claws of Anguish (Infectious Claws morph)	Active	Enemies
Dragonknight	Ardent Flame	Dragonknight Standard	Ultimate	Area
Dragonknight	Ardent Flame	Shifting Standard (Dragonknight Standard morph)	Ultimate	Area
Dragonknight	Ardent Flame	Standard of Might (Dragonknight Standard morph)	Ultimate	Area
Nightblade	Assassination	Death Stroke	Ultimate	Enemy
Nightblade	Assassination	Incapacitating Strike (Death Stroke morph)	Ultimate	Enemy
Nightblade	Assassination	Soul Harvest (Death Stroke morph)	Ultimate	Enemy
Templar	Dawn's Wrath	Dark Flare (Solar Flare morph)	Active	Enemies
Warden	Green Balance	Corruption Pollen (Healing Seed morph)	Active	Enemies

ENERVATION

Minor Enervation: Reduces Critical Damage done by 12%

Major Enervation: (Unavailable)

ENERVATION

Currently, Minor Enervation is only available through Alchemy recipes; there are no available sources of Major Enervation.

FRACTURE

Minor Fracture: Decreases Physical Resistance by 1320

Major Fracture: Decreases Physical Resistance by 5280

Abilities with Minor Fracture

Class	Skill Line	Ability	Ability Type	Buff Target
Any	Bow	Focused Aim (Snipe morph)	Active	Enemy
Templar	Dawn's Wrath	Power of the Light (Backlash morph)	Active	Enemy

Abilities with Major Fracture

Class	Skill Line	Ability	Ability Type	Buff Target
Any	One Hand and Shield	Puncture	Active	Enemy
Any	One Hand and Shield	Ransack (Puncture morph)	Active	Enemy
Any	One Hand and Shield	Pierce Armor (Puncture morph)	Active	Enemy
Dragonknight	Ardent Flame	Noxious Breath (Fiery Breath morph)	Active	Enemies
Nightblade	Assassination	Mark Target	Active	Enemy
Nightblade	Assassination	Piercing Mark (Mark Target morph)	Active	Enemy
Nightblade	Assassination	Reaper's Mark (Mark Target morph)	Active	Enemy
Nightblade	Shadow	Surprise Attack (Veiled Strike morph)	Active	Enemy
Warden	Animal Companions	Subterranean Assault (Scorch morph)	Active	Enemies

LIFESTEAL

Minor Lifesteal: Hits landed on afflicted target heal attackers for 600 Health every one second

Major Lifesteal: (Unavailable)

LIFESTEAL VARIABLES

The amount of Health granted by Lifesteal can be increased via effects that boost healing done or received. This makes Minor Lifesteal the only debuff that varies from caster to caster.

Abilities with Minor Lifesteal

Class	Skill Line	Ability	Ability Type	Buff Target
Any	Undaunted	Blood Alter	Active	Area
Any	Undaunted	Sanguine Alter (Blood Altar morph)	Active	Area
Any	Undaunted	Overflowing Altar (Blood Alter morph)	Active	Area
Any	Restoration Staff	Force Siphon	Active	Enemy
Any	Restoration Staff	Siphon Spirit (Force Siphon morph)	Active	Enemy
Any	Restoration Staff	Quick Siphon (Force Siphon morph)	Active	Enemy
Warden	Green Balance	Leeching Vines (Living Vines morph)	Active	Enemies

MAGICKASTEAL

Minor Magickasteal: Hits landed on afflicted target grant attackers 400 Magicka every one second

Major Magickasteal: (Unavailable)

Abilities with Minor Magickasteal

Class	Skill Line	Ability	Ability Type	Buff Target
Any	Destruction Staff	Elemental Drain (Weakness to Elements morph)	Active	Enemy
Any	Restoration Staff	Siphon Spirit (Force Siphon morph)	Active	Enemy
Templar	Restoring Light	Restoring Aura	Active	Enemies
Templar	Restoring Light	Radiant Aura (Restoring Aura morph)	Active	Enemies

MAIM

Minor Maim: Decreases damage done by 15%

Major Maim: Decreases damage done by 30%

Abilities with Minor Maim

Class	Skill Line	Ability	Ability Type	Buff Target
Any	One Hand and Shield	Low Slash	Active	Enemy
Any	One Hand and Shield	Deep Slash (Low Slash morph)	Active	Enemies
Any	One Hand and Shield	Heroic Slash (Low Slash morph)	Active	Enemy
Dragonknight	Draconic Power	Choking Talons (Dark Talons morph)	Active	Enemies
Nightblade	Shadow	Mass Hysteria (Aspect of Terror morph)	Active	Enemies
Nightblade	Shadow	Summon Shade	Active	Enemies
Nightblade	Shadow	Dark Shades (Summon Shade morph)	Active	Enemies
Nightblade	Shadow	Shadow Image (Summon Shade morph)	Active	Enemies

Abilities with Major Maim

Class	Skill Line	Ability	Ability Type	Buff Target
Templar	Dawn's Wrath	Nova	Ultimate	Area
Templar	Dawn's Wrath	Solar Prison (Nova morph)	Ultimate	Area
Templar	Dawn's Wrath	Solar Disturbance (Nova morph)	Ultimate	Area
Warden	Winter's Embrace	Frozen Device	Active	Area

MANGLE

Minor Mangle: Reduces Maximum Health by 10%

Major Mangle: (Unavailable)

Abilities with Minor Mangle

Class	Skill Line	Ability	Ability Type	Buff Target
Any	Destruction Staff	Pulsar (Impulse morph)	Active	Area

UNCERTAINTY

Minor Uncertainty: Reduces Critical Chance by 657

Major Uncertainty: (Unavailable)

ALTERNATIVE SOURCES: MINOR UNCERTAINTY

Currently, Minor Uncertainty is only available through Alchemy recipes; there are no available sources of Major Uncertainty.

VULNERABILITY

Minor Vulnerability: Increases damage taken by 8%

Major Vulnerability: (Unavailable)

MINOR VULNERABILITY

Currently, Minor Vulnerability is only available through Alchemy recipes and gear set bonuses; there are no available sources of Major Vulnerability.

MUNDUS STONES

Mundus Stones are ancient monuments imbued with the power of the constellations, and visiting one of these stones allows your character to benefit from an Attribute-enhancing boon.

Each Mundus Stone offers a different boon, but a character can only have one boon at a time. A claimed boon never fades, but it can be replaced by the effect of a different Mundus Stone.

There are no Mundus Stones in Vvardenfell, but these useful objects can be found scattered throughout the rest of Tamriel.

Location

Mundus Stone	Boon Effect	Aldmeri Dominion	Daggerfall Covenant	Ebonheart Pact
The Apprentice	Increases Spell Damage by 167	Reaper's March	Bangkorai	The Rift
The Atronach	Increases Magicka Recovery by 198	Greenshade	Rivenspire	Shadowfen
The Lady	Increases Physical Resistance by 1980	Auridon	Glenumbra	Stonefalls
The Lord	Increases Maximum Health by 1452	Grahtwood	Stormhaven	Deshaan
The Lover	Increases Spell Resistance by 1980	Auridon	Glenumbra	Stonefalls
The Mage	Increases Maximum Magicka by 1320	Grahtwood	Stormhaven	Deshaan
The Ritual	Increases healing received by 10%	Malabal Tor	Alik'r Desert	Eastmarch
The Serpent	Increases Stamina Recovery by 198	Greenshade	Rivenspire	Shadowfen
The Shadow	Increases Critical Damage by 12%	Greenshade	Rivenspire	Shadowfen
The Steed	Increases movement speed by 5% and Health Recovery by 198	Reaper's March	Bangkorai	The Rift
The Thief	Increases Critical Chance by 11%	Malabal Tor	Alik'r Desert	Eastmarch
The Tower	Increases Maximum Stamina by 1320	Grahtwood	Stormhaven	Deshaan
The Warrior	Increases Weapon Damage by 167	Malabal Tor	Alik'r Desert	Eastmarch

Apart from the Lord, all Mundus Stones can also be found in Cyrodiil.

CHAMPIONS

Character progression doesn't stop at Level 50. Max-level characters become Champions capable of earning powerful new Passive Abilities. High-ranking Champions can make use of better equipment and consumables, and all Champions have access to more difficult game content.

VETERAN CONTENT

Difficulty settings for Dungeons and Trials can be found in the Group Menu. While in a group, only the group leader's settings will be used.

THE CHAMPION SYSTEM

UNLOCKING THE CHAMPION SYSTEM

When your first character reaches Level 50, the Champion System is unlocked across your entire account. Once this happens, all of your characters—even those you might create down the line—have access to the Champion System. Use the Champion System menu to review available Passives and manage your character's Champion Points.

A TRUE CHAMPION

While low-level characters can benefit from the Champion System, a character only becomes a Champion after reaching Level 50.

CHAMPION POINTS

When your character reaches Level 50, they receive a Champion Bar. The Champion Bar works much like the Experience Bar it replaces: it fills as your character performs actions like killing monsters and completing quests. Each time the Champion Bar reaches capacity, your character receives a Champion Point (CP). The Champion Bar then resets, and the process starts over.

Champion Points come in three color-coded varieties. Each time you receive a Champion Point, you begin working toward the next color in the sequence:

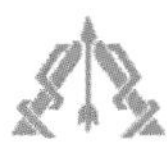

Green Champion Points can only be spent within the Thief Constellation Group.

Blue Champion Points can only be spent within the Mage Constellation Group.

Red Champion Points can only be spent within the Warrior Constellation Group.

Use earned Champion Points to unlock and upgrade the Passive Abilities found within the Champion System menu.

CHAMPION POINT SCALING

As your character progress through the Champion System, the Experience needed to earn a Champion Point increases—the more points you have, the more Experience you'll need to advance.

Each time a Champion Bar reaches capacity, all the characters on your account receive the indicated Champion Point. This doesn't mean Champion Points are shared between characters—each character has its own pool of points to spend.

Only Level 50 characters can earn Champion Points, but all of your characters can use them to unlock Passive Abilities in the Champion System menu.

A HEAD START

When you first unlock the Champion System, all of your characters receive 10 Champion Points.

CHAMPION POINT CAP

While there's no limit to the number of Champion Points you can earn, there are limits on how many points are available for use within the Champion System menu. Currently, you can spend a maximum of 630 Champion Points:

- 210 green Champion Points (for use in the Thief Constellation Group)
- 210 blue Champion Points (for use in the Mage Constellation Group)
- 210 red Champion Points (for use in the Warrior Constellation Group)

Earned: 211/210 **Available:** 203

Once you reach the Champion Point Cap, any additional points you earn are reflected in the Champion System's point tallies. If the Cap is raised in a future game update, your extra points will be made available for use.

CHAMPION RANK

Champion Rank serves the same purpose as your character's level. It indicates general progression and determines the equipment and consumables your character can use.

A character's Champion Rank is a reflection of the total number of Champion Points that can be (or have been) spent in the Champion System menu. When your first character reaches Level 50, it's automatically granted Champion Rank 10. Each additional Champion Point raises your character's rank by one level.

Due to the Champion Point Cap, Champion 630 is currently the highest rank a character can achieve.

ENLIGHTENMENT

Unlocking the Champion System also unlocks Enlightenment. While active, Enlightenment boosts Experience gains earned by Champion characters.

Enlightenment accumulates when you're offline. Your account can store up to 12 days of Enlightenment (1,200,000 points) at one time.

Available Enlightenment is indicated by a translucent glow within your character's Champion Bar. As your Champion earns Experience, your supply of Enlightenment is depleted.

SHARING RESOURCES

Enlightenment is an account-wide resource. It can't be used by low-level characters, but earning Experience with any Champion will deplete your supply.

CHAMPION SYSTEM MENU

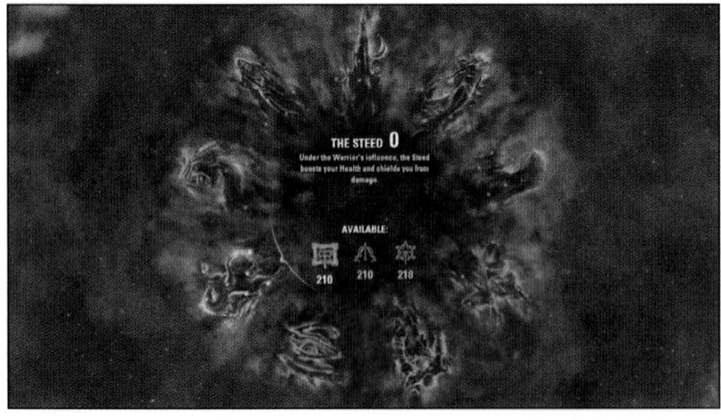

The Champion System menu allows you to convert your hard-earned Champion Points into powerful Passive Abilities. The menu's main screen features available Champion Points surrounded by three color-coded Constellation Groups:

The Thief: Green Constellations feature effects that improve utility. Investing in any green Constellation also boosts Maximum Stamina.

The Mage: Blue Constellations feature effects that improve damage output. Investing in any blue Constellation also boosts Maximum Magicka.

The Warrior: Red Constellations feature effects that improve defense. Investing in any red Constellation also boosts Maximum Health.

Each Constellation Group consists of three Minor Constellations. Highlight a Minor Constellation of your choice, and then zoom in to review the Passives it offers.

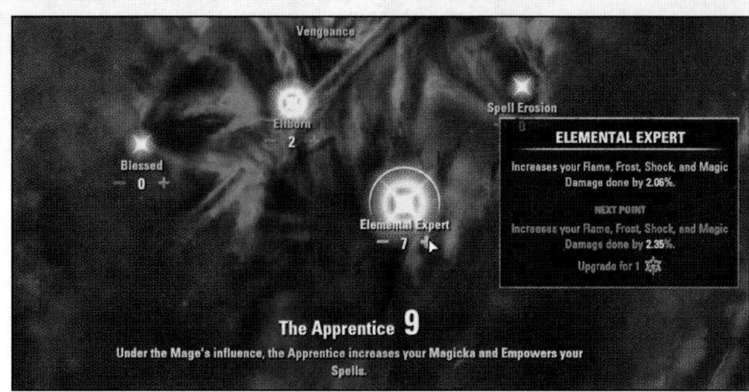

Once inside a Minor Constellation, you'll find eight stars. Four of these stars feature variable Passives—each time you invest a Champion Point in one of these stars, its effect becomes more potent.

DIMINISHING RETURNS

You can spend up to 100 Champion Points on a single star. Once you've done so, your character receives the star's greatest possible effect. However, as you invest in a star, each Champion Point you spend has less of an impact.

The remaining stars represent bonus effects that become active as the Minor Constellation increases in rank:

- At Rank 10, the first bonus effect is activated.
- At Rank 30, the second bonus effect is activated.
- At Rank 75, the third bonus effect is activated.
- At Rank 120, all four bonus effects are active.

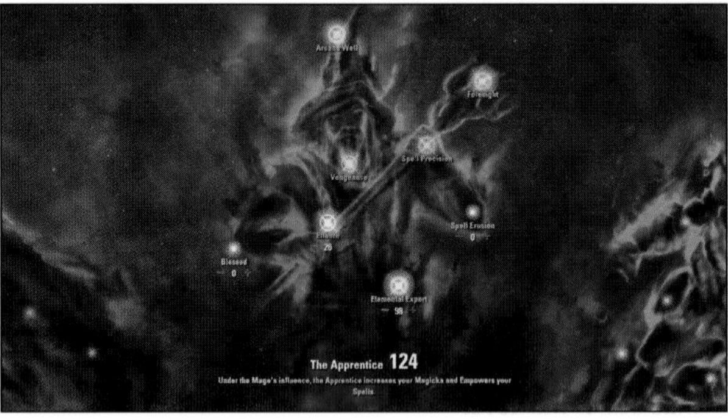

Each Champion Point you spend within a Minor Constellation increases its rank by one level, which means activating all of a Constellation's bonus effects requires an investment of at least 120 Champion Points.

REDISTRIBUTING CHAMPION POINTS

If you want to reclaim spent Champion Points, you can do so through the Champion System menu. Redistribution carries a flat fee of 3,000 gold, regardless of how many points you've earned or invested.

PASSIVE EFFECTS

The Champion System's Passive Abilities can be very powerful, but they also require a heavy investment—it takes 100 appropriately colored Champion Points to receive the full benefit of a single Passive Ability, which brings up some potentially difficult choices.

Should you maximize the effects of a small number of Passive Abilities? Would it be better to invest in a variety of less potent Passives? Is it worth sticking with a Minor Constellation to receive all of its bonus effects? In the end, it all comes down to a matter of personal preference.

It can take quite a while to reach the Champion Point Cap, giving you plenty of time to evaluate the effects of each point you spend. Whether you use your points to bolster your character's strengths or mitigate weaknesses, it can take a lot of trial and error to find the most useful combination of Passive Abilities.

CONSTELLATION GROUP: THE THIEF

THE TOWER

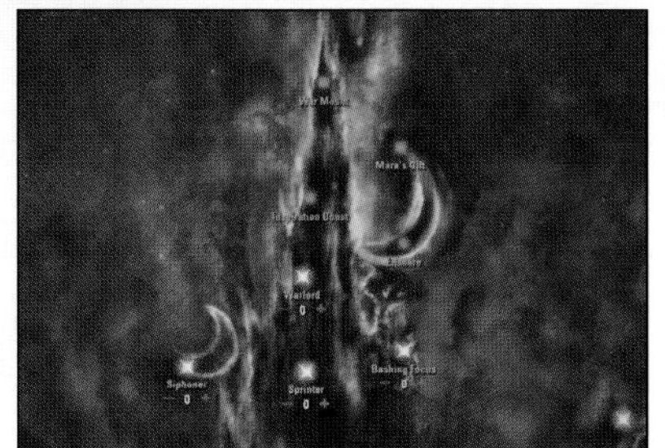

The Tower raises Maximum Stamina and improves the efficiency of basic actions:

Bashing Focus: Reduces the cost of Bash by up to 35%.

Siphoner: When you deal damage with a light or heavy attack, you decrease the enemy's Health, Magicka, and Stamina Recovery by up to 15% for three seconds.

Sprinter: Reduces the cost of Sprint by up to 35%.

Warlord: Reduces the cost of Break Free by up to 25%.

Bonus Stars: The Tower

Minimum Rank	Name	Effect
The Tower Rank 10	Ensnare	When you use Bash, you have a 33% chance to reduce the enemy's movement speed by 20% for three seconds.
The Tower Rank 30	Inspiration Boost	Increases your crafting Inspiration gained by 20%.
The Tower Rank 75	Mara's Gift	When you die, you heal all allies within eight meters of you for 3300 Health.
The Tower Rank 120	War Mount	Improves your mastery with mounts, removing all mount Stamina costs outside of combat.

THE LOVER

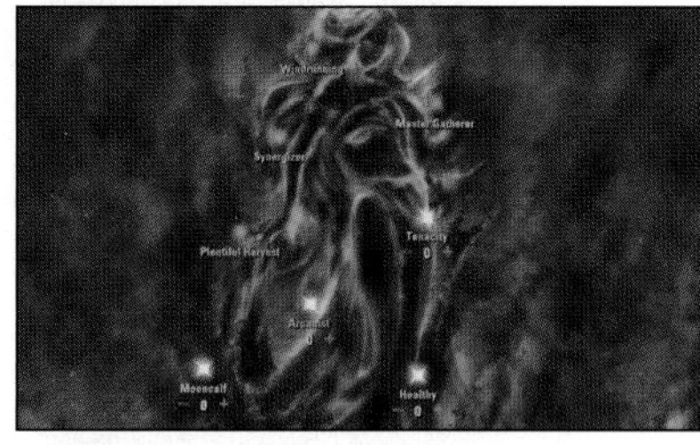

The Lover raises Maximum Stamina and accelerates resource generation:

Arcanist: Increases your Magicka Recovery by up to 15%.

Healthy: Increases your Health Recovery by up to 15%.

Mooncalf: Increases your Stamina Recovery by up to 15%.

Tenacity: Increases the Magicka and Stamina your fully charged heavy attacks restore by up to 15%.

Bonus Stars: The Lover

Minimum Rank	Name	Effect
The Lover Rank 10	Plentiful Harvest	You have a 10% chance to gain double the yield from normal resource nodes.
The Lover Rank 30	Synergizer	When you activate a Synergy ability, you generate 2 Ultimate.
The Lover Rank 75	Master Gatherer	Reduces your gathering time by 50%.
The Lover Rank 120	Windrunning	Increases your movement speed and mounted speed by 2%. Increases your Health and Magicka Recovery by 10% while sprinting.

THE SHADOW

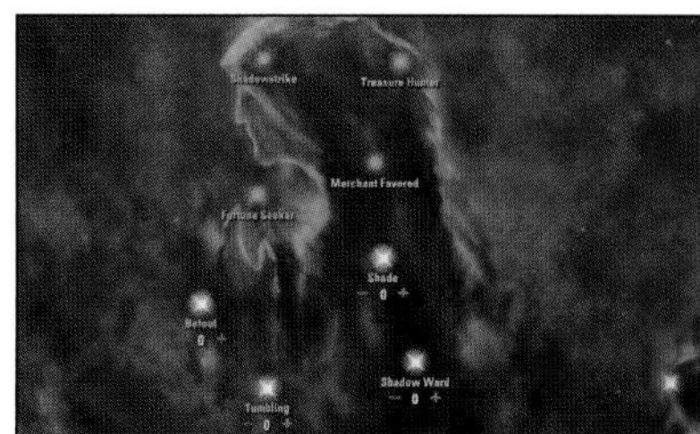

The Shadow raises Maximum Stamina and improves the efficiency of basic actions:

Befoul: Increases the effectiveness of your healing reduction abilities by up to 55%.

Shade: Reduces the cost of Sneak by up to 35%.

Shadow Ward: Reduces the cost of Block by up to 25%.

Tumbling: Reduces the cost of Roll Dodge by up to 25%.

Bonus Stars: The Shadow

Minimum Rank	Name	Effect
The Shadow Rank 10	Fortune Seeker	Increases the amount of gold you find in treasure chests and Safeboxes by 50%.
The Shadow Rank 30	Merchant Favored	Reduces the cost of repairing your armor by 10%.
The Shadow Rank 75	Treasure Hunter	Increases the quality of items you find in treasure chests.
The Shadow Rank 120	Shadowstrike	When you kill an enemy with a heavy attack, you become invisible for 2.5 seconds. This effect can occur once every five seconds.

CONSTELLATION GROUP: THE MAGE

THE APPRENTICE

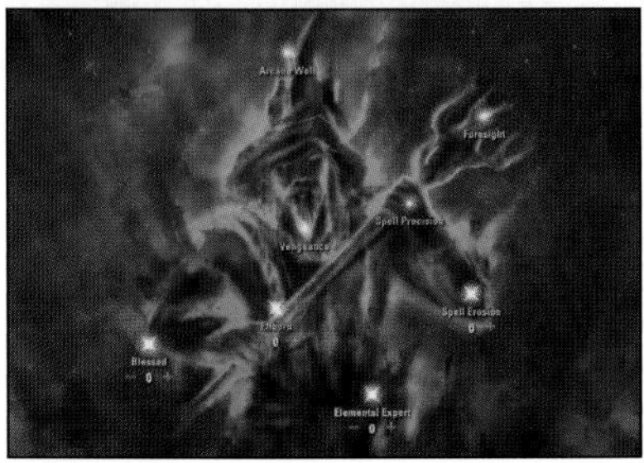

The Apprentice raises Maximum Magicka and improves spellcasting:

Blessed: Increases your healing done by up to 15%.

Elemental Expert: Increases your Flame, Shock, and Magic Damage done by up to 15%.

Elfborn: Increases the damage and healing of your Critical Strikes with Magicka abilities by up to 25%.

Spell Erosion: Increases your Spell Penetration by up to 5280.

Bonus Stars: The Apprentice

Minimum Rank	Name	Effect
The Apprentice Rank 10	Vengeance	When you block three spells within 10 seconds of each other, your next Magicka ability used within five seconds will always be a Critical Strike.
The Apprentice Rank 30	Spell Precision	Increases your Spell Critical by 12%.
The Apprentice Rank 75	Foresight	When you drink a potion, the cost of your next Magicka ability used within seven seconds is reduced by 80%.
The Apprentice Rank 120	Arcane Well	When you kill an enemy, you have a 20% chance to restore 1150 Magicka for up to three friendly targets within 2.5 meters of the enemy.

THE ATRONACH

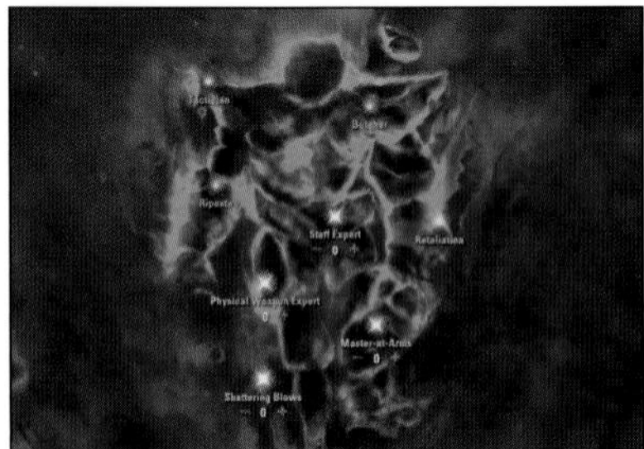

The Atronach raises Maximum Magicka and increases the damage done by basic attacks:

Master-at-Arms: Increases your damage done with direct-damage attacks by up to 25%.

Physical Weapon Expert: Increases your damage done with light and heavy attacks for Two-Handed, One Hand and Shield, Dual Wield, and bow weapons by up to 35%.

Shattering Blows: Increases your damage done to enemies with a damage shield by up to 25%.

Staff Expert: Increases your damage done with light and heavy attacks for destruction and restoration staves by up to 35%.

Bonus Stars: The Atronach

Minimum Rank	Name	Effect
The Atronach Rank 10	Retaliation	When you block a heavy attack, your next light attack used within seven seconds deals an additional 30% damage.
The Atronach Rank 30	Riposte	When you block an attack, you have a 15% chance to deal 2437 Physical Damage to the enemy. This effect can occur once every five seconds.
The Atronach Rank 75	Butcher	Increases your damage done with light and heavy attacks by 5% to enemies below 25% Health.
The Atronach Rank 120	Tactician	When you use dodge roll to dodge an attack, you set the enemy off-balance.

THE RITUAL

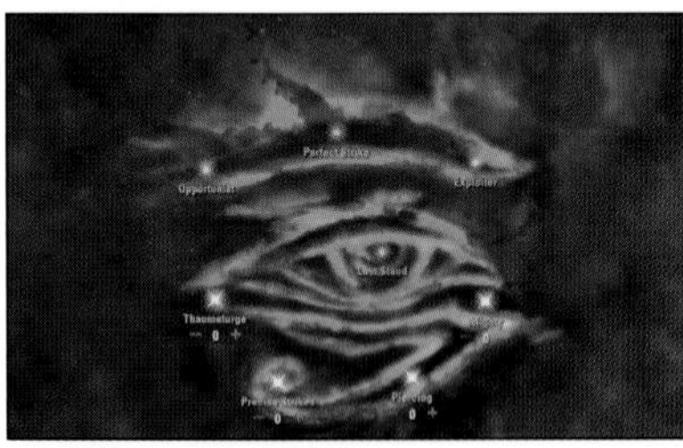

The Ritual raises Maximum Magicka while enhancing physical attacks and damage over time:

Mighty: Increases your Physical, Poison, and Disease Damage done by up to 15%.

Piercing: Increases your Physical Penetration by up to 5280.

Precise Strikes: Increases the damage and healing of your Critical Strikes with Stamina abilities by up to 25%.

Thaumaturge: Increases your damage done with damage-over-time effects by up to 25%.

Bonus Stars: The Ritual

Minimum Rank	Name	Effect
The Ritual Rank 10	Opportunist	When you interrupt an enemy, your next Physical Damage ability used within seven seconds deals an additional 15% damage.
The Ritual Rank 30	Perfect Strike	Increases your Weapon Critical by 12%.
The Ritual Rank 75	Exploiter	Increases your damage done against off-balance enemies by 10%.
The Ritual Rank 120	Last Stand	When you fall below 20% Health, you gain Major Heroism, granting 3 Ultimate every 1.5 seconds for eight seconds. This effect can occur once every 20 seconds.

CONSTELLATION GROUP: THE WARRIOR

THE STEED

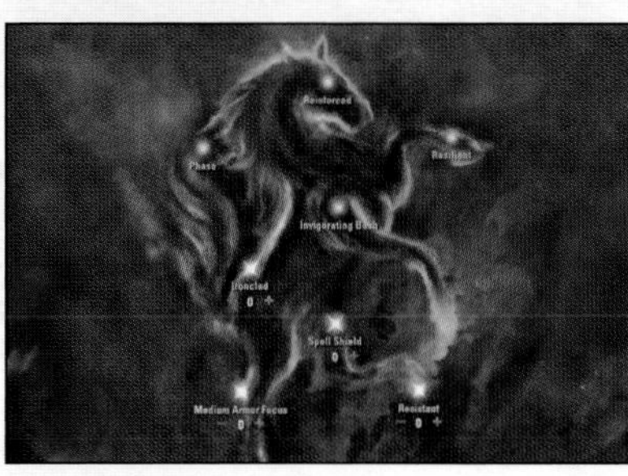

The Steed raises Maximum Health and shields you from damage:

Ironclad: Reduces your damage taken against direct-damage attacks by up to 25%.

Medium Armor Focus: Increases your Physical Resistance by up to 5281 while wearing five or more pieces of Medium Armor.

Resistant: Increases your Critical Resistance by up to 1650.

Spell Shield: Increases your Spell Resistance by up to 5280.

Bonus Stars: The Steed

Minimum Rank	Name	Effect
The Steed Rank 10	Invigorating Bash	When you use Bash, you have a 20% chance to heal for 589 Health.
The Steed Rank 30	Phase	When you use Roll Dodge, your Physical and Spell Resistance are increased by 660 for three seconds.
The Steed Rank 75	Resilient	When you take Critical Damage, you heal for 117 Health.
The Steed Rank 120	Reinforced	When you activate Block, you gain a damage shield that absorbs 1254 damage for three seconds. This effect can occur once every 10 seconds.

THE LADY

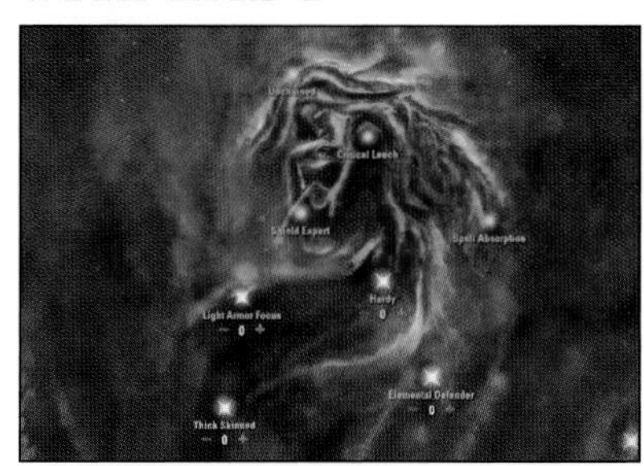

The Lady raises Maximum Health and protects you from negative effects:

Elemental Defender: Reduces your damage taken from Flame, Frost, Shock, and Magic Damage by up to 15%.

Hardy: Reduces your damage taken from Physical, Poison, and Disease Damage by up to 15%.

Light Armor Focus: Increases your Physical Resistance by up to 5280 while wearing five or more pieces of light armor.

Thick Skinned: Reduces your damage taken from damage-over-time effects by up to 25%.

Bonus Stars: The Lady

Minimum Rank	Name	Effect
The Lady Rank 10	Spell Absorption	When you take Flame, Frost, Shock, Magic, or Oblivion Damage equal to 30% of your Maximum Health, you restore 3465 Magicka. This effect can occur once every 10 seconds.
The Lady Rank 30	Shield Expert	Increases the armor of any shield you equip by 75%.
The Lady Rank 75	Critical Leech	When you deal direct Critical Damage, you heal for 330 Health. This effect can occur once every five seconds.
The Lady Rank 120	Unchained	When you use Break Free, the cost of your next Stamina ability used within five seconds is reduced by 80%.

THE LORD

The Lord raises Maximum Health and improves your Vitality:

Bastion: Increases the effectiveness of your damage shields by up to 25%.

Expert Defender: Reduces your damage taken from light and heavy attacks by up to 35%.

Heavy Armor Focus: Increases your Physical Resistance by up to 5280 while wearing five or more pieces of heavy armor.

Quick Recovery: Increases your healing received by up to 15%.

Bonus Stars: The Lord

Minimum Rank	Name	Effect
The Lord Rank 10	Field Physician	While you're resurrecting another player, your damage taken is reduced by 15%.
The Lord Rank 30	Infusion	When you resurrect another player, you increase their Magicka Recovery by 230 for eight seconds.
The Lord Rank 75	Revival	When you're resurrected by another player, you gain a damage shield that absorbs 10230 damage for five seconds.
The Lord Rank 120	Determination	When you drink a potion, you gain a damage shield that absorbs 1287 damage for 15 seconds.

CURSES: VAMPIRES AND WEREWOLVES

The game contains two cursed afflictions: Vampirism and Lycanthropy. Each of these afflictions grants access to exclusive skill lines, and each curse offers its own mix of positive and negative effects.

Curses are featured in some very effective builds, but they aren't for everyone. It's up to you to weigh the potential benefits against the drawbacks. If you're unsure whether a character would benefit from one of these afflictions, there are few things you might consider:

- Each curse benefits from different Attributes. Vampirism is a popular choice for Magicka-heavy builds; Lycanthropy is generally preferred for Stamina-heavy builds.
- Curses are curable, but they can only be removed with help from a specialist. You can acquire and cure these afflictions as many times as you like.
- A character can only have one curse at a time.
- The Fighters Guild skill line features abilities that do extra damage against Undead, Daedra, and Werewolves. Players with Vampirism are always considered Undead; players with Lycanthropy are only considered Werewolves while they're transformed. Neither of these afflictions prevents a character from joining the Fighters Guild.

VAMPIRISM

Vampires use powerful magic to damage, stun, and elude their enemies. With high damage potential, effective damage reduction, and some very nice stealth Passives, Vampirism has a lot to offer.

OVERVIEW

Developing the Vampire skill line takes a bit of time and a good number of Skill Points. A new Vampire won't receive many benefits from their curse, but those who stick with it have access to:

- Powerful new Magicka/Ultimate abilities
- Up to 10% additional Magicka/Stamina Recovery
- Multiple options for damage reduction
- Improved stealth movement speed
- The ability to transmit Vampirism to willing players

Of course, Vampirism has a few drawbacks. Afflicted players can expect:

- Up to 25% more damage taken from flame attacks
- Up to 75% less Health Recovery
- Up to 20% more damage taken from Fighters Guild abilities

Most of these benefits and penalties are affected by the stage of your Vampirism—a value that changes based on how often you feed and/or use Vampire abilities. Put simply, you must accept harsher penalties to enjoy greater benefits.

ACTIVE EFFECTS

The Vampire skill line features only a few Active Effects:

- **Bat Swarm** is a damage-focused Ultimate Ability that blends area-of-effect and damage-over-time effects.
- **Drain Essence** is a channeled attack that also serves as a self-heal and single-target stun.
- **Mist Form** grants a brief window of powerful damage reduction and immunity to all Disabling Effects (including roots and snares).

All of these abilities can be morphed to improve or augment their effects, but the Vampire skill line essentially offers a powerful, damage-focused Ultimate Ability, a channeled self-heal, and a uniquely powerful escape ability.

STAGES OF VAMPIRISM

As a Vampire's need for blood increases, the effects of Vampirism become more potent:

Stage 1: Your thirst is sated. Apart from your status as Undead, your affliction carries no penalties or benefits.

Stage 2: You suffer a 25% penalty to Health Recovery and take 15% more damage from fire. However, the casting cost of all Vampire abilities is reduced by 7%.

Stage 3: You suffer a 50% penalty to Health Recovery and take 20% more damage from fire. The casting cost of all Vampire abilities is reduced by 14%.

Stage 4: You suffer a 75% penalty to Health Recovery and take 25% more damage from fire. The casting cost of all Vampire abilities is reduced by 21%.

Several of the Vampire Passive Abilities also have stage requirements. This means that higher Vampirism stages grant additional benefits as you progress (and invest in) the Vampire skill line.

LOOKING THE PART

Stage progression is also reflected in your character's appearance.

STAGE MANAGEMENT

Vampirism progresses by one stage every six hours, but using any Vampire ability advances the stage timer by 30 minutes.

Feeding lowers Vampirism by one full stage. To do this, sneak up behind a humanoid target and press your designated Synergy key (or buttons).

FEEDING WITH THE BLADE OF WOE

The process of feeding is much like using the Dark Brotherhood's Blade of Woe. If you have both abilities, your distance from the target determines whether you'll feed or perform an assassination.

Stay back to feed; move close to activate the Blade of Woe.

Proper stage management is an important part of being an effective Vampire. For example, reverting to Stage 1 is a great way to prepare for dungeons or Trials that feature excessive Flame Damage. With each new situation, try to weigh the benefits of Vampirism against its drawbacks, and then make any adjustments that might serve to improve your performance.

LYCANTHROPY

Swift and savage, Werewolves slash, bite, and tear through their enemies. They're strongest in packs, but even a lone Werewolf can send its enemies running in terror.

OVERVIEW

Compared to Vampirism, Lycanthropy is very much an all-or-nothing affliction. Transforming into a Werewolf grants you a number of benefits and penalties. Outside of Werewolf form, Lycanthropy has little effect on your character.

PERSISTENT EFFECTS

There are only two Werewolf-related effects that don't require an active transformation:

- Immunity to Vampirism
- A 15% bonus to Stamina Recovery (if a Werewolf Ultimate is ability-slotted)

TRANSFORMATION EFFECTS

Getting the most out of the Werewolf skill line takes a great deal of time—and more than a few Skill Points—but even new Werewolves are granted powerful benefits during a transformation:

- 9966 additional Physical Resistance
- 9966 additional Spell Resistance
- Light attacks that inflict Bleeding
- Increased sprint speed

Heavy investment in the Werewolf skill line grants even greater benefits:

- Powerful new abilities
- Longer-lasting transformations
- Up to 100% more Stamina generated from heavy attacks
- Up to 18% more Weapon Damage
- The ability to transmit Lycanthropy to willing players

The penalties associated with Lycanthropy are active during all transformations, regardless of how heavily you invest in the Werewolf skill line. Whenever you're in Werewolf form, you can expect:

- 25% more damage taken from Poison Attacks
- Up to 20% more damage taken from Fighters Guild abilities
- The inability to use weapons or non-Werewolf skills

ACTIVE EFFECTS

For the most part, Werewolf abilities can only be used while Werewolf form is active—the exception being the Ultimate Ability, which triggers the transformation. Luckily, this skill line contains all the abilities you'll need for an effective transformation:

- **Werewolf Transformation** changes your character into a savage beast for a short time. While slotted, this Ultimate Ability also increases Stamina Recovery by 15%.
- **Pounce** is a direct-damage gap closer.
- **Hircine's Bounty** is a Magicka-based instant heal.
- **Roar** serves as a short-range area-of-effect fear.
- **Piercing Howl** combines heavy single-target damage with a Stun effect.
- **Infectious Claws** is a cone area-of-effect attack with a considerable damage-over-time effect.

As a whole, Werewolf abilities offer a good mix of damage, crowd control, and self-healing. Available morphs feature a variety of useful effects, adding considerable utility to an already well-rounded skill set. An appropriately built Werewolf can buff allies, debuff enemies, produce Synergies, and more.

WEREWOLF TRANSFORMATION

The Werewolf Transformation ability carries a heavy Ultimate cost, and because the Werewolf skill line progresses fairly slowly, Lycanthropy represents a serious investment. If you intend to embrace this affliction, take steps to ensure you make the most of each transformation:

Most Werewolf abilities are Stamina-based, so your damage scales Maximum Stamina, Weapon Damage, and Weapon Critical. Effective Werewolves generally focus on these stats.

Transforming into a Werewolf activates a new Action Bar. Avoid placing any non-Werewolf abilities in these slots.

Killing monsters while you're in Werewolf mode is the only way to rank up the Werewolf skill line. If you hope to gain access to new Werewolf abilities, transform as often as possible.

While you're in Werewolf form, a thin bar appears just below your Magicka pool. This extra bar indicates the time left until the transformation ends.

Staying near a Werewolf ritual site allows you to remain in Werewolf Mode indefinitely. Keep this in mind if you want to rearrange skills on your Werewolf Action Bar.

OBTAINING CURSES

Whether you're interested in Vampirism or Lycanthropy, there are three ways to afflict your character with the desired curse:

OPTION 1: BATTLE INFECTIOUS MONSTERS

If you're hoping to contract a curse on your own, you'll need to pick a fight with an appropriately cursed monster. Some Bloodfiends are capable of transmitting Noxiphilic Sanguivoria, a mysterious disease that can lead to Vampirism. Some Werewolves are capable of transmitting Sanies Lupinus, an ailment that can lead to Lycanthropy.

Infectious monsters are very rare—most of the Vampires and Werewolves you'll encounter out in the wild are incapable of transmitting curses.

To maximize the chance of infection, you should:

- **Pick the right zone.** Limit your search to Bangkorai, Reaper's March, or the Rift. Infectious Bloodfiends and Werewolves only appear in these areas.
- **Search at night.** Monsters capable of transmitting curses rarely (if ever) appear during daylight hours.
- **Look for paired enemies.** Infectious monsters are typically found in teams of two.
- **Keep moving.** When these rare monsters appear, they do so at randomly selected locations. Traveling up and down a zone's main road is often more effective than staking out one known (or suspected) spawn point.
- **Be patient.** Finding a rare spawn is largely a matter of luck. If your enthusiasm wanes, focus on other tasks. Complete quests, gather crafting materials, or search for chests and skyshards—anything that keeps you in the area improves your chances of stumbling across an infectious monster.

If you suspect you've found an infectious monster, move in and let it attack you. Curses are spread through bites and scratches, so resist the urge to defend yourself. Absorb as many attacks as you can tolerate, then retreat or retaliate. After the encounter, check the Character menu to see if you've gained the desired affliction.

Once you've contracted Noxiphilic Sanguivoria or Sanies Lupinus, you can begin the related quest line. Head to the zone's primary town (Evermore in Bangkorai, Rawl'kha in Reaper's March, or Riften in the Rift) and seek out the appropriate quest giver. Follow their instructions to develop your affliction into a full-fledged curse.

KINDRED SPIRITS

Players with Sanies Lupinus should look for Thoreki; players with Noxiphilic Sanguivoria should look for Vorundil. Check the area in and around the town—as long as you have the required affliction, the related quest giver should be marked with a Repeatable Quest icon.

OPTION 2: BEFRIEND A CURSED PLAYER

The Vampire and Werewolf skill lines both contain Passive Abilities that allow cursed players to infect willing victims. The Blood Ritual Passive Ability allows Vampire players to infect one target every seven days; the Blood Moon Passive Ability allows Werewolf players to infect one target every seven days.

This method is more predictable than searching for rare spawns, but there are a few caveats:

- The cursed player must have invested in the required Passive Ability.
- The cursed player must have avoided infecting anyone for at least seven days.
- The target player must not have an existing curse.
- Both players must be standing near a curse-related ritual site.

Once you've been infected, head to the zone's primary town and begin the process of developing your affliction into a full curse.

RITUAL SITES

Bangkorai, Reaper's March, and the Rift each contain one Vampire ritual site and one Werewolf ritual site.

OPTION 3: VISIT THE CROWN STORE

If you wish, you can simply purchase Vampirism or Lycanthropy from the Crown Store. Doing so instantly curses your character, allowing you to enjoy the benefits (and drawbacks) of your chosen affliction without completing the related quests.

REMOVING CURSES

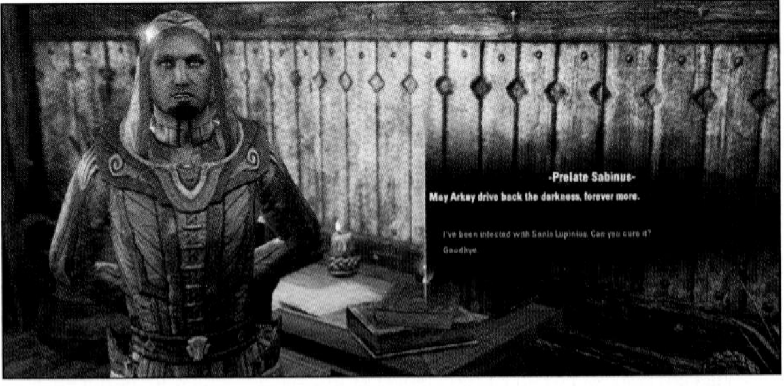

If you decide to remove an existing curse, you can do so in Evermore (Bangkorai), Rawl'kha (Reaper's March), or Riften (the Rift). Once you've settled on a location, visit the town's Mages Guild and enlist the services of Prelate Sabinus.

In exchange for a small fee, Sabinus will remove all traces of the cursed affliction—including the related skill line. You're then free to remain as you are, seek out a different curse, or reacquire your previous curse.

RECLAIMING A CURSE

Curing a curse doesn't erase the progress you've made toward ranking up the related skill line or abilities. If you choose to reclaim a curse, you can pick up right where you left off.

REDEDICATE BEFORE REMOVAL

Before you cure yourself of a curse, visit a Rededication Shrine to reclaim any Skill Points you've spent in the curse-related skill line.

SKILLS

OVERVIEW

More than anything else in the game, skills are what define a character. They determine how your character battles enemies, whether they can heal or offer group support, how they interact with NPCs, the type and quality of items they can make—virtually everything about the way a character performs is determines by the skills you choose to invest in.

SKILL LINES AND ABILITIES

The Skills menu contains all of the skill lines currently available to your character. Each skill line contains a selection of specific abilities. Every ability in the game falls into one of three basic categories:

Ultimate Abilities are uniquely powerful abilities that slowly charge as your character performs light/heavy attacks, heals allies in combat, and dodges/ blocks attacks. Once you've generated enough Ultimate, you can use the ability to devastating (or miraculous) effect. Your Action Bar can only hold one Ultimate Ability at a time.

Active Abilities account for the bulk of your character's damage, healing, and utility. Activating one of these abilities usually consumes either Magicka or Stamina. Your Action Bar can hold five Active Abilities at a time.

Passive Abilities affect your character in subtler ways. A Passive Ability might boost your character's Attributes, change the way an Active Ability functions, or trigger new dialogue options while conversing with NPCs. Some Passive Abilities grant persistent bonuses, while others only grant benefits when certain conditions are met. Passive Abilities are never placed on your Action Bar—they simply provide the specified benefits.

Finding the right mix of Ultimate, Active, and Passive Abilities is the first step toward discovering your playstyle.

UNLOCKING SKILLS

A new character begins with only a few skill lines. You can unlock additional skill lines by meeting certain conditions. Each skill line has its own perquisites. Some skill lines are unlocked when you complete certain quests; others are unlocked by equipping items or speaking to NPCs.

SKILL PROGRESSION

Just as your character gains levels, skill lines and the abilities they hold can progress during your time in the game. As a skill line progresses through available ranks, more of its abilities become available. Once a desired ability becomes available, you can unlock it by spending a Skill Point.

You can progress most skill lines by earning Experience with one or more of its abilities slotted on your Action Bar. However, some skill lines only progress under specific conditions.

ABILITY PROGRESSION

Like skill lines, slotted abilities can be ranked up to offer new benefits. With the exception of Werewolf abilities (which only progress during Werewolf Transformations), ranking up a slotted ability is just a matter of earning Experience—as long as the ability is on your Action Bar, it advances each time you gain Experience.

In most cases, abilities gain slight improvements as they increase in rank. A Rank 2 ability might do slightly more damage, last a bit longer, or gain a bit of range. The changes are subtle, but they add up over time.

At Rank 4, an ability can be morphed in exchange for a Skill Point. Morphing an ability can dramatically change its function. A damage effect might morph into a heal; a channeled ability might become an instant cast. In many cases, a Magicka ability can morph into a Stamina ability. Each time you morph an ability, you're able to choose between two possible results.

While all Ultimate Abilities and Active Abilities can be progressed (and morphed), this isn't the case for Passive Abilities.

If a Passive Ability features more than one rank, it simply means you can invest additional Skill Points to increase its effect. To do so, you must first progress the skill line until the Passive's next rank becomes available.

SECOND THOUGHTS

If you come to regret any of your Skill Point investments, you can reclaim them at any Rededication Shrine. When doing so, you have two options: you can pay the full fee to refund all of your spent Skill Points, or you can pay a smaller fee to refund just the Skill Points you've spent on morphs.

The fee increases based on the number of Skill Points returned.

Which abilities you unlock—and how you use them—are entirely up to you. Experimenting on your own will often yield better results than trying to utilize another player's build. However, a few common practices might be of some benefit to new players:

- Unlock and slot at least one ability from each of your class skill lines. As you grow more familiar with the game, you might find your preferences have changed or that a game update has made a specific skill more appealing. Keep your character prepared and your options open.
- Unlock all armor skill lines as early as possible by equipping three pieces of each weight. Continue to level the skill line by having at least one piece of each armor type while you level your character. Progressing all three armor skill lines makes it much easier to adjust your Attributes or experiment with new builds.
- Seek out Skill Points. *The Elder Scrolls Online: Morrowind* currently contains 379 Skill Points—only 11 of those are to be found in Vvardenfell. Complete the main quest, along with quests for factions and guilds. Explore delves and dungeons, collect skyshards, and spend time in Cyrodiil. The more Skill Points you collect, the more flexibility your character will have.

CLASS SKILL LINES

Every new character has access to three class-exclusive skill lines, and the abilities they contain are all that distinguish one class from another. Each class skill line has its own focus—and all class skill lines have their uses—but no character is defined by these skill lines alone. For more information about these skill lines, refer to **Classes** chapter. For information about other available skill lines, read on.

WEAPON SKILL LINES

Weapon skill lines offer a variety of combat-related abilities. Because every character uses some type of weapon, most effective character builds include at least one weapon skill.

Each weapon type (and its related skill line) supports a different playstyle. Before you commit to a weapon type, consider factors like attack speed, range, damage type, and resource consumption.

The **Two-Handed**, **One Hand and Shield**, **Dual Wield**, and **Bow** skill lines all feature Stamina-based abilities, and performing a heavy attack with any of these weapons generates Stamina.

The **Destruction Staff** and **Restoration Staff** feature Magicka-based abilities; staff heavy attacks regenerate Magicka.

It's also important to know that every weapon ability is tied to a specific weapon type. For example, Bow abilities can only be used while a while a bow is equipped. Equipping a different type of weapon will prevent you from activating any currently slotted Bow abilities.

New players are advised to experiment with different weapons, but Skill Points should always be handled with care. Once you've found your preferred weapon, work toward advancing its skill line and unlocking desired abilities.

BE ACTIVE WITH PASSIVES

Once you've settled on a primary weapon skill line, plan to invest in all of the available Passive Abilities. You'll have plenty of time to earn Skill Points as you rank up the skill line, and a full complement of weapon-related Passives is rarely a bad investment.

TWO-HANDED

Maximum Rank: Two-Handed Rank 50

Maximum Investment: 22 Skill Points

UNLOCKING AND PROGRESSING TWO-HANDED

The Two-Handed skill line is unlocked when you strike a killing blow while holding a two-handed melee weapon.

Progress the skill line by earning Experience with one or more Two-Handed abilities slotted on your Action Bar.

Slotting multiple Two-Handed abilities accelerates skill line progression.

The Two-Handed skill line has a great mix of hard-hitting melee abilities and basic utility. Along with some excellent attacks, you'll find a gap closer, an execute, and a self-heal that grants a damage buff—nearly everything a melee-focused player could want on one Action Bar.

Two-Handed Active Abilities are Stamina-based. To improve their effects, invest in Maximum Stamina, Stamina Recovery, Weapon Damage, and Weapon Critical.

ULTIMATE ABILITY

BERSERKER STRIKE

Berserker Strike deals heavy Physical Damage that ignores your target's mitigation, granting you Physical and Spell Resistance equal to the amount ignored for a short time.

While the base ability offers a nice mix of direct damage and defensive buffs, the utility offered by its morphs is what really makes Berserker Strike a contender for that valuable Action Bar slot.

AVAILABLE MORPHS

NAME	NEW EFFECT
ONSLAUGHT	Killing an enemy with this ability immediately refunds the Ultimate cost.
BERSERKER RAGE	You are immune to all Disabling, Snare, And Immobilization Effects for the duration.

ACTIVE ABILITIES

UPPERCUT

Its one-second cast time makes Uppercut a relatively slow but extremely powerful attack. If you plan to use a two-handed melee weapon, this will likely be your primary damage ability.

AVAILABLE MORPHS

NAME	NEW EFFECT
DIZZYING SWING	Stuns and knocks back the enemy hit.
WRECKING BLOW	Grants you Empower, increasing the damage of your next attack.

CRITICAL CHARGE

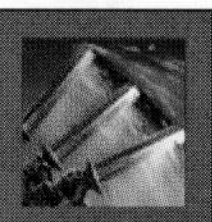

Although Critical Charge is a guaranteed Critical Strike, its popularity is due to its use as a gap closer. It's handy in PvE, but many players consider it an essential Two-Handed ability for PvP builds. Following up a Critical Charge with an Uppercut is one of the most common Two-Handed tactics.

AVAILABLE MORPHS

NAME	NEW EFFECT
STAMPEDE	Reduces the enemy's movement speed.
CRITICAL RUSH	Deals more damage based on the distance traveled.

CLEAVE

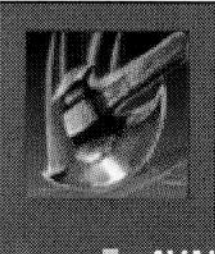

Cleave's combination of area-of-effect damage and damage over time makes it an important tool for Two-Handed DPS, and the utility offered by its morphs makes it a difficult skill to pass up.

AVAILABLE MORPHS

NAME	NEW EFFECT
CARVE	Grants Minor Heroism, increasing your Ultimate generation.
BRAWLER	Grants a damage shield that increases in strength for each enemy hit.

REVERSE SLASH

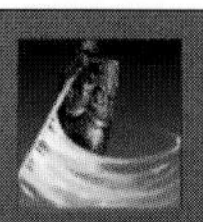

As a straightforward execute, Reverse Slash is a great way to boost your burst damage and overall DPS. Once your target reaches 35% health use this as your primary damage ability for the greatest effect, as it produces a 90% damage bonus.

AVAILABLE MORPHS

NAME	NEW EFFECT
REVERSE SLICE	Other enemies nearby take a percentage of the damage inflicted to the primary target.
EXECUTIONER	Increases the amount of bonus damage to low-Health targets.

MOMENTUM

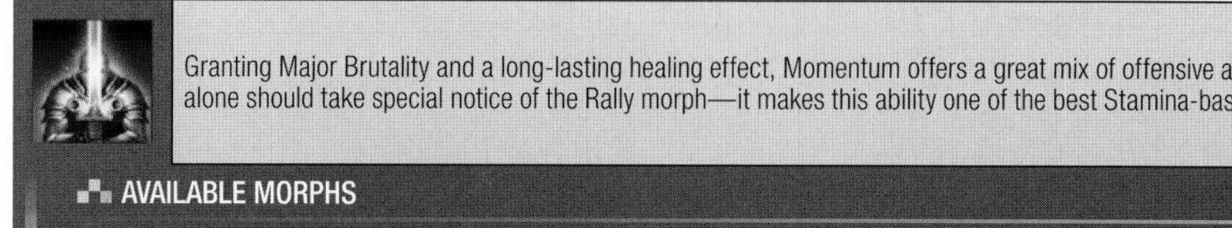

Granting Major Brutality and a long-lasting healing effect, Momentum offers a great mix of offensive and defensive utility. Those who plan to adventure alone should take special notice of the Rally morph—it makes this ability one of the best Stamina-based self-heals available to most classes.

AVAILABLE MORPHS

NAME	NEW EFFECT
FORWARD MOMENTUM	Reduces the cost and provides a brief immunity to snares and immobilizations.
RALLY	Also heals you when the effect expires.

PASSIVE ABILITIES

The Two-Handed skill line features five Passive Abilities, each of which has two ranks.

None of the available Passives are tied to specific abilities. If you utilize a two-handed weapon, it's recommended that you invest in all Two-Handed Passives.

PASSIVE REQUIREMENTS

You can only benefit from a Two-Handed Passive Ability while a two-handed weapon is equipped.

Two-Handed Passive Abilities

Name	Effect
Forceful	Your light and heavy attacks damage up to two additional enemies for a percentage of the damage inflicted to the primary target.
Heavy Weapons	Grants a specific bonus based on the type of weapon equipped.
Balanced Blade	Reduces the Stamina cost of your Two-Handed abilities.
Follow Up	A successful, fully charged heavy attack increases the damage of your next attack.
Battle Rush	Increases Stamina Recovery for 10 seconds after killing a target.

ONE HAND AND SHIELD

Maximum Rank: One Hand and Shield Rank 50

Maximum Investment: 22 Skill Points

UNLOCKING AND PROGRESSING ONE HAND AND SHIELD

The One Hand and Shield skill line is unlocked when you strike a killing blow while holding a one-handed melee weapon and a shield.

Progress the skill line by earning Experience with one or more One Hand and Shield abilities slotted on your Action Bar.

Slotting multiple One Hand and Shield abilities accelerates skill line progression.

The One Hand and Shield skill line leans heavily toward defensive abilities. With one of the game's only taunts and plenty of options for damage mitigation, this skill line serves as the foundation of many tanking builds. Of course, it's a viable option for anyone who wants to boost survivability during close combat. An appropriately built shield specialist can both absorb and deal significant damage.

One Hand and Shield features Stamina abilities. If you're looking to maximize your damage, focus on Maximum Stamina, Stamina Recovery, Weapon Damage, and Weapon Critical.

ULTIMATE ABILITY

SHIELD WALL

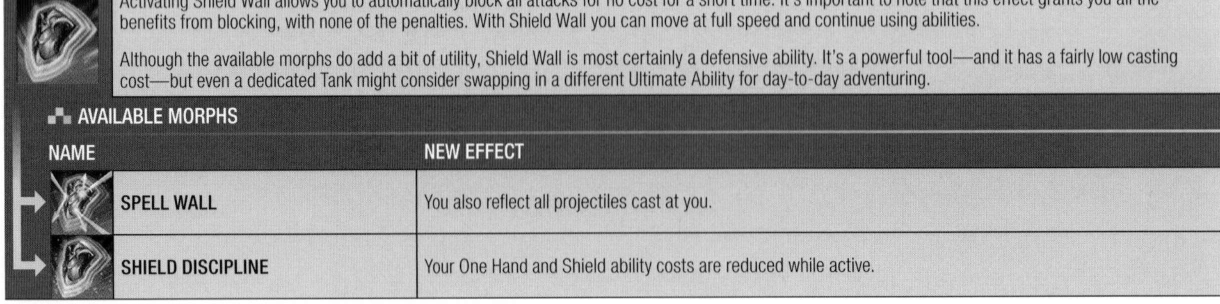

Activating Shield Wall allows you to automatically block all attacks for no cost for a short time. It's important to note that this effect grants you all the benefits from blocking, with none of the penalties. With Shield Wall you can move at full speed and continue using abilities.

Although the available morphs do add a bit of utility, Shield Wall is most certainly a defensive ability. It's a powerful tool—and it has a fairly low casting cost—but even a dedicated Tank might consider swapping in a different Ultimate Ability for day-to-day adventuring.

AVAILABLE MORPHS

NAME	NEW EFFECT
SPELL WALL	You also reflect all projectiles cast at you.
SHIELD DISCIPLINE	Your One Hand and Shield ability costs are reduced while active.

ACTIVE ABILITIES

PUNCTURE

It does a bit of direct damage, but the fact that it's one of the game's only taunts is what makes Puncture such a valuable tanking ability—of course, the inclusion of Major Fracture is a nice bonus.

AVAILABLE MORPHS

NAME	NEW EFFECT
RANSACK	You also gain Minor Resolve, increasing your Physical Resistance.
PIERCE ARMOR	Also afflicts the enemy with Major Breach, reducing their Spell Resistance.

LOW SLASH

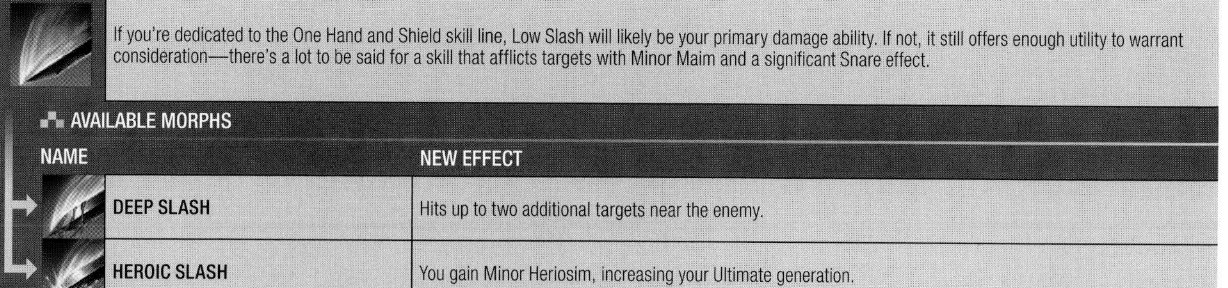

If you're dedicated to the One Hand and Shield skill line, Low Slash will likely be your primary damage ability. If not, it still offers enough utility to warrant consideration—there's a lot to be said for a skill that afflicts targets with Minor Maim and a significant Snare effect.

AVAILABLE MORPHS

NAME	NEW EFFECT
DEEP SLASH	Hits up to two additional targets near the enemy.
HEROIC SLASH	You gain Minor Heriosim, increasing your Ultimate generation.

DEFENSIVE POSTURE

Defensive Posture is useful as a spell-reflect, but its slotted bonus is what makes it an excellent tanking ability. As long as Defensive Posture is on your Action Bar, your blocks are more effective and more efficient.

AVAILABLE MORPHS

NAME	NEW EFFECT
DEFENSIVE STANCE	The reflected spell projectile also stuns the attacker.
ABSORB MAGIC	Absorb the spell projectile and heal yourself instead of reflecting it.

SHIELD CHARGE

Shield Charge is a standard gap closer. It does a bit of damage, but primarily it offers shield bearers some welcome mobility. Follow it up with a Low Slash to keep your target from escaping.

AVAILABLE MORPHS

NAME	NEW EFFECT
SHIELDED ASSAULT	Gain a damage shield after the attack.
INVASION	Stuns longer based on the distance traveled.

POWER BASH

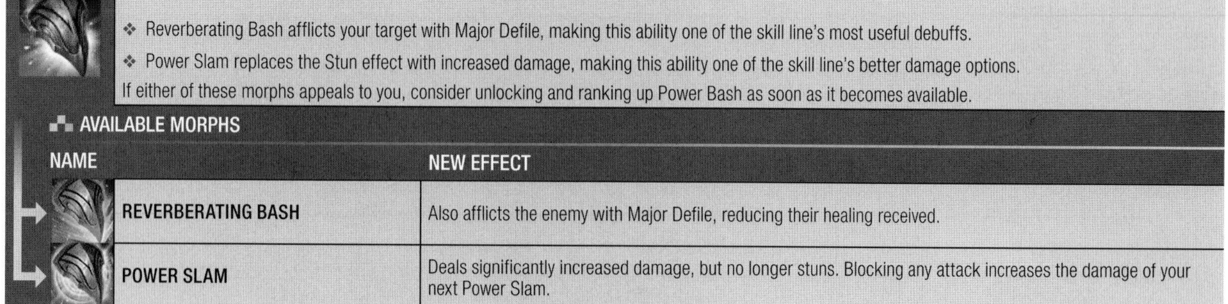

Power Bash serves as a low-damage interrupt, but the available morphs dramatically change the nature of this ability:

- Reverberating Bash afflicts your target with Major Defile, making this ability one of the skill line's most useful debuffs.
- Power Slam replaces the Stun effect with increased damage, making this ability one of the skill line's better damage options.

If either of these morphs appeals to you, consider unlocking and ranking up Power Bash as soon as it becomes available.

AVAILABLE MORPHS

NAME	NEW EFFECT
REVERBERATING BASH	Also afflicts the enemy with Major Defile, reducing their healing received.
POWER SLAM	Deals significantly increased damage, but no longer stuns. Blocking any attack increases the damage of your next Power Slam.

PASSIVE ABILITIES

The One Hand and Shield skill line features five Passive Abilities, each of which has two ranks.

None of the available Passives are tied to specific abilities, so any shield bearer should plan to invest in all of them. If you're running low on Skill Points, prioritize **Fortress** and **Sword and Board** for some extra damage, defense, and efficiency.

PASSIVE REQUIREMENTS

You can only benefit from a One Hand and Shield Passive Ability while a one-handed weapon and shield are equipped.

One Hand and Shield Passive Abilities

Name	Effect
Fortress	Reduces the Stamina cost of your One Hand and Shield abilities. Reduces the cost of blocking.
Sword and Board	Increases your Weapon Damage and the amount of damage you can block.
Deadly Bash	Improves your standard Bash attacks. Bashing deals additional damage and costs less Stamina.
Deflect Bolts	Increases the amount of damage you can block from projectiles.
Battlefield Mobility	Increases your movement speed while blocking.

DUAL WIELD

Maximum Rank: Dual Wield Rank 50

Maximum Investment: 22 Skill Points

UNLOCKING AND PROGRESSING DUAL WIELD

The Dual Wield skill line is unlocked when you strike a killing blow while holding two one-handed melee weapons.

Progress the skill line by earning Experience with one or more Dual Wield abilities slotted on your Action Bar.

Slotting multiple Dual Wield abilities accelerates skill line progression.

The Dual Wield skill line has some good options for one-on-one combat, but it really shines when it comes to area-of-effect damage. If you're looking for some versatile, high-damage weapon skills, this is a great place to start.

Dual Wield features Stamina abilities. Invest in Maximum Stamina, Stamina Recovery, Weapon Damage, and Weapon Critical if you're looking to boost your DPS. Thanks to one of the available Passive Abilities, Dual Wield is also an appealing option for DPS casters. If you're not relying on other skill lines for damage, you'll likely prioritize other Attributes.

ULTIMATE ABILITY

LACERATE

Lacerate is a multi-target damage-over-time ability featuring a nice healing effect. It lacks an instant-damage component, so it won't do much for burst damage, but it's a great option for overall DPS and survivability.

AVAILABLE MORPHS

NAME	NEW EFFECT
REND	Significantly increases the effect's duration.
THRIVE IN CHAOS	Each enemy hit increases your damage done.

ACTIVE ABILITIES

FLURRY

If you're relying on the Dual Wield skill line, Flurry is a solid choice for a primary damage ability. This channeled attack is a reliable source of single-target damage with a hard-hitting finish.

Flurry's channeling time makes it very easy to weave heavy attacks into your rotation: just hold down your heavy attack and activate Flurry each time your character draws its arm back. This doesn't maximize your DPS, but it does generate plenty of Stamina during prolonged battles.

AVAILABLE MORPHS

NAME	NEW EFFECT
RAPID STRIKES	Each hit increases the damage of the subsequent hit.
BLOODTHIRST	Heals you for 60% of the damage caused.

TWIN SLASHES

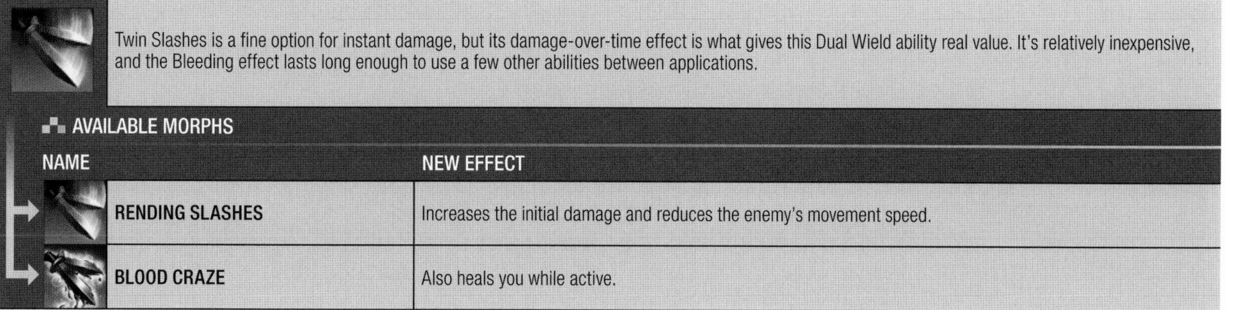

Twin Slashes is a fine option for instant damage, but its damage-over-time effect is what gives this Dual Wield ability real value. It's relatively inexpensive, and the Bleeding effect lasts long enough to use a few other abilities between applications.

AVAILABLE MORPHS

NAME	NEW EFFECT
RENDING SLASHES	Increases the initial damage and reduces the enemy's movement speed.
BLOOD CRAZE	Also heals you while active.

WHIRLWIND

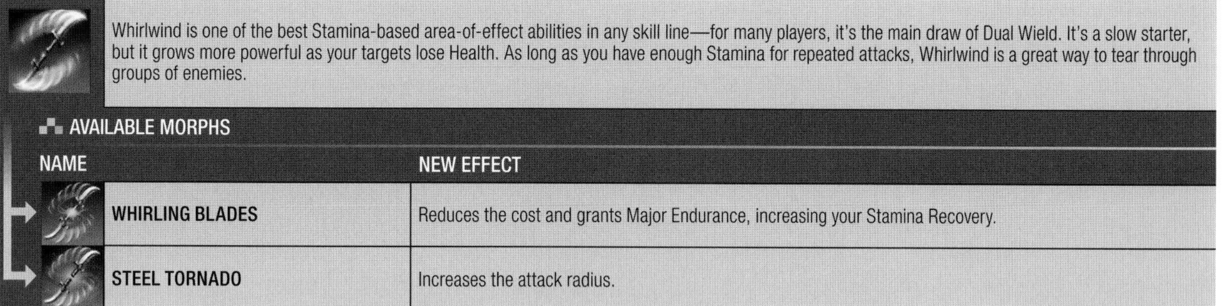

Whirlwind is one of the best Stamina-based area-of-effect abilities in any skill line—for many players, it's the main draw of Dual Wield. It's a slow starter, but it grows more powerful as your targets lose Health. As long as you have enough Stamina for repeated attacks, Whirlwind is a great way to tear through groups of enemies.

AVAILABLE MORPHS

NAME	NEW EFFECT
WHIRLING BLADES	Reduces the cost and grants Major Endurance, increasing your Stamina Recovery.
STEEL TORNADO	Increases the attack radius.

BLADE CLOAK

Blade Cloak offers a good mix of area and damage-over-time effects, but it also reduces the damage you take from area-of-effect attacks. When you're charging into a pack of enemies, you'd be hard-pressed to find a better combination than Blade Cloak and Whirlwind.

AVAILABLE MORPHS

NAME	NEW EFFECT
QUICK CLOAK	For a brief period after activation, you gain Major Expedition, increasing your movement speed by 30%.
DEADLY CLOAK	Increases the damage done.

HIDDEN BLADE

Hidden Blade is a long-range direct-damage attack that buffs you while snaring your target. What's not to like? It's a particularly good skill for Stamina builds that use melee weapons with both Action Bars—without a bow, Hidden Blade's range is a real asset.

AVAILABLE MORPHS

NAME	NEW EFFECT
SHROUDED DAGGERS	The dagger bounces up to two times, dealing increased damage with each bounce.
FLYING BLADE	Increases the damage and the range.

PASSIVE ABILITIES

The Dual Wield skill line features five Passive Abilities, each of which has two ranks.

None of the available Passives are tied to specific abilities—if you're relying on Dual Wield abilities for damage, it's recommended that you invest in each Passive as it becomes available.

THE DUEL SWORD SPELLCASTER

The **Twin Blade and Blunt** Passive grants different bonuses on the type of weapons you've equipped. At Rank 2, this Passive Ability grants an additional 2.5% damage done for each sword your character's holding. This potential 5% damage bonus applies to all attacks—including Magicka abilities.

PASSIVE REQUIREMENTS

You can only benefit from a Dual Wield Passive Ability while two one-handed weapons are equipped.

Dual Wield Passive Abilities

Name	Effect
Slaughter	Dual Wield abilities do more damage to low-Health enemies.
Dual Wield Expert	Increases Weapon Damage by a percentage of the your off-hand weapon's base damage.
Controlled Fury	Reduces the cost of Dual Wield abilities.
Ruffian	Dual Wield abilities do more damage against enemies that are stunned, immobilized, disoriented, or silenced.
Twin Blade and Blunt	Grants a specific bonus based on the type of weapon equipped.

BOW

Maximum Rank: Bow Rank 50

Maximum Investment: 22 Skill Points

UNLOCKING AND PROGRESSING BOW

The Bow skill line is unlocked when you strike a killing blow while holding a bow.

Progress the skill line by earning Experience with one or more Bow abilities slotted on your Action Bar.

Slotting multiple Bow abilities accelerates skill line progression.

The Bow skill line allows any character to utilize Stamina-based ranged abilities. In terms of DPS, Bow abilities fall a bit short of most weapon skill lines, but they can add a lot of versatility to a build.

Sometimes, you need a ranged attack. Whether you're trying to finish off a fleeing enemy or avoiding area-of-effect damage, a bit of range can make all the difference.

Unlike staves, bows can be fired from stealth. This allows for long-range, high-damage sneak attacks that aren't otherwise possible.

The Bow skill line features several options for Poison Damage. They're great damage-over-time options for general use, and they're particularly good for dealing with enemy Werewolves in PvP. In some cases, it's worth swapping to a bow in the middle of melee combat—just long enough to reapply a fading damage-over-time effect.

At any rate, if you're interested in bow use, plan to place at least a few of these abilities on the appropriate Action Bar. If you want to increase the effectiveness of your Bow abilities, prioritize Maximum Stamina, Stamina Recovery, Weapon Damage, and Weapon Critical.

ULTIMATE ABILITY

RAPID FIRE

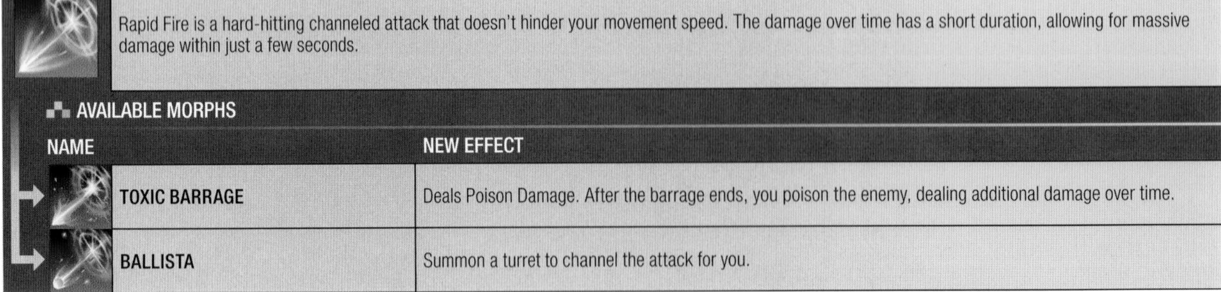

Rapid Fire is a hard-hitting channeled attack that doesn't hinder your movement speed. The damage over time has a short duration, allowing for massive damage within just a few seconds.

AVAILABLE MORPHS

NAME	NEW EFFECT
TOXIC BARRAGE	Deals Poison Damage. After the barrage ends, you poison the enemy, dealing additional damage over time.
BALLISTA	Summon a turret to channel the attack for you.

ACTIVE ABILITIES

SNIPE

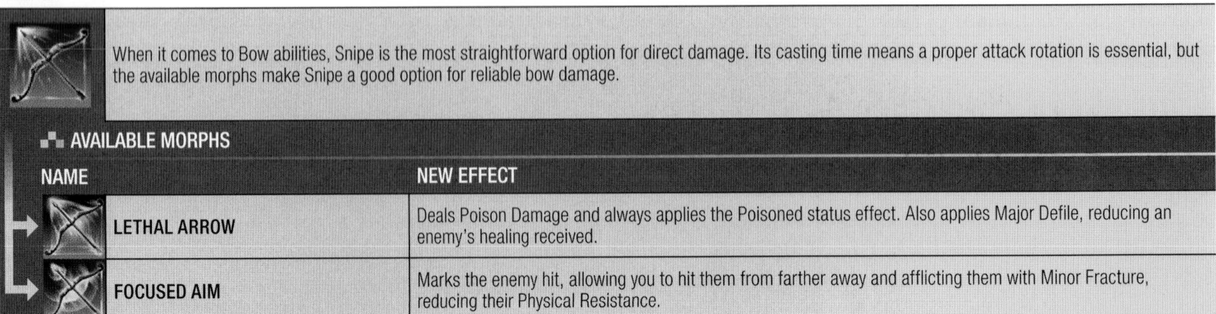

When it comes to Bow abilities, Snipe is the most straightforward option for direct damage. Its casting time means a proper attack rotation is essential, but the available morphs make Snipe a good option for reliable bow damage.

AVAILABLE MORPHS

NAME	NEW EFFECT
LETHAL ARROW	Deals Poison Damage and always applies the Poisoned status effect. Also applies Major Defile, reducing an enemy's healing received.
FOCUSED AIM	Marks the enemy hit, allowing you to hit them from farther away and afflicting them with Minor Fracture, reducing their Physical Resistance.

VOLLEY

Volley produces a shower of arrows for a combined AoE/DOT attack. It has a good range but a fairly small radius—and because it takes a while for the attack to resolve, it's often best used on enemies that are immobilized, distracted, or otherwise likely to stay put. It synergizes well with Arrow Spray to snare enemies.

AVAILABLE MORPHS

NAME	NEW EFFECT
ENDLESS HAIL	Increases the duration and reduces the cost.
ARROW BARRAGE	Increases the range and radius.

SCATTER SHOT

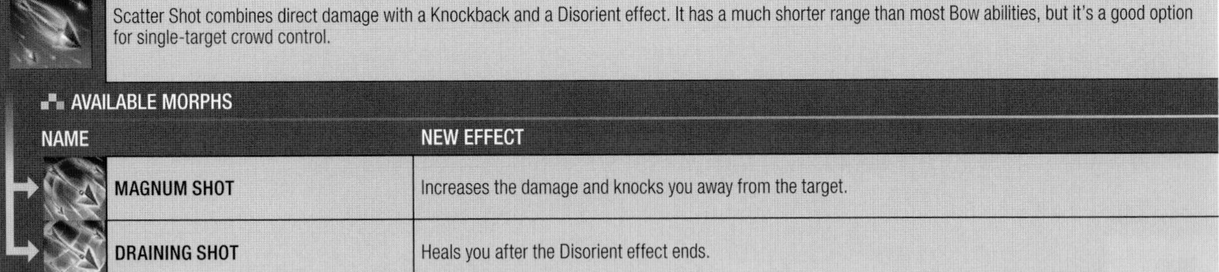

Scatter Shot combines direct damage with a Knockback and a Disorient effect. It has a much shorter range than most Bow abilities, but it's a good option for single-target crowd control.

AVAILABLE MORPHS

NAME	NEW EFFECT
MAGNUM SHOT	Increases the damage and knocks you away from the target.
DRAINING SHOT	Heals you after the Disorient effect ends.

ARROW SPRAY

Arrow Spray is an instant attack with a nice spread, but its Snare effect is the ability's real selling point. If your Action Bar could benefit from some area-of-effect crowd control, Arrow Spray is an excellent option.

AVAILABLE MORPHS

NAME	NEW EFFECT
BOMBARD	Also immobilizes enemies hit.
ACID SPRAY	Deals Poison Damage and adds additional damage over time.

PASSIVE ABILITIES

The Bow skill line features five Passive Abilities, each of which has two ranks.

None of the available Passives are tied to specific abilities. If you opt to use a bow, consider investing in all Bow Passive Abilities.

PASSIVE REQUIREMENTS

You can only benefit from a Bow Passive Ability while a bow is equipped.

Bow Passive Abilities

Name	Effect
Long Shots	Bow abilities do more damage to enemies at longer range.
Accuracy	Increases Weapon Critical rating.
Ranger	Reduces the Stamina cost of Bow abilities.
Hawk Eye	Dealing damage with a light or heavy attack temporarily increases the damage of your Bow abilities.
Hasty Retreat	Using Dodge Roll grants you a Major Expedition, temporarily increasing your movement speed by 30%.

DESTRUCTION STAFF

Maximum Rank: Destruction Staff Rank 50

Maximum Investment: 22 Skill Points

UNLOCKING AND PROGRESSING DESTRUCTION STAFF

The Destruction Staff skill line is unlocked when you strike a killing blow while holding a Destruction Staff (Flame, Frost, or Lightning).

Progress the skill line by earning Experience with one or more Destruction Staff abilities slotted on your Action Bar.

Slotting multiple Destruction Staff abilities accelerates skill line progression.

Of the two Magicka-based weapon skill lines, Destruction Staff is easily the better option for Damage-Dealers. With options for direct damage, area-of-effect damage, and damage over time, plus a bit of utility, this skill line has plenty to offer.

Most Destruction Staff abilities change based on your currently equipped staff. Inferno Staves, Ice Staves, and Lightning Staves can have wildly different effects—especially once you've invested in the available Passive Abilities. When you're trying to figure out whether a Destruction Staff ability deserves a slot on your Action Bar, make sure you review all of the available effects.

The Destruction Staff skill line features Magicka abilities. If damage is your priority, invest in Maximum Magicka, Magicka Recovery, Spell Damage, and Spell Critical.

ULTIMATE ABILITY

ELEMENTAL STORM

Elemental Storm is a very powerful long-range AoE/DOT attack. It's best used against stationary targets, but it has a fair radius and an impressive damage-tick. Your currently equipped staff determines the type of damage featured in the attack, as well as the bonus effect granted by the Elemental Rage morph.

AVAILABLE MORPHS

NAME	NEW EFFECT
ELEMENTAL RAGE	Increases the damage and gains a new effect depending on your staff type.
EYE OF THE STORM	The storm is cast above you instead, and follows you wherever you move.

ACTIVE ABILITIES

FORCE SHOCK

Dealing Flame Damage, Frost Damage, and Shock Damage with each attack, Force Shock is an excellent option for your primary damage ability. It works well in virtually any spell rotation, and the available morphs make it a popular ability with DPS casters.

AVAILABLE MORPHS

NAME	NEW EFFECT
CRUSHING SHOCK	Interrupts spells, putting the caster off-balance.
FORCE PULSE	Deals increased damage, and damages nearby enemies that are burning, chilled, or concussed.

WALL OF ELEMENTS

Wall of Elements is an AoE/DOT attack that features different effects based on your currently equipped staff. It only affects a narrow area in front of you, and it has a fairly short duration, but it can deal a lot of damage to enemies that favor close combat.

AVAILABLE MORPHS

NAME	NEW EFFECT
UNSTABLE WALL OF ELEMENTS	The wall explodes with it expires, dealing additional damage.
ELEMENTAL BLOCKADE	Increases the size and duration of the wall.

DESTRUCTIVE TOUCH

Destructive Touch mixes direct-damage, damage-over-time, and crowd-control effects. Depending on your currently equipped staff, you can inflict Knocked Back, Immobilized, or Stunned. If you're looking for a versatile single-target crowd-control ability, Destructive Touch is worth considering.

AVAILABLE MORPHS

NAME	NEW EFFECT
DESTRUCTIVE CLENCH	Each element gains additional effects.
DESTRUCTIVE REACH	Increases the range.

WEAKNESS TO ELEMENTS

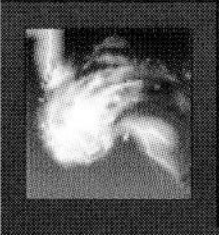

Weakness to Elements is a straightforward debuff ability that afflicts your target with Major Breach, reducing their Spell Resistance by 5280. It's also an instant, long-range ability with no casting cost. If you can spare the Action Bar slot, there's no reason to avoid using this ability.

AVAILABLE MORPHS

NAME	NEW EFFECT
ELEMENTAL SUSCEPTIBILITY	Any damage you deal to the enemy refreshes the effect to its maximum duration.
ELEMENTAL DRAIN	Also applies Minor Magickasteal to the enemy.

IMPULSE

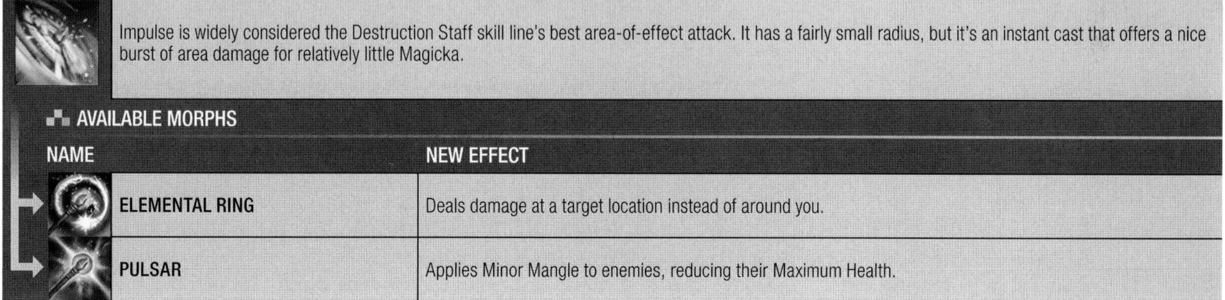

Impulse is widely considered the Destruction Staff skill line's best area-of-effect attack. It has a fairly small radius, but it's an instant cast that offers a nice burst of area damage for relatively little Magicka.

AVAILABLE MORPHS

NAME	NEW EFFECT
ELEMENTAL RING	Deals damage at a target location instead of around you.
PULSAR	Applies Minor Mangle to enemies, reducing their Maximum Health.

PASSIVE ABILITIES

The Destruction Staff skill line features five Passive Abilities, each of which has two ranks.

While none of the available Passives are tied to specific abilities, two Destruction Staff abilities are greatly affected by the type of staff you're using. The value offered by **Tri Focus** and **Ancient Knowledge** may change based on the equipment available to you, but it's recommended that Destruction Staff users invest in all of this skill line's Passive Abilities.

FROST STAFF TANKING

Thanks to some versatile Passives, the Destruction Staff skill line makes it possible to tank with a Frost Staff equipped:

Tri Focus causes fully charged frost heavy attacks to taunt your target while granting you a damage shield. It also causes blocking to consume Magicka instead of Stamina while a Frost Staff is equipped.

Ancient Knowledge reduces the cost of blocking and increases the amount of damage you can block while you have a Frost Staff equipped and a Destruction Staff ability slotted.

PASSIVE REQUIREMENTS

You can only benefit from a Destruction Staff Passive Ability while a Destruction Staff (Flame, Frost, or Lightning) is equipped.

Destruction Staff Passive Abilities

Name	Effect
Tri Focus	Grants a bonus effect based on your staff type.
Penetrating Magic	Your Destruction Staff abilities ignore a percentage of the enemy's Spell Resistance.
Elemental Force	Increases your chance to apply the Burning, Concussion, and Chilled effects while you have a Destruction Staff equipped.
Ancient Knowledge	Gain bonus effects based on your staff type while you have a Destruction Staff ability slotted.
Destruction Expert	You restore Magicka when you kill an enemy with a Destruction Staff ability.

RESTORATION STAFF

Maximum Rank: Restoration Staff Rank 50

Maximum Investment: 22 Skill Points

UNLOCKING AND PROGRESSING RESTORATION STAFF

The Restoration Staff skill line is unlocked when you strike a killing blow while holding a Restoration Staff.

Progress the skill line by earning Experience with one or more Restoration Staff abilities slotted on your Action Bar.

Slotting multiple Restoration Staff abilities accelerates skill line progression.

The Restoration Staff skill line allows any character to serve as a group Healer, but it also features options for damage shields and defensive buffs. It won't do much for DPS, but this skill line is a great option for any player interested in survivability or group support.

Restoration Staff abilities are Magicka-based, so focus on Maximum Magicka, Magicka Recovery, Spell Damage, and Spell Critical if you want to make the most of this this skill line.

ULTIMATE ABILITY

PANACEA

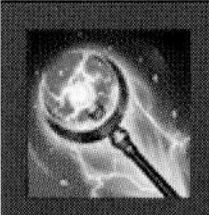

Panacea is a heal-over-time ability that can affect you or a nearby ally. The base ability offers a powerful healing effect, but the available morphs add some very useful defensive buffs.

As Ultimate Abilities go, Panacea has a low casting cost. With regular use, this ability can do a lot of healing over the course of an encounter.

AVAILABLE MORPHS

NAME	NEW EFFECT
LIFE GIVER	Also automatically casts Regeneration, Blessing of Protection, and Steadfast Ward.
LIGHT'S CHAMPION	Any friendly target healed gains Major Force and Major Protection, increasing Critical Damage and reducing damage taken.

ACTIVE ABILITIES

GRAND HEALING

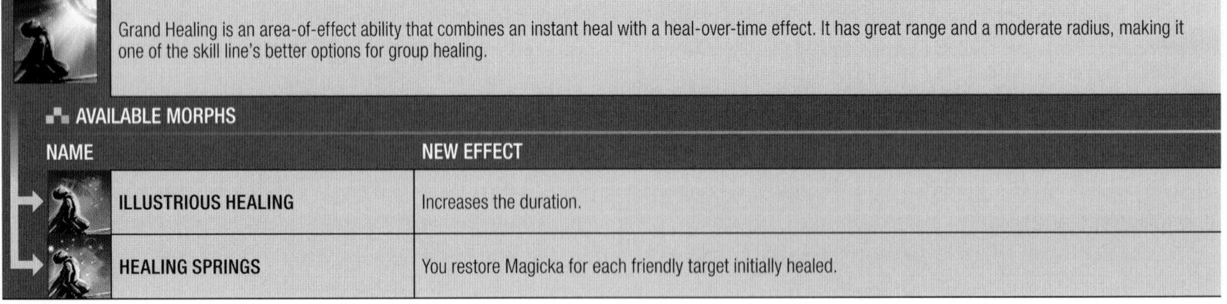

Grand Healing is an area-of-effect ability that combines an instant heal with a heal-over-time effect. It has great range and a moderate radius, making it one of the skill line's better options for group healing.

AVAILABLE MORPHS

NAME	NEW EFFECT
ILLUSTRIOUS HEALING	Increases the duration.
HEALING SPRINGS	You restore Magicka for each friendly target initially healed.

REGENERATION

Regeneration allows you to grant yourself and up to two nearby allies a lengthy heal-over-time effect. It restores a significant amount of Health, but the effect's duration means that it's best used as a preventative measure or a secondary source of healing.

AVAILABLE MORPHS

NAME	NEW EFFECT
RAPID REGENERATION	The heal-over-time effect is shorter, but ticks faster and more often.
MUTAGEN	If you or your allies are low on Health, the heal-over-time effect is consumed to heal immediately and remove a harmful effect.

BLESSING OF PROTECTION

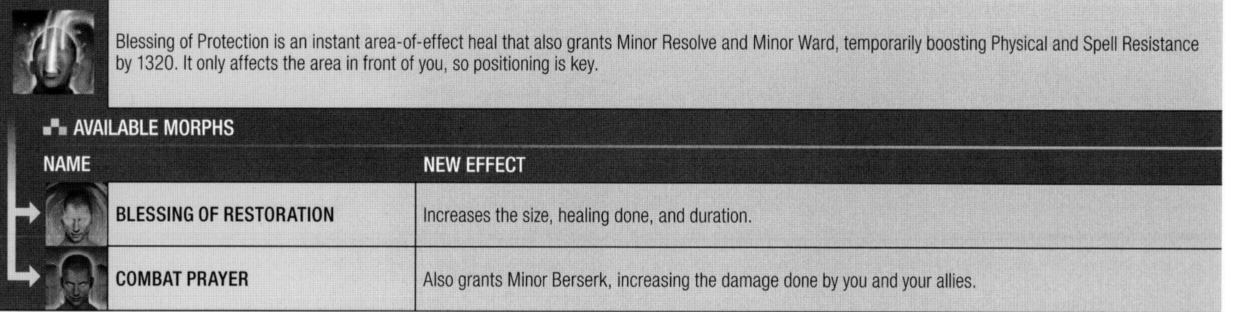

Blessing of Protection is an instant area-of-effect heal that also grants Minor Resolve and Minor Ward, temporarily boosting Physical and Spell Resistance by 1320. It only affects the area in front of you, so positioning is key.

AVAILABLE MORPHS

NAME	NEW EFFECT
BLESSING OF RESTORATION	Increases the size, healing done, and duration.
COMBAT PRAYER	Also grants Minor Berserk, increasing the damage done by you and your allies.

STEADFAST WARD

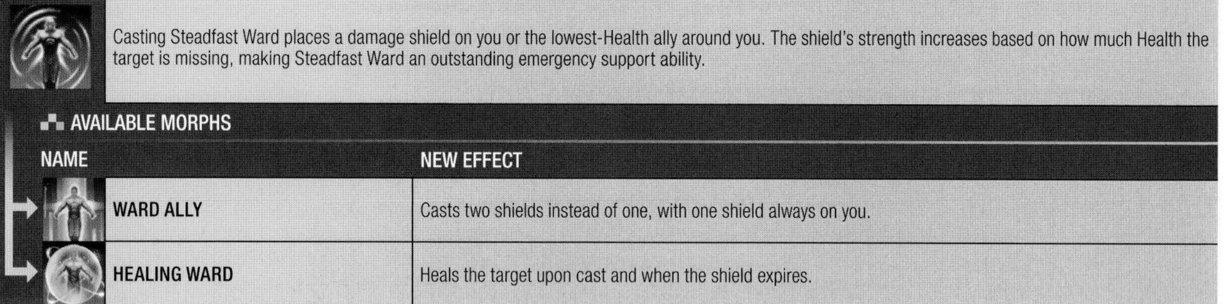

Casting Steadfast Ward places a damage shield on you or the lowest-Health ally around you. The shield's strength increases based on how much Health the target is missing, making Steadfast Ward an outstanding emergency support ability.

AVAILABLE MORPHS

NAME	NEW EFFECT
WARD ALLY	Casts two shields instead of one, with one shield always on you.
HEALING WARD	Heals the target upon cast and when the shield expires.

FORCE SIPHON

Force Siphon applies Minor Lifesteal to an enemy, granting small bursts of healing to all of the target's attackers. Though it has a bit of a cast time, it features a lengthy duration and a fairly low Magicka cost. Unless a teammate has a similar ability, consider Force Siphon for some low-maintenance group support.

AVAILABLE MORPHS

NAME	NEW EFFECT
SIPHON SPIRIT	Also applies Minor Magickasteal to the enemy.
QUICK SIPHON	Removes the cast time.

PASSIVE ABILITIES

The Restoration Staff skill line features five Passive Abilities, each of which has two ranks.

None of the Restoration Staff Passive Abilities are tied to specific abilities, and they're all very useful. If you use any Restoration Staff abilities, it's highly recommended that you invest in all available Passives.

PASSIVE REQUIREMENTS

You can only benefit from a Restoration Staff Passive Ability while a Restoration Staff is equipped.

Restoration Staff Passive Abilities

Name	Effect
Essence Drain	A fully charged heavy attack grants Major Mending, temporarily increasing your healing done by 25%. You also heal yourself or a target ally for a percentage of the damage inflicted by the final hit of the fully charged heavy attack.
Restoration Expert	Increases your healing done on low-Health allies.
Cycle of Life	Restores additional Magicka when you complete a heavy attack.
Absorb	Restores Magicka when you block a spell.
Restoration Master	Increases healing with Restoration Staff spells.

ARMOR SKILL LINES

The Passive Abilities found in armor skill lines rank among the best Skill Point investments you can make. It's fair to say that each armor type (light, medium, and heavy) is defined less by the protection it offers than by its related Passive Abilities.

In general:

- Light Armor Passives benefit Magicka-focused builds.
- Medium Armor Passives benefit Stamina-focused builds.
- Heavy Armor Passives benefit Health-focused builds.

Of course, players often mix and match armor types to great effect. But enjoying the benefits granted by any armor Passive means progressing—and investing in—the related skill line.

Each armor skill line also offers its own Active Ability. Once unlocked, you can slot and use an armor Active Ability no matter which armor type is equipped.

LIGHT ARMOR

Maximum Rank: Light Armor Rank 50

Maximum Investment: 13 Skill Points

UNLOCKING AND PROGRESSING LIGHT ARMOR

The Light Armor skill line is unlocked when you equip three or more pieces of light armor.

Progress the skill line by earning Experience with at least one piece of light armor equipped.

Equipping multiple pieces of light armor accelerates skill line progression.

If you're looking for a quick boost to your Magicka proficiency, this skill line is a great place to start.

ACTIVE ABILITY

ANNULMENT

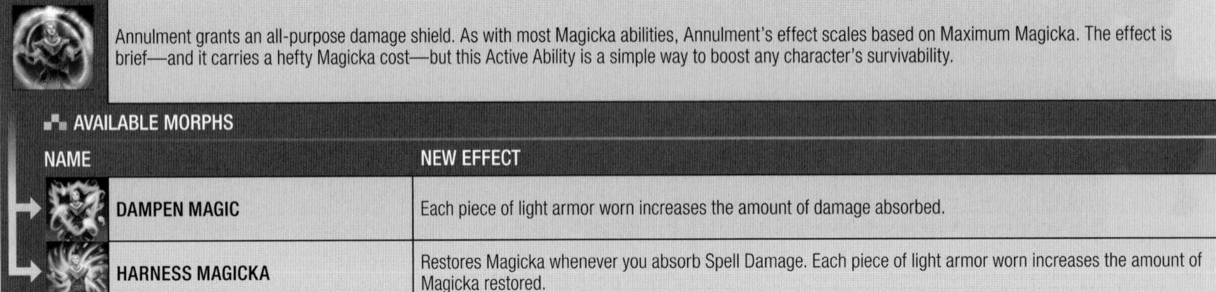

Annulment grants an all-purpose damage shield. As with most Magicka abilities, Annulment's effect scales based on Maximum Magicka. The effect is brief—and it carries a hefty Magicka cost—but this Active Ability is a simple way to boost any character's survivability.

AVAILABLE MORPHS

NAME	NEW EFFECT
DAMPEN MAGIC	Each piece of light armor worn increases the amount of damage absorbed.
HARNESS MAGICKA	Restores Magicka whenever you absorb Spell Damage. Each piece of light armor worn increases the amount of Magicka restored.

PASSIVE ABILITIES

The Light Armor skill line contains five Passive Abilities. **Recovery** features three ranks; all other Light Armor Passives offer two ranks.

Recovery, **Evocation**, and **Spell Warding** can all offer aid to anyone using at least one piece of light armor, but equipping more pieces improves their effects.

PASSIVE REQUIREMENTS

You must have at least one piece of light armor equipped to receive any bonuses from Light Armor Passives. **Prodigy** and **Concentration** only grant bonuses while five or more pieces of light armor are equipped.

Light Armor Passive Abilities

Name	Effect
Recovery	Increases your Magicka Recovery by up to 4% for each piece of light armor equipped.
Evocation	Reduces the Magicka cost of your abilities by up to 2% for each piece of light armor equipped.
Spell Warding	Increases your Spell Resistance by up to 363 for each piece of light armor equipped.
Prodigy	Increases your Spell Critical rating by up to 2191 when five or more pieces of light armor are equipped.
Concentration	Increases your Spell Penetration by up to 4884 when five or more pieces of light armor are equipped.

MEDIUM ARMOR

Maximum Rank: Medium Armor Rank 50

Maximum Investment: 13 Skill Points

UNLOCKING AND PROGRESSING MEDIUM ARMOR

The Medium Armor skill line is unlocked when you equip three or more pieces of medium armor.

Progress the skill line by earning Experience with at least one piece of medium armor equipped.

Equipping multiple pieces of medium armor accelerates skill line progression.

If you rely on mobility and/or Physical Damage, make the Medium Armor skill line a priority.

ACTIVE ABILITY

EVASION

Activating this ability grants Major Evasion, increasing your Dodge Chance by 15%. Because Major Evasion is a standardized effect, this ability doesn't scale with Maximum Stamina—though it does feature a fairly high Stamina cost.

AVAILABLE MORPHS

NAME	NEW EFFECT
SHUFFLE	Each piece of medium armor worn removes and grants immunity to snares and immobilizations for a short time.
ELUDE	Each piece of medium armor worn increases the effect's duration.

PASSIVE ABILITIES

The Medium Armor skill line contains five Passive Abilities. **Recovery** features three ranks; all other Medium Armor Passives offer two ranks.

Dexterity, **Wind Walker**, **Improved Sneak**, and **Athletics** can all offer aid to anyone using at least one piece of medium armor, but equipping more pieces improves their effects.

PASSIVE REQUIREMENTS

You must have at least one piece of medium armor equipped to receive any bonuses from Medium Armor Passives. You must equip at least five medium armor pieces to receive any benefit from **Agility**.

Medium Armor Passive Abilities

Name	Effect
Dexterity	Increases your Weapon Critical rating by up to 328 for each piece of medium armor equipped.
Wind Walker	Increases your Stamina Recovery by up to 4% for each piece of medium armor equipped; reduces the Stamina cost of your abilities by up to 2% for each piece of medium armor equipped.
Improved Sneak	Reduces the cost of Sneak by up to 7% for each piece of medium armor equipped; reduces the size of your detection area while sneaking by up to 5% for each piece of medium armor equipped.
Agility	Increases your Weapon Damage by up to 12% when five or more pieces of medium armor are equipped.
Athletics	Increases the movement speed bonus of Sprint by up to 3% for each piece of medium armor equipped; reduces the cost of Dodge Roll by up to 4% for each piece of medium armor equipped.

HEAVY ARMOR

Maximum Rank: Heavy Armor Rank 50

Maximum Investment: 13 Skill Points

UNLOCKING AND PROGRESSING HEAVY ARMOR

The Heavy Armor skill line is unlocked when you equip three or more pieces of heavy armor.

Progress the skill line by earning Experience with at least one piece of heavy armor equipped.

Equipping multiple pieces of heavy armor accelerates skill line progression.

Investing in the Heavy Armor skill line is an easy choice for any who prize survivability.

ACTIVE ABILITY

IMMOVABLE

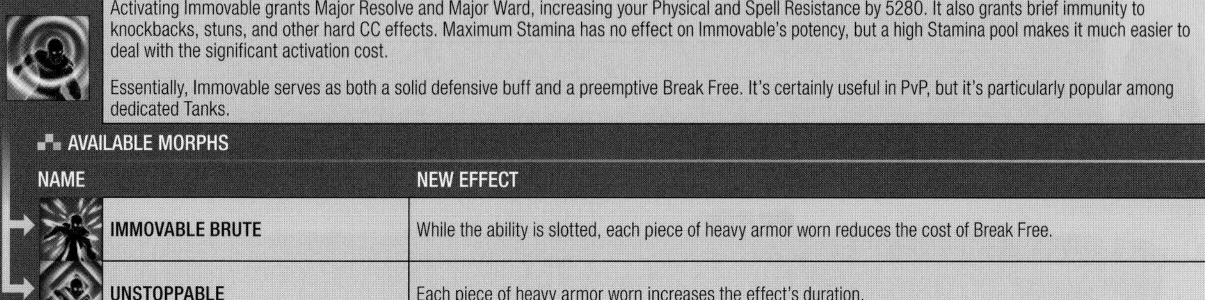

Activating Immovable grants Major Resolve and Major Ward, increasing your Physical and Spell Resistance by 5280. It also grants brief immunity to knockbacks, stuns, and other hard CC effects. Maximum Stamina has no effect on Immovable's potency, but a high Stamina pool makes it much easier to deal with the significant activation cost.

Essentially, Immovable serves as both a solid defensive buff and a preemptive Break Free. It's certainly useful in PvP, but it's particularly popular among dedicated Tanks.

AVAILABLE MORPHS

NAME	NEW EFFECT
IMMOVABLE BRUTE	While the ability is slotted, each piece of heavy armor worn reduces the cost of Break Free.
UNSTOPPABLE	Each piece of heavy armor worn increases the effect's duration.

PASSIVE ABILITIES

The Heavy Armor skill line contains five Passive Abilities. **Resolve** features three ranks; all other Heavy Armor Passives offer two ranks.

Resolve, **Constitution**, and **Juggernaut** can all offer aid to anyone using at least one piece of heavy armor, but equipping more pieces improves their effects.

PASSIVE REQUIREMENTS

You must have at least one piece of heavy armor equipped to receive any bonuses from Heavy Armor Passives. You must equip at least five heavy armor pieces to receive any benefit from **Wrath** or **Rapid Mending**.

Heavy Armor Passive Abilities

Name	Effect
Resolve	Increases your Physical and Spell Resistance by up to 362 for each piece of heavy armor equipped.
Constitution	Increases your Health Recovery by up to 4% for each piece of heavy armor equipped. You restore 108 Magicka and Stamina when you take damage for each piece of heavy armor equipped. This effect can occur once every four to eight seconds.
Juggernaut	Increases your Maximum Health by up to 2% for each piece of heavy armor equipped.
Wrath	Increases your Weapon and Spell Damage by up to 10 for five seconds when you take damage. This effect can stack a maximum of 20 times.
Rapid Mending	Increases your healing received by up to 8%; increases the Magicka or Stamina your heavy attacks restore by up to 25%.

WORLD SKILL LINES

World skill lines contain vastly different abilities. Between them, you'll find a selection of useful abilities that might benefit any character.

SOUL MAGIC

Maximum Rank: Soul Magic Rank 6

Maximum Investment: 10 Skill Points

UNLOCKING AND PROGRESSING SOUL MAGIC

The Soul Magic skill line is unlocked when you complete one of the game's tutorial missions, or when you choose to skip the tutorial on a new character.

Progress the skill line by advancing through the base game's main quest line. These quests are typically granted by the Prophet after he summons you to the Harborage.

Soul Magic is a relatively small but very important skill line tied to the game's main quest. It's available to all but the newest characters, and the few abilities it contains are worth consideration.

ULTIMATE ABILITY

SOUL STRIKE

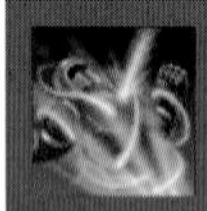

Soul Strike combines a channeled damage-over-time effect with a single-target snare. It also prevents the affected enemy from entering stealth or turning invisible. The effect has a short duration, but it can be very useful in PvP.

Soul Strike has great range and a fairly low Ultimate cost, making it a versatile option for single-target damage.

AVAILABLE MORPHS

NAME	NEW EFFECT
SOUL ASSAULT	The ability has a slightly longer duration.
SHATTER SOUL	If the target is killed, it explodes and damages nearby enemies.

ACTIVE ABILITY

SOUL TRAP

Soul Trap inflicts your target and up to one additional enemy with a damage-over-time effect. If an affected enemy dies, its essence fills an empty Soul Gem (if there's one in your inventory).

The damage component is certainly welcome, but Soul Trap's ability to fill Soul Gems is what makes it so important. It's also one of the only Active Abilities that doesn't require a Skill Point: as soon as you unlock the Soul Magic skill line, Soul Trap can be slotted on your Action Bar.

Every character should make use of Soul Trap during earlier levels. It won't take long for your Action Bar to reach capacity, but there's no reason to remove Soul Trap until it does. Use this time to rank up the ability and fill any Soul Gems you might recover.

AVAILABLE MORPHS

NAME	NEW EFFECT
SOUL SPLITTING TRAP	The ability affects an additional target.
CONSUMING TRAP	Also restores Health, Magicka, and Stamina if the enemy dies while affected.

PASSIVE ABILITIES

Soul Magic offers three Passive Abilities, each of which has two ranks.

Soul Shatter offers a bit of emergency damage, while Soul Summons and Soul Lock are both convenient tools for gem management.

Soul Magic Passive Abilities

Name	Effect
Soul Shatter	(Requires a slotted Soul Magic ability) If your Health drops below 20%, your soul explodes, dealing Magic Damage to nearby enemies. This effect can only be triggered once every two minutes.
Soul Summons	Allows you to revive once every one to two hours without spending a Soul Gem.
Soul Lock	Killing an enemy with a weapon ability has a chance of automatically filling an empty Soul Gem.

LEGERDEMAIN

Maximum Rank: Legerdemain Rank 20

Maximum Investment: 20 Skill Points

UNLOCKING AND PROGRESSING LEGERDEMAIN

The Legerdemain skill line is unlocked the first time you successfully pick a lock, pick a pocket, or use a Fence to launder or sell stolen goods.

Progress the skill line by picking locks, picking pockets, and laundering/selling stolen goods.

The Legerdemain skill line contains five Passive Abilities, each of which has four available ranks. It features no options for Active Abilities.

Essentially, the Legerdemain skill line serves to make your character a better thief. Heavy investment makes it much easier to acquire and profit from stolen goods. However, the benefits of **Improved Hiding** extend far beyond criminal activities—even those who prefer to stay on the right side of the law might consider this ability a worthy investment.

PASSIVE REQUIREMENTS

Once you invest in a Legerdemain Passive, its effects are always active.

Legerdemain Passive Abilities

Name	Effect
Improved Hiding	Reduces the Stamina cost of sneaking by up to 40%.
Light Fingers	Increases the chance of successfully pickpocketing by up to 50%.
Trafficker	Increases the number of Fence interactions you can use each day by up to 180% (140 item transactions).
Locksmith	Improves your chances of forcing locks by up to 70%.
Kickback	Reduces the Bounties you willingly pay to guards and Fences by 20%.

VAMPIRE

Maximum Rank: Vampire Rank 10

Maximum Investment: 15 Skill Points

UNLOCKING AND PROGRESSING VAMPIRE

The Vampire skill line is unlocked when you complete the Vampire quest line, which becomes available if you're infected by a Bloodfiend or by an infected player.

Vampirism is not available to characters currently afflicted with Lycanthropy.

Progress the skill line by earning Experience after gaining Vampirism.

As a cursed affliction, Vampirism carries a mix of benefits and drawbacks—and all the benefits are tied to the Vampire skill line. Whether or not you care to slot Vampire abilities, you'd be well advised to invest in at least a few of the available Passives.

Both of the skill line's Active Abilities are Magicka-based, and the Ultimate Ability deals Magic Damage. For more potent Vampire abilities, focus on Maximum Magicka, Spell Damage, and Spell Critical.

ULTIMATE ABILITY

BAT SWARM

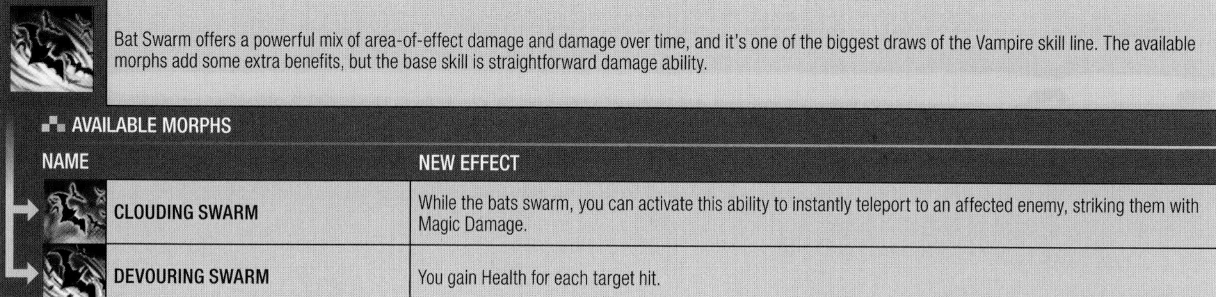

Bat Swarm offers a powerful mix of area-of-effect damage and damage over time, and it's one of the biggest draws of the Vampire skill line. The available morphs add some extra benefits, but the base skill is straightforward damage ability.

AVAILABLE MORPHS

NAME	NEW EFFECT
CLOUDING SWARM	While the bats swarm, you can activate this ability to instantly teleport to an affected enemy, striking them with Magic Damage.
DEVOURING SWARM	You gain Health for each target hit.

ACTIVE ABILITIES

DRAIN ESSENCE

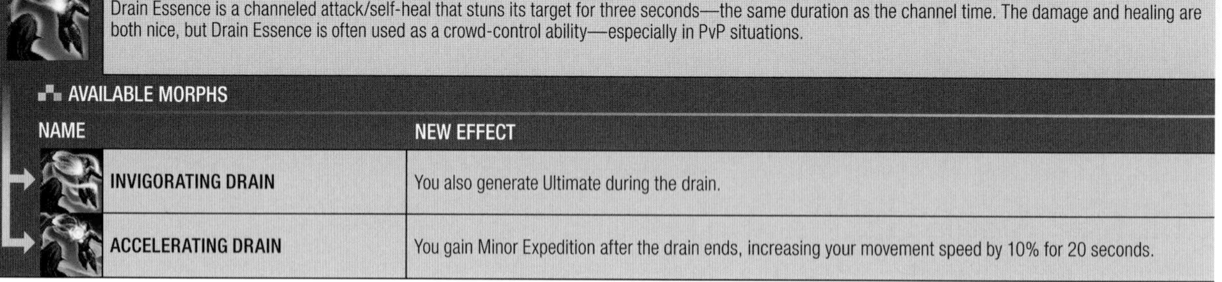

Drain Essence is a channeled attack/self-heal that stuns its target for three seconds—the same duration as the channel time. The damage and healing are both nice, but Drain Essence is often used as a crowd-control ability—especially in PvP situations.

AVAILABLE MORPHS

NAME	NEW EFFECT
INVIGORATING DRAIN	You also generate Ultimate during the drain.
ACCELERATING DRAIN	You gain Minor Expedition after the drain ends, increasing your movement speed by 10% for 20 seconds.

DRAIN ESSENCE TO DRAIN STAMINA

Blocking will end Drain Essence's channeled effect, leaving you free to use other abilities before your target recovers. If your target uses Break Free, you've forced them to sacrifice a good chunk of Stamina. If not, your follow-up attack is a sure hit.

MIST FORM

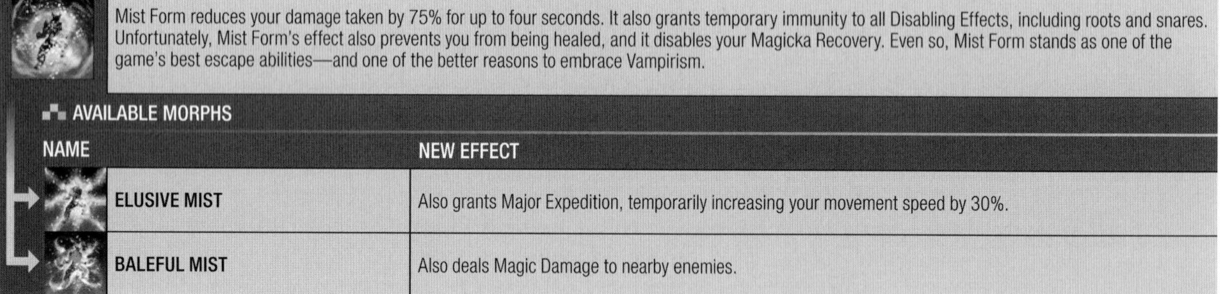

Mist Form reduces your damage taken by 75% for up to four seconds. It also grants temporary immunity to all Disabling Effects, including roots and snares. Unfortunately, Mist Form's effect also prevents you from being healed, and it disables your Magicka Recovery. Even so, Mist Form stands as one of the game's best escape abilities—and one of the better reasons to embrace Vampirism.

AVAILABLE MORPHS

NAME	NEW EFFECT
ELUSIVE MIST	Also grants Major Expedition, temporarily increasing your movement speed by 30%.
BALEFUL MIST	Also deals Magic Damage to nearby enemies.

MIST OPPORTUNITIES

Remember: Mist Form's damage mitigation is impressive, but it isn't absolute. If you wait too long to use it, incoming damage will likely finish you off.

PASSIVE ABILITIES

The Vampire skill line contains six Passive Abilities. **Savage Feeding**, **Supernatural Recovery**, and **Undeath** each feature two ranks. **Blood Ritual**, **Unnatural Resistance**, and **Dark Stalker** are all single-rank Passives.

Vampire Passive Abilities go a long way toward ensuring that the benefits of Vampirism outweigh the drawbacks. If you choose to accept this affliction, plan to invest in all available Passives.

PASSIVE REQUIREMENTS

You can only receive the benefits of **Supernatural Recovery** once you reach Vampirism Stage 2. Vampirism Stage 3 is required for **Undeath** to take effect, and **Dark Stalker** can only be active at Vampirism Stage 4.

Vampire Passive Abilities

Name	Effect
Savage Feeding	After feeding, your target is set off-balance and stunned for up to four seconds.
Supernatural Recovery	At Vampirism Stage 2 or higher, your Magicka and Stamina Recovery are increased by up to 10%.
Blood Ritual	Allows you to infect another player with Noxiphilic Sanguivoria once every seven days by returning to a Vampire ritual site. Players with Lycanthropy cannot be infected.
Undeath	At Vampirism Stage 3 or higher, your damage taken is reduced when your Health drops too low (30% to 50% of Maximum Health). The effect increases based on the amount of missing Health, reducing up to 33% of your damage taken.
Unnatural Resistance	Reduces the severity of the Health Recovery detriment in Vampirism Stages 2 through 4.
Dark Stalker	Allows you to ignore the movement speed penalty while in Crouch. Decreases the time it takes to crouch by 50% during the night.

WEREWOLF

Maximum Rank: Werewolf Rank 10

Maximum Investment: 21 Skill Points

UNLOCKING AND PROGRESSING WEREWOLF

The Werewolf skill line is unlocked when you complete the Werewolf quest line, which becomes available if you're infected by a Werewolf or by an infected player.

Lycanthropy is not available to characters currently afflicted with Vampirism.

Progress the skill line by killing enemies while in Werewolf form.

Like Vampirism, Lycanthropy grants powerful benefits while inflicting significant penalties. A character with Lycanthropy can ignore the affliction without consequence, but if you plan to utilize the Werewolf form, a heavy investment in the Werewolf skill line is recommended.

While transformed into a Werewolf, you only have access to Werewolf abilities; outside of transformations, only the Werewolf Ultimate Ability can be used.

While it does contain one Magicka ability, the Werewolf skill line clearly favors Stamina use. Invest in Maximum Stamina, Stamina Recovery, Weapon Damage, and Weapon Critical if you want to make the most of Werewolf transformations.

ULTIMATE ABILITY

WEREWOLF TRANSFORMATION

True to its name, Werewolf Transformation is what allows your character to transform into a Werewolf—if you want to take advantage of Lycanthropy, this ability *must* be slotted on your Action Bar.

While in Werewolf form, your light attacks inflict the Bleeding effect, your Physical and Spell Resistance are dramatically improved, your sprint speed is increased, and your unlocked Werewolf abilities appear on your Action Bar. Activating Werewolf Transformation also fears nearby enemies.

While Werewolf Transformation is slotted, your Stamina Recovery is increased by 15%. This bonus is applied whether or not your character is in Werewolf form.

Remember: Werewolf Transformation carries a very high Ultimate cost, and the effect has a fairly short duration. It also increases your vulnerability to Poison Damage, so take all necessary precautions.

AVAILABLE MORPHS

NAME	NEW EFFECT
PACK LEADER	Also summons two wolf companions to fight by your side.
WEREWOLF BERSERKER	Increases the Bleeding Damage inflicted by your light attacks.

A SKILL POINT SAVED

Werewolf Transformation is currently the only Ultimate Ability that doesn't require a Skill Point investment—the ability is automatically unlocked when you complete the Werewolf skill line. However, it still costs a Skill Point to morph the ability.

ACTIVE ABILITIES

POUNCE

Pounce is a hard-hitting gap closer that stuns the target enemy for two seconds if they were already set off-balance. It's a solid attack and an important part of Werewolf mobility.

AVAILABLE MORPHS

NAME	NEW EFFECT
BRUTAL POUNCE	Deals additional damage to the target and other nearby enemies.
FERAL POUNCE	Pouncing from at least 10 meters away extends the duration of your transformation.

HIRCINE'S BOUNTY

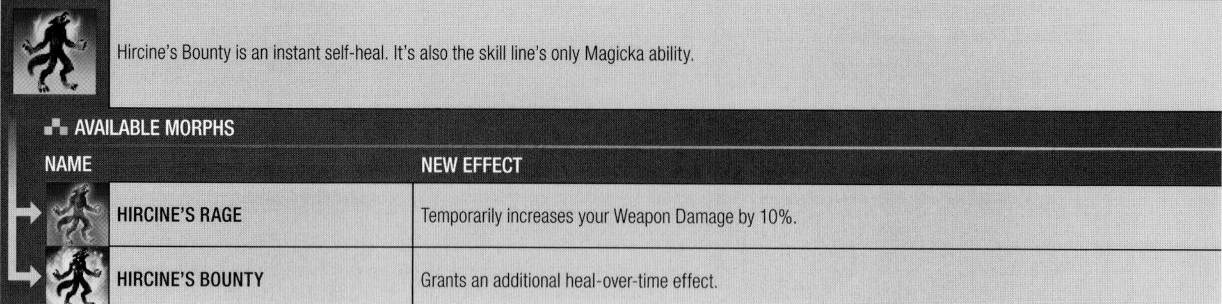

Hircine's Bounty is an instant self-heal. It's also the skill line's only Magicka ability.

AVAILABLE MORPHS

NAME	NEW EFFECT
HIRCINE'S RAGE	Temporarily increases your Weapon Damage by 10%.
HIRCINE'S BOUNTY	Grants an additional heal-over-time effect.

ROAR

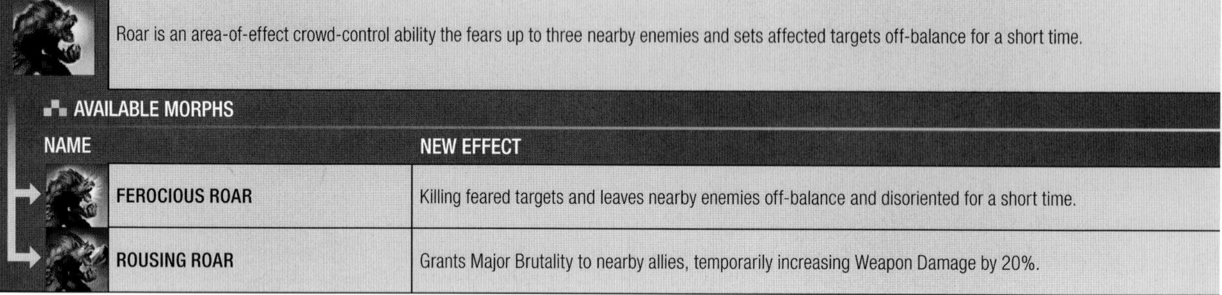

Roar is an area-of-effect crowd-control ability the fears up to three nearby enemies and sets affected targets off-balance for a short time.

AVAILABLE MORPHS

NAME	NEW EFFECT
FEROCIOUS ROAR	Killing feared targets and leaves nearby enemies off-balance and disoriented for a short time.
ROUSING ROAR	Grants Major Brutality to nearby allies, temporarily increasing Weapon Damage by 20%.

PIERCING HOWL

Piercing Howl is a powerful direct-damage attack that also features a Stun effect—one of your better options for single-target damage.

AVAILABLE MORPHS

NAME	NEW EFFECT
HOWL OF DESPAIR	Adds the Feeding Frenzy Synergy, allowing your allies to increase the damage of their light and heavy attacks.
HOWL OF AGONY	Increases your damage done to feared enemies.

INFECTIOUS CLAWS

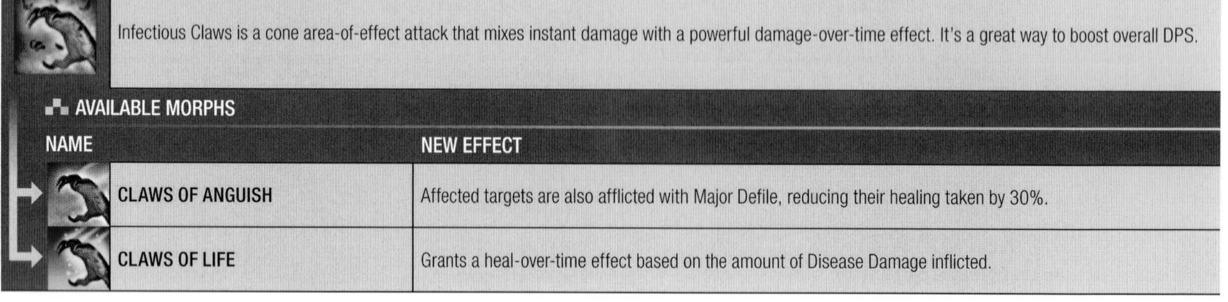

Infectious Claws is a cone area-of-effect attack that mixes instant damage with a powerful damage-over-time effect. It's a great way to boost overall DPS.

AVAILABLE MORPHS

NAME	NEW EFFECT
CLAWS OF ANGUISH	Affected targets are also afflicted with Major Defile, reducing their healing taken by 30%.
CLAWS OF LIFE	Grants a heal-over-time effect based on the amount of Disease Damage inflicted.

PASSIVE ABILITIES

The Werewolf skill line contains six Passive Abilities. **Devour** and **Blood Moon** are single-rank Passives; all other Werewolf Passives offer two ranks.

Simply slotting Werewolf Transformation represents a large investment in the Werewolf skill line, and all available Passives help ensure that you get the most out of this Ultimate Ability. Still, it takes a lot of Skill Points to unlock all available Werewolf abilities—you might face some tough choices when it comes to the skill line's Passives.

Consider prioritizing **Pursuit** and **Savage Strength**. Most of the remaining Werewolf Passives affect the duration of your transformation, so it's best to choose options that best suit your playstyle.

PASSIVE REQUIREMENTS

You can only receive benefits from Werewolf Passive Abilities while in Werewolf form.

Werewolf Passive Abilities

Name	Effect
Pursuit	Increases the Stamina your heavy attacks restore by up to 100%.
Devour	Allows you to devour corpses. Each feeding increases the duration of your Werewolf Transformation by 12 seconds.
Blood Rage	Increases the duration of your Werewolf Transformation by up to three seconds each time you take damage. This effect can occur once every three to five seconds.
Blood Moon	Allows you to infect another player with Lycanthropy once every seven days by returning to the Werewolf ritual site. Players afflicted with Vampirism cannot be infected.
Savage Strength	Increases your Weapon Damage by up to 18%.
Call of the Pack	Reduces the cost of remaining in your Werewolf Transformation based on the number of transformed Werewolves in your group.

GUILD SKILL LINES

Tamriel is home to a number of NPC guilds, each of which has its own unique purpose. Join them all to access new adventures, earn new rewards, and (perhaps most importantly) unlock new skill lines.

As you rank up various guild skill lines, unlock whatever abilities might benefit your character.

FIGHTERS GUILD

Maximum Rank: Fighters Guild Rank 10

Maximum Investment: 19 Skill Points

UNLOCKING AND PROGRESSING FIGHTERS GUILD

The Fighters Guild skill line is unlocked when you complete the first step of the Fighters Guild quest line, or when you speak to a recruiting Fighters Guild member and agree to join.

Progress the skill line by completing Fighters Guild quests, destroying Dark Anchors, and killing Undead and Daedra enemies.

The Fighters Guild skill line offers a selection of powerful Stamina abilities, making it a popular line for players focused on Physical Damage. If you plan to use any of these skills, consider prioritizing Maximum Stamina, Stamina Recovery, Weapon Damage, and Weapon Critical.

It can take quite a while to progress the Fighters Guild skill line. Join up as early as possible to ensure that you receive the full benefit of killing Undead, Daedra, and Werewolf enemies.

ULTIMATE ABILITY

DAWNBREAKER

Dawnbreaker has long been a top-pick Ultimate Ability for Stamina DPS, and it's not hard to see why. This cone area of effect follows a heavy burst of Physical Damage with a powerful damage-over-time effect. It has decent range, a relatively low cost, and a particularly popular morph that grants a Passive Weapon Damage bonus.

AVAILABLE MORPHS

NAME	NEW EFFECT
FLAWLESS DAWNBREAKER	Increases your Weapon Damage by 5%.
DAWNBREAKER OF SMITING	Deals increased damage and knocks down affected enemies.

ACTIVE ABILITIES

SILVER BOLTS

Silver Bolts is a long-range attack that features a nice Snare effect. It's a great option for Stamina builds that don't utilize Bow skills.

AVAILABLE MORPHS

NAME	NEW EFFECT
SILVER SHARDS	Deals less damage, but hits up to five additional enemies.
SILVER LEASH	Deals more damage. Can be activated a second time to pull yourself to the target.

CIRCLE OF PROTECTION

Circle of Protection is an area-of-effect buff that grants you and nearby allies Minor Protection and Minor Endurance, reducing your damage taken by 8% and increasing your Stamina Recovery by 10%.

Circle of Protection affects a relatively small area—and it carries a considerable activation cost—but it's a nice group-support option for Stamina-heavy builds.

AVAILABLE MORPHS

NAME	NEW EFFECT
TURN UNDEAD	Fears Undead, Werewolves, and Daedra when activated. Increases the duration of the effect.
RING OF PRESERVATION	Reduces Stamina cost of Dodge Roll for allies within the ring.

EXPERT HUNTER

Activating Expert Hunter reveals any stealthed or invisible enemies within six meters. Exposed enemies cannot return to stealth or invisibility for three seconds. While this ability is slotted, you also receive Major Savagery, increasing your Weapon Critical rating by 2191.

Expert Hunter is a great tool in PvP, but its slotted bonus makes it useful in any situation. Take special note of the **Camouflaged Hunter** morph—it's popular choice players who favor sneak attacks.

AVAILABLE MORPHS

NAME	NEW EFFECT
EVIL HUNTER	While active, the effect also reduces the Stamina cost of Fighters Guild abilities.
CAMOUFLAGED HUNTER	Critical hits while crouched grant Minor Berserk, temporarily increasing attack damage by 8%.

TRAP BEAST

Trap Beast places a trap on the ground, damaging and immobilizing the first enemy to step onto it. It also grants you Minor Force, temporarily increasing your Critical Damage done by 10%.

While the damage-over-time effect is nice, Trap Beast is a great utility skill. It takes a while for the trap to arm, but it can be very effective in crowded areas.

AVAILABLE MORPHS

NAME	NEW EFFECT
REARMING TRAP	The trap resets once after being triggered.
LIGHTWEIGHT BEAST TRAP	The trap can be placed up to 28 meters away.

PASSIVE ABILITIES

The Fighters Guild skill line contains five Passive Abilities. **Slayer** and **Banish the Wicked** each feature three ranks. The remaining Passives are single-rank abilities.

Intimidating Presence lowers the Stamina cost of all Fighters Guild abilities, but it's also a handy Passive during basic questing. **Banish the Wicked** and **Skilled Tracker** are helpful in many PvE areas, but they grant excellent bonuses in PvP—Vampires and Werewolves can often be found among enemy players.

PASSIVE REQUIREMENTS

While some of these Passives have uses outside the skill line, you'll receive no benefits from **Slayer** or **Skilled Tracker** unless you slot at least one Fighters Guild ability.

Fighters Guild Passive Abilities

Name	Effect
Intimidating Presence	Allows you to intimidate NPCs in conversation, and reduces the Stamina cost of your Fighters Guild abilities by 15%.
Slayer	Increases your Weapon Damage by up to 3% for each Fighters Guild ability slotted.
Banish the Wicked	Grants you up to an extra 9 Ultimate when you kill an Undead, Daedra, or Werewolf.
Skilled Tracker	Your Fighters Guild abilities deal an additional 20% damage to Undead, Daedra, and Werewolves.
Bounty Hunter	Allows you to accept Bounty quests from the Fighters Guild in Cyrodiil.

MAGES GUILD

Maximum Rank: Mages Guild 10

Maximum Investment: 19 Skill Points

UNLOCKING AND PROGRESSING MAGES GUILD

The Mages Guild skill line is unlocked when you complete the first step of the Mages Guild quest line or speak to a recruiting Mages Guild member and agree to join.

Progress the skill line by completing Mages Guild quests and collecting Lorebooks.

The Mages Guild skill line offers a variety of useful Magicka abilities, making it an excellent skill line for players focused on spellcasting. If you plan to utilize Mages Guild abilities, prioritize Maximum Magicka, Magicka Recovery, Spell Damage, and Spell Critical.

CREDIT WHERE CREDIT'S DUE

While there's no reason to put off joining the Mages Guild, rest assured that any Lorebooks you collect before signing up will be applied to the Mages Guild skill line once you become a member. If you spot a Lorebook, don't hesitate to add it to your collection.

ULTIMATE ABILITY

METEOR

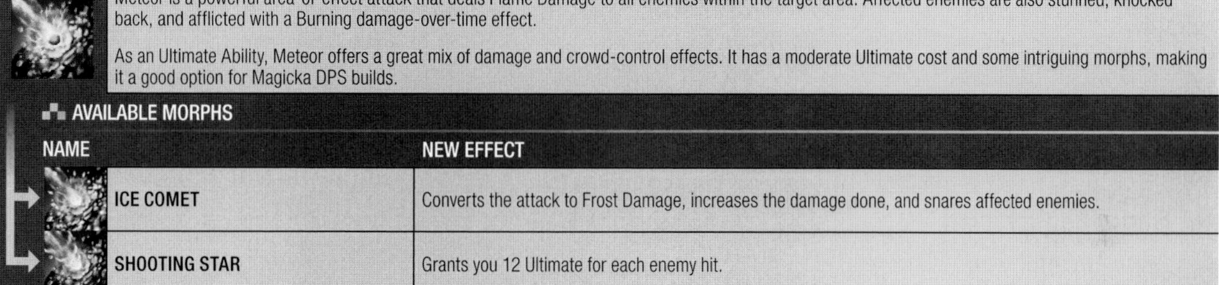

Meteor is a powerful area-of-effect attack that deals Flame Damage to all enemies within the target area. Affected enemies are also stunned, knocked back, and afflicted with a Burning damage-over-time effect.

As an Ultimate Ability, Meteor offers a great mix of damage and crowd-control effects. It has a moderate Ultimate cost and some intriguing morphs, making it a good option for Magicka DPS builds.

AVAILABLE MORPHS

NAME	NEW EFFECT
ICE COMET	Converts the attack to Frost Damage, increases the damage done, and snares affected enemies.
SHOOTING STAR	Grants you 12 Ultimate for each enemy hit.

ACTIVE ABILITIES

MAGELIGHT

Activating Magelight reveals any stealthed or invisible enemies within six meters. Exposed enemies cannot return to stealth or invisibility for three seconds. While this ability is slotted, you also receive Major Prophecy, increasing your Weapon Critical rating by 2191.

Magelight is a great tool in PvP, but its slotted bonus makes it useful in any situation—and both of the available morphs improve the benefits of slotting this ability.

AVAILABLE MORPHS

NAME	NEW EFFECT
INNER LIGHT	Also increases Maximum Magicka.
RADIANT MAGELIGHT	Reduces the cost and increases the radius of the reveal. Also prevents the Stun effect and reduces the damage taken from incoming stealth attacks.

ENTROPY

Entropy combines a lengthy damage-over-time effect with a bit of healing. It also grants you Major Sorcery, increasing your Spell Damage by 20% for 20 seconds. Put simply, Entropy is a low-cost spell with some great utility.

AVAILABLE MORPHS

NAME	NEW EFFECT
DEGENERATION	Your light and heavy attacks against the target have a chance to heal you.
STRUCTURED ENTROPY	While slotted, your Maximum Health is increased.

FIRE RUNE

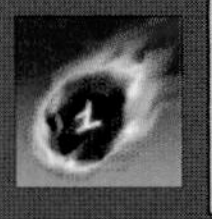

Fire Rune is essentially a damage trap—it takes two seconds for the rune to arm itself, after which it lasts up to 30 seconds. When (and if) it's triggered, the rune deals Flame Damage to all enemies within the target area.

This ability is most useful in PvP; use it to hinder invading armies, or to help protect key locations during siege warfare.

AVAILABLE MORPHS

NAME	NEW EFFECT
VOLCANIC RUNE	The enemy is knocked into the air.
SCALDING RUNE	Enemies also take Flame Damage over time.

EQUILIBRIUM

Activating Equilibrium sacrifices a portion of your Health to restore Magicka. The exchange renders you unable to heal yourself for four seconds—though you can still receive healing from other players.

Equilibrium's Health cost might be an issue for more fragile builds, but it's a great resource-management tool for well-defended casters.

AVAILABLE MORPHS

NAME	NEW EFFECT
SPELL SYMMETRY	Reduces the cost of your next spell.
BALANCE	Adds 5280 Physical and Spell Resistance.

PASSIVE ABILITIES

The Mages Guild skill line contains five Passive Abilities. **Persuasive Will** is a single-rank Passive; all other Mages Guild Passives offer two ranks.

Persuasive Will can be a time-saver when you're out questing, but it doesn't have any effect on combat performance. This makes it a better fit for leveling builds than for characters used in Veteran content.

The remaining Passives offer great benefits to those who favor Mages Guild abilities. If you plan to make use of this skill line, consider investing in all combat-related Passives.

PASSIVE REQUIREMENTS

Apart from **Persuasive Will**, this skill line's Passives provide no benefits unless at least one Mages Guild ability is available for use on your Action Bar.

Mages Guild Passive Abilities

Name	Effect
Persuasive Will	Allows you to persuade NPCs in conversation.
Mage Adept	Reduces the Magicka and Health costs of Mages Guild abilities by up to 15%.
Everlasting Magic	Increases the duration of Mages Guild abilities by up to 20%.
Magicka Controller	Increases your Maximum Magicka and Magicka Recovery by up to 2% for each Mages Guild ability slotted.
Might of the Guild	Casting a Mages Guild ability grants you a chance to cause Empower, increasing the damage of your next attack by 20% as long as it's activated within five seconds.

UNDAUNTED

Maximum Rank: Undaunted Rank 10

Maximum Investment: 14 Skill Points

UNLOCKING AND PROGRESSING UNDAUNTED

The Undaunted skill line is unlocked when you speak to a recruiting Undaunted member and agree to join.

Progress the skill line by earning Dungeon Achievements, and by completing the daily Undaunted Pledges that become available at Character Level 45.

The Undaunted skill line features a mix of Magicka and Stamina abilities, all with a heavy focus on group support. It contains options for damage, defense, healing, and crowd control, along with one of the game's few taunts.

The skill line doesn't include an Ultimate Ability, but every Undaunted Active Ability features a Synergy component. If you plan to participate in dungeons and Trials, consider the abilities offered by this skill line.

ACTIVE ABILITIES

BLOOD ALTAR

Activating Blood Altar afflicts nearby enemies with Minor Lifesteal—a debuff that grants Health to anyone attacking an affected target. Allies can also activate the Blood Funnel Synergy to heal themselves for 40% of their Maximum Health.

Blood Alter is a Magicka ability with a moderate radius and a bit of a cast time. It's an excellent support ability for Healers and Magicka DPS—especially for those who join the Undaunted early. As long as you have an available Skill Point, Blood Altar can be unlocked the moment you join the guild.

AVAILABLE MORPHS

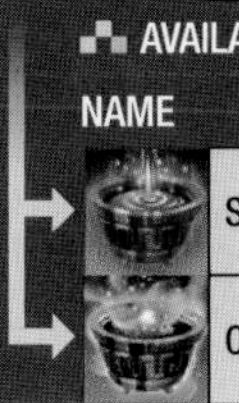

NAME	NEW EFFECT
SANGUINE ALTAR	Increases the altar's duration.
OVERFLOWING ALTAR	Increases the healing done by the Blood Feast Synergy.

TRAPPING WEBS

Trapping Webs is an area-of-effect snare that erupts after five seconds, dealing Poison Damage to enemies in the area. Allies can activate the Spawn Broodlings Synergy against any snared enemy, dealing additional Poison Damage over time.

This Stamina ability has great range but a small radius, so placement is important. It's a handy crowd-control option, and the available Synergy has excellent damage potential when multiple allies are in range.

AVAILABLE MORPHS

NAME	NEW EFFECT
SHADOW SILK	The Synergy summons more powerful black widow spiders, which deal additional damage over time.
TANGLING WEBS	The Synergy also fears the enemy.

INNER FIRE

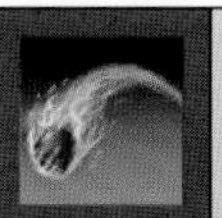

Inner Fire serves as a long-range taunt that deals Magicka damage to its target. It also grants a 15% chance that allies targeting the taunted enemy can activate the Radiate Synergy, causing additional damage over time and area-of-effect damage. It's a great skill for Magicka Tanks, but it's a viable option for any tanking build.

Inner Fire is a Magicka ability, but it offers a Stamina morph—because it maintains the base ability's range, **Inner Beast** is very popular among Stamina Tanks.

AVAILABLE MORPHS

NAME	NEW EFFECT
INNER RAGE	Increases the chance of a Synergy opportunity.
INNER BEAST	(Stamina morph) The ability has a reduced cost and scales off of Weapon Damage and Maximum Stamina.

BONE SHIELD

Bone Shield is a Stamina-based damage shield that scales off of the caster's Maximum Health. Allies can activate the Bone Wall Synergy, absorbing damage they'd otherwise take. This effect scales based on the allies' Maximum Health. The wall lasts 10 seconds and affects up to four nearby allies.

Basically, Bone Shield is another solid option for damage mitigation. For Tanks, its usefulness comes down to how many damage shields they already have access to and the resources they have available. However, its value as a support ability makes it well worth considering.

AVAILABLE MORPHS

NAME	NEW EFFECT
SPIKED BONE SHIELD	Returns damage to melee attackers.
BONE SURGE	The Synergy also grants Minor Vitality, increasing allies' healing received by 8%.

NECROTIC ORB

Necrotic Orb is a Magicka-based, area-of-effect, damage-over-time attack that moves slowly along a straight path. It also allows a nearby ally to activate the Combustion Synergy, causing a burst of area-of-effect Magic Damage while restoring the ally an amount of Magicka or Stamina (depending on which resource has the biggest pool).

Like most Undaunted abilities, Necrotic Orb's true value lies with the featured Synergy. It's a great way to deal some damage while supporting depleted allies.

AVAILABLE MORPHS

NAME	NEW EFFECT
MYSTIC ORB	Deals increased damage.
ENERGY ORB	Heals allies instead of damaging enemies.

PASSIVE ABILITIES

The Undaunted skill line contains two Passive Abilities, each of which has two ranks.

The available Passives aren't tied to Undaunted abilities, so they can benefit any build.

PASSIVE REQUIREMENTS

Once you've invested in an Undaunted Passive, its effect is always active. However, equipping at least one piece of each armor type is the only way to receive the full benefit of **Undaunted Mettle.**

Undaunted Passive Abilities

Name	Effect
Undaunted Command	Activating an ally's Synergy restores up to 4% of your Maximum Health, Stamina, and Magicka.
Undaunted Mettle	Increases your Maximum Health, Stamina, and Magicka by up to 2% for each type of armor (heavy, medium, and light) you have equipped.

THIEVES GUILD

Maximum Rank: Thieves Guild Rank 12

Maximum Investment: 11 Skill Points

UNLOCKING AND PROGRESSING THIEVES GUILD

The skill line is unlocked when you open a Thieves Trove or enter Hew's Bane (both actions require access to the Thieves Guild DLC pack).

Progress the skill line by finishing Thieves Guild quests, completing heists, and committing crimes posted within the Thieves Guild hideout.

The Thieves Guild skill line contains six Passive Abilities. **Swiftly Forgotten** and **Haggling** each offers four ranks. Remaining abilities are single-rank Passives.

Finders Keepers, which allows you to open Thieves Troves, doesn't require a Skill Point; it becomes active as soon as the skill line is unlocked.

Appropriately, the Thieves Guild skill line focuses on making criminal activities less risky and more profitable. The Passives have little effect outside of crime and the Justice System, but they're very useful bonuses for anyone who relies on less savory sources of income.

PASSIVE REQUIREMENTS

Once you invest in a Thieves Guild Passive Ability, its benefits are always active.

Thieves Guild Passive Abilities

Name	Effect
Finders Keepers	(Default Passive) Thieves Troves are caches located all over Tamriel. They can only be opened by members of the Thieves Guild.
Swiftly Forgotten	Bounty is decreased by up to 115 after three minutes. Heat is decreased by up to 64 after three seconds.
Haggling	Stolen items sold at a Fence are worth up to 10% more. This value does not apply to laundering.
Clemency	When a guard accosts you, you may use Clemency once per day. If used, the guard will not arrest you or take your money and stolen goods. Additionally, guards will not attempt to accost you for one minute after you use Clemency unless you commit other crimes.
Timely Escape	When you have Bounty and are in combat, you have a chance to spot a "Footpad" in a town with an Outlaws Refuge. Interacting with the Footpad will transport you safely into the nearest Refuge.
Veil of Shadows	Decreases detection range of witnesses and guards by 10%. Witnesses are thus less likely to notice crimes, while guards won't challenge until they get closer.

DARK BROTHERHOOD

Maximum Rank: Dark Brotherhood Rank 12

Maximum Investment: 11 Skill Points

UNLOCKING AND PROGRESSING DARK BROTHERHOOD

The Dark Brotherhood skill line is unlocked when you complete **Quest: Voices in the Dark** (requires access to the Dark Brotherhood DLC pack).

Progress the skill line by completing Dark Brotherhood story quests, contract quests, and Sacrament quests.

The Dark Brotherhood skill line contains six Passive Abilities. **Scales of Pitiless Justice** and **Padomaic Sprint** each offers four ranks. All remaining Passives are singe-rank abilities.

Blade of Woe does not require a Skill Point. It becomes available as soon as the Dark Brotherhood skill line is unlocked.

Dark Brotherhood Passive Abilities generally deal with assassinating NPCs. However, the **Shadow Rider** Passive is an excellent option for day-to-day adventuring or resource-gathering.

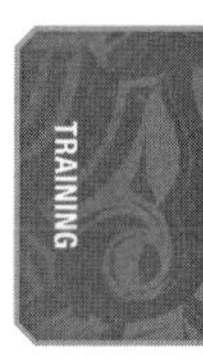

PASSIVE REQUIREMENTS

Once you invest in a Dark Brotherhood Passive, its effects are always active.

Dark Brotherhood Passive Abilities

Name	Effect
Blade of Woe	Call the weapon of the Dark Brotherhood to your hand and deliver a killing blow to an unsuspecting target. Experience from this target is reduced by 75%. Does not work on players or difficult targets.
Scales of Pitiless Justice	Bounty and Heat resulting from a witnessed murder or assault are reduced by up to 50%.
Padomaic Sprint	Grants Major Expedition, increasing your movement speed by 30% for up to 12 seconds after killing a Justice NPC.
Shadowy Supplier	A contact from the Brotherhood provides beneficial items once per day.
Shadow Rider	Aggression radius from hostile monsters is decreased by 50% while mounted.
Spectral Assassin	Grants a 15% chance to shroud you when using the Blade of Woe, shielding you from being witnessed and receiving a Bounty.

ALLIANCE WAR SKILL LINES

Alliance War skill lines offer additional options for damage, healing, and utility. While all of these abilities are useful in PvP, many of them perform just as well in PvE content.

ASSAULT

Maximum Rank: Assault Rank 10

Maximum Investment: 16 Skill Points

UNLOCKING AND PROGRESSING ASSAULT

The Assault skill line is unlocked when you earn your first Alliance Point reward.

Progress the skill line by continuing to earn Alliance Points.

The Assault skill line contains abilities meant to improve your offensive capabilities in Cyrodiil. While the line's Active Abilities can be useful in any situation, Assault Passive Abilities only provide benefits in PvP content.

Assault leans heavily toward Stamina abilities, but it does offer one Magicka ability.

ULTIMATE ABILITY

WAR HORN

War Horn is an excellent group buff that boosts Maximum Magicka and Maximum Stamina by 10%; it also grants Minor Toughness, increasing Maximum Health by 10%.

War Horn is a powerful buff with a large radius and some great morph effects. It has a high activation cost, but this Ultimate Ability is always welcome in group content. Keep in mind that these bonuses don't stack—coordinate with your teammates to maximize active buffs.

AVAILABLE MORPHS

NAME	NEW EFFECT
AGGRESSIVE HORN	Also grants Major Force, temporarily increasing Critical Strike Damage by 30%.
STURDY HORN	Increases the duration and grants 1320 Physical Resistance and Spell Resistance for the duration of the effect.

ACTIVE ABILITIES

RAPID MANEUVER

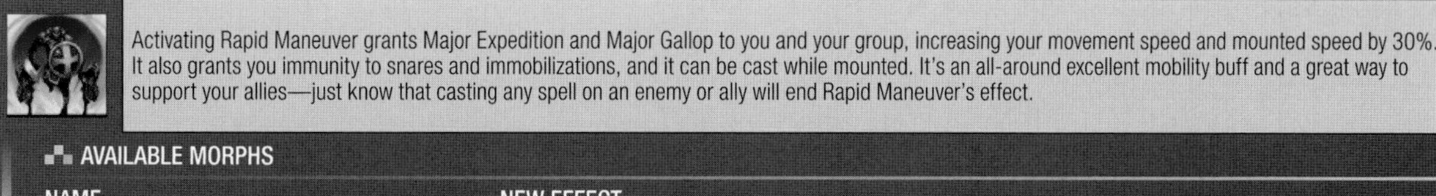

Activating Rapid Maneuver grants Major Expedition and Major Gallop to you and your group, increasing your movement speed and mounted speed by 30%. It also grants you immunity to snares and immobilizations, and it can be cast while mounted. It's an all-around excellent mobility buff and a great way to support your allies—just know that casting any spell on an enemy or ally will end Rapid Maneuver's effect.

AVAILABLE MORPHS

NAME	NEW EFFECT
RETREATING MANEUVER	Also removes all snares and immobilizations previously applied to you and your group.
CHARGING MANEUVER	Also grants Minor Expedition when the effect ends, temporarily increasing your movement speed by 10%.

VIGOR

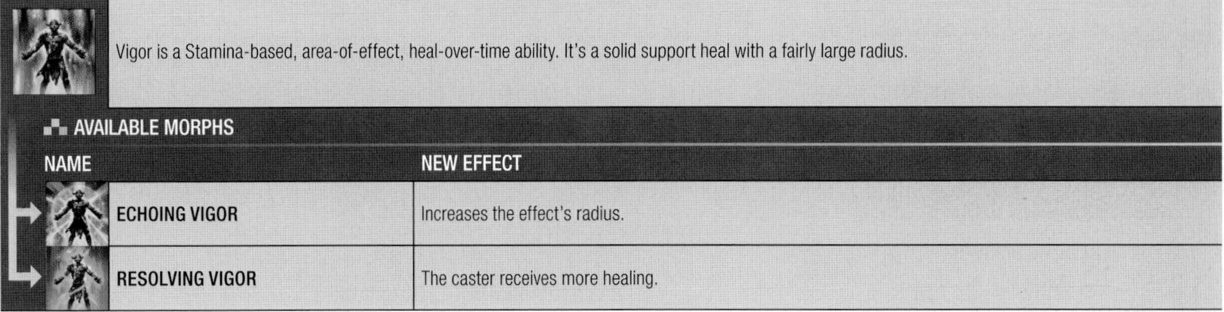

Vigor is a Stamina-based, area-of-effect, heal-over-time ability. It's a solid support heal with a fairly large radius.

AVAILABLE MORPHS

NAME	NEW EFFECT
ECHOING VIGOR	Increases the effect's radius.
RESOLVING VIGOR	The caster receives more healing.

CALTROPS

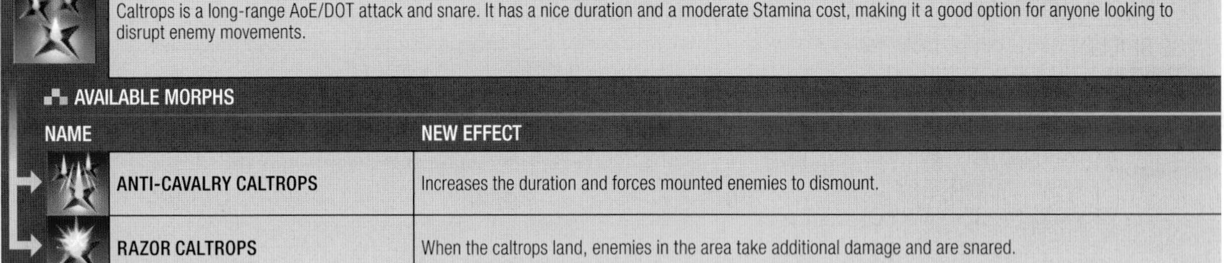

Caltrops is a long-range AoE/DOT attack and snare. It has a nice duration and a moderate Stamina cost, making it a good option for anyone looking to disrupt enemy movements.

AVAILABLE MORPHS

NAME	NEW EFFECT
ANTI-CAVALRY CALTROPS	Increases the duration and forces mounted enemies to dismount.
RAZOR CALTROPS	When the caltrops land, enemies in the area take additional damage and are snared.

MAGICKA DETONATION

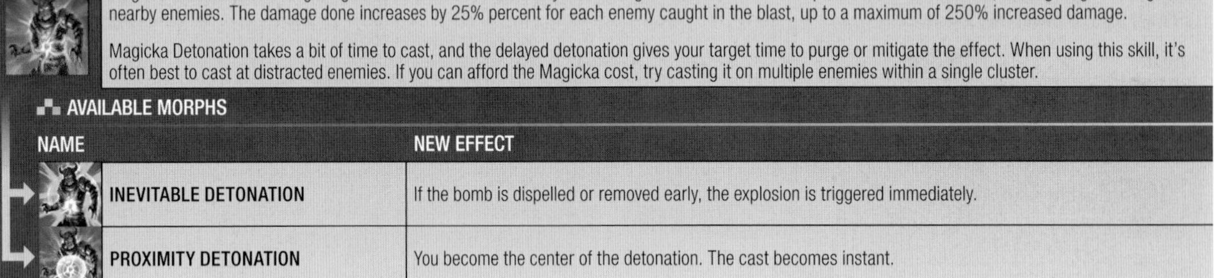

Magicka Detonation is a long-range attack that curses an enemy with a magical bomb. The bomb explodes after four seconds, dealing Magic Damage to all nearby enemies. The damage done increases by 25% percent for each enemy caught in the blast, up to a maximum of 250% increased damage.

Magicka Detonation takes a bit of time to cast, and the delayed detonation gives your target time to purge or mitigate the effect. When using this skill, it's often best to cast at distracted enemies. If you can afford the Magicka cost, try casting it on multiple enemies within a single cluster.

AVAILABLE MORPHS

NAME	NEW EFFECT
INEVITABLE DETONATION	If the bomb is dispelled or removed early, the explosion is triggered immediately.
PROXIMITY DETONATION	You become the center of the detonation. The cast becomes instant.

PASSIVE ABILITIES

The Assault skill line contains three Passive Abilities, each of which offers two ranks.

PASSIVE REQUIREMENTS

Assault Passive Abilities are very useful in Cyrodiil, but they don't grant any benefits outside of PvP.

Assault Passive Abilities

Name	Effect
Continuous Attack	Increases your Weapon and Spell Damage by up to 10%, and Magicka and Stamina Recovery by up to 20% for 10 minutes after you capture a lumber mill, farm, mine, or keep.
Reach	Increases the range of long-range abilities by up to five meters while near a keep. Any ability with a range greater than 15 meters is affected.
Combat Frenzy	You generate up to 20 Ultimate when you kill an enemy player.

SUPPORT

Maximum Rank: Support Rank 10

Maximum Investment: 16 Skill Points

UNLOCKING AND PROGRESSING SUPPORT

The Support skill line is unlocked when you earn your first Alliance Point reward.

Progress the skill line by continuing to earn Alliance Points.

The Support skill line features abilities meant to improve your defensive capabilities in Cyrodiil. Most of the skill line's Active Abilities can be useful in any situation, but only one of the available Passives grants any benefits outside of PvP.

Support contains several Magicka abilities and one Stamina ability.

ULTIMATE ABILITY

BARRIER

Barrier conjures damage-absorbing wards for you and nearby allies. It has a fairly high Ultimate cost, but Barrier is a defensive ability.

AVAILABLE MORPHS

NAME	NEW EFFECT
REVIVING BARRIER	Shielded allies gain Health Recovery.
REPLENISHING BARRIER	Each time a ward dissolves, you restore Ultimate and Magicka.

ACTIVE ABILITIES

SIEGE SHIELD

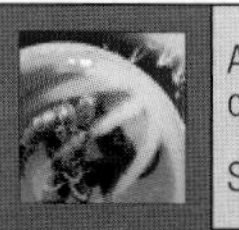

Activating Siege Shield creates a protective bubble around your location, reducing incoming Siege Weapon Damage by 35%. It may not be as versatile as other Support abilities, but it's very useful during large-scale battles.

Siege weapons often determine the winning side from the losing side, so limiting their effects is always a good strategy.

AVAILABLE MORPHS

NAME	NEW EFFECT
SIEGE WEAPON SHIELD	Allied siege weapons in the bubble take reduced damage from other siege weapons.
PROPELLING SHIELD	Costs less, and allies in the shield gain increased range.

PURGE

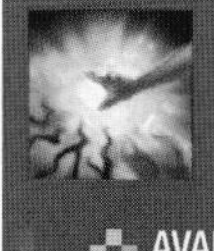

Purge allows you to cleanse yourself and your group, removing two negative effects and reducing the duration of any further negative effects by 50% for a short time.

It's a fairly expensive ability, but Purge has a large radius and a very useful effect.

AVAILABLE MORPHS

NAME	NEW EFFECT
EFFICIENT PURGE	Reduces the casting cost.
CLEANSE	If a negative effect is removed, the target is healed.

GUARD

Guard allows you to create a life bond between yourself and an allied player. While bonded, 30% of the damage your ally takes is instead delivered to you.

Guard is an instant-cast Stamina ability that remains active until you recast the spell or move more than 15 meters away from your ally. It's an easy way for heartier characters to support fragile allies, and the available morphs feature some particularly useful buffs.

AVAILABLE MORPHS

NAME	NEW EFFECT
MYSTIC GUARD	You and your bonded ally also gain Minor Vitality, increasing your healing received by 8%.
STALWART GUARD	You and your bonded ally also gain Minor Force, increasing your Critical Strike Damage.

REVEALING FLARE

Revealing Flare allows you to reveal stealthed and invisible enemies within a target area. Those exposed have their movement speed reduced by 50% and cannot return to stealth or invisibility for three seconds.

The ability has a fairly wide radius and an impressive range. It also boasts a low Magicka cost, making it possible to search large areas for hidden enemies.

AVAILABLE MORPHS

NAME	NEW EFFECT
LINGERING FLARE	The flare lingers at the target area, revealing enemies that enter it.
SCORCHING FLARE	Exposed enemies take damage over time.

PASSIVE ABILITIES

The Support skill line contains three Passive Abilities, each of which offers two ranks.

Support Passives are all useful in Cyrodiil, but only **Magicka Aid** offers a potential benefit outside of PvP.

PASSIVE REQUIREMENTS

Magicka Aid only grants a benefit while one or more Support abilities are slotted. **Combat Medic** and **Battle Resurrection** have no effect outside of PvP.

Passive Abilities

Name	Effect
Magicka Aid	Increases your Magicka Recovery by up to 10% for each Support ability slotted.
Combat Medic	Increases your healing done by 10% when you're near a keep.
Battle Resurrection	Reduces the time it takes to resurrect another player by 15% while you're in a PvP area.

RACIAL SKILL LINES

Every character has a selection of race-specific Passive Abilities that grant increased Attributes and other useful effects. With 10 races to choose from, the game includes a total of 10 racial skill lines.

Each of these skill lines contains a default Passive Ability—a minor benefit that becomes active once you reach Level 5. While this Passive is free, unlocking and improving the rest of the skill line requires a lot of time and a good supply of Skill Points.

It's recommended that you invest in all of your character's racial abilities. Doing so requires ranking the skill line to 50 and investing nine Skill Points.

Progressing your racial skill line is simply a matter of leveling your character. At Level 50, your character's racial skill line reaches its maximum rank.

For information about the Passive Abilities available to each race, please refer to **Races and Factions** chapter.

CRAFT SKILL LINES

Every character has access to six crafting-related skill lines, each of which features its own selection of Passive Abilities:

- Alchemy
- Blacksmithing
- Clothing
- Enchanting
- Provisioning
- Woodworking

You can unlock each of these skill lines by interacting with a related crafting station. Crafting skill lines progress as you earn Inspiration from actions like refining materials, creating items, deconstructing items, and completing crafting writs. As a crafting skill line ranks up, it grants access to Passives that serve to improve your crafting in one way or another.

Investing in all available crafting Passive Abilities requires 139 Skill Points—a costly feat by any measure. Of course, you can pick and choose Passives as you see fit. Or you can focus on priority crafting skills. You can even visit a Rededication Shrine to reclaim spent Skill Points after mastering a craft.

For more information on crafting skills (and crafting in general), refer to the guide's **Crafting** section.

ARCHETYPES

OVERVIEW

If you're having trouble settling on your new character, you might benefit from a quick look at the following archetype builds.

Each of these characters was designed to support a specific playstyle, but they represent only the smallest fraction of class/race/role combinations.

Note that archetype titles like "Zealot," "Beastmaster," and "Dragonscale" are meant to hint at each build's basic theme. They don't appear in the game, and they in no way limit the options available to you.

Archetypes are not offered as "best" builds. They're simply meant to give you a glimpse of the abilities and playstyles that you're bound to discover during your time in Tamriel.

While a certain set of abilities with certain gear should—in theory—yield certain results, the truth of the matter is that the way a character's played is far more important than the way a character is built.

Whether or not you model your character after an archetype, make sure you experiment with new abilities, equipment, and playstyles. If your character isn't living up to your expectations, use a Rededication Shrine to reclaim Skill Points or invest in different Attributes.

UNDERSTANDING CHARACTER ARCHETYPES

The provided archetypes are divided into four categories:

- **Magicka DPS:** Character builds that focus on dealing damage with spells
- **Stamina DPS:** Character builds that focus on dealing damage with melee weapons and bows
- **Tanks:** Character builds that prioritize survivability
- **Healers:** Character builds that focus on sustaining allies

While these categories indicate an archetype's role, they don't define it. Some DPS characters are designed to deal heavy, sustainable damage against formidable dungeon bosses; others are built for quick bursts of damage. Some Tanks are intended to lead their teammates in battle, while others are simply meant to survive alone in the wilds. Luckily, any character can be made to fill any role—all you need to do is find the right combination of abilities and equipment.

Nothing about an archetype is set in stone. From race and weapon selection to Attributes and Mundus Stone boons, every aspect of an archetype can be changed to suit your tastes.

CORE PASSIVES

Virtually every effective build requires heavy investment in Passive Abilities from skill lines that relate to class, race, armor, and weapons. These are considered "core" Passives that should be unlocked as they become available.

MAGICKA DPS

THE MAGE

Class: Sorcerer	Race: High Elf	Attribute Focus: Magicka	Weapon Types: Destruction Staves	Armor Focus: Light	Mundus Stone: The Thief

BAR 1: DESTRUCTION STAFF (FLAME STAFF)

KEY ABILITIES

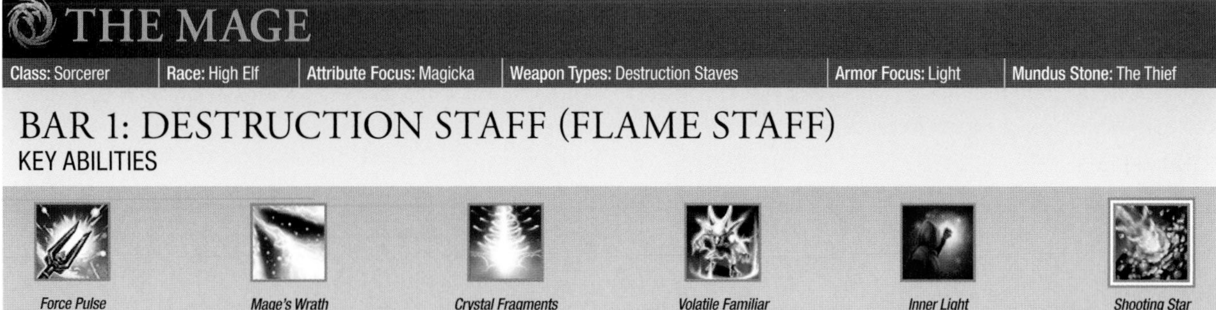

Force Pulse — *Mage's Wrath* — *Crystal Fragments* — *Volatile Familiar* — *Inner Light* — *Shooting Star*

Force Pulse: Morphed from **Force Shock** (Destruction Staff). This is your main ability for single-target damage.

Mage's Wrath: Morphed from **Mage's Fury** (Sorcerer > Storm Calling). A powerful execute ability. Use it when the target's Health drops below 20%.

Crystal Fragments: Morphed from **Crystal Shard** (Sorcerer > Dark Magic). Casting any other Magicka ability has a chance of reducing this spell's cost, eliminating its cast time, and increasing its damage. Use it only when this effect is triggered.

Volatile Familiar: Morphed from **Unstable Familiar** (Sorcerer > Daedric Summoning). This minion can add a good amount of single-target damage, and it has a great area-of-effect pulse.

Inner Light: Morphed from **Magelight** (Mages Guild). Slot this to boost your Maximum Magicka and Spell Critical. Use it when you need to reveal a stealthed player.

Shooting Star: Morphed from **Meteor** (Mages Guild). Use this powerful Ultimate Ability during boss encounters.

This is your main attack Bar. Use it while your longer-lasting abilities are in place and dealing damage. **Volatile Familiar** needs to be placed on both Action Bars, so it's taking up what would normally be a flex slot.

BAR 2: DESTRUCTION STAFF (FLAME STAFF)

KEY ABILITIES

Liquid Lightning

Haunting Curse

Elemental Blockade

Volatile Familiar

FLEX SLOT

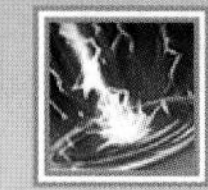
Elemental Rage

Liquid Lightning: Morphed from **Lightning Splash** (Sorcerer > Storm Calling). This powerful AoE/DOT ability should be kept up for the duration of any fight. While it's active, allies can use the Conduit Synergy to deal additional Shock Damage to nearby enemies.

Haunting Curse: Morphed from **Daedric Curse** (Sorcerer > Daedric Summoning). A powerful single-target attack with some area-of-effect splash damage. Recast as needed.

Elemental Blockade: Morphed from **Wall of Elements** (Destruction Staff). A very damaging ability that should be active at all times during any encounter.

Volatile Familiar: Morphed from **Unstable Familiar** (Sorcerer > Daedric Summoning). This ability is slotted on both Action Bars to prevent your minion from vanishing each time you swap weapons. Remember to pulse its area-of-effect attack as needed.

Elemental Rage: Morphed from **Elemental Storm** (Destruction Staff). This Ultimate Ability changes based on your staff type, but it hits hard with Flame Staves. Use it to clear out groups of weaker enemies.

This is your AoE/DOT Bar. Use it to initiate or maintain longer-lasting attacks, then swap back to your main Action Bar. If you're looking for more survivability, consider placing **Bound Aegis** in your flex slot. Otherwise, use any ability you feel is helpful.

PRIORITY PASSIVES

No surprises here. Invest in all of your core Passives as they become available.

CHAMPION POINT SUGGESTIONS

Thief: Invest heavily in Arcanist (Lover) and Tenacity (Lover).

Mage: Invest heavily in Elemental Expert (Apprentice) and Thaumaturge (Ritual). Elfborn (Apprentice) should also be a priority.

Warrior: Anything that helps your survivability should prove useful.

EQUIPMENT RECOMMENDATIONS

WEAPONS

Priority Trait: Sharpened

Priority Enchantment: Spell Damage

When it comes to maximizing your damage, stick with Flame Staves—preferably those featuring the **Sharpened** trait. Until you're able to obtain a set piece or something from the Maelstrom, use the best Flame Staves available to you.

Given the choice, look for staves that include Spell Damage enchantments.

ARMOR

Priority Trait: Divines

Priority Enchantment: Maximum Magicka

Always equip at least five pieces of light armor. The related Passives grant you some very important benefits. If you've invested in the **Undaunted Mettle** Passive Ability, remember to equip medium/heavy armor pieces in the remaining slots.

Equipment that grants suitable set bonuses is always your best option. Look for light armor that offers Maximum Magicka enchantments as you work toward obtaining high-level gear. Divines tends to be the most useful trait for Damage-Dealers, so keep an eye out for any options that cross your path.

JEWELRY

Priority Trait: Arcane

Priority Enchantment: Spell Damage

Until you manage to track down useful set pieces, use anything that increases Maximum Magicka and Spell Damage.

ARCHETYPE ADVICE

While using your main Action Bar, stick to **Force Pulse** until your target is below 20% Health. Once that happens, start using **Mage's Wrath**. **Crystal Fragments** should only be used when the instant cast procs (watch for the glow that appears on your character's hands).

The **Thief Mundus Stone** generally yields the greatest DPS gains, but you can still deal good damage without it. Don't hesitate to exchange it for any boon you think might be useful for a given situation.

Volatile Familiar can add a lot of damage over the course of a battle, but it's not right for every encounter. If you decide to replace this ability, make sure you pull it from both Action Bars.

Elemental Rage (or **Fiery Rage**, when a Flame Staff is equipped) does massive damage, but it's best avoided during boss encounters. Due to its lower Ultimate cost, **Shooting Star** is the better option for lengthy battles.

THE FLAMEBLADE

Class: Dragonknight | **Race:** Dark Elf | **Attribute Focus:** Magicka | **Weapon Types:** Dual Swords, Destruction Staff | **Armor Focus:** Light | **Mundus Stone:** The Atronach

BAR 1: DUAL WIELD (SWORDS)

KEY ABILITIES

Burning Embers

Engulfing Flames

Molten Whip

Flames of Oblivion

FLEX SLOT

Standard of Might

Burning Embers: Morphed from **Searing Strike** (Dragonknight > Ardent Flame). Used mostly for its healing effect, but the Flame Damage over time certainly helps DPS. Use it as soon as you're in range, and reapply as needed.

Engulfing Flames: Morphed from **Fiery Breath** (Dragonknight > Ardent Flame). A multi-target flame attack that applies damage over time while rendering affected targets more vulnerable to Flame Damage.

Molten Whip: Morphed from **Lava Whip** (Dragonknight > Ardent Flame). This is your primary single-target damage ability, and slotting it boosts the damage of all Ardent Flame abilities.

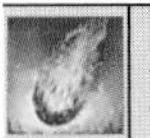

Flames of Oblivion: Morphed from **Inferno** (Dragonknight > Ardent Flame). Slotting this ability grants Major Prophecy and Major Savagery, which is the main reason it's on the Bar. Activate it as needed to maximize your DPS.

Standard of Might: Morphed from **Dragonknight Standard** (Dragon Knight > Ardent Flame). This Ultimate Ability deals Flame Damage while reducing the damage you take. A great option for difficult encounters.

This is your primary damage Bar. Use it when you're able to charge into the thick of the action. Get in close and apply those damage-over-time effects, then use **Molten Whip** to burn your enemies to the ground. You can boost your potential damage by slotting another Flame Damage-over-time effect. Otherwise, use the empty slot for additional utility or a more reliable heal.

BAR 2: DESTRUCTION STAFF (FLAME STAFF)

KEY ABILITIES

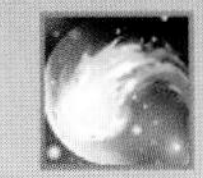

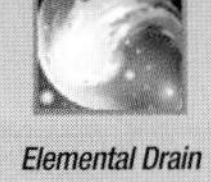

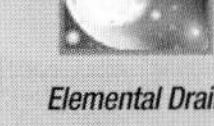

Elemental Drain

Force Pulse

Degeneration

Eruption

FLEX SLOT

Shooting Star

Elemental Drain: Morphed from **Weakness to Elements** (Destruction Staff). A free cast that inflicts your target with Major Breach and Minor Magickasteal. It's a great way to kick off any fight, and it's a big help with resource management during prolonged encounters.

Force Pulse: Morphed from **Force Shock** (Destruction Staff). This is your primary ranged attack.

Degeneration: Morphed from **Entropy** (Mages Guild). A ranged damage-over-time skill with some nice healing effects. Slotting it also grants Major Sorcery, boosting your Spell Damage.

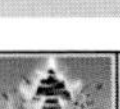

Eruption: Morphed from **Ash Cloud** (Dragonknight > Earthen Heart). This long-range flame attack includes a Snare effect.

Shooting Star: Morphed from **Meteor** (Mages Guild). This long-range Ultimate Ability combines heavy area-of-effect Flame Damage with a bit of crowd control. It also generates Ultimate based on the number of enemies hit. A great way to deal with swarming enemies.

This is your ranged Bar. Use it to apply **Elemental Drain** to a target, then swap to your swords and charge into the fray. Swap back when you need to reapply Elemental Drain or put some distance between yourself and your enemies, or when you find yourself low on Magicka. Place an ability of your choice in the remaining Bar slot.

PRIORITY PASSIVES

Make sure you invest in **Twin Blade and Blunt** (Dual Wield) to increase your damage done while two swords are equipped. It's the only reason this build favors swords for damage. The remaining Dual Wield Passives won't be as useful. **Dual Wield Expert** gives a small boost to your melee attacks, but avoid anything that only affects Dual Wield abilities. Other than that, invest in each of your core Passives as they become available.

CHAMPION POINT SUGGESTIONS

Thief: Invest heavily in Arcanist (Lover) for improved Magicka Recovery. Tenacity (Lover) can also be very helpful.

Mage: Invest heavily in Elemental Expert (Apprentice) and Thaumaturge (Ritual) for great damage gains.

Warrior: The combination of Elemental Defender (Lady) and Hardy (Lady) is always a good option, but you can spend these points wherever you like.

EQUIPMENT RECOMMENDATIONS

WEAPONS	ARMOR	JEWELRY
Priority Trait: Sharpened	**Priority Trait:** Divines	**Priority Trait:** Arcane
Priority Enchantment: Spell Damage	**Priority Enchantment:** Maximum Magicka	**Priority Enchantment:** Spell Damage
Stick with swords for dual-wielding—at least once you unlock the **Twin Blade and Blunt** Passive Ability. **Sharpened** is your best trait for overall damage, but don't shy away from any good sword with a useful trait.	Even on the front lines, you'll want to equip at least five pieces of light armor to take advantage of the skill line's Passives. If you've invested in the **Undaunted Mettle** Passive Ability, remember to equip medium/heavy armor pieces in the remaining slots.	Until you manage to track down useful set pieces, use anything that increases Maximum Magicka and Spell Damage.
For your main hand, look for something with a Spell Damage enchantment. You'll want to go for something different on your off-hand weapon, but there are plenty of useful options out there.	Equipment that grants suitable set bonuses is always your best option. Look for light armor that offers Maximum Magicka enchantments as you work toward obtaining high-level gear. **Divines** tends to be the Damage-Dealer's best option, so make it your priority armor trait.	

ARCHETYPE ADVICE

When it comes to race selection, the Dark Elf's boost to Flame Damage is the main consideration, but the XP gain in the Dual Wield skill line also makes it easier to obtain the **Twin Blade and Blunt** Passive Ability.

The use of swords raises your damage potential, but it doesn't help with sustainability. Swap to your Flame Staff and fire off a few heavy attacks when you need to recover some Magicka.

Don't forget to use the occasional light attack while dual-wielding. It won't do much damage with this build, but it's essential for Ultimate generation.

The **Atronach Mundus Stone** is selected to help with Magicka Recovery during basic adventuring. If sustainability isn't an issue for you, switch it out for a boon that improves your damage or survivability.

Your damage Bar should be enough to tear through common enemies, but get used to swapping weapons during difficult battles. Practice your attack rotation to maximize damage, sustainability, and survivability.

THE BLOODMAGE

Class: Nightblade	**Race:** Breton	**Attribute Focus:** Magicka	**Weapon Types:** Destruction Staves	**Armor Focus:** Light	**Mundus Stone:** The Thief

BAR 1: DESTRUCTION STAFF (FLAME STAFF)

KEY ABILITIES

Swallow Soul

Elemental Blockade

Impale

Crippling Grasp

Soul Harvest

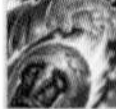	**Swallow Soul:** Morphed from **Strife** (Nightblade > Siphoning). This is your primary attack and a solid source of healing. Slotting it also grants Minor Vitality, increasing your healing received by 8%.
	**Elemental Blockade:** Morphed from **Wall of Elements** (Destruction Staff). A powerful area-of-effect skill that should be kept up at all times.
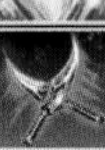	**Impale:** Morphed from **Assassin's Blade** (Nightblade > Assassination). A great ranged execute. Use it whenever your target's Health drops below 25%.
	Crippling Grasp: Morphed from **Cripple** (Nightblade > Siphoning). This is your main damage-over-time attack, but it also offers a bit of utility.
	Soul Harvest: Morphed from **Death Stroke** (Nightblade > Assassination). This is slotted to help with Ultimate generation, but it's also a great way to boost your **Impale** attacks.

This is your main damage Bar. Use it for the bulk of your attack rotation. The remaining slot can be used to hold any ability you like, but consider selecting a stronger heal or something that offers additional utility.

BAR 2: DESTRUCTION STAFF (LIGHTNING STAFF)

KEY ABILITIES

Siphoning Attacks

Twisting Path

Merciless Resolve

Harness Magicka

Elemental Rage

	**Siphoning Attacks:** Morphed from **Siphoning Strikes** (Nightblade > Siphoning). Causes your light and heavy attacks to restore Health and Magicka for 20 seconds.
	**Twisting Path:** Morphed from **Path of Darkness** (Nightblade > Shadow). Another solid AoE/DOT attack. Bring it into your attack rotation during longer battles.
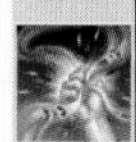	**Merciless Resolve:** Morphed from **Grim Focus** (Nightblade > Assassination). This long-lasting buff grants Minor Berserk, boosting your damage done by 8% for 20 seconds. It allows the use of a spectral bow. Cast at the start of each encounter and refresh as needed.
	**Harness Magicka:** Morphed from **Annulment** (Light Armor). A damage shield that mitigates incoming damage while restoring Magicka for each spell it absorbs. Use it when you're in danger of taking heavy damage.
	**Elemental Rage:** Morphed from **Elemental Storm** (Destruction Staff). A powerful area-of-effect skill that changes based on your staff type. It's chosen to keep a Destruction Staff ability on the Action Bar, but it's also the Ultimate Ability you'll use in most situations.

This is something of a utility Bar, but it's responsible for a lot of your damage. Use it to activate and refresh your longer-lasting abilities as needed. It's also the Action Bar you'll favor for Ultimate use.

The remaining slot can be used for whatever you like, but consider slotting something for group support.

PRIORITY PASSIVES

Investing in core Passives is a good start; branch out as you gain the Skill Points to explore other skill lines.

One Destruction Staff Passive, **Ancient Knowledge**, deserves special mention. This Passive Ability is the reason a Lightning Staff is your backup weapon—it's also the reason you need a Destruction Staff ability slotted on your backup Bar. Snatch it up as soon as you can to make the most of this build.

CHAMPION POINT SUGGESTIONS

Thief: Invest heavily in Arcanist (Lover). Tenacity (Lover) is a good choice for additional points.

Mage: Invest heavily in Elemental Expert (Apprentice) and Elfborn (Apprentice). Thaumaturge (Ritual) is also helpful.

Warrior: Invest heavily in Elemental Defender (Lady) and Hardy (Lady). Quick Recovery (Lord) is a great place to put your remaining points.

EQUIPMENT RECOMMENDATIONS

WEAPONS

Priority Trait: Sharpened

Priority Enchantment: Spell Damage

For your main weapon, use the best Flame Staff available to you. Try for something that includes the **Sharpened** trait and a Spell Damage enchantment.

For your backup weapon, go with the best Lightning Staff you can find. Again, the **Sharpened** trait and a Spell Damage enchantment allow for maximum damage

ARMOR

Priority Trait: Divines

Priority Enchantment: Maximum Magicka

Use at least five pieces of light armor at all times. The related Passives grant you some very important benefits. If you've invested in the **Undaunted Mettle** Passive Ability, equip medium/heavy armor pieces in the remaining slots. Otherwise, a full set of light armor is likely your best option.

In lieu of useful set bonuses, look for light armor that offers Maximum Magicka enchantments as you work toward obtaining high-level gear. Getting seven pieces with the **Divines** trait is a big step toward reaching your damage potential.

JEWELRY

Priority Trait: Arcane

Priority Enchantment: Spell Damage

Until you manage to track down useful set pieces, use anything that increases Maximum Magicka and Spell Damage.

ARCHETYPE ADVICE

The Breton's racial Passives support a more durable, efficient build. If you're after raw damage, feel free to go with a High Elf or a Dark Elf.

Use your backup Bar to cast **Merciless Resolve** and **Siphoning Attacks** at the start of every fight, then swap weapons and focus on damage until it's time to activate the spectral bow or reapply fading effects.

To fire **Merciless Resolve**'s spectral bow, you need to land four light attacks before the effect ends. Weave these between your main damage attacks, and it will be ready in no time.

Keep **Elemental Blockade** active throughout every fight. Use **Swallow Soul** as your main attack ability until your target drops below 25% Health, then switch to **Impale** for serious damage—just remember that you won't have **Swallow Soul**'s healing effect during this time.

THE FANATIC

Class: Templar	Race: Dark Elf	Attribute Focus: Magicka	Weapon Types: Dual Swords, Destruction Staff	Armor Focus: Light	Mundus Stone: Thief

BAR 1: DUAL WIELD (SWORDS)

KEY ABILITIES

Toppling Charge

Puncturing Sweep

Radiant Glory

Structured Entropy

Crescent Sweep

Toppling Charge: Morphed from **Focused Charge** (Templar > Aedric Spear). This is your gap closer. Use it to get into melee range.

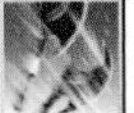

Puncturing Sweep: Morphed from **Puncturing Strikes** (Templar > Aedric Spear). This is your primary damage ability. It hits multiple targets and heals you based on damage done.

Radiant Glory: Morphed from **Radiant Destruction** (Templar > Dawn's Wrath). A channeled damage-over-time effect that serves as your execute ability. Start using it when your target's Health drops below 50%.

Structured Entropy: Morphed from **Entropy** (Mages Guild). Slot it to boost your Maximum Health. Use it as an attack and a damage buff.

Crescent Sweep: Morphed from **Radial Sweep** (Templar > Aedric Spear). This is a quick and inexpensive Ultimate Ability. It does fair area-of-effect damage, but it's most effective against enemies in front of you.

This is your damage Bar. Activate Toppling Charge to get into melee range, then use Puncturing Sweep as your primary attack. Remember that your heavy attacks generate Stamina rather than Magicka, so switch weapons as needed. Consider using **Inner Light** (Mages Guild) in the remaining slot. Otherwise drop in any ability you've come to enjoy.

BAR 2: DESTRUCTION STAFF
KEY ABILITIES

Breath of Life

Ritual of Retribution

Vampire's Bane

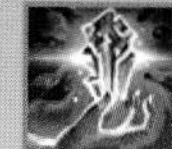
Destructive Clench

Shooting Star

Breath of Life: Morphed from **Rushed Ceremony** (Templar > Restoring Light). This Magicka ability heals you or a wounded ally. It also grants a smaller heal to an additional target. It's a great tool for emergencies.

Ritual of Retribution: Morphed from **Cleansing Ritual** (Templar > Restoring Light). An excellent support tool that adds a good amount of DPS. It's best used when you need to purge negative effects, but it also has a nice heal-over-time effect.

Vampire's Bane: Morphed from Sun Fire (Templar > Dawn's Wrath). This ability offers a bit of direct damage with a nice damage-over-time effect. Use it as your opening attack before you go charging in. Refresh as needed.

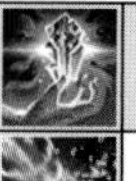
Destructive Clench: Morphed from **Destructive Touch** (Destruction Staff). This combines direct damage and damage over time with a bit of crowd control.

Shooting Star: Morphed from **Meteor** (Mages Guild). This is a powerful, long-range Ultimate Attack. A good option for boss encounters.

This is your utility Bar. It's mostly used to apply damage over time and healing, but it's also important for your Magicka Recovery. When you find yourself low on Magicka, swap to this Bar and perform a few heavy attacks. Place a desired ability in the remaining slot. The Templar has some excellent utility abilities, so you shouldn't have any trouble finding something you like.

PRIORITY PASSIVES

Remember that **Twin Blade and Blunt** is the only Dual Wield Passive Ability you really need (although **Dual Wield Expert** improves your melee attacks a bit). You want that 5% damage boost from your equipped swords. Other than that, invest in each of your core Passives as they become available.

CHAMPION POINT SUGGESTIONS

Thief: Invest heavily in Arcanist (Lover) and Tenacity (Lover).

Mage: Invest heavily in Elemental Expert (Apprentice). Elfborn (Apprentice) and Thaumaturge (Ritual) are also useful.

Warrior: Elemental Defender (Lady), Hardy (Lady), and Quick Recovery (Lord) are all good options.

EQUIPMENT RECOMMENDATIONS

WEAPONS

Priority Trait: Sharpened

Priority Enchantment: Spell Damage

Once you unlock the **Twin Blade** and Blunt Passive Ability, swords are all you want to use for dual-wielding. Until you find suitable set items, look for anything with the **Sharpened** trait.

For your main hand, Spell Damage is the preferred enchantment. Choose whatever you like for your off-hand weapon.

ARMOR

Priority Trait: Divines

Priority Enchantment: Maximum Magicka

Always equip at least five pieces of light armor to take advantage of the skill line's Passives. If you've invested in the **Undaunted Mettle** Passive Ability, equip medium/heavy armor pieces in the remaining slots.

While you hunt down desired set items, stick with light armor that features the **Divines** trait. If damage is your priority, Maximum Magicka generally yields the best results.

JEWELRY

Priority Trait: Arcane

Priority Enchantment: Spell Damage

Until you manage to track down useful set pieces, use anything that increases Maximum Magicka and Spell Damage.

ARCHETYPE ADVICE

The Dark Elf Passives help boost damage, but they don't help with Magicka Recovery. If you're looking for a bit more efficiency or sustainability, consider going with a High Elf or a Breton.

Try to open every fight with **Vampire's Bane**, then swap to your main Action Bar and hit **Toppling Charge**. Use **Puncturing Sweep** until your target's Health drops below 50%, and then finish them off with **Radiant Glory**. Of course, you should swap back to your staff whenever you need to heal or recover Magicka.

Vampire's Bane is your main damage-over-time effect, but **Destructive Clench** is a good way to boost damage over time. Neither of these effects lasts very long, though, and frequent applications can burn through your Magicka fairly quickly. Remember to use those heavy attacks during longer encounters.

Crescent Sweep is best used for grinding or adventuring. Rely on **Shooting Star** when you need a high-damage Ultimate Ability.

THE NATURALIST

Class: Warden | Race: High Elf | Attribute Focus: Magicka | Weapon Types: Destruction Staves | Armor Focus: Light | Mundus Stone: Thief

BAR 1: DESTRUCTION STAFF (FLAME STAFF)

KEY ABILITIES

Screaming Cliff Racer

Elemental Blockade

Fetcher Infection

Bird of Prey

Northern Storm

Screaming Cliff Racer: Morphed from **Dive** (Warden > Animal Companions). This is your primary attack. Use it from maximum range for more damage.

Elemental Blockade: Morphed from **Wall of Elements** (Destruction Staff). As long as you can stay in range, this Destruction Staff area-of-effect attack should be active for the duration of any fight.

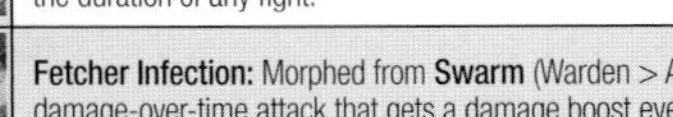

Fetcher Infection: Morphed from **Swarm** (Warden > Animal Companions). A nice damage-over-time attack that gets a damage boost every second time you cast it.

Bird of Prey: Morphed from **Falcon's Swiftness** (Warden > Animal Companions). An excellent utility skill. It boosts movement speed and Stamina Recovery, but it's mostly used as a source of Minor Berserk. Activate it often for a good damage boost.

Northern Storm: Morphed from **Sleet Storm** (Warden > Winter's Embrace). This Ultimate Ability offers a nice mix of area-of-effect damage, crowd control, and protection. It damages and snares nearby enemies while granting nearby allies Major Protection. Slotting it also increases your Maximum Magicka by 8%.

This is your main damage Bar. It provides a solid mix of direct damage, damage over time, and area-of-effect damage, so make the most of your attack rotation. Use the remaining Action Bar slot for whatever ability you think might be helpful.

BAR 2: DESTRUCTION STAFF (LIGHTNING STAFF)

KEY ABILITIES

Blue Betty

Lotus Blossom

Enchanted Growth

Winter's Revenge

Elemental Rage

Blue Betty: Morphed from **Betty Netch** (Warden > Animal Companions). Restores Magicka, grants Major Sorcery for a boost to Spell Damage, and purges one negative effect. This ability has a great duration and no casting cost. Keep it active at all times.

Lotus Blossom: Morphed from **Lotus Flower** (Warden > Green Balance). Allows your light and heavy attacks to heal you or a nearby ally for a percentage of the damage done. Also grants you Major Prophecy, increasing Spell Critical. This ability has a nice duration, and should be refreshed as often as needed.

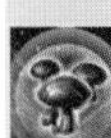

Enchanted Growth: Morphed from **Fungal Growth** (Warden > Green Balance). This instant ability heals you and all allies within your frontal cone. All affected targets also gain Minor Intellect and Minor Endurance, increasing Magicka and Stamina Recovery. It's a useful ability and a great way to support your group.

Winter's Revenge: Morphed from **Impaling Shards** (Warden > Winter's Embrace). This ability is a ranged AoE/DOT attack with a nice Snare effect. Use it when you need some extra damage or a bit of crowd control.

Elemental Rage: Morphed from **Elemental Storm** (Destruction Staff). This is your ranged Ultimate Ability. Use it to deal heavy damage from a safe distance. Slotting it also ensures that a Destruction Staff ability remains on your Bar.

This is your utility Bar. Use it to buff, heal, and provide a bit of crowd control.

If you're looking for some extra damage, consider installing a strong area-of-effect ability in the remaining slot. Otherwise add whatever ability you feel is useful.

PRIORITY PASSIVES

Invest in all core Passives, but take special note of those found in the Animal Companions, Winter's Embrace, and Destruction Staff skill lines. Selections from these skill lines are included on both Action Bars specifically to keep key Passives in play.

CHAMPION POINT SUGGESTIONS

Thief: Invest heavily in Arcanist (Lover) and Tenacity (Lover). Healthy (Lover) is a good option for remaining points.

Mage: Invest heavily in Elfborn (Mage) and Elemental Expert (Mage). Thaumaturge (Ritual) is also a worthy investment.

Warrior: Hardy (Warrior) and Elemental Defender (Warrior) are probably your best options, but Quick Recovery (Lord) is also worth considering.

EQUIPMENT RECOMMENDATIONS

WEAPONS

Priority Trait: Sharpened

Priority Enchantment: Spell Damage

For maximum damage, use a Flame Staff as your main weapon. A Lightning Staff is recommended as your backup weapon. In both cases, look for options that include the **Sharpened** trait and a Spell Damage enchantment.

ARMOR

Priority Trait: Divines

Priority Enchantment: Maximum Magicka

Equip at least five pieces of light armor at all times—especially once you've invested in the related skill line. If you're using the **Undaunted Mettle** Passive Ability, equip medium/heavy armor pieces in the remaining slots. Otherwise, a full set of light armor can be very effective.

When it comes to DPS, Divines is a difficult armor trait to beat. Prioritize light armor that features Maximum Magicka enchantments as you go about collecting desired set items.

JEWELRY

Priority Trait: Arcane

Priority Enchantment: Spell Damage

Until you manage to track down useful set pieces, use anything that increases Maximum Magicka and Spell Damage.

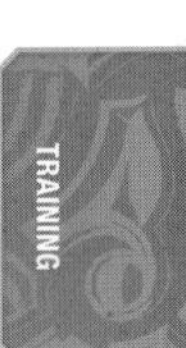

ARCHETYPE ADVICE

Before you engage a target, use your backup weapon to cast **Blue Betty** and **Lotus Blossom**. The combined buffs do wonders for your damage and sustainability. They also last a fairly long time, making it reasonably easy to work them into your attack rotation.

Screaming Cliff Racer is an instant cast, but the attack does have a bit of a delay—don't let this put you off using it. Properly used, it deals solid damage for relatively little Magicka.

Once you've invested in the **Ancient Knowledge** Passive Ability (Destruction Staff), using a Lightning Staff as your backup weapon helps boost the area-of-effect damage from **Winter's Revenge** and **Elemental Rage**.

Every second cast of **Fetcher Infection** does 75% more damage than the base ability. When applying multiple damage-over-time effects, prioritize targets to make sure your high-damage casts are put to the best possible use.

STAMINA DPS

THE ASSASSIN

Class: Nightblade | **Race:** Khajiit | **Attribute Focus:** Stamina | **Weapon Types:** Dual Wield, Bow | **Armor Focus:** Medium | **Mundus Stone:** Thief

BAR 1: DUAL WIELD

KEY ABILITIES

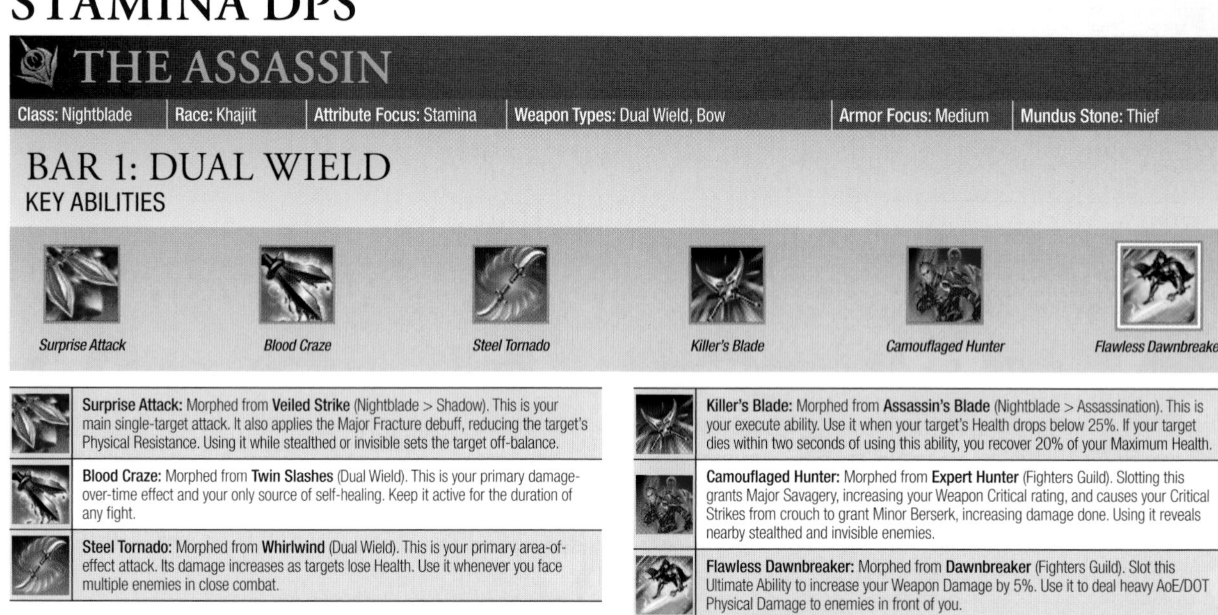

Surprise Attack | *Blood Craze* | *Steel Tornado* | *Killer's Blade* | *Camouflaged Hunter* | *Flawless Dawnbreaker*

Surprise Attack: Morphed from **Veiled Strike** (Nightblade > Shadow). This is your main single-target attack. It also applies the Major Fracture debuff, reducing the target's Physical Resistance. Using it while stealthed or invisible sets the target off-balance.

Blood Craze: Morphed from **Twin Slashes** (Dual Wield). This is your primary damage-over-time effect and your only source of self-healing. Keep it active for the duration of any fight.

Steel Tornado: Morphed from **Whirlwind** (Dual Wield). This is your primary area-of-effect attack. Its damage increases as targets lose Health. Use it whenever you face multiple enemies in close combat.

Killer's Blade: Morphed from **Assassin's Blade** (Nightblade > Assassination). This is your execute ability. Use it when your target's Health drops below 25%. If your target dies within two seconds of using this ability, you recover 20% of your Maximum Health.

Camouflaged Hunter: Morphed from **Expert Hunter** (Fighters Guild). Slotting this grants Major Savagery, increasing your Weapon Critical rating, and causes your Critical Strikes from crouch to grant Minor Berserk, increasing damage done. Using it reveals nearby stealthed and invisible enemies.

Flawless Dawnbreaker: Morphed from **Dawnbreaker** (Fighters Guild). Slot this Ultimate Ability to increase your Weapon Damage by 5%. Use it to deal heavy AoE/DOT Physical Damage to enemies in front of you.

This is your main damage Bar. Use it during close combat or when you're attacking from stealth.This loadout uses every slot on the Action Bar. Camouflaged Hunter is probably the least vital Active Ability, but removing it will likely cause a noticeable drop in DPS.

BAR 2: BOW

KEY ABILITIES

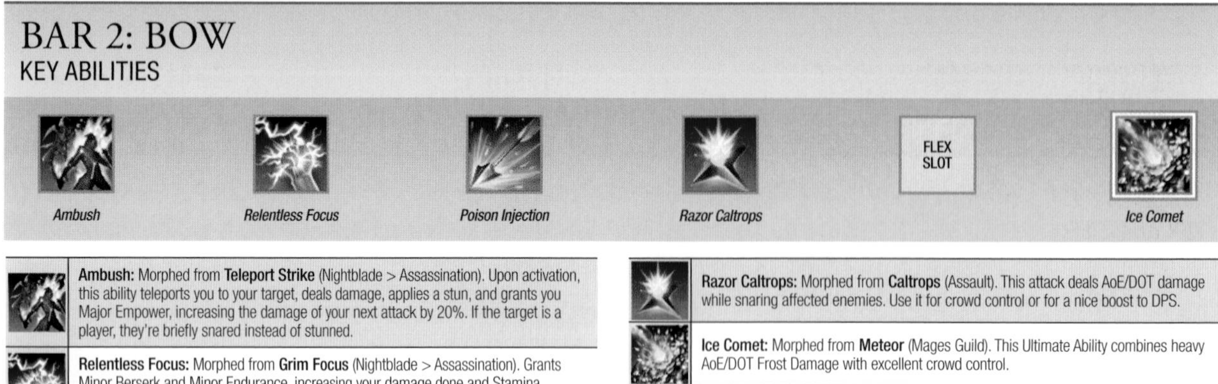

Ambush | *Relentless Focus* | *Poison Injection* | *Razor Caltrops* | *Ice Comet*

Ambush: Morphed from **Teleport Strike** (Nightblade > Assassination). Upon activation, this ability teleports you to your target, deals damage, applies a stun, and grants you Major Empower, increasing the damage of your next attack by 20%. If the target is a player, they're briefly snared instead of stunned.

Relentless Focus: Morphed from **Grim Focus** (Nightblade > Assassination). Grants Minor Berserk and Minor Endurance, increasing your damage done and Stamina Recovery for 20 seconds. It can also be used to fire a spectral bow for heavy damage.

Poison Injection: Morphed from **Poison Arrow** (Bow). This is your primary ranged attack and damage-over-time effect. It deals bonus Poison Damage to enemies below 50% Health, so it also serves as something of a ranged execute ability.

Razor Caltrops: Morphed from **Caltrops** (Assault). This attack deals AoE/DOT damage while snaring affected enemies. Use it for crowd control or for a nice boost to DPS.

Ice Comet: Morphed from **Meteor** (Mages Guild). This Ultimate Ability combines heavy AoE/DOT Frost Damage with excellent crowd control.

This is your ranged/utility Bar. Use it to buff yourself, attack from a distance, or impede your pursuers. It also contains a nice damage-over-time attack, so expect to do a fair amount of weapon swapping during prolonged encounters. Use the remaining Bar slot for any ability you feel is useful.

PRIORITY PASSIVES

Core Passives are your priority, but make sure you invest in **Improved Hiding** (Legerdemain). It's an important part of stealthy playstyles. **Dark Stalker** (Vampire) is also an appealing option, but the penalties of Vampirism can outweigh the benefits. Passive Abilities from the Assault skill line can be safely ignored outside of PvP.

CHAMPION POINT SUGGESTIONS

Thief: Mooncalf (Lover) is always useful, but Shade (Shadow) warrants some investment. Sprinter (Tower), Warlord (Tower), and Tumbling (Shadow) can all be useful.

Mage: Invest heavily in Mighty (Ritual) and Precise Strikes (Ritual). Master-at-Arms (Atronach) is also worth considering.

Warrior: Invest heavily in Elemental Defender (Lady) and Hardy (Lady). Thick Skinned (Lady) is also helpful.

EQUIPMENT RECOMMENDATIONS

WEAPONS

Priority Trait: Sharpened

Priority Enchantment: Weapon Damage

Your best weapon options come from the Maelstrom Arena or high-level sets. Until you manage to obtain such weapons, use the highest-quality versions you can find.

Once you've invested in the Dual Wield Passives, each weapon type provides a different bonus. The Weapon Critical bonus from daggers will probably result in the greatest damage gain, but find the combination that works for you.

Sharpened is the trait that most Damage-Dealers prefer, but **Precise** is also quite good. As for enchantments, favor Weapon Damage for your main hand. A **Crushing** enchantment would be a good choice for your off-hand weapon.

The combination of **Sharpened** and Weapon Damage also works well for your bow.

ARMOR

Priority Trait: Divines

Priority Enchantment: Maximum Stamina

Always equip at least five pieces of medium armor. The related Passives grant you some very important benefits. If you've invested in the **Undaunted Mettle** Passive Ability, you'll probably want to equip light and heavy armor pieces in the remaining slots.

Equipment that grants suitable set bonuses is always your best option. Look for medium armor that offers Maximum Stamina enchantments as you work toward obtaining high-level gear. **Divines** tends to be the most useful trait for PvE content, but **Infused** can be very effective on head, chest, and leg pieces.

JEWELRY

Priority Trait: Robust

Priority Enchantment: Weapon Damage

Until you manage to track down useful set pieces, use anything that increases Weapon Damage.

ARCHETYPE ADVICE

Whenever possible, open a fight with a **Surprise Attack** from stealth. It does great damage, applies Major Fracture, and sets your target off-balance. Follow up with a powerful attack, or use the time to switch Action Bars to activate buffs and apply **Poison Injection**.

Against a single target, use **Surprise Attack** for direct damage until your enemy's Health drops below 25%—then switch to **Killer's Blade** to finish them off. In multi-target situations, **Steel Tornado** should be your attack of choice.

Blood Craze is the closest thing you have to a self-heal, so try to keep it active on all enemies, at all times. Of course, the best way to mitigate damage is to avoid taking it. Make good use of stealth, ranged attacks, and crowd-control abilities.

Flawless Dawnbreaker is a fairly inexpensive Ultimate Ability. Use it often to boost your overall DPS; use **Ice Comet** when you need to attack from range or escape from dangerous situations.

THE BEASTMASTER

Class: Warden	Race: Wood Elf	Attribute Focus: Stamina	Weapon Types: Bow, Two-Handed	Armor Focus: Medium	Mundus Stone: Thief

BAR 1: BOW

KEY ABILITIES

Poison Injection | *Cutting Dive* | *Bull Netch* | *Green Lotus* | FLEX SLOT | *Wild Guardian*

Poison Injection: Morphed from **Poison Arrow** (Bow). This is your ranged damage-over-time effect. It deals bonus Poison Damage to enemies below 50% Health, but it's almost always worth using.

Cutting Dive: Morphed from **Dive** (Warden > Animal Companions). This is your primary ranged attack. Use it once your damage-over-time effect is in place.

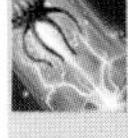

Bull Netch: Morphed from **Betty Netch** (Warden > Animal Companions). This free-cast ability grants Major Brutality and Major Sorcery, increasing Weapon and Spell Damage by 20%. It also restores Stamina for the duration of the effect. It lasts quite a while, so keep it active during any fight.

Green Lotus: Morphed from **Lotus Flower** (Warden > Green Balance). This Magicka ability restores Health to you or a nearby ally, based on the damage done by your light and heavy attacks. It also grants you Major Savagery, increasing your Weapon Critical for the duration of the effect.

Wild Guardian: Morphed from **Feral Guardian** (Warden > Animal Companions). This Ultimate Ability summons a grizzly to fight by your side. While the grizzly is active, the ability converts to **Guardian's Savagery**—activating it causes the grizzly to deal heavy Physical Damage to its target. Targets under 25% Health take twice the damage. It's placed on both Action Bars to prevent the grizzly from vanishing when you swap weapons.

This is your ranged-attack Bar. It also contains some long-lasting buff abilities. Consider placing **Arrow Spray** (Bow) or one of its morphs in the remaining slot. The combination of damage and crowd control can be very useful. **Bird of Prey** (Warden > Animal Companions) is also a good choice. Otherwise, add any ability you like.

BAR 2: TWO-HANDED

KEY ABILITIES

Wrecking Blow

Brawler

Subterranean Assault

Soothing Spores

FLEX SLOT

Wild Guardian

Wrecking Blow: Morphed from **Uppercut** (Two-Handed). This is your main short-range attack. It deals heavy damage and grants Empower, increasing the damage of your next attack by 20%.

Brawler: Morphed from **Cleave** (Two-Handed). This short-range multi-target attack applies Bleeding to all affected enemies. It also grants you a damage shield that increases in strength based on the number of enemies it hits. Use it to improve your DPS and survivability during close combat.

Subterranean Assault: Morphed from **Scorch** (Warden > Animal Companions). This area-of-effect ability deals Poison Damage to enemies in front of you. It also applies Major Breach and Major Defile to all affected targets, reducing their Spell Resistance and Physical Resistance.

Soothing Spores: Morphed from **Fungal Growth** (Warden > Green Balance). This instant-cast Stamina ability heals you and any allies in your frontal cone. Allies standing less than eight meters away receive more Health. It's a great self-heal and a good way to support your group.

Wild Guardian: Morphed from **Feral Guardian** (Warden > Animal Companions). This Ultimate Ability summons a grizzly to fight by your side. While the grizzly is active, the ability converts to **Guardian's Savagery**—activating it causes the grizzly to deal heavy Physical Damage to its target. Targets under 25% Health take twice the damage. It's placed on both Action Bars to prevent the grizzly from vanishing when you swap weapons.

This is your close-combat Bar. Use it when your enemies move into range or when you need to heal yourself. Again, **Bird of Prey** (Warden > Animal Companions) is a good option for the remaining slot, but the Two-Handed skill line has a few abilities also worth considering. Of course, you're free to slot anything you feel might be of use.

PRIORITY PASSIVES

Whether or not you add a Winter's Embrace ability to your Bar, make sure you invest in the **Icy Aura** and **Piercing Cold** Passives. For Green Balance, **Maturation** will probably be the most useful. It's fairly safe to delay (or even avoid) further investments in those skill lines. Other than that, try to invest in all core Passives as they become available.

CHAMPION POINT SUGGESTIONS

Thief: Invest heavily in Mooncalf (Lover). Tumbling (Shadow) and Warlord (Tower) are also quite useful.

Mage: Invest heavily in Mighty (Ritual). Precise Strikes (Ritual) and Piercing (Ritual) are also worth considering.

Warrior: Investing in Hardy (Lady) and Elemental Defender (Lady) is usually a safe bet.

EQUIPMENT RECOMMENDATIONS

WEAPONS

Priority Trait: Sharpened

Priority Enchantment: Weapon Damage

Until you obtain something from the Maelstrom Arena or a high-level set, use the highest-quality weapons you can find.

Look for weapons that feature the **Sharpened** trait—they tend to yield the most overall damage. **Precise** is also worth considering. As for enchantments, favor Weapon Damage for both your bow and your backup weapon.

ARMOR

Priority Trait: Divines

Priority Enchantment: Maximum Stamina

You'll want to wear at least five pieces of medium armor at all times. You must also equip light/heavy armor pieces to take advantage of the **Undaunted Mettle** Passive Ability, but there's nothing wrong with going for a full suit of medium armor.

The bonuses offered by various armor sets are well worth chasing, but you'll always benefit from using the best options available to you. Look for medium armor that offers Maximum Stamina enchantments as you work toward obtaining high-level gear. **Divines** is the most popular trait for PvE content, but **Infused** can be very effective on head, chest, and leg pieces.

JEWELRY

Priority Trait: Robust

Priority Enchantment: Weapon Damage

Until you manage to track down useful set pieces, use anything that increases Maximum Stamina and Weapon Damage.

ARCHETYPE ADVICE

The Wood Elf is chosen for its bonuses to Stamina Recovery. If burst damage is your priority, go with a Khajiit instead.

Bull Netch and **Green Lotus** both provide powerful, long-lasting buffs. Use both abilities before you engage enemies, and remember to refresh them as needed.

You have solid damage potential at any range, so don't be afraid to mix things up. Use your bow to attack approaching enemies, or use it to attack them while you move into melee range. In either case, utilizing both of your Action Bars is the best way to maximize your damage output.

Subterranean Assault is an instant cast, but it takes three seconds for the attack to occur. Activate it before you're in melee range, then follow up with **Brawler** and **Wrecking Blow** just after the Shalks appear.

Placing **Wild Guardian** in both of your Ultimate Ability slots makes it a huge investment, so put that grizzly to good use. It costs nothing to summon, and it can do a lot of damage over the course of a battle. Activating **Guardian's Savagery** costs you 75 Ultimate, but it does considerable damage to weakened enemies.

THE DEPRAVED

Class: Dragonknight | **Race:** Reguard | **Attribute Focus:** Stamina | **Weapon Types:** Dual Wield, Bow | **Armor Focus:** Medium | **Mundus Stone:** Warrior

BAR 1: DUAL WIELD

KEY ABILITIES

Noxious Breath

Venomous Claw

Bloodthirst

Flames of Oblivion

FLEX SLOT

Corrosive Armor

Noxious Breath: Morphed from **Fiery Breath** (Dragonknight > Ardent Flame). This multi-target attack applies Poison Damage over time and Major Fracture, reducing the Physical Resistance of afflicted enemies. Use it as soon as you get into range. Reapply as needed.

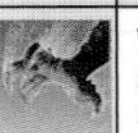
Venomous Claw: Morphed from **Searing Strikes** (Dragonknight > Ardent Flame). This single-target poison attack inflicts Poison Damage over time. Apply to individual targets after using **Noxious Breath**.

Bloodthirst: Morphed from **Flurry** (Dual Wield). This is your primary single-target attack. It also heals you for a percentage of the damage done by the attack's final blow. Use it once your damage-over-time effects are in place.

Flames of Oblivion: Morphed from **Inferno** (Dragonknight > Ardent Flame). While slotted, this ability grants Major Savagery, increasing your Weapon Critical rating. It's a Magicka ability, but its Flame Damage scales off of your highest resource. Activate it for a nice boost in DPS.

Corrosive Armor: Morphed from **Magma Armor** (Dragonknight > Earthen Heart). This Ultimate Ability greatly reduces incoming damage, deals AoE/DOT Poison Damage, and allows your attacks to ignore an enemy's Physical Resistance. Use it to boost your damage and survivability when you're on the front lines.

This is your main attack Bar. Use it to deal damage when you're in or near melee range. Afflict your enemies with poison effects, then use **Bloodthirst** to deal direct damage. Use the remaining Bar slot to add utility or additional damage over time.

BAR 2: BOW

KEY ABILITIES

Igneous Weaponst

Green Dragon Blood

Poison Injection

Acid Spray

FLEX SLOT

Toxic Barrage

Igneous Weapons: Morphed from **Molten Weapons** (Dragonknight > Earthen Heart). This popular group buff grants Major Sorcery and Major Brutality, increasing both Spell and Weapon Damage. Try to keep it active for the duration of any fight.

Green Dragon Blood: Morphed from **Dragon Blood** (Dragonknight > Draconic Power). This Magicka ability restores a percentage of your missing Health. It also grants you Major Fortitude, increasing your Health Recovery and Stamina Recovery by 20%, and Major Vitality, increasing your healing received by 8%. It's a good self-heal with some long-lasting buffs.

Poison Injection: Morphed from **Poison Arrow** (Bow). This ranged attack deals a good amount of Poison Damage over time, but it gets considerably more powerful when the target's Health drops below 50%. Use it to weaken your target as you move into melee range, when you need to keep your distance, or when you need a damage boost against low-Health enemies.

Acid Spray: Morphed from **Arrow Spray** (Bow). This ranged attack poisons and snares multiple enemies. The damage is a nice bonus, but it's mostly used for crowd control.

Toxic Barrage: Morphed from **Rapid Fire** (Bow). This channeled Ultimate Ability deals heavy Poison Damage over time. It's a devastating ranged attack that's sure to come in handy.

This is your ranged/support Bar. Use it to apply buffs, heal yourself, and poison enemies from a distance. Depending on how often you use ranged attacks, consider placing **Flames of Oblivion** in the remaining Bar slot. Doing so ensures you always benefit from Major Savagery.

PRIORITY PASSIVES

While you should invest in all of your core Passives, take special note of **Mountain's Blessing** (Dragonknight > Earthen Heart). In addition to improving Ultimate generation, this Passive Ability grants Minor Brutality to you and all nearby allies whenever you activate an Earthen Heart ability. Investing in this Passive makes **Igneous Weapons** an even more powerful buff.

CHAMPION POINT SUGGESTIONS

Thief: Invest heavily in Mooncalf (Lover). Healthy (Lover), Warlord (Tower), and Sprinter (Tower) are all worth consideration.

Mage: Thaumaturge (Ritual) is your priority. Mighty (Ritual) and Precise Strikes (Ritual) are also useful.

Warrior: Invest heavily in Elemental Defender (Lady) and Hardy (Lady).

EQUIPMENT RECOMMENDATIONS

WEAPONS
Priority Trait: Sharpened
Priority Enchantment: Weapon Damage
Once you've invested in the Dual Wield Passives, the Weapon Critical bonus from daggers will probably result in the greatest damage gain. However, every weapon type has its benefit, so it's worth experimenting with different combinations.
Your best weapon options come from the Maelstrom Arena or high-level sets. Until you manage to get ahold of top-tier items, use the highest-quality versions you find, buy, or craft.
Sharpened and **Precise** are both great traits, and you'd do well to consider any level-appropriate weapon that features one of them. As for enchantments, favor Weapon Damage for your main hand. A **Crushing** enchantment would be a good choice for your off-hand weapon.
The combination of **Sharpened** and Weapon Damage also works well for your bow.

ARMOR
Priority Trait: Divines
Priority Enchantment: Maximum Stamina
Equip no fewer than five pieces of medium armor once you've invested in the related Passives. Unless you're taking advantage of the **Undaunted Mettle** Passive Ability, seven pieces of medium armor should help maximize your damage output.
Equipment that grants suitable set bonuses is always your best option. If crafting isn't possible, look for medium armor that offers Maximum Stamina enchantments as you track down more powerful gear. **Divines** tends to be the most useful trait for PvE content, but consider using head, chest, and leg pieces that offer the **Infused** trait.

JEWELRY
Priority Trait: Robust
Priority Enchantment: Weapon Damage
Until you manage to track down useful set pieces, use anything that increases Weapon Damage.

ARCHETYPE ADVICE

Try to cast **Igneous Weapons** just before a fight begins. Use **Poison Injection** as your opening attack, then swap weapons and use Noxious Breath and **Venomous Claw** to apply additional damage-over-time effects. Poison Damage over time accounts for most of your DPS, so make sure you refresh these effects as needed.

When you use **Bloodthirst**, see it through to the end. Interrupting the attack before its final strike hurts your DPS and survivability.

If you need to pull back from a fight, hit your enemies with **Acid Spray** before you attempt to retreat—the snare should make escaping much easier. This ability can also be used as an additional Poison Damage-over-time attack during tougher fights.

Green Dragon Blood is your best option for emergency healing, but it also provides lingering bonuses to Health Recovery and Stamina Recovery. Try to keep it active during difficult encounters.

Activating **Flames of Oblivion** increases your damage, but it also consumes Magicka you might need for **Green Dragon Blood**. During each fight, prioritize damage or survivability and spend your Magicka accordingly.

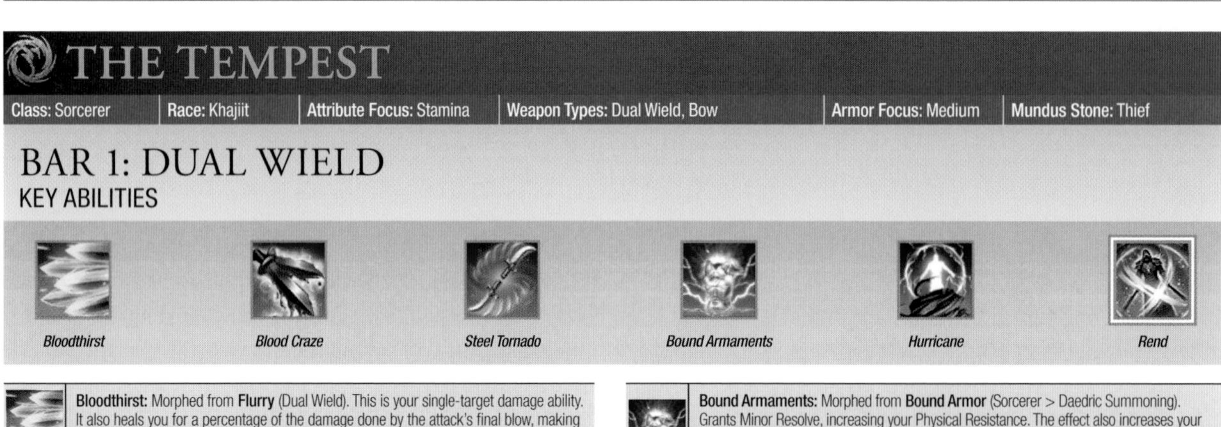

THE TEMPEST

Class: Sorcerer | **Race:** Khajiit | **Attribute Focus:** Stamina | **Weapon Types:** Dual Wield, Bow | **Armor Focus:** Medium | **Mundus Stone:** Thief

BAR 1: DUAL WIELD

KEY ABILITIES

Bloodthirst | *Blood Craze* | *Steel Tornado* | *Bound Armaments* | *Hurricane* | *Rend*

Bloodthirst: Morphed from **Flurry** (Dual Wield). This is your single-target damage ability. It also heals you for a percentage of the damage done by the attack's final blow, making it an important part of your survivability.

Blood Craze: Morphed from **Twin Slashes** (Dual Wield). This is your single-target damage-over-time attack and another source of self-healing. Keep it active for the duration of every fight.

Steel Tornado: Morphed from **Whirlwind** (Dual Wield). This is your primary area-of-effect attack. It has impressive range, and its damage increases as targets lose Health. Use it whenever you face multiple enemies.

Bound Armaments: Morphed from **Bound Armor** (Sorcerer > Daedric Summoning). Grants Minor Resolve, increasing your Physical Resistance. The effect also increases your Maximum Stamina by 8% and your damage done by heavy attacks by 11%. This ability is kept on both Action Bars to ensure that the effect remains active when you swap weapons.

Hurricane: Morphed from **Lightning Form** (Sorcerer > Storm Calling). This attack deals damage to all nearby enemies for 15 seconds. Over the course of the effect, the damage field grows in size and power. It also grants you Major Resolve and Major Ward, dramatically increasing your defense, and the Minor Expedition buff, which increases your movement speed.

Rend: Morphed from **Lacerate** (Dual Wield). This Ultimate Ability does heavy Physical Damage over time to nearby enemies in front of you. It also heals you for 50% of the damage done. It's the Ultimate you want to use in most situations.

This is your main damage Bar. Use it whenever your targets are within range of your abilities. In order to keep **Bound Armaments** on both Action Bars, this loadout leaves no slots for additional abilities.

BAR 2: BOW

KEY ABILITIES

Poison Injection

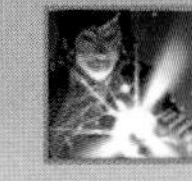
Critical Surge

Dark Deal

Bound Armaments

FLEX SLOT

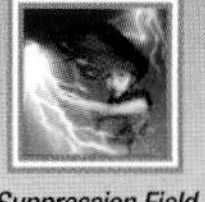
Suppression Field

Poison Injection: Morphed from **Poison Arrow** (Bow). This ranged attack deals a good amount of Poison Damage over time, but it gets much more powerful when the target's Health drops below 50%. This is your primary ranged-attack ability.

Critical Surge: Morphed from **Surge** (Sorcerer > Storm Calling). Grants Major Brutality, increasing Weapon Damage by 20%. While the ability is active, your Critical Strikes grant you Health. This effect can happen up to once per second.

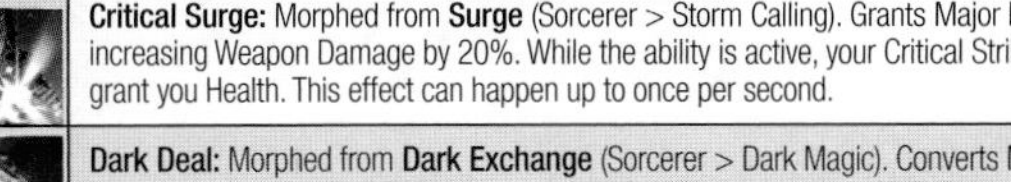
Dark Deal: Morphed from **Dark Exchange** (Sorcerer > Dark Magic). Converts Magicka into Health and Stamina. This ability has a brief cast time, but it's an excellent tool for sustainability.

Bound Armaments: Morphed from **Bound Armor** (Sorcerer > Daedric Summoning). Grants Minor Resolve, increasing your Physical Resistance. The effect also increases your Maximum Stamina by 8% and your damage done by heavy attacks by 11%. This ability is kept on both Action Bars to ensure that the effect remains active when you swap weapons.

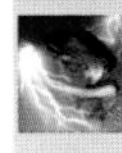
Suppression Field: Morphed from **Negate Magic** (Sorcerer > Dark Magic). This ranged Ultimate Ability creates a globe of magic suppression, damaging and stunning all NPCs within the target area. Enemy players will be silenced rather than stunned. It's a powerful crowd-control option that should be used sparingly.

This is your ranged/utility Bar. Use it when you need to activate buffs or attack from range. Consider placing **Arrow Spray** (Bow) or one of its morphs in the remaining slot. Otherwise, use the remaining slot for an ability you find useful.

PRIORITY PASSIVES

Useful Passives should become available at a manageable rate. Invest in your core Passives before moving on to less essential skill lines.

CHAMPION POINT SUGGESTIONS

Thief: Invest heavily in Mooncalf (Lover) and Warlord (Tower). Tenacity (Lover) can also be handy if Stamina management is an issue.

Mage: Invest heavily in Mighty (Ritual) and Precise Strikes (Ritual).

Warrior: Elemental Defender (Lady) and Hardy (Lady) tend to be very useful.

EQUIPMENT RECOMMENDATIONS

WEAPONS

Priority Trait: Sharpened

Priority Enchantment: Weapon Damage

Once you've invested in the Dual Wield Passives, each weapon type offers its own benefits. Experiment with different combinations until you find one that suits you.

Your best weapon options come from the Maelstrom Arena or high-level sets. Of course, it takes a fair amount of effort to obtain top-shelf items. Until you manage to do so, use the highest-quality versions you can get your hands on.

Sharpened is the Damage-Dealer's most useful weapon trait. **Precise** is also worth considering. As for enchantments, favor Weapon Damage for your main hand. A **Crushing** enchantment would be a good choice for your off-hand weapon.

The combination of **Sharpened** and Weapon Damage also works well for your bow.

ARMOR

Priority Trait: Divines

Priority Enchantment: Maximum Stamina

Once you've invested in the related Passives, keep at least five pieces of medium armor equipped. The **Undaunted Mettle** Passive Ability rewards wearing a mix of armor types, but it's hard to go wrong with a full suit of high-quality medium armor.

Aim for equipment that grants helpful set bonuses, but always use the best equipment available to you. Prioritize medium armor that offers Maximum Stamina enchantments. **Divines** is a popular trait outside of PvP, but consider using head, chest, and leg pieces that offer the **Infused** trait to make the most of your enchantments.

JEWELRY

Priority Trait: Robust

Priority Enchantment: Weapon Damage

Until you manage to track down useful set pieces, use anything that increases Weapon Damage.

ARCHETYPE ADVICE

Between **Hurricane** and **Steel Tornado**, area effects are your strength. Don't shy away from taking on groups of enemies—you have a lot of tools to keep you healthy.

Use **Blood Craze** whenever possible. It does great damage over time, and its healing effect is an important part of your survivability.

Hurricane serves as a great area-of-effect attack and an essential defensive buff. Keep it active during close combat, but don't refresh it too early—it's at its strongest just before it ends. Keep **Bound Armor** and **Critical Surge** active for the duration of any fight.

Your various healing effects should be enough to keep you going in most situations, but **Dark Deal** is an excellent tool for resource management. While adventuring, use it between battles to minimize downtime.

Bloodthirst is your best option for single-target damage, but it also provides a nice healing effect when it resolves. Once you start the attack, make sure you let it finish.

THE ZEALOT

Class: Templar	**Race:** Orc	**Attribute Focus:** Stamina	**Weapon Types:** Two-Handed, Bow	**Armor Focus:** Medium	**Mundus Stone:** Serpent

BAR 1: TWO-HANDED

KEY ABILITIES

Rally

Critical Rush

Biting Jabs

Reverse Slice

Flawless Dawnbreaker

Rally: Morphed from **Momentum** (Two-Handed). This ability grants Major Brutality and restores a nice bit of Health. Use it to buff Weapon Damage and improve survivability.

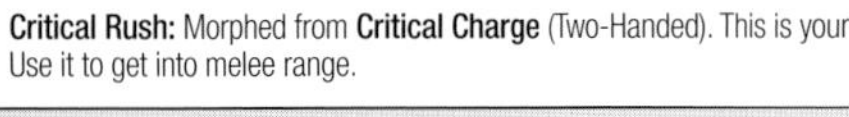

Critical Rush: Morphed from **Critical Charge** (Two-Handed). This is your gap closer. Use it to get into melee range.

Biting Jabs: Morphed from **Puncturing Strikes** (Templar > Aedric Spear). This is your primary damage ability. It's a multi-target attack, but the closest enemy takes increased damage and suffers a brief snare.

Reverse Slice: Morphed from **Reverse Slash** (Two-Handed). This is your execute ability. Use it when a target's Health drops below 50%. Nearby enemies take 65% of the damage inflicted, making this another good multi-target attack.

Flawless Dawnbreaker: Morphed from **Dawnbreaker** (Fighters Guild). Slot this Ultimate Ability to increase your Weapon Damage by 5%. Use it to deal heavy AoE/DOT Physical Damage to enemies in front of you.

This is your main attack Bar. Use it when you're within melee range of a target. During basic adventuring, consider using the remaining slot for **Repentance**, which is morphed from **Restoring Aura** (Templar > Restoring Light). Slotting it grants Minor Fortitude, Minor Endurance, and Minor Intellect; using it consumes nearby corpses to restore Health and Stamina. Otherwise, choose any ability you feel might be of use.

BAR 2: BOW

KEY ABILITIES

Power of the Light

Poison Injection

Endless Hail

Binding Javelin

Solar Disturbance

Power of the Light: Morphed from **Backlash** (Templar > Dawn's Wrath). This attack deals Physical Damage and applies Minor Fracture and Minor Breach to the target. It also copies their damage taken for six seconds, applying up to 20% of it as additional Physical Damage when the effect ends. It's most useful during group content, but it can sometimes be handy during solo adventuring.

Poison Injection: Morphed from **Poison Arrow** (Bow). This is your primary damage-over-time attack. It deals bonus Poison Damage to enemies below 50% Health, but it should be used whenever DPS is important.

Endless Hail: Morphed from **Volley** (Bow). This is your ranged area-of-effect skill. Use it accordingly.

Binding Javelin: Morphed from **Piercing Javelin** (Templar > Aedric Spear). This is a long-range attack that stuns and knocks back your target. Use it mainly for crowd control, but don't shy away from working it into any ranged-attack rotation.

Solar Disturbance: Morphed from **Nova** (Templar > Dawn's Wrath). This ranged Ultimate Ability deals AoE/DOT damage and reduces the damage done by affected enemies. It also snares enemies and allows an ally to use the Supernova Synergy.

This is your ranged-attack Bar. Use it when you need to keep your distance, and when you want to apply the debuffs granted by **Power of the Light**.

If you opt to slot **Repentance** on your first Action Bar, consider doing the same thing here. Otherwise, use the remaining slot to add any ability you enjoy.

PRIORITY PASSIVES

Unless you add one of its abilities to an Action Bar, Restoring Light is your lowest-priority Templar skill line. It has a lot to offer, but it won't benefit you as much as your other core skill lines. Invest accordingly.

CHAMPION POINT SUGGESTIONS

Thief: Invest heavily in Mooncalf (Lover). Depending on your equipment, Tenacity (Lover) and Healthy (Lover) can also be valuable.

Mage: Invest heavily in Mighty (Ritual) and Precise Strikes (Ritual).

Warrior: Elemental Defender (Lady) and Hardy (Lady) will likely be your best options.

EQUIPMENT RECOMMENDATIONS

WEAPONS
Priority Trait: Sharpened
Priority Enchantment: Weapon Damage
Your best weapon options come from the Maelstrom Arena or high-level sets. Until you're able to find or craft such items, use the highest-quality weapons you can find.
Once you've invested in the Dual Wield Passives, each weapon type provides a different bonus. Consider using daggers for a boost in Weapon Critical, but try out any decent weapon you can get your hands on.
Sharpened is the trait that most Damage-Dealers prefer, but **Precise** is also quite good. As for enchantments, favor Weapon Damage for your main hand. A **Crushing** enchantment would be a good choice for your off-hand weapon.
The combination of **Sharpened** and Weapon Damage also works well for your bow.

ARMOR
Priority Trait: Divines
Priority Enchantment: Maximum Stamina
To maximize your damage, equip at least five pieces of medium armor. If you've invested in the **Undaunted Mettle** Passive Ability, it's probably best to equip light and heavy armor pieces in the remaining slots.
Until you can find or craft a useful armor set, look for medium armor that offers Maximum Stamina enchantments. **Divines** is considered the best trait for PvP content, but **Infused** can be very effective on head, chest, and leg pieces.

JEWELRY
Priority Trait: Robust
Priority Enchantment: Weapon Damage
Until you manage to track down useful set pieces, use anything that increases Weapon Damage.

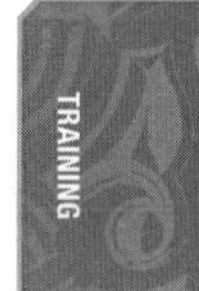

ARCHETYPE ADVICE

Power of the Light is most useful when you're part of a group, but it can always be used to boost your damage output. Cast it just before you charge an enemy to make the most of your opening attacks.

Keep **Rally** up for the duration of any battle. It's an important part of your DPS and your main tool for survivability. Cast it before you engage the enemy; refresh it as often as needed.

Biting Jabs is your main damage ability, but remember to use **Reverse Slice** whenever your target's Health drops below 50%. This powerful Two-Handed ability can do serious damage to grouped enemies.

Binding Javelin is a great way to interrupt enemy casters. It can also help create the distance you need to initiate a **Critical Rush**.

TANKS

THE CRUSADER

Class: Templar	Race: Imperial	Attribute Focus: Health/Stamina	Weapon Types: One Hand and Shield	Armor Focus: Heavy	Mundus Stone: Ritual

BAR 1: ONE HAND AND SHIELD

KEY ABILITIES

Pierce Armor

Heroic Slash

Channeled Focus

Absorb Magic

Breath of Life

Aggressive Horn

Pierce Armor: Morphed from **Puncture** (One Hand and Shield). This is your main taunt and debuff ability. It applies Major Fracture and Major Breach, reducing the target's Physical Resistance and Spell Resistance. Keep the effects up, but don't overuse the ability—in single-target situations, try to wait at least 10 seconds between uses.

Heroic Slash: Morphed from **Low Slash** (One Hand and Shield). This is your main damage ability and single-target snare. It applies Minor Maim, reducing the target's damage done, and grants you Minor Heroism, increasing your Ultimate generation.

Channeled Focus: Morphed from **Rune Focus** (Templar > Restoring Light). Using this Magicka ability places a protective rune at your feet. This rune grants you Major Resolve and Major Ward, increasing your Physical Resistance and Spell Resistance. It also boosts your Magicka Recovery.

Absorb Magic: Morphed from **Defensive Posture** (One Hand and Shield). While slotted, this ability increases the amount of damage you can block and reduces the Stamina cost for blocking, making it an important tool for survivability and sustainability. Activating this ability allows you to absorb an impressive amount of damage from the next spell projectile cast at you, healing you for a percentage of your Maximum Health.

Breath of Life: Morphed from **Rushed Ceremony** (Templar > Restoring Light). This Magicka ability heals you or a wounded ally. It also grants a smaller heal to an additional target. Use it for self-healing, but be aware of any allies who might benefit from its secondary effect.

Aggressive Horn: Morphed from **War Horn** (Assault). Increases the Maximum Magicka, Health, and Stamina of you and your allies by 10%. Affected targets also gain Major Force, temporarily increasing the damage and healing done by Critical Strikes. Use this Ultimate Ability during group content.

This is your main Bar. It contains your most frequently used abilities. To benefit from **Absorb Magic**'s slotted effect, prioritize use of this Action Bar. This loadout offers no empty Bar slots.

BAR 2: ONE HAND AND SHIELD

KEY ABILITIES

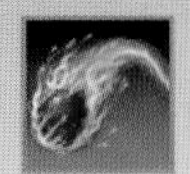
Inner Beast

Bone Surge

Blazing Shield

Power of the Light

FLEX SLOT

Solar Disturbance

Inner Beast: Morphed from **Inner Fire** (Undaunted). This is your long-range taunt. It does a nice amount of damage, but it's one of your more expensive Stamina abilities. Use it when you need to taunt from a distance.

Bone Surge: Morphed from **Bone Shield** (Undaunted). Grants you a damage shield that scales based on your Maximum Health. Also allows allies to activate the Spinal Surge Synergy, granting them Minor Vitality and a damage-absorbing wall. This is a solid defensive ability and a good option for group support.

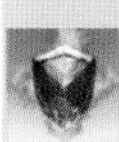
Blazing Shield: Morphed from **Sun Shield** (Templar > Aedric Spear). Grants you a damage shield that scales based on your Maximum Health. The shield grows stronger based on the number of enemies near you when the ability is activated. When the shield expires, it explodes outward, dealing a percentage of the damage it absorbed to nearby enemies.

Power of the Light: Morphed from **Backlash** (Templar > Dawn's Wrath). This attack deals Physical Damage and applies Minor Fracture and Minor Breach to the target. It also copies their damage taken for six seconds, applying up to 20% of it as additional Physical Damage when the effect ends. It's most useful during group content, but it can sometimes be handy during solo adventuring.

Solar Disturbance: Morphed from **Nova** (Templar > Dawn's Wrath). This ranged Ultimate Ability deals AoE/DOT damage and reduces the damage done by affected enemies. It also snares enemies and allows an ally to use the Supernova Synergy. Use this Ultimate Ability while you're adventuring alone.

This is your backup Bar. Use it to taunt from range, apply damage shields, and offer group support. The remaining slot can be used for any ability you find helpful, depending on the situation.

PRIORITY PASSIVES

Other than those found in the Assault skill line, invest in all of your core Passives. Move on to other skill lines as Skill Points become available.

CHAMPION POINT SUGGESTIONS

Thief: Invest heavily in Shadow Ward (Shadow) and Tenacity (Lover).

Mage: Invest heavily in Blessed (Apprentice).

Warrior: Elemental Defender (Lady) and Hardy (Lady) tend to be the most effective investments. Quick Recovery (Lord) and Resistant (Steed) can also be helpful.

EQUIPMENT RECOMMENDATIONS

WEAPONS

Priority Trait: Defending

Priority Enchantment: Crushing

You want to have a one-handed melee weapon and a shield equipped at all times. Early on, use the highest-quality weapon/shield combinations you can find. Prioritize one-handed melee weapons that feature the **Defending** trait.

For your shields, Reinforced and Sturdy are both good traits. Favor enchantments that boost Maximum Health or Maximum Stamina as needed.

ARMOR

Priority Trait: Sturdy or Infused

Priority Enchantment: Maximum Health or Maximum Stamina

Heavy armor should be your priority. Never tank with fewer than five pieces of heavy armor equipped. In many cases, it's best to forgo the **Undaunted Mettle** Passive Ability and don a full set of heavy armor. You'll need as much protection as you can get, and the Heavy Armor skill line's Passive Abilities contribute a lot to your survivability.

If you're serving as a group's main Tank, try to assemble a collection of high-quality armor sets. Your preferred balance of stats is sure to change from encounter to encounter, and the more options you have, the better off you'll be. You have a bit more freedom during solo adventuring, but your survivability is always your greatest asset.

Until you've acquired at least one Tank-friendly armor set, favor heavy armor pieces that offer a mix of Maximum Health and Maximum Stamina enchantments. Choose the highest-quality armor you can find for your level, but look for pieces that feature the **Sturdy** trait. Once you're comfortable with your Stamina management, aim for head, chest, and leg pieces that feature the **Infused** trait to get the most out of your enchantments.

JEWELRY

Priority Trait: Healthy

Priority Enchantment: Shielding

Until you collect a set you find useful, prioritize jewelry items that increase your Maximum Health and reduce the Stamina cost for blocking.

ARCHETYPE ADVICE

The **Ritual Mundus Stone** makes **Breath of Life** a more effective self-heal, so it's a nice option for any situation. Still, don't hesitate to exchange it for any boon that might serve you better.

With high-level gear, this build makes for a solid main Tank. However, it doesn't offer much in the damage department. Even during basic adventuring, combat is more a matter of outlasting your enemies than overpowering them.

The use of **Channeled Focus** limits your mobility—the effects linger for a bit if you leave the rune, but staying put is an important part of your Magicka management.

Health will likely be your primary Attribute, so **Stamina** management can be an issue. Perform a heavy attack at every opportunity to help support your Stamina abilities.

Bone Surge has a fairly heavy Stamina cost and should be used sparingly. **Blazing Shield** is a Magicka ability; use it every so often to reduce blocking-related Stamina consumption. Neither effect lasts long, so proper timing is important.

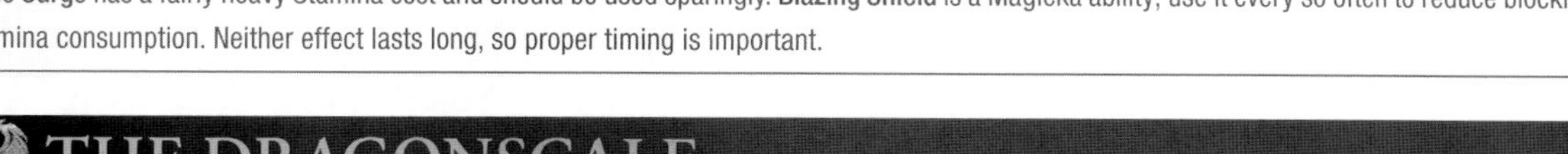

THE DRAGONSCALE

Class: Dragonknight | **Race:** Imperial | **Attribute Focus:** Health/Stamina/Magicka | **Weapon Types:** One Hand and Shield | **Armor Focus:** Heavy | **Mundus Stone:** Atronach

BAR 1: ONE HAND AND SHIELD

KEY ABILITIES

Pierce Armor

Heroic Slash

Absorb Magic

Green Dragon Blood

Unrelenting Grip

Standard of Might

Pierce Armor: Morphed from **Puncture** (One Hand and Shield). This is your main taunt and debuff ability. It applies Major Fracture and Major Breach, reducing the target's Physical and Spell Resistance. Time your rotation to avoid over-taunting.

Heroic Slash: Morphed from **Low Slash** (One Hand and Shield). This is your main damage ability and single-target snare. It applies Minor Maim, temporarily reducing the damage done by the target. Each use also grants Minor Heroism, increasing your Ultimate generation for nine seconds.

Absorb Magic: Morphed from **Defensive Posture** (One Hand and Shield). Slotting this Stamina ability increases the amount of damage you can block and reduces the Stamina cost for blocking. Activating it allows you to absorb an impressive amount of damage from the next spell projectile cast at you, healing you for a percentage of your Maximum Health.

Green Dragon Blood: Morphed from **Dragon Blood** (Dragonknight > Draconic Power). This Magicka ability restores a percentage of your missing Health. It also grants you Major Fortitude, increasing your Health Recovery and Stamina Recovery by 20%, and Major Vitality, increasing your healing received by 8%. It's a good self-heal with some long-lasting buffs.

Unrelenting Grip: Morphed from **Fiery Grip** (Dragonknight > Ardent Flame). This Magicka ability pulls the target to your location. It also inflicts a burst of Flame Damage and grants you Major Expedition for a temporary boost to movement speed. If the target can't be pulled, the Magicka cost is refunded.

Standard of Might: Morphed from **Dragonknight Standard** (Dragon Knight > Ardent Flame). This Ultimate Ability deals Flame Damage while reducing the damage you take. It's a great combination of offensive and defensive effects and a big help during solo adventuring.

This is your main Bar. It contains your most frequently used abilities. To benefit from **Absorb Magic**'s slotted effect, prioritize use of this Action Bar. This loadout offers no empty Bar slots.

BAR 2: SWORD AND SHIELD

KEY ABILITIES

Hardened Armor

Inner Rage

Choking Talons

Igneous Shield

FLEX SLOT

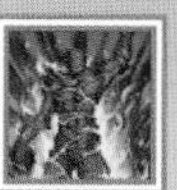

Magma Shell

Hardened Armor: Morphed from **Spiked Armor** (Dragonknight > Draconic Power). This Magicka ability grants you Major Resolve and Major Ward, increasing your Physical and Spell Resistance. You also gain a brief damage shield that scales off of your Maximum Health. While active, the armor returns Magic Damage to melee attackers. Try to keep this running for the duration of any tough fight.

Inner Rage: Morphed from **Inner Fire** (Undaunted). This Magicka attack is your long-range taunt. It also grants a chance that allies targeting the affected enemy can activate the Radiate Synergy, dealing extra damage to the target. Use it to taunt from range or as a Magicka-based alternative to your primary taunt.

Choking Talons: Morphed from **Dark Talons** (Dragonknight > Draconic Power). This Magicka ability damages and immobilizes nearby enemies. Affected targets are also afflicted with Minor Maim, temporarily reducing their damage done by 15%. While enemies are held, allies can activate the Impale Synergy to deal additional Magic Damage. Use it for a nice mix of damage, damage mitigation, and crowd control.

Igneous Shield: Morphed from **Obsidian Shield** (Dragonknight > Earthen Heart). This Magicka ability creates a damage shield for you and nearby allies. You also gain Major Mending, temporarily increasing your healing done by 25%.

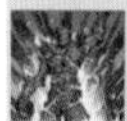

Magma Shell: Morphed from **Magma Armor** (Dragonknight > Earthen Heart). Caps incoming damage at 3% of your Maximum Health. Also grants nearby allies a powerful damage shield and deals Flame Damage to nearby enemies. This is an outstanding defensive Ultimate Ability that makes you nearly impossible to kill for nine seconds.

This is your backup Bar. Use it to taunt from range, activate damage shields, and apply group snares. The remaining slot can be used for any ability you find helpful, depending on the situation.

PRIORITY PASSIVES

Invest in all core Passives. The effects offered by One Hand and Shield, Heavy Armor, and your racial/class skill lines are more than nice boosts—they're essential to your survival.

CHAMPION POINT SUGGESTIONS

Thief: Invest heavily in Shadow Ward (Shadow) and Tenacity (Lover). Arcanist (Lover) is also worth considering.

Mage: Invest heavily in Blessed (Apprentice). Elfborn (Apprentice) is also useful.

Warrior: Invest heavily in Elemental Defender (Lady) and Hardy (Lady). Bastion (Lord) can also be very useful.

EQUIPMENT RECOMMENDATIONS

WEAPONS

Priority Trait: Infused

Priority Enchantment: Crushing

You want to have a one-handed melee weapon and a shield equipped at all times. Early on, use the highest-quality weapon/shield combinations you can find. Prioritize one-handed melee weapons that feature the **Infused** trait and the **Crushing** enchantment. Consider using something with **Decisive** as your backup weapon.

For your shields, **Reinforced** and **Sturdy** are both good traits. Favor enchantments that boost Maximum Health, Maximum Magicka, or Maximum Stamina as needed.

ARMOR

Priority Trait: Sturdy or Infused

Priority Enchantment: Maximum Health, Maximum Magicka, or Maximum Stamina

If you're serving as a group's main Tank, equip at least five pieces of heavy armor. Try to collect different sets so you can adapt to various encounters. If you're going for the **Undaunted Mettle** Passive Ability, make sure your light/medium armor pieces offer suitable set bonuses.

Until you've assembled your tanking sets, look to heavy armor pieces that shore up your stats. Health is your priority, but you need a good amount of Stamina and a fair bit of Magicka. Choose the highest-quality armor you can find for your level. Look for head, chest, and leg pieces that feature the **Infused** trait to get the most out of your enchantments. For the remaining pieces, prioritize the **Sturdy** trait.

For basic adventuring, you can probably do with swapping the bulk of your heavy armor for medium armor pieces—just make sure you invest in Medium Armor Passives. Otherwise, there's little point in compromising your survivability.

JEWELRY

Priority Trait: Healthy

Priority Enchantment: Shielding

Until you find a set you find useful, prioritize jewelry items that increase your Maximum Health and reduce the Stamina cost for blocking. As you obtain better gear, consider looking for jewelry that increases Magicka Recovery.

ARCHETYPE ADVICE

Even with the best available gear, resource management is an issue. Although Maximum Health should be your first priority, the goal is to balance all of your Attributes. Experiment with available equipment to find out just how much Health you need. The more you can invest in other resources, the better off you'll be.

Ultimate generation is a key part of your damage and survivability, but the Dragonknight's **Battle Roar** Passive Ability also makes it a big part of your sustainability. **Heroic Slash** is one of your most important Ultimate-generation tools, so make sure you use it.

Choking Talons is an efficient area-of-effect crowd-control tool, but it carries a high Magicka cost. Only use it when you're near enough enemies to make it worthwhile.

Unrelenting Grip is a great way to pull enemies away from vulnerable teammates or into area-of-effect damage—and using it on a target that can't be pulled grants a full refund of its Magicka cost. Most bosses are immune to being pulled, so use this ability as a quick (and essentially free) attack against formidable enemies.

THE STORMSHIELD

Class: Sorcerer	Race: Redguard	Attribute Focus: ealth/Stamina/Magicka	Weapon Types: One Hand and Shield	Armor Focus: Heavy	Mundus Stone: Atronach

BAR 1: ONE HAND AND SHIELD

KEY ABILITIES

Heroic Slash

Boundless Storm

Dark Deal

Absorb Magic

Bound Aegis

Spell Wall

Heroic Slash: Morphed from **Low Slash** (One Hand and Shield). This is your main single-target attack and snare. It applies Minor Maim, temporarily reducing the damage done by the target. Each use also grants Minor Heroism, increasing your Ultimate generation for nine seconds.

Boundless Storm: Morphed from **Lightning Form** (Sorcerer > Storm Calling). This Magicka ability grants important defensive buffs that should be kept active for the duration of any fight. It deals Shock Damage to nearby enemies while granting you Major Resolve, Major Ward, and Major Expedition.

Dark Deal: Morphed from **Dark Exchange** (Sorcerer > Dark Magic). Converts Magicka into Health and Stamina. This ability has a brief cast time, so proper timing is essential.

Absorb Magic: Morphed from **Defensive Posture** (One Hand and Shield). Slotting this Stamina ability increases the amount of damage you can block and reduces the Stamina cost for blocking. Activating it allows you to absorb an impressive amount of damage from the next spell projectile cast at you, healing you for a percentage of your Maximum Health.

Bound Aegis: Morphed from **Bound Armor** (Sorcerer > Daedric Summoning). Toggling this Magicka ability grants you Minor Resolve and Minor Ward, increasing your Physical and Spell Resistance. It must be placed on both Action Bars to prevent it from vanishing when you swap weapons.

Spell Wall: Morphed from **Shield Wall** (One Hand and Shield). Allows you to automatically block all attacks at no cost and reflect incoming projectiles. Use this Ultimate Ability when you need extra protection or when you're in danger of running out of Stamina.

This is your main Bar. It holds your most frequently used abilities and should be used for the bulk of any encounter. Because Bound Aegis should be placed on both Action Bars, this loadout doesn't feature a free slot.

BAR 2: ONE HAND AND SHIELD

KEY ABILITIES

Pierce Armor

Echoing Vigor

Critical Surge

Bound Aegis

Absorption Field

Pierce Armor: Morphed from **Puncture** (One Hand and Shield). This is your main taunt and debuff ability. It applies Major Fracture and Major Breach, reducing the target's Physical and Spell Resistance. Keep the effects up while tanking, but avoid over-taunting.

Echoing Vigor: Morphed from **Vigor** (Assault). This Stamina ability provides a nice heal-over-time effect for you and nearby allies.

Critical Surge: Morphed from **Surge** (Sorcerer > Storm Calling). Grants Major Brutality, increasing Weapon Damage by 20%. While this Magicka ability is active, dealing a Critical Strike grants you Health. This healing effect can happen up to once per second. It's an important source of self-healing, so try to keep it active.

Bound Aegis: Morphed from **Bound Armor** (Sorcerer > Daedric Summoning). Toggling this Magicka ability grants you Minor Resolve and Minor Ward, increasing your Physical and Spell Resistance. It must be placed on both Action Bars to prevent it from vanishing when you swap weapons.

Absorption Field: Morphed from **Negate Magic** (Sorcerer > Dark Magic). This ranged Ultimate Ability creates a globe of magic suppression, healing you and nearby allies while stunning all NPCs within the target area. Enemy players will be silenced rather than stunned. It's a powerful crowd-control tool and a useful group-healing ability.

This is your utility Bar. In addition to buffs and healing effects, it also holds your taunt ability. Use the remaining slot to add whatever ability you find useful.

PRIORITY PASSIVES

Because this build doesn't include any of Daedric Summoning's minion abilities, the **Rebate** and **Expert Summoner** Passives don't provide any benefits. Other than those, invest in all core Passives and move on from there.

CHAMPION POINT SUGGESTIONS

Thief: Invest heavily in Shadow Ward (Shadow). Arcanist (Lover) and Tenacity (Lover) are also useful.

Mage: Invest heavily in Blessed (Apprentice). Thaumaturge (Ritual) and Precise Strikes (Ritual) are also worth considering.

Warrior: Invest heavily in Elemental Defender (Lady) and Hardy (Lady). Spell Shield (Steed) and Quick Recovery (Lord) can also be useful.

EQUIPMENT RECOMMENDATIONS

WEAPONS

Priority Trait: Infused

Priority Enchantment: Crushing

You want to have a one-handed melee weapon and a shield equipped at all times. Prioritize one-handed melee weapons that feature the **Infused** trait and the **Crushing** enchantment. For your backup weapon, consider something that features the **Defending** trait. Early on, use the highest-quality weapon/shield combinations you can find. As you acquire more gear, look for combinations that offer useful set bonuses.

For your shields, **Reinforced** and **Sturdy** are both good traits. Favor enchantments that boost Maximum Health, Maximum Magicka, or Maximum Stamina as needed.

ARMOR

Priority Trait: Sturdy or Infused

Priority Enchantment: Maximum Health, Maximum Magicka, or Maximum Stamina

This build is best suited for basic tanking duties, so make sure you equip at least five pieces of heavy armor. There are many useful tanking sets out there, so try to collect a few that appeal to you. If you're going for the **Undaunted Mettle** Passive Ability, place light/medium armor pieces in your remaining equipment slots.

Until you've assembled your tanking sets, look to heavy armor pieces that offer a nice balance of stats. Health is your priority, but you need a plenty of Stamina and Magicka. Choose the highest-quality armor you can find for your level. Look for head, chest, and leg pieces that feature the **Infused** trait to get the most out of your enchantments. For the remaining pieces, prioritize the **Sturdy** trait to reduce the cost of blocking.

JEWELRY

Priority Trait: Healthy

Priority Enchantment: Shielding

Until you acquire a set you find useful, prioritize jewelry items that increase your Maximum Health and reduce the Stamina cost for blocking. As you obtain better gear, consider looking for jewelry that increases Magicka Recovery.

ARCHETYPE ADVICE

If you plan to serve as a main Tank, start ranking up abilities like **Inner Fire** (Undaunted) and **War Horn** (Assault), then invest in the most useful morphs. Most groups consider these abilities to be essential tanking tools.

This build doesn't feature many damage abilities, so consider alternative Ultimate Abilities for basic adventuring. **Dawnbreaker** (Fighters Guild) is a particularly good option that offers some powerful morphs.

Dark Deal is a useful tool for self-healing and Stamina management, but you're extremely vulnerable during its one-second cast time. Use it only when you have sufficient time between incoming attacks.

A large Magicka pool supports frequent use of **Boundless Storm** and **Critical Surge**, but Stamina management should be your priority. Blocking accounts for the bulk of your mitigation, so don't hesitate to divert resources as needed.

THE ICEBREAKER

Class: Warden	Race: Nord	Attribute Focus: Health/Magicka/Stamina	Weapon Types: One Hand and Shield, Destruction Staff	Armor Focus: Heavy	Mundus Stone: Lord

BAR 1: ONE HAND AND SHIELD

KEY ABILITIES

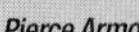
Pierce Armor

Heroic Slash

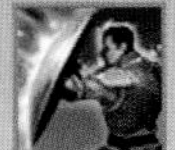
Absorb Magic

Deceptive Predator

Arctic Blast

Northern Storm

Pierce Armor: Morphed from **Puncture** (One Hand and Shield). This is your main taunt and debuff ability. It applies Major Fracture and Major Breach, reducing the target's Physical and Spell Resistance. Keep the effects up while tanking, but plan your rotation to avoid over-taunting.

Heroic Slash: Morphed from **Low Slash** (One Hand and Shield). This Stamina ability is your single-target attack and snare. It applies Minor Maim, temporarily reducing the damage done by the target. Each use also grants Minor Heroism, providing a bit of Ultimate generation over nine seconds.

Absorb Magic: Morphed from **Defensive Posture** (One Hand and Shield). Slotting this Stamina ability increases the amount of damage you can block and reduces the Stamina cost for blocking. Activating it allows you to absorb an impressive amount of damage from the next spell projectile cast at you, healing you for a percentage of your Maximum Health.

Deceptive Predator: Morphed from **Falcon's Swiftness** (Warden > Animal Companions). This Magicka ability grants Major Expedition, increasing movement speed by 30%, and Major Endurance, increasing Stamina Recovery by 20%. It also grants Minor Evasion, increasing your Dodge Chance by 5%. Most importantly, slotting it keeps an Animal Companions ability on your main Bar.

Arctic Blast: Morphed from **Arctic Wind** (Warden > Animal Companions). This Magicka ability heals you for 10% of your Maximum Health, after which it grants the same amount as a heal-over-time effect. It also deals Frost Damage to nearby enemies, making it both your self-heal and primary area-of-effect attack.

Northern Storm: Morphed from **Sleet Storm** (Warden > Winter's Embrace). This Ultimate Ability offers a nice mix of area-of-effect damage, crowd control, and protection. Slotting it also increases your Maximum Magicka by 8% and ensures that a Winter's Embrace ability remains on your Bar. It contributes a lot to your damage potential, so use it often.

This is your main Bar. It contains the bulk of your attack abilities and should be used as much as possible. This loadout doesn't feature an empty Bar slot.

BAR 2: DESTRUCTION STAFF (FROST STAFF)

KEY ABILITIES

Ice Fortress

Shimmering Shield

Gripping Shards

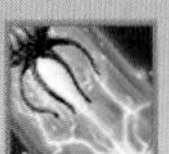
Bull Netch

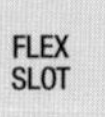

Elemental Rage

Ice Fortress: Morphed from **Frost Cloak** (Warden > Winter's Embrace). This Magicka ability grants you and nearby allies Major Resolve and Major Ward, increasing Physical and Spell Resistance. It also grants the caster Minor Protection, reducing incoming damage by 8% for the duration of the effect.

Shimmering Shield: Morphed from **Crystalized Shield** (Warden > Winter's Embrace). This Magicka ability creates a shield of ice that absorbs up to three projectiles over six seconds. Each successful absorption grants you Major Heroism, increasing Ultimate gain for six seconds.

Gripping Shards: Morphed from **Impaling Shards** (Warden > Winter's Embrace). This Magicka ability summons icy shards that deal damage each second the effect lasts. It also immobilizes enemies caught in the initial blast, after which it snares enemies who enter the area. The damage done scales based on your Maximum Health, making it a versatile ability for hardier builds.

Bull Netch: Morphed from **Betty Netch** (Warden > Animal Companions). This free-cast ability restores Stamina over 25 seconds. It also grants you Major Brutality and Minor Sorcery, increasing Weapon Damage and Spell Damage by 20% for the duration of the effect. Try to keep it active whenever you're in combat.

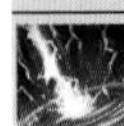
Elemental Rage: Morphed from **Elemental Storm** (Destruction Staff). This is your ranged Ultimate Ability. Use it to deal heavy damage from a safe distance. Slotting it also ensures that your Bar includes a Destruction Staff ability.

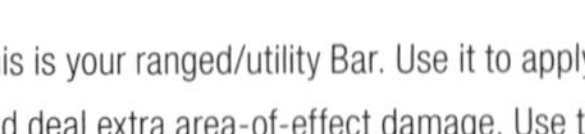
This is your ranged/utility Bar. Use it to apply and refresh buffs, attack from range, and deal extra area-of-effect damage. Use the remaining Bar slot for any ability you think you might need.

PRIORITY PASSIVES

Unless you opt to include a Green Balance ability, there's not much to be gained from investing in that skill line's Passive Abilities. Otherwise, invest in all core Passives and move on from there. Don't forget about the Destruction Staff Passives—**Tri Focus** and **Ancient Knowledge** are what make the Frost Staff a useful backup weapon.

It's also worth noting that **Savage Beast** (Animal Companions) is an important part of your Ultimate generation, and **Flourish** (Animal Companions) is a considerable help with sustainability.

CHAMPION POINT SUGGESTIONS

Thief: Invest heavily in Shadow Ward (Shadow) and Tenacity (Lover).

Mage: Invest heavily in Blessed (Apprentice). Elemental Expert (Apprentice) and Elfborn (Apprentice) can also be useful.

Warrior: Invest heavily in Hardy (Lady) and Elemental Defender (Lady). Quick Recovery (Lord) is also recommended.

EQUIPMENT RECOMMENDATIONS

WEAPONS
Priority Trait: Decisive
Priority Enchantment: Crushing
For your main Action Bar, you'll need a one-handed melee weapon and a shield. Early on, use the highest-quality weapon/shield combinations you can find. Prioritize one-handed melee weapons that feature the **Decisive** trait and the **Crushing** enchantment.
For your shield, **Sturdy** is probably the most useful trait. Favor enchantments that boost Maximum Health, Maximum Magicka, or Maximum Stamina as needed.
When it comes to your backup Bar, you'll generally want to use the highest-quality Frost Staff you can find. **Defending** is probably your best trait option, but **Sharpened** is useful if you add another attack ability to the Bar.
Remember that once you've invested in **Tri Focus**, your Frost Staff's fully charged heavy attacks also serve as long-range taunts. If you're not a group's designated Tank, consider switching to a Lightning Staff to avoid unwanted attention.

ARMOR
Priority Trait: Sturdy or Infused
Priority Enchantment: Maximum Health, Maximum Magicka, or Maximum Stamina
This isn't a main-Tank build, so you have a fair amount of freedom when it comes to equipment. Heavy armor should still be your focus, but there's nothing wrong with taking advantage of the Passives found in other armor skill lines. As you work toward assembling your tanking sets, experiment with different gear options to find a balance that works for you.
Look for head, chest, and leg pieces that feature the Infused trait to get the most out of your enchantments. For the remaining pieces, prioritize the Sturdy trait to reduce the cost of blocking.
When it comes to enchantments, focus on Maximum Health, then start experimenting with Magicka and Stamina enchantments. Of course, a Prismatic enchantment is always the best option.

JEWELRY
Priority Trait: Healthy
Priority Enchantment: Shielding
Until you collect a set you find useful, prioritize jewelry items that increase your Maximum Health and reduce the Stamina cost for blocking. As you obtain better gear, consider looking for jewelry that increases Magicka Recovery.

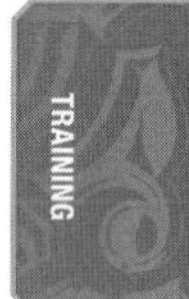

ARCHETYPE ADVICE

This build has a lot of survivability, but it lacks some of the most widely used tanking skills. If you hope to one day serve as a group's main Tank, start ranking up abilities like **Inner Fire** (Undaunted) and **War Horn** (Assault), then invest in the most useful morphs. You might also consider exchanging your Frost Staff for another weapon/shield combination.

You don't have many options for single-target damage, but you have some great tools for dealing with grouped enemies. **Arctic Blast** combines self-healing and area-of-effect damage, and **Northern Storm** combines great protection buffs with a nice damage effect. On your backup Bar, you have **Gripping Shards** and **Elemental Rage**.

Considering its resource needs, this build has fairly good sustainability. By switching weapons, you can use heavy attacks to regenerate Magicka or Stamina as needed without a huge drop in survivability—just remember that a fully charged heavy attack from your Frost Staff also serves as a long-range taunt.

Bull Netch is a versatile tool and should be a regular part of your attack rotation. At Rank 2, the **Savage Beast** Passive Ability grants 4 Ultimate each time you activate an Animal Companions ability (with a cooldown of eight seconds). **Bull Netch** is a cost-free cast, it grants multiple damage buffs, and it restores Stamina even while you're blocking.

THE REAPER

Class: Nightblade | **Race:** Argonian | **Attribute Focus:** Health/Magicka/Stamina | **Weapon Types:** One Hand and Shield, Destruction Staff | **Armor Focus:** Heavy | **Mundus Stone:** Atronach

BAR 1: ONE HAND AND SHIELD

KEY ABILITIES

Pierce Armor

Heroic Slash

Swallow Soul

Sap Essence

Refreshing Path

Soul Harvest

Pierce Armor: Morphed from **Puncture** (One Hand and Shield). This Stamina ability is your main taunt. It also applies Major Fracture and Major Breach, reducing the target's Physical and Spell Resistance. Use it when needed, but be mindful of the Stamina cost.

Heroic Slash: Morphed from **Low Slash** (One Hand and Shield). This is your priority Stamina ability. It applies Minor Maim, reducing the target's damage done, and grants you Minor Heroism, increasing your Ultimate generation. It also serves as a single-target snare.

Swallow Soul: Morphed from **Strife** (Nightblade > Siphoning). This Magicka ability is your primary attack and a reliable source of healing over time. Slotting it also grants Minor Vitality, increasing your healing received by 8%.

Sap Essence: Morphed from **Drain Power** (Nightblade > Siphoning). This Magicka ability serves as an area-of-effect attack and a potential group heal. As long as the attack hits an enemy, you gain Major Brutality and Major Sorcery, increasing your Weapon Damage and Spell Damage for 20 seconds.

Refreshing Path: Morphed from **Path of Darkness** (Nightblade > Shadow). Activate this Magicka ability to deal AoE/DOT damage to enemies within the target area. While in the affected area—and for up to two seconds after leaving it—you and your allies receive healing over time. Casting it also grants you Major Expedition, increasing your movement speed by 30%. It's useful, but it's slotted specifically to keep a Shadow ability on the Action Bar.

Soul Harvest: Morphed from **Death Stroke** (Nightblade > Assassination). This is slotted to help with Ultimate generation, but it's a cost-effective Ultimate Ability and a good option for single-target damage as well. It's also chosen to keep an Assassination ability on the Bar.

This is your main Bar. It holds your main attack and both of your One Hand and Shield abilities. This loadout does not feature an empty slot.

BAR 2: DESTRUCTION STAFF (FROST STAFF)

KEY ABILITIES

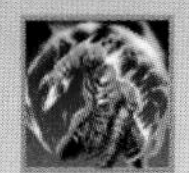

Mirage

Siphoning Attacks

Elemental Blockade

Lotus Fan

Veil of Blades

Mirage: Morphed from **Blur** (Nightblade > Assassination). This Magicka ability grants you Minor Evasion, Minor Resolve, and Minor Ward, increasing your Dodge Chance and your Physical and Spell Resistance for 26 seconds. Refresh as needed.

Siphoning Attacks: Morphed from **Siphoning Strikes** (Nightblade > Siphoning). This Magicka ability causes your light and heavy attacks to restore Health and Magicka for 20 seconds. With some basic weaving, this ability serves as another self-heal with a nice return on resources. Slotting also keeps a Siphoning ability on your Bar.

Elemental Blockade: Morphed from **Wall of Elements** (Destruction Staff). This Magicka ability is a good source of area-of-effect damage. Try to keep it active for the duration of any fight.

Lotus Fan: Morphed from **Teleport Strike** (Nightblade > Assassination). Activate this Magicka ability to teleport to your target, damaging and snaring them. When you arrive, you also afflict nearby enemies with Magic Damage over time.

Veil of Blades: Morphed from **Consuming Darkness** (Nightblade > Shadow). This Ultimate Ability snares nearby enemies, deals Magic Damage over time, and grants you and your allies Major Protection, reducing your damage taken by 30% for the duration of the effect. Low-Health allies can also activate the Hidden Refresh Synergy, granting them invisibility, increased speed, and a heal-over-time effect.

This is your backup Bar. Use it to cast buffs, use your gap closer, and generate additional area-of-effect damage.

Use the remaining slot to add any ability you feel is helpful.

PRIORITY PASSIVES

While you should invest in all core Passives, your class-based Passives are particularly important. Some of the chosen abilities are slotted specifically to keep these Passives active.

Again, **Tri Focus** and **Ancient Knowledge** are what make the Frost Staff a useful backup weapon—don't forget about the Destruction Staff Passives.

CHAMPION POINT SUGGESTIONS

Thief: Invest heavily in Shadow Ward (Shadow) and Tenacity (Lover).

Mage: Invest heavily in Blessed (Apprentice). Elemental Expert (Apprentice) and Elfborn (Apprentice) are also helpful.

Warrior: Invest heavily in Hardy (Lady) and Elemental Defender (Lady). Quick Recovery (Lord) is also recommended.

EQUIPMENT RECOMMENDATIONS

WEAPONS

Priority Trait: Defending

Priority Enchantment: Crushing

For your main Action Bar, you'll need a one-handed melee weapon and a shield. Early on, use the highest-quality weapon/shield combinations you can find. It's usually best to look for one-handed melee weapons that feature the **Defending** trait and the **Crushing** enchantment.

For your shield, **Sturdy** is probably the most useful trait. Favor enchantments that boost Maximum Health, Maximum Magicka, or Maximum Stamina as needed.

When it comes to your backup Bar, you'll generally want to use the highest-quality Frost Staff you can find. **Defending** is probably your best trait option, but **Sharpened** is useful if you favor a bit of extra damage.

Remember that once you've invested in **Tri Focus**, your Frost Staff's fully charged heavy attacks also serve as long-range taunts. If you're not a group's designated Tank, consider switching to a Lightning Staff to avoid unwanted attention.

ARMOR

Priority Trait: Sturdy or Infused

Priority Enchantment: Maximum Health, Maximum Magicka, or Maximum Stamina

This isn't a main-Tank build, but mitigation is still important. Heavy armor should still be your focus. You'll generally want to use at least five pieces of heavy armor, but consider equipping two pieces of light armor. This prevents you from taking advantage of the **Undaunted Mettle** Passive Ability, but the Light Armor Passives can sometimes prove more useful.

Look for head, chest, and leg pieces that feature the **Infused** trait to boost your most powerful enchantments. For the remaining pieces, prioritize the **Sturdy** trait to reduce the cost of blocking.

When it comes to enchantments, Maximum Health is the best way to get started. Experiment with Magicka and Stamina enchantments once you feel your survivability is acceptable. Eventually, you'll want to utilize **Prismatic** enchantments, but that should be put off until you're satisfied with your armor set.

JEWELRY

Priority Trait: Healthy

Priority Enchantment: Shielding

Until you collect a set you find useful, prioritize jewelry items that increase your Maximum Health and reduce the Stamina cost for blocking. As you obtain better gear, consider looking for jewelry that increases Magicka Recovery.

ARCHETYPE ADVICE

This build has considerable survivability, but it lacks some key tanking skills. If you plan to tank beyond basic group dungeons, start ranking up abilities like **Inner Fire** (Undaunted) and **War Horn** (Assault), then invest in the most useful morphs. You might also consider exchanging your Frost Staff for another weapon/shield combination.

The Argonian was selected primarily for its bonus to healing received. This helps make the most of your various Siphoning abilities.

By switching weapons, you can use heavy attacks to regenerate Magicka or Stamina as needed without a huge drop in survivability—just remember that a fully charged heavy attack from your Frost Staff also serves as a long-range taunt.

Once you've invested in Rank 2 of the **Shadow Barrier** Passive Ability (Nightblade > Shadow), casting **Refreshing Path** also grants you Major Ward and Major Resolve. When combined with the Minor Resolve, Minor Ward, and Minor Evasion granted by **Mirage**, your survivability is significantly improved.

HEALERS

THE DEVOTED

Class: Templar | **Race:** Breton | **Attribute Focus:** Magicka | **Weapon Types:** Destruction Staff, Restoration Staff | **Armor Focus:** Light | **Mundus Stone:** Atronach

BAR 1: DESTRUCTION STAFF (LIGHTNING STAFF)

KEY ABILITIES

Puncturing Sweep

Elemental Blockade

Purifying Light

Breath of Life

FLEX SLOT

Solar Prison

Puncturing Sweep: Morphed from **Puncturing Strikes** (Templar > Aedric Spear). This short-range attack can affect multiple targets, healing you based on the damage done. The nearest enemy takes increased damage and suffers a brief snare. It's your primary attack, and slotting it keeps a useful Aedric Spear ability on your Action Bar.

Elemental Blockade: Morphed from **Wall of Elements** (Destruction Staff). This area-of-effect ability greatly increases your damage potential. Keep it active whenever possible.

Purifying Light: Morphed from **Backlash** (Templar > Dawn's Wrath). This attack deals a bit of Magic Damage, but it also copies all damage the target takes for six seconds, applying up to 20% of it as additional Magic Damage when the effect ends. It's a great way to contribute to your group's DPS.

Breath of Life: Morphed from **Rushed Ceremony** (Templar > Restoring Light). This ability heals you or a wounded ally. It also grants a smaller heal to an additional target. Use it as needed, but be mindful of the Magicka cost.

Solar Prison: Morphed from **Nova** (Templar > Dawn's Wrath). This ranged Ultimate Ability deals Magic Damage to enemies within the targeted area. It also afflicts enemies with Minor Maim, reducing their damage done by 30% for the duration of the effect. Additionally, an ally can activate the Gravity Crush Synergy, damaging and stunning all enemies in the area.

This is your attack Bar. It also holds one of your more useful healing abilities. Whether you're on your own or healing for a group, try to spend the bulk of your time using these abilities. Use the remaining slot to add any ability you feel is helpful.

BAR 2: RESTORATION STAFF

KEY ABILITIES

Blazing Spear

Ritual of Retribution

Rapid Regeneration

Combat Prayer

FLEX SLOT

Aggressive Horn

Blazing Spear: Morphed from **Spear Shards** (Templar > Aedric Spear). This ranged area-of-effect attack does a bit of damage, but it's really used for its featured Synergy. While the effect is active, an ally can use Blessed Shards to restore a good amount of Magicka or Stamina, depending on their highest resource. It's one of your most important support skills, so make good use of it.

Ritual of Retribution: Morphed from **Cleansing Ritual** (Templar > Restoring Light). Cleanses you of up to two harmful effect and heals you and nearby allies for the duration of the effect. Additionally, enemies in the area take Magic Damage, and allies can activate the Purify Synergy. This allows them to cleanse themselves of all harmful effects and receive additional healing.

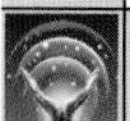

Rapid Regeneration: Morphed from **Regeneration** (Restoration Staff). Grants a heal-over-time effect to you or up to two nearby allies.

Combat Prayer: Morphed from **Blessing of Protection** (Restoration Staff). Use this ability to heal yourself and allies in front of you. Those affected also gain Minor Berserk, Minor Resolve, and Minor Ward, increasing damage done, Physical Resistance, and Spell Resistance.

Aggressive Horn: Morphed from **War Horn** (Assault). Increases the Maximum Magicka, Health, and Stamina of you and your allies by 10%. Affected targets also gain Major Force, temporarily increasing the damage and healing done by Critical Strikes. This is an excellent support skill, and should be your Ultimate Ability of choice during boss encounters.

This is your support Bar. Use it to apply buffs, share resources, and initiate heal-over-time effects. The remaining slot can be used to add any ability you might find helpful.

PRIORITY PASSIVES

The **Light Weaver** Passive Ability only affects specific Restoring Light abilities—none of which are used in the default loadout. Other than that, invest in all core Passives and move on from there.

CHAMPION POINT SUGGESTIONS

Thief: Invest heavily in Arcanist (Lover) and Tenacity (Lover).

Mage: Invest heavily in Blessed (Apprentice) and Elemental Expert (Apprentice). Elfborn (Apprentice) is another good option.

Warrior: Invest heavily in Elemental Defender (Lady) and Hardy (Lady). Quick Recovery (Lord) is also worth considering.

EQUIPMENT RECOMMENDATIONS

WEAPONS

Priority Trait: Sharpened

Priority Enchantment: Spell Damage

For your main weapon, use the best Lightning Staff you can find. The **Sharpened** trait is your best option for damage—and a Spell Damage enchantment would be nice—but any high-quality staff should help you do reliable damage until you're able to obtain a nice set piece or something from the Maelstrom.

You'll always want a Restoration Staff as your backup weapon. Given the choice, look for staves that feature traits like **Precise**, **Powered**, or **Decisive**. As far as enchantments go, **Absorb Magicka** tends to be useful.

ARMOR

Priority Trait: Divines

Priority Enchantment: Maximum Magicka

Always equip at least five pieces of light armor. The related Passives grant you some very important benefits. If you've invested in the **Undaunted Mettle** Passive Ability, you'll probably want to equip medium/heavy armor pieces in the remaining slots.

Equipment that grants suitable set bonuses is always your best option. Look for light armor that offers Maximum Magicka enchantments as you work toward obtaining high-level gear. **Divines** tends to be the most useful trait for PvE content, but **Infused** can be very effective on head, chest, and leg pieces.

JEWELRY

Priority Trait: Arcane

Priority Enchantment: Reduce Spell Cost

Until you manage to track down useful set pieces, use anything that reduces the Magicka cost of your spells.

ARCHETYPE ADVICE

Before each encounter, cast **Rapid Regeneration** on all of your allies. Each use only affects two targets, so move quickly to get everyone covered. When the battle begins, cast **Ritual of Retribution** for additional healing over time. These abilities should account for the bulk of your healing—use **Breath of Life** only when it's needed.

Unless you're actively healing or buffing your group, you should try to deal damage. Once you've applied your heal-over-time effects, switch to your attack Bar and go to work. **Breath of Life** allows you to heal priority targets without swapping Bars, so don't be afraid to indulge in a little offense.

Combine **Elemental Blockade** with **Puncturing Sweep** to help clear out weaker enemies, and use **Purifying Light** to contribute during boss encounters. If resource management is an issue, perform a few extra heavy attacks to replenish your Magicka.

Don't be stingy with **Blazing Spear**. It's in your best interest to support your teammates. The occasional Blessed Shard Synergy can do wonders for your Tank or Damage-Dealers.

THE DRUID

Class: Warden	Race: Argonian	Attribute Focus: Magicka	Weapon Types: Destruction Staff, Restoration Staff	Armor Focus: Light	Mundus Stone: Thief

BAR 1: DESTRUCTION STAFF

KEY ABILITIES

Screaming Cliff Racer

Growing Swarm

Winter's Revenge

Expansive Frost Cloak

Enchanted Growth

Northern Storm

Screaming Cliff Racer: Morphed from **Dive** (Warden > Animal Companions). This is your main single-target attack. Use it from maximum range for more damage.

Growing Swarm: Morphed from **Swarm** (Warden > Animal Companions). Use this ability to infect a target with Fetcherflies, causing damage over time. When the effect ends, the Fetcherflies infect up to six new targets.

Winter's Revenge: Morphed from **Impaling Shards** (Warden > Winter's Embrace). This ability is a ranged AoE/DOT attack with a nice Snare effect. Use it when you need some extra damage or a bit of crowd control.

Expansive Frost Cloak: Morphed from **Frost Cloak** (Warden > Winter's Embrace). Grants Major Resolve and Major Ward to you and nearby allies, increasing your Physical and Spell Resistance by 5280 for the duration of the effect.

Enchanted Growth: Morphed from **Fungal Growth** (Warden > Green Balance). This instant ability heals you and all allies within your frontal cone. All affected targets also gain Minor Intellect and Minor Endurance, increasing Magicka and Stamina Recovery. Its quick heal provides a small boost to resource generation.

Northern Storm: Morphed from **Sleet Storm** (Warden > Winter's Embrace). This Ultimate Ability offers a nice mix of area-of-effect damage, crowd control, and protection. Slotting it also increases your Maximum Magicka by 8% and ensures that a Winter's Embrace ability remains on your Action Bar.

This is your damage Bar. It also contains some of your healing and support abilities. This loadout uses all available Bar slots.

BAR 2: RESTORATION STAFF

KEY ABILITIES

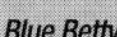
Blue Betty

Lotus Blossom

Rapid Regeneration

Budding Seeds

Leeching Vines

Enchanted Forest

Blue Betty: Morphed from **Betty Netch** (Warden > Animal Companions). Restores Magicka, grants Major Sorcery for a boost to Spell Damage, and purges one negative effect. This ability has a great duration and no casting cost. Keep it active at all times.

Lotus Blossom: Morphed from **Lotus Flower** (Warden > Green Balance). Allows your light and heavy attacks to heal you or a nearby ally for a percentage of the damage done. Also grants you Major Prophecy, increasing Spell Critical. This ability has a nice duration, and should be refreshed as often as needed.

Rapid Regeneration: Morphed from **Regeneration** (Restoration Staff). Grants a heal-over-time effect to you or up to two nearby allies.

Budding Seeds: Morphed from **Healing Seed** (Warden > Green Balance). Activate this ability to initiate a delayed area-of-effect heal. Activate it again at any time during the six-second delay to end the effect for an instant heal. While the effect lasts, allies can activate the Healing Seed Synergy to restore Health.

Leeching Vines: Morphed from **Living Vines** (Warden > Green Balance). Casting this ability places a cluster of vines on you or the lowest-Health ally in front of you. While active, the vines heal the target each time they take damage—this effect can happen once every second. The vines also apply Minor Lifesteal to enemies that damage the target, allowing allies to regain Health while attacking afflicted enemies.

Enchanted Forest: Morphed from **Secluded Grove** (Warden > Green Balance). This Ultimate Ability grants an instant heal to you or a nearby ally, after which it continues to heal all friendly targets within the area. You gain 20 Ultimate if the ability is used to heal an ally under 50% Health.

This is your support Bar. Use it to apply buffs and cast area-of-effect heals. This loadout uses all available Bar slots.

PRIORITY PASSIVES

Passives from Green Balance and Restoration Staff have the greatest effects on your healing spells. However, it's worth noting that the Animal Companions skill line has an excellent Passive Ability for resource management: Rank 2 **Flourish** increases your Magicka and Stamina Recovery by 12%.

CHAMPION POINT SUGGESTIONS

Thief: Invest heavily in Arcanist (Lover) and Tenacity (Lover).

Mage: Invest heavily in Blessed (Apprentice) and Elfborn (Apprentice). Thaumaturge (Ritual) is also helpful.

Warrior: Invest heavily in Elemental Defender (Lady) and Hardy (Lady). Quick Recovery (Lord) is also worth considering.

EQUIPMENT RECOMMENDATIONS

WEAPONS

Priority Trait: Sharpened

Priority Enchantment: Spell Damage

For your main weapon, use the best Destruction Staff you can find—just avoid Frost Staves once you've invested in the **Tri Focus** Passive Ability. Look for something with the **Sharpened** trait and a Spell Damage enchantment until you're able to obtain a Maelstrom staff or a suitable set item.

You'll always want a Restoration Staff as your backup weapon. Given the choice, look for staves that feature traits like **Precise**, **Powered**, or **Decisive**. When it comes to enchantments, **Absorb Magicka** is likely your best option.

ARMOR

Priority Trait: Divines

Priority Enchantment: Maximum Magicka

Always equip at least five pieces of light armor. Add a piece of medium armor and heavy armor if you've invested in the **Undaunted Mettle** Passive Ability. Otherwise, it's often best to stick with seven pieces of light armor.

Armor sets offer the most useful bonuses, but look for light armor that offers Maximum Magicka enchantments until you find something better. **Divines** tends to be the most useful trait, but **Infused** can be very effective on head, chest, and leg pieces.

JEWELRY

Priority Trait: Arcane

Priority Enchantment: Reduce Spell Cost

Until you manage to track down useful set pieces, use anything that reduces the Magicka cost of your spells.

ARCHETYPE ADVICE

Blue Betty and **Lotus Blossom** should be kept active for the duration of any encounter. Maintaining **Expansive Frost Cloak** can also reduce the amount of healing you need to do.

Keep **Rapid Regeneration** active, but consider **Budding Seeds** your primary heal. You can let your allies take advantage of the Healing Seed Synergy, or you can double-cast it for a near-instant heal.

Enchanted Growth is a nice heal, but it's a fairly expensive cast. Use it for the buffs it provides or as burst healing while wounded allies activate the Healing Seed Synergy.

Enchanted Forest has a low Ultimate cost and the potential to return 20 Ultimate each time it's used. Cast it only on allies below 50% Health for maximum efficiency.

Growing Swarm is a great way to contribute damage during hectic encounters. Toss it onto the occasional enemy and let the Fetcherflies do their work.

THE INVOKER

Class: Sorcerer | **Race:** Breton | **Attribute Focus:** Magicka | **Weapon Types:** Destruction Staff, Restoration Staff | **Armor Focus:** Light | **Mundus Stone:** Thief

BAR 1: DESTRUCTION STAFF (LIGHTNING STAFF)

KEY ABILITIES

Force Pulse

Liquid Lightning

Mage's Wrath

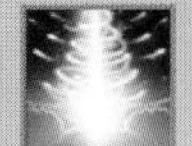

Crystal Fragments

Summon Twilight Matriarch

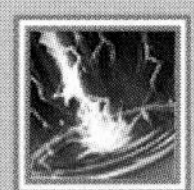

Elemental Rage

Force Pulse: Morphed from **Force Shock** (Destruction Staff). This is your main ability for single-target damage.

Liquid Lightning: Morphed from **Lightning Splash** (Sorcerer > Storm Calling). This is your main AoE/DOT ability. While it's active, allies can use the Conduit Synergy to deal additional Shock Damage to nearby enemies.

Mage's Wrath: Morphed from **Mage's Fury** (Sorcerer > Storm Calling). Use this powerful execute ability whenever your target's Health drops below 20%.

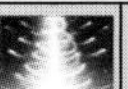

Crystal Fragments: Morphed from **Crystal Shard** (Sorcerer > Dark Magic). Casting any other Magicka ability has a chance of reducing this spell's cost, eliminating its cast time, and increasing its damage. Use it only when this effect is triggered.

Summon Twilight Matriarch: Morphed from **Summon Winged Twilight** (Sorcerer > Daedric Summoning). While summoned, this minion fights by your side, dealing Shock Damage to its chosen target. Activating the Twilight Matriarch's special ability causes it to heal itself and up to two nearby allies. This ability is kept on both Action Bars to prevent your minion from vanishing when you swap weapons.

Elemental Rage: Morphed from **Elemental Storm** (Destruction Staff). This is your offensive Ultimate Ability. Use it to deal heavy area-of-effect damage over time.

This is your attack Bar. It contains all of your offensive abilities. Use it whenever you're free to deal damage. Because Twilight Matriarch is featured on both Action Bars, this loadout uses all available slots. Of course, this also means that your minion's activated heal is always available.

BAR 2: RESTORATION STAFF

KEY ABILITIES

Mutagen

Healing Springs

Combat Prayer

Summon Twilight Matriarch

FLEX SLOT

Absorption Field

Mutagen: Morphed from **Regeneration** (Restoration Staff). Grants healing over time for you or up to two nearby allies. If an affected target's Health drops below 20%, the spell is consumed, removing one negative effect and granting an instant heal.

Healing Springs: Morphed from **Grant Healing** (Restoration Staff). This area-of-effect ability grants an instant heal to you and any allies located within the target area. Remaining in the area grants additional healing for a short time. You also restore Magicka based on the number of friendly targets affected by the initial heal.

Combat Prayer: Morphed from **Blessing of Protection** (Restoration Staff). Use this ability to heal yourself and allies in front of you. Those affected also gain Minor Berserk, Minor Resolve, and Minor Ward, increasing damage done, Physical Resistance, and Spell Resistance.

Summon Twilight Matriarch: Morphed from **Summon Winged Twilight** (Sorcerer > Daedric Summoning). While summoned, this minion fights by your side, dealing Shock Damage to its chosen target. Activating the Twilight Matriarch's special ability causes it to heal itself and up to two nearby allies. This ability is kept on both Action Bars to prevent your minion from vanishing when you swap weapons.

Absorption Field: Morphed from **Negate Magic** (Sorcerer > Dark Magic). This ranged Ultimate Ability conjures a globe of magic suppression. Enemies within the targeted area are stunned or silenced for 10 seconds; enemy-placed effects within the target area are immediately dispelled. The globe also heals friendly targets for the duration of the effect.

This is your support Bar. Use it to apply buffs and cast heals. You can use the remaining slot for any ability you find helpful, but consider choosing another heal or an ability that helps with resource management.

PRIORITY PASSIVES

Invest in all of your core Passives, then look to other skill lines for useful abilities.

CHAMPION POINT SUGGESTIONS

Thief: Invest heavily in Arcanist (Lover) and Tenacity (Lover).

Mage: Invest heavily in Blessed (Apprentice) and Elfborn (Apprentice). Elemental Expert (Apprentice) is another good option.

Warrior: Invest heavily in Elemental Defender (Lady) and Hardy (Lady). Light Armor Focus (Lady) is also worth considering.

EQUIPMENT RECOMMENDATIONS

WEAPONS
Priority Trait: Sharpened
Priority Enchantment: Spell Damage
For your main weapon, use the best Lightning Staff you can find. Look for something that features the **Sharpened** trait and a Spell Damage enchantment until you obtain a top-tier staff.
You'll always want a Restoration Staff as your backup weapon. Given the choice, look for staves that feature traits like **Precise**, **Powered**, or **Decisive**. An **Absorb Magicka** enchantment is always a good option.

ARMOR
Priority Trait: Divines
Priority Enchantment: Maximum Magicka
Always equip at least five pieces of light armor. The related Passives grant you some very important benefits. If you've invested in the **Undaunted Mettle** Passive Ability, it's often best to equip medium/heavy armor pieces in the remaining slots. Still, a complete set of light armor works well in most cases.
Equipment that grants suitable set bonuses is always your best option. Until you find something you like, look for light armor that offers Maximum Magicka enchantments. **Divines** is a popular choice, but **Infused** can be very effective on head, chest, and leg pieces.

JEWELRY
Priority Trait: Arcane
Priority Enchantment: Reduce Spell Cost
Until you manage to track down useful set pieces, use anything that reduces the Magicka cost of your spells.

ARCHETYPE ADVICE

This build features a nice balance of damage and healing, but it doesn't offer much utility. If you intend to heal beyond basic content, consider trading at least one of your attacks for something that adds a bit of group support.

Apply **Mutagen** to all of your teammates before each encounter. Once the battle begins, use **Combat Prayer** for its buffs and additional healing. If you're the group's main Healer, aim to keep both of these abilities active at all times.

Unless you add a tool for resource management, you'll need to rely on heavy attacks to keep your Magicka in order. Weave them between your abilities as often as needed.

Remember that you can still utilize the **Twilight Matriarch**'s healing ability while you're dealing damage. It's a great emergency heal if you mind your positioning, and it has the chance to proc **Crystal Fragments**.

THE FLAMEKEEPER

Class: Dragonknight | **Race:** Argonian | **Attribute Focus:** Magicka | **Weapon Types:** Restoration Staff, Destruction Staff | **Armor Focus:** Light | **Mundus Stone:** Thief

BAR 1: RESTORATION STAFF

KEY ABILITIES

Igneous Shield

Healing Springs

Healing Ward

Quick Siphon

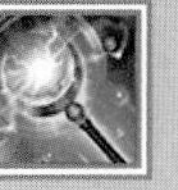
Light's Champion

Igneous Shield: Morphed from **Obsidian Shield** (Dragonknight > Earthen Heart). This Magicka ability creates a damage shield for you and nearby allies. You also gain Major Mending, temporarily increasing your healing done by 25%.

Healing Springs: Morphed from **Grant Healing** (Restoration Staff). This area-of-effect ability grants an instant heal to you and any allies located within the target area. Remaining in the area grants additional healing for a short time. You also restore Magicka based on the number of friendly targets affected by the initial heal.

Healing Ward: Morphed from **Steadfast Ward** (Restoration Staff). Grants you or the lowest-Health ally around you a damage shield. The shield also grants a heal when it appears; when it expires, the target is healed based on the shield's remaining strength.

Quick Siphon: Morphed from **Force Siphon** (Restoration Staff). Use this ability to apply Minor Lifesteal to an enemy. This debuff allows you and your allies to regain Health by attacking the target.

Light's Champion: Morphed from **Panacea** (Restoration Staff). This Ultimate Ability grants you or a nearby ally a brief but powerful heal-over-time effect. Any friendly target you heal gains Major Force and Major Protection, temporarily increasing their Critical Damage and reducing their damage taken.

This is your healing Bar. Use it to apply damage shields, heal-over-time effects, and the Minor Lifesteal debuff. Use the Bar's remaining slot to add any ability you feel would be helpful.

BAR 2: DESTRUCTION STAFF

KEY ABILITIES

Force Pulse

Elemental Blockade

Pulsar

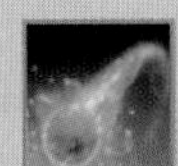
Energy Orb

Aggressive Horn

Force Pulse: Morphed from **Force Shock** (Destruction Staff). This is your main ability for single-target damage.

Elemental Blockade: Morphed from **Wall of Elements** (Destruction Staff). This tried-and-true area-of-effect ability is a great way to deal extra damage.

Pulsar: Morphed from **Impulse** (Destruction Staff). Activate this ability to hit nearby enemies with a burst of Magic Damage. Affected enemies are afflicted with Minor Maim, temporarily reducing their Maximum Health by 10%.

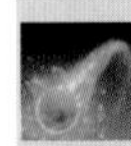
Energy Orb: Morphed from **Necrotic Orb** (Undaunted). Conjures a floating orb that moves through the area, healing nearby allies. An ally can also activate the Combustion Synergy to recover Health and Magicka. The amount of Magicka an ally gains scales off the number of targets the orb has healed.

Aggressive Horn: Morphed from **War Horn** (Assault). This Ultimate Ability increases the Maximum Magicka, Health, and Stamina of you and your allies by 10%. Affected targets also gain Major Force, temporarily increasing the damage and healing done by Critical Strikes.

This is your damage Bar, but it does contain a useful support ability. Dealing damage is an important part of any encounter, so use this Action Bar as often as your healing duties allow. Use this Bar's remaining slot to include any ability you might find handy in a given situation.

PRIORITY PASSIVES

Until you slot abilities from the Ardent Flame and Draconic Power skill lines, you may not find much use for the Passives they offer. Invest in your core Passives and branch out from there.

CHAMPION POINT SUGGESTIONS

Thief: Invest heavily in Arcanist (Lover) and Tenacity (Lover).

Mage: Invest heavily in Blessed (Apprentice) and Elemental Expert (Apprentice). Elfborn (Apprentice) is another good option.

Warrior: Invest heavily in Elemental Defender (Lady) and Hardy (Lady).

EQUIPMENT RECOMMENDATIONS

WEAPONS	ARMOR	JEWELRY
Priority Trait: Precise	**Priority Trait:** Divines	**Priority Trait:** Arcane
Priority Enchantment: Spell Damage	**Priority Enchantment:** Maximum Magicka	**Priority Enchantment:** Reduce Spell Cost
You'll always want a Restoration Staff as your main weapon. Given the choice, look for staves that feature traits like **Precise, Powered,** or **Decisive.** An **Absorb Magicka** enchantment is always a good option.	Depending on the available gear, a full set of light armor may be your best option. Of course, if you'd rather make use of the **Undaunted Mettle** Passive Ability, there's nothing wrong with boosting your resource pools.	Until you manage to track down useful set pieces, use anything that reduces the Magicka cost of your spells. Once you've got a handle on Magicka management, look into boosting your Spell Damage.
For your backup weapon, stick to Lightning or Flame Staves. Look for something that features the **Sharpened** trait and a Spell Damage enchantment until you obtain a top-tier staff.	Equipment that grants suitable set bonuses is always your best option. Until you find something you like, look for light armor that offers Maximum Magicka enchantments. **Divines** is always a good choice, but **Infused** can be very effective on head, chest, and leg pieces.	

ARCHETYPE ADVICE

You'll need some fairly good gear to serve as a main Healer, even in entry-level dungeons. Once you get the hang of Magicka management, focus on increasing your Spell Critical.

The damage shields provided by **Igneous Shield** can certainly be useful, but the fact that it grants you Major Mending is what really makes it a valuable tool. When incoming damage is outpacing your healing effects, cast Igneous Shield to boost your next few spells.

Quick Siphon has a fairly long duration, and it can be a big help during tough encounters. Whenever your team is focused on a single target, make sure this ability is active.

Healing Ward serves as your emergency heal. It's much more effective when used on low-Health targets. If you just want to mitigate a bit of incoming damage, use Igneous Shield instead.

THE SHADOWPRIEST

Class: Nightblade	**Race:** High Elf	**Attribute Focus:** Magicka	**Weapon Types:** Restoration Staff, Destruction Staff	**Armor Focus:** Light	**Mundus Stone:** Mage

BAR 1: RESTORATION STAFF

KEY ABILITIES

Rapid Regeneration

Blessing of Restoration

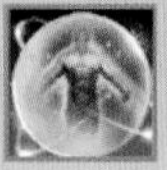
Healing Ward

Sap Essence

FLEX SLOT

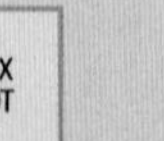
Soul Siphon

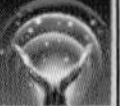
Rapid Regeneration: Morphed from **Regeneration** (Restoration Staff). Grants a heal-over-time effect to you or up to two nearby allies.

Blessing of Restoration: Morphed from **Blessing of Protection** (Restoration Staff). Use this ability to heal yourself and allies in front of you. It also grants Minor Resolve and Minor Ward, boosting Physical and Spell Resistance for all affected targets.

Healing Ward: Morphed from **Steadfast Ward** (Restoration Staff). Grants you or the lowest-Health ally around you a damage shield. The shield also grants a heal when it appears; when it expires, the target is healed based on the shield's remaining strength.

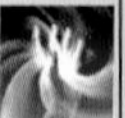
Sap Essence: Morphed from **Drain Power** (Nightblade > Siphoning). This Magicka ability serves as an area-of-effect attack and a potential group heal. As long as the attack hits an enemy, you gain Major Brutality and Major Sorcery, increasing your Weapon Damage and Spell Damage for 20 seconds.

Soul Siphon: Morphed from **Soul Shred** (Nightblade > Siphon). Activate this Ultimate Ability to heal yourself and nearby allies. All affected friendly targets are granted Major Vitality, briefly increasing healing received by 30%. An ally can target an affected enemy to activate the Soul Leech Synergy for additional healing.

This is your healing Bar. Use it to heal and apply heal-over-time effects. Use the remaining slot to add an ability of your choice.

BAR 2: DESTRUCTION STAFF (LIGHTNING STAFF)

KEY ABILITIES

Funnel Health

Refreshing Path

Elemental Blockade

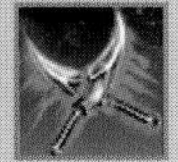

Impale

FLEX SLOT

Veil of Blades

Funnel Health: Morphed from **Strife** (Nightblade > Siphoning). Use this ability to deal Magic Damage to a target enemy. You and one nearby ally are then healed for 25% of the damage inflicted over the next 10 seconds.

Refreshing Path: Morphed from **Path of Darkness** (Nightblade > Shadow). Activate this Magicka ability to deal AoE/DOT damage to enemies within the target area. While in the affected area—and for up to two seconds after leaving it—you and your allies receive healing over time. Casting it also grants you Major Expedition, increasing your movement speed by 30%.

Elemental Blockade: Morphed from **Wall of Elements** (Destruction Staff). This area-of-effect ability is a great source of damage. Keep it active whenever possible.

Impale: Morphed from **Assassin's Blade** (Nightblade > Assassination). A great ranged execute. Use it whenever your target's Health drops below 25%.

Veil of Blades: Morphed from **Consuming Darkness** (Nightblade > Shadow). This Ultimate Ability snares nearby enemies, deals Magic Damage over time, and grants you and your allies Major Protection, reducing your damage taken by 30% for the duration of the effect. Low-Health allies can also activate the Hidden Refresh Synergy, granting them invisibility, increased speed, and a heal-over-time effect.

This is your damage Bar. Thanks to the Nightblade's class skill lines, several of these abilities can also be used to heal. Utilize this Action Bar as much as possible for a nice mix of damage and healing. The remaining Bar slot can be used to hold any ability you find helpful.

PRIORITY PASSIVES

Invest in your core Passives to make the most of these abilities—all of them are useful, and most of them will serve to make you a more effective Healer.

CHAMPION POINT SUGGESTIONS

Thief: Invest heavily in Arcanist (Lover) and Tenacity (Lover).

Mage: Invest heavily in Blessed (Apprentice) and Elfborn (Apprentice).

Warrior: Invest heavily in Elemental Defender (Lady) and Hardy (Lady). Quick Recovery (Lord) is also worth considering.

EQUIPMENT RECOMMENDATIONS

WEAPONS

Priority Trait: Precise

Priority Enchantment: Spell Damage

You'll always want a Restoration Staff as your main weapon. Look for any high-quality staff that features a trait like **Precise**, **Powered**, or **Decisive**. **Absorb Magicka** is usually the best enchantment for healing.

For your backup weapon, it's best to use a Lightning Staff. Look for something that features the **Sharpened** trait and a Spell Damage enchantment until you obtain a Maelstrom offering or something from a suitable set.

ARMOR

Priority Trait: Divines

Priority Enchantment: Maximum Magicka

Always wear at least five pieces of light armor. Unless you've invested in the **Undaunted Mettle** Passive Ability, consider equipping light armor in all of your armor slots.

Equipment that grants suitable set bonuses is always your best option. Until you find something you like, look for light armor that offers Maximum Magicka enchantments. **Divines** is usually the best trait for PvE, but **Infused** can be very effective on head, chest, and leg pieces.

JEWELRY

Priority Trait: Arcane

Priority Enchantment: Reduce Spell Cost

Until you manage to track down useful set pieces, use anything that reduces the Magicka cost of your spells. Once you have a handle on Magicka management, look into boosting your Spell Damage.

ARCHETYPE ADVICE

Funnel Health should serve as your favored attack and your primary heal. Try to use it whenever your heal-over-time effects are in place.

Blessing of Restoration is a useful group heal, but it also provides some nice buffs. As long as your Magicka can support it, try to keep its effects active during difficult fights.

Combining **Elemental Blockade** and **Refreshing Path** can be very effective. Of course, proper placement is important.

Impale is a high-damage execute ability, but once you invest in Rank 2 of the **Executioner** Passive Ability (Assassination), it also has great potential for efficiency. When used as a killing blow, it can restore more Magicka than it takes to cast.

COMBAT

It is imperative that you learn the most proficient methods of slaying the wealth of horrors lurking across Tamriel, through the dispatching of foes. For this, a primer on maximizing your melee, ranged, or magical combat potential is necessary.

INITIAL COMBAT TACTICS

At the most basic level, there are strikes you always attempt that are open to any type of character, without the need of skill-learning, though you can augment these with Passive Abilities.

LIGHT ATTACKS

Lightly damaging and swift, the attack most often used in battles across Tamriel.

These are swift strikes that you can inflict with any equipped weapon. Tap the Attack button to attempt a light attack. The damage caused scales to your Maximum Stamina (unless you're using staves, in which case it's related to Magicka), but performing the attack doesn't use Stamina (or Magicka for a staff).

ANIMATION CANCELING: "WEAVING"

This technique requires timing. When you're about to use one of your Active Effects, tap a light attack immediately beforehand. This grants you a small additional damage bonus between more powerful attacks. With proper timing, the light attack actually strikes after the ability animation has started, hence the technique's other name, negating the problems associated with cast times.

This only works if your target is within attack range, so some players may find staves excellent to use for this. The timing requires practice—try executing the light attack, then the Active Effect in time with your own heartbeat.

This is an excellent exploit, allowing seamless and frequent light attacks along with a favored Active Effect that adds to the damage you cause. It also shortens the time you need to wait before recharging your Ultimate Ability.

HEAVY ATTACKS

A mightier wallop, inflicting more damage, but with the risk of being interrupted as you charge up your strike.

These are slow-building strikes you must charge by holding down your Attack button, before releasing to inflict a greater amount of harm than a light attack. Accurate timing is necessary—for example, move to an enemy while holding this strike until you're within range, and then let go. During the buildup, you're prone to a foe bashing or interrupting you. The exact buildup time—before a weapon inflicts damage after release—can vary depending on your weapon, so experiment. As with light attacks, heavy attacks also replenishes your Stamina (or Magicka) when the attack is over, though the attack must be fully charged.

HEAVY ATTACK HELPFULNESS

Are you about to deplete your Stamina (or Magicka, if using staves)? Then execute a heavy attack, and recharge this resource quickly, as well as inflicting damage. Note that the amount of restored resources depends on the time it takes to complete the heavy attack. So a shorter attack, as from a dagger, restores fewer resources than a longer attack, as from a two-handed blade, though the latter is easier to interrupt.

Heavy attacks are also prone to knocking foes off-balance, down to the ground, or stunning them—depending on your weapon, the strength of the enemy, and other factors. This is helpful during PvE, but less so in PvP, as a human foe is more likely to interrupt your heavy attack midway through its buildup.

STAFF DAMAGE

Are you wielding a staff? Then your damage scales to your Maximum Magicka, not Stamina. Staves also deal Spell Damage rather than Weapon Damage, so if you're focusing on using these, you may wish to increase your Magicka more often than your Stamina. For all other weapons (one-handed, two-handed, shields, bows, and dual-wielding), Stamina scaling and Weapon Damage are used to calculate the damage caused by your actions.

When using a staff during a heavy attack, remember the weapon begins to damage a foe as the attack is charging, rather than at the end, like Stamina-based weapons. This means you can't focus all your damage on a massive and mighty wallop as you would with a two-handed weapon, for example, at the end of the charge. Therefore, a foe notices you earlier, which can be a problem if you're worried about interruptions.

DEALING LESS DAMAGE

Although each weapon you wield lists the damage it inflicts on a foe, remember that an enemy may be using a shield, wearing armor, or using spells with a resistance. All of these protections soak up the damage your weapon inflicts, so don't expect your sword to deal its entire damage unless you foe is completely unprotected.

RECHARGING ULTIMATES

When you strike with a light or heavy attack, you charge your Ultimate Abilities, building them up to unleash a suitably devastating strike. The Ultimate you're actively using takes up the sixth slot on your control panel (called the Action Bar, Skills Bar, or Hotkey Bar).

BLOCKING

Defending yourself from an attacker, understanding the timing involved, and learning to watch for an enemy's defenses and exploit them are keys to longevity in Tamriel. Blocking uses Stamina.

The biggest benefit to blocking is the reduction in damage; usually at least half of the power of an enemy's attack is negated, though the value varies depending on a number of factors (disabling secondary effects the enemy may use such as knockbacks, roots, snares or stuns, or whether you're blocking with a shield or a weapon). You can increase your protection, and reduce damage taken, by choosing certain skills.

A block can counter secondary effects an enemy attempts to harm you with. With correct timing, you can also interrupt an enemy attempting a heavy attack on you (see the following "Observe and Counter" section). Indeed, the blocking of an incoming heavy attack is perhaps the best use of the blocking technique, as it usually absorbs the most damage in the shortest amount of time.

NO STAMINA RECOVERY

While you're blocking, your Stamina does not regenerate, so you can't simply wade into a location and permanently block. Instead, rely on correct timing and countering.

A CHIP OFF THE OLD BLOCK

If you're a Dragonknight, choose **Iron Skin**. If you're a Templar, look into **Spear Wall**. If you're focusing on One-Hand and Shield skills, think about acquiring **Deflect Bolts**, **Defensive Posture**, and **Sword and Board**. All help to further reduce incoming damage while you block, though some help only under certain circumstances. Other plans, including enchanted jewelry, **Block Expertise** (Champion), **Bracing** (Heavy Armor), **Fortress**, and **Defensive Posture** (One-Hand and Shield), all help reduce the Stamina needed to block. Also try Active Effects like **Venom Arrow**, which acts like a bash without additional Stamina expenditure.

The best way to protect yourself? Invest in a shield until you become familiar with fighting.

THE RHYTHM OF COMBAT

Attempt to learn how long it takes you to perform a block, bash, light attack, heavy attack, and (optionally) any channeled attacks with your chosen equipment. Then learn how long it takes an enemy to do the same. As your timing improves, you can more proficiently decide when it's appropriate to attack or defend.

BASHING (INTERRUPTING)

It's always a good idea to attempt a bit of offense with your defense, and the bash, which is a light attack while you're blocking, is an excellent way to inflict harm on a foe even though you're defending. This is usually used to interrupt an enemy at melee range, and sometimes leads to staggering them. If your foe has a special ability (a channeled attack is the best example), then bash them before they launch this dangerous strike.

OBSERVE AND COUNTER

You can take down enemies more proficiently if you observe their actions and choose an appropriate counter. For most battles, at a rudimentary level, try the following:

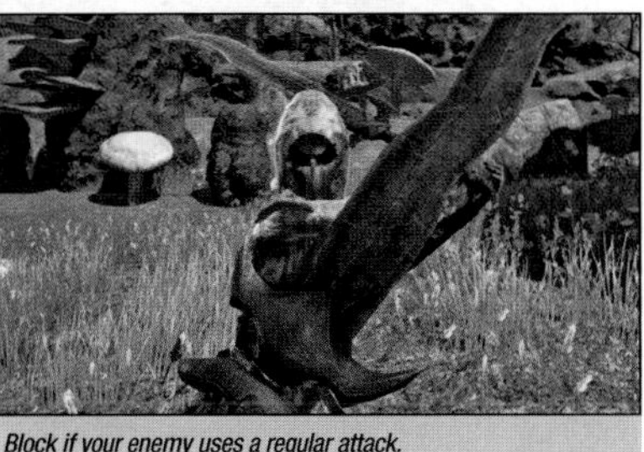

Block if your enemy uses a regular attack.

Bash (light attack) if your enemy tries a heavy attack or channeled attack, to quickly interrupt and stagger them.

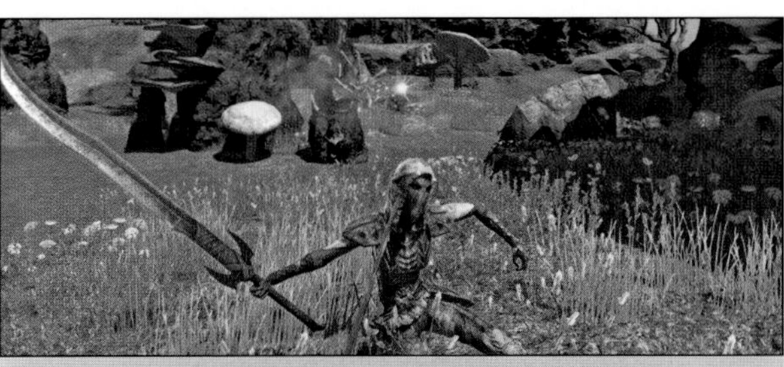

Inflict a heavy attack if your enemy is blocking, so you break their block and stagger them.

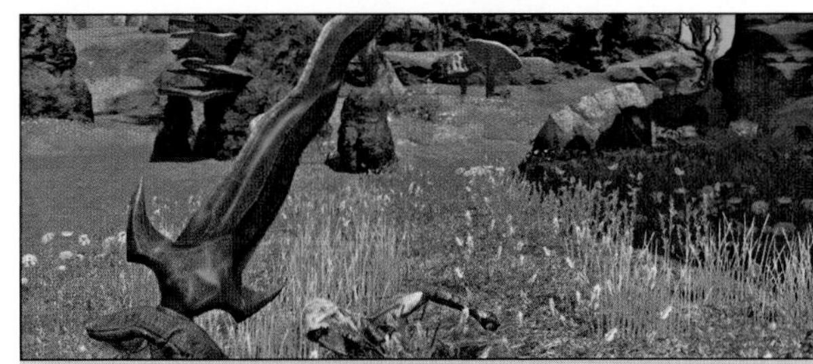

Attack quickly if your enemy is staggered, to instantly deal damage and possibly cut them down.

DODGING

Also known as roll dodging or dodge rolling, this defensive technique is used along with movement in a certain direction—rolling forward, backward, to the sides, or any angle in between. This is different from blocking in that you're (theoretically) maneuvering completely out of the way of an opponent's attack so no damage or secondary effects are inflicted on you. Dodging isn't used all the time, due to the high cost of Stamina needed to attempt it over the course of multiple occasions.

When a foe is attempting an area-of-effect attack, a quick way to retreat is the dodge roll.

When an enemy attempts an area-of-effect attack (usually indicated by a red glow on the ground near or around the foe's body), root effect, or a weighty heavy attack known to be highly damaging, execute a roll. Keep doing this (at the cost of Stamina) until you're outside the area of effect, or away from the enemy's strike.

DODGE FATIGUE

You can't dodge continuously, as the costs to Stamina increases—an effect known as dodge fatigue. Simply stop dodging to prevent this, or amass a large enough amount of Stamina to enable multiple dodging.

DODGE CHANCE

If you're perfecting your Evasion (Medium Armor) skill, or you're using an item with a similar effect, you can increase the "dodge chance," or ability to avoid being struck from an attack. This prevents a foe from damaging you, just as a dodge would, but you don't need to expend Stamina or even execute a dodge, making it extremely useful.

SIDESTEPPING

If your foe is taking too long to launch an attack you usually dodge, you can strafe around to the enemy's side if the focus of the effect is to the front, or step in and counter before the attack is launched. Timing is everything. These simpler maneuvers don't use Stamina.

RANGED COMBAT AND TARGETING

The target reticule is helpful when situating yourself toward a certain foe. Produce a bow and strike the target from range; a quite generous hit area enables arrows to hit home even if the foe moves slightly out of your central view. The target shrinks when you're directly targeting an enemy, and the enemy takes on a red glow about it. Don't forget you can also block using a bow, as well as cancel an arrow you're about to fire.

Use ranged targeting to perfect your bow-based takedowns, or to coax a foe into moving toward you.

CYCLING TARGETS

You can cycle through all nearby enemies within range. This is doable whether you're attacking from range or with a melee weapon. Don't like the foe you've targeted? Then quickly cycle through to find another. This is usually helpful if you're ignoring a weaker enemy in favor of concentrating an attack on a greater threat.

ADDITIONAL COMBAT TACTICS

As you progress, you should learn to focus your combat prowess on a specific weapon capability in order to perfect it and become much more competent. During this time, learning the nuances of the Action Bar, Synergy attacks, and weapon swapping becomes of paramount importance.

FOOD AND DRINK

Don't overlook the use of food, drink, and potions during your adventuring. Enjoying food and drink increases your Health, Magicka, and Stamina, as well as recovery of these stats. Make sure you also explore the different potions you can swig. They provide a wide range of abilities depending on the specific potion, from increasing your Critical Strike Chance to granting temporary invisibility.

WEAPON SWAPPING

When you reach Level 15, you gain the option of weapon swapping. This has a couple of major benefits and should be utilized whenever it suits your purposes. It takes about a second to swap from your usual weapon (or weapons) to a "backup" set of weaponry. The best news is that your Action Bar can also be swapped, leading to the following possibilities:

WHY WEAPON-SWAP?

It's a great idea to weapon-swap for a number of reasons, as you then essentially have two different combat-ready weapon sets (main and off-hand), as well as abilities to utilize under different circumstances:

Archer and Melee: Choose a bow and abilities to help with ranged combat as you first encounter the enemy. Then switch to melee-centric weaponry and abilities as you close in.

Assassin and Bludgeoner: Why not sneak up to a foe with assassin-friendly weaponry and abilities, get in a stealth strike for additional damage, then switch to two-handed (or other) weaponry and abilities once you're seen?

One-Hand and One-Hand: You can choose two sets of similar weapons, with identical abilities, in case you find a combination of armaments and augmentations you don't want to change.

Enchanted Weapons: Even if you choose two sets of similarly effective weapons and abilities, you should enchant each set differently. For example, have one deal mainly fire-based damage while the other inflicts frost-based damage.

Ability Longevity: Picking your abilities for the first and "swapped" Action Bars is also worth pondering. You can use an ability that lasts a while, swap to your alternate set of abilities, and still have the effects of the first ability active.

Finally, remember that swapping weapons and abilities uses up a small amount of Magicka and Stamina during combat, so only do so if you have the necessary reserves. Outside of combat, weapon swapping does not sap Magicka and Stamina.

ACTION BAR ABILITIES

The Action Bar (also known as the Abilities Bar, Combat Bar, Hotkey Bar, or Skills Bar) appears at the bottom of your screen. It has five slots for different abilities you can quickly access, and a sixth slot for your Ultimate Ability. These skills are interchangeable and are almost exclusively used during combat. When you reach Level 15, you're able to weapon-swap and create a second Action Bar to use with your alternate weaponry (which can be the same, or a completely different set of skills), bringing your total available abilities to 12 (10 usual and two Ultimate). Abilities fall into one or more of the following general categories:

An Action Bar, fully resplendent with a perfect combination of complementary abilities, turns you into a true master of combat.

ACTIVE (ACTIVATED) EFFECTS

These are usually the most beneficial and well-used in your Action Bar, and cost Magicka or Stamina. They typically perform a damage-based attack on a target, add to the potency of the weapon you're holding or armor you're wearing, or provide some other bonus. Some abilities require you to manually select a foe, while others have an area of effect the enemy must be in to be harmed by the attack's effects. Some may need to be aimed by selecting a location in your field of vision.

Example: Evasion (Medium Armor): This increases your dodge chance by 20% for 20 seconds, but only after you trigger it. You cast it on yourself.

PASSIVE (SLOTTED) ABILITIES

These are abilities that may be Active, Toggled, or Ultimate, but which also grants you a bonus. They don't have to be slotted into your Action Bar, and they usually entail specific applications. For example, Passive weapon bonuses are only applied when you have a specific weapon equipped. Passive Abilities possess equipment or slotting requirements that must be met before you can enjoy the benefits of the ability. Your end goal is to have as many of these abilities active at once as you're able, especially with the Champion System, as they're essentially free bonuses you don't *actively* have to worry about!

Example: Magicka Controller (Mages Guild): This increases your Maximum Magicka and Magicka Recovery by 1% for each Mages Guild ability slotted.

TOGGLED (ON-OFF) ABILITIES

Some abilities have a reasonably clear "on" and "off" functionality, remaining inactive until you enable them. Some may require a constant sapping of Stamina or Magicka, may lower these stats during the time they're active, or may require a single additional cost when enabled. They're disabled if you weapon-swap.

Example: Magelight (Mages Guild): This enhances your spellcasting when you cast on yourself, at the cost of Magicka.

ULTIMATE ABILITY

The sixth slot in your Action Bar is reserved for an Ultimate Ability. As the name suggests, these are extremely powerful, with impressive and devastating effects, employed occasionally, and are used once your character has obtained them. They aren't initially available to you, becoming unlocked as you advance your Experience through a specific skill line or character class. Ensure your Ultimate complements your other abilities, both Passive and in your Action Bar.

The resource that powers Ultimate Abilities is called Ultimate. Currently you can store up to 500 Ultimate. This resource is generated for several seconds after you land a light or heavy attack. Pair this with the Heroism buff, as it provides additional Ultimate generation (as do a few Passive Abilities) to fill up your Ultimate more quickly. This is the reason why weaving (aka "animation canceling") is so valuable; it generates Ultimate without slowing down your attack rotation.

Example: Berserker Strike (Two-Handed): Become more proficient and unlock more skills in this skill line to deliver a truly vicious blow to an enemy. You also gain Spell and Physical Resistance.

A WINNING COMBINATION

Reading Is Fundamental: It's imperative you know exactly how each Active Effect works. There's no point in launching an attack that requires you to pinpoint an area of ground if you fail to select the terrain, or in conjuring a frost-based attack on a foe who's impervious to the cold. Read ability descriptions thoroughly.

The Correct Combination: When you've chosen a main weapon you're happy with, ensure the Action Bar abilities you choose are picked to improve this particular weapon as you level up. Proficiency in your main weapon, and skills to augment it, is a worthwhile use of Skill Points early in your adventure.

A Winning Combination: Be sure to utilize any racial, class-based, equipment (weapon and armor), guild, and skill tree abilities along with the Action Bar abilities you use the most, to achieve the most potent, damaging, and helpful buffs while engaging in combat.

SYNERGY (COORDINATED ATTACKS)

Though lone warriors can gain greatness, a faster way to defeat foes is to play well with a team. Certain skills have a "synergetic" component, which allows others in your party to add to the effects of an attack. This may create a more potent form of the original attack, or imbue teammates with increased damage or hit potential.

Need an unstoppable method of felling foes? Then coordinate so that one of your party launches an attack, after which all other party members receive a message that a Synergy is available. These should then be launched, providing you have the necessary abilities, as well as the Stamina or Magicka to do so. Synergy attacks have a recharge period, so your party can't use them constantly, and are most beneficial when you're adventuring through public dungeons (instances) and encounter particularly troublesome monsters.

SYNERGY SKILLS

Any skill or ability that can be synergized includes notes to this effect in its description. When the Synergy is available to others, a notice appears on-screen for others to join in.

INCOMING ENEMY ATTACK!

Enemies also have coordinated Synergy attacks, so beware. React by cutting down the number of foes who can coordinate attacks to minimize any group damage a cluster of foes is capable of inflicting.

SYNERGY TYPES AND EXAMPLES

Undaunted: Though many skill lines have abilities that can be used in unison with teammates, the Undaunted skills are the most plentiful.

Example 1 (Skill Synergy): Blood Altar (Blood Funnel and Blood Feast): This heals you and your allies by a percentage of the damage you inflict. Allies can cast Blood Funnel or Blood Feast to increase the healing potential as combat continues.

Example 2 (Synergetic Actions): Teammates with different skills can work together. One places an immobilizing trap on the ground, while another sets fire to the area around the trap. Now an enemy caught in this trap suffers additional Fire Damage.

Example 3 (Instances): Certain Synergies are only available during specific battles, such as the Brace for Impact Synergy you're able to access during the Lord Warden Dusk fight in the Imperial City Prison. These appear only during occasional, and usually tough, battles, and it's almost always worth activating the Synergy to bolster your chances of victory.

DAMAGE TYPES AND POTENCY

It's worth remembering the type of damage each general set of items and equipment employs, as well as understanding the optimal methods of increasing the damage you inflict.

STAMINA-BASED DAMAGE

Any ability using Stamina scales with Weapon Damage and your Maximum Stamina, and also increases at higher ranks (I to IV). To enhance the level and quality of your weapons (except staves), use item sets, jewelry enchantments, potions, certain buffs (Brutality, Endurance, Savagery, Force, Empower, or Fracture), and better-quality weapons. To enhance your Maximum Stamina, use Attribute Points, certain armor enchantments, the Robust jewelry trait, items sets, and food.

MAGICKA-BASED DAMAGE

Any ability using Magicka scales with Spell Damage and your Maximum Magicka, and also increases at higher ranks (I to IV). To enhance the level and quality of your spells and staff weapons, use item sets, jewelry enchantments, potions, certain buffs (Sorcery, Intellect, Prophecy, Ward, or Breach), and better-quality weapons. To enhance your Maximum Magicka, use Attribute Points, certain armor enchantments, the Arcane jewelry trait, item sets, and food.

CRITICAL STRIKES

There's an initial 10% chance that each strike you land may inflict half as much damage again, thanks to a Critical Strike. This occurs whether you're using weapon-based (Stamina) or spell-based (Magicka) attacks. Employ item sets, potions, and certain buffs (Savagery or Prophecy, depending on whether you use Stamina or Magicka) to enhance your Critical Chances and Damage.

INCREASING DAMAGE A LOT, THEN A LITTLE

As you progress, you receive a diminishing set of returns for the expenditures to your damage rating. Begin by improving your Maximum Stamina or Magicka and your Weapon or Spell Damage, then work on your Critical Strike improvements while concurrently collecting enchantments, items, and buffs. Don't forget to up your armor enchantments so you're more proficient at surviving the enemy, too.

You should also learn the different character archetypes (builds) and employ the recommendations to create a more well-rounded character, as sometimes focusing purely on increasing damage ratings at the expense of every other aspect of your build isn't the wisest plan. Why have amazing Weapon Damage if your armor rating is so low that you're cut down in seconds?

CROWD CONTROL: VULNERABILITIES AND DEATH

While the majority of this Combat section is devoted to inflicting damage and winning the fight, it's important to know what to do when you're weakened, disabled, or prone to attack. Death comes to us all; here's how to react to the various non-beneficial statuses prior to it, as well as a description of the effects, which also apply to enemies if you inflict Disabling Effects on them. The all-encompassing term for vulnerabilities is "crowd control" (CC).

DISABLING EFFECTS

These result in your character becoming temporarily sluggish, or losing control to varying degrees. They occur after a particularly brutal or specific enemy attack. Look for information on enemy attacks, or weapons and spells if you're in a PvP battle, to learn the likelihood of being debilitated by one of the following:

Learn to correctly counter any Disabling Effect you can, or face additional unwanted damage.

DISORIENTED

Description: The target is dizzied, unable to move or perform actions, usually after being struck by a weapon with an ability. Example: Scatter Shot (Bow skill).

Counteract: You need to break free of this effect, which costs you Stamina.

FEARED

Description: The target randomly runs away from the entity employing this effect, and cannot perform actions during the flee. Example: Roar (Werewolf skill).

Counteract: You need to break free of this effect, which costs you Stamina.

IMMOBILE (ROOTED)

Description: The target cannot move from their position (unless they teleport), but is able to attack, block, and utilize spells. Example: Stampede (Two-Handed).

Counteract: Escape by dodge rolling, or use a Purge skill or Synergy.

KNOCKED BACK

Description: The target is pushed back approximately five meters, possibly incurring additional Disabling Effects, depending on the spell or item used. Example: Piercing Javelin (Templar skill).

Counteract: You need to break free of this effect, which costs you Stamina.

KNOCKED DOWN

Description: The target falls and is completely prone, unable to perform actions for up to five seconds. Example: Stonefist (Dragonknight skill).

Counteract: You need to break free of this effect, which costs you Stamina.

OFF-BALANCE

Description: The target is dizzied for approximately five seconds, a shorter amount of time than caused by "disoriented" attacks. Consecutive attacks afterward can lead to the target being knocked down. This usually occurs if the victim blocks a heavy attack, or a number of class and weapon skills. Example: Lava Whip (Dragonknight skill).

Counteract: You need to break free of this effect, which costs you Stamina.

PULLED

Description: The target is pulled to the entity employing this effect, during which time the target cannot perform actions or move. Example: Silver Leash (Fighters Guild).

Counteract: You need to break free of this effect, which costs you Stamina.

SILENCED

Description: The target is stopped from casting spells or using Magicka-based abilities, but can move and utilize other attacks. Example: Negate Magic (Sorcerer skill).

Counteract: You need to break free of this effect, which costs you Stamina.

SNARED

Description: The target's movement is slowed, but they can employ attacks and other maneuvers. Example: Sun Fire (Templar skill).

Counteract: Utilize a Purge skill or Synergy. Example: Purifying Ritual (Templar skill).

STUNNED

Description: The target falls to their knees and is not able to perform actions. Follow up with further attacks if you're the entity performing the stun. Example: Crystal Shard (Sorcerer skill).

Counteract: You need to break free of this effect, which costs you Stamina.

ELEMENTAL VULNERABILITIES

These effects not only tend to damage you in a specific manner, but damage you for a specific length of time afterward and make you even more vulnerable to additional attacks of the same type. They may also apply previously listed Disabling Effects.

BURNED (FIRE)

Description: The target is set on fire for up to three seconds. Example: Ardent Flame (Dragonknight skill).

Counteract: Adorn armor and jewelry with fire-resistant enchantments or buffs.

CHILLED (FROST)

Description: The target suffers Frost Damage for up to three seconds and movement is slowed, like with a snare. Example: Ice Comet (Mages Guild).

Counteract: Adorn armor and jewelry with frost-resistant enchantments or buffs.

CONCUSSED (SHOCK)

Description: The target suffers Shock Damage for up to four seconds and inflicts reduced damage. Example: Storm Calling (Sorcerer skill).

Counteract: Adorn armor and jewelry with shock-resistant enchantments or buffs.

OTHER VULNERABILITIES

The following additional vulnerabilities have different and wide-ranging effects that should be studied.

BLINDED

Description: A rarely seen effect (no pun intended) where the target is more apt to miss an attack for a number of seconds. Only a few foes use this attack. Example: Akatosh's Blessed Armor (set), used when blocking.

Counteract: You need to break free of this effect, which costs you Stamina.

BLEEDING

Description: The target is struck by a (usually sharp) weapon and suffers additional damage over a period of time, not typically longer than ten seconds. Example: Damage from an axe.

Counteract: React to the attack by blocking or avoiding to prevent bleeding. Adorn armor and jewelry with resistant enchantments or buffs.

DISEASED

Description: The target takes damage and has less potency when attempting to heal. Your Health Recovery is halved for a few seconds. Example: Werewolf claw attacks.

Counteract: React to the attack by blocking or avoiding to prevent becoming diseased. Adorn armor and jewelry with resistant enchantments or buffs.

IMMOVABLE

Description: The target becomes immune to knockback and other Disabling Effects. Example: Immovable (Heavy Armor skill).

Counteract: Attack the target before Immovable is cast.

POISONED

Description: Inflicts additional Poison Damage on a target for a number of seconds. Often damages in conjunction with reduced healing for the target. Example: Lethal Arrow (Bow skill).

Counteract: React to the attack by blocking or avoiding to prevent becoming poisoned. Adorn armor and jewelry with resistant enchantments or buffs.

TAUNTED

Description: Used during PvE combat. The target is forced to attack the caster for approximately 15 seconds, usually when the target is at a disadvantage—weakened, suffering from effects, or otherwise incapacitated. Example: Inner Fire (Undaunted skill).

Counteract: Retreat from the caster. If you're the attacker, pick the weakest foe, or maneuver an enemy you wish to attack you, so your party can help finish them off.

VISUAL VULNERABILITIES

Just as you can identify some effects by sight, such as an area-of-effect attack or dodge fatigue, many vulnerable states (like being off-balance) have visual cues. Learn them to quickly determine what's affecting you and those around you. For example, characters who are snared show a cloud around their feet. You can also view your Status Bar, which provides a variety of visual cues for certain vulnerabilities, as well as empowerments.

Enable "Combat Text" (Interface menu) if you wish to read the types of damage deployed by you and those around you. This usually allows for quicker assessment of your situation, including identification of threat types.

DEATH

Should you succumb to your wounds, your corpse remains where you fall for a few moments, as you view the reasons why you died. You then have a choice of where to resurrect yourself:

You (or another player) can utilize a Soul Stone and so you resurrect at your current position.

You can resurrect at the nearest Wayshrine.

You can resurrect at the entrance to a delve or public dungeon, if you died inside one.

During PvP, you can choose to resurrect at a keep controlled by your alliance, so long as it has a resource under your alliance's control and isn't currently being attacked. Or you can spawn at a forward camp, if you're close by. Or you can be resurrected by an ally.

Any equipped items lose durability, forcing you to utilize a Repair Merchant or a Repair Kit. These are worth completing before you begin your adventuring again, as you require the most durable equipment to survive in treacherous Tamriel.

STEALTH AND SNEAKING

For those of a nefarious disposition, who wish to maneuver without sound or surreptitiously, be they members of the infamous Thieves Guild or otherwise, with the plan to assassinate a target unaware of their presence, the use of stealthy actions is encouraged. Note that any character has the ability to sneak and be stealthy—they're the same type of activity. However, there are certain character classes with a predisposition toward stealth.

SNEAKING

Go from a normal standing position to a crouch by entering Sneak Mode. Note the on-screen target transformation and description of how successful you are at staying out of sight. Your noise levels are reduced as well as your visibility, and you're better able to avoid being detected. This comes at the expense of your speed. The following on-screen cues are of importance:

The eye of stealth: Instead of a crosshair, your display becomes an eye, which changes depending on your status:

- **"Hidden":** This word and a line underneath indicate you are properly hidden from enemies.
- **"Eye-Opening":** If a foe is attempting to search for you, or you're closing in on an enemy, the eye begins to open. You're seen when it fully opens, so evade to remain hidden.
- **"Detected":** An open eye with this word means you're seen by a nearby foe. It's usually worth standing up at this point!
- **Stamina:** Note your Stamina bar depletes while you're crouched, so bear this in mind when attempting stealth maneuvers and attacks. Mitigate this Stamina-sapping by utilizing some sets.

Certain abilities can only be activated while you're sneaking.

STEALTH COMBAT: SNEAK ATTACKS

When you attack an enemy who doesn't know you're there, you can inflict up to three times (3x) the normal amount of damage. So what constitutes a sneak attack? It involves remaining crouched and hidden, then striking from behind or the flanks of the enemy, and inflicting the blow before you're seen. It's also important to note the following:

If a foe never sees your attack coming, it deals exceptionally more damage.

- **Weapon Types:** The bonus of a sneak attack applies no matter the type of weapon you're using. Therefore, it's possible to inflict a stealth-based attack bonus using bows and two-handed weapons, as well as the one-handed daggers you'd normally expect to use for this sort of attack.
- **Skills:** If you have a skill that increases the damage inflicted by a weapon, that stat is also "stacked," or multiplied, by three.
- **Stunning:** The attack may also stun your foe, which is obviously helpful.
- **No Effect:** Enchantments and poisons added to your weapon are not affected by the multiplier, though they still inflict the normal amount of damage.
- **Sneak Completion:** Once the attack occurs, you stand up out of the sneak, thus allowing you to fight normally, or flee.
- **Detection:** As soon as the sneak attack is finished, you become visible to the enemy if they survive the strike. This even occurs at range (if you used arrows, for example).
- **Subsequent Sneaking:** Assuming you aren't actively being watched, you can then crouch again and repeat these actions.

STEALTH-CENTRIC TIPS

If you want a more general plan to improving your sneaking, ensure you employ any or all of the following tips:

Gaining Perspective: Try using the third-person view, as it's easier to see foes patrolling than in first-person view.

In the Shadows: The enemy's line of sight is most important when determining whether they can spot you. If you're behind cover, a low wall, or a tree, it's easier to remain hidden.

Drawing Out Foes: Enemies react to sounds, like an arrow impacting a nearby area. Use sound to coax an enemy into the open, or to a secluded spot where you can sneak-slay them without attracting attention.

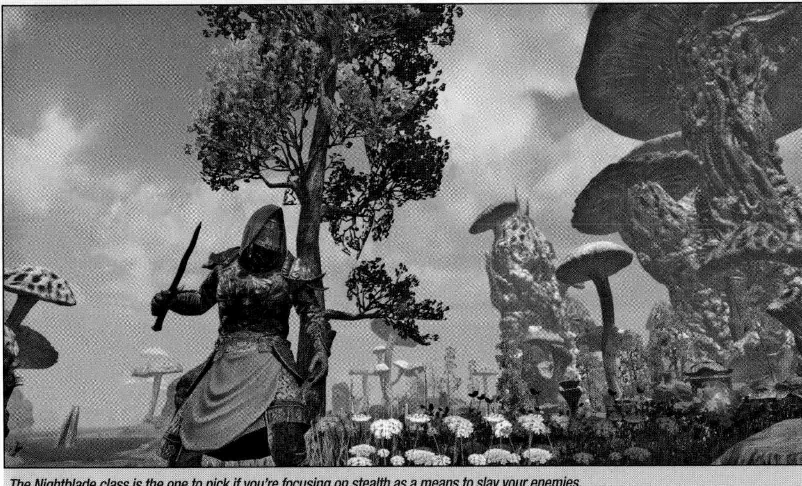

The Nightblade class is the one to pick if you're focusing on stealth as a means to slay your enemies.

Invisibility: This magical effect (**Invisible Potion**) grants you this temporary lack of detection, though it doesn't reduce noise. Use it if you need to reach a foe quickly without sneaking, or need to pass through an enemy-infested area before reverting to Sneak Mode. As you're already hidden while sneaking, invisibility isn't necessary, though it helps you stay hidden if foes walk in on you and your nefarious actions! Note the **Shadow Cloak** skill also grants invisibility.

Racial Bonuses: Pick a **Bosmer** or **Khajiit** for their innate racial bonuses that are tied to stealth.

Skills: At lower levels, invest in **Improved Hiding** (Legerdemain) to reduce the Stamina cost of your sneaking. **Improved Sneak** (Medium Armor) also helps, assuming you're wearing the appropriate armor. The Nightblade-only Assassination skills (**Master Assassin**) increase both your Weapon and Spell Damage during stealth attacks. **Dark Stalker** (Stage 4 Vampirism) removes the movement penalty while crouching. For Thieves Guild members, **Veil of Shadows** increases the range at which you can remain undetected.

Sets: There are a number of equipment sets that benefit the stealth-inclined. **Archer's Mind** (Bosmer Medium Armor) increases Critical Damage when using stealth attacks. **Night Mother's Embrace** (Daedric Medium Armor) reduces your detection radius and the Stamina cost of sneaking, and increases Weapon Damage. **Night Terror** (Daedric Medium Armor) reduces your detection radius and the Stamina cost of sneaking (three items). **Shadow Dancer's Raiment** (Thieves Guild Light Armor) ignores the movement slowdown during sneaking and adds Stamina Recovery. **Shadow Walker** (Argonian Medium Armor) restores Health and Stamina if you're hidden and stationary. **Stygian** (Draugr Medium Armor) increases your Maximum Magicka and Spell Damage if you're sneaking. **Vicecanon of Venom** (Argonian Armor) inflicts additional Poison Damage, then heals you by the same amount, if you inflict a Critical Strike during a sneak attack.

Craftable Sets: Night's Silence (Blacksmith, Clothing, or Woodworking) ignores the movement slowdown during sneaking.

The Shadow (Champion): This constellation is thief-related and has two perks. **Shade** reduces Stamina loss while crouched, and **Shadowstrike** lets you enter stealth after killing a target using a heavy attack, repeatable every five seconds.

Nightblade Assassin: If you plan to utilize a character that benefits the most from stealth, read up on the **Archetypes** section of this guide and pick a Nightblade class. Then build your character up to be the ultimate assassin.

Negating Sneaking Foes: If you're attempting to reveal an enemy who may be sneaking, there are a number of skills to help. **Magelight**, **Expert Hunter**, **Revealing Flare**, and **Mark Target** are all good examples.

This section details the ad-hoc-style activities you can engage in when attempting group activities. Such events are distinct from content you attempt with player guilds; these are usually quickly accessed romps through delves and dungeons for battles, treasure, and Experience. This section offers some examples of group activities, along with recommendations on adjusting your style of play.

WINNING FRIENDS

There is no alliance restriction to the group you can join. Indeed, the linking of up to four like-minded individuals into a group (including yourself) awards you with a 10% XP bonus. A chosen leader is indicated by a crown icon, while other members of the group created are indicated by an arrow icon. At this point, you're able to begin exploration.

Enter the Group menu to access group dungeons, both random and specific, as well as Alliance War content.

Group Menu: Access the Grouping Finder to invite friends, create your group, pick the Normal or Veteran version of a dungeon, and choose the role you wish for yourself (Tank, Healer, or Damage-Dealer). Then you can choose the type of dungeon you wish to explore, be it random or specific. After that, simply enter the queue until you join up, and head out.

Dungeon Finder: Click on a random dungeon to view the random daily reward crate and XP reward you will receive for completion. Click on a specific dungeon or dungeons you wish to enter, especially if you're interested in the daily Pledge rewards on offer, and you're transported to any of them when a group is available.

You're able to contact your friends and launch a random dungeon with them—either one friend or up to three others, providing you've chosen one Tank, one Healer, and two Damage-Dealers. Just invite them and join the queue.

Follow the Leader: The leader chooses whether to enter a dungeon in Normal or Veteran Mode. The latter becomes available once the leader reaches Level 50. All players and content scales to CP 160, allowing lower-level characters to participate.

Alliance War: The Alliance War (AvA) content, which takes place in Cyrodiil (for 8-24 players) or the Imperial City (4-12 players) and is detailed elsewhere in this chapter, is also available.

INFLUENCING PEOPLE (KNOW YOUR ROLE)

Now that you've chosen a general type of character (known colloquially as Tank, Healer, or Damage-Dealer), it's important to know and play your role effectively for the good of the group, and to increase your chances at victory. Heed the following advice:

A dash through a particularly thrilling dungeon should result in victories and spoils, not constant party death and argumentative shouting.

GENERAL ADVICE

The Holy Trinity: Your party should be properly balanced, with one Tank, one Healer, and two Damage-Dealers (DPS), though you can tweak this setup, providing you have one of each type of player. Wading in with four players of the same type means you're likely to cripple yourself during combat, simply because a greater variety of options isn't available to you.

First We Feast!: Ensure that you're fully equipped for the dangers that lie ahead. Though you may need help from your group, your safety is usually of paramount concern. Check your equipment and eat a food item—ensuring that your Health, Stamina, and Magicka are as high as possible. Bring along potions to use as you progress.

Local Knowledge: If you're new to the dungeon you're wandering through, spend time researching the location, and converse with your team about the dangers and how the larger enemies should be fought. Forewarned is forearmed!

Swapping Roles: Once you reach Level 15, you have the ability to weapon-swap, and this flexibility allows certain party members a "dual personality." For example, if your style of play calls for a Tank the majority of the time, but a Damage-Dealer if you weapon-swap, you can change roles based on the need and situational threats.

Exceptional Synergy: Explained earlier in this chapter, the use of Synergies (group attack abilities) enables your party to more easily protect yourselves and create greater damage potential during combat. Not only do you receive bonuses like resource restoration for using Synergies, you inflict greater damage. The advantages are numerous; there's never been a better time to be an Undaunted!

TANK ADVICE

Crowd Control and Taunts: Your main task is to beckon enemies into attacking you instead of the others in your group by taunting them. You must decide which mobs are the most dangerous to the group and keep them taunted. There is no need to taunt all enemies as DPS and healers can survive some monsters solo. Learning which enemies to deal with and keeping their attention is vital to being an effective tank. Taunting every five seconds or so is usually sufficient to ensure your foe doesn't ignore you and attack teammates. Be sure to intercept your targets if their attention sways before they inflict real damage on your friends.

Leader by Example: As you're likely to be the first one into battle, and usually pick the enemies to fight first, it makes sense that you become the leader of the group. You're here to scout the unexplored areas, bear the brunt of enemy attacks, and explain to the group how to tackle a particularly troublesome foe with specific takedown needs.

Faith in the Healer: As a Tank, it's assumed you have impressive reserves of Stamina. Pick the biggest foe and bring them down quickly and effectively. You're relying on your Healer to help you maintain your Health (though not exclusively), but if something massive and terrifying is charging your party's way, the Tank should be the one to step in and intercept it.

Block (and Bash) Around the Clock: Learn to block continuously to deflect damage before bashing (aka "interrupting") to disorient foes, stopping many from retaliating or casting spells. Effective against all types of foes, but particularly enemy mages and bowmen, this is another way to minimize the enemy's aggressions.

HEALER ADVICE

Feeling Flexible: A wide variety of classes can make the most of the healing abilities and spells on offer (the Templar especially), but if you're not used to the carnage-filled combat of group dungeon exploration, you may find you haven't set yourself up with enough healing power. Ensure you have at least two Action Bar slots filled with healing abilities, and learn what healing capabilities your team members have so you know who to focus on once the damage is being taken. Also, you have enough Magicka, right?

Healing First and Fast: Be the first to cast healing spells, rather than waiting until your friends are struggling. Spells that give continuous healing over a period of time (known as "healing over time") should be cast just before engaging the enemy, and again just as it finishes attacking, until the fight is over. In addition, these spells—plus spells cast on the ground and spells allowing your teammates to step to an area to be healed—are more helpful than spells focused on a single teammate, or spells that shield them. Those usually cost more to perform and are a less proficient use of your time and Magicka.

Other Actions: When you're not healing, your secondary actions (without compromising your Magicka needed for any subsequent healing needs) should include abilities that back up your Tank and Damage-Dealers. These include Synergies, buffs, and stuns. If combat is progressing well with little need for healing, weapon-swap to a more combat-support Action Bar.

Non-Class Skills: Take into consideration alterative skill lines that can assist in your task as the healer. Select skills from Restoration Staff, Undaunted (Bone Shield, Blood Altar, and Energy Orb), Assault (Vigor, War Horn), Support (Purge), and Fighters Guild (Circle of Protection) to give an added boost to healing.

DAMAGE-DEALER (DPS) ADVICE

Sometimes, You're on Your Own: Don't rely on your Healer to consistently keep you alive, or your Tank to bear the brunt of every attack. Instead, balance your team and independent actions, using your dodging and blocking to maintain your health, and use the techniques you've developed to slay foes in other game modes. You may wish to forgo spells that have an area of effect, as they can cause multiple enemies to engage you.

The Order of Death: You're here to properly prioritize your targets, especially with the Tank usually going for the most ferocious entity. Depending on the situation and the state of your teammates, you should provide combat support to your Tank. Otherwise, target ranged foes (archers) first, then spellcasters, then the weaker enemies, and finally the foe the Tank is tussling with. However, every encounter is different, so alter or ignore this order as the situation demands.

Prioritize and Protect: Your obvious advantage is the damage you can deal, but this may not be the best way to support your team. Situational awareness is a must; make full use of dodging and blocking so the Healer isn't constantly having to expend Magicka to keep you alive. Similarly, keep an eye on your Healer; take some of the enemy's attacks off them so the Healer can use up Magicka on you and the Tank rather than themself.

The Nimble Resurrection: You're the default teammate in charge of resurrecting teammates who've died. This must be done as soon as possible, especially as the Healer and Tank have more focused and protective roles. You should be saving your friends both before and after they drop.

OVERVIEW

Join a player guild if you're looking to adventure with a number of like-minded players, you're Level 10 or higher in Experience, or you're seeking to perfect your character, purchase helpful or valuable items, learn more about the game from veterans, and generally socialize. You can choose up to five player guilds to be part of, and guilds can be accessed by players of any alliance affiliation. Note, however, that when fighting in the Alliance War (PvP content), you must be in the guild's affiliation to benefit from resource claims and bonuses. The five guilds you can join are related to your ESO account, not each character, so any of your characters can join the five guilds, despite any differing alliances.

WHY JOIN A PLAYER GUILD?

Some guilds require an extensive résumé, while others offer a more straightforward recruitment process. The reasons for joining a guild vary depending on how you wish to socialize within Tamriel. Are you interested in group dungeons or the Alliance War (PvE or PvP activities)? Perhaps you're drawn to a guild that shares your interests (all female or all Orc, for example). Most of all, you should join a guild to make a new online family of friends who can teach you how to better yourself. Need crafting advice? Information on a particular skill line? Want to find a band of jesters who only converse in lore-approved banter? There's a guild out there for you!

After joining a guild, research what's expected of you. Be sure to read their "About Us" and "Message of the Day" sections to understand their expected goals and help achieve them. Expect to join in on message boards, chats, and other non-game-related information to converse and plan with your guild members.

Obviously, adventuring, both in small groups and larger PvP alliances, is the main reason to join. Be sure to check your Guild Roster to see who's online and where.

THE GUILDMASTER AND RANKS

The creator of a player guild is known as the Guildmaster (aka guild leader). This seasoned player is in charge of the guild, hands out different permissions to trusted guild members, and changes the different ranks of guild members. Initially, a leader can grant one of four ranks, each with a different set of permissions. This number can be increased to ten ranks and named however you like. Permissions include the ability to chat with others of the same or lower ranks; monitor alliance, bank, and store resources; and promote, demote, or remove members to maintain a cohesive and pleasant atmosphere.

THE GUILD BANK

Once the guild you're a member of has acquired ten or more members, a bank can be created. Find any Tamriel Banker to access it. Provided your rank allows it, you and your guild can store up to 500 items and unlimited gold. Think of banks as unsafe storage repositories, as anyone of an appropriately high rank can store or take any item in the bank. However, assuming your members are trustworthy, this is another location to place and take equipment. Use it to pick up items left by a fellow member, or deposit goods for someone who needs them but isn't online to more easily trade with you. If you want to make some gold in this type of bartering, sell items through the Guild Store instead.

THE GUILD STORE

Once the guild you're a member of has acquired 50 or more members, a Guild Store can be created. Locate any Banker in Tamriel to access the store—unless a Guild Trader has been hired, in which case they can be accessed as well. Assuming you have the permission, you can sell up to 30 items within this store, each available for a period of 30 days to be purchased by anyone accessing the store. If the item does not sell in 30 days from posting, it is returned. Expect a small tax to be applied to the sale that goes into the Guild's bank. Initially, the store is only available to members of your guild, but if you utilize the services of a Guild Trader—or a Quartermaster if your guild controls a Cyrodiil Keep during the Alliance War—anyone can buy your wares. Similarly, you can view the items of any other guild.

GUILD TRADER

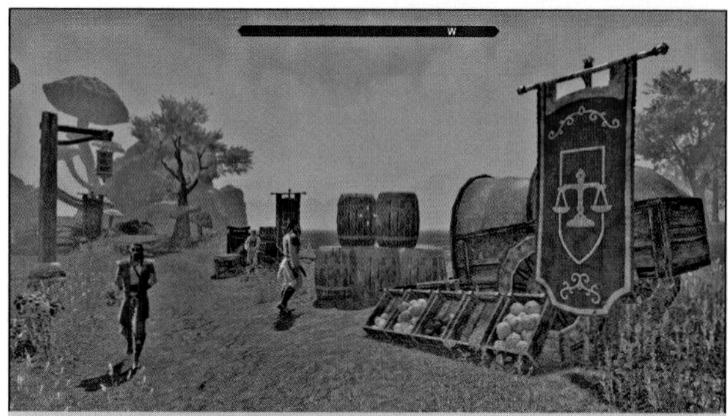

Quality merchandise at sometimes unaffordable prices! Hire a Guild Trader, like these fine fellows in Vivec City, to ply your wares.

Throughout Tamriel, Guild Traders are available to sell guild items to any adventurer, whether a guild member or not. Your guild simply bids the most gold (compared to other guilds) to utilize the services of the Guild Trader for a single real-world week. The funds come from the Guild Bank, and a small portion of each sale a Guild Trader provides goes back as tax on the item into Guild Bank coffers.

WHY HIRE A GUILD TRADER?

Your guild should hire a Guild Trader in order to sell quality and hard-to-find items to a much wider audience. It's worth asking a more experienced member of your guild how to make the most of hiring a specific trader. For example, those in the most well-populated areas, like Mournhold, are likely to sell your goods for the most gold. Unfortunately, they're also likely to be more expensive to hire. Through trial and error, you can find the sweet spot and hire a trader who isn't too expensive, but is still located in an area with high foot traffic.

GUILD HERALDRY

Once the guild you're a member of has acquired 10 or more members, the Guildmaster can purchase, create, and change your guild's insignia—a tabard with a variety of designs and colors to choose from. Each member can then purchase a tabard frrom the guild store at any banker by searching the Guild Items category. This way, your guild can become more uniform in appearance. Your heraldry is also displayed above a keep that your guild controls in the Alliance War.

Set in the center of Tamriel, Cyrodiil is rife with conflict, as the three alliances battle it out for the coveted Ruby Throne. Alliance bases have been set up in the three corners of the triangular zone, where players enter the campaign. Advancing inward, combatants battle for control of resources, keeps, towns, the Elder Scrolls, and ultimately the throne. Only one player can hold the title of Emperor, with great benefits bestowed on the leader.

JOINING A CAMPAIGN

When players reach Level 10, an invitation to join the battle is sent to their mailboxes. Select the Alliance War tab from the menu to find a list of available campaigns. Players are allowed to choose one as their home campaign, where they're eligible for the leaderboards. Note that if you're in a guild, your leader may have assigned the group to a specific campaign.

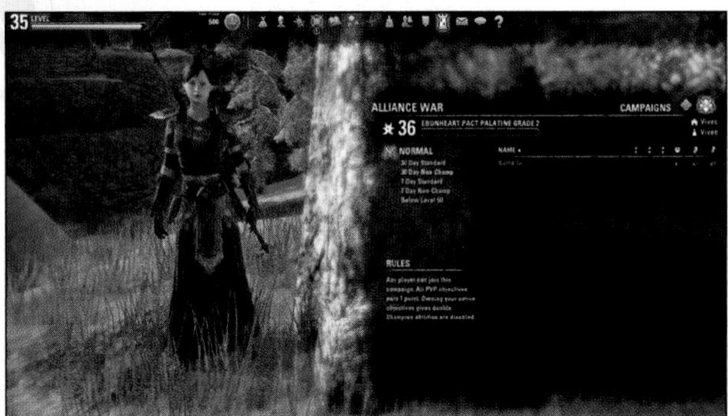

A player may also enter a second campaign as a guest, but is not eligible for leaderboard placement, and Alliance Points gained do not count toward campaign rewards. Switching your home and guest campaigns may only be done after a set period of time, and a fee is charged in order to do so. You can pay this fee in Alliance Points or gold.

If grouped with other players and your home and guest campaigns are assigned, you can still follow the group into another campaign. This is shown in the campaign listing.

After selecting a campaign, choose to enter it to join the queue. Once a position is available, you may travel to the campaign.

ALLIANCE BORDER KEEPS

Alliance	Border Keep
Aldmeri Dominion	Eastern Elsweyr
	Western Elsweyr
Daggerfall Covenant	Northern High Rock
	Southern High Rock
Ebonheart Pact	Northern Morrowind
	Southern Morrowind

Players enter the campaign at one of two border keeps that belong to their alliance. The Aldmeri Dominion set up on the south side of Cyrodiil, with the Daggerfall Covenant in the northwest and the Ebonheart Pact to the northeast. These bases are basically the staging areas—providing Merchants, mission boards, and a means of travel within and outside the zone.

EXITING CYRODIIL

To exit Cyrodiil and the Alliance War, travel back to one of your border keeps and find the nearby Wayshrine. This allows fast travel to any unlocked Wayshrine in Tamriel, just like outside of Cyrodiil. You can return to the war through the Alliance War tab. The campaign may be abandoned in the same manner it was joined once outside Cyrodiil.

Speak to the quest givers as you enter a campaign for the first time, and play through the introductory quests to learn the ins and outs of warfare. This is worthwhile simply for getting the hang of moving around and seizing enemy strongholds.

ALLIANCE POINTS AND RANKINGS

Participating in the Alliance War by defeating enemies, capturing/defending keeps and resources, confiscating Elder Scrolls, and completing quests earns Alliance Points (AP). This currency can be used at Merchants within Cyrodiil on exclusive items, such as elite gear and siege equipment. Player-versus-player (PvP) combat is not necessary to earn AP; defeat mobs that roam the zone and complete quests, though you should always watch your back for the opposition.

Alliance Points also go toward your Alliance War skill line, Alliance War Rank, and leaderboard position for the current campaign. The first AP earned in the Alliance War or Battlegrounds unlocks the Assault and Support skill lines.

From the starting rank of Citizen, there are 50 ranks to achieve as you make your way to Grand Overlord Grade 2—25 titles, each with two grades. The highest rank requires over 60 million Alliance Points, so a lot of time is required on the battlefield to max it out. This can be well worth the time, as each rank earns the player a Skill Point, and some higher-level gear is restricted by rank.

Alliance War Ranks

Rank	Title	AP to Next Rank	Total AP for Rank
0	Citizen	700	0
1	Volunteer Grade 1	901	700
2	Volunteer Grade 2	6400	1601
3	Recruit Grade 1	14400	8001
4	Recruit Grade 2	25600	22401
5	Tyro Grade 1	40000	48001
6	Tyro Grade 2	57600	88001
7	Legionary Grade 1	78400	145601
8	Legionary Grade 2	102400	224001
9	Veteran Grade 1	129600	326401
10	Veteran Grade 2	160000	456001
11	Corporal Grade 1	193600	616001
12	Corporal Grade 2	230400	809601
13	Sergeant Grade 1	270400	1040001
14	Sergeant Grade 2	313600	1310401
15	First Sergeant Grade 1	360000	1624001
16	First Sergeant Grade 2	409600	1984001
17	Lieutenant Grade 1	462400	2393601
18	Lieutenant Grade 2	518400	2856001
19	Captain Grade 1	577600	3374401
20	Captain Grade 2	640000	3952001
21	Major Grade 1	705600	4592001
22	Major Grade 2	774400	5297601
23	Centurion Grade 1	846400	6072001
24	Centurion Grade 2	921600	6918401
25	Colonel Grade 1	1000000	7840001
26	Colonel Grade 2	1081600	8840001
27	Tribune Grade 1	1166400	9921601
28	Tribune Grade 2	1254400	11088001
29	Brigadier Grade 1	1345600	12342401
30	Brigadier Grade 2	1440000	13688001
31	Prefect Grade 1	1537600	15128001
32	Prefect Grade 2	1638400	16665601
33	Praetorian Grade 1	1742400	18304001
34	Praetorian Grade 2	1849600	20046401
35	Palatine Grade 1	1960000	21896001
36	Palatine Grade 2	2073600	23856001
37	August Palatine Grade 1	2190400	25929601
38	August Palatine Grade 2	2310400	28120001
39	Legate Grade 1	2433600	30430401
40	Legate Grade 2	2560000	32864001
41	General Grade 1	2689600	35424001
42	General Grade 2	2822400	38113601
43	Warlord Grade 1	2958400	40936001
44	Warlord Grade 2	3097600	43894401
45	Grand Warlord Grade 1	3240000	46992001
46	Grand Warlord Grade 2	3385600	50232001
47	Overlord Grade 1	3534400	53617601
48	Overlord Grade 2	3686400	57152001
49	Grand Overlord Grade 1	3841600	60838401
50	Grand Overlord Grade 2	—	64680001

Assault and Support Skill Line Ranks

Skill Line Rank	Total AP Required
1	1
2	700
3	8000
4	38000
5	98000
6	188000
7	308000
8	488000
9	758000
10	1158000

CAMPAIGN SCORE

After you join a campaign, the Alliance War tab displays the status of the war. Each alliance begins with six keeps, an outpost, 18 resources, and two Elder Scrolls. At set intervals, the campaign score is evaluated and each alliance is given points based on the amount of these locations it possesses.

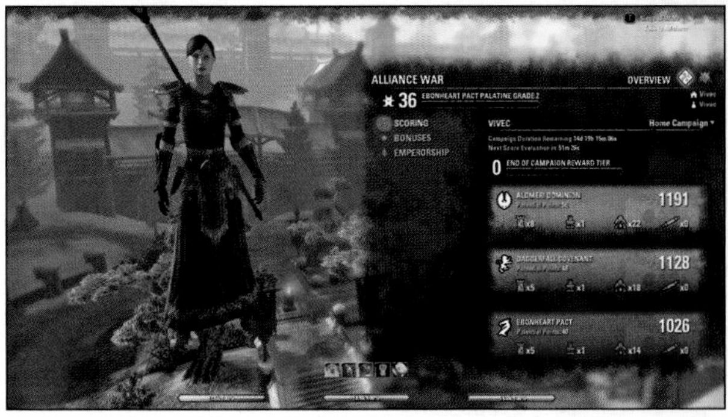

There are two possible scoring bonuses, dependent upon how alliances are performing. If an alliance falls way behind or suffers from low population, scores and Alliance Points are given a boost.

At the end of a campaign, players are rewarded based on Alliance Points earned in the home campaign. Alliance Points, gold, Repair Kits, and exclusive items are possible rewards.

ALLIANCE BONUSES

Bonuses are available for holding enemy keeps, enemy Elder Scrolls, and the emperorship. All home keeps or scrolls must be held to gain the corresponding bonuses.

Bonus	Alliance Holds	Effect
Home Keep Bonus	All Home Keeps	Increases Experience, Alliance Points, and gold by 5% while in PvP locations.
Enemy Keep Bonus I	1 Enemy Keep	Increases Experience, Alliance Points, and gold by 7% while in PvP locations.
Enemy Keep Bonus II	2 Enemy Keeps	Increases Experience, Alliance Points, and gold by 7%. Increases Weapon Critical and Spell Critical by 2% while in PvP locations.
Enemy Keep Bonus III	3 Enemy Keeps	Increases Experience, Alliance Points, and gold by 9%. Increases Weapon Critical and Spell Critical by 2% while in PvP locations.
Enemy Keep Bonus IV	4 Enemy Keeps	Increases Experience, Alliance Points, and gold by 9%. Increases Weapon Critical and Spell Critical by 4% while in PvP locations.
Enemy Keep Bonus V	5 Enemy Keeps	Increases Experience, Alliance Points, and gold by 11%. Increases Weapon Critical and Spell Critical by 4% while in PvP locations.
Enemy Keep Bonus VI	6 Enemy Keeps	Increases Experience, Alliance Points, and gold by 11%. Increases Weapon Critical and Spell Critical by 6% while in PvP locations.
Enemy Keep Bonus VII	7 Enemy Keeps	Increases Experience, Alliance Points, and gold by 13%. Increases Weapon Critical and Spell Critical by 6% while in PvP locations.
Enemy Keep Bonus VIII	8 Enemy Keeps	Increases Experience, Alliance Points, and gold by 13%. Increases Weapon Critical and Spell Critical by 8% while in PvP locations.
Enemy Keep Bonus IX	9 Enemy Keeps	Increases Experience, Alliance Points, and gold by 15%. Increases Weapon Critical and Spell Critical by 8% while in PvP locations.
Defensive Scroll Bonus I	1 Enemy Elder Scroll	Increases armor rating by 5% while in PvP locations.
Defensive Scroll Bonus II	2 Enemy Elder Scrolls	Increases Spell Resistance and armor rating by 5% while in PvP locations.
Offensive Scroll Bonus I	1 Enemy Elder Scroll	Increases Spell Power by 5% while in PvP locations.
Offensive Scroll Bonus II	2 Enemy Elder Scrolls	Increases Weapon Power and Spell Power by 5% while in PvP locations.
Emperorship Bonus	The Emperorship	Increases Maximum Health by +35 per character level while in PvP locations. (Self Cast)

EXPLORING CYRODIIL

Location/Item	Number in Cyrodiil
Delves	18
Dolmens	10
Mundus Stones	12 (all but the Lord)
Rare Fish	12
Skyshards	46

Many of the same locations and items are discoverable in Cyrodiil as in every other zone. Skyshards, Mundus Stones, rare fish, Dolmens, and a variety of dungeons can be collected and completed. Explore the area cautiously, as most of Cyrodiil is open to PvP combat.

TRANSITUS NETWORK

The Transitus Network has been set up throughout the zone for fast travel, though movement is limited to locations under your alliance's control, and there must be a connection between your current location and your destination. Travel is performed between Transitus Shrines, which are found inside every keep.

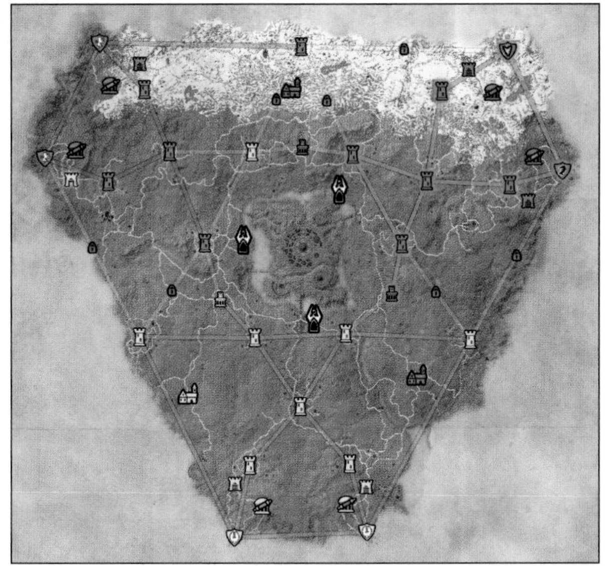

Approach and activate a Transitus Shrine, such as the one found at the border keep at which you begin. This brings up a map of Cyrodiil, displaying the full network of keeps and the links between them. Keeps, temples, outposts, resources, gates, and towns are given a color based on the alliance that currently controls them. A location outlined with a starburst means that it's under attack.

Lines connect all keeps and outposts and are displayed in red, green, or blue, depending on which alliance can use them. If a keep along the path is captured by an opposing alliance, the line is broken and it can no longer be used for fast travel. A lock indicates that only one alliance may travel along that line. Otherwise, as long as there is an unbroken connection between your current location and destination, travel is possible.

SAFE ZONES

There are limited safe zones in Cyrodiil, where players are safe from PvP gameplay. Public dungeons are completely PvE, allowing players to take on the bosses alongside members of opposing alliances. Each town has a safe house, where members of the ruling alliance may take refuge away from the war.

CAPTURE POINTS

The main objective of the Alliance War is to capture resources and keeps for your alliance. The resources add benefits to the nearby keep for your side, while keeps provide an added bonus for all players of the ruling alliance. Capture all six interior keeps, and the leader of your alliance becomes the Emperor, providing yet another bonus. Plus, all ownership adds to the campaign score.

To seize these Capture Points, you must turn all associated flags to your alliance. To do so, wipe out the nearby guards and take their place next to the flag. This brings up a meter that is filled with the color of the current owner. This slowly depletes as you remain in the area, and then fills with your team's color. With one player, this takes a long time and you're extremely vulnerable. But as more players stand guard, the meter depletes and fills at a faster rate.

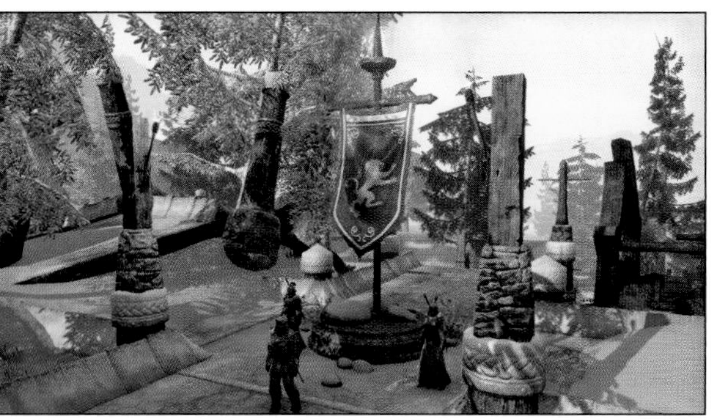

Icons denoting the flags at each point are shown on the compass when facing their way. The color indicates who currently controls the flag, while a highlight means that alliance is currently attempting to take it over.

GUARDS

Guards for the ruling alliance protect all structures and flags and must be dealt with before the flags can be turned. They are powerful foes, and taking them all down typically requires a group of players.

Only the defenders who stand next to a flag need to be removed, but a patrolling guard may take interest in your desire to overtake the Capture Point. Guards also stand outside keeps/outposts and attempt to keep players from getting inside.

KEEP

➤ **Number of Flags: 2**

The Keeps

Original Alliance	Keep	Required for Emperorship?	Artifact Gate/Temple Protected
Aldmeri Dominion	Castle Alessia	Yes	—
	Castle Black Boot	No	Altadoon
	Castle Bloodmayne	No	Mnem
	Castle Brindle	No	—
	Castle Faregyl	No	Altadoon, Mnem
	Castle Roebeck	Yes	—
Daggerfall Covenant	Fort Aleswell	Yes	—
	Fort Ash	Yes	—
	Fort Dragonclaw	No	—
	Fort Glademist	No	Alma Ruma, Ni-Mohk
	Fort Rayles	No	Alma Ruma
	Fort Warden	No	Ni-Mohk
Ebonheart Pact	Arrius Keep	No	Chim, Ghartok
	Blue Road Keep	Yes	—
	Chalman Keep	Yes	—
	Drakelowe Keep	No	—
	Farragut Keep	No	Ghartok
	Kingscrest Keep	No	Chim

There are 18 keeps in Cyrodiil, with each alliance controlling six at the start of the campaign. All six interior keeps are required to gain the emperorship, as well as strategic advantage for advancement.

The two keeps nearest an Artifact Gate must be captured in order to open the gate and get at the corresponding temple. Note that the two keeps need not be ruled by the same alliance, just not the original.

Siege weaponry must be used to get inside a keep. Use it to attack a door or wall, as well as the guards on duty. Focus all siege weapons on the same wall to limit the time required. A battering ram can be used to bust down a door, but best results require up to six players, and operators are susceptible to dropped oil and enemy players. Be sure to have part of the group protecting the siege weapons, since they're also vulnerable to enemy players.

Once through the outer wall, players should move inside to eliminate any opposition. As you finish off the first wall, the defending alliance is most likely setting up for your assault. Now the attacking group should concentrate fire on the inner wall, repeating the same process as with the outside.

Once inside the keep, clear out the guards and enemy alliance on the first floor, as well as any stragglers above, who are likely set up with ranged weapons and flaming oil. Turn the two flags to your alliance to capture the structure. The ruling alliance may continue to assault the keep throughout this process, so remain vigilant.

Holding an Elder Scroll on a keep's scroll pedestal bestows a bonus for every member of that alliance.

Controlling the surrounding resources is beneficial in keeping the structure repaired and guards strong. The longer the resources are held, the greater the benefit for the keep. There are five levels of benefits for each resource, which continually increase as long as the associated resource is held.

Benefits Bestowed on Keep with Captured Resources

Level	Wood Benefits	Food Benefits	Ore Benefits
1	Doors get 15000 more HP.	Your keep guards are more resistant to magical damage and siege weapons.	Guards have thicker armor. Walls get 35000 more HP.
2	Doors regenerate HP when not in combat.	Guards do more damage.	Walls regenerate HP when not in combat. Keep corners get an extra build-out section.
3	Keep mages gain more powerful versions of some of their abilities. Doors get 15000 more HP.	Melee guards gain more powerful versions of some of their abilities. Guards have more HP.	Various wall sections have more protective locations. Walls get 35000 more HP.
4	Keep menders gain more powerful versions of some of their abilities. Doors regenerate 50% more HP.	Keep archers gain more powerful versions of some of their abilities.	Keep honor guards gain more powerful versions of some of their abilities. Walls regenerate 50% more HP.
5	Walls and doors regenerate HP faster. Doors get 15000 more HP.	Mages and archers have longer range on their abilities.	Walls get 35000 more HP.

Visit the Warfront Mission Board for quests that require capturing a keep.

RESOURCES

➤ **Number of Flags: 1 Each**

Resources

Resource	Benefit of Capture
Farm	The food increases the strength of NPC soldiers guarding the keep.
Lumbermill	Allows players to strengthen the doors of the keep.
Mine	The ore is required to upgrade and repair the keeps.

Production and Defense Bonuses for Owned Resources

Level	Production	Defense
1	Your gatherer NPCs collect more resources per trip.	Walls regenerate HP when not in combat. Your keep guards are more resistant to magical damage and siege weapons. The tower overwatching the resource has more HP.
2	The base amount of resources earned is increased by 25%.	Melee guards gain more powerful versions of some of their abilities. Guards have more HP.
3	Your gatherer NPCs collect more resources per trip.	Keep mages gain more powerful versions of some of their abilities. The tower overwatching the resource has more HP.
4	The base amount of resources earned is increased by 25%.	Keep menders gain more powerful versions of some of their abilities. Walls regenerate 50% more HP.
5	Your gatherer NPCs collect more resources per trip.	Keep honor guards gain more powerful versions of some of their abilities. The tower overwatching the resource has more HP.

A farm, lumbermill, and mine surround each of the 18 keeps in Cyrodiil. Capture a resource by killing off enough of the opposition so that your side outnumbers them. One flag must be turned to your alliance to gain control. Controlling these resources gives the keep an added benefit as stated in the above table. There are five levels of upgrades per resource, which are unlocked over time. Therefore, the longer you hold the resources, the better they become.

Visit the Battle Mission Board for quests that require capturing specific resources.

OUTPOSTS

➤ **Number of Flags: 2**

Near the center of Cyrodiil, three outposts sit along the Transitus Network between pairs of keeps. Each alliance controls one of these outposts at first, which sit between one of their own keeps and an opposing keep. This is the front line of the war, and because of their position, they may change hands frequently.

An outpost is smaller than a keep, with no outer wall, but still holds a pair of flags inside the structure. Use siege weaponry to get inside the building, and flip the two flags to gain control of the outpost.

ARTIFACT GATES

➤ **Number of Flags: 0**

Artifact Gates are the last line of defense before reaching an opponent's temple. Initially, an Artifact Gate is closed to all players except for the original ruling alliance. In order to get it open, the two nearest keeps must be captured by the remaining alliances. A number of guards protect the gate; so once it's open, it must still be assaulted in order for players to get through to the temple. Refer to the previous keep table to see which keeps are required to open each gate.

TOWNS

➤ **Number of Flags: 3**

Initial Alliance	Town	Quartermaster / Reward Container Armor Sets	Typical Weight of Armor
Aldmeri Dominion	Vlastarus	Alessian Order Bastion of the Heartland Beckoning Steel Blessing of the Potentates Crest of Cyrodiil Deadly Strike Elf Bane Ravager The Juggernaut	Heavy
Daggerfall Covenant	Bruma	Eagle Eye Hawk's Eye Kyne's Kiss Item Sentry Shadow Walker Shield of the Valiant The Morag Tong Vengeance Leech Ward of Cyrodiil	Medium
Ebonheart Pact	Cropsford	Almalexia's Mercy Buffer of the Swift Curse Eater Desert Rose Grace of the Ancients Light of Cyrodiil Robes of Alteration Mastery The Arch-Mage Wrath of the Imperium	Light

Three Cyrodiil towns can be captured: Vlastarus, Bruma, and Cropsford. Each alliance begins the campaign controlling one of them. Each town possesses a normal Merchant who is accessible to all players. A Quartermaster, who sells exclusive equipment sets, and a Siege Merchant are available to the ruling side. A spawn point is also available for players who die near the town, though they must belong to the ruling alliance.

Numerous quests are available at each town for all players, whether they belong to the alliance that controls the town or not. Of course, the guards who protect the flags and patrol the town may have something to say about it.

There are three flags that must be turned in order to capture a town. Three guards protect one of the flags and two stand guard at the second, while the third is undefended. You must flip all three flags to take advantage of the Quartermaster, Siege Merchant, and spawn point.

SIEGE AND DEFEND

Siege Merchant Goods

Equipment	Description	Toughness (HP)	Cost (AP/Gold)
Ballista	Creates a ballista siege weapon whose bolt causes great damage to structures and enemies.	100000	1,800/—
Battering Ram	Creates a battering ram that can be used to destroy doors.	200000	1,800/—
Fire Ballista	Creates a ballista siege weapon whose bolt causes Flame Damage to structures and also damages foes over time.	100000	1,200/450
Fire Trebuchet	Creates a trebuchet weapon whose fireball causes Flame Damage to structures and foes.	200000	1,800/450
Iceball Trebuchet	Creates a trebuchet weapon whose iceball causes damage and ensnares players.	200000	1,800/—
Lightning Ballista	Creates a ballista siege weapon whose electrically charged bolt ensnares enemies and drains their Magicka.	100000	1,200/—
Meatbag Catapult	Creates a catapult siege weapon that fires a bag of diseased meat at its targets.	150000	1,200/—
Oil Catapult	Creates a catapult siege weapon that fires a jar of oil at its targets, ensnaring them and draining their Stamina.	150000	1,200/—
Scattershot Catapult	Creates a catapult siege weapon whose mass of small rocks causes damage to foes in a wide area.	150000	1,200/—
Stone Trebuchet	Creates a trebuchet weapon whose stones cause great damage to structures and foes.	200000	1,800/—
Flaming Oil	Very effective weapon against rams and players operating a ram.	100000	800/—

In order to get inside keeps and outposts, you must use siege equipment to bust down the doors and walls. Siege weaponry is available from Siege Merchants at the alliance bases and captured towns. Battering rams, ballistae, trebuchets, and catapults are all available for purchase.

- **Battering Ram:** Can only be used to attack a keep door, and requires a big enough flat space next to the door. Standing next to the ram causes it to move toward the door and attack. The weapon becomes more effective with more players, up to a maximum of six. Operators are extremely susceptible from flaming oil above and enemy players, so stay alert during deployment.

- **Ballista:** Shoots a firebolt, electrically charged bolt, or standard bolt in a low arc at its target. The firebolt damages over time, the lightning shot ensnares enemies and drains Magicka, and the standard bolt is effective on a wall.

- **Catapult:** Launches a meatbag, jar of oil, or scattershot. These projectiles do not quite have the range of a trebuchet, but are capable of high damage. Use a firebolt or fireball on a meatbag to cause serious trouble for the enemy. The oil snares players, while the scattershot hits a wide area.

- **Trebuchet:** Bombards its target with a fireball, iceball, or stone. These weapons have the longest range and are best for taking down a wall. The fireball damages players over time, the iceball snares a hit enemy, and the stone is best used on a wall.

- **Flaming Oil:** From the upper level of a keep or outpost, spill the oil on assaulting enemies. This is extremely effective against battering ram operators, but can also be dropped onto players as they attempt to capture a flag.

To deploy a siege weapon, place the item into a quickslot and use it. Find a flat area to accommodate the machine—a green circle signifies a usable location—and press Fire. Interact with a ballista, catapult, trebuchet, or flaming oil to bring up a green arc, showing the intended path of the projectile. Aim at the structure or player(s) you wish to target, and fire the shot. At this point, the arc turns red for a short time, as the next round is prepared. Stow the weapon by pressing the indicated button.

You are extremely vulnerable while using siege weapons, so pay careful attention to your Health. The weapons are also susceptible, as enemies may set them on fire. Assigning players to protect these weapons is often a good idea.

The more players focusing on the same wall or door, the quicker it comes down, so work as a team to bust your way inside. The big weapons take some time to turn, so try not to rotate too much when aiming.

REPAIR KITS

Siege Merchant Repair Kits

Equipment	Description	Cost (AP/Gold)
Keep Door Woodwork Repair Kit	Repairs 5,000 points of damage to a door.	200/90
Keep Wall Masonry Repair Kit	Repairs 5,000 points of damage to a keep wall.	300/90
Siege Repair Kit	Repairs a siege weapon for 20000 HP.	200/90

Siege weapons, as well as the doors and walls targeted by them, have a set amount of Health points. Once these points are depleted, the weapon or structure is destroyed. Repair Kits, received as rewards for completing objectives and available for purchase from Siege Merchants, can be used to mend the weapons and structures.

Equip the kit in a quickslot and use it when next to the damaged structure. You may want to clear out any enemies in the area before attempting the repair.

FORWARD CAMP

A forward camp allows teammates to respawn at its location and can be placed anywhere in Cyrodiil, as long as the site is flat enough. Players who die near a forward camp have the opportunity to respawn at that site. It can be purchased from a Siege Merchant for 20,000 AP. Use the item from a quickslot and find a flat, suitable spot; a red X indicates that the site is unsuitable.

You must be Alliance Rank 6 or higher to purchase a forward camp, and it only allows for 20 soldiers to respawn. You may not use the forward camp if you have used it recently. Press the Interact button to dismantle an enemy's forward camp.

TEMPLES AND THE ELDER SCROLLS

The Six Temples and Scrolls Held at Each

Alliance	Temple/Elder Scroll	Nearest Border Keep	Type of Scroll
Aldmeri Dominion	Altadoon	Western Elsweyr	Offensive
	Mnem	Eastern Elsweyr	Defensive
Daggerfall Covenant	Alma Ruma	Southern High Rock	Defensive
	Ni-Mohk	Northern High Rock	Offensive
Ebonheart Pact	Chim	Northern Morrowind	Defensive
	Ghartok	Southern Morrowind	Offensive

A temple sits just inside each border keep. Each temple holds an offensive or defensive Elder Scroll at the start of the campaign. The Elder Scroll is well-protected by alliance guards, as well as by a nearby Artifact Gate. This gate cannot be opened by opposing alliances without first capturing the two nearest keeps.

Each alliance begins with two Elder Scrolls, one offensive and one defensive. Another alliance may capture a scroll and store it upon a scroll pedestal inside one of their own keeps, with a bonus awarded to every player of that alliance. In order to capture another alliance's scroll, your side must control its own scroll of the same type. A scroll originally stored at an alliance's temple must be returned to that temple. Refer to the bonuses table earlier in this chapter for details on the bonuses given.

TYPES OF QUESTS

There are numerous quests available in Cyrodiil.

Mission Type	Description
Introductory Quests	Three quests teach you the basics of the Alliance War, from traveling around the zone to operating the siege equipment.
Scouting Missions	Scout resource locations and report on the enemy's defenses.
Battle Missions	Quests from the Battle Mission Board require the player to capture resources around enemy keeps. Join other players in order to defeat the guards who protect these locations.
Warfront Missions	The Warfront Mission Board asks players to capture a specific keep for the alliance. Find a group of players and help them seize the indicated keep.
Elder Scrolls Missions	Each scroll has an associated quest that asks the player to steal or return the scroll. Use the map to find each scroll's current location.
Settlement Quests	PvE quests are available in Bruma, Cheydinhal, Chorrol, Cropsford, Vlastarus, and Weynon Priory. Bruma, Cropsford, and Vlastarus are ruled by one of the alliances, but can still be visited by the other side.
Wilderness Quests	More PvE quests are available out in the wild, so keep your eye out for quest givers.

IMPERIAL CITY DLC

By owning the Imperial City DLC or being a member of ESO Plus, players may enter the Imperial City Sewers through three gates in the middle of Cyrodiil. No matter which gate is entered, you are led directly to your alliance's base, where more quests and Merchants are found.

There are six districts of the Imperial City: Arboretum, Arena, Elven Gardens, Memorial, Nobles, and Temple. The city is open PvP, with quests available in each district once the Imperial City story quests are complete.

MORROWIND: BATTLEGROUNDS (PVPVP)

Introduced with the release of *The Elder Scrolls Online: Morrowind*, the Battlegrounds, located in the heart of Vvardenfell, offers quick, 15-minute games of Team Deathmatch, Capture the Flag, and Domination. Three teams of four players face off at one of three battlefields: Ald Carac, the Foyada Quarry, or Ularra.

ENTERING A BATTLEGROUND

At the Gladiator's Quarters in Vivec City and outside each of the Battlegrounds gates, read the flyer posted on the Bulletin Board to begin a quest called "For Glory!" that leads you to Battlemaster Rivyn, who is found nearby. He rewards the player with Experience and gold after completing a Battleground.

To enter a Battleground, open the Activity Finder and navigate to Battlegrounds. Here you'll see the option to join Battlegrounds and the current playlists available. Select the desired game to jump into the queue and continue with your game; a message notifies you when there are enough players to join the Battleground.

Select between two level ranges of 10-49 and 10-50. Characters are battle-leveled the same way as in Cyrodiil.

GAMEPLAY

At the start of a Battleground, you're assigned to one of three teams: Fire Drakes, Pit Daemons, or Storm Lords; there are no Alliance ties in Battlegrounds. Each team has an associated color, which corresponds to the objectives.

KNOW YOUR MAP

Each spawn point has multiple paths into the battlefield. Running straight ahead is often not the best option.

Battlegrounds Teams

	Team	Color
	Fire Drakes	Red
	Pit Daemons	Green
	Storm Lords	Purple

All games in Battlegrounds last a maximum of 15 minutes, with points awarded to teams for completing the appropriate objective. Kill opposing players in Deathmatch, seize the enemy's relic in Capture the Flag, and control Capture Points in Domination. The first team to 500 points, or the team in the lead after 15 minutes, wins the match.

WAITING TO BE RESURRECTED

Before using a Soul Gem or reviving at your team's spawn point, give your teammates a chance to resurrect you. This is often the best play, allowing you to get back in the game quicker.

Your HUD provides everything necessary to keep track of game progress:

- White chevrons on the compass keep you in contact with teammates.
- Icons for each relic and flag in the objective game modes allow you to quickly find them as they are seized and dropped.
- A scoreboard on the right side of the screen keeps track of each team's progress. Objectives are shown above progress bars, indicating who possesses each one.
- Health bars for each teammate appear on the left for easy status updates.

BATTLE ROLES

TANK
Absorbs damage from enemies and prevents allies from being attacked.

HEALER
Heals and protects allies, keeping them alive throughout the battle.

DAMAGE-DEALER
Focuses on dealing damage against enemies that pose a threat.

Though you don't have much control of your team makeup, roles can be a consideration if taking a group of four players into the Battlegrounds.

Tanks are a great choice for carrying the relic or defending a Capture Point, with their uncanny ability to take punishment for lengths of time. A Healer is important in the two objective-based games, in order to keep others alive while capturing the other team's relic or flag. DPS players are vital to racking up the kills in Team Deathmatch and grabbing an objective. Each role can be an asset no matter the mode, though it's best to realize your strengths when entering a battle.

GAME MODES

TEAM DEATHMATCH

Objective: Kill Opposing Players

"Team Deathmatch has always been popular. All that ceaseless bloodshed really gets the heart pumping! Just go into the field and attack as many players as possible. The more hits you get in, the more points your team scores."

- Battlemaster Rivyn

Scoring

ACTION	SCORE
Kill a player on an opposing team	15

Team Deathmatch pits the three teams against one another, with each kill adding to the team's score. The first team to accumulate 500 points wins the match. If no one reaches this mark before the 15-minute time limit, the team with the most points wins.

There's a variety of strategies that can be deployed in Team Deathmatch. Support your teammates by moving around as a group, teaming up on the opposition. Send out a scout to find the enemy's position and move in for the kill. Split up and take on as many of your rivals as you can within the time limit.

It's the killing blow that gets the points for your team, so stealing kills from other squads is encouraged and can be the key to victory.

CAPTURE THE FLAG

Objective: Capture Opposing Team's Relic

"Capture the Relic is one of our simpler games. You must seize your enemy's relic and return it to your base, all while protecting your own relic as well. Teamwork is the key to victory in this game, as you'll need a strong defense and offense."

- Battlemaster Rivyn

Team Relics

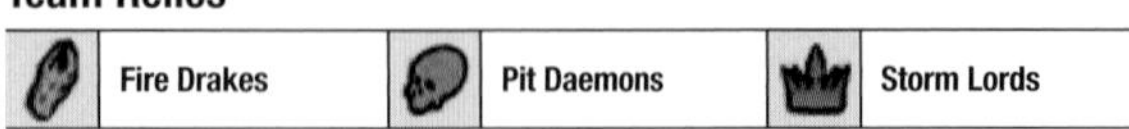

Fire Drakes	**Pit Daemons**	**Storm Lords**

Scoring

ACTION	SCORE
Deliver an opponent's relic to your base	100

Each team has a relic that sits atop a pedestal at its home base, glowing a color that matches the team: red, green, or purple. The objective is to swipe one of the opponent's relics and return it to your base for a successful capture. Your team's relic must currently reside at your home base in order to get the score. Otherwise, the carrier of the enemy's relic must wait for it to be returned. Icons displayed on the compass and scoreboard are also color-matched and give you a quick indication of their locations.

A graphic on the right side of the screen displays progress bars for each team, along with the three relics above. These icons change color depending on who currently holds them. Notification messages also appear on-screen to indicate changes.

Each successful capture earns the team 100 points, and the first team to achieve this five times, or score 500 points, wins the game. Good offensive skills are required in order to get to the opponent's relic, as well as defensive abilities to keep the opposition from getting your relic. Decide as a team whether you move around as a group and hope for the best at your home base, or split up into offensive and defensive groups.

STAY ON TASK

Don't forget your main objective. In Capture the Flag and Domination, points are rewarded for capturing and defending relics and banners, not for player kills.

When a relic is dropped, it's returned to its original location after ten seconds.

DOMINATION

Objective: Capture and Control Flags

"Anyone can claim a Capture Point, but it's a true test of skill to master Domination. Seize and protect as many Capture Points as you can. The team with the most territory in the end wins. In this game you must dominate your rivals, or be dominated!"

- Battlemaster Rivyn

The Flags

	ALD CARAC	FOYADA QUARRY	ULARRA
	Central	Central	Central
	Centurion	Storm Pit	Mushroom
	Forge	Fire Storm	Altar
	Engine	Fire Pit	Waterfall

Scoring

ACTION	SCORE
Capture a flag	8
Every 10 consecutive seconds a flag is controlled	8

A simple land-grab game, Domination requires teams to capture and maintain control of four Capture Points. Points are rewarded for gaining control of a flag and every 10 seconds a flag is under a team's control. The first team to 500 points, or the team that leads after 15 minutes, is the winner.

Once within range of a banner, a horseshoe-shaped graphic pops up on your HUD, representing ownership of the location. The controlling team's logo appears in the middle with their color filling the meter. To take control of the flag, the opposing team's color must fully drain before filling with your own. If not under anyone's control yet, the meter is empty and immediately begins to fill with your team's color.

TAKE ADVANTAGE OF THE SCORE TRACKER

Banners shown above the score tracker on the right side of the HUD show not only ownership, but also who currently attacks or defends each one. If a banner has a white outline, no one is defending or attacking that capture point.

If opposing teams stand near a flag, the capture progress will not change until one team remains or has more players than enemy teams. Flags are captured at a faster rate when more team members are near it.

Moving as a foursome makes quick work of the Capture Points, staking your claim in no time at all. Plus, this allows the team to be ready for ambushes and confrontations. It can be tempting to sneak out on your own and capture a flag, but without your team, you're extremely vulnerable to the opposition that moves as a pack. On the other hand, splitting up allows a team to cover more ground and, if they can avoid the big groups, grab more flags. Stay on the move and try not to get so caught up in big fights that you lose track of the main objective.

BATTLEFIELDS

ALD CARAC

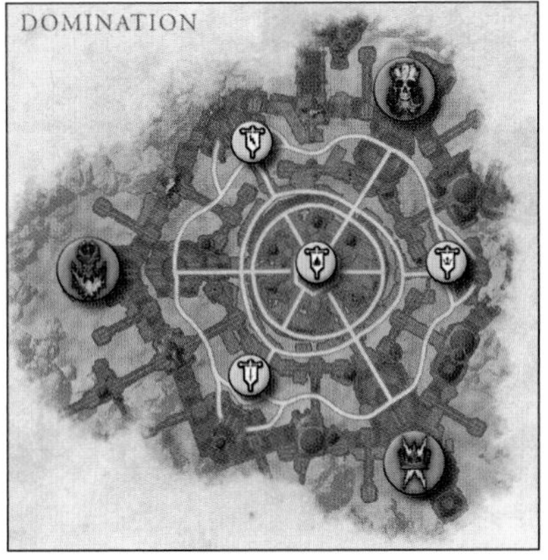

The crumbling Dwarven fortifications of Ald Carac are said to date to the time of the War of the First Council, early in the First Era.

ULARRA

The ruins of Ularradallaku are all that remain of an ancient temple complex devoted to the dread Daedric Prince Mehrunes Dagon.

FOYADA QUARRY

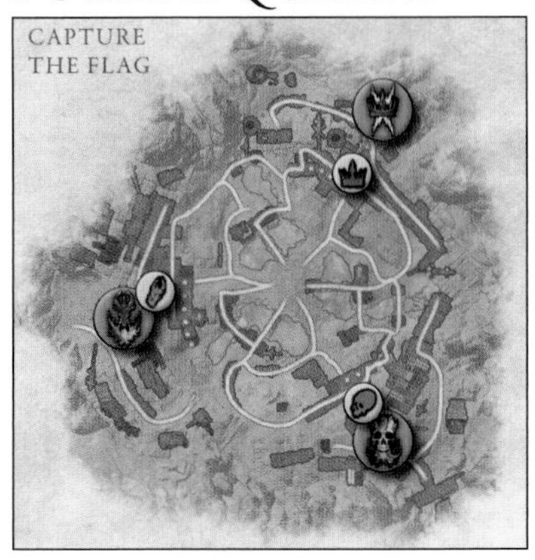

This quarry on the southern slopes of Red Mountain is the source of the granite being used to construct Vivec City—or it was, until the volcano awoke and began once more pouring lava down its foyadas.

REWARDS

At the conclusion of each game of Battlegrounds, Experience, Alliance Points, and possibly items are presented to the players. Team placement, along with personal medals, determines the value of the reward.

Spend Alliance Points at Battleground and Elite Gear Merchants, found in Vivec City and outside the three Battleground gates, to purchase gear from PvP-focused equipment sets. Apparel from one of the Battleground sets is occasionally rewarded for stellar gameplay. These sets include Coward's Gear, Knight Slayer, Vanguard's Challenge, and Wizard's Riposte.

ALLIANCE WAR SKILL LINE

Alliance Points are earned in the Battlegrounds for kills and match completion. These points increase your Alliance War skill line. Spend Skill Points on an assortment of assault and support abilities that are geared toward group, PvP gameplay.

MEDALS

Medals are handed out after each Battleground match for completing actions that support the type of game played, such as killing an opponent in Deathmatch and capturing the objective in Capture the Flag or Domination. The following table lists available medals. Points are tallied on weekly leaderboards for each game mode. The "Note" column indicates whether a medal can be earned multiple times per match or if only one player earns the medal each time. If no note, each player may earn the medal once per game.

TEAM DEATHMATCH MEDALS

Team Deathmatch Medals

MEDAL	DESCRIPTION	NOTE
First Strike	First Kill	One Player Per Match
Double Kill	Get 2 kills within 20 seconds	Repeatable in Match
Triple Kill	Get 3 kills within 20 seconds	Repeatable in Match
Quadrupule Kill	Get 4 kills within 20 seconds	Repeatable in Match
Killing Blow	Earn 1 killing blow	Repeatable in Match
Furious Strikes	Earn 10 killing Blows	—
Bruiser	Deal 5,000 damage	—
Fearsome Fighter	Deal 25,000 damage	—
Medal Gladiator	Deal 50,000 damage	—
Medal Champion	Deal 500,000 damage	—
Minor Mender	Heal 5,000 damage	—
Heroic Healer	Heal 25,000 damage	—
Medic	Heal 50,000 damage	—
Fearless Physician	Heal 500,000 damage	—
Critical Heal	Heal 10,000 damage at once	Repeatable in Match
Rapid Recovery	Heal 20,000 damage at once	Repeatable in Match
Heavy Hitter	Deal 10,000 damage at once	Repeatable in Match
Crushing Blow	Deal 15,000 damage at once	Repeatable in Match
Assist	Signifigantly Aid in the killing or healing of players in Combat	Repeatable in Match

DOMINATION MEDALS

Domination Flag Capture

MEDAL	DESCRIPTION	NOTE
Dominator	Capture 1 Banner	Repeatable in Match
Vigilant Defender	Defend Banners under attack for at least 500 contribution	Repeatable in Match
Gleaming Guardian	Take 15,000 Damage	—
Dauntless Defender	Take 30,000 Damage	—
Valiant Vanguard	Take 60,000 Damage	—
Steady Centurion	Take 250,000 Damage	Repeatable in Match
Iron Soul	Take 10,000 Damage in one hit	Repeatable in Match
Steel Skin	Take 15,000 Damage in one hit	Repeatable in Match
Defensive Execution	Kill an Attacking player while defending a Banner	Repeatable in Match
Offensive Execution	Kill a Defending player while attacking a Banner	Repeatable in Match
Humble Protector	Heal 5,000 Damage at a Banner	—
Devoted Protector	Heal 25,000 Damage at a Banner	—
Sublime Protector	Heal 50,000 Damage at a Banner	—
Divine Protector	Heal 500,000 Damage at a Banner	—
Helping Hand	Heal 5,000 Damage in one heal at a Banner	Repeatable in Match
Blessed Assistance	Heal 15,000 Damage in one heal at a Banner	Repeatable in Match

CAPTURE THE FLAG MEDALS

Capture the Flag Medals

MEDAL	DESCRIPTION	NOTE
First Relic	First Flag Capture	One Player Per Match
Relic Runner	Capture a relic	Repeatable in Match
Relic Hunter	Kill a Flag Carrier	Repeatable in Match
Humble Protection	Heal a flag carrier for 5,000 damage in one hit	—
Critical Healer	Heal a flag carrier for 10,000 damage in one hit	—
Relic Protector	Heal flag carriers for 50,000 damage	—
Devoted Protection	Heal flag carriers for 250,000 damage	—
Divine Guardian	Heal flag carriers for 500,000 damage	—
Relic Crushing Blow	Deal 15,000 damage to a flag carrier in one hit	—
Relic Bruiser	Deal 5,000 damage to flag carriers	—
Relic Fearsome Fighter	Deal 25,000 damage to flag carriers	—
Relic Gladiator	Deal 50,000 damage to flag carriers	—
Relic Champion	Deal 500,000 damage to flag carriers	—

CRAFTING

Adventuring through Tamriel isn't just about hunting down beasts and slaying them. There are other activities to try, and the six crafting professions, also known as trade skills, are the most beneficial and lucrative. The six professions are:

 Alchemy

 Blacksmithing

 Clothing

 Enchanting

 Provisioning

 Woodworking

Anyone can take up crafting, but you need to spend Skill Points in a specific craft if you wish to create more impressive items, and become more profitable if this hobby turns into a trade. Crafting requires the gathering of ingredients, items, and other materials from across the world, whether looted from foes, found naturally, bought from traders, or converted from raw materials. New items are then crafted at a crafting station specific to your profession.

Crafting is rewarding in a number of ways. You're able to create new items relying solely on your own competence rather than depending on others, you can sell these items for fun and profit, and you can choose to keep and use a wealth of items to become self-sufficient instead of purchasing them.

Some of the most potent items available anywhere are available to craft, provided you have the necessary ingredients, components, and competence.

WHERE ARE MY CRAFTING STATIONS?

Need to see where your nearest specific crafting station is? Check your in-game map! Each apothecary, smithy, clothier, chironasium, camp, inn, and carpentry location is shown.

Don't overlook crafting. Although it doesn't seem initially as helpful as mastering a weapon, armor, or magic-based skill line, it's worth starting to investigate one or two of the six professions as you gain Experience, if only to augment the quality of your equipment. Conversely, be warned that attempting to master all six professions with a single character usually results in one that is unimpressive in all of them and lacks combat skills to properly survive, as all points are poured into crafting. This is unwise, so stick to professions that directly benefit your character build. For example, Blacksmithing can help you forge better weapons.

SEEKING INSPIRATION

The six crafting professions use an Experience-like system known as Inspiration for leveling. Once you reach a certain number of Inspiration Points, you gain a crafting rank (from 1 to 50). The higher the quality of the item, the more Inspiration you receive. Generally, you receive Inspiration for completing any of the following activities:

- Creating an item from base components
- Improving an item you've acquired or already crafted
- Extracting elements from an item
- Refining an item
- Completing crafting writs

INSPIRATION FAVORS FRIENDSHIP

It's worth palling around with a fellow player who's looking to improve the same crafting trade skill as you, so you can craft items and then deconstruct each other's creations. The reason is simple: you're awarded the most Inspiration for such endeavors and can therefore level up your crafting professions much more quickly.

IT'S THE LORE

Good news! There are Lorebooks dotted around Tamriel that grant you a level in one of the six trade skills. Seek them out if you wish to level up a profession more quickly.

CERTIFICATION AND CRAFTING WRITS

Are you still reticent about learning one of these "non-combative" professions? Then put your love of killing things to good use by completing crafting writs—a number of repeatable quests that reward you with Experience, gold, supplies, and other valuables!

BECOMING CERTIFIED

These types of quests are only open to those who've been certified in a particular profession. Becoming certified involves fulfilling a set of criteria (usually reaching Level 6), and then finding a master in your chosen profession and completing a training quest for them. You can also start a certification quest by reading the Writ Board, located in every major city. Note there are two types of board: one relating to writs for equipment (Blacksmithing, Clothing, and Woodworking), and the other for consumables (Alchemy, Enchanting, and Provisioning).

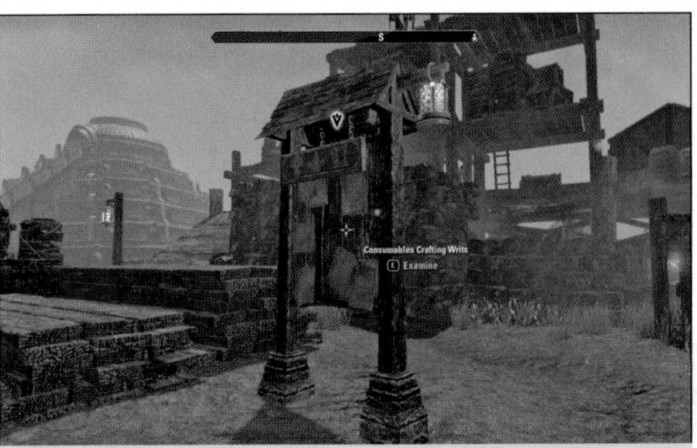

Find a Writ Board in any major city if you want to become certified or start a crafting writ.

WHY BECOME CERTIFIED?

Becoming certified in a particular crafting profession should be undertaken as soon as possible, and is thoroughly recommended for the following reasons:

This is an easy way to accrue Experience at Level 6 or higher.

Certification is straightforward and quick. The master crafter guides you through the process of finding materials you need, and you're shown how to craft the elements into something desirable. Simply put, this is a comprehensively helpful in-game tutorial for any profession you wish to perfect.

If you're already at Inspiration Rank 10 or higher for a skill related to the profession you're seeking to be certified in, you can simply skip the process and receive almost instant certification.

COMPLETING A CRAFTING WRIT

Once you've completed a crafting writ, expect to receive a survey report, unless you're Provisioning.

Once you're certified, return to either a Consumable Writ Board (for Alchemy, Enchanting, or Provisioner writs) or an Equipment Writ Board (for Blacksmithing, Clothing, or Woodworking writs). Take a writ you're interested in, and fulfill the contract stated on it. This is almost always the locating of products, goods, or items; the possible creation of those things; and the delivery of them to the individual requesting them.

As well as receiving Inspiration and other possible minor rewards, finishing a crafting writ may give you a survey report. Like maps to treasure, these show some high-yield harvest nodes only available to you, now that you've finished the writ. Go there and grab them! Provisioners do not receive survey reports; instead, they have a chance of obtaining a new recipe.

MASTER WRITS

When you've mastered your trade skill, you can expect to receive a Master Writ, which is a slightly more involved writ compared to a crafting writ. While a crafting writ usually involves your Homestead, Master Writs are awarded more often to those supremely dedicated to their craft, though they may also be given out upon completion of crafting writs.

For Alchemists: The larger the number of translated runes, the higher the probability of being awarded a Master Writ.

For Enchanters: The larger the number of reagents you've learned the effects from, the higher the possibility you'll receive a Master Writ.

For Blacksmiths, Clothiers, and Woodworkers: If you have excellent knowledge of styles (Racial Motifs, especially the more esoteric ones like the Celestial or Minotaur Motifs) and are well into your trait researching, expect a Master Writ.

For Provisioners: If you have a good knowledge of the higher-quality (purple and gold) recipes, expect a higher number of Master Writs to be awarded.

Master Writs require you to complete a similar contract to a crafting writ; for example, you may receive an Alchemy writ requiring you to make a specific poison. The difference is the reward: you receive Writ Vouchers. Master Writs are also sealed, so they can be stored, sold, or traded as you wish—or undertaken, of course!

Finish a Master Writ, claim your Writ Vouchers (a non-transferable currency), and spend them at a trader in any large city that sells items for your Homestead. Need a Blacksmithing Station? How about some Legendary plans for furniture? Spend your Writ Vouchers to obtain this booty!

CRAFTING HOMESTEAD FURNISHINGS

Now that you're able to own a Homestead in Tamriel, the six crafting trade skills gain a number of additional advantages. You can start making furnishings for your dwelling from Alchemy Formulas, Blacksmithing Diagrams, Clothing Patterns, Enchanting Praxises, Provisioning Designs, and Woodworking Blueprints. Find out more about this features in the guide section on **Homestead**.

TRAITS

Wait! Research traits now! You'll be glad you did!

For adventurers considering one of the three equipment trade skills (Blacksmithing, Clothing, or Woodworking), it's worth understanding that certain gear items can have particular properties, or "traits," added. Traits grant specific effects, but different gear types may not be created in the same way; for example, a bow with a damage bonus requires a different trait plan compared to a sword. Traits tend to improve if an item's quality—the color-coding from Common/white to Legendary/gold—is higher.

Additionally, it's worth noting that you can ignore traits completely, or craft equipment with traits added as a final, extra step. It takes time, but for those wanting the most powerful equipment of all, it's a worthwhile task. Keep in mind that only one trait can be added to a single piece of equipment, though you can use armor and weapons and wear jewelry that have all been researched, with a trait applied to each.

ITEMS WITH TRAITS IMBUED

The key to researching traits is to find an item with a trait imbued that can be destroyed during the research process. These are occasionally found throughout Tamriel, looted from enemies, or created during crafting. They can also be purchased from traders, but the easiest method of obtaining an item with a trait is from a friendly guild member.

RESEARCHING TRAITS

To create an item with a trait, you first need to research it at a crafting station specific to the gear type:

Heavy armor and **metal-based weapons** are researched at a Blacksmithing Station. There are over 125 different research traits for all the heavy armor and weapons, mainly because each individual piece of armor requires its own trait research, even if the trait is identical to another section of heavy armor.

Light armor and **medium armor** are researched at a Clothing Station. There are over 125 different research traits for these armor types, mainly because each individual piece of armor requires its own trait research, even if the trait is identical to another section of light or medium armor.

Bows, **shields**, and **staves** are researched at a Woodworking Station. There are over 50 different research traits for this equipment, spread across the three types.

THIS WAY MADNESS LIES!

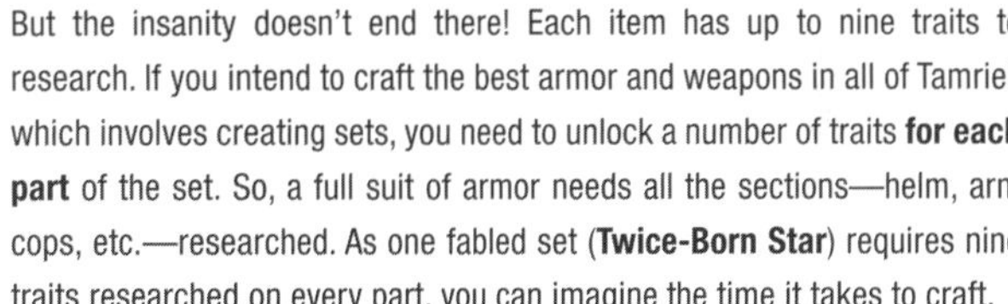

But the insanity doesn't end there! Each item has up to nine traits to research. If you intend to craft the best armor and weapons in all of Tamriel, which involves creating sets, you need to unlock a number of traits **for each part** of the set. So, a full suit of armor needs all the sections—helm, arm cops, etc.—researched. As one fabled set (**Twice-Born Star**) requires nine traits researched on every part, you can imagine the time it takes to craft.

Go to the station with an item in your inventory that already has the trait you wish to research. Research it by destroying that item, and wait a specific number of real hours or days.

MINIMIZING RESEARCH TIME

The first time you research an item, it takes six hours of real time. For the second trait of the same trade skill, that time is doubled. This means that if you're researching the eighth trait at a Blacksmithing Station, you'll need to wait 32 entire days for the research to complete!

Shorten this time frame by placing points into the following Passive Abilities capable of reducing the research time by 5-25%, and which allow two to three traits to be researched at the same time:

Metallurgy (Blacksmithing) | **Stitching (Clothier)** | **Carpentry (Woodworking)**

How much does this help? Well, if you've reached Level 42 and can access Rank 4 of Metallurgy, this (like Stitching and Carpentry) caps the days needed at 30, nearly halving the time for higher-level researching. This still takes a considerable amount of time (almost a year of real time!), so you're encouraged to bergin researching traits as soon as possible.

You can research your different trade skills simultaneously without any penalties, so with Rank 3 or 4 in Metallurgy, Stitching, and Carpentry, you can have as many as nine traits researching at the same time.

TRAIT GEMS

Once research is complete, certain dyes may be unlocked as by-products of the research, as well as some Achievements. The trait itself is bound to a specific type of gem. These need to be acquired if you wish to use a Trait Gem when crafting an item with that trait. So, if you want the Charged trait for your weapons, you need a supply of amethysts. Find Trait Gems by:

- Refining raw materials (there's a chance a random Trait Gem appears)
- Looting containers across Tamriel
- Deconstructing items with a trait (sometimes)
- Buying them from traders, or fellow players
- Receiving them from Hirelings

The following tables show the available traits and their associated gems for each of the nine armor traits (for shields and light, medium, and heavy armor) and weapon traits (for metal and non-metal weaponry).

TRAIT GEMS (ARMOR)

TRAIT	GEM		EFFECTS
DIVINES*		SAPPHIRE	Increases Mundus Stone effects
IMPENETRABLE*		DIAMOND	Increases Critical Resistance, and item takes 50% less durability damage
INFUSED*		BLOODSTONE	Increases armor enchantment effect
NIRNHONED		FORTIFIED NIRNCRUX	Increases Physical and Spell Resistance
PROSPEROUS		GARNET	Increases gold gained from looting enemies
REINFORCED*		SARDONYX	Increases item's armor value
STURDY		QUARTZ	Reduces block cost
TRAINING*		EMERALD	Increases Experience gained from kills
WELL-FITTED		ALMANDINE	Reduces the cost of sprinting and dodge rolling

** Recommended traits to try first.*

TRAIT GEMS (WEAPONS)

TRAIT	GEM		EFFECTS
CHARGED		AMETHYST	Increases chance to apply status effects
DECISIV		CITRINE	Chance to gain an additional Ultimate when an Ultimate is gained
DEFENDING		TURQUOISE	Increases Physical and Spell Resistance
INFUSED		JADE	Increases weapon enchantment effect and reduces enchantment cooldown by 40%
NIRNHONED		POTENT NIRNCRUX	Increases Weapon Damage
POWERED*		CHYSOLITE	Increases healing
PRECISE*		RUBY	Increases Weapon and Spell Critical values
SHARPENED*		FIRE OPAL	Increases Physical and Spell Penetration
TRAINING		CARNELIAN	Increases Experience gained from kills

** Recommended traits to try first.*

WHAT ABOUT CRAFTING STYLES (MOTIFS)?

The appearance of your weapons and armor can also change, though the differences are purely cosmetic. Any crafting skill that involves creating this type of equipment has a style you can craft too, be it racial or not. Styles are created with Style Gems and specific style items. *Morrowind*-related Motifs are covered later in this chapter. For an overview of styles for Blacksmithing, Clothing, and Woodworking, consult this chapter's corresponding sections.

CRAFTING SITES AND SETS

In addition to the crafting stations for each profession, there are special stations available at specific crafting sites across Tamriel, indicated by the icon shown. These are of particular importance, as you can craft sets of items, which enable additional bonuses (usually combat-related) to be imbued. Only certain crafting sites allow the creation of craftable sets, and sets are only available to the Blacksmithing, Clothing, and Woodworking professions.

Need to create sets of items? Then locate a crafting site. This is why learning traits is so important; you need to have researched up to nine traits before all sets become accessible.

Depending upon your alliance, specific locations allow the creation of certain sets, usually one site per alliance territory, or neutral zones for other set types. After researching a given number of traits, you utilize the crafting site and craft the effects of the set for your chosen equipment. Note the minimum number of traits you need to craft a set is two, and the maximum is nine.

There are other craftable sets, available once you've completed quests for certain guilds, such as the Fighters Guild or Mages Guild.

NON-CRAFTABLE SETS OF ITEMS

There are other sets of items you can obtain: Arena Sets, Dungeon Sets, Monster Helm Sets, Overland Sets, PvP Sets, and Trial Sets. These are found or purchased while undertaking the activities denoted in their titles. For example, Dungeon Sets are found after tackling underbosses and bosses in a particular dungeon.

EXAMPLE CRAFTING SET: DEATH'S WIND

You've decided you wish to take advantage of the bonuses of the Death's Wind set. You've researched two traits and can therefore create this set. You're part of the Aldmeri Dominion alliance, so you journey to the Eastshore Islets Camp in Auridon, where the specific crafting site for making this set resides. You can then add the effects of this set to two to five items of equipment you're wearing or using. You receive bonuses to your Physical Resistance (two items) and Maximum Health (three and four items), and acquire automatic Knockback and Stun effects against enemies if you're under 35% Health during melee combat (five items). This is in addition to the trait's effects you may choose to imbue each part of the set with!

HIRELINGS HELPFULNESS

Certain crafts (all but Alchemy) have a passive ability where a Hireling is acquired to forage base materials on your behalf, allowing you to tend to other adventuring matters. There are three ranks to this passive ability, enabling you to receive some relevant goods (as well as rare items related to your craft) once every 24 hours (Ranks 1 and 2) and 12 hours (Rank 3). Note that you must **actively retrieve** the item from the Hireling via the message you receive from them, rather than simply read the message, to begin the timer again. Be warned: You won't start the 24 or 12 hour countdown until you do!

MORROWIND CRAFTING MOTIFS AND SETS

What's new in Vvardenfell? Well, there are new craftable sets of equipment, and some unique crafting Motifs to find on your travels. Here's what to look for:

CRAFTABLE EQUIPMENT SETS

Uncover some special crafting tables to create three new and unique sets of equipment. Some tables are shown at the Randas Ancestral Tomb.

There are three new craftable sets of equipment (armor and weapons) to be found, each at a unique set of crafting tables in a specific location. These are:

Shacklebreaker set at the Vvardenfell location Zergonipal.

Assassin's Guile set at the Vvardenfell location Marandas.

Daedric Trickery set at the Vvardenfell location Randas Ancestral Tomb.

Need to know where these three locations are? Consult the **Atlas of Morrowind**, found later in this guide.

CRAFTABLE EQUIPMENT SETS

Got a cool 500,000 Alliance Points to spend? Then pay a visit to the Battleground Elite Merchant in Vivec City and claim the Militant Ordinator Motif! All sales final!

CRAFTING MOTIFS

There are four new styles (Motifs) to uncover across Vvardenfell. These are:

ASHLANDER

This style's Motif chapters are found by completing the relic and the hunting daily quests in Vvardenfell. The style item, Ash Canvas, is picked up during those same activities, more commonly than the chapters.

BUOYANT ARMIGER

This Motif's chapters are found by opening treasure chests. While exceptionally rare, they will appear more often for players who've completed Vvardenfell's main quest line and restored Vivec's power, or for players who've completed the museum quest line. Completing both will result in the best possible chance of finding these Motif chapters, but even then they will be quite the rare find indeed.

The style item's raw component, Viridian Dust, can be found by harvesting cloth, metal, and wood throughout Vvardenfell. The more chapters of the Buoyant Armiger style you know, the more likely you'll be to find Viridian Dust, but even if you don't know anything about how to craft Buoyant Armiger, you'll still have a chance to find some. Once you've found 10 of the raw material, refine it at any equipment crafting station to craft Volcanic Viridian, which can then be used to craft in this style.

MILITANT ORDINATOR

The chapters for this style are exclusively sold by Colotarion, the Battleground Elite Merchant, in the Vivec City Battlegrounds camp. The chapters cost a significant amount of AP (Alliance Points), earned through PvP combat, both in Cyrodiil and the Imperial City, or in Battlegrounds. The chapters cost as much as 500,000 AP.

The style item is sold by the same Merchant in its raw form, Dull Sphalerite, for 5,000 AP apiece. You must obtain 10 of these, refine them into Lustrous Sphalerite at an equipment crafting station, and then use that to craft an item in this style.

MORAG TONG

This Motif's chapters can be found by completing the world boss and delve boss daily quests in Vvardenfell. They drop rarely, so they're not a guarantee. The style item, Boiled Carapace, is found the same way, but more commonly.

CRAFTING PROFESSIONS

The six types of crafting professions you can attempt are as follows:

 Alchemy  Blacksmithing  Clothing  Enchanting  Provisioning  Woodworking

ALCHEMY

Learn the art of combining ingredients in the form of reagents and solvents to create beneficial potions or debilitating poisons. Find your crafting station at apothecaries, usually where an Alchemist vendor resides.

If you value the thrill of arcane experimentation by mixing a variety of (sometimes foul-smelling) reagents and solvents to create elixirs or deadly poisons, seek out Alchemy as a pastime.

Alchemy is the creation of potions that grant enhancements to your stats for a short amount of time, and poisons that inflict detriments on an enemy's stats. The potency of such liquids is usually higher than that of, say, drinks you would create in Provisioning crafting, but it doesn't last nearly as long.

WHY BECOME AN ALCHEMIST?

The crafting is initially straightforward, and the more complex ingredient combinations can yield highly potent results. These can add substantially to your combat prowess. They can also be sold to make money.

To craft a potion or poison, there are two important elements you need to combine. These are reagents and solvents, which are combined at an Alchemy Station. This sounds rather simple, and initially it is, but it becomes more complicated once you attempt to combine ingredients to learn their properties, or craft poisons.

The key to mastering this trade skill is experimentation. When you smith or enchant an item, you already know what the end result is going to be. Not so with Alchemy. You often have no idea what you're making, which leads to excitement at the possibility of discovering a powerful new potion or effect.

Reagents are the base ingredients for a potion or poison, and are the by-products of certain animals, flowers, fungi, or herbs. They're naturally occurring throughout Tamriel, and combining different reagents gives you a wide variety of results. Scour the lands, collecting every reagent you see, including those previously picked (found in scenery); the wider your variety of ingredients, the more quickly your skill advances. If you have the gold, you can also purchase ingredients from traders.

Solvents are a variety of waters and oils that combine with two or more reagents to create the potion or poison. Solvents have a level associated with them, which determines the potency of the end product. You'll find solvents in waterlogged areas of Tamriel such as rivers and streams (denoted by a small splash disturbance), as well as in bottles and Water Skins, and sitting in or on scenery. Need higher-level solvents? Find them in higher-level zones. Solvents can also be bought from traders.

In summary, the process of Alchemy involves foraging for ingredients (reagents), learning their effects, combining them with solvents, and experimenting with combinations to make potions and poisons.

REAGENTS

Take to the hills, valleys, and less-desirable countryside in search of flowers to pick, small animals to bludgeon, and reagents to gather.

The key to perfecting your potions and poisons is to learn the variety of effects each reagent grants you, both positive and negative. Since our guide lets you skip the trial and error of the experimentation process, you can (and should) start making potions that combine two or more reagents with the same effect. Potions are usually used on you or a friendly character, which means you need to minimize a reagent's harmful effects. To start with, don't combine reagents with two identical detrimental effects.

The following table lists all available reagents and their effects. Those marked with a "(+)" are positive effects. Those marked with a "(-)" are negative effects.

ALCHEMY: REAGENTS EFFECTS

REAGENT	EFFECT 1	EFFECT 2	EFFECT 3	EFFECT 4	GENERAL LOCATION FOUND
BEETLE SCUTTLE	(-) Lower Spell Resistance	(+) Protection	(+) Increase Armor	(+) Vitality	Looted from Assassin Beetles, Beetles, Shalks, and Thunderbugs
BLESSED THISTLE	(+) Restore Stamina	(+) Increase Weapon Power	(-) Ravage Health	(+) Speed	Harvested throughout the lands
BLUE ENTOLOMA	(-) Ravage Magicka	(-) Lower Spell Power	(+) Restore Health	(+) Invisible	Harvested throughout the lands
BUGLOSS	(+) Increase Spell Resistance	(+) Restore Health	(-) Lower Spell Power	(+) Restore Magicka	Harvested throughout the lands
BUTTERFLY WING	(+) Restore Health	(+) Sustained Restore Health	(-) Lower Spell Critical	(+) Vitality	Looted from Butterflies
COLUMBINE	(+) Restore Health	(+) Restore Magicka	(+) Restore Stamina	(+) Unstoppable	Harvested throughout the lands

REAGENT	EFFECT 1	EFFECT 2	EFFECT 3	EFFECT 4	GENERAL LOCATION FOUND
CORN FLOWER	(+) Restore Magicka	(+) Increase Spell Power	(-) Ravage Health	(+) Detection	Harvested throughout the lands
DRAGONTHORN	(+) Increase Weapon Power	(+) Restore Stamina	(-) Lower Armor	(+) Weapon Critical	Harvested throughout the lands
EMETIC RUSSULA	(-) Ravage Health	(-) Ravage Magicka	(-) Ravage Stamina	(-) Stun	Harvested throughout the lands
FLESHFLY LARVA	(-) Ravage Stamina	(-) Creeping Ravage Health	(-) Vulnerability	(+) Vitality	Looted from Fleshflies and Zombies
IMP STOOL	(-) Lower Weapon Power	(-) Ravage Stamina	(+) Increase Armor	(-) Lower Weapon Critical	Harvested throughout the lands
LADY'S SMOCK	(+) Increase Spell Power	(+) Restore Magicka	(-) Lower Spell Resistance	(+) Spell Critical	Harvested throughout the lands
LUMINOUS RUSSULA	(-) Ravage Stamina	(-) Lower Weapon Power	(+) Restore Health	(-) Reduced Speed	Harvested throughout the lands
MOUNTAIN FLOWER	(+) Increase Armor	(+) Restore Health	(-) Lower Weapon Power	(+) Restore Stamina	Harvested throughout the lands
MUDCRAB CHITIN	(+) Increase Spell Resistance	(+) Protection	(+) Increase Armor	(-) Defile	Looted from Mudcrabs
NAMIRA'S ROT	(+) Spell Critical	(+) Speed	(+) Invisible	(+) Unstoppable	Harvested throughout the lands
NIGHTSHADE	(-) Ravage Health	(-) Creeping Ravage Health	(+) Protection	(-) Defile	Harvested throughout the lands
NIRNROOT	(-) Ravage Health	(-) Lower Spell Critical	(-) Lower Weapon Critical	(+) Invisible	Harvested throughout the lands
SCRIB JELLY	(-) Ravage Magicka	(-) Vulnerability	(+) Speed	(+) Sustained Restore Health	Looted from Kwamas and Scribs
SPIDER EGG	(-) Reduced Speed	(+) Sustained Restore Health	(+) Invisible	(-) Defile	Looted from Spiders
STINKHORN	(-) Lower Armor	(-) Ravage Health	(+) Increase Weapon Power	(-) Ravage Stamina	Harvested throughout the lands
TORCHBUG THORAX	(-) Lower Armor	(-) Lower Weapon Critical	(+) Detection	(+) Vitality	Looted from Torchbugs
VIOLET COPRINUS	(-) Lower Spell Resistance	(-) Ravage Health	(+) Increase Spell Power	(-) Ravage Magicka	Harvested throughout the lands
WATER HYACINTH	(+) Restore Health	(+) Spell Critical	(+) Weapon Critical	(-) Stun	Harvested throughout the lands
WHITE CAP	(-) Lower Spell Power	(-) Ravage Magicka	(+) Increase Spell Resistance	(+) Detection	Harvested throughout the lands
WORMWOOD	(+) Weapon Critical	(-) Reduced Speed	(+) Detection	(+) Unstoppable	Harvested throughout the lands

Knowing the effects of the available reagents, you can start to combine them to concoct appropriately potent potions and poisons. However, you still need to learn all the reagents' effects in-game; indeed, doing so is recommended, as this adds to your Inspiration. Learn the first effect of each reagent by using it. Learn the subsequent effects by mixing it with other reagents and solvents. Also consider investing Skill Points into the Laboratory Use Alchemy Attribute, which enables you to combine more reagents to create more complex potions.

EXAMPLE: A RUDIMENTARY HEALTH POTION

After harvesting a Butterfly Wing and a Spider Egg, combining them with a solvent at an Alchemy Station allows you to utilize the Sustained Restore Health effect these reagents share. Now, if you had a Scrib Jelly, you can craft a potion that's even more potent!

EXAMPLE: THE BEST REAGENTS

Study the table and you'll see that Columbine, Mountain Flower, and Namira's Rot have a variety of potent effects, making them highly collectible. Focus on these ingredients as you first begin to harvest reagents.

Keen Eye: Reagents (the Alchemy Passive Ability) is recommended when searching for these materials, as the glow they give off is more pronounced with the ability purchased.

POTION OR POISON?

As the previous table indicates, most reagents have both positive and negative effects. In the same way that two reagents with the same positive effect can be combined, so can reagents with identical negative effects. Such effects are well-suited to crafting poisons, as explained later.

SOLVENTS

Scoop out the contents of rivers and streams, or check barrels or Water Skins, and use the water types to make increasingly potent potions and poisons.

While reagents grant you the type of positive or negative effect(s) of a potion or poison, the solvent determines the potency. This liquid is combined with one or more reagents, and the level of the potion is given. The higher the level, the more potent the potion, and usually the more difficult it is to obtain the proper solvent. Find higher-level solvents in higher-level adventure zones.

It's important to remember that the Solvent Proficiency Attribute, which has eight ranks to unlock, is the key to concocting higher-level potions and poisons. The following tables indicate the different waters (for potions) and oils (for poisons) you can obtain.

ALCHEMY: SOLVENTS (WATER-BASED) FOR POTIONS

SOLVENT	SOLVENT LEVEL*	POTION LEVEL**
NATURAL WATER	1	3
CLEAR WATER	1	10
PRISTINE WATER	2	20
CLEANSED WATER	3	30
FILTERED WATER	4	40
PURIFIED WATER	5	CP 10
CLOUD MIST	6	CP 50
STAR DEW	7	CP 100
LORKHAN'S TEARS	8	CP 150

ALCHEMY: SOLVENTS (OIL-BASED) FOR POISONS

SOLVENT	SOLVENT LEVEL*	POTION LEVEL**
GREASE	1	3
ICHOR	1	10
SLIME	2	20
GALL	3	30
TEREBINTHINE	4	40
PITCH-BILE	5	CP 10
TARBLACK	6	CP 50
NIGHT OIL	7	CP 100
ALKAHEST	8	CP 150

** Solvent level indicates the rank of Solvent Proficiency you need in order to make a potion or poison with this solvent.*
*** Potion level indicates the strength of the potion or poison; the higher, the better, and the more Inspiration you receive from making it. "CP" refers to Champion Point levels needed to make the concoction.*

At this point, armed with a complete list of all reagents and solvents, you can begin to craft potions and poisons specifically tailored to your needs. Remember to increase the potency by combining two or more reagents with the same effects, and solvents of the highest levels you can find.

SCAVENGING FOR WATER AND OIL

Find waters from water skins, occasionally from containers, and from pure water locations in bodies of water. For oils, you'll have to attack revolting beasts such as Daedroths, Giants, Mammoths, Netches, Ogres, Ogrims, Trolls, and Wamasus. In addition, you may wish to join the Dark Brotherhood guild to make full use of poisons, along with quests that grant further rewards. The level of solvent found is equally based on your current level and the rank of the Solvent Proficiency Passive.

PASSIVE ABILITIES

There are six Alchemy Passive Abilities:

NAME	DESCRIPTION	PREREQUISITE
SOLVENT PROFICIENCY	This enables you to utilize higher-level waters and oils, which in turn give you more potent effects. Raise this to the general level you're adventuring in; only raise it to Rank 8 if you're easily able to obtain Lorkhan's Tears and Alkhest, or the rank goes to waste.	Eight Ranks at Levels 1, 10, 20, 30, 40, 48, 49, and 50
KEEN EYE	Only spend Skill Points on this luxury if you're really "keen" to become an Alchemist as early as possible and you can afford to forgo skills in other areas, such as weapons and armor (which isn't recommended when you're just starting out).	Reagents (Three Ranks at Levels 2, 6, and 17
MEDICINAL USE	Spend Skill Points here to extend the benefits and bonuses your potions give you. This only applies to potions, and grants a lengthier effect (from 10-30%). If you use a potion with a cooldown period, which stops you from spamming and stacking the effects of potions, Medicinal Use helps your potion outlast the cooldown. This means you get the potion's bonus without the threat of the potion running out before the cooldown period ends. Imagine, for example, the benefits of invisibility, immobility, or speed potions, without the worry that the potion will run out before you can use it again.	Three Ranks at Levels 3, 12, and 32
CHEMISTRY	This allows you to create an additional one, two, or three potions and four, eight, or 12 poisons for each rank. No additional reagents or solvents are needed, making this an excellent choice if you have the additional Skill Points to hand, you're selling potions or poisons, or you've found a potent potion you use constantly. You may wish to make use of this later into your adventure, when more helpful Alchemy skills allowing you to power-level up faster are available.	Three Ranks at Levels 12, 30, and 47
LABORATORY USE	This must-have should be taken as soon as possible. It enables you to craft three-reagent potions and poisons instead of the normal two. As three-reagent creations are more potent, this proves extremely useful.	One Rank at Level 15
SNAKEBLOOD	The biggest downside of creating potions is the negative effects associated with some reagents. This skill reduces those effects by 50%, 80%, and 100%. If you've created a potion where the negative effects are already negligible, this isn't as effective. Make use of this luxury if you're not getting the benefits of a potion.	Three Ranks at Levels 23, 33, and 43

INITIAL CONCOCTIONS

The following table provides some two-reagent examples of potions and poisons you can craft, before you spend a Skill Point on Laboratory Use. The potions don't have any major harmful effects. Start your Alchemy career with any of these concoctions:

ALCHEMY: RUDIMENTARY POTIONS AND POISONS

PRIMARY EFFECT BONUS	SECONDARY EFFECT BONUS(ES)	REAGENT 1	REAGENT 2
DETECTION	None	Cornflower	Wormwood
HEALTH	None	Bugloss	Mountain Flower
HEALTH	None	Columbine	Water Hyacinth
HEALTH	None	Mountain Flower	Water Hyacinth
HEALTH	Magicka Recovery	Bugloss	Columbine
HEALTH	Stamina Recovery	Columbine	Mountain Flower
INVISIBILITY	None	Nirnroot	Blue Entoloma
MAGICKA	None	Bugloss	Lady's Smock
MAGICKA	None	Columbine	Cornflower
MAGICKA	None	Columbine	Lady's Smock
MAGICKA	Spell Damage	Cornflower	Lady's Smock
MAGICKA	Health Recovery	Bugloss	Columbine
RAVAGE ARMOR (NEGATIVE)	Weapon Damage	Dragonthorn	Stinkhorn
SPEED	None	Blessed Thistle	Namira's Rot
SPELL CRITICAL	None	Lady's Smock	Water Hyacinth
STAMINA	None	Blessed Thistle	Columbine
STAMINA	None	Columbine	Dragonthorn
STAMINA	None	Dragonthorn	Mountain Flower
UNSTOPPABLE	None	Columbine	Namira's Rot
UNSTOPPABLE	None	Namira's Rot	Wormwood
WEAPON CRITICAL	None	Dragonthorn	Water Hyacith
WEAPON CRITICAL	None Dragonthorn	Wormwood	Dragonthorn
WEAPON DAMAGE	Stamina Recovery	Blessed Thistle	Dragonthorn
RAVAGE HEALTH (POISON)	None	Blessed Thistle	Nirnroot
RAVAGE HEALTH (POISON)	None	Stinkhorn	Violet Coprinus
RAVAGE HEALTH (POISON)	None	Cornflower	Nirnroot
RAVAGE MAGICKA (POISON)	None	Violet Coprinus	White Cap
RAVAGE SPELL CRITICAL (POISON)	None	Nirnroot	White Cap
RAVAGE STAMINA (POISON)	None	Luminous Russula	Water Hyacinth
RAVAGE WEAPON CRITICAL (POISON)	None	Imp Stool	Nirnroot

THE MOST POTENT POTIONS AND POISONS

The following table provides some recommended reagents and solvents to mix together in order to create some particularly impressive potions. Note that the effects of the potion are bolstered by higher-level water (solvents), and the Laboratory Use Attribute allows three reagents to be combined.

ALCHEMY: THE BEST POTIONS

POTION PRIMARY EFFECT BONUS	SECONDARY EFFECT BONUS(ES)	REAGENT 1	REAGENT 2	REAGENT 3
ARMOR (WEAPON DAMAGE REDUCED)	None	Imp Stoll	Mountain Flower	White Cap
DETECTION INCREASE	Magicka Recovery, Spell Damage	Cornflower	Lady's Smock	Wormwood
INVISIBILITY	None	Blue Entoloma	Namira's Rot	Nirnroot
INVISIBILITY	Health Recovery	Blue Entoloma	Luminous Russula	Namira's Rot
HEALTH	None	Columbine	Imp Stool	Water Hyacinth
HEALTH	Stamina, Magicka	Bugloss	Columbine	Mountain Flower
MAGICKA	None	Bugloss	Cornflower	Lady's Smock
RAVAGE SPELL POWER (NEGATIVE)	Health Recovery, Spell Resistance	Bugloss	Columbine	White Cap
SPEED	Stamina Recovery	Blessed Thistle	Mountain Flower	Namira's Rot
SPELLS (DAMAGE)	None	Columbine	Violet Coprinus	Water Hyacinth
SPELLS (INCREASES CRITICAL AMOUNT AND DURATION)	None	Lady's Smock	Namira's Rot	Water Hyacinth
SPELLS (INCREASES CRITICAL AMOUNT AND DURATION)	Health and Magicka Recovery	Bugloss	Lady's Smock	Water Hyacinth
SPELLS (INCREASES CRITICAL AMOUNT AND DAMAGE)	Magicka Recovery	Cornflower	Lady's Smock	Water Hyacinth
SPELLS (PROTECTION FROM SPELL PROTECTION)	None	Bugloss	Cornflower	White Cap
STAMINA	None	Blessed Thistle	Columbine	Mountain Flower
UNSTOPPABLE (IMMUNITY TO KNOCKBACK)	Columbine	Namira's Rot	Wormwood	
WEAPON (INCREASES CRITICAL)	None	Dragonthorn	Stinkhorn	Wormwood
WEAPON (INCREASES CRITICAL)	Health and Stamina Recovery	Dragonthorn	Mountain Flower	Water Hyacinth

The following table provides some recommended concoctions to mix up to create some harmful poisons. These are not ingested by you, but applied to your weapon. When the weapon strikes, there's a 20% chance of the poison's effects being applied. Expect the effects to last no more than 10 seconds. Note that the effects of the poison are bolstered by higher-level oil (solvents), and the Laboratory Use Attribute allows three reagents to be mixed together. Note that with the changes in Morrowind that effect Magicka and Stamina recovery, poisons that give the player Magicka or Stamina with every hit are incredibly useful.

ALCHEMY: THE DEADLIEST POISONS

POISON PRIMARY EFFECT BONUS	SECONDARY EFFECT BONUS(ES)	REAGENT 1	REAGENT 2	REAGENT 3
RAVAGE HEALTH	None	Blessed Thistle	Cornflower	Emetic Russula
RAVAGE HEALTH	None	Cornflower	Nirnroot	Stinkhorn
RAVAGE HEALTH	Ravage Magicka	Stinkhorn	Violet Coprinus	White Cap
RAVAGE HEALTH	Ravage Stamina	Imp Stool	Stinkhorn	Violet Coprinus
RAVAGE HEALTH	Ravage Stamina and Magicka	Emetic Russula	Stinkhorn	White Cap
RAVAGE HEALTH	Ravage Stamina, Reduce Weapon Critical	Imp Stool	Nirnroot	Stinkhorn
RAVAGE HEALTH	Reduce Weapon Critical	Imp Stool	Nirnroot	Violet Coprinus
RAVAGE MAGICKA	Ravage Stamina	Emetic Russula	Luminous Russula	Violet Coprinus
RAVAGE MAGICKA	Ravage Stamina	Emetic Russula	Luminous Russula	White Cap
RAVAGE STAMINA	None	Imp Stool	Luminous Russula	Stinkhorn

POISON PRIMARY EFFECT BONUS	SECONDARY EFFECT BONUS(ES)	REAGENT 1	REAGENT 2	REAGENT 3
RAVAGE STAMINA	Reduce Weapon Damage	Emetic Russula	Imp Stool	Luminous Russula
RAVAGE WEAPON DAMAGE	None	Emetic Russula	Luminous Russula	Mountain Flower
STUN	Ravage Magicka	Emetic Russula	Water Hyacinth	White Cap
STUN	Ravage Stamina, Ravage Magicka	Emetic Russula	Imp Stool	Water Hyacinth

BLACKSMITHING

Learn the art of creating metal-based weapons and heavy armor, accomplished through a series of progressive improvements. Find your crafting station at smithies, usually where a Blacksmith vendor resides.

Blacksmithing is the art of forging quality heavy armor and metallic weaponry for fun and profit. Before you seek out a Blacksmithing Station (an anvil) that can forge the items you want, you must mine a reasonable supply of raw materials from the mountains of Tamriel. Combining different ingots, ores, and tempers makes the crafting of a variety of heavy armor and weaponry possible.

Any metal-based armor and weaponry can be deconstructed at a Blacksmithing Station for the raw materials and the traits they possess. Once these are further improved and traits added, you can create an ultimate suit of armor or metal weapon you can be justly proud of.

WHY BECOME A BLACKSMITH?

If your combat style requires you to use metal-based weapons, you favor heavy armor, and you want to create your own exceptional and augmented metallic items, then Blacksmithing is for you. The number of items you can make is also impretssive, and these can be sold, sets created, and money made.

CONSIDER YOUR OPTIONS

The crafting process for Blacksmithing is similar to Clothing and Woodworking, utilizing the following steps: acquiring of raw materials, refinement, creation, improvement, deconstruction, and researching traits.

Need to craft heavy armor or weapons made from metal? Choose Blacksmithing as a trade skill. Need to craft light or medium armor? The Clothier trade skill might suit you best. Want to craft bows, staves, and shields? Pick Woodworking.

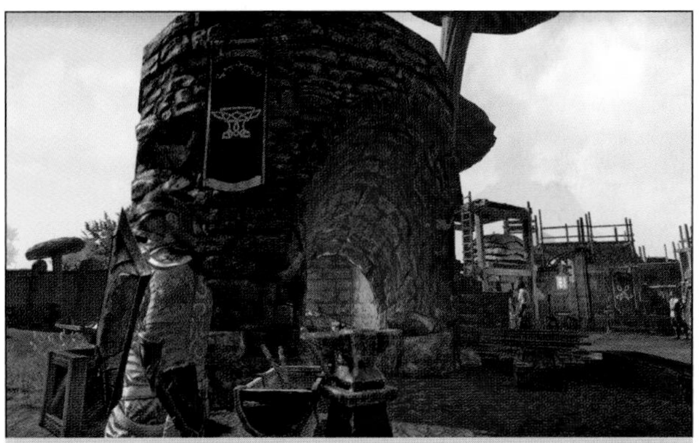

If you enjoy the sound of hammer on anvil and you have a penchant for creating heavy armor and metal weaponry, choose Blacksmithing.

PASSIVE ABILITIES

There are six Blacksmithing Passive Abilities:

NAME	DESCRIPTION	PREREQUISITE
METALWORKING	This allows access to the better-quality ingot types, from the relatively common Iron to the very rare Rubedite. If you want your items to be of increasingly better quality, and want to create items from a wider variety of ore, this is the main ability to pick from and constantly add points to.	10 Ranks at Levels 1, 5, 10, 15, 20, 25, 30, 35, 40, and 50
KEEN EYE	When mining for ore, if you're within 20, 30, or 40 meters of an ore deposit, it emits a glow—especially illuminating at night. To mine ore more quickly, or if you find ore-location tricky, pick this.	Three Ranks at Levels 2, 9, and 30
MINER HIRELING	Once per day (every 24 hours Ranks 1-2, and every 12 hours at Rank 3), and every time you log back in to your game (assuming a day has passed), your Hireling sends you ore and other random items related to improving your Blacksmithing, like tempers. This is helpful, and it's another source of raw materials.	Three Ranks at Levels 3, 12, and 32
METAL EXTRACTION	Pick this to increase the chances of extracting a greater amount of ingots, tempers, and trait materials from each refinement action.	Three Ranks at Levels 4, 22, and 32
METALLURGY	To research two traits for a weapon or heavy armor at once—or three once Rank 3 is unlocked—and lessen the research time by up to 25%, this is a must-have skill. Grab this when you're fully committed to trait research.	Four Ranks at Levels 8, 22, 28, and 42
TEMPER EXPERTISE	When you're improving an item, there's a chance of failure. This mitigates that problem somewhat, increasing the chances of improving items with tempers. Since the higher-value tempers are difficult to come by and this allows you to more easily improve items without risking their destruction, it's well worth picking.	Three Ranks at Levels 10, 25, and 40

SCAVENGING: LOCATING ORE

Chip away at the vast ore deposits of Tamriel, and don't halt until you have 10 of the same type.

Those wishing to forge metal items should check the foothills of rocky outcrops, the insides of caves, and other rocky areas throughout Tamriel for the necessary raw materials. These take the form of ore from different rock deposits. There are 10 varieties, beginning with Iron. Look for small clumps of rock rich with veins of the ore material you seek. You produce a pick-axe (which doesn't have to be bought; it's automatically used), chip the ore out of the deposit, and receive around three to four of a specific ore type in your inventory. Keep chipping at different deposits until you have at least 10 of the same type, the minimum needed to forge into ingots during the refining process.

Once you've gone on an ore-mining field trip, you need to refine your ore. Thus the creation of ingots begins. The type of ore found in the wild improves as your level increases, as well as by upgrading your Metalworking Passive Ability. Half of the nodes that you come across are scaled to your combat level, while the other half meets the rank of this passive ability. The following table lists the available ores and when they are found:

SEEING THE ORE FROM THE ROCKS

Keen Eye: Ore (the Blacksmithing Passive Ability) is recommended when searching for raw materials, as the glow they give off is more pronounced, especially at night, with the ability purchased.

Remember that each ore type can also be obtained from Hirelings (Miner Hireling Passive Ability), or as a reward when completing Blacksmithing writs.

BLACKSMITHING: RAW MATERIALS

TYPE	AVAILABLE	METALWORKING SKILL RANK REQUIRED
IRON ORE	Level 1-14	1
HIGH IRON ORE	Level 16-24	2
ORICHALC ORE	Level 26-34	3
DWARVEN ORE	Level 36-44	4
EBONY ORE	Level 46-50	5
CALCINIUM ORE	Champion Rank 10-30	6
GALATITE ORE	Champion Rank 46-60	7
QUICKSILVER ORE	Champion Rank 70-80	8
VOIDSTONE ORE	Champion Rank 90-140	9
RUBEDITE ORE	Champion Rank 150-160	10

REFINING: PROCESSED MATERIALS

Find a Blacksmithing Station, and melt these lumps of ore into ingots so they're ready to be crafted into metal heavy armor or a variety of weapons.

Refined ore in the form of ingots is collectively known as processed material. It takes 10 pieces of raw ore to create 7-10 ingots. Ingots are then utilized in the creation of heavy armor and metallic weaponry. The type of ore indicates the level and quality of the equipment. To start with, transform the ore you've collected into ingots, and begin the crafting of items. Refining ore also has a chance to provide trait stones and tempers and is a great source for the materials.

CLOTHING

Learn the craft of combining certain animal hides and plants to create medium and light armor, accomplished through a series of progressive improvements. Find your crafting station at smithies or clothiers (not tailors).

Craft using plant-based cloth and animal hides, and create light and medium armor for yourself to wear or sell. Welcome to the fine arts of Clothing.

Becoming a Clothier involves scouring the lands for creature hides and plants that can be turned into leather and cloth, respectively, and tailored into wearable light and medium armor. This occurs at a Clothing Station. Before the items are sewn together, though, a supply of raw materials needs to be secured. Search for and harvest plants (cloth for light armor) and animals (leather for medium armor). Combining cloth or leather and tannins makes the crafting of a variety of light and medium armor possible.

Any cloth- and leather-based armor can be deconstructed at a Clothing Station for the raw materials and the traits they possess. Once these are further improved and traits added, you can create the ultimate outfit. Compared to the metal-based heavy armor of the Blacksmithing trade skill, these items offer lower defense, but a higher maneuverability.

WHY BECOME A CLOTHIER?

If your combat requires you to wear light or medium armor and you wish to sew your own robes, hats, or other outfits, then Clothing is for you. There's a variety of wearable items, which can also be sold for profit.

PASSIVE ABILITIES

There are six Clothier Passive Abilities:

NAME	DESCRIPTION	PREREQUISITE
TAILORING	This allows access to the better-quality cloth and leather types, from the relatively common Jute (cloth) and Rawhide (leather) to the very rare Ancestor Silk (cloth) and Rubedo (leather). If you want your outfits to be of increasingly better quality, and want to create items from a wider variety of cloth and leather, this is the main ability to pick from and constantly add points to.	10 Ranks at Levels 1, 5, 10, 15, 20, 25, 30, 35, 40, and 50
KEEN EYE: CLOTH	When searching for fibrous plants to collect prior to cloth-refining, if you're within 20, 30, or 40 meters of such a plant, it emits a glow—especially illuminating at night. To pick plants more quickly, or if you find plant-location tricky, pick this. Note this only helps when searching for cloth, not leather. Ignore this skill if you're only interested in crafting medium armor.	Three Ranks at Levels 2, 9, and 30
OUTFITTER HIRELING	Once per day (every 24 hours Ranks 1-2, and every 12 hours at Rank 3), and every time you log back in to your game (assuming a day has passed), your Hireling sends you cloth, leather, and other random items related to improving your Clothing, like tannins. This is helpful, and it's another source of raw materials.	Three Ranks at Levels 3, 12, and 32
UNRAVELING	Pick this to increase the chances of extracting a greater amount of clothing ingredients, better tannins, and trait materials from a single raw material.	Three Ranks at Levels 4, 22, and 32
STITCHING	To research two traits for your armor item at once—or three once Rank 3 is unlocked—and lessen the research time by up to 25%, this is a must-have skill. Grab this when you're fully committed to trait research.	Four Ranks at Levels 8, 18, 28, and 45
TANNIN EXPERTISE	When you're improving an item, there's a chance of failure. This mitigates that problem somewhat, increasing the chances of improving items with tannins. Since the higher-value tannins are difficult to come by and this allows you to more easily improve items without risking their destruction, it's well worth choosing.	Three Ranks at Levels 10, 25, and 40

SCAVENGING: LOCATING RAW MATERIALS FOR CLOTH AND LEATHER

Search the zones of Tamriel for level-appropriate fibrous plant life, and harvest it until you acquire enough raw materials for light armor fabrication.

SEPARATING THE FLAX FROM THE GRASS

Keen Eye: Cloth (the Clothier Passive Ability) is recommended when searching for plant-based raw materials for light armor, as the glow they give off is more pronounced, especially at night, with the ability purchased.

Remember that each cloth or leather type can also be obtained from Hirelings (Outfitter Hireling Passive Ability), or as a reward when completing Clothing writs.

Battle animal-like beasts across Tamriel for level-specific leather, cut from the hides of these foes. Then use the leather when sewing together your medium armor.

Slightly different methods exist for obtaining the necessary raw materials to create light armor versus medium armor. For light armor, items from fibrous plants must be refined into various types of cloth. For medium armor, items from animal hides must be refined into various types of leather. There are 10 varieties of cloth and 10 varieties of leather. The former are simply harvested by locating an appropriate fibrous plant and picking it. The latter are looted from the corpses of animals, such as wolves, that provide leather in the form of their skin. Find such a raw material to receive around three to four of its type in your inventory. Keep searching until you have 10 or more of the same type—the minimum required to sew into cloth or leather during the refining process.

Once you've done a good bit of plant-picking and animal-rustling, you need to refine your raw materials, and the creation of cloth and leather begins. The following table lists the available raw materials, and the level at which you can expect to find both the cloth and leather. The material found is equally based on your current level and Tailoring Passive Ability rank.

CLOTHING: RAW MATERIALS (LIGHT ARMOR)

TYPE	AVAILABLE	TAILORING SKILL RANK NEEDED
JUTE	Level 1-14	1
FLAX	Level 16-24	2
COTTON	Level 26-34	3
SPIDERSILK	Level 36-44	4
EBONTHREAD	Level 46-50	5
KRESHWEED	Champion Rank 10-30	6
IRONWEED	Champion Rank 46-60	7
SILVERWEED	Champion Rank 70-80	8
VOID BLOOM	Champion Rank 90-140	9
ANCESTOR SILK	Champion Rank 150-160	10

CLOTHING: RAW MATERIALS (MEDIUM ARMOR)

TYPE	AVAILABLE	TAILORING SKILL RANK NEEDED
RAWHIDE	Level 1-14	1
HIDE	Level 16-24	2
LEATHER	Level 26-34	3
THICK LEATHER	Level 36-44	4
FELL HIDE	Level 46-50	5
TOPGRAIN HIDE	Champion Rank 10-30	6
IRON HIDE	Champion Rank 46-60	7
SUPERB HIDE	Champion Rank 70-80	8
SHADOWHIDE	Champion Rank 90-140	9
RUBEDO HIDE	Champion Rank 150-160	10

REFINING: PROCESSED MATERIALS

Locate a Clothing Station, and craft this plant and animal material into cloth and leather, so they're ready to be made into light and medium armor, respectively.

Refined plants suitable for crafting take the collective name "cloth," while refined animal skins take the collectible name "leather" or "hide." Both are collectively known as processed materials. It takes 10 pieces of raw material to create 7-10 pieces of cloth or leather, which is then used in the creation of light or medium armor. The type of cloth or leather indicates the level and quality of the armor you'll be making. To start with, sew one selection of raw materials into either cloth or leather, and then start crafting armor sections afterward.

ENCHANTING

Learn the art of imbuing an item with magical runes or glyphs powered by soul energy, to grant additional effects to jewelry, weapons, and armor. Your crafting station is an Enchanting Table, usually found at a chironasium where an Enchanter vendor resides.

If you need your equipment and jewelry to really shine with magical imbuements, pick Enchanting as a profession and craft glyphs.

This trade skill enables you to gather a number of different runes from across Tamriel and hone them into glyphs with particularly helpful bonuses. The glyphs are then set into your armor, weaponry, and jewelry. This occurs at an Enchanting Table and works a little like reagents used in the Alchemy trade skill. The combination of runes you use in the Enchanting process determines the effects and impressiveness of the glyph.

To begin with, you need three different rune stones to craft a glyph. These are gathered throughout the lands at resource nodes, which look like tiny shrines and appear in a variety of colors related to the rune type. They can also be purchased from other players. Potency runes are available from Enchanters you may encounter. In addition, any of the three rune types can be obtained from a Hireling, or as an Enchanting writ reward.

The three types of runes are Aspect, Essence, and Potency. Each time you find a Runestone node, you automatically pry out an Aspect and Essence rune, and you have about a one-in-three chance of gaining a Potency rune. The runes you find are usually around the same level as either your character or your Enchanting trade skill. This means that if your character's level is high but your Enchanting level is low, you may find runes you can't use yet.

When crafted into new glyphs, your obtained runes are translated and their effects learned.

WHY BECOME AN ENCHANTER?

The crafting of runes into glyphs is reasonably straightforward. Finding the optimal trio of runes to combine has the potential to yield some impressive effects and bonuses. These effects can usually be stacked, if appropriate. They can be applied to armor, weapons, and jewelry, allowing multiple similar or different effects at once, and adding substantially to your combat prowess. Runes and glyphs can also be sold to make money.

RUNES

All runes have a strange, secretive language carved onto them, and once each rune is translated, that code is translated into a magical effect, which you can add to your created glyph. As you find runes, you'll see they come in three shapes, or types:

Aspect: These are circular in shape and affect the quality (also known as rarity) of the glyph you make. There are five variants, and the quality works in a similar way to the color-coding of other materials (white, green, blue, purple, and gold). The better the quality, the rarer the rune, and the better the final glyph will be.

Example: You find a Denata rune. It translates to "Superior" (blue) quality.

Essence: These appear to be triangular in shape, with the corners sliced off. They determine the precise Attribute or bonus the Enchanting effect will give you. There are around 20 types of Essence runes, which give you a variety of single bonuses to Health, Stamina, or Magicka (or other statistics).

Potency: This appears as a square or cube-shaped rune, and determines how powerful the effects of the glyph will be, along with the level you need to be to craft it. Potency runes are divided into two sub-groups, each including around 16 Runestones: **Additive** and **Subtractive**. As you might expect, in general terms an Additive Potency rune grants you a bonus, while a Subtractive Potency rune gives you a negative power, usually a resistance.

Example: You find a Jora rune. It translates to "Develop" and a "Trifling" title, and can be placed on Level 1-10 gear. If you combine the Makkoma Essence rune with the Jora rune, you create a Trifling Glyph of Magicka Recovery, if applied to jewelry gear.

Now that you have a basic understanding of the three types of runes, consult the following tables to learn all the variations these runes offer:

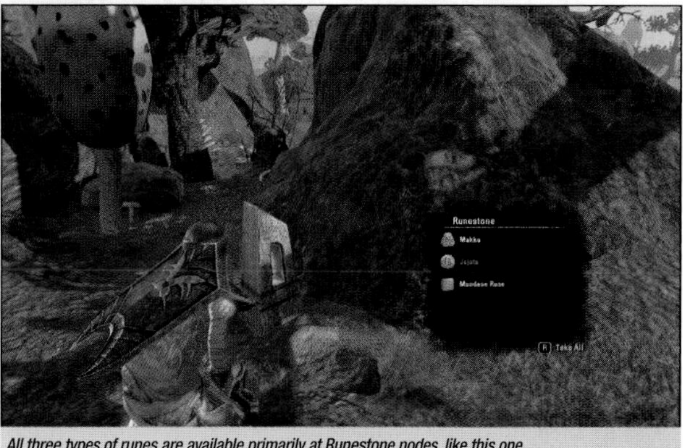

All three types of runes are available primarily at Runestone nodes, like this one.

ENCHANTING: ASPECT RUNES

NAME	TRANSLATION	GLYPH QUALITY
TA	Common	White
JEJOTA	Fine	Green
DENATA	Superior	Blue
REKUTA	Artifact	Purple
KUTA	Legendary	Gold

ENCHANTING: ESSENCE RUNES

NAME	TRANSLATION	EXAMPLE EFFECTS (ADDITIVE/SUBTRACTIVE)*
DAKEIPA	Frost	Frost Damage/Resistance
DENI	Stamina	Stamina Recovery/Maximum Stamina Improvement
DENIMA	Stamina Recovery	Stamina Recovery/Reduced Stamina Cost
DETERI	Armor	Shield Damage/Target's Armor Reduced
HAKEIJO	Prism	Prismatic Defense (Maximum Health, Stamina, Magicka)/Magic Damage to Daedra and Undead
HAOKO	Disease	Disease Damage/Disease Resistance
JAEDI	Shield	Reduced Bash and Blocking Cost (Subtractive only)**
KADERI	Shield	Reduced Bash and Blocking Cost (Subtractive only)
KUOKO	Poison	Poison Damage/Poison Resistance
LIRE	Physical Harm	Weapon Damage/Greater Armor Resistance**

NAME	TRANSLATION	EXAMPLE EFFECTS (ADDITIVE/SUBTRACTIVE)*
MAKDERI	Spell Harm	Spell Damage/Spell Resistance
MAKKO	Magicka	Magic Damage and Recovery/Maximum Magicka Improvement
MAKKOMA	Magicka Recovery	Magicka Recovery/Reduced Magicka Spell Cost
MEIP	Shock	Shock Damage/Shock Resistance
OKO	Health	Health Recovery/Maximum Health Improvement
OKOMA	Health Recovery	Damage (ignoring defenses) /Health Recovery
OKORI	Power	Increased Power (wearer)/Reduced Power (target)
ORU	Alchemist	Potion Effect Improvement/Reduced Potion Cooldown
RAKEIPA	Fire	Fire Damage/Fire Resistance
TADERI	Physical Harm	Weapon Damage/Greater Armor Resistance

** These are examples of the general effect you should expect, though there are more, and variations depend on the type of Potency rune and whether the glyph you create is placed on armor, weapons, or jewelry.*
*** These runes are usually no longer used in Enchanting, and should be kept as keepsakes or sold.*

ENCHANTING: POTENCY RUNES (ADDITIVE AND SUBTRACTIVE)

ADDITIVE NAME (TRANSLATION)	SUBTRACTIVE NAME (TRANSLATION)	GLYPH PREFIX	POTENCY LEVEL	EQUIPMENT LEVEL*
JORA (DEVELOP)	JODE (REDUCE)	Trifling	1	Levels 01-10
PORADE (ADD)	NOTADE (SUBTRACT)	Inferior	1	Levels 05-15
JERA (INCREASE)	ODE (SHRINK)	Petty	2	Levels 10-20
JEJORA (RAISE)	TADE (DECREASE)	Slight	2	Levels 15-25
ODRA (GAIN)	JAYDE (DEDUCT)	Minor	3	Levels 20-30
POJORA (SUPPLEMENT)	EDODE (LOWER)	Lesser	3	Levels 25-35
EDORA (BOOST)	POJODE (DIMINISH)	Moderate	4	Levels 30-40
JAERA (ADVANCE)	REKUDE (WEAKEN)	Average	4	Levels 35-45
PORA (AUGMENT)	HADE (LESSEN)	Strong	5	Levels 40-50
DENARA (STRENGTHEN)	IDODE (IMPAIR)	Major	5	Levels CP 10-30
RERA (EXAGGERATE)	PODE (REMOVE)	Greater	6	Levels CP 30-50
DERADO (EMPOWER)	KEDEKO (DRAIN)	Grand	7	Levels CP 50-70
REKURA (MAGNIFY)	REDE (DEPRIVE)	Splendid	8	Levels CP 70-90
KURA (INTENSIFY)	KUDE (NEGATE)	Monumental	9	Levels CP 100-140
REJERA (INTENSIFY)	JEHADE (NEGATE)	Superb	9	Level CP 150
REPORA (INTENSIFY)	ITADE (NEGATE)	Truly Superb	9	Level CP 160

** Your gear must at least meet this range of levels in order to imbue it with the resulting glyph.*

Once you know the general effects of the three types of runes, you can begin to enchant them into appropriately potent glyphs for your various gear

PASSIVE ABILITIES

There are five Enchanting Passive Abilities:

NAME	DESCRIPTION	PREREQUISITE
ASPECT IMPROVEMENT	This is important when enchanting with the various Aspect Runestones, as it allows you to utilize the better-quality, color-coded types: Standard/green, Superior/blue, Artifact/purple, and finally Legendary/gold. The higher the quality, the better the statistical bonuses of your glyph. Invest in this as soon as you can, or the moment you receive a more potent Aspect Runestone and you have enough levels to do so. Four Ranks at Levels 1, 6, 16, and 31	10 Ranks at Levels 1, 5, 10, 15, 20, 25, 30, 35, 40, and 50
POTENCY IMPROVEMENT	This is arguably the key to enchanting better glyphs. It enables you to unlock the use of the more impressive Potency Runestones, increasing the level of the glyph you enchant. Simply put, if you don't invest in this skill, you can't access the better Potency Runestones listed in the previous table, and your glyphs won't be nearly as powerful. This is also the key to power-leveling as an Enchanter.	10 Ranks at Levels 1, 5, 10, 15, 20, 25, 30, 35, 40, and 50
KEEN EYE: RUNESTONES	This enables you to spot Runestone nodes more easily, especially at night, as a glow emits from them at 20, 30, or 40 meters. However, as these nodes are reasonably easy to spot, this ability isn't really necessary, unless you're a completionist.	Three Ranks at Levels 2, 7, and 14
HIRELING	A Hireling will do the Runestone rummaging and searching for you, returning once every 24 hours (at Ranks 1 and 2) with a number of Runestones, possibly including some rarer ones. At Rank 3, the Hireling becomes an Enchanter who gathers Runestones every 12 hours. What's better than free Runestones? Free Runestones you don't have to search for!	Three Ranks at Levels 3, 12, and 32
ASPECT EXTRACTION	The most proficient way to gain Inspiration when enchanting is to break down, or deconstruct, a glyph a fellow adventurer has made, separating it into its component parts. Though there's a chance the runes will be destroyed during the process, this ability increases the chances of successful extraction by up to 10%. This becomes more helpful when you're hoping for rarer or more powerful Runestones.	Three Ranks at Levels 4, 19, and 29

GLYPHS

With a basic understanding of every rune type, head to an Enchanting Table and begin crafting glyphs! Even though your character may not know the effects of some runes in-game, you can still combine one of each type and create a glyph as if the effects are known, assuming you've unlocked any necessary Enchanting Passive Abilities.

ADDING TO YOUR GEAR

Once you've translated the runes, place one of each type to display the glyph you're about to create. Some differences apply when creating an armor, weapon, or jewelry glyph. Armor glyphs are only craftable using Additive Potency runes. Weapon and jewelry glyphs can be created using either Additive or Subtractive Potency runes. Note the shape and color of the glyph icon in the middle menu box, and craft away.

Afterward, choose the apparel you want to enchant (remember, you need to have armor, weapons, or jewelry to fit an enchantment on!), and make sure you enchant the glyph you favor onto it. Now the glyph becomes active and useful.

Prior to completion, make sure to compare the before-and-after stats of your gear so you know whether the enchantment is worthwhile. You don't, for example, want to enchant a Champion-level sword with a Trifling glyph, now, do you?

Armor glyphs are particularly potent, as you can add this type to every single part of your protective gear. However, you only receive the full benefit of the statistical increases if you place your glyph on your head, chest, legs, or shield armor. Your shoulders, hands, waist, and feet armor only receive a portion of the effect, and should therefore be augmented later.

RECHARGING GLYPHS: SOUL GEMS

Glyph enchantments have an energy bar associated with them, shown on the gear you place the glyph on. These glyphs work at the same strength until the bar is depleted, and then stop working completely. They need to be recharged using Soul Gems. The better the enchantment, the higher the quality of Soul Gem needed. Buy Soul Gems at the Mages Guild, or receive them for killing bosses in dungeons, or for trapping souls using spells from the Soul Magic skill line.

The following table lists the available glyphs you're able to create, along with their general effects. To find the rune you need to make a glyph, consult the tables earlier in this section of the guide.

ENCHANTING: AVAILABLE GLYPHS

TYPE	NAME	EFFECTS
Armor	Glyph of Health	Maximum Health Improvement
Armor	Glyph of Magicka	Maximum Magicka Improvement
Armor	Glyph of Prismatic Defense	Health, Magicka, Stamina Improvements
Armor	Glyph of Stamina	Maximum Stamina Improvement
Jewelry	Glyph of Bashing	Increased Bash Damage
Jewelry	Glyph of Decreased Physical Harm	Increased Armor
Jewelry	Glyph of Decreased Spell Harm	Increased Spell Resistance
Jewelry	Glyph of Disease Resistance	Increased Disease Resistance
Jewelry	Glyph of Fire Resistance	Increased Fire Resistance
Jewelry	Glyph of Frost Resistance	Increased Frost Resistance
Jewelry	Glyph of Health Recovery	Increased Health Recovery
Jewelry	Glyph of Increased Magical Harm	Increased Spell Damage
Jewelry	Glyph of Increased Physical Harm	Increased Weapon Damage
Jewelry	Glyph of Magicka Recovery	Increased Magicka Recovery
Jewelry	Glyph of Poison Resistance	Increased Poison Resistance
Jewelry	Glyph of Potion Boost	Increased Potion Potency
Jewelry	Glyph of Potion Speed	Reduced Potion Cooldown
Jewelry	Glyph of Reduced Feat Cost	Reduced Stamina Cost for Abilities
Jewelry	Glyph of Reduced Spell Cost	Reduced Magicka Cost for Spells
Jewelry	Glyph of Shielding	Reduced Bashing and Blocking Cost
Jewelry	Glyph of Shock Resistance	Increased Shock Resistance
Jewelry	Glyph of Stamina Recovery	Increased Stamina Recovery
Weapon	Glyph of Absorb Health	Health Recovery and Magic Damage
Weapon	Glyph of Absorb Magicka	Magicka Recovery and Magic Damage
Weapon	Glyph of Absorb Stamina	Stamina Recovery and Magic Damage
Weapon	Glyph of Crushing	Decreases Enemy's Armor Temporarily
Weapon	Glyph of Decrease Health	Inflicts Unresistable Damage
Weapon	Glyph of Fire	Inflicts Fire Damage
Weapon	Glyph of Foulness	Inflicts Disease Damage
Weapon	Glyph of Frost	Inflicts Frost Damage
Weapon	Glyph of Hardening	Grants Damage Shield Temporarily
Weapon	Glyph of Poison	Inflicts Poison Damage
Weapon	Glyph of Prismatic Onslaught	Deals Magic Damage to Daedra and Undead
Weapon	Glyph of Rage	Increases Your Power Temporarily
Weapon	Glyph of Shock	Inflicts Shock Damage
Weapon	Glyph of Weakening	Decreases Enemy Power Temporarily

EXTRACTING GLYPHS

The Enchanting Table has an Extraction menu where you can take glyphs you've acquired, either by making them yourself or obtaining them from traders or other players, and deconstruct them into separate runes. There's a chance you'll receive one or more runes, or nothing at all. Increase the chances of obtaining runes by spending points in the Aspect Extraction Passive Ability. The main reason for extracting glyphs is to gain Inspiration; extraction grants you the most leveling potential in a trade skill that is otherwise lengthy to level up.

PROVISIONING

Learn the craft of studying recipes, then combining and converting base ingredients into consumable food and drink, usually to grant temporary buffs. Your "crafting station" is simply a Cooking Fire, typically found at camps or inns.

From the lowly Fishy Stick to the Legendary Psijic Ambrosia, the art of cooking up base ingredients into long-lasting Attribute-boosting meals is an excellent way to perfect a trade skill.

Provisioning is the crafting of delicious food and drink consumables that enhance your stats for a finite amount of time. The effects of food and drink last longer than Alchemy-based consumables, and continue to function even if you die.

WHY BECOME A PROVISIONER?

The crafting is straightforward. The benefits of food and drink are long-lasting. The profitability when selling food and drink is high, especially as you gain Inspiration and craft higher-level consumables.

To craft food or drink, you need a recipe—instructions on how to make a particular consumable—and a number of base ingredients. The number depends on the complexity of the recipe, ranging from one to four.

Recipes can be found in scenery (desks, crates, barrels, chests), gained from other characters, looted from foes, awarded for completing crafting writs, or purchased from traders. Simply look at the recipe in your inventory to learn it; the recipe then appears when you use a Cooking Fire.

Ingredients can be found growing, obtained by hunting or fishing, slaying animals, receiving deliveries from your Hirelings, searching the same type of scenery as for finding recipes, completing crafting writs, or purchased from traders.

The quality of recipes and ingredients you scavenge depends on two factors: your location and level. You can also purchase items from traders and Guild Stores, which is helpful in sourcing rarer items, or ones you're not easily able to find.

The created consumable provides a beneficial effect. It also has an appropriate level related to its recipe. Such levels grant you more Inspiration, but crafting the best recipes requires ranks of the Recipe Improvement Passive Ability. In general, the higher the recipe level, the more potent the effects of the consumable created.

Generally speaking, food grants buffs to your Attributes: Health (meat), Stamina (vegetables), and Magicka (fruit). Drink, meanwhile, grants buffs to your recovery: Health (alcohol), Stamina (tonics) and Magicka (teas).

COLOR-CODED RECIPES

In order to make more useful items from your base ingredients, you require better recipes. These are color-coded: Normal/white, Magic/green, Arcane/blue, Artifact/purple, and Legendary/gold (for making Psijic Ambrosia).

Make note of the color of the recipe you find or purchase; there's a color-coding to these creations!

Aside from Normal, the easiest recipes are green, which usually require two different items and grant you a reasonably good end product to use or sell when starting out.

Blue recipes require a combination of three items, while purple recipes require four. Balance the time it takes to find these ingredients with the additional Inspiration you gain from making more complex recipes. For example, it's sometimes easier to craft multiple green or blue recipes, compared to one or two purple ones if you're only concerned with Inspiration leveling.

Locate a Cooking Fire to see the list of items you're able to create. You can select them by ingredients or skills. When you choose an item, be sure to view its level, and craft the item with the highest available level your Recipe Improvement skill rank allows. Higher-level recipes grant more potent effects and gain you more Inspiration.

PASSIVE ABILITIES

There are seven Provisioning Passive Abilities:

NAME	DESCRIPTION	PREREQUISITE
RECIPE QUALITY	This is important for unlocking blue recipes, as it gives you a better rate of return on the quality of your food and drink, as well as more Inspiration.	Four Ranks at Levels 1, 10, 35, and 50
RECIPE IMPROVEMENT	Max this out, as it enables you to concoct the very best recipes.	Six Ranks at Levels 1, 20, 30, 40, 50, and 60
GOURMAND AND CONNOISSEUR	These are worth considering once you fully commit to being a Provisoner. They add duration to the effects of any consumed food or drink, respectively, that you make. For consumables such as the fabled Psijic Ambrosia, a drink that adds significantly to your XP, the duration bonus is particularly beneficial.	Gourmand:Three Ranks at Levels 3, 14, and 43 Connoisseur: Three Ranks at Levels 5, 25, and 47
CHEF AND BREWER	an extra serving to each food and drink consumable, respectively, that you craft. They're worth considering, but only if you intend to make Provisioning a primary trade skill and can spare the Skill Points. The bonus these skills offers is obvious, though!	Chef: Three Ranks at Levels 7, 23, and 33 Brewer: Three Ranks at Levels 9, 25, and 36
HIRELING	A Provisioner Hireling brings you a package of food and drink ingredients every 24 or 12 hours (every 24 hours Ranks 1-2, and every 12 hours at Rank 3).	Three Ranks at Levels 28, 38, and 48

ENDGAME: GOLD RECIPES

One of the best Legendary recipes is for the fabled Psijic Ambrosia. Acquiring this one takes time and patience, as the recipe comes in seven fragments, and the three ingredients needed are also difficult to come by. Each fragment is randomly awarded once you've completed the following:

Time to take up fishing! One of the ingredients for this fabled drink is Perfect Roe, found randomly once you fillet a fish at Master Provisioner level.

- Increased your Recipe Quality skill to Rank 4 (maximum)
- Increased your Recipe Improvement skill to Rank 6 (maximum)
- Reached Level 50, a Master Provisioner
- Become certified, and continuously completed Provisioning crafting writs until the seven pieces of the recipe are randomly awarded to you

Two of the three ingredients, Bervez Juice and Frost Mirriam, are found as rewards randomly given to you at the end of crafting writs, just like the fragments of the recipe. Or you can loot them or purchase them from traders.

The Perfect Roe is randomly found by filleting fish you've caught at a Fishing Hole. This takes time, usually minutes or hours, so try for patience, and perhaps perfect your fishing by attempting to achieve the Master Angler title at the same time.

Another option is to team up with like-minded guild members to obtain Psijic Ambrosia recipe fragments and ingredients within a shorter time frame. You can also use multiple characters to heighten your chances, and share the loot between them, turning specific characters into Provisioning machines you can then share goods with. Or you can purchase the completed Psijic Ambrosia recipe from a Guild Store, if you have the gold.

Psijic Ambrosia itself is a drink that grants you a 50% Experience Point bonus from all sources for 30 minutes. Before you create this incredible elixir, think about purchasing the Brewer Passive Ability to create additional servings, and Connoisseur to add more time to the effects.

WOODWORKING

Learn the art of carving untreated wood from across the land into bows, shields, and staves. Your crafting station is found at carpentries, usually where a Carpenter vendor resides.

Woodworking involves the crafting of different types of wood, extracting ingredients from this wood, refining raw materials, optionally adding resins to create improved items, deconstructing items, and destroying finished, wood-based items to research a trait. All of this is done at a Woodworking Station.

WHY BECOME A WOODWORKER?

If you're focusing on archery or the use of staves, you can create your own, impressively augmented weapons as well as some fine protective shields. The Skill Point expenditure is low to begin with, and only wood of various types is used, meaning fewer raw ingredients to forage for.

PASSIVE ABILITIES

There are six Woodworking Passive Abilities:

NAME	DESCRIPTION	PREREQUISITE
WOODWORKING	This allows access to the better-quality wood types, from the lowly Maple to the coveted Ruby Ash. If you want your items to be of increasingly better quality, and want to create items from a wider variety of wood, this is the main ability to pick from and constantly add points to.	10 Ranks at Levels 1, 5, 10, 15, 20, 25, 30, 35, 40, and 50
KEEN EYE	If you're within 20, 30, or 40 meters of logs in the wild when collecting lumber, they emit a glow—especially illuminating at night. Pick this to grab rough logs more quickly, or if you find log-location tricky.	Three Ranks at Levels 2, 9, and 30
LUMBERJACK HIRELING	Once per day, and every time you log back in to your game (assuming a day has passed), your Hireling sends you wood and other random items related to improving your Woodworking, like resins (once every 24 hours Ranks 1-2, and every 12 hours at Rank 3). This is helpful, and it's another source of raw materials.	Three Ranks at Levels 4, 12, and 32
WOOD EXTRACTION	Pick this to increase the chances of extracting a greater amount of wood, resins, and trait materials from each refinement attempt.	Three Ranks at Levels 6, 18, and 32
CARPENTRY	To research two traits for a wooden bow or other item at once—or three once Rank 3 is unlocked—and lessen the research time by up to 25%, this is a must-have skill. Grab this when you're fully committed to trait research.	Four Ranks at Levels 8, 22, 28, and 45
RESIN EXPERTISE	When you're improving an item, there's a chance of failure. This mitigates that problem somewhat, increasing the chances of improving items with resins. Since the higher-value resins are difficult to come by and this allows you to more easily improve items without risking their destruction, it's well worth picking.	Three Ranks at Levels 10, 25, and 40

SCAVENGING: LOCATING ROUGH WOOD

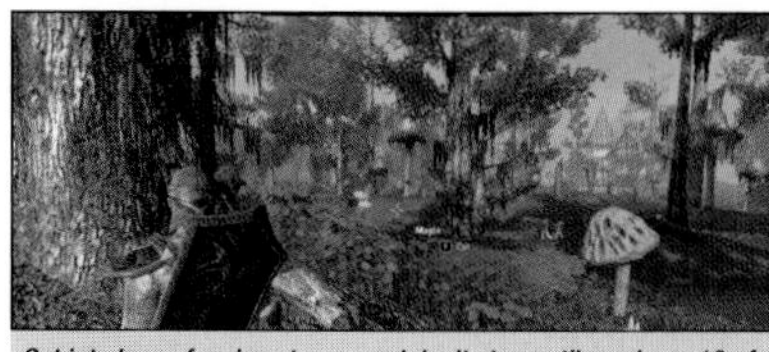

Cut into logs of various types, and don't stop until you have 10 of the same type.

To craft with wood, start with raw materials. These are logs from a varieties of trees, beginning with Maple. There are 10 varieties, and they can be found, as you'd expect, in the wooded areas and forests across Tamriel, as well as on the outskirts of settlements, the sides of roads, and dotted around rivers and streams. You're not looking to fell trees, but for large log sections of different wood varieties. Take out your axe (which doesn't have to be bought; it's automatically used), cut into these wood deposits, and you receive around three to four "rough" logs in your inventory. Keep going until you have at least 10 of the same type, as that's what's needed to create a "sanded" version in the refining process.

SEEING THE WOOD FROM THE TREES

Keen Eye: Wood (the Woodworking Passive Ability) is recommended when searching for raw materials, as the glow they give off is more pronounced, especially at night, with the ability purchased.

Remember that each wood type can also be obtained from Hirelings (Lumberjack Hireling Passive Ability), or as a reward when completing Woodworking writs.

Now, you can't create a bow by simply adding a piece of string to a log, so the rough raw materials need to be refined to create sanded versions. The following table lists the available woods, and the level at which you can expect to find raw materials. The wood found depends equally on your current level and the rank of your Woodworking Passive Ability.

REFINING: PROCESSED MATERIALS

Sanded sections of wood are collectively known as processed materials, and it takes 10 pieces of rough wood to make 7-10 sanded pieces. Sanded wood is then used as an ingredient to craft wooden weapons and shields. The type of wood indicates the level of the bow, staff, or shield. Simply use up the rough wood you've collected, and turn it into sanded varieties so you can start crafting items.

WOODWORKING: RAW MATERIALS

TYPE	AVAILABLE	WOODWORKING SKILL RANK NEEDED
ROUGH MAPLE	Level 1-14	1
ROUGH OAK	Level 16-24	2
ROUGH BEECH	Level 26-34	3
ROUGH HICKORY	Level 36-44	4
ROUGH YEW	Level 46-50	5
ROUGH BIRCH	Champion Rank 10-30	6
ROUGH ASH	Champion Rank 46-60	7
ROUGH MAHOGANY	Champion Rank 70-80	8
ROUGH NIGHTWOOD	Champion Rank 90-140	9
ROUGH RUBY ASH	Champion Rank 150-160	10

EQUIPMENT PROFESSIONS: YOUR GEAR'S LIFE CYCLE

The three equipment trade skills—Blacksmithing, Clothing, and Woodworking—share a number of processes and features. This section seeks to detail the stages through which your gear progresses, from the creation of a piece of equipment, through any improvements you wish to make, all the way to its eventual deconstruction, which provides you with parts to start the cycle anew.

ITEM CREATION

PART 1: TYPE AND MATERIAL

At a Blacksmithing Station, Clothing Station, or Woodworking Station, access the Creation menu. You should notice sub-menus for Type, Material, Style, and Trait. To begin with, focus on the type and material of equipment you're about to make.

Type: This is the type of creation you end up crafting. You might forge a metal sword or axe at a Blacksmithing Station, or a protective hat or robe at a Clothing Station. Or maybe a Woodworking creation like a bow or shield is more your speed.

You can add to the variety of gear you craft by applying different styles and adding traits. When you're starting out, it's a good idea to focus on this menu, picking equipment best suited to how you fight.

Material: This is the inventory of all the materials you've processed. If you've spent Skill Points in your crafting station's corresponding skill (Metalworking, Tailoring, or Woodworking), a variety of available, previously acquired materials appears here, ready for combining. If you haven't spent points in one of these skills, only the most basic material type is available—plus any materials you may have scavenged, bought, or been given by a Hireling.

A range of levels exists for creating items, even when using the same type of material. This is because you can add more of the same material in your Material menu and create a higher-level item, up to the maximum allowed. For example, to forge a High Iron Axe at a Blacksmithing Station, the base level would be 16. However, if you add more High Iron Ore ingots, you can raise the level up to 24. The higher the level, the better the item quality, at the expense of your raw materials.

BUILDING THE BASICS

Blacksmiths, Clothiers, amd Woodworkers can each forge two groups of gear. Consult the following tables:

Blacksmith Rudimentary Equipment

WEAPONS		HEAVY ARMOR
One-handed:	**Two-handed:**	**Head:** Helm
Axe	Battle Axe	**Chest:** Cuirass
Sword	Greatsword	**Waist:** Girdle
Hammer	Maul	**Shoulders:** Pauldrons
Dagger		**Hands:** Gauntlets
		Legs: Greaves
		Feet: Sabatons

These types of gear can be made in one of the 49 racial styles, and can be crafted with one or more of nine traits.

Clothier Rudimentary Outfits

LIGHT ARMOR	MEDIUM ARMOR
Head: Hat	**Head:** Helmet
Chest: Robe	**Chest:** Jack
Chest: Jerkin	**Waist:** Belt
Waist: Sash	**Shoulders:** Arm Cops
Shoulders: Epaulets	**Hands:** Bracers
Hands: Gloves	**Legs:** Guards
Legs: Breeches	**Feet:** Boots
Feet: Shoes	

Woodworking Rudimentary Equipment

WEAPONS	ARMOR
Two-handed:	**One-handed:**
Bows	Shields
Staves	

BUILDING BETTER

The level of the equipment you create is the same as the type of material used, so check the Raw Materials table. For example, to create a Hickory Bow at a Woodworking Station, you need Sanded Hickory, Level 36-44. Spend Skill Points on Passive Abilities to access rarer ores, cloth, and woods that allow you to craft better gear.

The other way to improve your item, which begins at Common quality, is through the use of improvement items: tempers for Blacksmithing, tannins for Clothing, and resins for Woodworking.

PART 2: STYLES

Style: One of the crafting menus you can choose from is Style. There are 14 styles to choose from, based on the various races in Tamriel. Your own character's race is unlocked. The others are unlocked when you find and read "Racial Motif" books found across the lands. Feel free to locate any and all of them, or buy them from other players. You also need the semi-precious stone associated with each race. These are primarily found on or in scenery, and aren't particularly rare.

Crafting gear with a different racial style from your own simply gives the item a different appearance. There are no other differing effects.

RACIAL STYLES FOR OTHER TRADE SKILLS

Good news! The books you find that unlock more racial styles apply to all three crafting professions focused on here: Blacksmithing, Clothing, and Woodworking.

PART 3: RESEARCHING AND TRAITS

Need the extra resistance to damage and spells when wading into combat? Research weapons with the Defending trait, and have Turquoise gems handy.

Is your cloth armor a little flimsy? Need to enhance its ability to resist enemy Critical Strikes? Research armor with the Impenetrable trait, and have Diamonds ready to go.

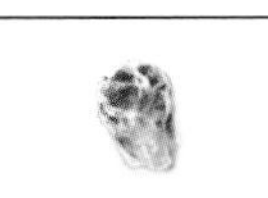

Need to fire a bow more quickly, like a fast-fingered elf? Research a bow with the Weighted trait, and prepare your Citrine gems.

Traits: The last Creation sub-menu you can access when crafting your gear is Trait. Traits are special bonuses you can add to an item when you create it, done at the same time when you're choosing the style, material, and item itself. Note that you must not only research the trait to unlock it, you need to have the material (a precious gem) on hand as well.

Researching: In order to unlock a trait, you need to research it. Traits are relevant only to the item you're creating. For example, if you're researching a trait for a weapon, you don't learn the traits for armor. You must find an item with the trait you wish to learn, and research it at the relevant crafting station. Then you wait a given amount of hours: six hours for the first trait, and double that for each additional trait for that specific item, up to 32 days for the final (eighth) trait.

Mitigate this length of time by starting research as soon as possible, and choose your profession's corresponding Passive Ability (Metallurgy, Stitching, or Carpentry) to reduce the time frame considerably. During research, the item with the trait you're learning from is destroyed, but the trait is learned and Inspiration is awarded, as well as the ability to add the trait to the item you're creating—provided you have the appropriate gem.

For a more in-depth look at traits, consult the **Traits** section, found earlier in this chapter.

BLACKSMITHS AND WOODWORKERS

In the Blacksmithing and Woodworking professions, there are distinct traits that apply to weapons (swords, bows, etc.) and armor (helmets, shields, etc.).

ITEM IMPROVEMENT: TEMPERS, TANNINS, AND RESINS

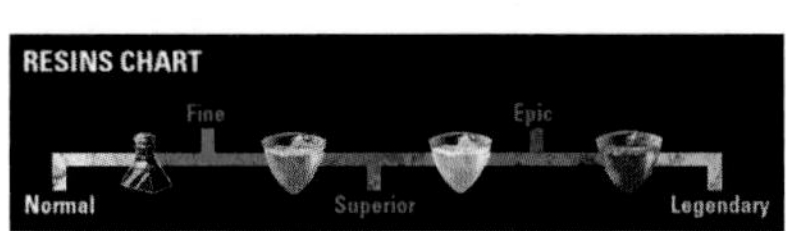

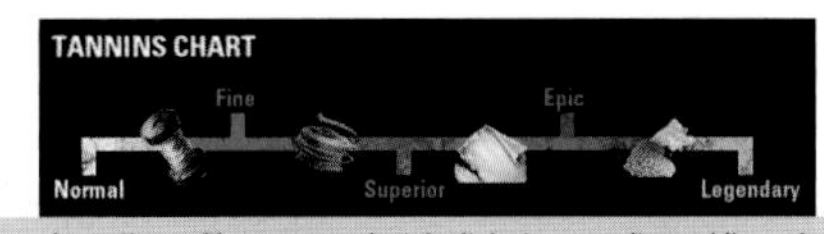

Increase the effectiveness of your gear by adding tempers, tannins, or resins to the crafting process. Just don't destroy your item while you're at it!

To begin with, any item you've created is listed as "Common" or "Normal," and is color-coded white. Access the Improvement menu to improve the quality of your chosen item by using tempers for Blacksmithing, tannins for Clothing, and resins for Woodworking. You must advance your item step by step, meaning you can't jump from Normal quality straight to Epic. The small chart at the bottom of the in-game menu indicates how improvement is achieved.

Improvement Items

QUALITY	COLOR	TEMPER USED TO ACHIEVE	TANNIN USED TO ACHIEVE	RESIN USED TO ACHIEVE	CHANCE OF SUCCESS
NORMAL	White	—	—	—	
FINE	Green	Honing Stone	Hemming	Pitch	20%
SUPERIOR	Blue	Dwarven Oil	Embroidery	Turpen	15%
EPIC	Purple	Grain Solvent	Elegant Lining	Mastic	10%
LEGENDARY	Gold	Tempering Alloy	Dreugh Wax	Rosin	5%

** Chance can be increased to 100% by adding the appropriate number of Improvement Items. Investing in the appropriate Expertise Passive Ability increases your odds even more.*

Improving items isn't as straightforward as adding a temper/tannin/resin and creating an improved version. A single improvement item gives you an added chance of success. This means there's a big chance that combining your item with an improvement item will fail, in which case the item and improvement item are both permanently destroyed. The more tempers/tannins/resins you use, the greater the chance of successfully improving your item.

You can get tempers, tannins, and resins in a number of ways:

- Acquired from a Hireling
- Bought from other players
- Randomly awarded when refining raw materials
- Randomly awarded when deconstructing equipment of the corresponding category
- Awarded at the end of crafting writs

LEAVING NOTHING TO CHANCE

It's worth giving yourself a 100% chance of improving an item, since a lower-percentage chance of success runs the risk of destroying the item. To avoid failure, acquire enough of each temper/tannin/resin to increase your chance to 100%. Also think about investing in the Temper Expertise, Tannin Expertise, or Resin Expertise skill to increase the chance of improving an item while using fewer improvement items.

WHY IMPROVE AN ITEM?

Improving your gear grants bonuses to any enchantments, traits, and base defenses, plus other possible advantages. This makes your gear more useful—and more impressive—in combat.

ITEM DECONSTRUCTION

Any piece of gear you craft or acquire on your travels can be deconstructed at the corresponding crafting station. Once this occurs, you receive some (but not all) of the materials previously utilized in the item's construction if you made it, or some new processed materials or other goodies if the item was acquired by other means. In addition, there's a chance the deconstruction may yield an improvement item, a racial stone based on the style of the item, and a precious stone related to the item's trait, if the item had a trait listed. If deconstructing an item well above your skill level, you may end up with no materials.

Even though there's a chance you'll net no materials or other items whatsoever, deconstruction is a good way to recycle items you've created or found. It's also a great way to find improvement items and other enhancements.

CONSTRUCTED DECONSTRUCTION

If you're seeking Inspiration in Blacksmithing, Clothing, or Woodworking, deconstructing the relevant gear gives you the highest number of points, compared to making these items. The higher the level and the finer the item quality, the more Inspiration Points awarded. You also get the bonus of extracting the raw materials.

The only potential problem is that deconstructing your own items (the ones you've made) nets you far fewer Inspiration Points than breaking down an identical item you find, or one a fellow player has created. So pal around with your guild friends and swap items to deconstruct for a greater Inspiration gain.

POWER-LEVELING

Once you've grasped the nuances of your chosen trade skill(s), it's time to put your knowledge into practice.

MASTER ALCHEMIST

To maximize your Alchemy prowess as quickly as possible, begin with a large repository of reagents and solvents, based on the previous tables indicating the most helpful potions and poisons—dozens of each solvent type up to Star Dew, and hundreds of the two to four most easily found reagents that you know combine with the same effect.

Start by making potions based on the previous recommended formulas, using the most common ingredients. It doesn't matter if the effects of the potion are beneficial or detrimental; you're at an Alchemy Station to create as many potions as you can, using the reagents you've found most easily. For this reason, think about using reagents such as Wormwood, which you may not normally employ.

As you create potions, your Inspiration level rises. It also rises when you discover the effects of the reagents you're mixing, though it isn't necessary to "unlock" all these effects. If you have Champion Points, be sure to access the Tower and Inspiration Boost for even more Inspiration-accruing while you're concocting.

Once you reach Alchemy Level 10, spend your Skill Points on the Solvent Proficiency skill. Continue creating simple two-reagent potions, but use better-quality water (Pristine) so the potions are Level 20. This gives you more Inspiration for each potion.

Continue with this technique, spending Skill Points on Solvent Proficiency as follows:

Alchemy Level 20: Rank 3, use Cleansed Water

Alchemy Level 30: Rank 4, use Filtered Water

Alchemy Level 40: Rank 5, use Purified Water

Alchemy Level 48: Rank 6, use Cloud Mist

Alchemy Level 49: Rank 7, use Star Dew

Keep pumping out the potions until you hit Alchemy Level 50 and unlock the Master Alchemist Achievement. Your potion reagents don't need to change unless you want to create more useful potions; power-leveling is done to get you to Level 50 as quickly as possible.

RESETTING YOUR SKILLS

You need six to seven Skill Points to raise your Solvent Proficiency. You also have the option of spending three more Skill Points to raise your Medicinal Use skill to Rank 3 once you hit Alchemy Level 50.

Feel free to re-spec your character at a Rededication Shrine if you aren't concerned with making any further potions. This removes the Solvent Proficiency Skill Points for use elsewhere. It's ideal to raise the Medicinal Use skill from Rank 1 to 3 and keep it active, so the effects of your potions last longer.

The Siphoning > Catalyst Passive Ability allows you to gain 6-12 Ultimate (depending upon rank) once you drink a potion—a great trick if you're a Nightblade.

MASTER BLACKSMITH, CLOTHIER, AND WOODWORKER

Leveling up the Blacksmithing, Clothing, and Woodworking trade skills all work pretty much the same way. Simply refining raw materials does not reward you with Inspiration, but there are methods to increase these skills.

Begin by gathering any appropriate materials you see in your adventures. These items might be simply lying around, but are more frequently found on enemies you've slain.

Another option is to find guild players willing to give (or sell) you these item types. If you can, work together as a team. Each member should gather and create a variety of items independently. Then swap collections for a greatly increased cache of items available for deconstruction.

Or you can join a trading company and, with enough gold, purchase their selection of items.

You need to amass a large number of these items. Instead of selling them, return to the appropriate crafting station and deconstruct them. Keep deconstructing, and watch your Inspiration Points increase!

You can also craft items. You should be doing this independently of power-leveling, so pick items that don't use up a lot of raw materials. However, nothing quickens your Inspiration Bar faster than breaking apart a newly discovered item!

Continue to locate different items and deconstruct them, along with researching traits, until you reach Level 50. As you level up, become certified, add a Hireling, and complete writs to obtain more esoteric gems you can imbue into your creations.

MASTER ENCHANTER

If you're hoping for a rapid ascension through the ranks of Enchanting to Level 50, exercise some patience. This trade skill is the most laborious of the lot! Although you'll spend a lot of time finding and learning the effects of runes, extracting glyphs always yields more Inspiration than creating them. Therefore, it's imperative you partner with another player, ideally one close to your own Enchanting level, and start to create glyphs of the maximum possible level, based on the Potency Rune table shown earlier in this chapter. Then trade glyphs with each other and extract them. This yields a lot more Inspiration compared to making and deconstructing them yourself. Crafting furnishings is an alternative for Enchanters that does not require a partner.

MASTER PROVISIONER

Here's an efficient plan for leveling up Provisioning quickly and effectively. It enables you to reach Level 50, Master Provisioner status, in the shortest amount of time:

First, be sure you have 13 or more Skill Points you can place into Provisioning Passive Abilities, but don't pick the abilities yet.

Instead, visit multiple Guild Stores at a frequented Merchant hub (visiting other traders also yields recipes and ingredients). Then peruse the recipes each trader has for sale.

Look for Arcane recipes (blue-colored), as these give you a better rate of return regarding Inspiration gains, compared to other colors. This tactic assumes you're concentrating solely on quickly leveling up Provisioning. Browse the list of recipes, and pay special attention to the "Ingredients" and "To Create" parts of the recipe information box.

"Ingredients" displays the base materials needed for the food or drink in question. Any you're carrying are listed in white text. Any missing ingredients are grayed out. Choose recipes with ingredients you have, or that you know are easy to find.

"To Create" lists the skills needed to make the recipe. The skills you have are color-coded green; those you don't are color-coded red. Though you can stick to creating hundreds of easier recipes and gradually gain Inspiration, a quicker way is to purchase a single recipe that requires the Recipe Improvement skill at Ranks 2-6, even if you haven't unlocked the whole skill line yet.

If you have Champion Points, be sure to access the Tower and Inspiration Boost for even more Inspiration-accruing while you're cooking.

At a Cooking Fire, consume all the recipes you've bought—assuming you've looted enough animals, barrels, drawers, and other scenery, and gathered the ingredients for the recipes you've bought.

Note the Provisioning level in your Skills > Craft > Provisioning menu. Make Normal/white recipes until you reach Level 1, then switch to Magic/green, then to Arcane/blue until you reach Level 20. Then switch to purple if you wish.

To start with, look at the Cook menu and choose the food you can create with the highest level, as this gives you the most Inspiration points. Create as many of these as your ingredients allow. As you're creating the dozens of consumables, keep an eye on your Provisioning rank at the top left of the screen. When this hits the rank numbers listed below, start spending your Skill Points! Here's what to get:

PROVISIONING POWER-LEVELING

PROVISIONING RANK	ABILITIES TO PURCHASE	ACTIONS
0-1	None	Normal (White) of highest level
At Rank 1	Recipe Quality Rank 1	Magic (Green) recipes now available
At Rank 1	Recipe Improvement Rank 1	Up to Level 19 recipes
1-10	None	Magic (Green) of highest level
At Rank 10	Recipe Quality Rank 2	Arcane (Blue) recipes now available
11-20	None	Magic (Green) or Arcane (Blue) of highest level
At Rank 20	Recipe Improvement Rank 2	Up to Level 29 recipes
21-30	None	Magic (Green) or Arcane (Blue) of highest level
At Rank 30	Recipe Improvement Rank 3	Up to Level 39 recipes
31-35	None	Magic (Green) or Arcane (Blue) of highest level
At Rank 35	Recipe Quality Rank 3	Artifact (Purple) recipes now available*
36-40	None	Magic (Green), Arcane (Blue), or Artifact (Purple) of highest level
At Rank 40	Recipe Improvement Rank 4	Up to Level 49 recipes*
41-50	None	Magic (Green), Arcane (Blue), or Artifact (Purple) of highest level
At Rank 50	Recipe Quality Rank 4	Legendary (Gold) recipes now available*
At Rank 50	None	Congratulations! You've reached Master Provisioner!

Optional. It's better to spend Skill Points ranking up your Recipe Improvement Passive Ability so you can craft consumables of higher and higher levels.

When you're creating dozens upon dozens of consumables, try to find recipes at the level you intend to reach. For example, when you reach Level 30, look for Level 35 recipes to quicken the filling of the Inspiration Bar.

Obviously, you'll need to constantly find ingredients—for the recipes you're continually creating, as well as new ingredients for recipes you access as your Recipe Improvement skill rank improves. As you purchase additional ranks, switch to the better recipes you've purchased earlier. They don't necessarily need to be purple.

You can spend points on other Provisioning abilities if you wish, but they aren't necessary if you're purely focused on leveling up this trade skill to reach Master Provisioner status and access Legendary/gold recipes as soon as possible.

When you reach Level 50, and Master Provisioner, keep creating recipes to unlock the last two ranks (5 and 6) of Recipe Improvement. Also consider purchasing the three ranks of Hireling to receive automatic ingredients. At this point, leave your cooking and become certified, and start a Provisioning crafting writ—a small quest detailed previously.

HOMESTEAD

After a long day's adventuring, it's worth returning to a dwelling of your very own, relaxing in the confines of an environment that you've furnished and personalized to your satisfaction. In the long term, you can invest in multiple homes across the entirety of the world. Welcome to Homestead!

ROOM AT THE INN: OBTAINING YOUR FIRST HOME

Begin your adventuring into real estate by grabbing the free housing brochure from the Crown Store. This is a straightforward set of tasks, undertaken after speaking to Canthion the Wood Elf Housing Broker. He resides at the bank in one of the following towns, depending on your alliance: Note that the Crown Store brochure is not necessary to begin the quest, as you just need to seek out Canthion.

Aldmeri Dominion: Vulkhel Guard Manor and Treasury, Vulkhel Guard, Auridon.

Daggerfall Covenant: Bank of Daggerfall, Daggerfall, Glenumbra.

Ebonheart Pact: Uveran Bank, Davon's Watch, Stonefalls.

Neutral: Foundations Rising, Vivec City, Vvardenfell

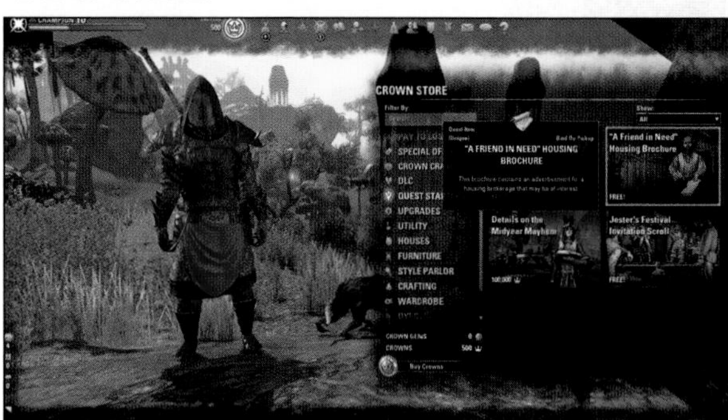

Canthion the Wood Elf holds the deeds to your first home—a humble chamber inside an inn located in a town related to your alliance.

You can also find out more about Canthion and the available houses by locating the Housing Brochure in any major city. Once the quest is completed, you receive the deed to an inn in your alliance's main settlement or in Morrowind. Congratulations! You now own your first home! Now you can furnish it, or buy additional dwellings.

NO QUEST FOR ME!

You can also ignore the quest and simply visit the Crown Store to preview all the available homes, with the exception of the four inn chambers. This allows you to own a home without learning through the tutorial that the quest provides.

FREE ROOM AND BOARD

The chamber you're rewarded with at the end of Canthion's quest is open to all your account characters. So, if you don't want to pay the 3,000 gold for the other inn rooms in the other alliance cities and/or Morrowind, simply complete the quest two more times, with characters of different alliances. or a new character in Morrowind.

EXAMPLE COSTS AND SIZES OF HOMES

Now that you've finished the quest and/or bought your first home, you have a new menu (Collections > Housing). As new houses are being added all the time, a complete list of homes isn't available, but it's worth looking around some example dwellings of each type so you know what it's going to take to own one. You can also access homes in the Crown Store, or walk to any of the dwellings in Tamriel and physically enter to preview it. Access the Housing menu to preview each home in an unfurnished or furnished state, to see if it's right for you. However, to purchase the home, you require the following:

- A certain Achievement must be met (if you aren't buying from the Crown Store).
- Completion of **Quest: A Friend in Need** (if you aren't buying from the Crown Store). It is only necessary to complete this quest with one character per account.
- You must have enough gold or crowns (from the Crown Store) to purchase (either unfurnished, or furnished at a greater cost). Furnished homes can only be purchased with Crowns.
- For Imperial-style homes, you need to own the Imperial Edition game to purchase with gold. Anyone may purchase them with Crowns.
- Access to the Crown Store for store-exclusive properties, which aren't available to purchase with gold.

Once the purchase requirements are met,, the house is yours!

HOUSE TYPES

Homes are divided into three categories: Staple, Classic, and Notable. Think of these as small (including inn rooms and single-room homes), medium, and large homes (including manors), respectively. There's usually one home type for each race, so pick the one most aesthetically pleasing to your eye. Note that each house type has a maximum set of items, trophies, special items, and visitors it can accommodate, listed as follows. Values in parentheses indicate the maximum if you have an ESO Plus account.

LOCATION, LOCATION, LOCATION

Before you pick a home, it's worth considering the amenities nearby. Is it close to a bank? Or a trader? Or a large settlement? Or is it in the wilds, away from everyone, or close to an ingredient you like to harvest? Does it have a yard? Be mindful of the area immediately around your abode, in case there are advantages to living close to certain landmarks.

Don't worry if you're keen on a trade skill like Blacksmithing but there's no crafting station near your house. Simply add one in your Homestead by buying one in game. (From other players, writ vouchers, vendors, or the Housing Editor's Purchase Tab.)

HOME EXAMPLE: STAPLE (INN ROOMS)

Though the noise from the Rosy Lion may interrupt your slumber, this room in the Daggerfall Inn is a place to rest your head, while you dream of bigger and better dwellings.

- **Furnishings: 15 (30)**
- **Trophy Busts: 1 (2)**
- **Assistants, Mounts, or Pets: 1 (2)**
- **Visitors: 2**

Extremely modest, bordering on meager living, the inn room you can obtain for free by completing **Quest: A Friend in Need** house little more than your personal belongings. However, this is a good place to test out the Housing Editor and furnishings you can make or purchase. There are four inn rooms available, though the one received from the quest depends on where it was completed: Vulkhel Guard, Daggerfall, Ebonheart, or Vivec City. The remaining inn rooms can be purchased for 3,000 gold.

HOME EXAMPLE: STAPLE (APARTMENTS)

Sheltered from the dreadful winds and blasting sands of the Alik'r Desert, the Sisters of the Sands Apartment offers tavern-based living for those with a modest income.

- **Furnishings: 50 (100)**
- **Trophy Busts: 1 (2)**
- **Assistants, Mounts, or Pets: 1 (2)**
- **Visitors: 6**

A step up from the inn is an apartment chamber, which offers an affordable alternative to a house. There are three to choose from, all alliance-based, and these allow you a comfortable living, assuming you like to live without copious amounts of furnishings. Prices range between 11,000-13,000 gold.

HOME EXAMPLE: STAPLE (SMALL)

It doesn't get much more compact than the Humblemud home, a daubed and rough affair with a single bedchamber and small exterior courtyard.

- **Furnishings: 100 (200)**
- **Trophy Busts: 5 (10)**
- **Assistants, Mounts, or Pets: 2 (4)**
- **Visitors: 6**

These homes offer cheap costs for small areas, and some lack exterior courtyards. These should be an initial purchase, especially if you haven't learned a craft or amassed enough gold to fill up the abode. There are 10, one for each race, so expect a home to suit your needs. Homes start at 40,000 gold if you aren't buying them from the Crown Store.

HOME EXAMPLE: CLASSIC (MEDIUM)

If you're seeking solace from the constant cold of Skyrim, come to Grymharth's Woe in Windhelm—a commodious townhome, but with no outdoor space.

- **Furnishings: 200 (400)**
- **Trophy Busts: 10 (20)**
- **Assistants, Mounts, or Pets: 3 (6)**
- **Visitors: 12**

If you'd like an assistant, mount, and pet to live in one home; you're starting to really get creative with your furnishing crafting; and you're expecting some guild members to come around for sweetrolls, why not purchase a roomier place with multiple levels? There are 11 initially to pick from. You'll need 190,000 gold at a minimum, though!

HOME EXAMPLE: CLASSIC (LARGE)

Found in Port Hunding, this Redguard palace is as ominous as it is spacious, and provides copious amounts of room, both indoors and out.

- **Furnishings: 300 (600)**
- **Trophy Busts: 20 (40)**
- **Assistants, Mounts, or Pets: 4 (8)**
- **Visitors: 12**

With a starting price of 760,000 gold, you'll need some sizable coffers to purchase one of these sprawling estates. Expect upward of two floors, expansive grounds, and a couple of unique features you can uncover during the preview. If you're throwing a party and you're a more seasoned adventurer with gold reserves to match, pick one of these 11 homes.

HOME EXAMPLE: NOTABLE (MANORS)

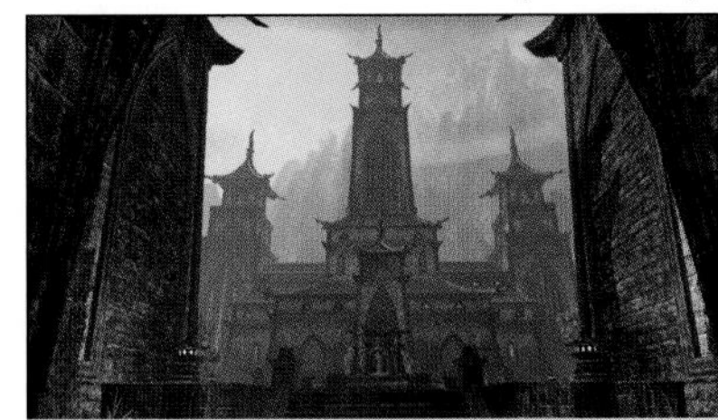

Ebonheart Chateau is a magnificent castle keep, with watchtowers, a large courtyard, and a sprawling interior, built on the side of an active volcano!

- **Furnishings: 350 (700)**
- **Trophy Busts: 40 (80)**
- **Assistants, Mounts, or Pets: 5 (10)**
- **Visitors: 24**

If wallowing in ostentatious grandeur is one of your life's goals, then the opulent manors of Tamriel should be on your list. Though simply speaking of the price of these palaces is considered gauche (don't expect much change from close to four million gold), you could hold a small army in the grounds.

HOME EXAMPLE: CROWN STORE (UNIQUE)

From time to time, additional homes exclusive to the Crown Store are available for purchase. Keep in mind that this is the only method of purchasing these; no gold is used. Such homes usually have a few esoteric or unique features to tempt you. Keep a lookout for these!

MORROWIND HOMES

If you've thought about living close to a gigantic active volcano, you'll be pleased to learn there are four initial home offerings on the island of Vvardenfell:

MORROWIND HOME #1: ALD VELOTHI HARBOR HOUSE

- **Requirement for Gold Purchase: Champion of Vivec Achievement**
- **Price (Gold/Crowns): 322,000/4,000**
- **Furnished Price (Crowns): 5,000**
- **Location: West of Ashalmawia Delve**
- **Type of Home: Classic (Medium)**

Purchase this using gold or crowns. Near a small set of docks along the northern coast of the West Gash region is an imposing harbor house known as Ald Velothi. Once a military outpost, this dwelling can be yours for the right price! This potential house features a small walled garden and two entrances, along with a multi-floor interior.

MORROWIND HOME #2: AMAYA LAKE MANOR

- **Requirement for Gold Purchase: Savior of Morrowind Achievement**
- **Price (Gold/Crowns): 1,300,000/7,000**
- **Furnished Price (Crowns): 8,800**
- **Location: Southwest side of Lake Amaya**
- **Type of Home: Classic (Large)**

Purchase this using gold or crowns. Close to the idyllic lake of the same name in the Ascadian Isles region of Vvardenfell, this impressive manor house with a large walled courtyard garden can be yours for the correct amount of crowns or gold! Think of the potential here. Plus, you're close to Vivec City for travel and goods!

MORROWIND HOME #3: SAINT DELYN PENTHOUSE

- **Requirement Awarded for Completing the Housing Quest, A Friend in Need**
- **Price (Gold/Crowns): Free**
- **Location: St. Delyn's Inn, Vivec City**
- **Type of Home: Staple (Inn Room)**

Obtain this for free after completing **Quest: A Friend in Need**. Though poky, this chamber is all you need if you're traveling light in the Vvardenfell area. Access it by visiting the St. Delyn Waistworks inside the Canton of St. Delyn the Wise in Vivec City.

FURNISHING YOUR HOME

There are well over 3,000 furnishings, and more added all the time. Make your house into a home and really show off your style!

Now that you've acquired one or more homes, think about adding your own furnished touches, provided you didn't buy the abode fully furnished—though you can still add touches to it. See the **Appendices** at the end of this book for a full list.

DIFFERENT FURNISHING TYPES AND CRAFTING

Any item you can place inside any of your homes is known as a furnishing and uses this identification in your inventory. Though many items are simply gathered to make your home look more pleasant, especially if you acquire scenery of the same or similar styles, there are some furnishings with special functionalities, such as:

- Living assistants, available whether you own a home or not, you can situate at a house to serve you or your guests.
- Seating objects you can sit on.
- Lights you can turn off and on.
- Books you can read, including almost 300 Mages Guild reprints of the collection from Shalidor's Library. Note that these do not increase your Mages Guild skill line.
- Target Dummies you can practice combat skills on. There are multiple types, including , a regular and a robust version. They're usually crafted after the plans are awarded to you by the Mastercraft Mediator Rolis Hlaalu, who does not appear unless you have a completed Master Writ to turn in or have done one before. Skeletons are also available from the Housing Editor's Purchase tab.
- Crafting stations to practice one of the six trade skills on. These can be purchased from Rolis Hlaalu, the Mastercarft Mediator, for Writ Vouchers or from the Housing Editor for Crowns
- Why not invite your friends to your home for a crafting session? It's far easier, more sociable, and quicker for creating furnishings, especially if you're interested in crafting item sets!
- Mundus Stones can be placed in your home with Morrowind, purchased directly from the Housing Editor's Purchase tab.

Are you close to the item limit for your home? Check the House Information panel in your Housing Editor for the maximum value for furnishings, as specified earlier in this section. ESO Plus doubles the amount of items that you can place in your home.

There are a number of methods of obtaining furnishings:

Home Goods Furnisher: Journey to a main city or capital to find these vendors, who offer stone and plants found in the given region, and a basic array of furniture and other items.

Achievement Furnisher: Throughout Tamriel, these merchants allow you to purchase special furnishings after completing specific quests and achievements. There's some fine statuary available, assuming you've adventured hard enough to unlock the sale of these!

Holiday Furnisher: Sells achievement furnishings associated with the regular Holiday events in Tamriel.

Luxury Furnisher: For the good stuff, visit Zanil Theran, found in Cicero's Food and General Goods Store in the Hollow City inside Coldharbour, for some premium and special items only available for a short time. Zanil is only present on the weekends.

Other: The Shadowy Supplier is a Dark Brotherhood skill that unlocks Remains-Silent in Outlaws Refuges and the Dark Brotherhood Sanctuary. This NPC provides the player with beneficial items once per day with a rare chance of being awarded a furnishing. A set of books can be purchased from the Magisters in the Mages Guilds once a collection has been discovered.

Crown Store (and Housing Editor): You can purchase furnishing items at the Crown Store, or for crowns once you're inside your home and using the Housing Editor to place scenery, but want to purchase an item you don't have yet. These items can't be traded for gold or sold to others.

Fishing: Try a Fishing Hole to randomly obtain some fish-themed objects for your home. The type differs depending on the type of Fishing Hole: fresh, salt, river, or foul.

Furnishing Crafting: You're able to craft a great many items for your home, with the added benefits of selling them to fellow players. Each type of trade skill has its own plans (a little like a Provisioning recipe), found in scenery throughout the lands, purchased, looted from foes, or stolen. Craft any plans you obtain at the appropriate crafting station, which doesn't need to be in your home, though it can be. To obtain higher-quality plans, raise your trade skill, and be warned that crafting quality items may require tannins, tempers, or resins. The following types of plans are available, which use some new materials, as well as others you'll be familiar with if you've crafted before:

Alchemy Formulas, using Alchemical Resin.
Blacksmithing Diagrams, using Regulus.
Clothier Patterns, using Bast and Clean Pelts.
Enchanting Praxes, using Mundane Runes.
Provisioning Designs, using Decorative Waxes.
Woodworking Blueprints, using Heartwood.

Craft these to add Inspiration to your chosen trade skill, and even if you don't have a home, you can still sell the finished items to other players. Thousands of plans are available, so get crafting mirrors, banners, lamps, bookcases, nightstands, barrels, pots, basins, braziers, hammocks, beds, pillows, vases, bottles, frying pans, trestle tables, shrines, tiles, totems, candles, and much, much more!

Master Crafting Writs: To buy crafting stations (both regular and set-related), plans for master-crafted furniture and furnishings, ebony-related items, Target Skeleton plans, and rare furnishing parcels, pay a visit to Rolis Hlaalu, the Mastercraft Mediator. Rolis, who can be found in Wayrest, Mournhold, or Elden Root, takes Master Writs if you've completed them. Look at the **Crafting** section for more information on Master Writs.

Other Activities: You can also find Undaunted busts when looting the final boss of any arena, Trial, or veteran dungeon. Tried murdering or pickpocketing someone for a recipe or other small furnishing item?

FURNISHING PLACEMENT

The Housing Editor is used to place the furnishing you've acquired. You can even buy (from the Crown Store) items from this Editor. The Editor is pretty self-explanatory, accessed via F5 (keyboard), D-Pad + Circle (PS4), or D-Pad + B (Xbox One). You can place items, purchase items, filter items by name, and find items you already placed by retrieving them.

HOMESTEAD VISITING AND VISITORS

For every home you own, you can set different or identical permissions to allow entry to only those you deem true friends. Simply access the Housing Editor and the Settings tab to tweak the guild members and other individuals you're able to let in. You can also give your friends different levels of access:

Primary Residence: If you own more than one home, you can pick one your friends and guild members automatically visit when you aren't in the game. The permissions you've given them remain, so ensure you want those with Decorator access to fiddle with your scenery!

Visitor Access: This permission enables you to visit a friend's home and interact with the furnishings without moving them.

Decorator Access: This permission enables you to reposition any scenery inside or out. This is a great idea, as you can optionally agree to decorate the interior of a friend's house (for free, or to make some gold), if you have the eye for design. Do those Redguard Pots go with that Throne of Cyrodiil? Only with the correct lighting!

Dueling: If your home has enough space (not inns, apartments, and smaller-sized rooms), you can challenge a player to a friendly duel. These are best attempted and watched in an outside courtyard or large hall.

Banned!: Finally, if you have a particularly troublesome guild member whose filthy feet aren't allowed to sully your hallowed halls, you can easily ban them from the Settings tab.

OTHER ACTIVITIES

This section of the Training chapter concludes with a thorough but by no means exhaustive look at the other, more minor explorations you can attempt on your travels through Tamriel. None are mandatory, but some may yield rewards, and all are entertaining.

EXPLORATION

This section is dedicated to the wanderlust evoked by adventuring across new and unexplored territories, and the minor activities you can engage in during this time.

TROPHIES

Claim the still-smoldering ember heart of a Flame Atronach as part of the Atronach Element Collector Achievement.

Certain Achievements require you to slay various entities and gather a special "trophy" loot drop from their remains. These collectibles are extremely rare and should always be gathered when possible to complete the various associated Achievements. For example, if you gather evidence that you've defeated all four types of Atronach (Smoldering Ember Heart for Flame, Fleshy Symbiont for Flesh, Everfrost for Frost, and Crackling Lodestone for Storm), you can receive the Atronach Element Collector Achievement.

OTHER TROPHY TYPES

There are other types of useful items that fall into the Trophy category, including treasure maps, survey reports, quest-related items, and the rarer fish you can catch.

GROUP BOSSES

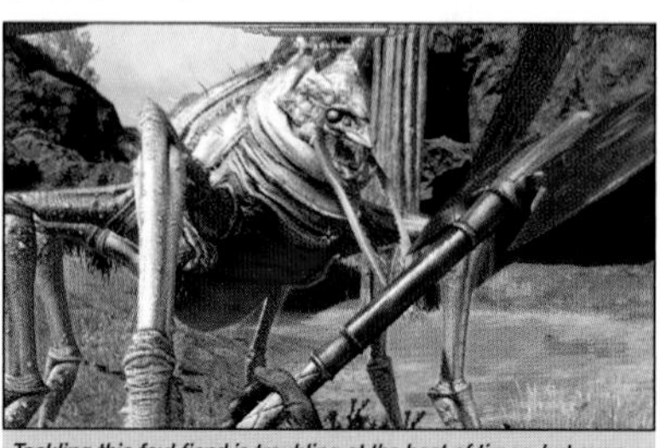

Tackling this foul fiend is troubling at the best of times, but even trickier when he's sporting special offensive capabilities!

Even though you may start off hunting small game for the animal skins, the real challenges in Tamriel takes place at a group boss location. Here, you'll find a particularly powerful variation of a large creature or entity you may have faced before, a juggernaut of a beast with special resistances and abilities. It's worth starting a hunting party to ensure the beast is slain. Most group bosses in Tamriel are balanced for four players.

LANDMARKS AND SIGHTSEEING

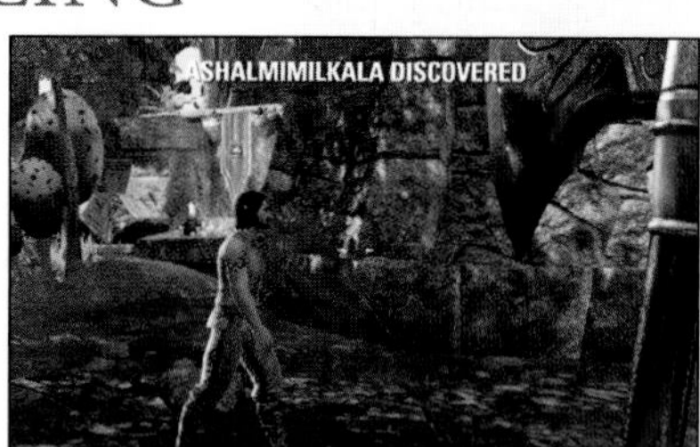

A strange Daedric ruin slowly sinking into the mire of the Bitter Coast of Vvardenfell. Search out locales with similar icons.

Consult this guide's **Atlas of Morrowind** to discover all the landmark locations. Find them all and you receive an Achievement. You may also wish to use such locations as anchor points—areas you become familiar with as you continue to explore.

TREASURE MAPS AND SURVEY MAPS

If you find a treasure map with a sketch of a location, try finding that area of landscape within the realm you're traversing, as shown.

If you uncover a map during your looting of a boss or opening of a chest, study the sketch carefully; it shows the location of a pile of dirt to dig up for impressive treasure! This guide's **Atlas** reveals the locations of every one, which are only accessible once you have the map in your hands. This guide's **Appendices** also demonstrate an image of each map paired with an image of the treasure location. Note that some treasure maps are Collector's Edition only.

Similarly, if you complete a daily crafting writ, there's a chance you may be rewarded with a survey report. This details an area of the world where a cluster of high-value nodes specific to your associated crafting skill can be found. Go there, gather the resources, and expect to receive bonus yields. Once again, such yields are only available once you have the survey report in your hands. Going to a node without the necessary map doesn't yield you any bonuses.

ASSISTANTS AND PETS

Human-sized and animal-shaped non-combat companions are available, usually after purchasing them from the Crown store, as a bonus for purchasing a pack, or after completing a specific action during a quest. Most assistants come with a specialized skill to make them useful to you, such as filling the role of Merchant, Banker, or smuggler. Most pets are simply delightful and/or cute. Find your Assistants and Pets at the Collections tab.

"Who's a good boy, then? You are! Yes, you are! Are you hungry? Wait...not the leg! Aaargh!"

What are these ne'er-do-wells up to? One of many small encounters means your adventuring never goes the same way twice.

WORLD ENCOUNTERS

While traversing Tamriel, you may encounter a small event that wasn't there the last time you visited a location. Interacting with one usually results in a small amount of Experience awarded, and sometimes a small amount of combat. For example, if you see a couple of bandits arguing over a locked chest, it may be worth your time to deal with them.. These are random and numerous, so don't overlook them.

MATERIAL GATHERING

LOCKPICKING

Once you've bought or found a supply of Lockpicks, you can attempt to open a locked chest or door, and with it, a small mini-game. Beware unlocking chests or doors in areas where others are present; if you're spotted and the unlock message is colored red, you're seen as technically attempting a crime, and a Bounty will be applied.

Locks have five difficulty levels:

- Trivial (25)
- Simple (25)
- Intermediate (20)
- Advanced (15)
- Master (12)

Bring a Lockpick, tinker with a locked chest, and if you're successful, the contents can be yours!

The number indicates the time you're given to unlock the mechanism. Fail, and you must wait a few moments for the lock to reset before you can attempt with another Lockpick.

You can also force the lock, after which your Lockpick breaks and the lock opens, if you're successful. Invest in Legerdemain to improving your ability to force a lock.

The lock itself has five different pins, which can be depressed downward. The highest setting is the starting position. Your aim is to push each of the five lock spring pins into the correct position within the time limit. Push each pin down one at a time, until it vibrates, then release it so the pin remains in the position. When it does, move to the next pin. If it doesn't, push the pin down again until it's set.

If you're intent on become a proficient lockpicker, you may wish to invest points into the Legerdemain skill line.

FISHING

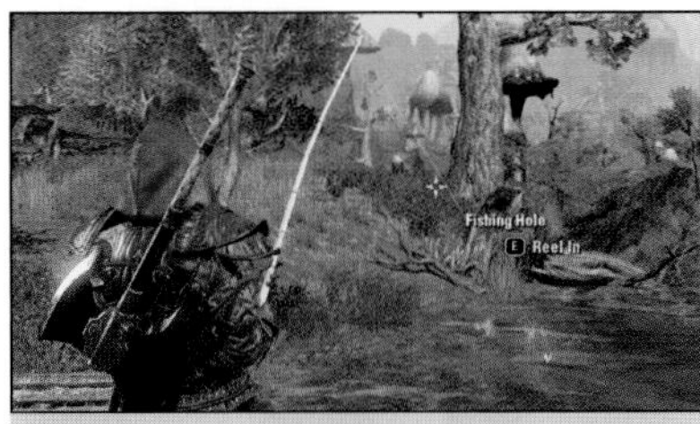

While away the hours with rod in hand, hoping to catch something impressive, rare, and valuable.

Fishing is more than a simple pastime; it allows you to feed yourself and catch rare fish you can sell. Plus, there's a chance to fillet a fish and discover Perfect Roe, an ingredient used in Provisioning to create the fabled Psijic Ambrosia.

The regions of Vvardenfell have Fishing Holes that allow fish from the four different types of water to be caught (fresh, foul, river, and salt). This guide's **Atlas** pinpoints every single one of them, and what rare and very rare fish to expect to catch at each!

Before reaching a Fishing Hole, obtain bait by looting insects or Undead foes, fishing in various locations, or purchasing from a trader. Then look for a Fishing Hole with visible signs of fish present. There are numerous Achievements available for catching rare fish. The number of players (up to three) at a fishing hole, as well as the type of bait used, increases the chances of catching a rare fish.

NODES

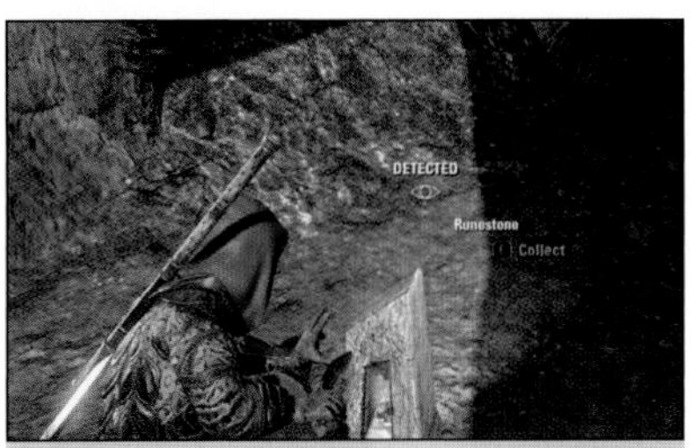

The collective term for a location where harvesting of any kind can occur is "node." Here's an example of gathering Runestones in the bleak landscape of Vvardenfell.

As specifically discussed throughout the **Crafting** section of this guide, each crafting skill requires some base ingredients to be harvested before the materials can be honed, brewed, smelted, or otherwise fiddled with, to create final items you can use or sell. However, if you're just starting out and you see environmental items that interest you, consult the following general information to learn what the item is useful for.

Logs: There's a variety of fallen trees in the form of logs, such as Maple, Yew, and Ruby Ash. These are used in the refining process for Woodworking.

Ore Veins: There's a number of particularly colorful veins of rock ore, such as Iron, Ebony, and Voidstone, which are used in the refining process for Blacksmithing.

Plants: There's a variety of plants, such as Columbine, Mountain Flower, and Nirnroot, that are used as reagents for Alchemy and clothing materials for Clothing. Occasionally, you may find worms or crawlers that can be used as fishing bait.

Runestones: These tiny shrine-like stones allow you to gather, when searched, a variety of runes that are used for Enchanting purposes.

Water: Water Skins and Pure Water, indicated by a splash, can be gathered and used in solvents for Alchemic purposes.

You can employ the Hireling and Keen Eye abilities specific to each crafting skill to allow easier gathering of base materials.

This guide's **Atlas** does not show every single node, due to the sheer number of harvestable materials.

Did you harvest ten thousand crafting nodes? Then you haven't acquired the Grand Master Crafting Harvester Achievement yet, have you?

ADVENTURING ACROSS TAMRIEL

There are plenty of activities to keep players busy as they explore the lands of Tamriel.

This portion of the *Morrowind* guide covers everything a player may discover while adventuring across Tamriel, from the variety of currencies that make the game's economy go round, to NPC factions that offer new and exciting quests and skills, to the Dark Anchors used by Molag Bal in an attempt to pull Nirn into Coldharbour.

In the cities and towns of Tamriel, NPCs offer an assortment of services for the player, providing upgrades, supplies, travel, and additional conveniences. Money is required to take advantage of many amenities, but there are numerous methods for acquiring currency.

Complete quests to receive gold, Experience, and items. Destroy Molag Bal's Dark Anchors for a sweet reward. Try your hand at thievery to acquire valuable treasure. Or take up a trade skill and sell your wares to fellow players.

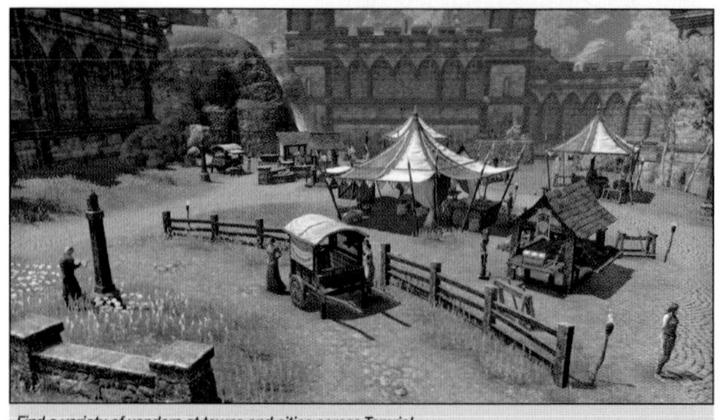

Find a variety of vendors at towns and cities across Tamriel.

This chapter seeks to prepare players for any situation they may face in the vast world of Tamriel.

CURRENCY AND HOLIDAY EVENTS

Five currencies are used in *Elder Scrolls Online*: gold, crowns, Alliance Points, Tel Var Stones, and Writ Vouchers. While gold is the primary money exchanged in PvE, the remaining four currencies give access to exclusive items and gear.

Elder Scrolls Online Currencies

Currency	Where Available	Earn	Spend
Gold	Throughout Tamriel	Complete quests, defeat enemies, steal treasure, and sell items.	Buy and sell items at Merchants across Tamriel.
Crowns	Online Stores and Retailers	Purchase separate from game.	Spend crowns at the Crown Store or in the Housing Editor's Purchase tab for exclusive content. Certain homes can be purchased with Crowns, bypassing the achievement requirement for a gold purchase.
Alliance Points	Cyrodiil	Participate in the Alliance War.	Spend points at Merchants in the Alliance War on siege equipment and exclusive PvP gear.
Tel Var Stones	The Imperial City	Complete quests and defeat monsters/Daedra, bosses, and players in the Imperial City.	Spend stones at Merchants on exclusive Imperial City gear.
Writ Vouchers	Major Cities	Complete Master Crafting Writs.	Spend at Mastercraft Mediator.

GOLD

Gold is collected in a number of ways, such as completing quests, looting mobs, selling items, and thievery. Most vendors of Tamriel accept gold for your adventuring needs.

CROWNS

Crowns are used at the Crown Store for DLC, exclusive items, and in-game upgrades. Buying the game earns 500 crowns, while an ESO Plus subscription gives 1500 crowns per month. Otherwise, crowns must be purchased from the *Elder Scrolls Online* PC/MAC Store, the PlayStation Store, Xbox Store, or Steam. Crowns are also available from retailers as a digital code.

Purchase Crown Crates from the Crown Store to receive a mystery collection of items. The selection of items from these crates changes quarterly. Due to the random nature of the Crown Crates, identical mounts, pets, costumes, and personalities are inevitable. Crown Gems are given in exchange for these duplicates. Certain items earned from Crown Crates can be converted to gems. These are used to purchase specific Crown Crate items at the Crown Store.

The Crown Store includes the following:

Crown Crates: Purchase a crate to receive a randomly selected item related to the current season.

DLC: New zones, quests, skills, rewards, and more are available with DLC. ESO Plus gives players access to all DLC as long as they are members.

Quest Starters: Occasionally, an item must be collected from the Crown Store to start a special quest, such as the housing introduction, **Quest: A Friend in Need**.

Upgrades: Play in the alliance of your choice with the Adventurer Pack, gain an additional character slot, purchase assistants, increase your inventory space, access the Vampire and Werewolf skill lines, and more in exchange for crowns.

Utility: Get a limited-time experience boost, reset Attributes or skills, or purchase supplies for your adventure.

Houses: Preview and purchase Staple, Classic, or Notable Homes around Tamriel.

Furniture: Use your crowns to furnish your homes with accessory, bedroom, kitchen, and living room sets.

Style Parlor: Visit the style parlor to add or change adornments, hairstyles, markings, and personalities.

Crafting: Crafting Motifs allow you to craft gear in new styles. Choose from an assortment of alliance and exotic styles. Buy Crown Mimic Stones, which can be used in place of any style items when crafting a weapon or apparel.

Wardrobe: Exclusive costumes, hats, and polymorphs are available from the Wardrobe section of the Crown Store.

Dyes: A rotating selection of dyes can be purchased from the Crown Store.

Mounts: Acquire a mount for quicker travel and increased storage space. A selection of exotic mounts and horses are available.

Non-Combat Pets: Non-combat pets provide companionship as you explore Tamriel. Choose from Daedric, domestic, and exotic pets.

ALLIANCE POINTS

Alliance Points are earned by participating in the Alliance War and Battlegrounds. Kill other players and mobs, complete PvP quests, help capture keeps and resources, and defend keeps to earn the currency. Spend Alliance Points at Alliance War Merchants on siege equipment, PvP gear, and more.

These points also decide your Alliance War Rank. Starting out as a Citizen, make your way all the way to Grand Overlord.

TEL VAR STONES

Earn Tel Var Stones in the Imperial City by completing quests, defeating Daedra and other players, and looting chests. Tel Var Stones dropped by an opponent are split evenly amongst anyone who contributes to the kill. The more stones you have, the more you earn with mob kills, thanks to an increasing multiplier shown in the lower-right corner.

Tel Var Stones Multiplier

Tel Var Stones Carried	Multiplier
0 – 100	x1
101 – 1,000	x2
1,001 – 10,000	x3
10,001+	x4

Tel Var Stones are dropped upon death; killing another player gives you the opportunity to collect your opponent's loot. You lose 50% of the Tel Var Stones you currently carry upon death. Note that unopened Tel Var Stone boxes, earned by completing quests, are not lost. Tel Var Stones can be deposited at the bank for safekeeping.

Spend Tel Var Stones at Merchants found in the Imperial City Sewers.

WRIT VOUCHERS

Complete a max-tier writ and open the reward for a chance to receive a Master Crafting Writ. Complete the typically complex writ to receive Writ Vouchers. These in turn can be spent at the Mastercraft Mediator, Rolis Hlaalu, who becomes available once you have Writ Vouchers in Elden Root, Wayrest, or Mournhold. He sells specialty furnishings for your house, Ebony Style Motif Chapters, furnishing plans, and more.

INCREASING ODDS OF MASTER WRITS

Note that Master Writs are dropped based on time invested in that crafting discipline.

Alchemy: Number of reagents with all four traits discovered

Blacksmithing / Clothing / Woodworking: Total Motif knowledge, especially those that require more effort to learn, and number of traits researched

Enchanting: Total Runestone translations discovered

Provisioning: Known Purple and Gold Recipes

HOLIDAY EVENTS

Celebrate with civilians of Tamriel during special Holiday Events. Special quests and rewards are available during the festivities. Look for more celebrations as we progress through the year.

Holiday Events

Holiday Event	Previous Dates	Description
Jester's Festival	March 23 – April 3, 2017	Celebrate absurdity with jesters and fools during the spring festival.
Anniversary	April 4 – April 18, 2017	Celebrate ESO's three-year milestone with acclaimed Chef Donolon.
Midyear Mayhem	July 22 – July 31, 2017	Celebrate the Whitestrake's slaughter of Elves at the Bridge Heldon at a summer festival in Cyrodiil.
Witches Festival	October 13 – November 1, 2016	Celebrate Tamriel's spooky autumn festival with exclusive quests and rewards.
New Life Festival	December 15 – January 4, 2016	Celebrate the new year with a series of quests and fun rewards.

MERCHANTS AND SERVICES

Exploring the world puts a strain on the Vestige, with its countless mobs and challenging dungeons—inventory space fills up and equipment becomes obsolete. Fortunately, the citizens of Tamriel offer numerous services to help out. Mostly found within the cities, NPCs allow the player to earn extra gold for unwanted items, repair and upgrade worn-out gear, and purchase supplies for the next outing.

BANKS AND MONEYLENDERS

Located in most major cities of Tamriel, a bank offers the ability to store items, gold, and Tel Var Stones for safekeeping. These items are accessible at all banks and by all of your characters. The initial allotment of 60 storage spaces is upgradable by 10 slots at a time, to a maximum of 240. Moneylenders offer access to your bank inside Outlaws Refuges.

Banks also allow access to your Guild Bank and Guild Store. Share loot and money, or buy and sell items between guildmates. A guild must have at least 10 members to enable the Guild Bank and 50 members for the Guild Store..

CRAFTING STATIONS

Armor, weapons, glyphs, potions, poisons, food, and drinks can be crafted at the appropriate crafting station. You must be certified in each discipline to unlock the corresponding crafting writs, and specific resources are required to create the items. These materials are gathered out in the wild, looted from mobs, collected from containers, and purchased from vendors.

Look for special crafting set stations outside of town. These locations include Blacksmithing, Clothing, and Woodworking Stations, allowing the player to create exclusive equipment sets.

CRAFTING STATION	CRAFT...
Alchemy Station	Potions, Poisons
Blacksmithing Station	One-Handed Weapons, Two-Handed Weapons, Heavy Armor
Clothing Station	Light Armor, Medium Armor
Cooking Fire	Food, Drinks
Enchanting Table	Glyphs
Woodworking Station	Destruction Staves, Restoration Staves, Bows, Shields

DYE STATIONS

Customize your armor and shield at Dye Stations, where up to three colors can be chosen per apparel item. Peruse all of the available colors, save sets of colors, and apply the dyes to your apparel. If you're an ESO Plus member, dyes can be applied to hats and costumes. Dyes are unlocked by completing Achievements. At a Dye Station, highlight a color to find out the required Achievement.

FENCES

Found inside Outlaws Refuges, Fences allow the player to sell or launder items that have been stolen from NPCs. Sell treasures or any loot you do not wish to keep. Launder stolen items that you wish to use or bank. Stolen consumables can be used without repercussions, so don't pay for the laundering if you plan to use the consumables soon. There's a daily limit to how many items can be fenced and laundered, which can be increased via the Ledgerdemain skill line.

MERCHANTS

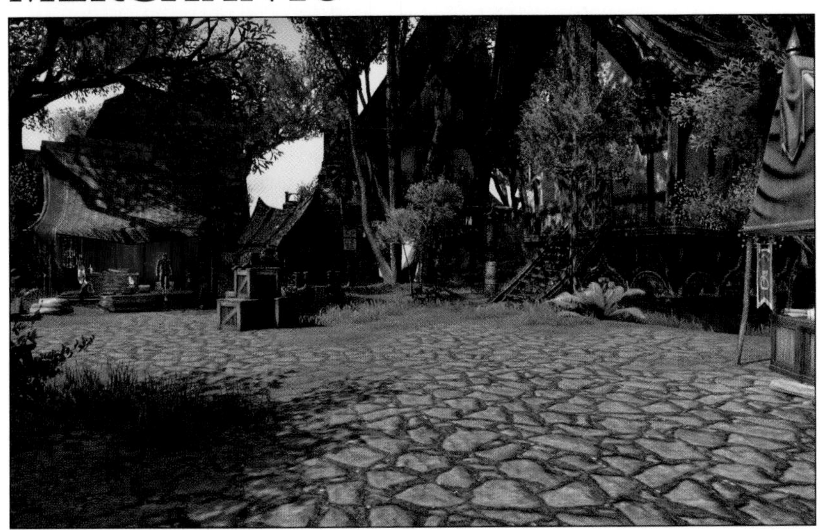

Merchants offer gear, supplies, and materials in exchange for gold. These vendors are typically found in the cities of Tamriel, but they can also be found in smaller towns and traveling between locations. Special vendors are found in Cyrodiil and the Imperial City, offering goods in exchange for Alliance Points and Tel Var Stones. Vendors also give you the opportunity to repair all of your armor in exchange for gold.

Merchants

MERCHANT	EXAMPLES OF ITEMS AVAILABLE
Achievement Furnisher	Furnishings (requires an Achievement to purchase corresponding furnishing)
Alchemist	Poisons, Potions
Armorer	Heavy Armor
Armsman/Weaponsmith	Weapons, Shields
Blacksmith	Style Materials, Unknown Heavy Armor/Metal Weapon Containers, Furnishing Diagrams
Brewer	Alcoholic Beverages, Tea Beverages, Tonic Beverages, Drink Recipes
Carpenter	Style Materials, Unknown Wooden Weapon Containers, Furnishing Blueprints
Chef/Grocer	Fruit Dishes, Meat Dishes, Vegetable Dishes, Food Recipes
Clothier	Style Materials, Unknown Light/Medium Armor Containers, Furnishing Patterns
Enchanter	Potency Runestones, Glyphs (Armor, Weapon, Jewelry)
Festival Merchants	Items related to current Holiday Event
General Goods (Innkeepers)	Lockpicks, Potions, Repair Kits
Guild Vendors	Guild-exclusive items
Home Goods Furnisher	Furnishings
Leatherworker	Medium Armor
Luxury Furnisher	Exclusive Furnishings only available on the weekend
Magus	Rings, Necklaces, Staves
Mastercraft Mediator	Exclusive content for Writ Vouchers
Mystic	Soul Gems (full and empty), Merethic Restorative Resin , book collections (once Mages Guild book collections are discovered)
Pack Merchant	Backpack Upgrades
Tailor	Light Armor
Woodworker	Bows, Shields, Staves

Cyrodiil Merchants

MERCHANT	EXAMPLES OF ITEMS AVAILABLE
Elite Gear Vendor	Unidentified Elite Armor Containers
The Golden (Weekend Only)	Epic PvE Gear
Regional Equipment Vendors	Unknown Item Containers (equipment pieces from home zone sets)
Siege Merchant	Siege Equipment, Siege/Keep Repair Kits, Soul Gems, General Goods
War Enchanter	Runestones
War Researcher	Ancient Scale, Eagle Feather, Motif Chapters

Imperial City Merchants

MERCHANT	EXAMPLES OF ITEMS AVAILABLE
Armorers	Epic Armor
General	Soul Gems, Runestones, Various Containers, Sigil of Imperial Retreat
Equipment Lockbox	Various Equipment Boxes (Epic-quality equipment)
Jewelry Lockbox	Various Jewelry Boxes (Legendary-quality jewelry)
Stylemaster	Style Materials

GUILD TRADERS

Look for Guild Traders, often found in groups, in the cities of Tamriel. These servants sell items put up for sale by members of a certain guild that owns that store. Search by item type, price range, level range, and quality.

Sometimes items sold by Guild Traders are overpriced and other times a great deal can be had, but they're a great convenience and can serve as one-stop shops. Depending on the guild's commitment to the store, a Guild Trader often holds a wide variety of items—including goods that are rare and hard to acquire.

Guilds participate in a blind bid that lasts one week to win a Guild Trader's services for the next full week. You can only bid on one trader at a time. If a trader is currently available, he or she can be hired through the week for a flat fee. A guild must have 50 members to hire this service.

NAVIGATORS

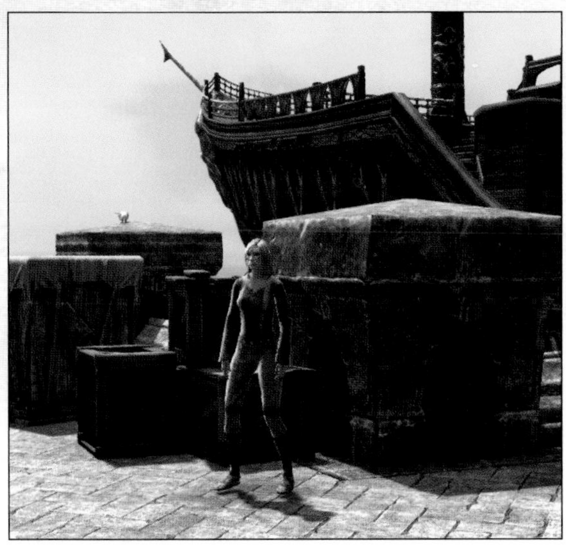

Boatswains and caravans, found in many cities, offer fast travel to cities and towns around Tamriel. These are typically found within cities, and provide transit to other major cities. This type of travel is free for the player, so look for these options when travel is necessary and a Wayshrine is unavailable.

CARAVANERS

In Vvardenfell, Caravaners occupy towers in several towns and cities, offering a quick trip to other locales within the zone—by way of a Silt Strider. A simple Achievement is earned once you talk to each caravaner.

SHRINES

There are three types of shrines that offer services within the major cities. These monuments go by different names, depending on where you are, providing the following amenities:

- Join a partner in a ceremony that earns both of you an Experience bonus when grouped and wearing Rings of Mara
- Reset your Attributes, if you want to switch between Magicka, Stamina, or Health builds
- Reset your skills, or just the morphs, if you would like to try a different build

STABLES

Find Stablemasters in most big cities of Tamriel, offering upgrades to your mount. Every 20 hours, visit the stable to increase your mount's speed, Stamina, or carrying capacity for a fee. Most of these vendors also have a small selection of mounts for sale.

MAKING MONEY

Early in your Tamriel adventures, gold may be tight. Purchasing supplies, upgrading gear, and paying for conveniences tend to run you through cash reserves quickly. Fear not, though, as there are a number of ways to make money in *Elder Scrolls Online*.

Loot Defeated Mobs: The gold and items looted from the corpses of defeated mobs may not be worth a whole lot at first, but they add up. Don't circumvent enemies as you traverse between quest givers and your objectives. Fill your bags with loot and unload what you don't want at local vendors. Look for Traveling Merchants along well-trafficked paths to eliminate the need to return to town.

Loot Containers: Containers—such as barrels, crates, pots, urns, and dressers—hold resources, basic gear, Lockpicks, and more. Grab everything you can and sell the goods at a vendor.

Treasure Chests: Keep an eye out for treasure chests that hide throughout Tamriel. A Lockpick can be used to get inside the chest and extract the loot. The higher the lock difficulty, the less time available to pick it, but its contents are typically more valuable.

Thieves Troves: Thieves Troves also provide valuable loot, but there's no need to pick a lock to get inside. The downside is that any items swiped from the container are marked as stolen, so they must be fenced or laundered. Thieves Troves require the Thieves Guild DLC to open.

Gather Resources: Gather resources as you explore the Tamriel wilderness, even if you don't plan to take part in crafting. Sell the materials to Merchants for a little gold, or better yet, sell them to other players for a bigger profit. As your level increases, higher-level resources are found, which in turn sell for more gold.

Fill Soul Gems: You may not want to make a business of it, but filling empty Soul Gems with enemy souls can make a decent profit. A filled gem sells for much more than an empty gem.

Complete Quests: Earn gold by simply completing quests. Story quests, zone quests, guild quests, and crafting writs are all rewarded with gold, Experience, and occasionally valuable items. Progressing through quest lines sends you to new locations, which provide more opportunities to earn money and experience.

Daily Quests: Numerous daily quests become available throughout Tamriel that offer new jobs each day. The Mages Guild, Fighters Guild, Dark Brotherhood, Thieves Guild, and Undaunted all offer repeatable quests. Cyrodiil and the Battlegrounds provide daily tasks in PvP areas. In Vvardenfell, find new daily quests in Ald'ruhn and Vivec City after following their respective vector quests.

Run Dungeons, Repeat: Exclusive equipment sets are available as drops in the dungeons of Tamriel. To complete the sets, though, you must run the dungeons multiple times. Sell unwanted gear for a decent profit. As a bonus, the multiple runs through the dungeons earn a great amount of Experience and gold.

Destroy the Dark Anchors: Keep an eye and ear out for active Dolmens around Tamriel. These world events are heard and seen from far away, and anyone in the area can participate. Help defeat three waves of Daedra and Undead to complete the event and receive a chest full of valuable loot.

Theft: For those who don't mind breaking the law, pickpocketing, trespassing, and burglary can net a decent profit. Visit a Fence at any Outlaws Refuge, where you can sell the treasures for 100% profit or launder them to keep them. Invest in the Legerdemain and Thieves Guild skill lines to improve thievery abilities. Get caught breaking the law and you could end up losing the stolen items and paying a fine.

Crafting: Crafting armor and weapons not only gives your character access to gear, but it can be lucrative selling the items to fellow players. The more trade skills you take part in, though, the more places you have to spend Skill Points.

Buy a Mount: A mount is expensive, but the travel time saved and increased storage space mean a mount can pay for itself over time. Use the mount and its Sprint ability to reach your destination quicker.

Player Guilds: Join guilds for the ability to sell and trade items with guildmates. Guilds with at least 50 members are able to open a Guild Store. Guilds also have the ability to bid on Guild Traders throughout Tamriel, allowing players in the group to sell items to all players. Due to the convenience of these traders, and with a good location, this can be incredibly lucrative. Players can join up to five guilds.

PvP: After reaching Level 10, players can participate in player-versus-player (PvP) combat in Cyrodiil. Play through the introductory quests to learn the basics of the Alliance War, gain some gold and Alliance Points, and receive a free forward camp. Alliance Points can be spent at Merchants in Cyrodiil for exclusive items.

Depraved deeds can be profitable, if done carefully.

A Justice System attempts to keep the peace in Tamriel. Get caught swiping an NPC's possessions or killing a citizen, and a Bounty is placed on your head. With enough heat, the Tamriel Guards pursue the player in an attempt to make an arrest. Once your infamy has reached the Infamy status level of "Fugitive,", orders are to kill on sight. Stealing treasure and selling it to a Fence can be lucrative, but it comes with consequences if you're not careful.

THE CRIMES

Crimes

Type	Crime	Description
PETTY	Pickpocket	Steal directly from a citizen NPC.
	Trespassing	Pick locked doors and enter guarded properties.
	Theft	Steal from Safeboxes or take things owned by NPCs.
	Killing Livestock	Kill livestock owned by a citizen.
MAJOR	Assault	Attack a citizen NPC.
	Murder	Kill a citizen NPC.
	Resisting Arrest	Attempt to flee an arrest.

A life of crime can be well worth the effort and time, but learning when and where, as well as what point to flee, improves your odds of making a profit and circumventing arrest. While major crimes result in high infamy, enough petty crimes can also push a player into Fugitive status as well. Being a wanted criminal has its drawbacks, but it can be a lucrative activity for the discerning outlaw.

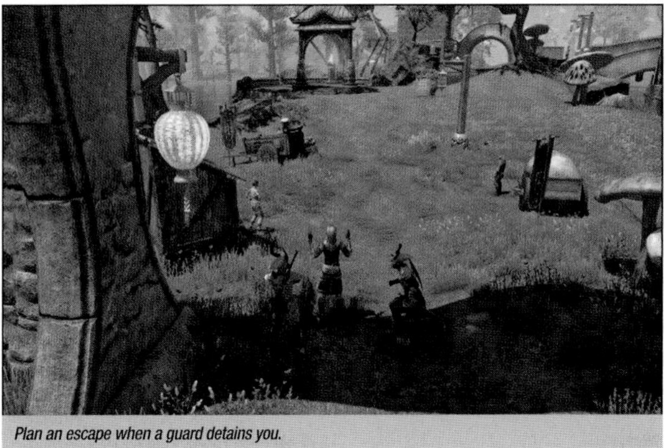
Plan an escape when a guard detains you.

Always have an escape plan, and take care not to get cornered. Guards cannot be defeated. Dodge their attempts to trap you, and run out of the city, where your pursuer eventually gives up. Slipping into the Outlaws Refuge is another great way to avoid being caught. Plus, stolen items can be unloaded while inside.

INFAMY METER

Infamy

Meter	Status	Consequences
	Upstanding	None. Meter goes away once upstanding.
	Disreputable	Guards attempt to arrest disreputable players who approach them.
	Notorious	Guards are more suspicious and arrest players at a greater range.
	Fugitive	Guards are ordered to kill Fugitives on sight. Most merchants do not interact with players who are Fugitives, either.

Some NPCs are unwilling to interact with a fugitive.

Once a crime is witnessed, the player's infamy level increases. This includes both the Bounty and Heat levels represented in the lower right corner of the UI HUD. The white portion of this meter is the Bounty, and the red portion of the meter is the Heat. In order to remove Bounty or Heat, the player can wait until it naturally decays, or they can pay their Bounty off at a Guard—provided they are not a Fugitive. If the player is a Fugitive, they should pay off their fine at a Fence in an Outlaws Refuge or acquire a Pardon Edict that will expunge a certain amount of your bounty.

Once a petty crime is committed and witnessed, your infamy increases. If a Guard witnesses the crime, they immediately attempt to arrest you. Citizen NPCs react differently according to their personalities—some scold you, others may attack you, some flee from you in terror. Their social class partially determines this behavior—citizen NPCs who are considered Nobles are more likely to gasp or flee from a murder than to attack the murderer.

Commit enough crimes, kill a civilian, or flee an arrest, and Fugitive status is achieved. The dagger in the middle of the meter turns red and you're treated as kill-on-sight status by the guards. At this point, it's a good idea to lie low or pay off the Bounty at a Fence. Once the meter slips back into Notorious, guards no longer kill on sight— unless you flee their grasp, which returns you to Fugitive status..

Note that if you pay your fine to a Guard, they take any stolen goods in your inventory as well. This is the cost of being an Upstanding citizen. You can alternatively pay your bounty to a Fence in order to keep your stolen items from being confiscated. You can also use a Bounty Pardon Edict to erase some or all of your fines.

There's no Justice in War! Cyrodiil enlists Fugitives regularly and Guards have been instructed to leave Fugitives alone in the area.

STEALTH

When crouched, your aiming reticle turns into an eyeball with the word "Hidden" or "Detected" above. Use this information to pull off unlawful lockpicking and burglaries around town. If hidden, thefts go unnoticed and a Bounty is not introduced. If detected attempting a crime, Bounty and Heat rise.

PICKPOCKET

Some NPCs can be pickpocketed by crouching, approaching the person from behind, and interacting when within range. Hostile NPCs or NPCs who offer conversation or a quest cannot be pickpocketed. A message appears on-screen when crouching near an eligible NPC. Once you're within range, if "Suspicious" or "Aware" appears, the crime cannot be committed. A percentage chance appears when a successful pickpocket is possible, indicating how likely you are to end up with an item. Try to find the sweet spot, where chances increase up to 20% if you are patient enough. If the victim becomes aware as the theft is attempted, Bounty is added and the NPC reacts to the situation. If the crime is a success, a treasure is added to your inventory.

The percentage chance of success is shown when attempting a pickpocket.

NPCs react differently to thieves. Some immediately attack, while others require a little prodding before doing so. If you are attacked first, killing the NPC does not count as murder.

LOCKPICKING

Lockpicking is a valuable skill for criminals. With a Lockpick, purchased from a Merchant or found inside containers, an NPC's locked door or Safebox can be opened through a short mini-game. The difficulty of the lock is shown next to the Unlock command.

Five pins are presented inside the lock mechanism, with your movable Lockpick just above. A timer counts down below the lock, which must be successfully cracked before the timer reaches zero. The difficulty of the lock determines the time limit, as well as how quick the tumblers move. If the lockpicking attempt fails, a short cooldown counts down before another attempt may be made.

The only Trivial locks exist during the two tutorials.

Move left and right to select a tumbler, and hold the Interact button to depress the pin. Listen for a rattling sound or look for the tumbler to vibrate, quickly releasing the button to set the tumbler in place. If you're not quick enough, the tumbler resets to its original position. If this happens, return to the point where the vibrating begins and release. The higher the difficulty, the more precise you must be in the positioning.

Higher difficulties do not give much time, so stay on the move, quickly locking each tumbler in place. Once all five are set, the door or box is opened—moving you inside or displaying the contents of the Safebox.

A Force Lock option is always available during a lockpicking by pressing the button shown at the bottom of the screen. Besides the lone Trivial lock, there is a small chance of success shown in our table; this can be improved with the Legerdemain Locksmith Passive Ability.

There are three things to remember when attempting a Force Lock:

- The Lockpick is always broken, whether successful or not.
- There is a cooldown period before the lock can be attempted again.
- No Experience is gained when the lock is forced open.

Note that you are vulnerable while picking a lock, so be sure enemies are cleared out before attempting. Also, a Bounty is placed on your head if you are seen picking the lock to a house or Safebox. Crouching when accessing the lock informs you whether you're hidden or not.

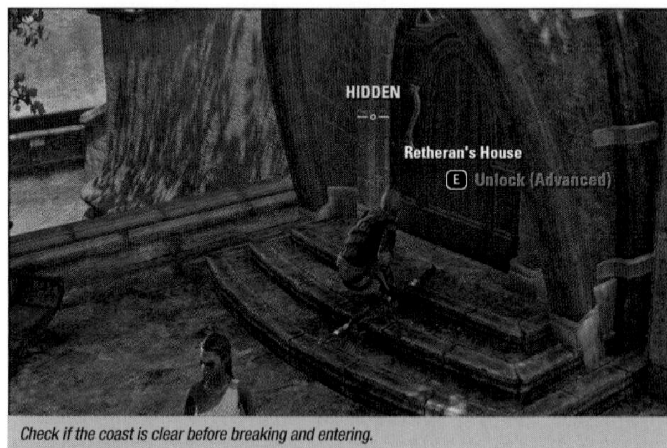

Check if the coast is clear before breaking and entering.

Lock Difficulty

Lock Difficulty	Time Limit	Force Lock Chance
Trivial	60 Seconds	100%
Simple	25 Seconds	15%
Intermediate	20 Seconds	10%
Advanced	15 Seconds	5%
Master	12 Seconds	0%

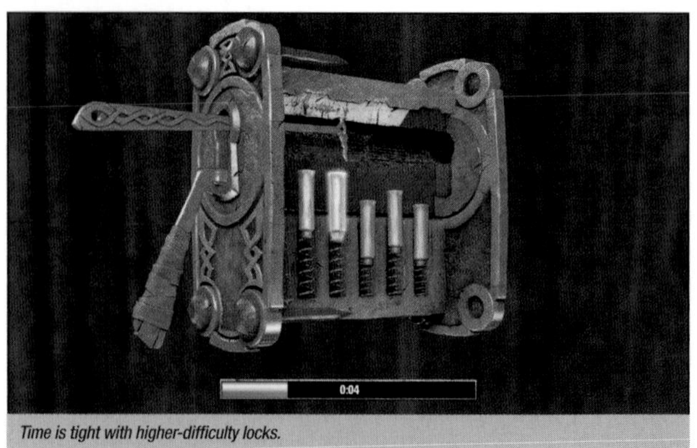

Time is tight with higher-difficulty locks.

BREAKING AND ENTERING

After successfully picking a locked door, the player enters the home. If there's a witness to the breaking-and-entering crime, a modest Bounty is added. Even if your crime goes unnoticed from outside, a civilian inside the home can act as a witness.

Picking an NPC's locked door risks adding a charge of breaking and entering to your record.

THEFT

When targeting an NPC's possessions, whether they're furnishings inside a home or containers sitting around town, the words "Steal From" appear in red text. This indicates the items inside are owned by a civilian and swiping the loot adds Bounty if detected. Feel free to examine an NPC's goods without worry, as a crime is not committed until the item is taken.

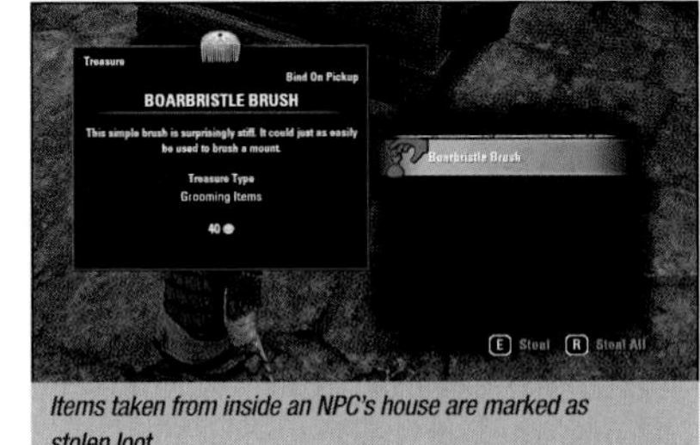

Items taken from inside an NPC's house are marked as stolen loot.

A red icon appears next to the item name, indicating it's considered stolen once taken. The same icon is shown in your inventory next to the stolen items. Note that they do not stack with like items until a Fence has laundered them.

When hidden, there's no harm in filling your inventory with stolen items. The only risk is the possibility of confiscation if stopped by a guard. If detected when taking the items, though, a Bounty is added with each offense.

If a guard is attacking you inside of a building, you must dodge their attacks without getting hit for a few seconds in order to exit through the door.

SAFEBOXES

Found inside numerous Tamriel buildings—including houses, Guild Halls, and shops—Safeboxes hold the townsfolk's most precious valuables. To get inside, the lock must be picked, just like a locked door or chest. Safeboxes are always guarded, so stealth is advised. Oftentimes, an NPC or two occupy the nearby area. Patiently wait for them to move away and quickly pick the lock. Once spotted, though, infamy is added and the citizen(s) may become hostile.

Safeboxes require a Lockpick in order to receive the valuable loot inside.

KILLING LIVESTOCK

Killing livestock owned by a citizen is a petty crime, with little reward. A small Bounty is added if caught, while items looted from the animal are marked as stolen.

SMUGGLING CONTRABAND

Guards do not stop a suspect for simply carrying stolen items, but the contraband is confiscated when caught. Paying Bounty to a guard or dying at the guard's hands not only costs the price on your head, but also any stolen items in your possession. Have the items fenced or laundered to avoid losing them.

It is possible to equip stolen items, but they're confiscated when you're accosted by a guard. Stolen consumables are usable just like their legitimate counterparts. Be sure to use them before they're confiscated, though. Stolen materials can be used as usual, though they do not stack with the normal resources and they are not added to the Craft Bag. Stolen items cannot be deposited at a bank. It's a good idea to have any items you wish to keep laundered.

ASSAULT AND MURDER

Attacking an NPC instantly adds Bounty and changes your status to Fugitive. Continuing to assault the civilian until death results in a big jump in Bounty. Anything looted from the body is considered stolen. Any assault committed against an NPC results in a kill-on-sight status with the Tamriel Guards, so clear out of the area to avoid their wrath. Join the Dark Brotherhood to receive the Blade of Woe, which gives the player the ability to kill humanoids in one shot—making it possible to get away with murder.

Assaulting a civilian instantly makes the suspect a fugitive.

TOGGLE PREVENT ATTACKING INNOCENTS

It is possible to turn off the ability to kill civilians in the game settings, though this does restrict progress toward the Dark Brotherhood. If you would rather not partake in the murderous ways of the Dark Brotherhood, go to the Gameplay Settings and find the option called Prevent Attacking Innocents. Turn it off to avoid accidently killing the citizens of Tamriel. Beware that this may restrict your ability to defend yourself or flee the scene. Steal an item in front of an aggressive NPC with nowhere to run and you may have to accept death.

AIDING IN A CRIME

If a fleeing criminal is healed, even accidently, from your spell, a modest Bounty is added. Be careful when casting spells in a city.

TRESPASSING

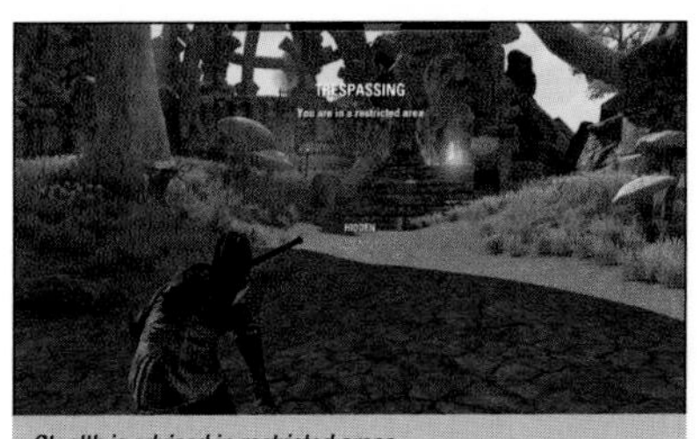
Stealth is advised in restricted areas.

There are restricted areas of Tamriel where Heat is maxed out upon entry. Any detection adds to the Bounty, and guards attempt to kill on sight.

TAMRIEL GUARDS: PAYING YOUR BOUNTY

Accosted By a Guard

Option	Description
Pay Bounty	Your Bounty comes out of your carried gold, and all stolen items are confiscated.
Clemency	With the Thieves Guild Clemency skill, guards leave you alone for a minute unless another crime is committed. Usable once a day.
Flee	A timer counts down your chance to flee the guard. Once selected, run away from your pursuer.

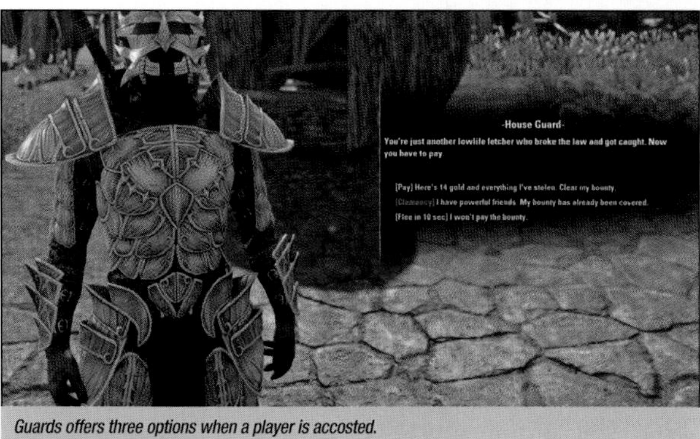

Guards offers three options when a player is accosted.

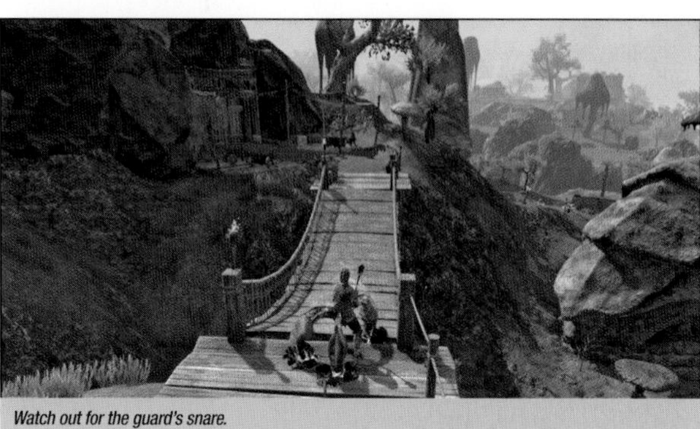

Watch out for the guard's snare.

Guards in each city enforce the law when a crime is committed. When Disreputable, you must approach a guard before he accosts you. At Notorious, guards pursue from farther away, with more guards joining in when nearby. At Fugitive, guards attempt to kill on sight—pursuing the suspect to the city limits. If they take you down, stolen items in your possession are confiscated.

With Infamy below Fugitive, a guard stops the suspect when nearby and provides the player with three options.

PAY BOUNTY

The simplest means to eliminate your wanted status is to pay your Bounty. The price is subtracted from your carried gold, stolen items are confiscated, and Infamy is reduced to Upstanding. If you do not have enough gold on you, the guard attempts to kill you. If you wish to pay the Bounty, go to a Fence or use the bank in the Outlaws Refuge to withdraw the required funds, before a guard has the chance to accost you.

CLEMENCY

The second option only becomes available with the Thieves Guild's Clemency Passive Ability. It requires Guild Rank 4, so you must spend some time with the guild to gain the ability. Once it's available, select the Clemency option to be released and left alone for one minute. Committing another crime within the minute cancels the reprieve. Clemency can only be used once a day.

FLEE: RESISTING ARREST

You only have a short time to flee, so decide quickly if a getaway is desired and use this time to plan an escape route. Once this option is selected, quickly sprint away from the hard-hitting guard. The guard cannot be defeated, so standing tall is futile. The guard possesses a couple spells that keep targets close. One stops you in your tracks, while a chain pulls you back. If you notice the guard casting, evade in the opposite direction to avoid the interruption.

Look for opportunities to hop over barriers and head for the edge of town, as the guard eventually stops pursuit. You're a fugitive at this point, so this is a great opportunity to spend some time adventuring outside of the city or visiting the Outlaws Refuge. Bounty decreases over time when logged out or playing alternate characters on the same account.

OUTLAWS REFUGE

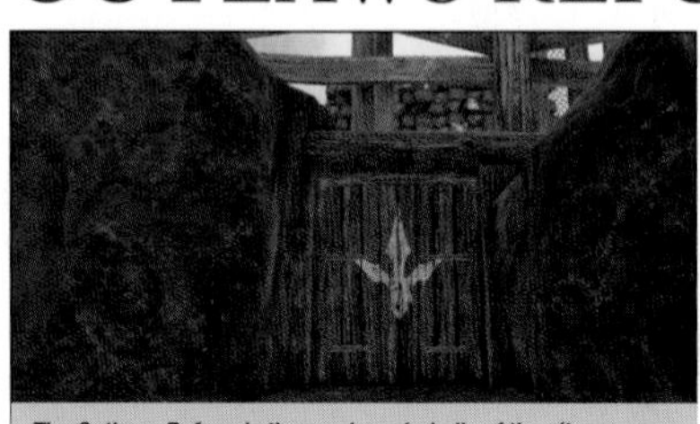

The Outlaws Refuge is the seedy underbelly of the city.

Each major city allows access to an Outlaws Refuge, where Tamriel criminals go to hide out. There's always an entrance hidden inside the city and another away from town. That way, if you're running from the law, you have a straight shot to freedom. Inside the refuge, Fences take care of your stolen items, a Merchant sells general goods, a Guild Trader deals in various products, and a Moneylender gives you access to your bank. Quest lines for the Thieves Guild and Dark Brotherhood are also available with the appropriate DLC.

FENCE

The Fence provides two valuable services for the player. Stolen items can be sold for gold or laundered, which removes the stolen status. There is no buy-back option, so be sure to launder any items you wish to keep.

There's a limit to the number of items that can be fenced and laundered, which starts out at 50 each. "Items Sold So Far" is shown below the item list when speaking with a Fence. After an item is laundered, this changes to "Items Laundered." Upgrade the Legerdemain Trafficker Passive Ability to increase these limits.

Note that stolen consumables may be used just as standard consumables. Stolen gear can be equipped, but can also be confiscated if not laundered. Materials marked as stolen can be used as normal, though they do not stack with their counterparts, nor can they be stored in the Craft Bag. No stolen items can be deposited at a bank. It's usually a good idea to launder any items you wish to hold on to, especially non-consumables. Stolen gear can be deconstructed, producing non-stolen materials.

TREASURE

Treasure Sell Price

Treasure Quality	Sell Price (Gold)
Normal	40
Fine	100
Superior	250
Epic	1,500

Treasure is often found by pickpocketing NPCs, and stealing their possessions from Safeboxes and containers in their homes. They can also be found in Thieves Troves and Hidden Panels. Sell these items at a Fence for some easy money. Be careful carrying too many of these objects through town, due to the risk of confiscation.

THIEVES TROVES

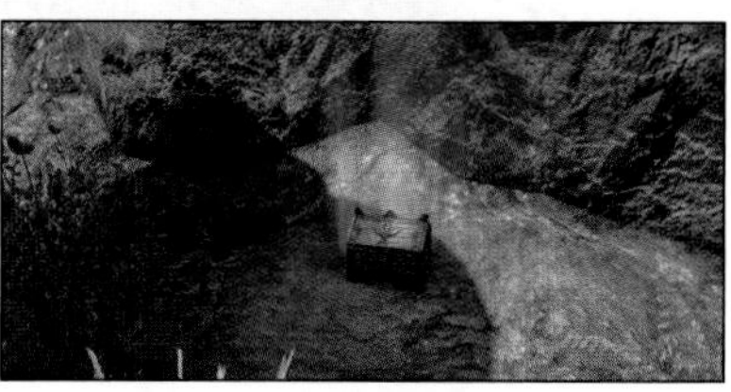

Thieves Troves hidden throughout Tamriel hold valuable NPC property. Attempting to open one with the Thieves Guild DLC installed automatically gives the player access to the skill line. Note that anything found inside is marked as stolen.

HELPFUL SKILLS

Three skill lines are helpful when committed to a life of crime: Legerdemain, Thieves Guild, and Dark Brotherhood.

LEGERDEMAIN

The Legerdemain skill line appears under the World Skills once the player has successfully stolen an item. Improve Legerdemain rank through fencing goods, pickpocketing, and picking locks.

Legerdermain Passive Abilities

Skill	Effect	Required Legerdermain Rank			
		I	II	III	IV
Improved Hiding	Reduces the Stamina cost of Sneaking.	1	6	11	16
Light Fingers	Increases the chance of a successful pickpocketing.	2	7	12	17
Trafficker	Increases the number of items sold and laundered to a Fence each day.	3	8	13	18
Locksmith	Improve chance of forcing locks.	5	9	14	19
Kickback	Reduces Bounty price willingly paid to guards and Fences.	6	10	15	20

THIEVES GUILD

The Thieves Guild skills show up under the Guild header once **Quest: Partners in Crime** is begun or interacting with a thieves trove. Improve Thieves Guild rank by committing crimes on the tip board, completing heists, and aiding guildmates.

Thieves Guild Passive Abilities

Skill	Effect	Required Thieves Guild Rank			
		I	II	III	IV
Finders Keepers	Thieves Troves, found throughout Tamriel, can only be opened by members of the Thieves Guild.	1	—	—	—
Swiftly Forgotten	Decreases bounty after three minutes and Heat decreased after three seconds	2	5	8	11
Haggling	Increases value of items sold at a Fence. Does not apply to laundering.	3	6	9	12
Clemency	When a guard accosts you, you may use Clemency once per day. If used, the guard will not arrest you or take your money and stolen goods. Additionally, guards will not attempt to accost you for one minute after you use Clemency unless you commit other crimes.	4	—	—	—
Timely Escape	When you have a Bounty and are in combat, you have a chance to spot a "Footpad" in a town with a Refuge. Interacting with the Footpad will transport the player safely into the nearest Refuge.	7	—	—	—
Veil of Shadows	Decreases the detection range of witnesses and guards by 10%. Witnesses are thus less likely to notice crimes, while guards won't challenge until they get closer.	10	—	—	—

DARK BROTHERHOOD

The Dark Brotherhood skills show up in Guild skills after you receive the Blade of Woe Passive Ability by completing **Quest: Voices in the Dark**. Improve Dark Brotherhood rank by completing Gold Coast story quests, performing contracts, and fulfilling Sacraments.

Dark Brotherhood Passive Abilities

Skill	Effect	Required Dark Brotherhood Rank			
		I	II	III	IV
Blade of Woe	Call the weapon of the Dark Brotherhood to your hand and deliver a killing blow to an unsuspecting target. Experience from this target is reduced by 75%. This ability does not work on players or difficult targets.	1	—	—	—
Scales of Pitiless Justice	Bounty and Heat resulting from a witnessed murder or assault are reduced.	2	5	8	11
Padomaic Sprint	Grants Major Expedition, increasing your movement speed for a short time after killing a Justice NPC.	3	6	9	12
Shadowy Supplier	A contact from the Brotherhood (located in the Sanctuary) provides beneficial items for assassins once per day.	4	—	—	—
Shadow Rider	Aggression radius from hostile monsters is decreased by 50% while mounted.	7	—	—	—
Spectral Assassin	Grants 15% chance of being shrouded when you use the Blade of Woe, shielding you from being witnessed and receiving a Bounty.	10	—	—	—

MOUNTS

Mounts provide a speedier means of transportation with a longer sprint time and increased storage space for the player. Anytime you are outdoors and not in combat, pressing the Toggle Mount button causes your character to hop onto your currently selected mount. Note that a mount cannot be ridden until it has been set as your active mount at the Collections tab. While you're riding, the mount can gallop and jump.

Horses are most common of the mounts, but there are various animals available for this purpose. All mounts are equivalent, with a limited number of Speed, Stamina, and Carrying Capacity upgrades available at any Stablemaster. Exclusive mounts are purchasable from the Crown Store.

AVAILABLE MOUNTS

Visit the Stablemaster or the Crown Store to purchase a mount.

Available Mounts

TYPE	MOUNT	COST	WHERE AVAILABLE
Stable Horses	Bay Dun Horse	42,700	Stablemaster
	Brown Paint Horse	42,700	Stablemaster
	Midnight Steed	42,700	Stablemaster
	Sorrel Horse	10,000	Stablemaster
Exotic	Cave Bear	1,800 Crowns	Crown Store
	Hammerfell Camel	1,800 Crowns	Crown Store
	Highland Wolf	1,800 Crowns	Crown Store
	Pride-King Lion	1,800 Crowns	Crown Store
	Tessellated Guar	1,300 Crowns	Crown Store
Horses	Piebald Destrier	900 Crowns	Crown Store
	White Mane Horse	900 Crowns	Crown Store
Special	Alliance War Horse	2,500 Crowns	Crown Store
	Nightmare Courser	2,500 Crowns	Crown Store

** The Crown Store rotates its stock of mounts, providing more options than are listed here.*

STABLES

Stables are available in most major cities and offer a few horses for sale, as well as training. Talk to the Stablemaster to see the list of mounts available and to train your riding skills.

TRAINING

Visit a Stablemaster every 20 hours for the ability to train your mount.

Once every 20 hours, the player can visit a Stablemaster and train in one of the following three riding skills for 250 gold. Riding Lessons are also available from the Crown Store for a set amount of Crowns. Each lesson allows the player to increase a stat by one, but still limited to the maximum of 60. There is no daily limit to these upgrades and you must own a mount to make the purchase.

Riding Skill

STAT	DESCRIPTION
Speed	Increases movement speed while mounted, up to a maximum of 60%.
Stamina	Increases your stamina while mounted, up to a maximum of 60, allowing your mount to sprint longer and take more hits before you become dismounted.
Carrying Capacity	Increases your carrying capacity, up to a maximum of 60.

ITEMS OF NOTE AND INTEREST

The thousands of items available from vendors, enemy drops, quest rewards, and containers can be overwhelming for a newcomer to *Elder Scrolls Online*. The goal of this section is to make sense of each item type, so you can make the best use of everything the game has to offer.

A player begins the game with 60 inventory spaces, with the option to upgrade at a Bag Merchant, found in most major cities. Add 10 slots at a time, up to a maximum of 140.

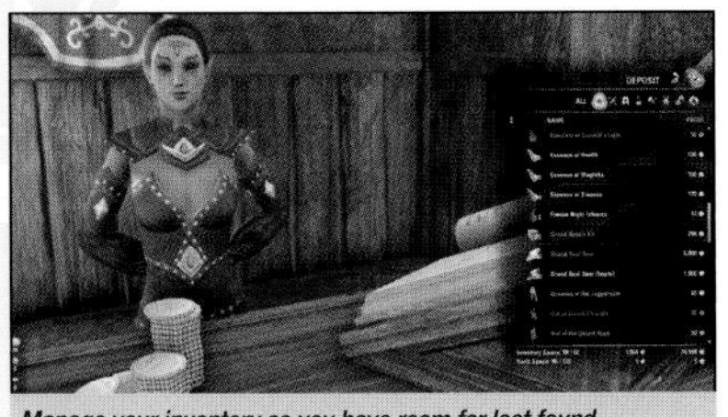
Manage your inventory so you have room for loot found in your adventures.

A bank, accessible at major cities, allows for an additional 60 items. ESO Plus members receive double the bank space with the Morrowind update. This too is upgradable, with the addition of 10 spaces per purchase, up to a maximum of 240. Note that these upgrades get more expensive the higher you go. This allows ESO Plus subscribers to reach 480 spaces.

With an active mount, upgrade carrying capacity at a Stablemaster to add one inventory space at a time, up to an additional 60.

It takes a whole lot of gold and time to reach maximum capacity, but even then, it's possible to fill up your storage—especially when participating in all crafting disciplines.

ESO PLUS CRAFT BAG

For ESO Plus subscribers, a Craft Bag allows for unlimited crafting material storage. Any legally collected materials go straight to the Craft Bag. Being able to gather all resources as you explore Tamriel, without worrying about bag capacity, is a huge asset since fewer trips back to town are required.

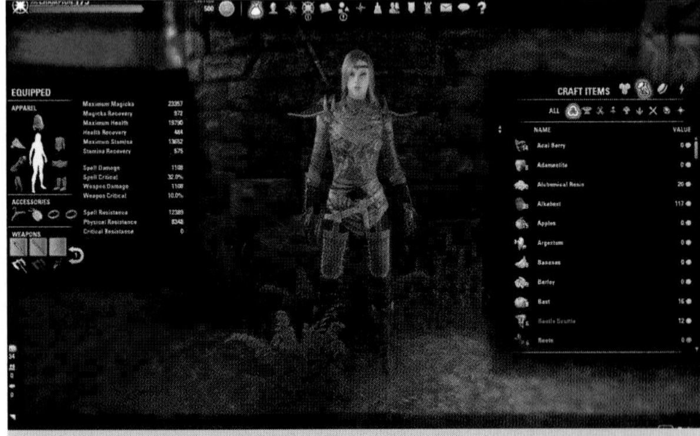
A Craft Bag is a huge asset during long expeditions through Tamriel.

Note that collected materials remain accessible from the Craft Bag after membership expires, though nothing can be added at that point. Stolen materials must be laundered before being added to Craft Bag.

CURRENCY

Five currencies are used in *Elder Scrolls Online*: gold, crowns, Alliance Points, Tel Var Stones, and Writ Vouchers. Gold is the primary money exchanged in PvE when buying and selling equipment, materials, and more.

Crowns must be purchased from the *Elder Scrolls Online* Store and other online retailers. Purchase exclusive content from the Crown Store. Alliance Points are exclusive to Cyrodiil and the Battleground, while Tel Var Stones are earned and spent in the Imperial City.

Writ Vouchers are a relatively new currency, received as a rare reward for completing Master Crafting Writs. Spend the vouchers at the Mastercraft Mediator.

Currency does not take up any room in your inventory and can be viewed at the Inventory screen by selecting the Coin icon. Gold and Tel Var Stones can be deposited in a bank.

WEAPONS

Focus on one or two weapon types to conserve Skill Points.

Tamriel is full of animals, evil individuals, and Daedra that attack players when they are near. Because of this, it's a good idea to carry around a weapon or two. At the start of the game, you may not have much choice which weapon to use since your selection is limited, but you should still decide early which weapon to focus on. Each type of weapon has an associated skill line, and Experience is gained toward those skills based on equipped weapons and abilities.

Once you reach Level 15, two weapon/ability setups are available, which can be toggled with the press of a button. Mixing a long- and short-range weapon setup can be worthwhile, so you're ready for any situation, but is not necessary. The same weapon(s) can be equipped on both setups with a different selection of abilities. Experiment and figure out which works best for you.

ONE HAND

One-handed weapons consist of axes, maces, swords, and daggers. They can be equipped into the main hand and/or off-hand. If you're using a shield, though, the weapon goes in the main hand. Mix or match two weapons to Dual Wield. These weapons are crafted at a Blacksmithing Station.

BOW

Bows are long-range weapons that cause high damage while keeping you out of harm's way. Combine with a melee option to handle any situation. Bows are crafted at a Woodworking Station.

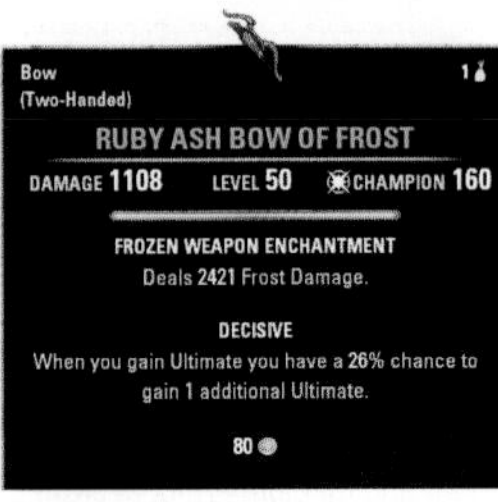

RESTORATION STAFF

A Restoration Staff does less damage than the Destruction Staff, but it has the ability to heal as it does so. Restoration Staves are crafted at a Woodworking Station.

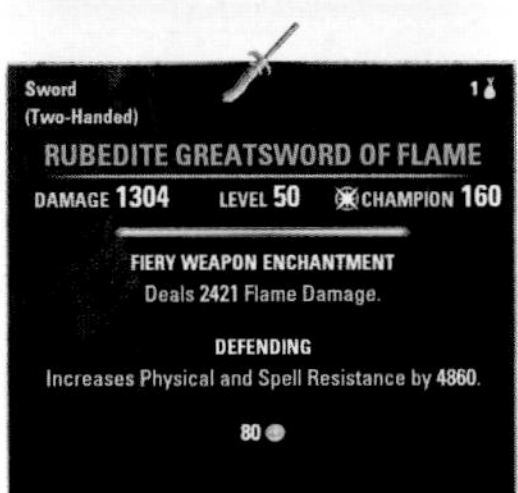

TWO-HANDED

Battle axes, mauls, and greatswords require two hands to wield. They are more powerful than equivalent one-handed weapons, but slower and more cumbersome. These weapons are crafted at a Blacksmithing Station.

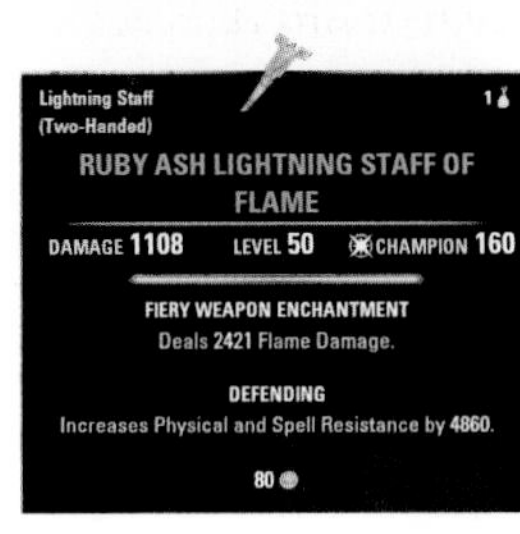

DESTRUCTION STAFF

Cast fire, ice, or lightning magic from a long distance with Destruction Staves. Ice Staves are good for tanking, fire works well for single-target DPS, and lightning excels at area DPS. Destruction Staves are crafted at a Woodworking Station.

APPAREL

SHIELDS

A shield, equipped in the off-hand opposite a one-handed weapon, gives added defense—especially when blocking. Shields are crafted at a Woodworking Station.

ARMOR

Equipped in seven slots at the inventory, armor provides extra protection for the player. Your level must be equal to or greater than the armor's level to wear it. Some armor comes with a trait and/or enchantment, which provides added benefits.

Chest
(Light Armor)
ANCESTOR SILK JERKIN OF MAGICKA
ARMOR 1316 LEVEL 50 CHAMPION 160
MAXIMUM MAGICKA ENCHANTMENT
Adds 763 Maximum Magicka.
STURDY
Reduces block cost by 3%.
60

Armor comes in three unique weights: light, medium, and heavy. The amount of protection increases the heavier the armor. The three armor types have a skill line that gives one Active Effect and five Passive Abilities. Your playstyle may dictate which type you wear, but mixing it up also has its advantages. Heavy armor is best for players in the front lines, medium works well for stamina users, and light armor is geared toward Magicka users.

Armor Slot	Light	Medium	Heavy
Head	Hat	Helmet	Helm
Chest	Robe	Jack	Cuirass
Hands	Gloves	Bracers	Gauntlets
Shoulders	Epaulets	Arm Cops	Pauldrons
Waist	Sash	Belt	Girdle
Legs	Breeches	Guards	Greaves
Feet	Shoes	Boots	Sabatons

Light and medium armor is crafted at a Woodworking Station. Heavy armor must be created at a Blacksmithing Station.

JEWELRY

Three more slots, the neck and two fingers, can be equipped with a necklace and rings. These items come with their own enchantments and traits. Jewelry cannot be crafted.

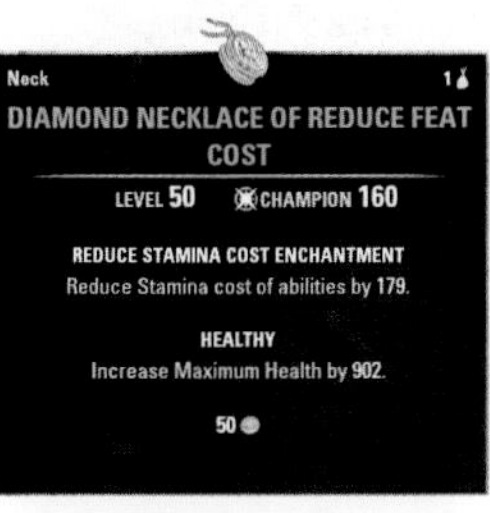

WEAPON AND ARMOR SETS

Equipping weapons and armor from the same set gives the player added stats as stated in the item's description. Most, but not all, item sets give bonuses for wearing up to five pieces from the same set. These items can be crafted, dropped by enemies, found in dungeons, and purchased from vendors in Cyrodiil.

CONSUMABLES

Consumables are removed from your inventory once they're expended. They can be used directly from your inventory, but quickslots allow for swifter access to many items. Potions, poisons, food, and drink are more effective when usable during a fight. This quick access makes this possible. Placing a treasure map in one of the slots allows you to reference the picture often while searching for the loot.

POTIONS AND POISONS

Potions provide a benefit to the player, such as restore Health/Magicka/Stamina, add a buff, or grant invisibility. Poisons cause a negative effect on your target, such as Poison Damage, increasing ability cost, or reducing movement speed. Quickslot some potions for easy usage against tougher opponents. Poisons must be applied to a weapon. Use Alchemy Stations to create your own potions and poisons.

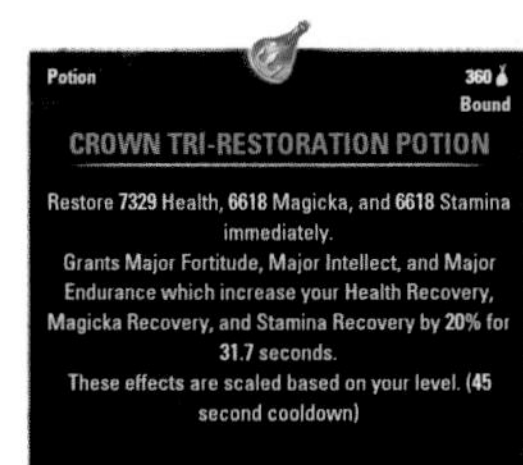

FOOD AND DRINK

Effects of Food and Drinks

FOOD/DRINK TYPE	EFFECT
Meat Dish	Increases Maximum Health
Fruit Dish	Increases Maximum Magicka
Vegetable Dish	Increases Maximum Stamina
Savoury Dish	Increases Maximum Health and Magicka
Ragout Dish	Increases Maximum Health and Stamina
Entremet Dish	Increases Maximum Magicka and Stamina
Gourmet Dish	Increases Health, Magicka, and Stamina
Alcohol Beverage	Increases Health Recovery
Tea Beverage	Increases Magicka Recovery
Tonic Beverage	Increases Stamina Recovery
Liqueurs Beverage	Increases Health and Magicka Recovery
Tinctures Beverage	Increases Health and Stamina Recovery
Cordial Tea Beverage	Increases Magicka and Stamina Recovery
Distillates Beverage	Increases Health, Magicka, and Stamina Recovery

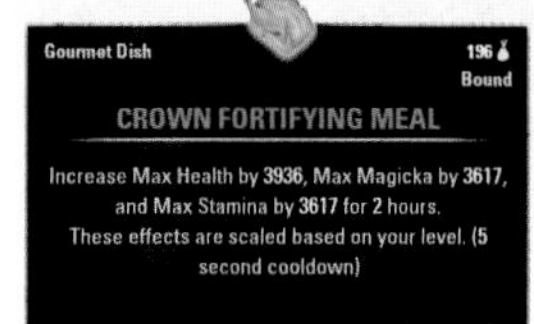

Foods increase your Maximum Health, Magicka, and/or Stamina for a period of time, while drinks increase recovery of the three. A selection of food and drinks can be purchased from Merchants, but most must be created at a Cooking Fire with the corresponding recipe. Purchase or find recipes and increase your Provisioning skill line for more powerful provisions.

FISH

Use bait to interact with Fishing Holes, located all around Tamriel, and catch fish. These fish can be sold to Merchants for a small chunk of change or used for fillets. These fillets are used in certain Provisioning recipes. There is a rare chance to receive Perfect Roe, used in crafting experience-boosting drinks, when filleting a fish.

CONTAINERS

UNIDENTIFIED EQUIPMENT

Found in shops and given as rewards, these containers hold an unidentified weapon or piece of armor. Blacksmiths, Clothiers, and Carpenters sell a selection of appropriate equipment containers. Special vendors, such as the Regional Equipment Vendor found in Cyrodiil, sell higher-level equipment inside containers. These are often from sets, while those from normal vendors are never set items. Your level must be equal to or greater than the level indicated on the item description to open the container. If indicated in the description, the contents are bound to your character once collected.

CRAFTING WRIT REWARDS

Crafting Writ Rewards

WRIT	CONTAINER
Alchemy	Alchemist's Vessel
Blacksmithing	Blacksmith's Crate
Clothing	Clothier's Satchel
Enchanting	Enchanter's Coffer
Provisioning	Provisioner's Pack
Woodworking	Woodworker's Case

After completing a consumable or equipment crafting writ, the goods must be delivered to the indicated location. The goods are exchanged for the appropriate container, which can be used to receive items related to that crafting discipline. If the reward is from a top-tier writ, a Master Writ may be rewarded.

SHIPMENTS OF MATERIALS

Materials are a popular reward from completed writs. Open the container to receive a load of the indicated raw material.

FURNISHING PLANS

Crafting Furnishings

CRAFT/STATION USED	PLAN	RAW MATERIAL (WHERE FOUND)
Alchemy	Formulae	Alchemical Resin (Mushrooms and Plants)
Blacksmithing	Diagrams	Regulus (Ore Nodes)
Clothing	Patterns	Bast (Plants) Clean Pelts (Animals)
Enchanting	Praxises	Mundane Runes (Runestones)
Provisioning	Designs	Decorative Wax (Crates, Barrels, etc.)
Woodworking	Blueprints	Heartwood (Wood)

Furnishing plans are found inside containers, purchased from Merchants, dropped by enemies, or by pickpocketing NPCs. These plans are used at the appropriate station to create furnishings for housing. Note that higher-quality plans may require multiple trade skills with required ranks in specific Passive Abilities.

CRAFTING MATERIALS

GATHERING MATERIALS

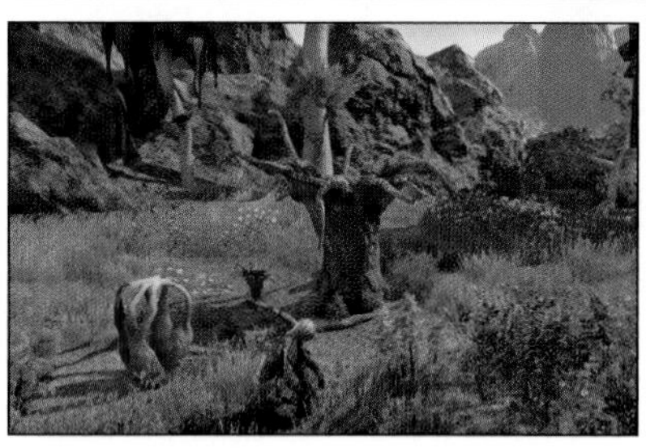

Alchemy solvents, Blacksmithing ores, Clothing materials, and Woodworking timbers are gathered from the appropriate nodes found throughout Tamriel and looted from mobs. The specific resources found are equally based on two factors: the player's current level and the rank of the corresponding crafting Passive Ability. This allows you to find materials needed to improve your crafting as well as upgrade your gear.

ALCHEMY

CRAFT	Potions, Poisons

SOLVENTS

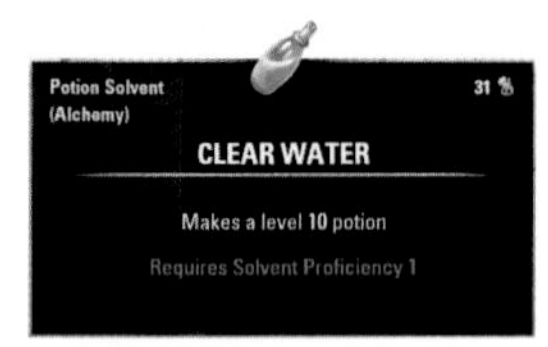

Solvents serve as the base when formulating potions and poisons at an Alchemy Station. Look for Water Skins and Pure Water spots in bodies of water to find Potion Solvents, while various enemies, such as Ogres and Trolls, drop Poison Solvents. As you progress through higher-level zones, the solvents found create more potent products, though you must upgrade your Solvent Proficiency Alchemy Passive Ability to use the higher solvents. Note that the solvents you find are based on your current level and Solvent Proficiency.

REAGENTS

Two or three reagents are added to a solvent to create potions and poisons. Each reagent has four traits that decide the effects of the mixture, but when first found, none are known. Use a reagent straight from the Inventory screen for a chance to learn a trait. Create a successful formula to learn that trait for all reagents used. Note that if all reagents used do not share a common trait, the formula fails and the items are lost.

Beetle Scuttle, Butterfly Wing, Fleshfly Larva, Mudcrab Chitin, Scrib Jelly, Spider Egg, and Torchbug Thorax are dropped by small creatures. The rest can be found growing in the wild.

BLACKSMITHING

CRAFT Metal Weapons, Heavy Armor

ORES AND INGOTS

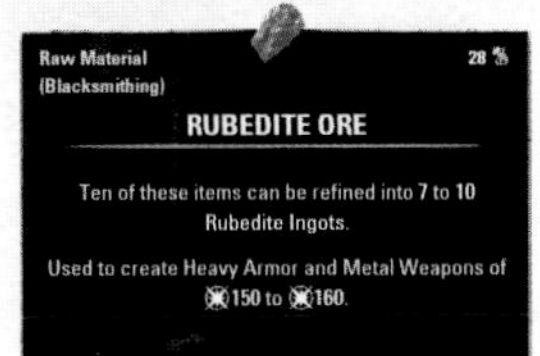

Blacksmithing allows the player to create metal weapons and heavy armor at Blacksmithing Stations. Mine ore nodes found throughout Tamriel and use the station to refine 10 ores into the matching ingots, which are then used in the production of the metal equipment. Your rank in the Metalworking Passive Ability and current level determine the type of ore available for mining and crafting.

TEMPERS

When improving heavy armor or metal weapons at a Blacksmithing Station, add tempers to improve the quality. Using one temper gives a small chance to successfully improve the item with the risk of losing the item if unsuccessful. Add tempers to improve the chances up to a 100% chance. Ranking up the Temper Expertise passive also improves your chances.

CLOTHING

CRAFT Light Armor, Medium Armor

CLOTHING MATERIALS

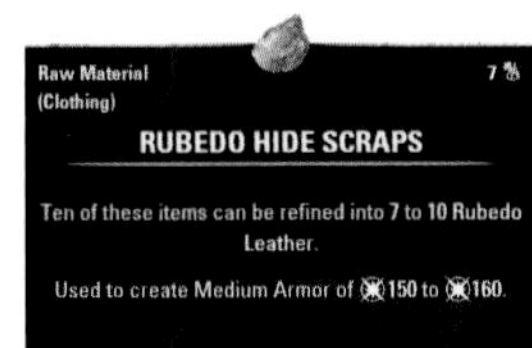

Collect raw materials and use a Clothing Station to refine them. Light armor raw materials, such as cloth, is found by harvesting plants, while medium armor raw materials, such as leather, are looted from certain monsters and critters. Then use the station to create light and medium armor pieces. Separate materials are used for light and medium armor. Your rank in the Clothing Tailoring Passive Ability and current level determine the type of material available for picking and crafting.

TANNINS

When improving light or medium armor at a Clothing Station, tannins are added to improve the quality. Using one tannin gives a small chance to successfully improve the item with the risk of losing the item if unsuccessful. Add tannins to improve the chances up to a 100% chance. Ranking up the Tannin Expertise passive also improves your chances.

ENCHANTING

CRAFT Glyphs

RUNESTONES

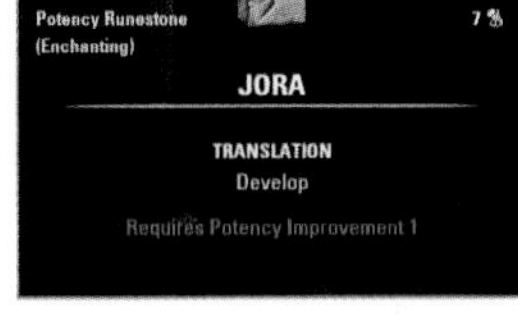

Chisel Potency, Essence, and Aspect Runestones out of rock Runestones scattered around Tamriel. Look for the red glow to light the way. Take the Runestones to an Enchanting Table, where they can be combined to create armor, jewelry, and weapon glyphs, which can be used to enchant your gear.

Start with a Potency Runestone to decide the equipment level and whether the glyph is additive or subtractive. An Essence Runestone decides the effect of the glyph. The Aspect Runestone gives the glyph its quality.

PROVISIONING

CRAFT Food, Drink

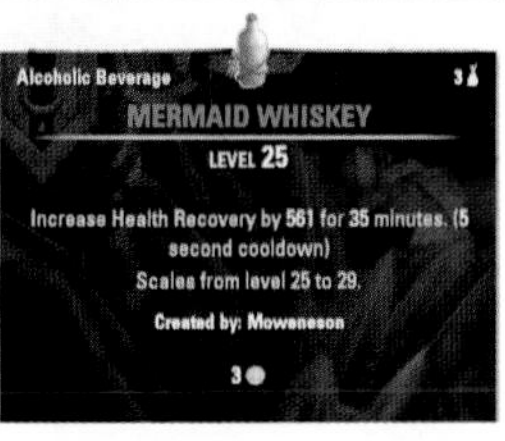

The Provisioning crafting skill allows the player to create food and drinks. Food increases Maximum Health, Stamina, and/or Magicka, while drinks increase recovery of the three. Provisions are created at Cooking Fires, which can be found in and outside of town.

RECIPES

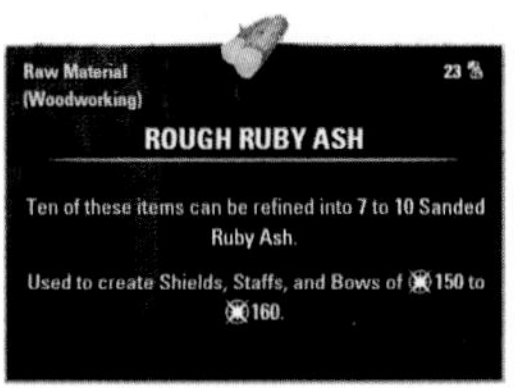

A recipe, purchased from Merchants or found around town, must be learned before it can be crafted at a Cooking Fire. Use the recipe to learn it, and then head to a fire with the required ingredient(s). Learning and crafting food and drinks adds Experience to the Provisioning skill line.

Upgrading the Recipe Quality Passive Ability allows for higher-quality recipes to be created, while Recipe Improvement decides the level of recipes that can be created.

WOODWORKING

CRAFT Bows, Staves, Shields

WOOD

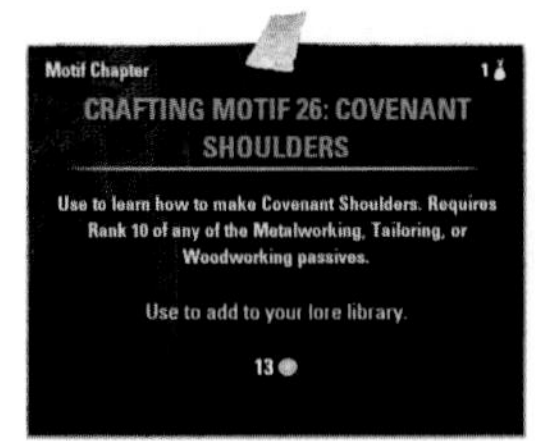

Collect woods in the wild, such as maple and ash, and refine it at a Woodworking Station. Use the station to create bows, staves, and shields with the refined woods. Your rank in the Woodworking Passive Ability and current level determine the type of material available for picking and crafting.

Raw Material (Woodworking) 23
ROUGH RUBY ASH
Ten of these items can be refined into 7 to 10 Sanded Ruby Ash.
Used to create Shields, Staffs, and Bows of 150 to 160.

RESINS

When improving bows, staves, and shields at a Woodworking Station, resins are added to improve the quality. Using one resin gives a small chance to successfully improve the item with the risk of losing the item if unsuccessful. Add resins to improve the chances up to a 100% chance. Ranking up the Resin Expertise passive also improves your chances.

MATERIALS

CRAFTING SKILL Blacksmithing, Clothing, Woodworking

When creating apparel or a weapon at a Blacksmithing, Clothing, or Woodworking Station, a style must be selected to create the equipment in that fashion. Each requires knowledge of that style gained by using the appropriate Motif Book and the corresponding style material. The initial 10 materials may be purchased at Blacksmiths, Carpenters, Clothiers, and Stylemasters for 15G each.

Use a Motif Book to learn a new crafting style. Many styles requires a specific rank in any of the metalworking, tailoring, or woodworking Passive Abilities.

Raw materials may be found for select styles that must be refined at a crafting station into the desired style material. For example, Coarse Chalk is refined into Fine Chalk, Dwemer Scraps become a Dwemer Frame, and Malachite Shards turn into Malachite.

GLASS STYLE

Ten Glass Style Motif Fragments and a Merethic Restorative Resin, available from Mystic Merchants, are required to create a random Glass Style Motif Chapter. The fragments are extremely rare rewards from high-end writs.

TRAIT ITEMS

CRAFTING SKILL	Blacksmithing, Clothing, Woodworking

Trait Items

TRAIT	TRAIT ITEM	EFFECT
ARMOR		
Divines	Sapphire	Increases Mundus Stone effects
Impenetrable	Diamond	Increases Critical Resistance, and this item takes less durability damage
Infused	Bloodstone	Increases armor enchantment effect
Nirnhoned	Fortified Nirncrux	Increases Physical and Spell Resistance
Prosperous	Garnet	Increases gold gained from looting enemies
Reinforced	Sardonyx	Increases this item's armor
Sturdy	Quartz	Reduces block cost
Training	Emerald	Increases Experience gained from kills
Well-Fitted	Almandine	Reduces cost of sprinting and dodge rolling
WEAPON		
Charged	Amethyst	Increases chance to apply status effects
Defending	Turquoise	Increases Physical and Spell Resistance
Decisive	Citrine	Chance to gain additional Ultimate when Ultimate gained
Infused	Jade	Increases weapon enchantment effect and reduces enchantment cooldown
Nirnhoned	Potent Nirncrux	Increases damage of this weapon
Powered	Chysolite	Increases healing done
Precise	Ruby	Increases Weapon and Spell Critical values
Sharpened	Fire Opal	Increases Physical and Spell Penetration
Training	Carnelian	Increases Experience gained from kills

Weapons, armor, and jewelry are not only improved with an enchantment; a trait can be added for another effect. Traits often come "pre-loaded" on dropped and purchased gear, but can also be applied at Blacksmithing, Clothing, and Woodworking Stations. Just as with enchanting, only one trait can be used per item.

Similar to adding a style, traits require a specific trait item and the knowledge to apply that trait. Each type of weapon and armor has a set of traits that must be researched at the appropriate station.

Things to remember when researching new traits:

- Researching a trait requires a weapon or piece of armor with that trait
- Only one item can be researched at a time per discipline, unless the appropriate Passive Ability is upgraded
- Researching is done separately for each type of weapon and armor
- The item is destroyed when researched
- Researching a trait takes a set amount of time to complete
- Each discipline has a Passive Ability that reduces research times and allows for more items to be researched at onc

BLACKSMITHING	Metallurgy
CLOTHING	Stitching
WOODWORKING	Carpentry

MISCELLANEOUS

SOUL GEMS

Empty Soul Gems are used to capture souls. This creates a full Soul Gem, which can be used to revive a player or fully charge a weapon. Purchase full and empty gems from a Mystic Merchant, or receive them as rewards.

When highlighting an enchanted weapon on the Inventory screen, a blue bar indicates its current charge. The enchantment is ineffective when this bar is depleted. At the Inventory screen, select the weapon and choose to charge the weapon. Select the Soul Gem and then charge to complete the process.

When defeated, the Vestige can use a full Soul Gem to revive at the current location. It can also be used to revive a recently deceased player, indicated by a white plus-sign icon. The dead player must accept the resurrection before the Soul Gem is consumed.

KEY FRAGMENT

Key Fragments are found in the Imperial City. Gathering 60 grants access to one of the city's hidden Trophy Vaults; gather 150 to open the Trophy Vaults in the Imperial City Prisons or the White-Gold Tower.

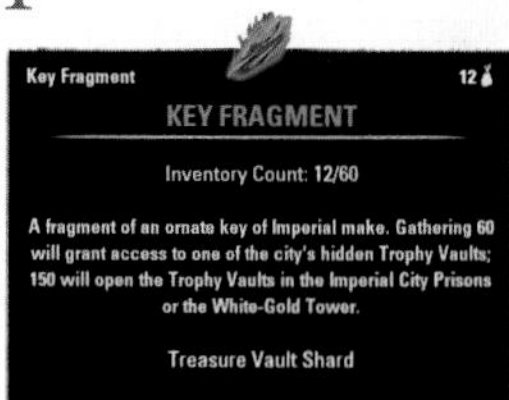

TREASURE MAPS

A treasure map shows a drawing of a specific location in Tamriel. The name of the treasure map tells you what zone to search in. Equip the map in a quickslot for easy reference. Once the spot is found, interact with the dirt mound to dig for the treasure. This consumes the map.

SURVEY REPORTS

A survey report is a random reward for completed writs. It's similar to a treasure map, but instead of getting a drawing of a certain spot, you get a map that leads you directly to the bounty. A group of materials is ready for you, and only you, to collect. Collecting the resources consumes the survey report.

MASTER WRITS

Master Writs are received as a rare reward after completing a maximum-tier writ. Use the Master Writ to start a new writ, where a relatively complex item must be completed to receive Writ Vouchers. These vouchers can be spent at the Mastercraft Mediator.

SCROLLS

Though many scrolls found around Tamriel simply provide lore, some are added to your inventory and provide valuable information or services. Outside of the inn rooms given after completing the housing quest, the *Anthology of Abodes Available for Acquisition* lists all purchasable houses. For members of the Thieves Guild, a Counterfeit Pardon Edict can often be found inside Thieves Troves.

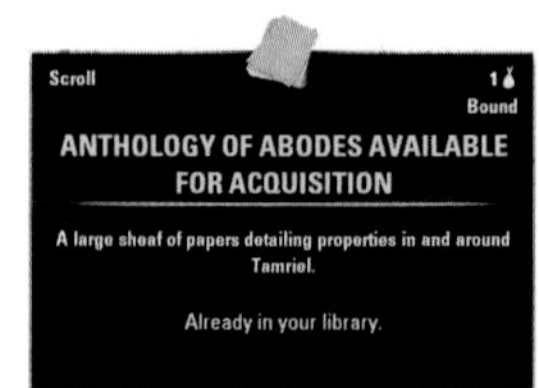

TREASURES

Find treasures on NPCs or in their possessions. They can only be obtained by pickpocketing and stealing, so they must be sold or laundered at a Fence. Get caught with these items and risk having them confiscated.

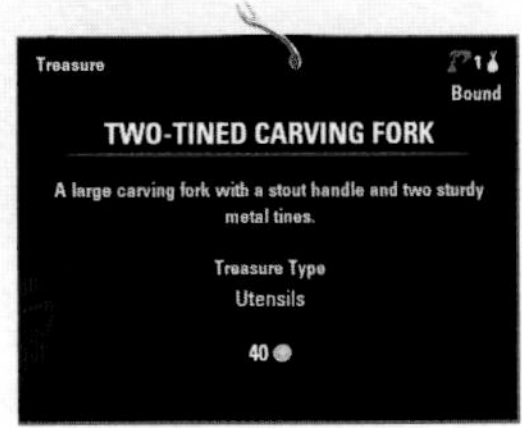

Find Kari's Hit List in the Thieves Guild in Abah's Landing to find locations of 16 Legendary Treasures. These are not worth any gold but can be displayed at the den to complete a quest and earn an Achievement.

MONSTER TROPHIES (COLLECTIBLE)

Monster Trophies

ACHIEVEMENT	COLLECT FROM	DROPPED TROPHIES	ACHIEVEMENT POINTS
ATRONACH ELEMENT COLLECTOR	Atronachs	Smoldering Ember Heart, Fleshy Symbiont, Everfrost, Crackling Lodestone	10
CHITIN ACCUMULATOR	Chitinous Creatures	Petrified Spider Egg, Calcified Cuttle, Razor-Edged Mandible, Luminous Blood Sac, Polished Shell Shard, Prized Barb, Multifaceted Eye, Gossamer Winglet	10
DWARVEN SECRETS GATHERER	Dwemer Constructs	Perfectly Balanced Gyro, Whirring Dynamo	10
MONSTROUS COMPONENT COLLECTOR	Monstrous Creatures	Werewolf's Cameo, Nose Shackle, Troll Skull, Ogre Toe Ring, Stony Heart, Second Skin, Flawless Tail Feather	10
NATURE COLLECTOR	Nature Spirits and Creatures	Primal Sproutling, Lashing Tentacle, Brass Anklets, Imp's Effigy, Icebound Vertebra, Knotted Heart, Glowing Remnant	10
OBLIVION SHARD GATHERER	Daedra	Banekin Horn, Daedric Dewclaw, Burning Daedroth Eye, Blighted Iron Collar, Spider's Crown	10
TAMRIEL BEAST COLLECTOR	Beasts	Shimmering Alit Bezoar, Magnificent Bat Pelt, Gnarled Bear Claw, Wolf's Tooth Necklace, Cat's Claw, Inert Egg, Malformed Kagouti Tusk, Huge Mammoth's Tooth, Buzzing Spine, Bile Gilt, Cruel Collar, Scaly Durzog Hide	10
UNDEAD HOARDER	Undead	Hand of Glory, Chattering Skull, Wraith Shackle, Crypt Jar, Twitching Draugr Hand, Ectoplasmic Discharge	10

Many slaughtered enemies randomly drop Monster Trophies. Drop rates vary greatly between mob types, so it can take hundreds of kills to get one. Collect all trophies from a type of enemy to earn the associated Achievements.

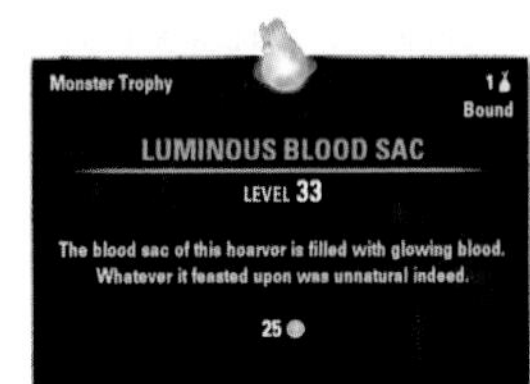

RELICS

An Orsinium quest directs the player to collect relics hidden throughout Wrothgar, to be displayed at the House of Orsimer Glories Museum.

FURNISHINGS

Furnishing Categories

FURNISHING CATEGORY	DESCRIPTION
Conservatory	Items for a garden such as plants, trees, and boulders.
Courtyard	Outdoor items such as fountains, wells, and statues.
Dining	Furniture for the dining room such as tables and chairs.
Gallery	Embellish the house with art, paintings, and other décor.
Hearth	A wide variety of items such as baskets, dishes, utensils, and more.
Library	For the academic, use shelving and desks to show off books and papers.
Lighting	From sconces to chandeliers, brighten the house with a wide selection of lighting products.
Miscellaneous	Some housing items do not fall in the other categories.
Parlor	Set up the parlor with comfy seating and decorate with banners, tapestries, and more.
Services	Add Assistants, Mundus Stones, Training Dummies, and Crafting Stations to o your home.
Structures	Add on to your property with building blocks, planks, and more.
Suite	Provide all essential furnishings for the bedroom, such as beds and dressers.
Undercroft	If you desire a crypt look for your house, a wide variety of items are available, such as urns, cages, and basins.
Workshop	Common tradeskill items, such as barrels, crates, and crafting props can be placed in your home.

Furnishings allow the player to decorate a house and are available for purchase from furnishers, or can be created with the appropriate plans and materials. Use the Housing Editor inside a house you own to place the items. There are many furnishings available for purchase with crowns inside the Housing Editor. This also allows you to preview items before purchasing or crafting them.

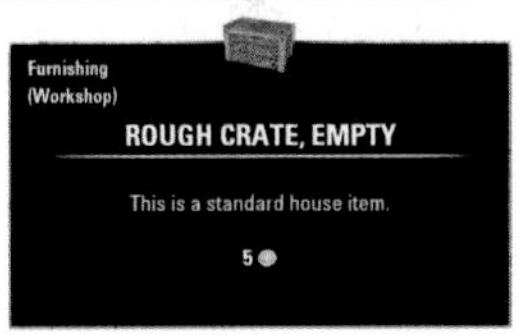

Many vendors, including Achievement Furnishers, provide unique furnishings that require the player to complete an Achievement before purchasing.

Note that assistants, mounts, and non-combat pets may also be placed inside a house. Defeated final bosses in some dungeons drop a collectible trophy bust, which can be shown off inside your house.

LOCKPICK

A Lockpick allows the player to pick a locked door, chest, or Safebox, with valuable loot as the reward. Lockpicks may be purchased for nine gold or looted from containers.

Five tumblers must be pushed down to a specific height within a set time limit to open the door or box; the higher the lock difficulty, the less time you have. Listen for a rattling sound or look for the tumbler to vibrate, and quickly release the button. If unsuccessful, remember the position and return the tumbler to that point. Lockpicks break periodically during the process, so always carry a few in your inventory.

A bounty is placed on your head if you're seen trespassing in a heavily guarded area or stealing from an NPC's Safebox. Crouching when accessing the lock indicates whether or not the player is hidden.

GLYPHS

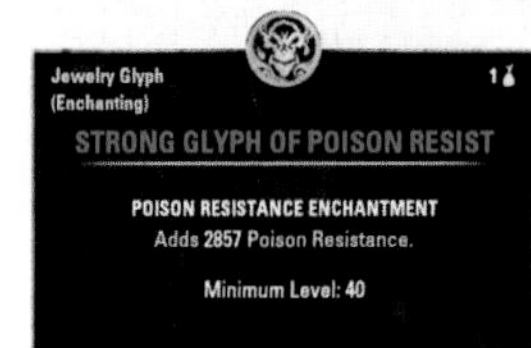

Glyphs are used to enchant weapons, armor, and jewelry with added stats—such as added Health, reduced Spell Resistance, or Magicka cost of spells. You must use the appropriate glyph for the type of item being enhanced, and only one may be applied at a time to each piece of equipment.

Use an Enchanting Table to create glyphs from Runestones, purchased from an enchanter or harvested from Runestones in the wild.

BAIT

Bait must be used at a Fishing Hole to fish that spot. Fishing Holes can be found throughout Tamriel at four types of water: foul water, streams, lakes, and the sea. There are preferred baits for each type.

Baits

BAIT	PREFERRED IN	WHERE FOUND
Chub	Sea	Fish out of lakes
Crawlers	Foul Water	Pick plants and loot small spiders
Fish Roe	Foul Water	Fish out of streams
Guts	Lakes	Loot small animals such as rats and rabbits
Insect Parts	Streams	Loot insects such as butterflies, fleshflies, and torchbugs
Minnow	Lakes	Fish out of sea
Shad	Streams	Fish out of foul water
Simple Bait	—	Purchase for 15G from Merchants
Used bait	Unusable	Failed fishing attempt
Worms	Sea	Pick plants and loot Zombies

RARE FISH (COLLECTIBLE)

Rare fish are rare collectibles fished out of the waters of Tamriel. These fish cannot be filleted, but they do count toward Achievements. Each zone offers an Achievement for collecting all rare fish from that zone. Completing all zones for each faction earns another three Achievements, while completing all fishing Achievements earns Master Fisher. Refer to the Achievements at the Journal tab for your progress.

REPAIR KIT

Repair Kits allow the player to repair damaged armor wherever they are. These are purchasable from General Merchants. It's a good idea to carry a couple close to your equipment levels. Select the damaged armor on the Inventory screen and choose to repair it. Select the Repair Kit to mend the item. A lower-level kit can be used, but it doesn't fully repair the item.

REPAIR KIT	MOST EFFECTIVE ON	COST (GOLD)
Petty Repair Kit	Levels 1 - 9	45
Minor Repair Kit	Levels 10 - 19	180
Lesser Repair Kit	Levels 20 - 29	255
Common Repair Kit	Levels 30 - 39	315
Greater Repair Kit	Levels 40 - 49	375
Grand Repair Kit	Levels 50+	420

PLEDGE OF MARA/RING OF MARA

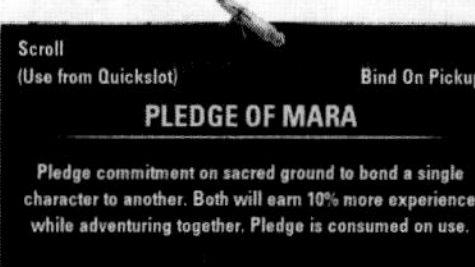

The Pledge of Mara may be purchased from the Crown Store or received from the Imperial Edition. Using this item at a Shrine to Mara with a second player grants a Ring of Mara to each player. An Experience bonus is granted when both players are grouped together and wearing the rings.

TRASH

Inevitably, enemies drop items labeled as trash. As you might guess, trash is typically not worth looting when the opportunity arises. It can be sold to vendors, but only nets you a little gold.

APPEARANCE

Receive hats, costumes, skins, and polymorphs by completing Achievements, from rare rewards, and by purchasing through the Crown Store. Slip these items on at the Collections tab to change your appearance. Note that polymorphs hide costumes, hats, and skins. Appearance items often hide armor, but stats are retained.

DISGUISES

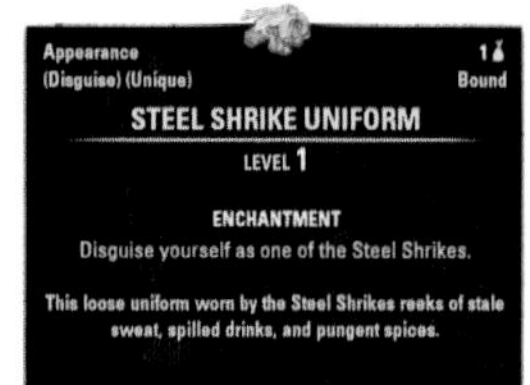

Disguises allow the player to blend into the current surroundings, typically in order to complete a quest. Once equipped, the disguise is placed in the Appearance slot of your apparel and changes your look. If your disguise is discovered, it is often confiscated and you must retrieve another to complete the objective.

QUEST ITEMS

Oftentimes, a quest leaves an item in your inventory. While in your possession, they show up under the Quest tab on the Inventory screen. Items such as books and scrolls can be read by using the item.

PVP SIEGE EQUIPMENT

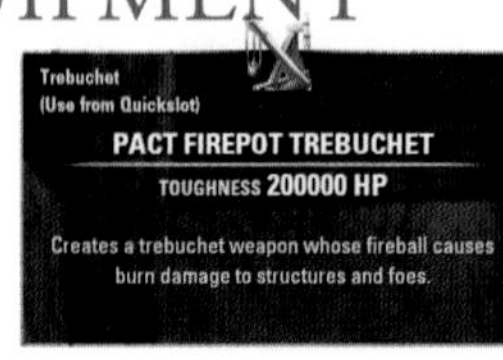

Look for Siege Merchants in Cyrodiil to purchase equipment specifically for the Alliance War. Siege weapons, such as ballistas, battering rams, catapults, and trebuchets, are used against rival factions in the war.

A forward camp creates a site at which 20 fellow teammates can respawn.

FACTIONS (MAJOR AND MINOR)

MAJOR GUILDS

Not to be confused with player-created guilds, there are five major NPC guilds in *Elder Scrolls Online*: Fighters Guild, Mages Guild, Dark Brotherhood, Thieves Guild, and the Undaunted. Joining each one unlocks a new quest line with unique rewards and skills.

Joining them all is not a bad idea, as each offers great quests, skills, and gear. But it's best to primarily focus on the one that matches your playstyle. If melee is your thing, follow the Fighters Guild quest line. If casting spells is more your speed, find the Mages Guild. The Thieves Guild concentrates on thievery, while the Dark Brotherhood is all about assassinations. The Undaunted offers group abilities that are beneficial in dungeons.

Guilds offer new quests, rewards, and skills.

FIGHTERS GUILD

Availability: Base Game

Headquarters: Major Cities

Rank Up By: Kill Undead and Daedra, Destroy Dark Anchors

Ultimate Ability: Dawnbreaker

Initial Quest Giver: Talk to the Hall Steward at the Fighters Guildhall in First Major City

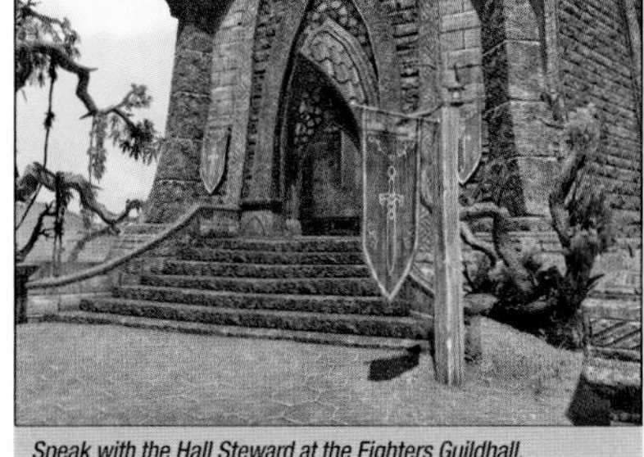

Speak with the Hall Steward at the Fighters Guildhall.

Examine the Fighters Guild Handbill that hangs in the first city of each starting zone. It directs you to talk to the quest giver inside the local Fighters Guildhall. By simply talking to a Hall Steward, you become a member of the guild and gain access to the Fighters Guild skills.

The Fighters Guild, including Guildmaster Sees-All-Colors, can be found at the guildhall in most major cities. Their primary purpose is to hunt down Daedra and their Dark Anchors. These enormous chains are attached to a Dolmen, as Daedra pour out of the portal.

Quest Giver

Alliance	City	Quest Giver
Aldmeri Dominion	Vulkhel Guard	Aicessar
Daggerfall Covenant	Daggerfall	Basile Fenandre
Ebonheart Pact	Davon's Watch	Hilan

The guild's first Passive Ability, Intimidating Presence, gives you the ability to intimidate NPCs in conversation, with a possibility of reducing the required legwork during certain quests. Earn reputation by completing daily quests offered by Cardea Gallus at Fighters Guild Halls in Elden Root, Mournhold, and Wayrest. Unlock the Bounty Hunter passive skill to unlock Bounty Quests in Cyrodiil, available at your Border Keeps.

MAGES GUILD

Availability: Base Game

Headquarters: Major Cities

Rank Up By: Find Lorebooks

Ultimate Ability: Meteor

Initial Quest Giver: Talk to the Magister at the Mages Guildhall in First Major City

Quest Giver

Alliance	City	Quest Giver
Aldmeri Dominion	Vulkhel Guard	Curinure
Daggerfall Covenant	Daggerfall	Nemarc
Ebonheart Pact	Davon's Watch	Rudrusa
Neutral	Vivec City	Tolendir Gals
Neutral	Balmora	Vilyn Veleth

Members seek out books, tomes, and ancient scrolls across Tamriel. At your alliance's first major city, enter the Mages Guildhall. Talking to the Magister begins their quest line and gives you access to the Mages Guild skills. The guild is joined once you speak with a Magister at any Mages Guild.

Collecting Lorebooks increases your rank in the guild. Look for the blue glow from the reading material that signifies it is a Lorebook. Even if you have not talked to the Magister, collecting one of these books places you in the Mages Guild with immediate access to the skills. Pick up the Mages Guild's first Passive Ability, Persuasive Will, for the ability to persuade NPCs during certain conversations. Doing so may reduce the legwork of a quest. Alvur Baren, found at the Mages Guild Halls in Elden Root, Mournhold, and Wayrest, offers daily quests for the guild—a great way to earn reputation.

DARK BROTHERHOOD

Availability: Dark Brotherhood DLC Game Pack

Headquarters: Anvil, Gold Coast

Rank Up By: Complete Quests, Contracts, and Sacraments

Initial Quest Giver: Talk to Amelie Crowe in any Outlaws Refuge, or Accept Quest on Collections Tab.

The player must kill an innocent in Anvil to become a member of the Dark Brotherhood.

Accept the Dark Brotherhood quest line from the Collections tab, or find Amelie Crowe in any Outlaws Refuge. This sends you to Anvil on the Gold Coast, where additional quests, Litany of Blood assassinations, and Sacraments—daily repeatable quests—become available.

You must receive the Blade of Woe Passive Ability by completing **Quest: Voices in the Dark** before gaining access to Dark Brotherhood skills.

Interact with the Bounty Board in Anvil or Kvatch for daily quests, though reputation is not earned toward the Dark Brotherhood. The Anvil board provides delve quests, while Kvatch offers a group boss quest, with XP earned for completion.

THIEVES GUILD

Availability: Thieves Guild DLC Game Pack

Headquarters: Abah's Landing, Hew's Bane

Rank Up By: Complete Quests and Jobs

Initial Quest Giver: Talk to Quen in any Outlaws Refuge, or Accept Quest on Collections Tab.

The Thieves Guild is headquartered in Abah's Landing, Hew's Bane.

The Thieves Guild DLC Game Pack is required to participate in the following additions. A quest line can be started directly from your Collections UI or by visiting any Outlaws Refuge and talking to Quen. Either way, the first quest, **Partners in Crime**, begins and access is granted to the Thieves Guild skills.

A new zone called Hew's Bane becomes available in southern Hammerfell. It is here, within the bustling city of Abah's Landing, where the Thieves Guild headquarters is located. Hone your pickpocketing and burglary skills with the justice system and the Thieves Guild Passive Abilities.

By joining the Thieves Guild, the player gains access to Thieves Troves, located throughout Tamriel. The valuables inside these small chests are the property of Tamriel citizens. Therefore, a petty crime is committed if a witness is present, and the items must be fenced or laundered.

Note that even if you have not started the first quest, simply picking up a Thieves Trove causes you to join the Thieves Guild, and the skill line instantly becomes available. Earn reputation towards the guild by completing larceny quests, available in the Thieves Den. Heists, guild jobs, and Rye's Reacquisitions are repeatable quests available to members of the guild.

THE UNDAUNTED

Availability: Base Game

Headquarters: Major Cities

Rank Up By: Explore Dungeons, Complete Pledges

Initial Quest Giver: Dependent on Alliance, Found in Local Tavern

Alliance	City	Tavern	Quest Giver	First Group Instance
Aldmeri Dominion	Vulkhel Guard	Salted Wings Tavern	Turuk Redclaws	The Banished Cells
Daggerfall Covenant	Daggerfall	The Rosy Lion	Mighty Mordra	Spindleclutch
Ebonheart Pact	Davon's Watch	The Fish Stink Tavern	Kailstig the Axe	Fungal Grotto

Though not one of the four major guilds, the Undaunted do offer quests and a skill line. After you talk to the initial quest giver, the next quest is **One of the Undaunted**, which challenges you to enter a nearby Group Instance. After discovering the dungeon, return to the quest giver to gain access to the Undaunted skills. This quest is also available outside the first dungeons. Reach Level 45 to unlock Undaunted daily quests with Veteran level dungeons introduced at Level 50.

Earn the "This One's On Me" Achievement by buying drinks for your Undaunted companions at each location.

Talk to Bolgrul at the Undaunted Enclave in Elden Root, Mournhold, or Wayrest for Undaunted daily quests.

MINOR FACTIONS

A Selection of the Minor Factions of Tamriel

There are a number of minor factions that do not offer quests or skills, but are present throughout Tamriel. Some are assisted as you adventure through the world, while others are targeted during your quests. While you join some as part of the quests, little is gained from it.

Faction	Location
Ash'abah	Alik'r Desert
Blackfeather Court	Crow's Wood, Stonefalls
Bloodthorn Cult	Betnikh
Brackenleaf's Briars	Grahtwood
Eyes of the Queen	Auridon
Maulborn	Deshaan
Morag Tong	Various

Faction	Location
Ordinators	Various
Shatul Clan	Wrothgar
Sixth House	Vvardenfell
Star-Gazers	Craglorn
Veiled Inheritance	Auridon
Worm Cult	Various

Exploring the vast lands of Tamriel is a huge part of *Elder Scrolls Online*, so it's wise to be comfortable with the numerous location types.

PROVINCES AND ZONES

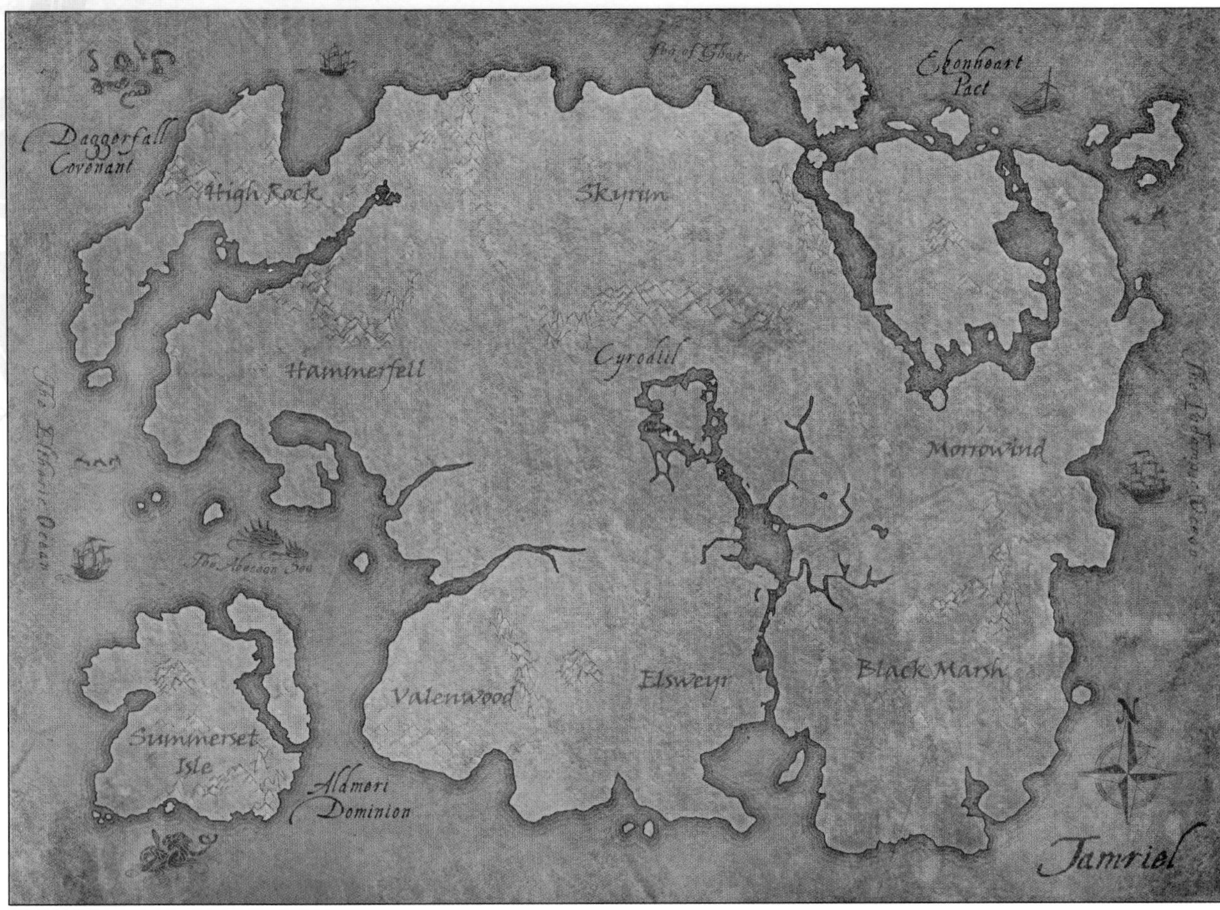

Players begin their journey in the Wailing Prison in Coldharbour, the only zone located outside of Tamriel, or Firemoth Island just off the coast of Vvardenfell. Once this tutorial is completed, you move into your starting zone, which is dependent upon the chosen faction. The tutorial can be skipped with subsequent characters. You return to Coldharbour later in the game.

Tamriel's nine Imperial Provinces are split into multiple zones, with the contested province of Cyrodiil sitting in the middle.

The Zones of Tamriel

Province	Faction	Zone
Black Marsh	Ebonheart Pact	Shadowfen
Cyrodiil	Neutral	Cyrodiil
		Gold Coast
Elsweyr	Aldmeri Dominion	Khenarthi's Roost (Starting Zone)
		Reaper's March
Hammerfell	Daggerfall Covenant	Alik'r Desert
		Bangkorai
		Stros M'Kai (Starting Zone)
	Neutral	Craglorn
	Neutral	Hew's Bane
High Rock	Daggerfall Covenant	Betnikh
		Glenumbra
		Rivenspire
		Stormhaven
	Neutral	Wrothgar

Province	Faction	Zone
Morrowind	Ebonheart Pact	Bal Foyen
		Bleakrock Isle (Starting Zone)
		Deshaan
		Stonefalls
	Neutral	Vvardenfell
Skyrim	Ebonheart Pact	Eastmarch
		The Rift
Summerset Isles	Aldmeri Dominion	Auridon
Valenwood	Aldmeri Dominion	Grahtwood
		Greenshade
		Malabal Tor
		Reaper's March

CITIES

Cities offer a number of amenities for the player, including banks, merchants, and crafting stations. Available services differ from city to city, though the biggest cities offer everything required of the player. Zones typically contain three cities, which means you don't need to go far to find one.

Faction Capital Cities

Faction	Capital City
Aldmeri Dominion	Elden Root (Grahtwood)
Daggerfall Covenant	Wayrest (Stormhaven)
Ebonheart Pact	Mournhold (Deshaan)

WAYSHRINES

Explore the expansive land of Tamriel to discover Wayshrines. Once discovered, these shrines appear on the map, providing a means of fast travel for the player. Interact with a Wayshrine to bring up the map, and then select a Wayshrine icon close to your desired destination. Moving between two Wayshrines in this manner does not cost anything. It is possible to quickly teleport to one of these points from anywhere, but it will cost a certain amount of gold, which is shown when highlighting the Wayshrine. This price increases greatly just after you use a Wayshrine, before cooling down to the regular amount, which is based on current level.

When the player dies, he/she is given the choice of reviving at the current location by using a full Grand Soul Gem, or reviving at the nearest Wayshrine. Wayshrines are also found inside dungeons to limit travel time back inside.

HOUSING

A diverse selection of houses is available for purchase once **Quest: A Friend in Need** is complete. Grab the free "A Friend in Need" Housing Brochure from the Crown Store to get started. A small room at the local inn is given to the player. Preview each of the nearly 40 homes by selecting it from the map. At this point you can see the purchase options—fully furnished or completely empty. Use gold or crowns to make the property your own. Select from thousands of unique furnishings to decorate your home and then invite friends and guildmates over for a housewarming party. Note that some homes require an Achievement before purchase. The Quest: A **Friend In Need** is not required to purchase houses with Crowns.

NAVIGATORS (BOATSWAINS AND CARAVANS)

Docks, found near the sea, and caravans that typically show up in town offer fast travel to another zone. This helps keep the player moving through Tamriel.

MERCHANTS

A variety of Merchants can be found in every city in Tamriel. Traveling General Goods Merchants roam the roads outside of town too, so keep an eye out if space is becoming a premium. The following table lists the items available from each type of Merchant.

Note that most Merchants also sell related furnishings, though each requires a specific Achievement to purchase.

Merchants

Merchant	Examples of Items Available
Achievement Furnisher	Furnishings (requires an Achievement to purchase corresponding furnishing)
Alchemist	Poisons, Potions
Armorer	Heavy Armor
Armsman/Weaponsmith	Weapons, Shields
Blacksmith	Style Materials, Unknown Heavy Armor/Metal Weapon Containers, Furnishing Diagrams
Brewer	Alcoholic Beverages, Tea Beverages, Tonic Beverages, Drink Recipes
Carpenter	Style Materials, Unknown Wooden Weapon Containers, Furnishing Blueprints
Chef/Grocer	Fruit Dishes, Meat Dishes, Vegetable Dishes, Food Recipes
Clothier	Style Materials, Unknown Light/Medium Armor Containers, Furnishing Patterns
Enchanter	Potency Runestones, Glyphs (Armor, Weapon, Jewelry)
General Goods (Innkeeper)	Lockpicks, Potions, Repair Kits
Home Goods Furnisher	Furnishings
Leatherworker	Medium Armor
Magus	Rings, Necklaces, Staves
Mystic	Soul Gems (full and empty), Merethic Restorative Resin
Pack Merchant	Backpack Upgrades
Prestige Furnisher	Special Furnishings
Tailor	Light Armor
Woodworker	Bows, Shields, Staves

CRAFTING STATIONS

Crafting stations are found in all major cities, allowing the player to create a number of helpful items, such as potions, armor, weapons, glyphs, and provisions. Each requires specific materials found at vendors and in the wild.

Crafting Stations

Crafting Station	Product	Materials
Alchemy	Poisons, Potions, Furnishings	Solvents, Reagents (Animal Parts, Fungus, Herbs)
Blacksmithing	Metal Weapons, Heavy Armor, Furnishings	Ingots (refined from ore), Style Materials, Trait Items, Tempers
Clothing	Light Armor, Medium Armor, Furnishings	Cloths and Leathers (refined raw material), Style Materials, Trait Items, Tannins
Enchanting Table	Glyphs, Furnishings	Potency, Essence, Aspect Runestones
Cooking Fire (Provisioning)	Food, Drinks, Furnishings	Food Additives
Woodworking	Shields, Wooden Weapons, Furnishings	Wood (refined raw materials), Style Materials, Trait Items, Resins

CRAFTING SETS

Special crafting stations are also found outside of town, which offer an exclusive set of creatable items. Explore Tamriel and keep an eye out for the Crafting Set icon to appear on the map. With the correct trait items, unique equipment can be created at these stations.

GUILD TRADERS

Each Guild Trader is owned by a player guild and allows anyone to buy items from members of that guild. Each vendor must be bid on by the guild to maintain control. The store can be searched by item type, price range, level range, and quality. Items are priced by the players who put them up for sale. Guild Traders offer a great convenience for someone looking for a particular, hard-to-find item.

BANKS

A bank, accessible at major cities, allows for an additional 60 storage spaces. This can be upgraded, with 10 spaces added per purchase, up to a maximum of 240. Note that these upgrades get more expensive the higher you go. Items and currencies deposited into the bank are accessible by all of your characters. In an Outlaws Refuge, a Moneylender offers access to the bank. ESO Plus subscribers get double the bank space for the duration of their subscriptions.

If you belong to a player-created guild, banks also grant access to the Guild Bank and Guild Store for that guild. Deposit items and money to share with the guild at the Guild Bank. The Guild Store allows a guild to buy and sell amongst its members. Guilds must have 10 members to enable the Guild Bank and 50 for the Guild Store.

STABLES

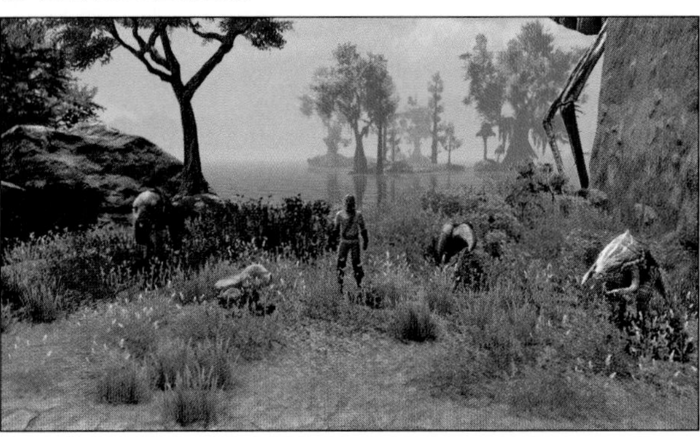

Stables, found in most major cities, sell a small selection of horses, which can be mounted and ridden throughout Tamriel. Visit the Stablemaster once every 20 hours to upgrade the following riding skills for 250 gold.

Riding Skills

Stat	Description
Speed	Increases movement speed while mounted, up to a maximum of 60%.
Stamina	Increases your Stamina while mounted, up to a maximum of 60, allowing your mount to sprint longer and take more hits before you become dismounted.
Carrying Capacity	Increases your carrying capacity, up to a maximum of 60.

DYE STATION

Dye Stations allow the player to customize their armor and shield with two or three colors per piece of equipment. There's a plethora of colors to choose from, though each must be unlocked by earning the corresponding Achievement.

OUTLAWS REFUGE

An Outlaws Refuge can be found in the major cities. Inside, the first quest givers can be found for the Thieves Guild and Dark Brotherhood DLCs. Fences, Moneylenders, Merchants, and Remains-Silent (with the Shadowy Supplier Dark Brotherhood skill) are also present.

FENCE

Fences are the only NPCs that deal with stolen items. Sell them or have them laundered if you wish to keep the items. There is a limit to the number of items that can be sold and laundered each day, indicated under your inventory list. This amount can be upgraded with the Legerdemain Trafficker Passive Ability.

GUILD HALLS

FIGHTERS AND MAGES GUILD HALLS

Join and participate in the Mages and Fighters Guilds at their headquarters found in most major cities. It's worthwhile to join both guilds, but concentrate on the one that matches your playstyle. Each comes with a related skill line. Fighters Guild skills focus on consuming Stamina to take down an opponent, while Mages Guild skills are all about Magicka. The first Fighters Guild Passive Ability allows the player to intimidate NPCs in conversation. For Mages, the Passive gives the ability to persuade NPCs.

THIEVES GUILD DEN

The Thieves Guild, headquartered in Abah's Landing in Hew's Bane, offers a number of interesting quests and six Passive Abilities—though these are inaccessible without the Thieves Guild DLC. Quests and skills are all about thievery, giving you the ability to earn money via less legitimate means.

Visit the Thieves Guild Den for the same amenities as an Outlaws Refuge—Fence, Moneylender, Merchant, and a Guild Trader.

DARK BROTHERHOOD SANCTUARY

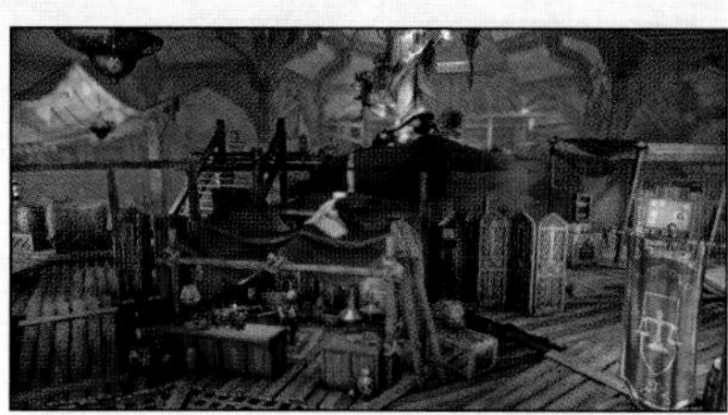

The Dark Brotherhood Sanctuary is found on the Gold Coast, between Anvil and Kvatch. Access related quests and vendors inside with the Dark Brotherhood DLC installed.

UNDAUNTED ENCLAVES

Undaunted Enclaves are found in Elden Root, Mournhold, and Wayrest, depending on Alliance affiliation. Receive Undaunted Pledges once you reach Level 45 and shop at special Undaunted vendors.

SHRINES

Shrine Locations

Shrine	Zone (City)		Effect
Shrine to Mara	Stonefalls (Davon's Watch) Deshaan (Mournhold) Glenumbra (Daggerfall)	Stormhaven (Wayrest) Auridon (Vulkhel Guard) Grahtwood (Elden Root)	Experience bonus for pair of players when wearing rings.
Shrine of Mother Morrowind	Morrowind (Vivec City)		
Shrine to Kyne	Deshaan (Mournhold)		Resets Attributes.
Shrine to Auriel	Grahtwood (Elden Root)		
Shrine of Akatosh	Stormhaven (Wayrest)		
Shrine of the Warrior-Poet	Morrowind (Vivec City)		
Shrine to Stuhn	Deshaan (Mournhold)		Resets skills or morphs.
Shrine of Stendarr	Grahtwood (Elden Root)	Stormhaven (Wayrest)	
Shrine of Father of Mysteries	Morrowind (Vivec City)		

RITUAL OF MARA

Shrines: Shrine to Mara, Shrine of Mother Morrowind

With the Pledge of Mara, purchased from the Crown Store or received from the Imperial Edition, a player may perform a Ritual of Mara with a partner. This rewards both players with a Ring of Mara. Whenever the two are grouped together and wearing the rings, an Experience bonus is earned.

RESET ATTRIBUTES

Shrines: Shrine to Kyne, Shrine to Auriel, Shrine of Akatosh, Shrine of the Warrior-Poet

Make a donation of a set amount of gold to be granted the ability to reset all Attribute Points. This allows you to alter your focus if you decide the current allocation is not to your liking.

RESET SKILLS OR MORPHS

Shrines: Shrine to Stuhn, Shrine of Stendarr, Shrine of Father of Mysteries

Donate a set amount of gold to earn the ability to reset your skills, or just the morphs, with the latter costing significantly less.

STRIKING LOCALES

An eye icon denotes points of interest around Tamriel. These are typically interesting locations that are worth checking out.

SETTLEMENTS, GROVES, TOWNS, CAMPFIRES

While you explore Tamriel, NPCs often ask for assistance from the player. This frequently entails completing quests to rid the area of a threat and bring the lives of the townsfolk back to normal. The black icon turns white once the quest line has been completed.

MUSEUMS

A museum in Wrothgar is accessible with the Orsinium DLC, while a second is added with Morrowind. Both require collecting specific items to be displayed at the museum, as well as completing new quests.

HOUSE OF ORSIMER GLORIES

Location: Orsinium (Wrothgar)

Collect relics across Wrothgar to be shown in the House of Orsimer Glories.

TEMPLE CANTON

Location: Vivec City (Morrowind)

The Curator of Temple Canton, Librarian Bradyn, needs help completing his model and finding the lost Library of Andule. Take rubbings at 30 ancestral tombs across Vvardenfell and deliver them to the Librarian.

KARI'S HIT LIST (THIEVES DEN)

Location: Thieves Den in Abah's Landing (Hew's Bane)

As a member of the Thieves Guild, steal legendary treasures, located throughout Tamriel, that are listed on Kari's Hit List. Once collected, put the treasures on display in the Thieves Den. There are 16 in all and earn an Achievement once all have been displayed.

LITANY OF BLOOD (DARK BROTHERHOOD SANCTUARY)

Location: Dark Brotherhood Sanctuary (Gold Coast)

As a member of the Dark Brotherhood, assassinate the targets listed in the book, Litany of Blood. There are 15 targets that must be disposed of with the Blade of Woe. Once they are killed, their souls appear back at the sanctuary.

DUNGEONS

GROUP DUNGEONS

Designed For: 4 Players

Group dungeons offer an instanced experience for a group of players. Enter one of these dungeons with a group of two lower-level players and you will probably get crushed.

PUBLIC DUNGEONS

Designed For: 2 Players

Since public dungeons are not instanced to each character, you may come across players inside. Therefore, it is possible to survive on your own, though content is balanced for two. Help out others and maybe they will join you throughout your time inside the dungeon.

DELVES

Designed For: 1-2 Players

Delves are small, public dungeons that can be completed alone or with a group. Find a skyshard in each delve, as well as a boss, which must be defeated to get credit for a completion. Group delves in Craglorn are instanced dungeons for two to four players.

TRIALS

Designed For: 12 Players

Join eleven players and take on some of the most challenging PvE encounters in Tamriel. Three Trials are found in Craglorn, one in Hew's Bane, and another in Morrowind. Leaderboards display the fastest times, with valuable loot going to anyone who completes the Trials. A Vitality bonus is awarded based on group revivals.

Trials

Zone	Trial
Craglorn	Aetherian Archive
Craglorn	Hel-Ra Citadel
Craglorn	Sanctum Ophidia
Reaper's March	Maw of Lorkhaj
Morrowind	Halls of Fabrication

A randomly selected Trial is chosen by the Undaunted to be the Weekly Trial. Receive a special reward each week by completing it.

GROUP BOSSES

Indicated by a skull and crossed swords on the map, group bosses are powerful enemies that necessitate a group of players to defeat. Though group bosses typically require about four players, those found in Gold Coast, Hew's Bane, and Wrothgar demand significantly more—up to a dozen players.

SPECIAL EVENTS

Special Holiday Events are indicated on the map with a Special Event icon. During the holidays, these locations provide exclusive quests.

DOLMENS (DARK ANCHORS)

Dolmens are found throughout Tamriel, with three instances in most zones, besides Cyrodiil, where there are 10. Note that there are no Dolmens in Morrowind, Craglorn, Wrothgar, Hew's Bane, and Gold Coast. These world events require waves of enemies to be dealt with by players in the area. The start of this event can be heard and seen from a long distance, giving you time to participate if nearby. Within a zone, one dolmen typically spawns at a time with the next beginning only after the previous one has been knocked down.

After you clear out the waves of Daedra, there's a chance for one of Molag Bal's generals to show up. Defeating the generals earns Achievements for the player. Once the Dark Anchor is destroyed, an instanced chest appears for each participant.

AYLEID OR AETHERIAL WELLS

Ayleid Wells, or Aetherial Wells in Auridon, provide the player with a 10-minute Maximum Health buff, called an Ayleid Health Bonus. After the well is activated, a cooldown period follows before the player can use it again. Besides in Cyrodiil, these wells are instanced. Note that this means everyone must wait out the cooldown after a well is used in Cyrodiil.

MUNDUS STONE

Scattered throughout Tamriel, 51 Mundus Stones offer the player a boon. There are 13 types of buffs available, with three of each found outside of Cyrodiil. Within the PvP zone, all but the Lord can be found. You may only have one boon at a time. There are no Mundus Stones in Morrowind, so plan accordingly.

Mundus Stone	Zones	Boon
The Apprentice	Bangkorai, Reaper's March, the Rift, Cyrodiil	Increases Spell Damage.
The Atronach	Greenshade, Rivenspire, Shadowfen, Cyrodiil	Increases Magicka recovery.
The Lady	Auridon, Glenumbra, Stonefalls, Cyrodiil	Increases Physical Resistance.
The Lord	Deshaan, Grahtwood, Stormhaven	Increases Maximum Health.
The Lover	Auridon, Glenumbra, Stonefalls, Cyrodiil	Increases spell resistance.
The Mage	Deshaan, Grahtwood, Stormhaven, Cyrodiil	Increases Maximum Magicka.
The Ritual	Alik'r Desert, Eastmarch, Malabal Tor, Cyrodiil	Increases healing effectiveness.
The Serpent	Greenshade, Rivenspire, Shadowfen, Cyrodiil	Increases Stamina Recovery.
The Shadow	Greenshade, Rivenspire, Shadowfen, Cyrodiil	Increases Critical Strike Damage.
The Steed	Bangkorai, Reaper's March, the Rift, Cyrodiil	Increases run speed and Health Recovery.
The Thief	Alik'r Desert, Eastmarch, Malabal Tor, Cyrodiil	Increases Critical Strike Chance.
The Tower	Deshaan, Grahtwood, Stormhaven, Cyrodiil	Increases Maximum Stamina.
The Warrior	Alik'r Desert, Eastmarch, Malabal Tor, Cyrodiil	Increases Weapon Damage.

CYRODIIL LOCATIONS

ALLIANCE WAR MERCHANTS

Note that some items, such as siege equipment, in Cyrodiil require Alliance Points to purchase. These are earned by participating in the Alliance War. The typical merchants can be found in Cyrodill, such as General Merchants and Chefs, along with specialty vendors, such as Elite Gear Vendors and Siege Merchants.

Tel Var Stones and Alliance Points are required to purchase many items from vendors inside the Imperial City Sewers. Complete quests and defeat enemies in the Imperial City to earn Tel Var Stones.

TRANSITUS SHRINES

Transitus Shrines allow the player to fast-travel in Cyrodiil. Interact with the shrine to travel to keeps or outposts fully controlled by your faction. Note that it must be connected to your current location.

BORDER KEEP

Border keeps are the entry points to the Alliance War, with two per alliance. These locations offer quests and vendors for the players. A Wayshrine at each location allows you to fast-travel out of Cyrodiil. A Transitus Shrine is also available, giving you quicker access to the front lines.

FORWARD CAMP

A forward camp allows teammates to respawn at its location and can be placed anywhere in Cyrodiil, as long as it is flat enough. Players who die near a forward camp have the opportunity to respawn at that site. It can be purchased from a Siege Merchant for 20,000 Alliance Points. Use the item from a quickslot and find a flat, suitable spot; a red X indicates that the site is unsuitable.

You must be Alliance Rank 6 or higher to purchase the item, and it only allows for 20 soldiers to respawn. You may not use the forward camp if you have used it recently. Press the Interact button to dismantle an enemy's forward camp.

KEEP

There are 18 keeps in Cyrodiil, with each alliance controlling six at the start of an Alliance War. Turn the two flags to your alliance to capture the structure. Controlling the surrounding resources is beneficial with keeping the structure repaired. Holding an Elder Scroll on a keep's scroll pedestal bestows a bonus for every member of that alliance.

RESOURCES

A farm, lumbermill, and mine surround each of the 18 keeps in Cyrodiil. Capture a resource by killing off enough of the opposition so that your side outnumbers them. One flag must be turned to your alliance to gain control. Controlling these resources gives the keep an added benefit for repair.

Resource		Benefit of Capture
	Farm	Increases the strength of NPC soldiers guarding the keep.
	Lumbermill	Allows players to strengthen the doors of the keep.
	Mine	Gathers the stone necessary for wall upgrade and repair.

TEMPLE

A temple sits just inside each border keep. A temple holds an Elder Scroll at the start of an Alliance War, which gives bonuses to every player of the alliance. Each alliance begins with an offensive and defensive scroll.

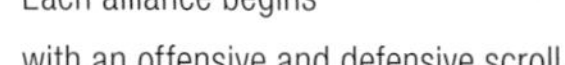

Alliance	Temple/Original Elder Scroll	Nearest Border Keep	Type of Scroll
Aldmeri Dominion	Altadoon	Western Elsweyr	Offensive
	Mnem	Eastern Elsweyr	Defensive
Daggerfall Covenant	Alma Ruma	Southern High Rock	Defensive
	Ni-Mohk	Northern High Rock	Offensive
Ebonheart Pact	Chim	Northern Morrowind	Defensive
	Ghartok	Southern Morrowind	Offensive

ELDER SCROLLS

Each alliance begins with two Elder Scrolls, one offensive and one defensive. These can be captured and taken to another alliance's keep or temple, where a bonus is awarded every player of that alliance. Click Bonuses on the Alliance War tab for details of the bonuses given.

ARTIFACT GATE

An Artifact Gate acts as a last line of defense, protecting each temple from outside threats. Two keeps must be captured to open a gate. The gates are given the same name as the temple it protects.

OUTPOST

Near the center of Cyrodiil, three outposts sit along the Transitus network between a pair of keeps. Use a nearby, friendly keep to travel to the outpost. A pair of flags inside the structure must be turned to apture it.

TOWN

Bruma, Cropsford, and Vlastarus sit near the perimeter of Cyrodiil, between opposing border keeps. A town can be captured, offering a safe location for players to respawn. Specialized equipment vendors are found within a friendly town.

BATTLE

Look for the Battle icon on the Cyrodiil map to discover where the action is taking place.

IMPERIAL CITY ENTRANCE

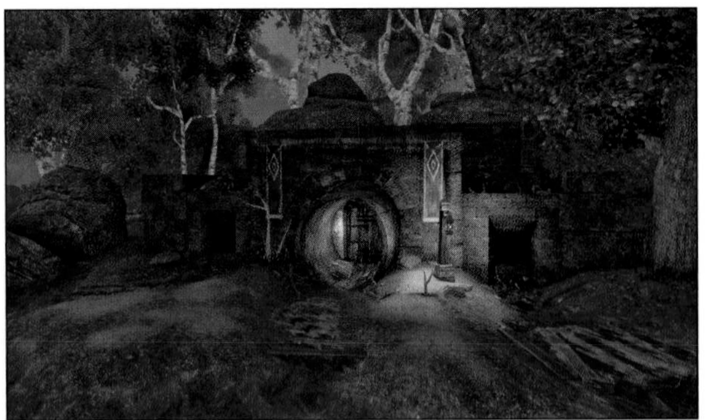

The Imperial City DLC is required to access the Imperial City entrances. Three gates offer entry points to the Imperial Sewers, from which you are sent to your alliance's base within the sewers.

IMPERIAL CITY LOCATIONS

By owning the Imperial City DLC or being an ESO Plus member, gain access to the Imperial City through the Imperial Sewers.

IMPERIAL DISTRICTS

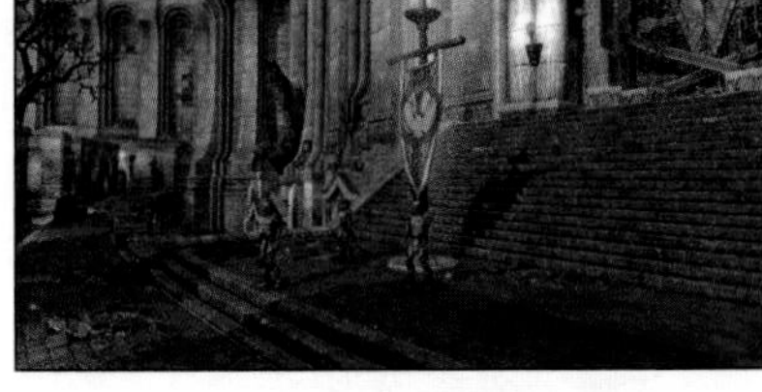

There are six districts of the Imperial City: Arboretum, Arena, Elven Gardens, Memorial, Nobles, and Temple. The city is open PvP, with quests available in each district once the Imperial City story quests are complete.

IMPERIAL CITY DOORS

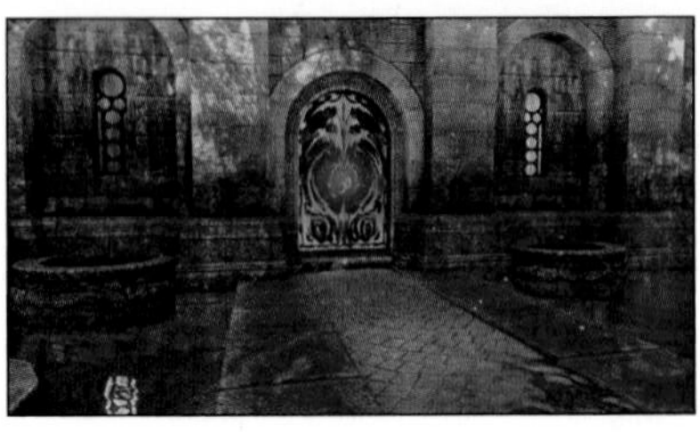

A Trophy Vault sits within each district and dungeon per our table. Collecting 60 Key Fragments from enemies in the Imperial City grants access to one of the city's hidden Trophy Vaults. Gather 150 to open the Trophy Vaults in the Imperial City Prison or the White-Gold Tower.

District/Dungeon	Trophy Vault
Arboretum	Clawed
Arena	Ethereal
Elven Gardens	Planar Armor
Memorial	Bone Shard
Nobles	Legionary
Temple	Monstrous Tooth
Imperial City Prison	Daedric Shackle
White-Gold Tower	Daedric Embers

SEWER ENTRANCE

Use sewer entrances to move between areas of the Imperial Sewers, as well as in and out of the six districts.

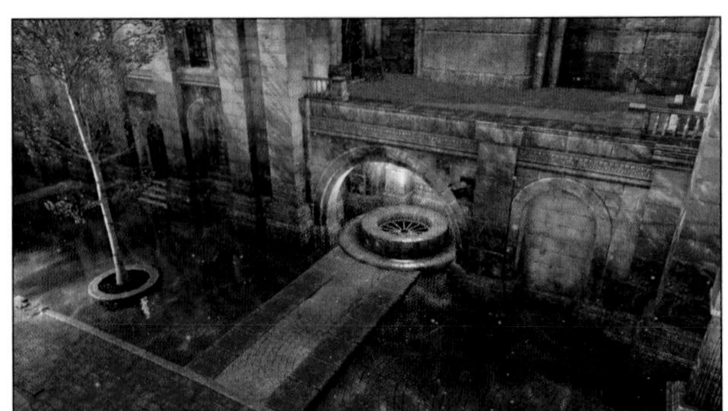

DARK ANCHORS (DOLMENS)

Molag Bal uses Dolmens, located throughout much of Tamriel, to fasten his Dark Anchors in an attempt to pull Nirn into Coldharbour. Worm Cultists perform a ritual at the site, bringing the Anchor crashing down in exchange for a sacrifice. Once attached, the cultists are randomly dragged into the air, eventually replaced with new followers. Any players in the area may take part in this world event, fighting the antagonists responsible for the invasion. This is the first of three phases, which, upon completion, rewards those who participated with an instanced chest.

Active Dark Anchors are visible from distant lands.

Three Dolmens exist within nearly every zone of Tamriel. Cyrodiil holds ten Dark Anchor points, while no Dolmens are found in the starter zones , Craglorn, Wrothgar, Hew's Bane, Gold Coast, and Vvardenfell.

The Fighters Guild offers daily quests that require the player to destroy three dolmens in a given zone.

Dolmens are activated when a player gets within range, beginning the Worm Cultists' ritual. A loud noise announces the incoming Dark Anchor with a scene that is visible from far away. Anyone may join the event, with an Achievement available for destroying all Dark Anchors in each zone. Completing these events also levels up your Fighters Guild rank and is required for their quest line.

DOLMENS LOCATIONS

ALDMERI DOMINION

AURIDON
Calambar Dolmen
Lluvamir Dolmen
Vafe Dolmen

GRAHTWOOD
Green Hall Dolmen
Long Coast Dolmen
Tarlain Heights Dolmen

GREENSHADE
Drowned Coast Dolmen
Green's Marrow Dolmen
Wilderking Court Dolmen

MALABAL TOR
Broken Coast Dolmen
Silvenar Vale Dolmen
Xylo River Basin Dolmen

REAPER'S MARCH
Dawnmead Dolmen
Jodewood Dolmen
Northern Woods Dolmen

DAGGERFALL COVENANT

ALIK'R DESERT
Hollow Waste Dolmen
Myrkwasa Dolmen
Tigonus Dolmen

BANGKORAI
Ephesus Dolmen
Fallen Wastes Dolmen
Mournoth Dolmen

GLENUMBRA
Cambray Hills Dolmen
Daenia Dolmen
King's Guard Dolmen

RIVENSPIRE
Boralis Dolmen
Eyebright Feld Dolmen
Westmark Moor Dolmen

STORMHAVEN
Alcaire Dolmen
Gavaudon Dolmen
Menevia Dolmen

EBONHEART PACT

DESHAAN
Lagomere Dolmen
Redolent Loam Dolmen
Siltreen Dolmen

EASTMARCH
Frostwater Tundra Dolmen
Giant's Run Dolmen
Icewind Peaks Dolmen

THE RIFT
Ragged Hills Dolmen
Smokefrost Peaks Dolmen
Stony Basin Dolmen

SHADOWFEN
Leafwater Dolmen
Reticulated Spine Dolmen
Venomous Fens Dolmen

STONEFALLS
Daen Seeth Dolmen
Varanis Dolmen
Zabamat Dolmen

NEUTRAL

CYRODIIL
Applewatch Wood Dolmen
Bruma
Cheydinhal Foothills Dolmen
Eastern Shore Dolmen
Great Forest Dolmen
Greenmead Dolmen
Niben Basin Dolmen
Nibenay Valley Dolmen
Winter's Reach Dolmen

Killing the Daedra and Undead fills the four Anchor Pinions, one at a time.

If left alone, the six Worm Cultists continue the ritual, with members being randomly pulled into the air, only to be replaced with more Worm Cultists. Killing these followers causes four Anchor Pinions to appear around the Dolmen. Normal- and elite-level Daedra and Undead drop in from the portal above, damaging players caught in their landing areas.

Defeating the Daedra and Undead fills up the first Anchor Pinion with their animi, with elite mobs adding twice as much per kill. The Pinion opens once full as the enemy spirits begin to fill the next pinion. A player must approach each open Anchor Pinion and interact with it to destroy it. Each time this is done, the Health, Magicka, and Stamina for all nearby players are fully restored. Destroying all four pinions completes the second phase of the event.

There's a chance that one of Molag Bal's generals makes an appearance during the final wave.

As Molag Bal taunts the players, a boss is summoned to the Dolmen with a complement of tougher Daedra and Undead. Instead of one of the standard bosses, there's a small chance that one of Molag Bal's generals makes an appearance. An Achievement is earned by defeating each general, and another for destroying them all. The spirits from this final wave fill the fifth and final Anchor Pinion at the base of the Dark Anchor. Destroying this trap reveals a chest, available to all players who participated.

Molag Bal's Generals

- Anaxes and Medrike, the Xivilai torturers
- The Dark Seducer sisters, Vika, Dylora, and Jansa
- Daedroth Hrelvesuu
- Destroy Ozzozachar, the favored Titan of Molag Bal
- Gedna Relvel, the Lich of Mournhold
- King Styriche of Verkarth and his companions, Fangaril and Zayzahad
- Lord Dregas Volar, the holder of the Daedric Crescent
- Menta Na, Molag Bal's most favored Daedroth
- Methats, Vonshala, and Sumeer, the Dremora travelers
- Molag Bal's torturers, Kathutet, Amkaos, and Ranyu
- Nomeg Haga, the giant Frost Atronach of Coldharbour
- Ogrim Brothers, Glut, Hogshead, and Stumble
- Rhagothan, the Devourer of Souls
- Velehk Sain, the Dremora pirate
- Yggmanei the Ever-Open Eye, Molag Bal's greatest spy
- Zymel Hriz, the giant Storm Atronach of Coldharbour

A TROVE OF TAMRIEL TIPS

SKYSHARDS

Look for the beam of light to spot the hidden skyshards.

Additional Skill Points are available by collecting skyshards found around Tamriel. Interact with three skyshards to earn one Skill Point. These shards can be found almost anywhere, including deep inside dungeons, so be attentive as you explore Tamriel. A light shines upward from the shard, making it visible from a distance. The Achievements section of the Journal offers tips for every skyshard in the game, as well as keeping track of those that you have found. Note that every delve and public dungeon has a skyshard.

Number of Skyshards Per Zone

FACTION	ZONE	# OF SKYSHARDS
Aldmeri Dominion	Khenarthi's Roost	6
	Auridon	16
	Grahtwood	16
	Greenshade	16
	Malabal Tor	16
	Reaper's March	16
Daggerfall Covenant	Stros M'Kai	3
	Betnikh	3
	Glenumbra	16
	Stormhaven	16
	Alik'r Desert	16
	Bangkorai	16
	Rivenspire	16

FACTION	ZONE	# OF SKYSHARDS
Ebonheart Pact	Bleakrock Isle	3
	Bal Foyen	3
	Stonefalls	16
	Deshaan	16
	Shadowfen	16
	Eastmarch	16
	The Rift	16
Neutral	Gold Coast	7
	Hew's Bane	6
	Coldharbour	16
	Craglorn	12
	Cyrodiil	46
	Morrowind	18

TIPS

Starting out in *Elder Scrolls Online* may seem daunting at first. A tutorial quest teaches the basics, and pop-up messages offer advice as new mechanics arise. Still, the ability to travel most anywhere and the sheer amount of quests available at the start can become overwhelming. Here are a handful of tips to keep in mind as you begin your adventures.

- During early levels, loot every enemy. Most items sell for at least one gold, and this money adds up.
- Lockpicks are often found, which can be used to procure more valuable loot.

- Be sure to visit a vendor and/or the bank before leaving town in order to free up space for new loot.
- Early in the game, equipment is found at a fairly quick pace, so don't waste money on repairs if you can help it. Repair becomes more practical later on as favorite gear is found and time between levels increases.
- Experience is not only earned by completing quests and other activities, but also for simply discovering new locations. Explore off the beaten path to earn extra XP. This is also a great way to find hidden loot and resources.
- Wayshrines are available throughout Tamriel, allowing for fast travel between zones. Traveling directly to a Wayshrine from the wild costs money, but traveling between two Wayshrines, by interacting with one, is free.. While money is tight, take the time to find a Wayshrine before travel.

- By placing a skill on the Action Bar, Experience is earned directly to that skill line, whether that ability is used or not. Earn Experience toward six different skill lines by placing an active ability of each on the Action Bar, including an Ultimate. It's even possible to level up a weapon without having that weapon equipped.
- Consider race and class carefully during character creation. Race provides four unique racial Passive Abilities, while class gives access to three skill lines, each with an assortment of Active Effects and Passive Abilities, as well as an Ultimate.
- A second Action Bar is unlocked at Level 15, allowing you to arrange two sets of abilities and weapon. Set up complementary weapons, such as a bow and daggers for long distance and melee combat, respectively. Or create two sets of abilities with the same weapon, giving you access to twice as many abilities.

- Typically Tank builds are best equipped in heavy armor, Stamina users in medium, and light armor is best for Magicka casters. This means your playstyle or role may dictate the type of armor worn, but there are advantages to mixing it up. Each weight has one Active Ability and five Passive Abilities, and wearing just one piece earns Experience toward that skill line. Early on, equip at least one of each type to gain access to these Passives.
- It is often wise to specialize in no more than three crafting disciplines. Attempting to take on all six can burn through Skill Points that can be used elsewhere. Decide early on which areas you wish to specialize in. Focusing on the three equipment trade skills or the three non-equipment skills, makes best use of similarities between them. Consider creating an alternate character with the sole purpose of crafting, making it possible to take on more disciplines.
- All your characters deposit and withdraw from the same bank account. This allows you to share between characters and use "mules" for extra storage space.
- Don't limit yourself to just the quests; Tamriel has a lot to offer. Group bosses, dungeons, and Dark Anchors all provide great Experience boosts, with chances to find valuable loot.
- Do not forget about your Soul Gems. Once it's available, place the Soul Trap Ability on the Action Bar and fill empty gems with enemy souls to keep your stock up.

- Examine all Lorebooks found in your travels, as they all add to your Mages Guild rank. Even if you're not currently participating in their quests, it's good practice.
- Always keep an eye out for the bright light emitted from skyshards throughout Tamriel. For every three collected, a valuable Skill Point is rewarded.
- Look for bookshelves inside city buildings as well as dungeons and other structures throughout Tamriel. Interact with each one to read a book. Occasionally one provides a boost in a related skill, so it's well worth the little time it takes. There's no need to actually read the entries.

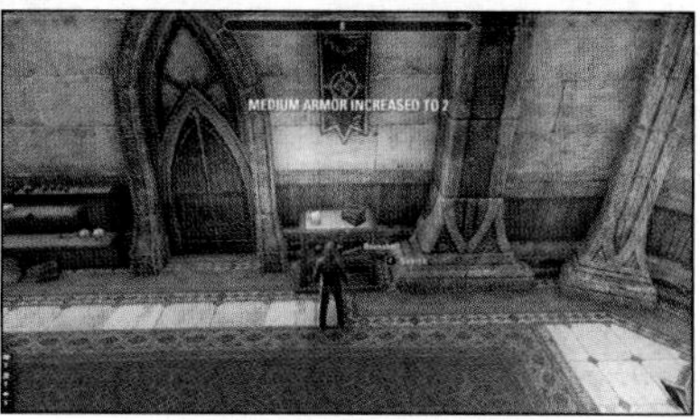

- The Alliance War in Cyrodiil becomes available once you reach Level 10. This unlocks new challenges and more opportunities to earn Experience and great items. Instead of gold, you're rewarded in Alliance Points, which can be used at specialized vendors at the alliance base. When entering Cyrodiil, your character is battle-leveled, allowing you to be more competitive when facing other players. Higher-level players have access to better abilities, so they still have an advantage.
- Take advantage of the introductory quests in Cyrodiil to learn the ins and outs of the Alliance War. Not only do you receive Alliance Points and Experience, but a free forward camp is also awarded.
- Start researching Traits early, even if you don't think you'll make use of the equipment-crafting tradeskills for a while. Trait research takes a lot of real-world time to complete, so starting early can save you weeks or even months down the line.

GLOSSARY

The following table lists useful terms used in and out of the game.

Adds	Additional mobs that attack while you fight another. Many boss fights introduce adds to create a tougher challenge. Crowd-control abilities become invaluable in these instances.
Aggro	To attract the attention of an enemy, or the amount of aggression generated from the mobs. It's best not to aggro too many enemies at once. Leave this task to melee fighters or, better yet, the Tanks, allowing weaker casters to remain out of harm's way.
Alt (alternate character)	A character that is not your main. Typically, this is a secondary character created for the purpose of handling another, mundane task, such as crafting or extra storage.
AoE (area of effect)	A skill that causes an effect over an area. When an enemy casts an AoE, a red shape appears on the ground to show the area that will be affected.
Buff	An effect on a player that temporarily improves an attribute or ability.
Boon	In *Elder Scrolls Online*, a boon is a permanent buff given from a Mundus Stone. There are 13 available boons in the game, but you can only possess one at a time.
CC (crowd control)	Abilities that allow the player to control an enemy's movement. A skill that stuns an opponent is an example of crowd control. This is an extremely important job when facing higher numbers of foes, such as while exploring dungeons.
COD (Cash on Delivery, via mail)	When trading through the in-game mail system, this setting means that money must be sent upon receiving the item. Note that there is a postage fee associated when using C.O.D.
CP (Champion Points)	A Champion Point is awarded each time the Champion Bar is filled after reaching Level 50. These points can be allocated into a constellation at the Champion screen, giving the player new powerful Passive Abilities. Currently, you can spend a maximum of 630 Champion Points.
Debuff	An effect placed on a player that temporarily lowers an attribute or ability.
DoT (damage over time)	An attack that continues to cause damage after the initial hit, usually with an applied status effect, such as Bleed.
DPS (damage per second)	The amount of damage that a player causes every second.
Instanced	A location or item that is duplicated for each player. For example, group dungeons are instanced for each group, isolating the team from other players. Clear a Dark Anchor and an instanced chest is awarded, allowing everyone involved to get their cut.
Main	This is your main character.
Mob	A computer-controlled enemy is often referred to as a mob.
NPCs (non-player characters)	Any characters that are controlled by the computer are NPCs, such as vendors, quest givers, Stablemasters, and Navigators.
PvE (player versus environment)	Any combat between a player or group of players and computer-controlled enemies. Outside the zone of Cyrodiil and the Battlegrounds in Vvardenfell, everything is PvE.
PvP (player versus player)	Any combat between human players. This is limited to Cyrodiil, the Imperial City, and the Battlegrounds in Vvardenfell.
Skill Line	A set of abilities that are improved together with earned Experience. Two-Handed weapons are an example of a skill line. The following categories have their own skill lines: race, class, guild, weapon, armor, world, Alliance War, and crafting.
Status Effect	Temporary change to a player's stats, typically caused by an enemy, though traps in the environment may also produce a status effect. Snared, Stunned, Defile, Bleed, and Silenced are all examples.
Tank	A character build set up to absorb damage. It's best for the player to keep the enemy's attention with an ability such as a Taunt.
Trash Mob	Weaker enemies the player faces between boss fights.
WTB (Want to Buy)	Commonly used in chat by a player who wishes to buy a specific item.
WTS (Want to Sell)	Commonly used in chat by a player who has an item that they wish to sell.
XP (Experience)	Gained by defeating enemies and completing quests. The player moves up a level with certain amounts of XP.

QUESTS

Elder Scrolls Online provides well over 1500 quests across Tamriel. The main story, alliance story lines, zone quests, the Alliance War, guilds, and expansions all provide unique experiences for the player.

Each of the three factions offers its own story line that ends in an attack against Coldharbour. Complete the story line for your chosen alliance to receive Cadwell's Almanac as a new tab in your Journal, which allows you to play through a second alliance and then the third in the following order.

Cadwell's Almanac

STARTING ALLIANCE	CADWELL'S SILVER	CADWELL'S GOLD
Aldmeri Dominion	Ebonheart Pact	Daggerfall Covenant
Daggerfall Covenant	Aldmeri Dominion	Ebonheart Pact
Ebonheart Pact	Daggerfall Covenant	Aldmeri Dominion

Here we list the types of quests available throughout Tamriel with a rough number of each type. In order to participate in DLC quests, you must own the corresponding DLC or be a member of ESO Plus. In this chapter, we provide detailed coverage of every quest available in Vvardenfell.

MAIN STORY

Number of Quests	15
Starting Location	The Harborage (After Soul Shriven in Coldharbour Tutorial)

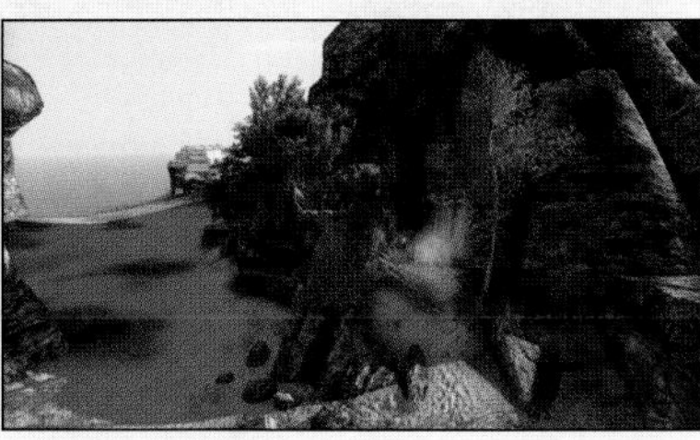

Beginning with **Tutorial: Soul Shriven in Coldharbour,** 15 quests follow the main story of ***Elder Scrolls Online***. Escape the Wailing Prison and meet up with the Prophet to learn of Molag Bal's threat to Nirn. Retrieve the Amulet of Kings and confront the Daedric Prince. Once Molag Bal is defeated, the player is given the opportunity to explore the other two alliances.

The Harborage

FACTION	LOCATION
Aldmeri Dominion	East of Vulkhel Guard
Daggerfall Covenant	Southeast of Daggerfall
Ebonheart Pact	West of Davon's Watch

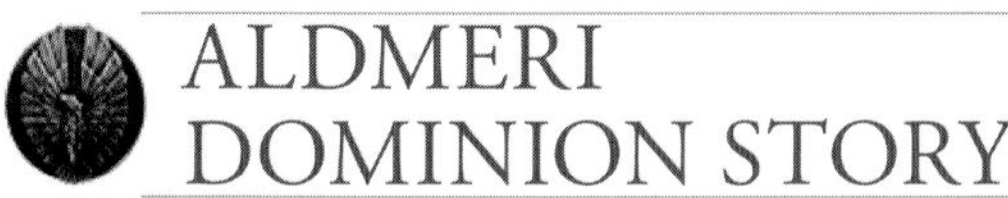

ALDMERI DOMINION STORY

Number of Quests	91
Starting Location	Khenarthi's Roost

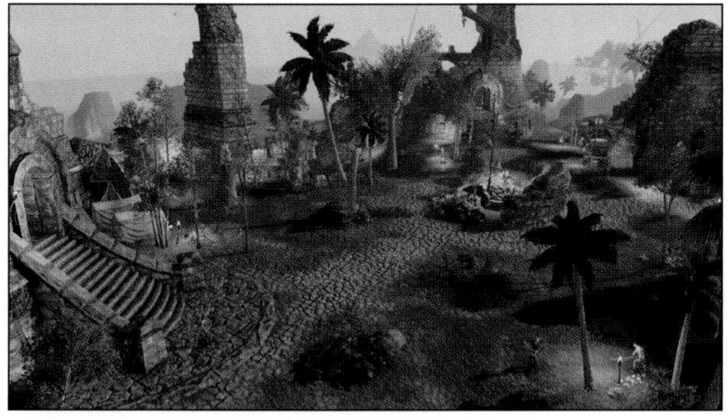

With assistance from Razum-dar, help Queen Ayrenn defend the region against the Sea Vipers and other worthy foes. Following the Aldmeri Dominion story line, the player travels through Khenarthi's Roost, Auridon, Grahtwood, Greenshade, Malabal Tor, and Reaper's March, before heading to Coldharbour—where the three alliances must be convinced to join forces and stop the Planemeld.

DAGGERFALL COVENANT STORY

Number of Quests	129
Starting Location	Stros M'Kai

After being washed ashore on the desert island of Stros M'Kai, the Daggerfall Covenant story line leads the player through Betnikh, Glenumbra, Stormhaven, Rivenspire, Alik'r Desert, and Bangkorai, before the three alliances must be convinced to join forces in Coldharbour. Assist High King Emeric and the Daggerfall Covenant against the many threats of northwestern Tamriel.

EBONHEART PACT STORY

Number of Quests	134
Starting Location	Bleakrock Isle

After escaping the Wailing Prison, the player starts out on Bleakrock Isle, before moving on to Bal Foyen and Stonefalls, where the Ebonheart Pact must be protected against a Daggerfall Covenant attack. The story continues through Deshaan, Shadowfen, Eastmarch, and the Rift. After completing the story quests in these zones, the player is tasked with convincing the other two alliances to join forces and attack Coldharbour.

ALLIANCE WAR (PVP)

Number of Quests	150
Starting Location	Cyrodiil

Complete the four introductory quests to learn about the Alliance War, and then assist your chosen alliance by completing scouting, capture, and bounty missions. Or retrieve one of six Elder Scrolls and return it to a keep under your alliance's control. Spend your well-earned Alliance Points on siege equipment, PvP gear, and more. As you earn more points, increase your Alliance War Rank from Citizen all the way to Grand Overlord.

Initial Quest Giver

FACTION	GATE	QUEST GIVER
Aldmeri Dominion	Eastern Elsweyr Gate	Arcarin
	Western Elsweyr Gate	Fangil
Daggerfall Covenant	Northern High Rock Gate	Zahreh
	Southern High Rock Gate	Veronard Liancourt
Ebonheart Pact	Northern Morrowind Gate	Olvyia Indaram
	Southern Morrowind Gate	Mirrored-Skin

CYRODIIL QUESTS (PVE)

Number of Quests	80
Starting Location	Cyrodiil

Like any zone in Tamriel, there is plenty to do in Cyrodiil, including numerous PvE quests. Towns require aid, dungeons need completing, and the Cyrodiil Fighters Guild needs assistance against resident foes.

IMPERIAL CITY (DLC)

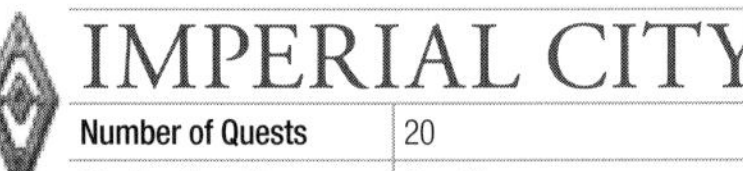

Number of Quests	20
Starting Location	Cyrodiil

For the Imperial City DLC, complete eight story quests within the city to thwart Molag Bal's plan. Depending on your alliance, speak to one of the captains listed or report directly to the general at the alliance base to get things started. Six districts provide additional quests.

Initial Quest Giver

FACTION	GATE/BASE	QUEST GIVER
Aldmeri Dominion	Eastern Elsweyr	Captain Mulamurr
	Western Elsweyr	Captain Sireril
	Aldmeri Dominion Base	General Nedras
Daggerfall Covenant	Northern High Rock	Captain Alesace
	Southern High Rock	Captain Durida
	Daggerfall Covenant Base	General Aklash
Ebonheart Pact	Northern Morrowind	Captain Rythe
	Southern Morrowind	Captain Veranim
	Ebonheart Pact Base	General Nesh-Tan

DARK BROTHERHOOD (DLC)

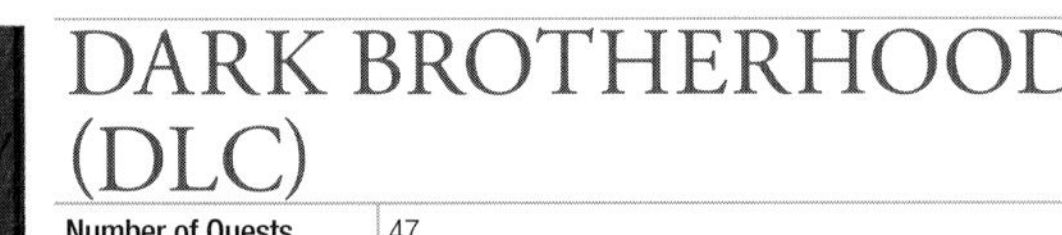

Number of Quests	47
Starting Location	Outlaws Refuge

With the Dark Brotherhood DLC activated, find Amelie Crowe in any Outlaws Refuge to begin the story quests. This sends you to Anvil on the Gold Coast, where Litany of Blood assassinations, daily Sacraments, and contracts become available. Once **Quest: Voices in the Dark** has been completed, the Blade of Woe Passive Ability allows for instant kills against normal-difficulty humanoid NPCs. Go stealth and use the blade on unsuspecting targets to complete contracts for the Dark Brotherhood.

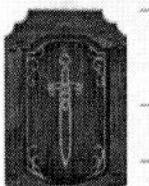

FIGHTERS GUILD

Number of Quests	27
Starting Location	First Major City

At any Fighters Guild, talk to the Hall Steward to join the Fighters Guild—giving you access to their skill line. Next, speak to Sees-All-Colors or Bera Moorsmith, depending on your location, at their guildhall to begin the first quest, **Anchors from the Harbour**. Story quests, bounties, and Dark Anchor daily quests are available from the guild. Increase your rank by killing Undead and Daedra and destroying Dark Anchors.

The guild's first Passive Ability, Intimidating Presence, gives you the ability to intimidate NPCs in conversation with a possibility of reducing required legwork during certain quests.

Quest Giver

FACTION	CITY	QUEST GIVER
Aldmeri Dominion	Vulkhel Guard	Aicessar
Daggerfall Covenant	Daggerfall	Basile Fenandre
Ebonheart Pact	Davon's Watch	Hilan

MAGES GUILD

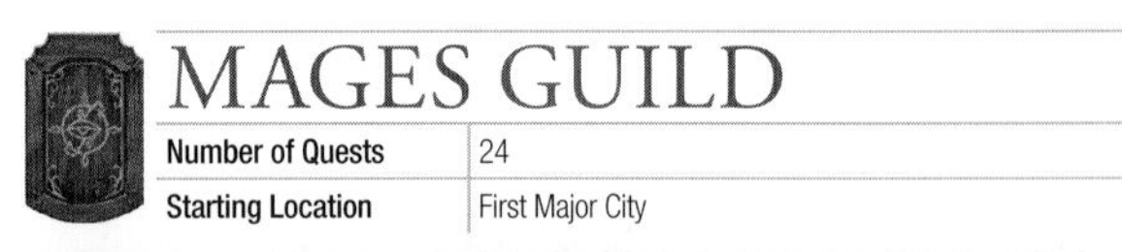

Number of Quests	24
Starting Location	First Major City

At any Mages Guild, speak with the Magister, or simply collect a Lorebook, to join the guild and gain access to their skills. Next, find Valaste or Adelle Montagne at a guildhall to begin the first quest, **Long Lost Lore**. Collecting Lorebooks increases your rank in the guild. Beyond the nine story quests, daily quests require you to retrieve an artifact from a random public dungeon.

Pick up the Passive Ability Persuasive Will for the ability to persuade NPCs during certain conversations. Doing so may reduce the legwork of a quest.

Quest Giver

FACTION	CITY	QUEST GIVER
Aldmeri Dominion	Vulkhel Guard	Curinure
Daggerfall Covenant	Daggerfall	Nemarc
Ebonheart Pact	Davon's Watch	Rudrusa

THIEVES GUILD

Number of Quests	29
Starting Location	Outlaws Refuge

With the Thieves Guild DLC activated, or as an ESO Plus member, talk to Quen inside any Outlaws Refuge to begin the first quest, **Partners in Crime**. The quest line leads you to Abah's Landing in Hew's Bane, where the guild is headquartered. Hone your pickpocketing and burglary skills with the justice system and the Thieves Guild Passive Abilities, which include Finders Keepers—allowing access to the valuable loot inside Thieves Troves located all over Tamriel.

UNDAUNTED

Number of Quests	78
Starting Location	First Major City

Speak to one of the associated quest givers to begin the first Undaunted quest, **One of the Undaunted**, which challenges you to enter a nearby Group Instance. Once the introductory quest is complete, explore more dungeons, delves, and Trials to earn reputation toward the guild. Starting at Level 45, complete Undaunted Pledges to earn keys that can be used on chests at an Undaunted enclave.

Quest Giver

FACTION	CITY	TAVERN
Aldmeri Dominion	Vulkhel Guard	Salted Wings Tavern
Daggerfall Covenant	Daggerfall	The Rosy Lion
Ebonheart Pact	Davon's Watch	Fish Stink Tavern
QUEST GIVER	**FIRST GROUP INSTANCE**	
Turuk Redclaws	The Banished Cells	
Mighty Mordra	Spindleclutch	
Kailstig the Axe	Fungal Grotto	

ALDMERI DOMINION SIDE QUESTS

Number of Quests	185
Starting Location	Auridon

Beyond the story quest, the zones of the Aldmeri Dominion hold nearly 200 quests. NPCs throughout Auridon, Grahtwood, Greenshade, Malabal Tor, and Reaper's March require aid from the Vestige.

DAGGERFALL COVENANT SIDE QUESTS

Number of Quests	194
Starting Location	Stros M'Kai

Take part in side quests throughout the zones of the Daggerfall Covenant, including Stros M'kai, Betnikh, Glenumbra, Stormhaven, Rivenspire, Alik'r Desert, and Bangkorai.

EBONHEART PACT SIDE QUESTS

Number of Quests	234
Starting Location	Bleakrock Isle

NPCs throughout the zones of the Ebonheart Pact require assistance from the player. Assist the citizens in Bleakrock Isle, Bal Foyen, Stonefalls, Deshaan, Shadowfen, Eastmarch, and the Rift.

COLDHARBOUR SIDE QUESTS

Number of Quests	22
Starting Location	Coldharbour

Revisit Coldharbour and complete side quests in Shrouded Plain, Black Garrison, and Fist of Stone.

CRAGLORN QUESTS

Number of Quests	32
Starting Location	Alliance Capital Cities

Craglorn is a neutral zone that sits northwest of Cyrodiil, with a mix of solo and group gameplay. The first quest, **The Star-Gazers**, can be started by talking to Star-Gazer Herald at an Alliance Capital City, or by traveling to Belkarth in Craglorn. Twelve story quests can be tackled within the zone, as well as daily, and a few Trial quests.

Quest Giver

FACTION	CITY	QUEST GIVER
Aldmeri Dominion	Elden Root	Star-Gazer Herald
Daggerfall Covenant	Wayrest	Star-Gazer Herald
Ebonheart Pact	Mournhold	Star-Gazer Herald
Neutral	Belkarth, Craglorn	Examine a Dire Warning

WROTHGAR QUESTS

Number of Quests	59
Starting Location	First Major City

The Orsinium DLC is required to unlock the Wrothgar zone. Begin the first quest, **Invitation to Orsinium**, by speaking to Stuga in Vulkhel Guard, Daggerfall, or Davon's Watch, or by traveling directly to Merchant's Gate, Orsinium. Nine quests allow the players to assist in reforging Orsinium. Numerous zone quests as well as daily quests are also available.

Quest Giver

FACTION	CITY	QUEST GIVER
Aldmeri Dominion	Vulkhel Guard	Stuga
Daggerfall Covenant	Daggerfall	Stuga
Ebonheart Pact	Davon's Watch	Stuga
Neutral	Merchant's Gate	Examine Orsinium Messenger

WORLD ENCOUNTERS

Number of Quests	14
Starting Location	Almost Anywhere

While exploring the Tamriel wilderness, keep an eye out for travelers in need or miscreants up to no good. Remedy the situation for a small Experience bonus. Activate a Celestial Rift in Craglorn to release waves of enemies, balanced for four players. Four events, exclusive to Wrothgar, present more opportunities for the player to assist the citizens of Tamriel.

CRAFTING

Number of Quests	21
Starting Location	First Major City

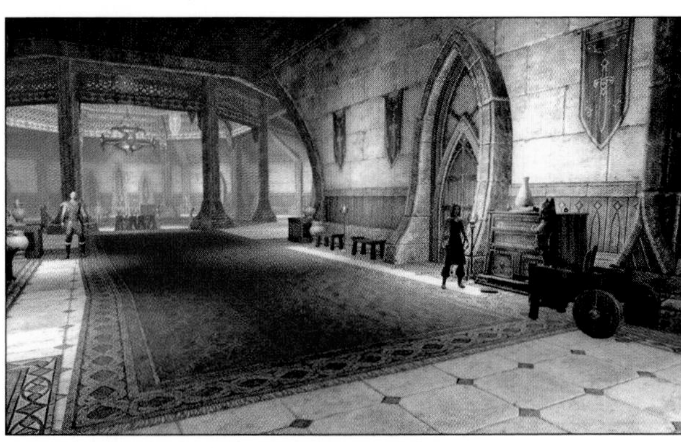

In order to take part in daily crafting writs, you must complete the corresponding certification. Find Millenith at the first major city for Blacksmithing, Clothing, and Woodworking. Danel Telleno offers certification in Alchemy, Enchanting, and Provisioning. Writs can be completed each day within all six disciplines by finding the crafting writs boards in most cities. Increase a crafting skill to progress through the various writs available for that discipline. Complete a max-tier writ for a chance to receive a Master Writ as a reward, which requires the player to craft a master item.

Crafting Certifications

FACTION	CITY	QUEST GIVER
Aldmeri Dominion	Vulkhel Guard	Millenith and Danel Telleno
Daggerfall Covenant	Daggerfall	Millenith and Danel Telleno
Ebonheart Pact	Davon's Watch	Millenith and Danel Telleno

HOLIDAY EVENTS

Number of Quests	19
Starting Location	Various

Celebrate Holiday Events in Tamriel by completing unique quests only available during the event. So far, the citizens of Tamriel have celebrated Witches Festival, New Life Festival, and Jester's Festival.

MISCELLANEOUS

Number of Quests	3
Starting Location	Various

Learn about Tamriel housing and receive your first home by completing **Quest: A Friend in Need**, available in Vulkhel Guard, Daggerfall, or Davon's Watch. Gain access to Werewolf and Vampire skills by completing **Quest: Hircine's Gift** and **Quest: Scion of the Blood Matron**, respectively.

MORROWIND QUESTS

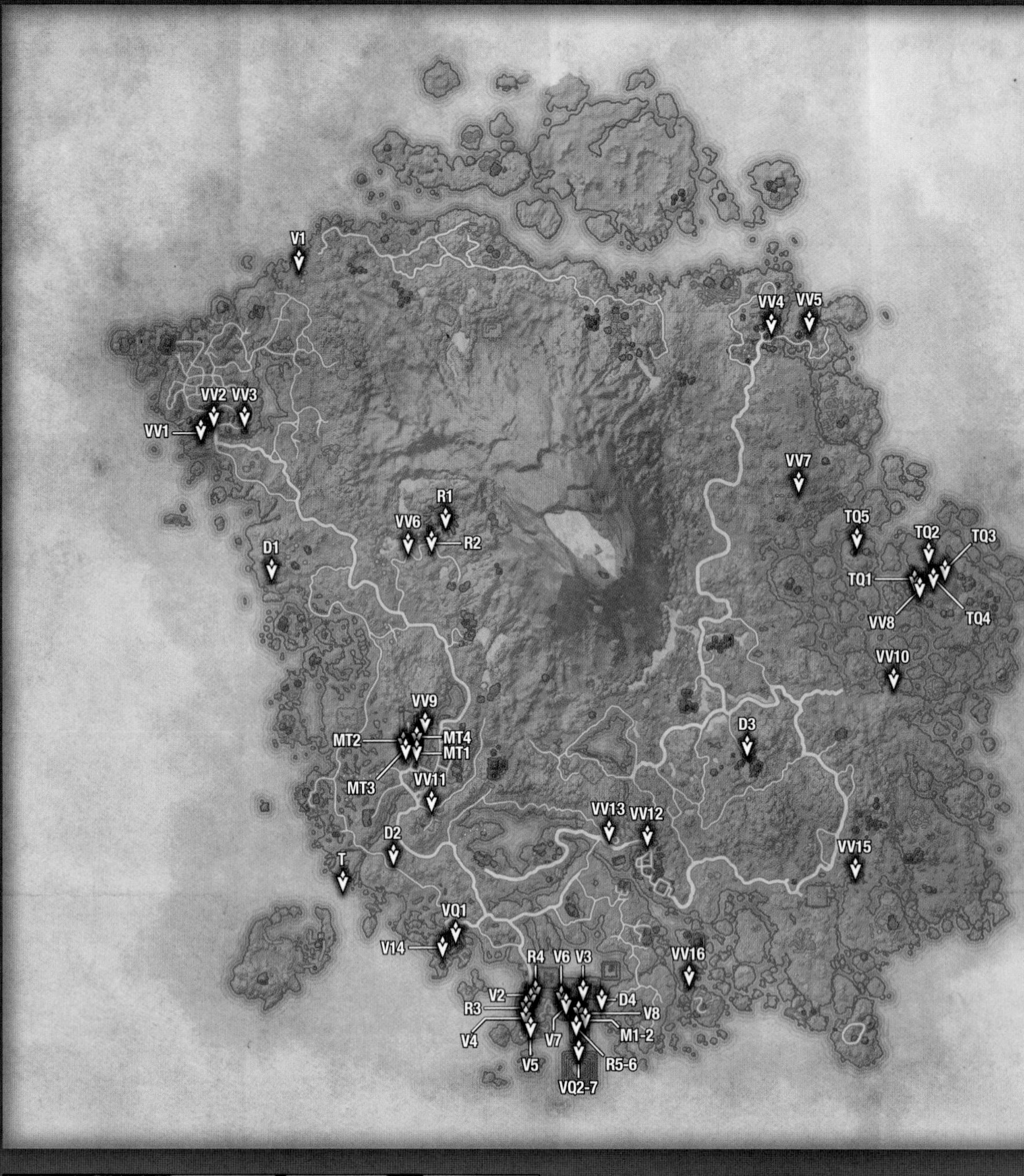

Skipping the Firemoth Island tutorial places the player at Seyda Neen.

Elder Scrolls Online: Morrowind provides a new zone, Vvardenfell, which sits in the middle of the Morrowind province in northeastern Tamriel. Dozens of new quests, two public dungeons, six delves, a Trial, and more become available for the player with the expansion.

A new tutorial starts the player on Firemoth Island off the western coast before disembarking at Seyda Neen. The main story line leads the player to Vivec City, while two side stories are based out of the cities of Balmora and Sadrith Mora.

At any point, you can jump to Wayshrines already revealed in major cities all around Tamriel. Boatswain Synda Imyam in Vivec City offers rides to Elden Root, Wayrest, and Mournhold. Likewise, players who own ***Morrowind*** may travel to Vivec City by talking to Captain Jenassa at the docks of most major cities.

A minimap at the start of each quest displays the locations visited during that quest with numbers indicating the order.

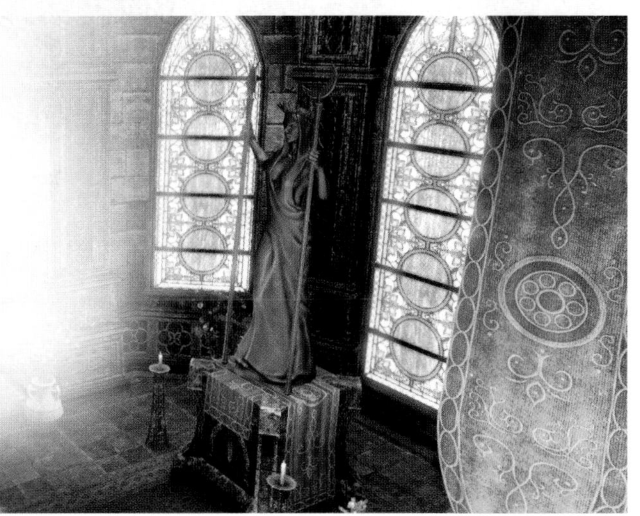

NEW QUEST

For existing players who might have missed it and those starting their journey in Vvardenfell, a new quest was recently added, called The Missing Prophecy. Speak with Rhea Opacarius at any inn. The clairvoyant servant of the Twilight Queen asks the player to visit Pariah Abbey and speak directly with Azura. Complete the quest to receive the Twilight Shard Memento.

VVARDENFELL MAIN STORY

T

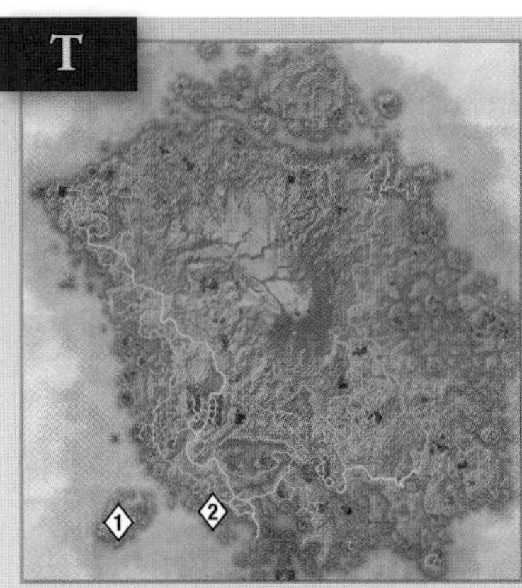

Broken Bonds (Tutorial)

Quest Giver	Good Travels Letter
Prerequisite	None
Quest Giver Location	Firemoth Island
Reward	Gold, Waterlogged Strong Box, Experience, 1 Skill Point

Greaves of the Faithful

STYLE	ITEM TYPE	ENCHANTMENT	TRAIT	SET NAME	QUALITY
Ashlander	Heavy Legs	Health	Divines	Warrior-Poet	Superior

Noteworthy Tasks

- Fight Naryu Virian
- Obtain the Gate Key and Slaver Clothes
- Gather Fire Salts and Kindlepitch
- Board the Slaver Ship
- Throw the Fire Bomb from a Safe Distance
- Escape the Slaver Ship
- Talk to Governor Salvi at Seyda Neen

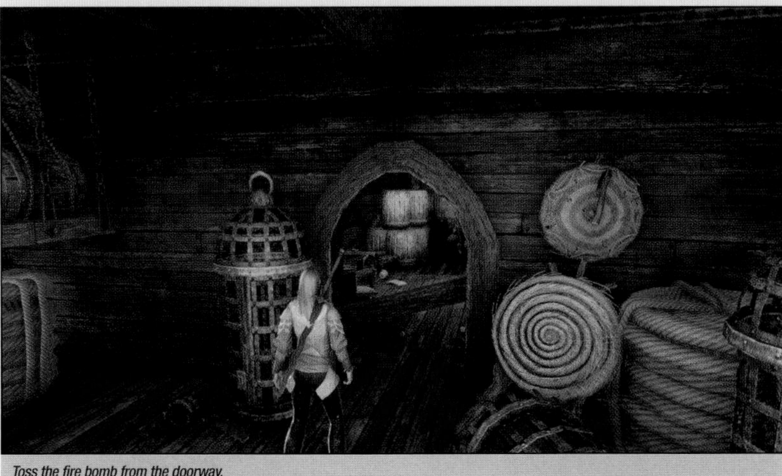

Toss the fire bomb from the doorway.

The Morrowind tutorial begins on Firemoth Island, just off the western coast of Vvardenfell. Examine "Good Travels" to begin the quest and add a Lorebook to your library. Various tasks lead the player to Seyda Neen in Vvardenfell as the game teaches gameplay mechanics, such as combat, lockpicking, and equipping gear. Note that the tutorial may be skipped with subsequent characters.

Use the compass and map to find the locations of quest items that must be collected to continue. Escape from the island and collect the bomb ingredients before boarding the slaver ship. After using the fire bomb on the lower deck, follow Naryu off the side of the boat. This leads you to Seyda Neen on the mainland.

OPTIONAL STEPS

Occasionally, Optional Steps are presented with the current objective. These tasks typically offer additional information beneficial to the quest, but also may offer the player an opportunity to further help allies. Optional Steps do not change the quest, but may lead to extra Experience along the way.

VQ1

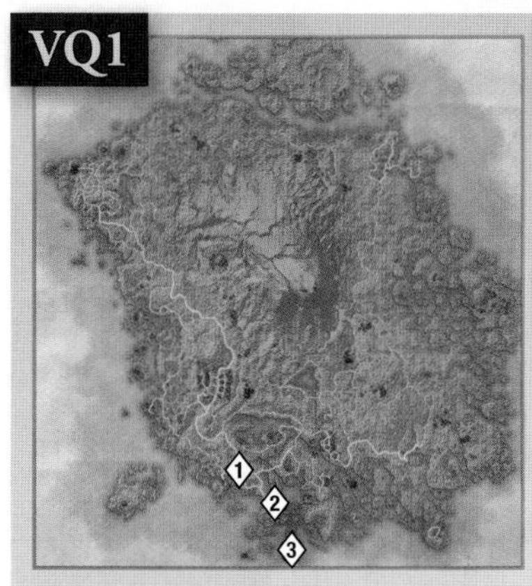

Divine Conundrum

Quest Giver	Alavesa Arethan
Prerequisite	None
Quest Giver Location	Seyda Neen
Reward	Gold, Canon's Staff of the Tribunal, Experience

Canon's Staff of the Tribunal

STYLE	ITEM TYPE	ENCHANTMENT
Buoyant Armiger	Frost Staff	Damage Health
TRAIT	SET NAME	QUALITY
Powered	—	Fine

Noteworthy Tasks

- Enter the Andrano Ancestral Tomb
- Escort Canon Llevule to the Summoning Chamber
- Talk to the Ancestral Spirit
- Talk to Lord Vivec in the Vivec City Palace
- Rescue Two Workers Inside the Construction Site
- Retrieve the Blessing Stone
- Perform the Divination Ritual

Canon Llevule requests your assistance inside the **Andrano Ancestral Tomb**. A variety of Skaafin mobs stand in the way, so take them down as you circle the tomb toward the **Summoning Chamber**. Attempt to pull enemies to your location to avoid being overwhelmed, limiting the number of mobs you fight at one time. Speak to the Ancestral Spirit before exiting the tomb.

Speak to the Ancestral Spirit inside the Andrano Ancestral Tomb.

This sends the player to **Vivec City**, the biggest city of Vvardenfell, located on the south side of the zone. After meeting Lord Vivec, you are asked to free two trapped workers at the construction site before collecting the Blessing Stone for Archcanon Tarvus. Back at the Palace Receiving Room, perform the Divination Ritual to complete the quest.

VQ2

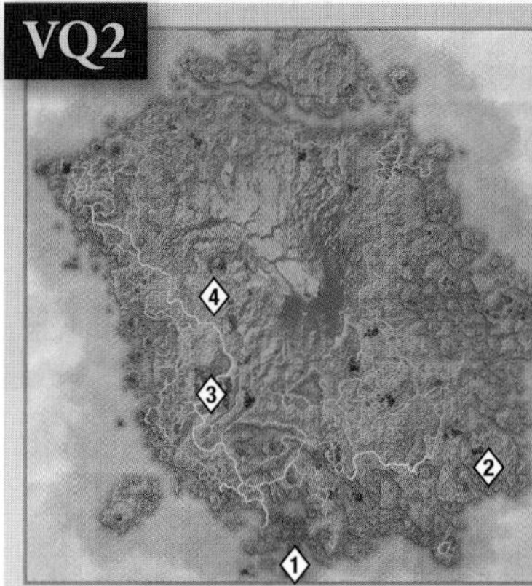

Divine Inquiries

Quest Giver	Lord Vivec
Prerequisite	Complete Divine Conundrum
Quest Giver Location	Vivec City (Palace Receiving Room)
Reward	Gold, Buoyant Armiger's Brogans, Experience

Buoyant Armiger's Brogans

STYLE	ITEM TYPE	ENCHANTMENT
Buoyant Armiger	Heavy Feet	Health
TRAIT	SET NAME	QUALITY
Sturdy	—	Fine

Noteworthy Tasks

- Talk to Archcanon Tarvus
- Investigate Barilzar's Tower
- Help Complete Barilzar's Experiment
- Investigate Balmora
- Gather Information (3) and Investigate Shulk Ore Mine
- Investigate Ald'ruhn
- Find Out What Happened to Chodala

Help Barilzar complete his experiment.

Find **Barilzar's Tower** east of Molag Mar, and help Barilzar complete his experiment by activating the crystals in the proper order, by shape or color. The correct order is Red Sphere, Yellow Tetrahedron, Green Square, Blue Diamond, Violet Octagon.

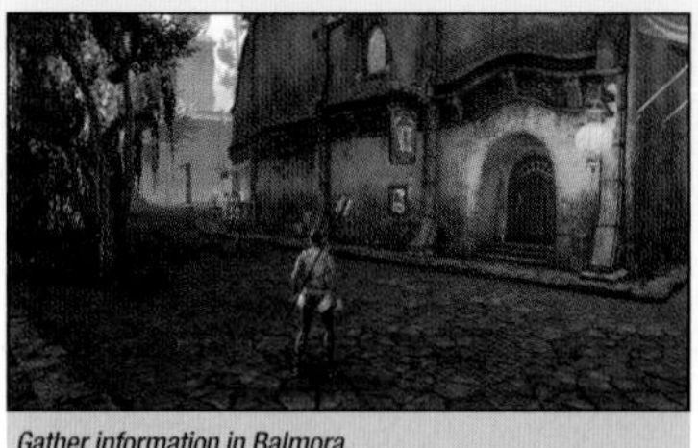

Gather information in Balmora.

At **Balmora**, northwest of Vivec City, enter the center of town to reveal three objective markers. Two townsfolk and a flyer offer up valuable information. It is possible to bribe the Randy Netch Inn barmaid, Milesa Relavel, to score two pieces of information, but it's not worth it. The miner, Renaku, by the water also has two helpful bits of information, but you must possess the Intimidate perk to get them both.

Once you have obtained three sources of information, find the crew chief southwest of Balmora, near the Shulk Ore Mine. Fight your way to the back of the mine, where Curate Erydno and five underlings attack once detected. Be careful not to become overwhelmed, though Erydno will sacrifice the others during the battle. This fight can be avoided altogether by sneaking along the right wall. Find a Nycotic Ritual Bag on the far side of the room.

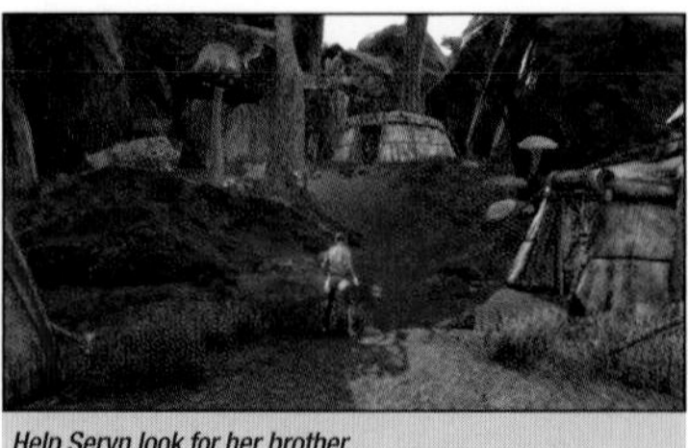

Help Seryn look for her brother.

Farther north, near **Ald'ruhn**, Seryn wants you to enter a Red Exile camp and look for her brother. Red Exile soldiers occupy the area, so be careful as you make your way to the far hut. Examine the scroll found inside and return to Seryn. Once the three tasks are complete, return to Archcanon Tarvus in Vivec City.

VQ3

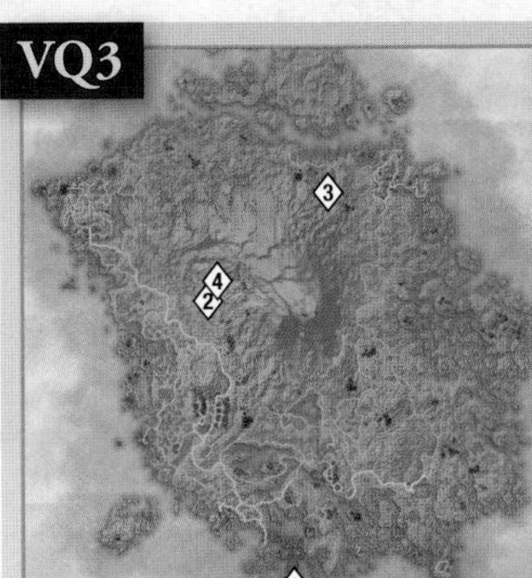

Divine Delusions

Quest Giver	Archcanon Tarvus
Prerequisite	Complete Divine Inquiries
Quest Giver Location	Vivec City (Palace Receiving Room)
Reward	Gold, Greaves of the Warrior-Poet, Experience

Greaves of the Warrior-Poet

STYLE	ITEM TYPE	ENCHANTMENT	TRAIT	SET NAME	QUALITY
Ashlander	Heavy Legs	Health	Divines	Warrior-Poet	Superior

Talk to Seryn before traveling to the far side of **Red Mountain** to the **Cavern of the Incarnate**. Wise Woman Dovrosi gives you the ability to commune with three spirits, who in turn hand over three scrolls. Return to Ald'ruhn and enter **Skar**. Hand Seryn the appropriate scroll dependent upon Chodala's argument.

➤ **Hand Seryn Incarnate Ranso's Scroll when Chodala states his power makes him the Nerevarine.**

➤ **When he claims he shall be victorious on the battlefield, give Seryn the Aduri's Scroll.**

➤ **Chodala says he needs no counsel but his own, so provide Seryn with Danaat's Scroll.**

A group of Red Exile mobs attack, so quickly take them down, before Gulakhan Yus-Zashten shows up. Once Gulakhan Yus-Zashten is defeated, talk to Seryn before returning to Vivec City.

Noteworthy Tasks

- Talk to Archcanon Tarvus
- Talk to Seryn in Ald'ruhn
- Enter the Cavern of the Incarnate
- Use Grave Dust on Incarnate Spirits
- Return to Ald'ruhn and Enter Skar
- Use Scrolls to Disprove Chodala's Three Claims
- Defeat the Red Exiles and Gulakhan Yus-Zashten

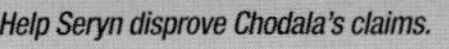

Help Seryn disprove Chodala's claims.

Watch out for Gulakhan Yus-Zashten's fiery breath.

VQ4

Divine Intervention

Quest Giver	Archcanon Tarvus
Prerequisite	Complete Divine Delusions
Quest Giver Location	Vivec City (Palace Receiving Room)
Collectible	Replica Tonal Inverter Memento—Complete Quest
Reward	Gold, Great Axe of the Defiler, Experience

Great Axe of the Defiler

STYLE	ITEM TYPE	ENCHANTMENT	TRAIT	SET NAME	QUALITY
Ashlander	Two-Handed Axe	Life Drain	Powered	Infector	Superior

Return to Barilzar's, head to the understructure, and defeat the Hunger. Find Barilzar in the next room and ask about a Tonal Inverter. In order to create the device, you must talk to Barilzar's three hirelings, who are found in Molag Mar. Leona Blassio is next to the Penitent Pilgrim Inn and sends you to the Nchuleft Delve. Volrina Quarra hangs out inside the Penitent Pilgrim Inn on the middle floor and mentions a component inside Galom Daeus. Finally Snorfin is found on the dock, east of the village, and remarks that you should search inside Arkngthunch-Sturdumz.

Gather information from Barilzar's hirelings.

Travel north to the **Nchuleft Delve**, near the town of Vos. Explore the interior, enter the Nchuleft Depths, and fight your way through Dwarven mobs, including Scary-difficulty Dwarven Centurions. Note that it is possible to drop to a lower floor, if you pick your jump point carefully. At the second floor from the bottom, take out the Centurion on the north and follow the rock path to find a Dwarven Chest. Find the Manual Clockwork Shaft inside.

Noteworthy Tasks

- Rescue Barilzar from the Hunger in the Tower Understructure
- Speak with Barilzar's Three Hirelings
- Retrieve Components from Nchuleft Delve, Arkngthunch-Sturdumz, and Galom Daeus
- Get the Tonal Inverter and Give It to Seryn
- Defeat Chodala in Kaushtarari
- Return to the Archcanon in Vivec City

Find **Galom Daeus** directly west of the Nchuleftingth Wayshrine. Explore the ruin until you reach the entrance to Galom Daeus Manufactory. Defeat the Dwarven Centurion before collecting Volrina's Notes and move inside. Search the Dwarven Spider to find the Galom Daeus Control Rod, and then use it on the Spiders that lie around the room until one activates the Inversion Conduit. Collect the item and exit the ruin.

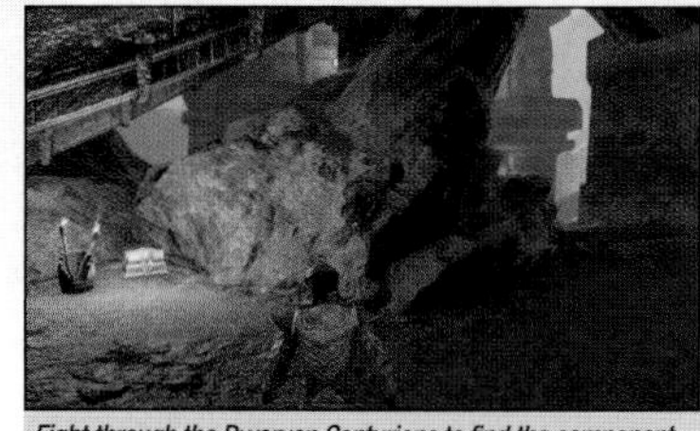

Fight through the Dwarven Centurions to find the component.

The **Arkngthunch-Sturdumz Ruin** is located in the northwestern corner of Vvardenfall. Read Snorfin's Notes (Lorebook) found just inside the entrance before exploring the ruin. Inside the final chamber, take care of the Centurion and then use the three Furnace Release Valves (Western, Eastern, and Northern) to allow access to another Dwarven Chest. Collect the Sonance Generator from inside.

Barilzar uses the components to create the Tonal Inverter. After visiting Vivec City, meet Seryn at **Kaushtarari**, south of Sadrith Mora. Fight through the Skaafins, talk to Renos Oran, and then enter **Malacath's Shrine** to find Chodala.

Use the control rod on the Spiders.

Use the release valves.

NORMAL SCARY HARD DEADLY

CHODALA

Abilities	Quick Strike, Cleave, Empowered Strike, Sunder's Echo

At the start of the fight, Seryn charges the Tonal Inverter, while the player fights off the Skaafin Bloodcleaver, Wretch, and Witchling summoned by Chodala. Once the Tonal Inverter is fully charged, stand in front of Seryn, aim toward Chodala, and activate the Synergy to remove his protective shield.

Take advantage of Chodala's vulnerability by hitting him with everything you've got. Block his Empowered Strike and avoid the Sunder's Echo attack while taking him down.

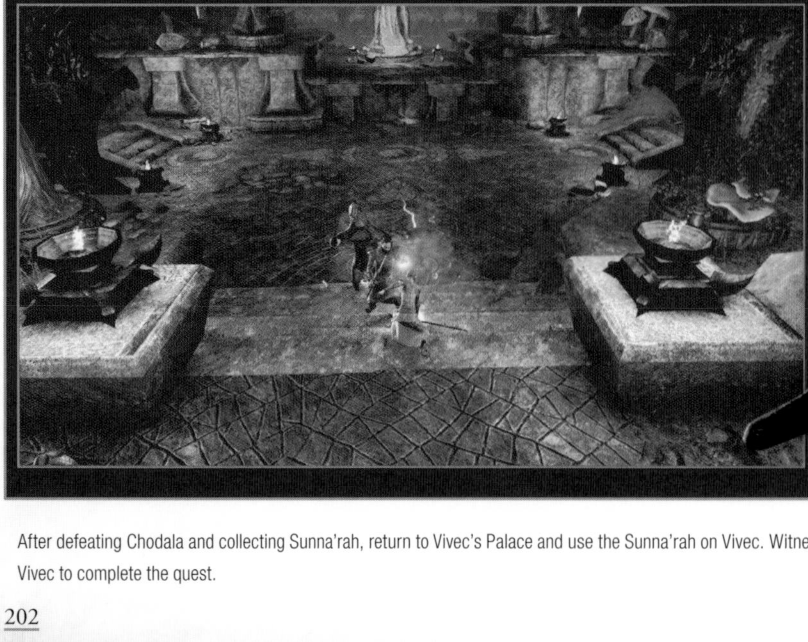

After defeating Chodala and collecting Sunna'rah, return to Vivec's Palace and use the Sunna'rah on Vivec. Witness the scene and talk to Seryn and Vivec to complete the quest.

VQ5

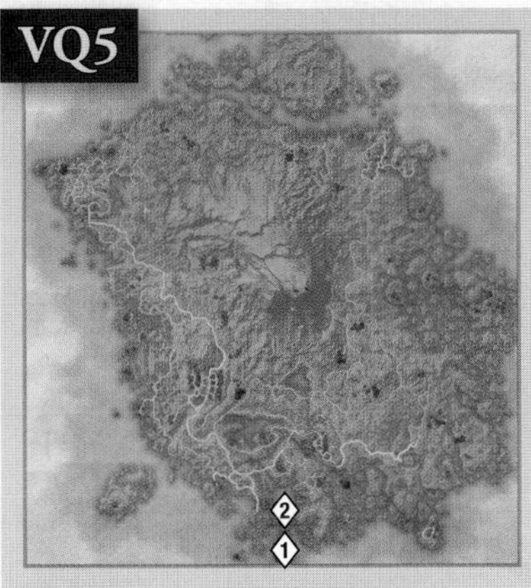

Divine Disaster

Quest Giver	Canon Llevule
Prerequisite	Complete Divine Intervention
Quest Giver Location	Vivec City (Lord Vivec's Chambers)
Reward	Gold, Buoyant Armiger's Chapeau, Buoyant Armiger's Cummerbund, Experience

Buoyant Armiger's Chapeau

STYLE	ITEM TYPE	ENCHANTMENT
Buoyant Armiger	Light Head	Magicka
TRAIT	**SET NAME**	**QUALITY**
Infused	—	Fine

Buoyant Armiger's Cummerbund

STYLE	ITEM TYPE	ENCHANTMENT
Buoyant Armiger	Medium Waist	Stamina
TRAIT	**SET NAME**	**QUALITY**
Infused	—	Fine

Noteworthy Tasks

- Find the Overseer
- Search the Construction Site
- Retrieve the Blessing Stone
- Return to Vivec's Chambers

Canon Llevule asks the player to retrieve a Blessing Stone that still sits at the ziggurat construction site. Find the overseer's wife, Varona Beloren, just outside **Canton of St. Delyn the Wise**. Enter the construction site through the gate and help Overseer Shirales fight off the bullies to receive the Third Canton Key. Enter the third canton to the east and wind your way through the site—avoiding the red warning circles that appear on the ground, which signify incoming rocks. Find the Blessing Stone on the west side, just below the third canton entrance. Return to Vivec's Chambers to complete the quest.

Search the construction site for the Blessing Stone.

VQ6

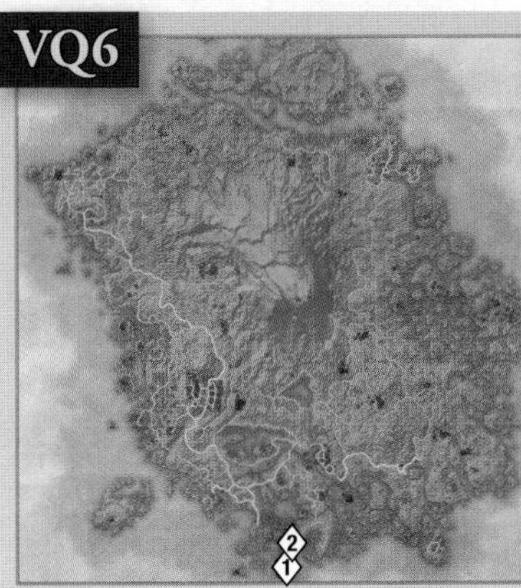

Divine Restoration

Quest Giver	Lord Vivec
Prerequisite	Complete Divine Disaster
Quest Giver Location	Vivec City (Lord Vivec's Chambers)
Reward	Gold, Blade of the Warrior-Poet, Experience

Blade of the Warrior-Poet

STYLE	ITEM TYPE	ENCHANTMENT
Buoyant Armiger	One-Handed Sword	Absorb Stamina
TRAIT	**SET NAME**	**QUALITY**
Decisive	Warrior-Poet	Superior

Noteworthy Tasks

- Talk to Azura
- Enter Barilzar's Portal
- Follow Barbas through Clockwork City
- Get Past the Gate
- Enter the Energy Reservoir
- Defeat Barbas
- Use Sunna'rah to Restore Vivec

Avoid the Whirring Blade Traps.

To reach Clockwork City, enter Barilzar's portal in the **Archcanon's Office**. A tough Clockwork Guardian must be taken down before exploring the city. Whirring Blade Traps present obstacles along the pathways. Watch their patterns and slip between or sprint through them to avoid taking too much damage. Added effects, Serrated Blade and Hamstrung, cause the player to bleed and slow down for a short time, respectively.

Destroy the Clockwork Mediators and the Clockwork Mediator Core.

Two Spring-Wound Gate Couplings, guarded by Factotum mobs, must be disabled before you proceed through the gate. Barbas disappears into the Viaduct, but it's inaccessible. Instead, follow the right walkway, which is blocked by Jovval Mortal-Bane. Dodge his Skaafin Flare attacks and take him down before entering the bridge.

Enter the **Divinity Atelier**, where three cores must be destroyed before you move on. First, eliminate the Defense Core that sits just ahead. To the south, activate the torsion clutch to access the Clockwork Mediator Core and three Clockwork Mediators. Quickly destroy the Mediators before taking care of the core.

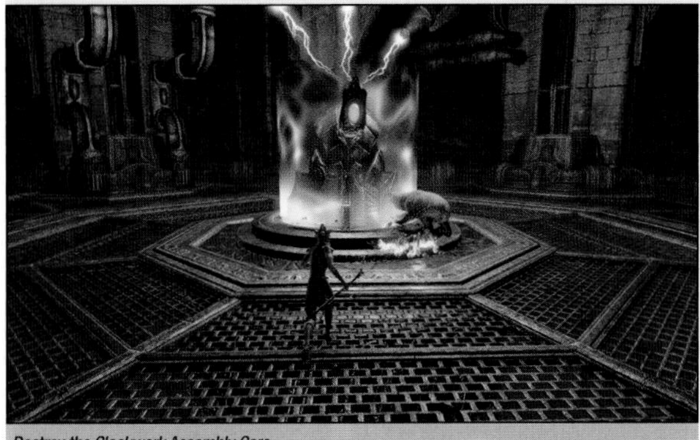

Destroy the Clockwork Assembly Core.

Next, activate the northern torsion clutch to reach the Clockwork Assembly Core. Kill the Fabricant Beetles as they're summoned and destroy the final core. With the three cores eliminated, activate another torsion clutch to find Barbas—the final and toughest fight in the Vivec quest line.

NORMAL SCARY HARD DEADLY

BARBAS

Abilities	Quick Strike, Lunge, Spinning Blades, Barbs, Divine Hijack

Find Barbas inside the **Energy Reservoir**, surrounded by four platforms. The boss sets up in the center of the room as he launches projectiles at the player. Dodge or block Barbs tossed your way, or risk getting knocked back. Possessing some kind of knockback resistance is extremely effective.

Divine Hijack presents the biggest challenge for the player, as explosive charges are launched outward along the ground. Detonating in a discernible pattern, they spiral in toward the boss before moving back out to the perimeter of the room. While the player is busy dodging the attack, Barbas steadily regenerates his Health. If available, hit him with a damage-over-time attack to negate the heal. Stay on the move throughout this attack, avoiding explosions with well-timed dodge rolls.

As the fight goes on, Barbas activates portals on four platforms around the perimeter. Skaafin Wretches periodically spawn from these portals. Deal with them during Barbas' Divine Hijack.

Reverse the energy flow by using the Divinity Reservoir before returning to Vivec's Palace. Use Sunna'rah to restore Vivec.

VQ7

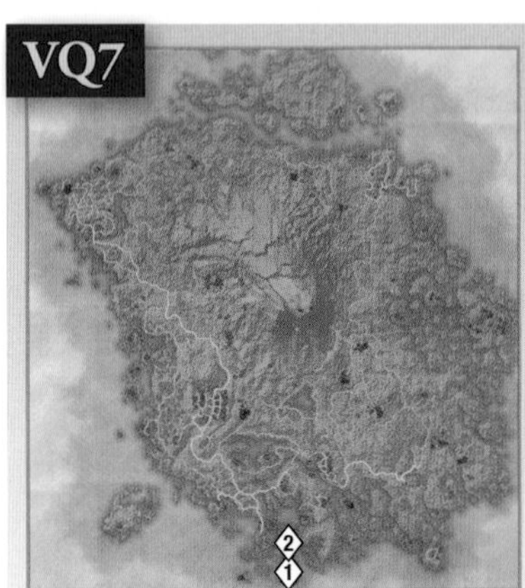

Divine Blessings

Quest Giver	Lord Vivec
Prerequisite	Complete Divine Restoration
Quest Giver Location	Vivec City (Lord Vivec's Chambers)
Collectible	Buoyant Armiger Body Tattoos Body Marking—Complete Quest
Reward	Gold, Breastplate of the Warrior-Poet, Experience, 1 Skill Point

Breastplate of the Warrior-Poet

STYLE	ITEM TYPE	ENCHANTMENT	TRAIT	SET NAME	QUALITY
Buoyant Armiger	Heavy Chest	Health	Infused	Warrior-Poet	Epic

Noteworthy Tasks

- Retrieve the Archcanon's Signet
- Meet Vivec
- Reward the Overseer, Barilzar, and Canon Llevule

Head to the **Archcanon's Office** and collect the Archcanon's Signet from the lockbox. While you are there, grab the Archcanon's Journal to score a Lorebook. Outside the Temple Canton, Vivec asks you to reward Overseer Shirales, Barilzar, and Canon Llevule. This completes **Quest: Divine Blessings** and the Vivec quest line.

MORAG TONG SIDE STORY

MT1

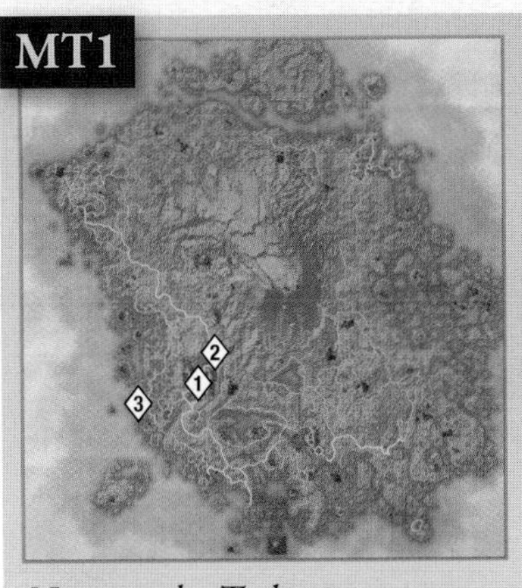

Fleeing the Past

Quest Giver	Sergeant Faldrus
Prerequisite	None
Quest Giver Location	Balmora
Reward	Gold, Redoran Honor Gauntlets, Experience

Redoran Honor Gauntlets

STYLE	ITEM TYPE	ENCHANTMENT
Redoran	Medium Hands	Stamina
TRAIT	**SET NAME**	**QUALITY**
Reinforced	—	Fine

Noteworthy Tasks

- Talk to Councilor Eris in the Redoran Kinhouse
- Track Veya's Friends Through Balmora
- Confront Drevis
- Defeat Ashur's Harassers
- Assist Naryu Virian

Track Veya's friends through Balmora.

Help Naryu defeat Olfrig.

Talk to Councilor Eris on the second floor of the **Redoran Kinhouse** in Balmora about a missing Dark Elf, Veya. Captain Brivan, who hangs out next to the river, suggests tracking her friends.

Find two friends on the east side of town and follow the one with the note. Get too close and the runner asks that you stop. Remain too close and the runner heads to a different house. If this happens, return to Captain Brivan to restart the task.

From a safe distance, tail the runners as the note is handed off twice. Follow the final runner into the **Randy Netch Inn** and confront Drevis on the second floor. If you possess the Passive Abilities, you can intimidate and persuade him for more information. No matter the questioning, you must find Ashur, just northeast of Balmora.

Defeat the three people who harass Ashur before learning of Veya's Mentor. Inside the **Ashurnibibi Ruins**, located on the water to the west, agree to help Naryu Virian with her writ. Fight your way through the ruins and join the assassin as she fights against Olfrig and other soldiers. Once they're defeated, talk to Naryu before returning to Councilor Eris.

MT2

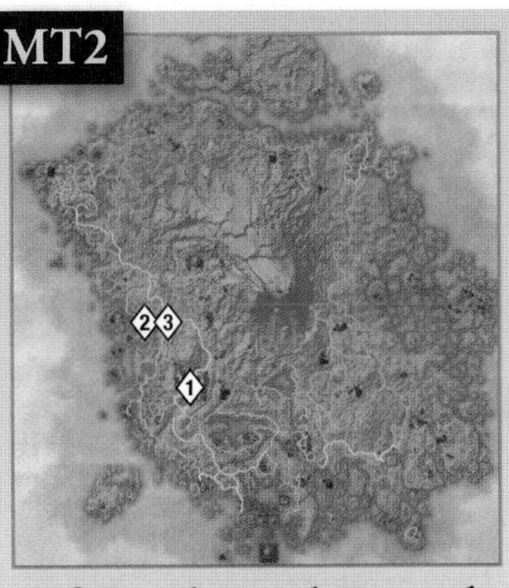

Of Faith and Family

Quest Giver	Councilor Eris
Prerequisite	Fleeing the Past
Quest Giver Location	Balmora (Redoran Kinhouse)
Reward	Gold, Warclaws Battle Bow, Experience

Warclaws Battle Bow

STYLE	ITEM TYPE	ENCHANTMENT
Khajiit	Bow	Weapon and Spell Damage
TRAIT	**SET NAME**	**QUALITY**
Decisive	—	Fine

Noteworthy Tasks

- Find a Way to Contact Veya
- Use Morag Tong Maps to Find Their Safe House
- Steal the Redoran Registry
- Search the Swamp for Veya
- Talk to Veya inside Mallapi Cave
- Search the Ashlander Camp
- Enter Kudanat Mine and Search for Clues

In order to find Naryu and question her further about Veya's whereabouts, you must find their hideout. Receive a Morag Tong Map from Ashur and use it to find the second map and a key, hidden in a broken crate below the northern Balmora bridge. Use this map to discover the safe house, which is found by entering the alley north of the well and west of the Randy Netch Inn. Descend into the **Abandoned Cellar** to find Naryu.

Find the Morag Tong safe house.

Naryu asks you to steal records from **Lord Drono's house**. Pick a simple lock to access his townhouse on the east side of the waterway. Wait for the Redoran soldier to move away from the steps before descending to the first floor.

When the Redoran Knight goes left, move in and swipe the House Redoran Registry (Lorebook) from the desk.

Swipe the registry from Lord Drono's townhouse.

With the registry in hand, Naryu directs the player to the swamp, northwest of Balmora. Find Brivan, who has gathered a group of Warclaws to search for Veya. Continue north to find her first. Defeat the waves of Warclaw mobs before entering nearby **Mallapi Cave** and talking to Veya and Naryu. Fight through the back tunnels to an alternate exit. Allow Veya to make an escape by confronting Councilor Eris, before heading to the **Ashlander Camp** to the southeast.

The Warclaw mobs in the camp can be taken out or avoided by sneaking around the outer edges. Examine the House Redoran Orders (Lorebook) that lie on the ground, and talk to Wise Woman Khamishi in the corner yurt. Next, grab the Kudanat Mine Key that sits inside the supply yurt, or loot the key from the Warclaw Irgazaar that patrols the center of camp.

Collect the Kudanat Mine Key from the Ashlander Camp.

Enter **Kudanat Mine** on the south side of camp, near Old Woman Khamishi. Defeat the Warclaw Zabaseh and Banobani before collecting Ulran's Speaking Stone at the back of the mine. Listen to the speaking stone after talking to Naryu to learn more about Veya's brother. Return to Councilor Eris to complete the quest.

MT3

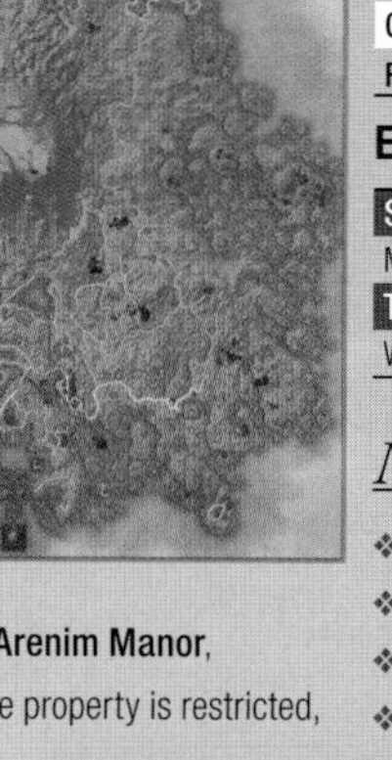

A Purposeful Writ

Quest Giver	Ashur
Prerequisite	Of Faith and Family
Quest Giver Location	Balmora (Outside Redoran Kinhouse)
Reward	Gold, Executioner's Helm, Experience

Executioner's Helm

STYLE	ITEM TYPE	ENCHANTMENT
Morag Tong	Medium Head	Stamina
TRAIT	**SET NAME**	**QUALITY**
Well-Fitted	—	Fine

Noteworthy Tasks

- Meet Naryu at Arenim Manor Northwest of Balmora
- Find a Way Into the Manor
- Search the Manor
- Confront Councilor Dolvara

Meet Naryu Virian at the **Arenim Manor**, northwest of Balmora. The property is restricted, so setting foot inside the wall is considered trespassing, and being detected adds Bounty to the Infamy Meter. An optional step suggests that you avoid killing Redoran soldiers.

Search the Arenim Manor.

There are a couple ways inside. The warehouse next to the dock gives access to the manor's cellar, which allows you to get inside the house. Or, from the front entrance, sneak over to the pile of crates ahead and use them to hop over the fence. Enter the manor and search for clues. The House Redoran Advisory (Lorebook) sits on a console table near the entrance.

Watch out for Redoran Knights and Templars as you sneak around to the left. Collect the Council Meeting Summons (Lorebook) off the wine rack. When the soldier moves to the far corner, sneak behind the Knight and head upstairs. Exit to the Manor Balcony and collect the Letter to Councilor Dolvara (Lorebook).

Move back inside, enter the **Councilor's Quarters**, and interrogate Councilor Dolvara. A Persuade option at the start of the conversation determines the Councilor's fate. Before leaving the room, examine the Hlaalu Letter (Lorebook), and Report from Captain Brivan (Lorebook). Return to Veya at the **Abandoned Cellar** to complete the quest.

Collect the Letter to Councilor Dolvara.

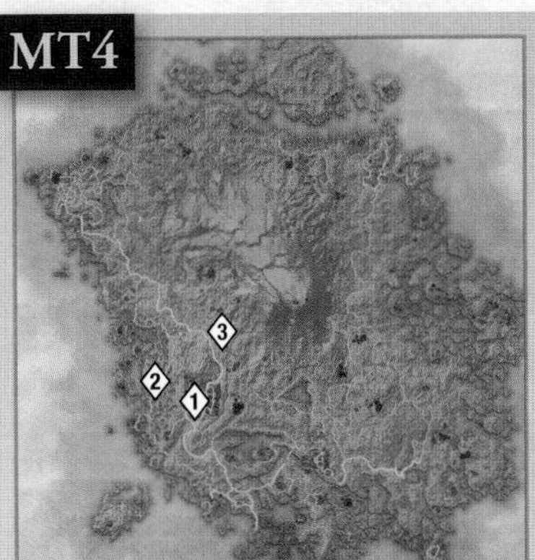

Family Reunion

Quest Giver	Veya Releth
Prerequisite	A Purposeful Writ
Quest Giver Location	Balmora (Abandoned Cellar)
Collectible	Morag Tong Face Tattoo—Complete Quest
Reward	Gold, Veya's Axe of the Defiler, Experience, 1 Skill Point

Veya's Axe of the Defiler

STYLE	ITEM TYPE	ENCHANTMENT
Morag Tong	One-Handed Axe	Poison
TRAIT	**SET NAME**	**QUALITY**
Infused	Infector	Superior

Noteworthy Tasks

- Meet Veya Near the Hlormaren Stronghold
- Find the Redoran Soldiers
- Find the Key and Enter the Stronghold
- Get the Key to Vatola Telem's Cell
- Investigate the Redoran Kinhouse
- Enter the Redoran Garrison
- Talk to Captain Brivan
- Stop Veya
- Talk to High Councilor Meriath

Deal with Curate Skaliz and grab the Cell Key.

Meet Veya near the **Hlormaren Stronghold**, directly west of Balmora. Three locations are marked on the map with Nycotic enemies throughout the area. Examine the Bedroll, Redoran Officer's Blade, and Corporal Darvel as you proceed toward the stronghold. Take out the enemies to find the Hlormaren Stronghold Key.

Enter the **Hlormaren Stronghold** and head left as more Nycotics patrol the halls. Make a right at the first opportunity to find Vatola Telem, being held in a cell. Return to the main hall and continue to the right. Inside a room on the right, the Cell Key sits on a table in the back, but Curate Skaliz stands nearby. It is possible to sneak around the perimeter of the room, snag the key, and exit the room. He will give chase, but if you exit the stronghold and go far enough away, he will cease. This does mean you must fight your way back inside, though, so it's a trade-off. If you stay and fight, watch out for Skaliz's Whirlwind attack and the Skaafin Witchlings he summons.

Return to Vatola Telem and decide whether he gets the key, before returning to the **Abandoned Cellar**. Investigate the **Redoran Kinhouse**, continue up to **Captain Brivan's Apartment**, and then head up more stairs to find out Brivan is at the Redoran Garrison, located north of Balmora. Talk to Naryu and then meet her in front of the garrison.

Fight the Warclaws as you search the Redoran Garrison.

Warclaws patrol the **Redoran Garrison**, so deal with them as you move through the building. Enter the Garrison Chambers and fight your way down the left hallway through the kitchen, or follow the second floor to reach Naryu. Talk to her, return to the first-floor hallway, and descend to the basement.

Stop Veya.

Eventually you run into a Warclaw Ferhara with two Warclaw fighters. Defeat them to find Captain Brivan. After the conversation, talk to Naryu and exit to the kitchen through the nearby doorway. Fight your way into the **Garrison Meeting Hall**, where you must fight Veya Releth, with her dual axes and Whirlwind skill. After defeating her, talk to High Councilor Meriath and then Naryu, who asks you to decide Veya's fate. Return to the **Abandoned Cellar** to complete the Morag Tong side story.

TELVANNI SIDE STORY

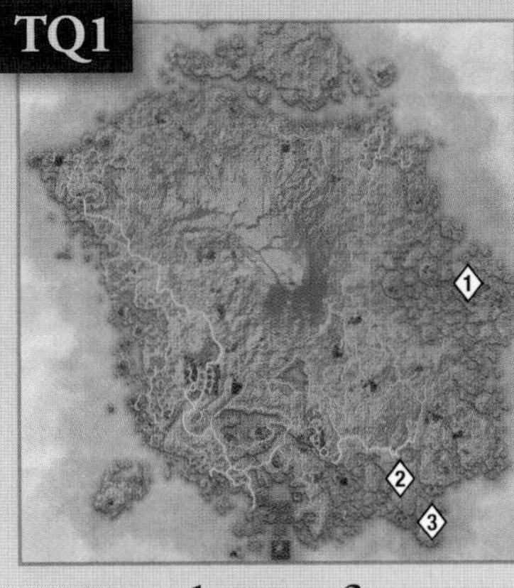

A Hireling of House Telvanni

Quest Giver	Eoki
Prerequisite	None
Quest Giver Location	Sadrith Mora (North of Wayshrine)
Reward	Gold, Robe of Ambition, Experience

Robe of Ambition

STYLE	ITEM TYPE	ENCHANTMENT
Telvanni	Light Chest	Magicka
TRAIT	**SET NAME**	**QUALITY**
Infused	—	Fine

Noteworthy Tasks

- Speak to Brelan Neloren inside Tel Naga
- Pickpocket the Bad Poem
- Take Magister Therana's Correspondence
- Talk to Sun-in-Shadow
- Enter Zaintiraris
- Find the Finger Bone of St. Felms
- Get Therana's Approval for Sun-in-Shadow in Tel Branora
- Deliver the Writ to Eraven Onthim in Sadrith Mora

After talking to Sun-in-Shadow inside Tel Naga, head to the **Council House** and enter **Eraven Othin's Chambers**. Brelan Neloren asks you to pickpocket a Bad Poem from Ethrandora, who is inside the **Wizards' Study**, also in the Council House. Return the poem to Brelan and grab Magister Therana's Correspondence (Lorebook) off the desk.

Pickpocket the Bad Poem.

Return to Sun-in-Shadow, who asks you to travel to the Daedric shrine, **Zaintiraris**. It's locked, so you must find a way to get inside. Eight braziers sit in a circle above the entrance, with a Scribbled Note (Lorebook) in the middle.

Read the note for clues to unlock Zaintiraris. Four of the braziers must be lit, with the number of skulls deciding the order. Count the skulls and light the brazier with two skulls first, followed by three skulls, five skulls, and then six skulls. Drop down and move inside.

Light the braziers in order to unlock Zaintiraris.

Deal with the Scamps and Seducers as you follow the path left or right. Be careful, as a Hunger hangs out along both routes, which can present a tough fight if you're not ready for it. When the paths meet again, enter the Inner Sanctum to find a powerful watcher named Izhavi the Petty guarding a Peculiar Key. Take the mob down or sneak around the perimeter of the room, and swipe the key off the stone pedestal. Watch out for water geysers along the way.

Grab the Peculiar Key in the Inner Sanctum.

Use the key to enter the **Central Chamber**, and fight through the Scamps that litter the room. Approach the Daedric Reliquary on the stone pedestal and collect the Finger Bone of St. Felms. Ascend the stairs and use the door switch to reach the exit. Travel to **Tel Branora** in far southeast Vvardenfell and talk to Magister Therana inside **Therana's Chambers**. Collect the Magister's Writ off the table and deliver it to Eraven Onthim in the **Sadrith Mora Council House**. Report to Sun-in-Shadow to complete the quest.

TQ2

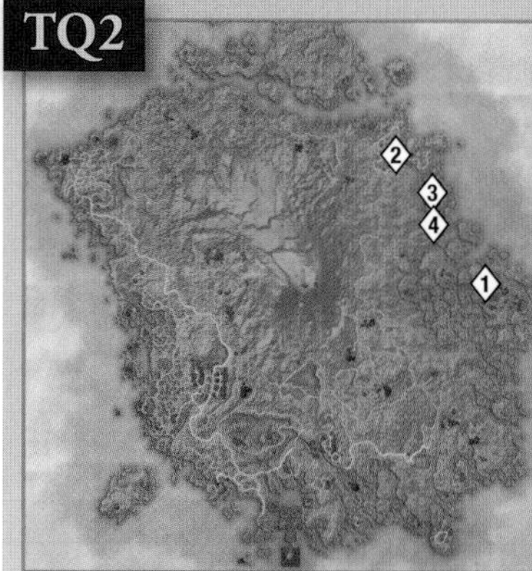

Rising to Retainer

Quest Giver	Sun-in-Shadow
Prerequisite	A Hireling of House Telvanni
Quest Giver Location	Sadrith Mora (Council House)
Reward	Gold, Telvanni Retainer's Ring, Experience

Telvanni Retainer's Ring

STYLE	ITEM TYPE	ENCHANTMENT
—	Ring	Spell Damage +
TRAIT	**SET NAME**	**QUALITY**
Arcane	—	Fine

Noteworthy Tasks

- Find Someone Willing to Sell Land Near Vos
- Find Seythen Rendo at the Esutanamus Shrine
- Talk to Barys Rendo
- Find Out What Mertis Othren Wants
- Get the Deed from Jinrisa
- Deliver the Deed to Master Firuth
- Deliver the Writ to Sun-in-Shadow

Search Mertis's bag.

Talk to Sun-in-Shadow at her house to learn that she needs to find someone willing to sell land near Vos, located to the north. Talk to Eoki or citizens in **Vos** to find out about Barys Rendo, located just north of town, who is willing to sell land in exchange for finding his boy Seythen.

Head southeast to **Esutanamus Shrine** to find Seythen Rendo. Fight the Winged Twilights while he escapes to the northwest. Return to Barys to discover that Mertis Othren has already bought the deed. Find Mertis to the northwest, defeat him, and grab a Letter to Mertis (Lorebook) from Mertis' bag.

After reporting in with Sun-in-Shadow, go to the **Adepts' Hall** in Tel Naga to retrieve the deed from Jinrisa. The hall is restricted, so watch the patrol patterns of those inside. If you're detected, the Adepts will attack on sight. Sneak over to the chest on the right and steal the Rendo Property Deed.

Update Sun-in-Shadow near the Wayshrine before delivering the deed to Master Firuth, who is located near **Hanud** to the northwest. Watch out for Flame Atronachs that occupy the area. Collect Firuth's Writ of Endorsement (Lorebook) off the table and bring it to Sun-in-Shadow just outside the **Council House**.

Deliver the deed to Master Firuth.

TQ3

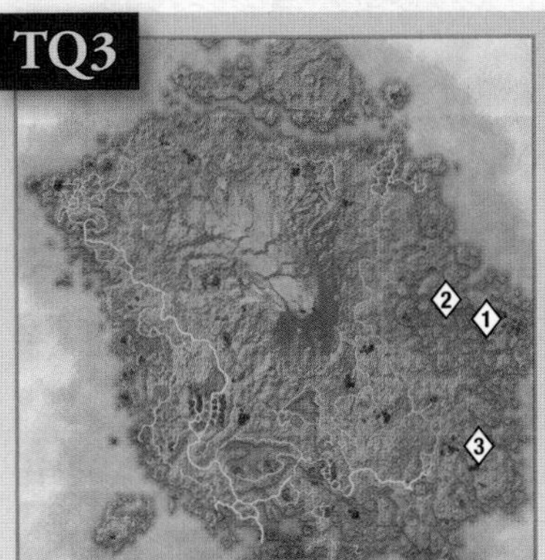

Objections and Obstacles

Quest Giver	Eoki
Prerequisite	Rising to Retainer
Quest Giver Location	Sadrith Mora
Reward	Gold, Magister's Elegant Boots, Experience

Magister's Elegant Boots

STYLE	ITEM TYPE	ENCHANTMENT	TRAIT	SET NAME	QUALITY
Telvanni	Medium Feet	Stamina	Prosperous	—	Fine

Noteworthy Tasks

- Talk to Angharal in the Council Audience Chamber
- Gain an Audience with Magister Gothren at Tel Aruhn
- Retrieve Stolen Goods from Shashpilamat
- Deliver Sun-in-Shadow's Gift to Ralasa in the Council House

Sun-in-Shadow wants you to appear before the council at the Council Audience Chamber. Let her know they rejected her petition before heading northwest to Tel Aruhn. Talking to Midiri Berathi outside **Tel Aruhn Tower** offers a chance to persuade him into letting you inside. Otherwise, you must find another way in.

One way or another, gain access to Tel Aruhn Tower.

Deal with Ralasa Delvi.

Kizmar suggests setting fire to crates of dried saltrice on the dock to distract the guards. This plan works, so enter Tel Aruhn Tower and head upstairs to **Gothren's Audience Chamber**. After you talk to Magister Gothren, Arith Sendrul asks for a favor—to retrieve stolen goods from thieves who fled to Shashpilamat.

Travel to **Shashpilamat** to the south and talk to Zashanti to find the whereabouts of the stolen goods; Captain Giravel shows up to put a stop to the retrieval. Report the bad news back to Sun-in-Shadow, who has a new plan. Depending on your response, either assassinate Ralasa Delvi or deliver Sun-in-Shadow's gift to her.

TQ4

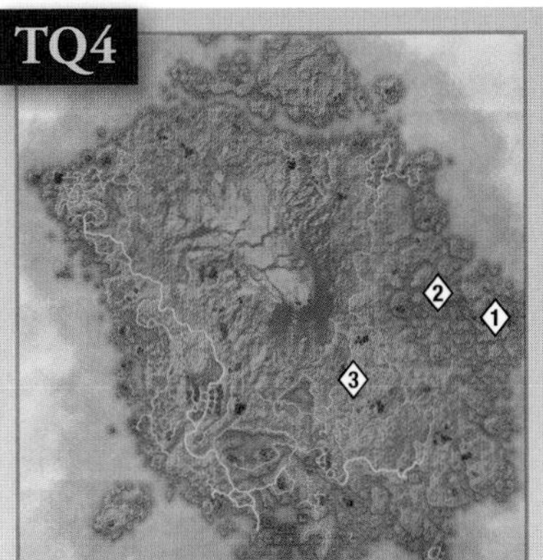

The Magister Makes a Move

Quest Giver	Sun-in-Shadow or Eoki
Prerequisite	Objections and Obstacles
Quest Giver Location	Sadrith Mora (After Completing Previous Quest) or at the Dock
Reward	Gold, Magister's Exquisite Gloves, Experience

Magister's Exquisite Gloves

STYLE	ITEM TYPE	ENCHANTMENT	TRAIT	SET NAME	QUALITY
Telvanni	Light Hands	Magicka	Prosperous	—	Fine

Noteworthy Tasks

- Examine Sun-in-Shadow's House and Talk to Arith Sendrul
- Steal Magister Otheri's Journal for Magister Gothren
- Explore the Zalkin-Sul Egg Mine
- Release the Dwarven Prism
- Return to Magister Gothren

Collect tools inside Mzanchend.

Inside Sun-in-Shadow's house, examine the Journal Page and the Scattered Items, and then talk to Florinna Avau. Arith Sendrul sends you to **Tel Aruhn** to talk to Magister Gothren, who orders you to steal Magister Otheri's notes in exchange for Sun-in-Shadow's release.

Enter Tel Naga in Sadrith Mora and ascend to the **Magister's Retreat**. The room is restricted, but no Bounty is added if you're caught; you're simply banished to the lower level. Wait for an opening, sneak over to the bookshelf against the right wall, and collect the Research Journal. Read the journal within your inventory for Lorebook Experience before delivering it to Arith Sendrul inside the **Council Hall**.

Next, Magister Gothren wants you to retrieve the Dwarven artifact from the **Zalkin-Sul Egg Mine** to the southwest. Two Foremen patrol the mine, but they can be avoided by sneaking between the hiding spots. The guards will attack if you're detected within the blue circle projected from their lanterns. The Kwama Workers throughout the first portion of the mine are non-combative.

Enter the **Mysterious Chamber** and talk to Lothnarth. Agree to hand over any notes you find or bribe him to skip this step. Move inside **Mzanchend**, where Dwarven mobs litter the area. Fight your way along the path, collecting the Dwarven Spur Gear, Dwarven Crank, and Dwarven Piston before entering **Magister Otheri's Laboratory**.

Avoid or fight the Mzanchend Guardian inside the laboratory.

A Mzanchend Guardian stands guard inside the lab and presents a challenge with its Steam Breath, powerful Hammer, and Sweeping Spin. Avoid the foe by giving it a wide berth. Collect the Dwarven Release Switch, if you agreed to collect them, from the coffer behind the machinery and read the Technical Logbook located on a pedestal at the back of the laboratory. Return to Lothnarth and use the Machine Base. Pull the lever, collect the prism, and escape through the **East Mine** as the mine begins to cave in. Fight through the Kwama mobs and return to **Tel Aruhn**, where Sun-in-Shadow is released.

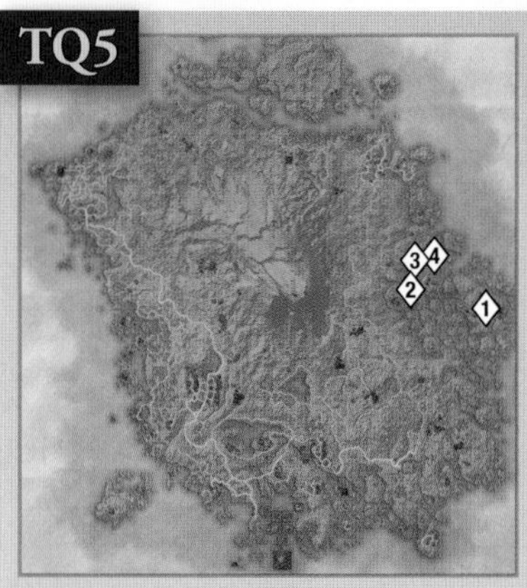

The Heart of a Telvanni

Quest Giver	Sun-in-Shadow or Arith Sendrul
Prerequisite	The Magister Makes a Move
Quest Giver Location	Tel Aruhn (After Completing Previous Quest) or Sadrith Mora (next to the Wayshrine)
Collectible	Telvanni Magister Personality—Complete Quest
Reward	Gold, Tear-Stained Staff of the War Maiden, Experience, 1 Skill Point

Tear-Stained Staff of the War Maiden

STYLE	ITEM TYPE	ENCHANTMENT
Telvanni	Healing Staff	Frost
TRAIT	**SET NAME**	**QUALITY**
Defending	War Maiden	Superior

Noteworthy Tasks

- Deliver Payment to the Ropefish Contact
- Deliver Payment to Bothamul
- Enter the Vassamsi Mine
- Defeat the Guards
- Help the Slaves in the Mine Escape
- Help Defeat Slavemaster Arenim

Deliver the payment to Bothamul.

After talking to Sun-in-Shadow at her house, visit Eoki on the docks. Take his payment to the Ropefish contact in the **Gateway Inn**. Atarga is unable to accept, so arrange a delivery to Bothamul. Either come clean about Eoki's plans or lie to Sun-in-Shadow before exiting the inn. Find a Ropefish camp just west of Tel Aruhn, where Lagdabash and Hazbur attempt to ambush you. Defeat them, read Bothamul's Orders, and head to the real Ropefish camp to the north. Talk to Bothamul and then find Eoki to the east.

He gives two options for dealing with the mine guards: knock them out with Rihnissi's powder bombs, or kill them all. Selecting the former gives you the ability to toss a bomb at the guards to take them down in a non-lethal manner. The option appears on-screen when available.

Knock the guards out with powder bombs or kill them.

Enter **Vassamsi Grotto**, take out the two guards ahead, and release the two slaves from the cages. Just ahead, Captain Flaeus attacks from the right, so knock him out with a powder bomb or kill him. Continue into the Mining Area and eliminate the remaining guards as you move toward the **Vassamsi Mine Escape Shaft**.

In the next area, take out the Warden, Slavemaster Arenim. Once Arenim is defeated, talk to Sun-in-Shadow to decide whether Eoki flees or stays in Sadrith Mora. Talk to her again to complete the quest line.

VVARDENFELL QUESTS

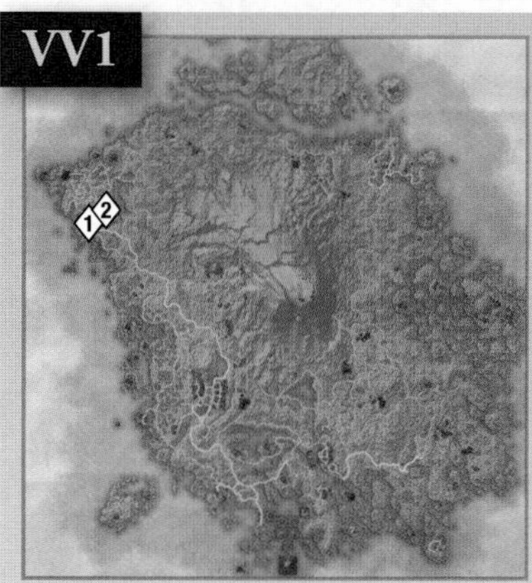

A Melodic Mistake

Quest Giver	Manore Mobaner
Prerequisite	None
Quest Giver Location	Gnisis (North of the Wayshrine)
Reward	Gold, Kwama-Cutter, Experience

Kwama-Cutter

STYLE	ITEM TYPE	ENCHANTMENT
Redoran	Two-Handed Sword	Reduce Armor
TRAIT	**SET NAME**	**QUALITY**
Sharpened	—	Fine

Noteworthy Tasks

- Talk to Foreman Lathdar
- Investigate the Disturbance in Gnisis Egg Mine
- Find a Way Past the Dwarven Barrier
- Fix the Dwarven Resonator
- Talk to Revus Demnevanni

The Dwarven Centurion Alpha stands in your way.

Foreman Lathdar mentions a disturbance in **Gnisis Egg Mine** that has placed a hex on the egg hands, so volunteer to investigate. Fend off Kwama Workers as you search for and talk to the two workers near the mine entrance. Deeper into the mine, examine the Kwama Queen and then talk to Destaine.

Defeat the Dwarven Spiders and tough Centurions as you explore farther into the mine. Inside the central chamber, the Dwarven Centurion Alpha poses the biggest threat of the quest, as a power core gives it an added buff. Take the big guy around the central pillar to break the connection. Watch out for Dwarven Spiders and Dwarven Spheres to join the fight.

After clearing out the mobs, use the Dwarven Tonal Focus to grab the Tonal Prism, and use it on the barrier that blocks the exit. It's possible to swipe the prism while the Centurion is busy on the other side of the pillar, allowing you to escape without defeating the sub-boss.

Continue to search for the source of the sound as you fight your way to the **Dwarven Sanctum** and talk to Revus Demnevanni, who attempts to fix the resonator. In order for Revus to repair the device, the five Tonal Valves must be set to the correct positions: up, down, or neutral. Flip them to neutral, down, up, up, down. Once you're happy with the settings, use the Resonator Release Valve in the middle of the room to play the sounds.

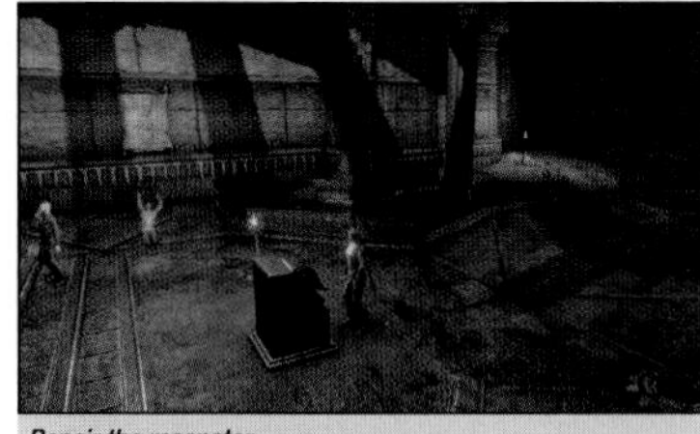

Repair the resonator.

Exit through the **Dwarven Tunnels** and talk to Revus before reporting to Foreman Lathdar, who stands just outside the **Resting Kwama**.

VV2

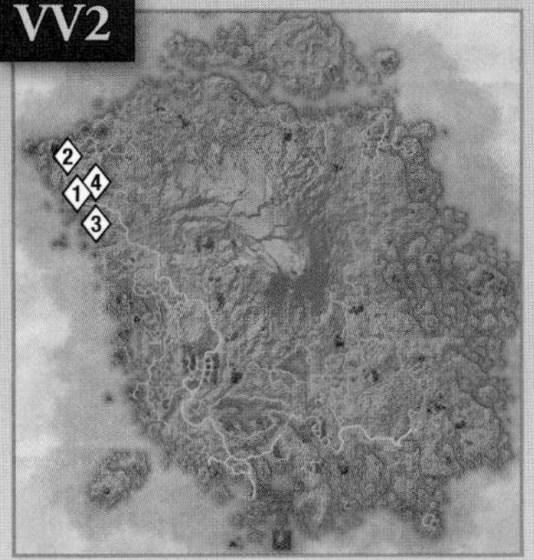

Hatching a Plan

Quest Giver	Foreman Lathdar
Prerequisite	A Melodic Mistake
Quest Giver Location	Gnisis (Outside the Resting Kwama)
Reward	Gold, Revus' Spare Staff of the War Maiden, Experience

Revus' Spare Staff of the War Maiden

STYLE	ITEM TYPE	ENCHANTMENT
Redoran	Lightning Staff	Crusher (Reduce Target's Resistances)
TRAIT	**SET NAME**	**QUALITY**
Precise	War Maiden	Fine

Noteworthy Tasks

- Find Revus at the Hatchery
- Mark the Egg-Heaps with Revus' Divining Stone
- Recruit Vigard the Sparrow
- Help Uncover the Royal Egg
- Hatch the Royal Egg in the Nursery

Foreman Lathdar wants you to find Revus Demnevanni at a **hatchery**, located to the north; cross the bridge to reach him. Revus admits to being responsible for the Kwama Queen's death, but he possesses a Royal Kwama Egg that may help fix the situation. Approach the three Cliff Strider Egg-Heaps marked on the map and place the stone on each. Return to the hatchery.

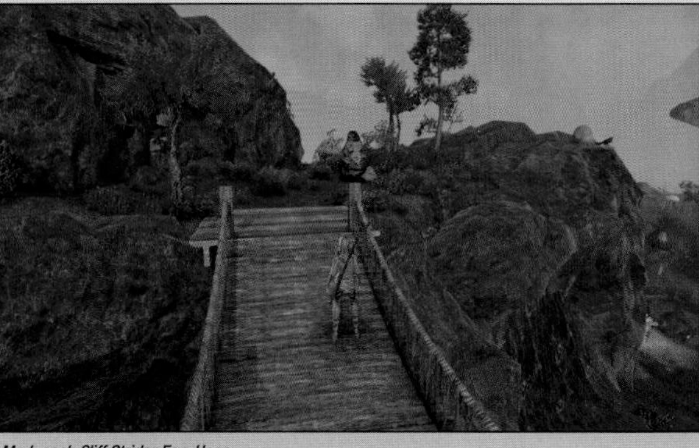

Mark each Cliff Strider Egg-Heap.

After reporting back to Revus, visit Foreman Lathdar outside the **Resting Kwama**. Next, Revus wishes you to recruit Vigard the Sparrow for his voice. Head south down the road to find him surrounded by three kagoutis. Take them out and convince the bard to return to **Gnisis** with you.

Manore Mobaner directs you to the west docks. Something goes terribly wrong with Revus' plan and an irate Cliff Strider shows up. Kill the beast and again talk to Revus, who has another, more dangerous, plan. Enter the **Gnisis Egg Mine** and talk to Revus again before moving inside the nursery. Approach the Egg Holder and signal Revus. Defend the Royal Egg from Kwama Workers and Warriors. Once that task is complete, report in with Foreman Lathdar, outside the mine, to complete the quest.

Signal Revus at the Egg Holder.

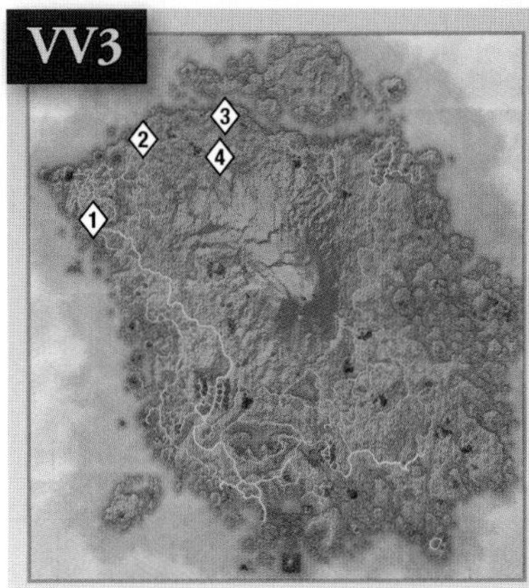

Haunted Grounds

Quest Giver	Theyo Prevette
Prerequisite	None
Quest Giver Location	Gnisis (Egg Mine Barracks Basement)
Reward	Gold, Spirit-Walker Leggings, Experience

Spirit-Walker Leggings

STYLE	ITEM TYPE	ENCHANTMENT	TRAIT	SET NAME	QUALITY
Hlaalu	Medium Legs	Stamina	Divines	—	Fine

Noteworthy Tasks

- Go to the Ashlander Urshilaku Camp
- Find the Ghost Hunters at Valenvaryon
- Find Farwen
- Set the Magical Wards
- Destroy Ghosts to Find a Potent Spirit Essence
- Defeat Galgalah

Talk to Theyo Prevette at the **Egg Mine Barracks** before heading northeast to the **Ashlander Urshilaku Camp**, where Lord Thanlen informs you that the Ghost Hunters have gone to Valenvaryon without your protection. Head east to find Theyo just south of **Valenvaryon** and warn him of Galgalah. Talk to Farwen and help her set up three magical wards. Defeat the pairs of Ghosts and then allow Farwen to set the wards. After Farwen is taken, activate the third ward and then talk to Theyo—concluding that Galgalah has taken control of Farwen.

Help Farwen set the magical wards.

Move up the hill ahead and destroy the Ghosts, being sure to take out the Ancient Spirit that appears from each one before moving on. Collect a Potent Spirit Essence off one of the Ghosts and return to the group. Talk to the Captive Spirit to find the location of Galgalah's lair. Choose whether Galgalah and Farwen live before heading south to his lair.

Defeat Galgalah.

At first Galgalah does not pose much of a threat, though its summoned Zombie and Fright Force skill have the ability to frustrate. Once defeated, though, he transforms into a more powerful mob with the following skills: Soul Cage, Defiled Ground, Soul Rupture, and Necrotic Spear.

Once Galgalah has been killed, talk to Farwen and decide her fate by choosing to finish her or encouraging her to fight the spirit. Return to Gnisis and talk to the Ghost Hunters at the **barracks**.

Reclaiming Vos

Quest Giver	Gray-Skies
Prerequisite	None
Quest Giver Location	Vos (East of Tel Mora Wayshrine)
Reward	Gold, Dratha's Epaulettes of the War Maiden, Experience

Dratha's Epaulettes of the War Maiden

STYLE	ITEM TYPE	ENCHANTMENT	TRAIT	SET NAME	QUALITY
Telvanni	Light Shoulders	Magicka	Infused	War Maiden	Fine

Noteworthy Tasks

- Find Evidence of Corruption Inside Savarak's Manse
- Meet with Nerandas
- Investigate the Base of Tel Mora Tower
- Follow Clues to Track Menwendel's Captors
- Defeat Nerandas
- Collect the Toxin Sample
- Defeat Savarak

Pay Savarak Fels a visit at the **Gathering House** before talking to Llayne Sadri inside Tel Mora. Return to central Vos and break into **Savarak's Manse**. Sneak downstairs and examine the Shipping Notice inside the first keg storage, the Freshly Penned Note on the desk at the corner, and the Letter to Savarak that sits on a workbench in the back room. Avoid detection by the personal guards who patrol the cellar.

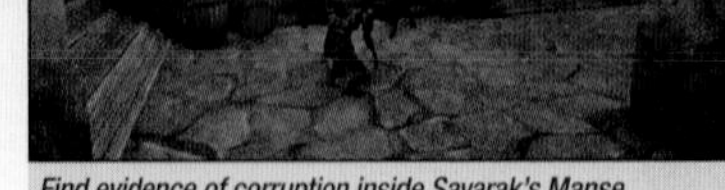
Find evidence of corruption inside Savarak's Manse.

Find Menwendel just inside Pinsun.

Check in with Llayne and then meet Nerandas at the wharf to learn of a plot against Mistress Dratha. Examine the Malignant Growth on the backside of **Tel Mora Tower**. Llayne asks you to visit **Menwendel's Nursery** next door, where Gray-Skies reveals that Menwendel has been taken.

Watch out for Black Snail mobs as you follow the trail south into **Pinsun**. A short way into the cave, slip through the narrow opening on the left to find Menwendel, who offers her help as long as the player acquires a sample of the poison.

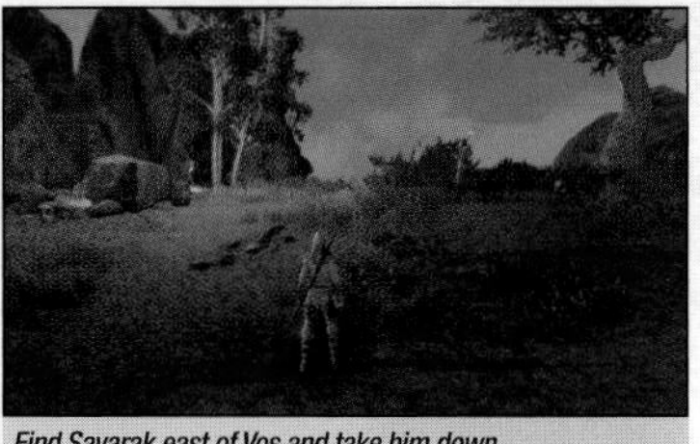
Find Savarak east of Vos and take him down.

Explore deeper inside Pinsun to find Nerandas. Defeat him, examine the Notice to Research Assistants that sits on a nearby workbench, and then collect the Fungal Toxin found on a crate in the higher portion of the cave to the east.

Deliver the sample to Menwendel in **Tel Mora** and then assist Llayne by defeating Savarak, who is found near the eastern coast. Return to Tel Mora to complete the quest.

VV5

At Any Cost

Quest Giver	Mistress Dratha
Prerequisite	Reclaiming Vos
Quest Giver Location	Tel Mora
Reward	Gold, Dark Staff of the War Maiden, Experience

Dark Staff of the War Maiden

STYLE	ITEM TYPE	ENCHANTMENT	TRAIT	SET NAME	QUALITY
Daedric	Flame Staff	Absorb Magicka	Infused	War Maiden	Superior

Noteworthy Tasks

- Retrieve the Stones of Cold Fire
- Defeat Xykenaz

Mistress Dratha asks the player to collect powerful magicked stones, the Stones of Cold Fire, at seven Daedric shrines around Vvardenfell. Visit the following shrines and collect a stone from each. All but one have an elite foe nearby, though said foes can be avoided at the outdoor locations.

DAEDRIC SHRINE	LOCATION	STONE	MINIBOSS
Ashalmawia	Inside Ashalmawia Delve, northwest Vvardenfell	Stone of Ashalmawia	Zylara
Bal Ur	Inside Bal Ur Underground, north of Suran	Stone of Bal Ur	Phylaraak
Esutanamus	Shrine, southeast of Vos	Stone of Esutanamus	Daedroth
Kushtashpi	Shrine, northwest of Vos	Stone of Kushtashpi	Daragaz
Ramimilk	Inside Ramimilk Shrine, south of Ald'ruhn	Stone of Ramimilk	None
Tusenend	Inside Tusenend Shrine, north of Molag Mar	Stone of Tusenend	Kythiirix
Yansirramus	Shrine, west of Sadrith Mora	Stone of Yansirramus	Brakuum

Return the stones to Dratha and then enter her portal to the **Prison of Xykenaz**. Defeat Xykenaz and report back to Dratha to complete the quest.

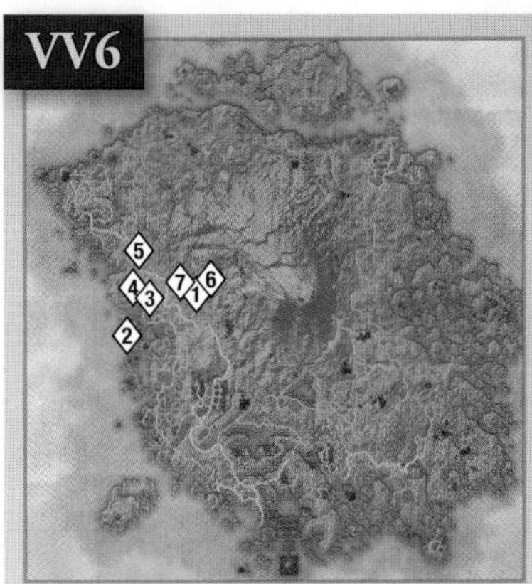

Ancestral Ties

Quest Giver	Drelyth Hleran
Prerequisite	None
Quest Giver Location	Ald'ruhn (Near the Wayshrine)
Reward	Gold, Seal of Hleran, Experience

Seal of Hleran

STYLE	ITEM TYPE	ENCHANTMENT
—	Neck	Bash & Block Cost -
TRAIT	**SET NAME**	**QUALITY**
Robust – Max Stamina +	Infector	Fine

Noteworthy Tasks

- Obtain an Ashen Fern
- Obtain the Weapon of an Exiled Ashlander
- Obtain the Bones of a Fallen Guar
- Obtain a Jeweled Cuttle
- Place the Four Offerings
- Search the Hleran Tomb
- Take Dranoth's Spear
- Deliver the Spear to Drelyth

Collect the Bones of a Fallen Guar east of Khartag Point.

Farseer Kuamta in **Ald'ruhn** wants you to obtain four items. These items can often be found elsewhere in Vvardenfell, but suggested locations are marked on the map. The Ashen Fern can be picked along the west coast, south of **Arenim Manor**. The Weapon of an Exiled Ashlander is a possible drop from any Red Exile mob. Find the Bones of a Fallen Guar at the objective marker east of **Khartag Point**, west of Ald'ruhn. A Jeweled Cuttle sits at the back of the **Ashimanu Cave**, northwest of the West Gash Wayshrine. Kwama Workers and Warriors occupy the cave.

Visit the four marked locations around Ald'ruhn and place the four offerings. Talk to Wise Woman Asani and then Drelyth Hleran before heading west toward the **Hleran Ancestral Tomb**. Hop across the rock in the middle of the lava lake to reach the far side. Follow the path and enter the tomb.

Pay your respects at the four shrines inside the Hleran Ancestral Tomb.

Watch out for the Hleran mobs as you explore the tomb. At the first room, kneel at the shrine ahead and another down the east hall, before following the path the other way. Find two more shrines as you circle to the northern side of the tomb, at which time the enemies become non-combative. Attack them, though, and they will return in kind.

Enter **Dranoth's Burial Chamber**, talk to Dranoth Hleran, and collect Dranoth's Spear. Examine Dranoth's Urn behind Dranoth to find a Lorebook. Deliver the spear to Drelyth next to the fire in **Ald'ruhn** to complete the quest and the Ald'ruhn objective.

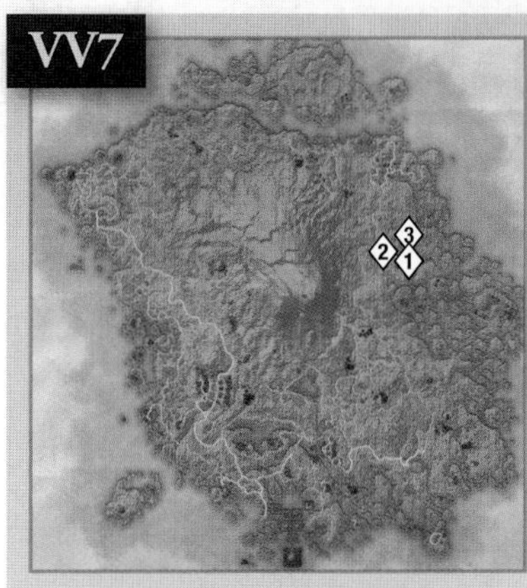

If the Spell Fits

Quest Giver	Stromgruf the Steady
Prerequisite	None
Quest Giver Location	Southwest of Hanud
Reward	Gold, Stromgruf's Ensorcelled Pants, Experience

Stromgruf's Ensorcelled Pants

STYLE	ITEM TYPE	ENCHANTMENT
Nord	Light Legs	Magicka
TRAIT	**SET NAME**	**QUALITY**
Divines	—	Fine

Noteworthy Tasks

- Search for the Witch
- Locate the Goblin Camp
- Recover Nerise's Pack and Sword
- Return the Items to Nerise Venim

Head west from Stromgruf and examine the series of bottles of mead to find Nerise Venim at a nearby campfire. She wants her stolen items before releasing Stromgruf. Go northeast to locate the goblin camp, where Ruinfang the Wicked guards Nerise's Pack. Defeat him and his animal companions to recover the bag. A Netch Gouger Ironskin stands over Nerise's Fine Elven Sword just west of the camp. Talk to Stromgruf before delivering the items to Nerise, who shows up nearby.

Defeat Ruinfang the Wicked to get Nerise's Pack.

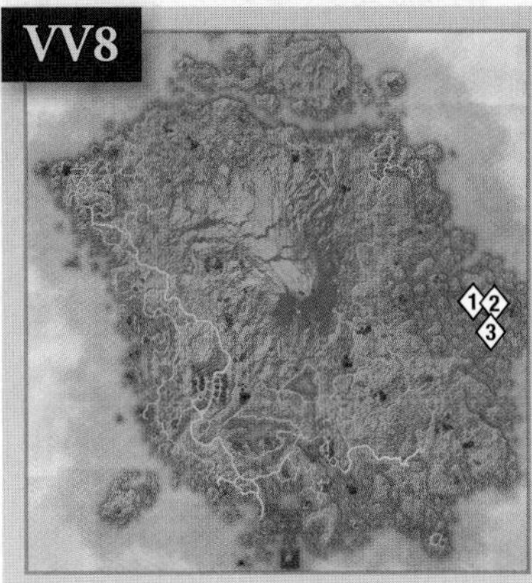

Bound by Love

Quest Giver	Llonas Givyn
Prerequisite	None
Quest Giver Location	Sadrith Mora (At the Wayshrine)
Reward	Gold, Star-Shell Dagger, Experience

Star-Shell Dagger

STYLE	ITEM TYPE	ENCHANTMENT
Telvanni	Dagger	Damage Shield
TRAIT	**SET NAME**	**QUALITY**
Infused	—	Fine

Noteworthy Tasks

- Talk to Faras Givyn
- Collect Three Red Star Shells
- Buy Tirwin for Llonas Givyn, or Steal Tirwin's Servitude Obligation
- Give Servitude Obligation to Tirwin

Agree to Faras Givyn's terms of three Red Star Shells in exchange for Tirwin. Find the shells by digging up three of the mud mounds south of town. Use the compass to find them. Talking to Tirwin opens two paths: continue with Llonas Givyn's plan, or steal Tirwin's Servitude Obligation.

Dig the Red Star Shells out of the mounds.

If you agreed to purchase Tirwin, return to Llonas Givyn and agree to buy her, then talk to Faras Givyn.

If you decided to steal the agreement, pick the simple lock at Givyn Tower. Sneak past three workers, using the baskets to hide if necessary. Enter the **basement** and move past two more workers to find the Servitude Obligation. Deliver it to Tirwin to complete the quest.

Steal the Servitude Obligation.

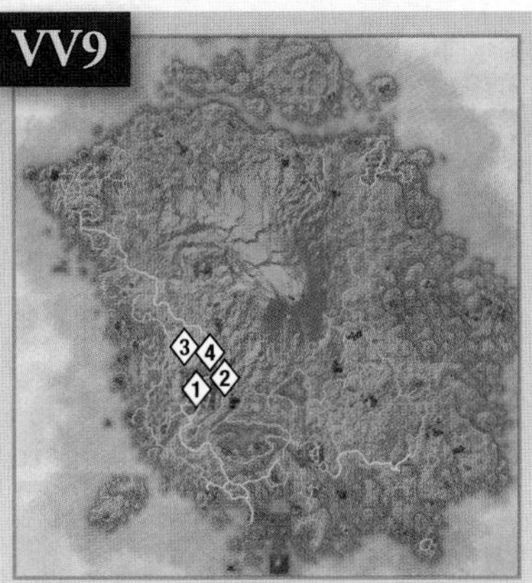

The Memory Stone

Quest Giver	Gilan Lerano
Prerequisite	None
Quest Giver Location	Balmora (Outside Lerano's House)
Reward	Gold, Belt of Notched Memories, Experience

Belt of Notched Memories

STYLE	ITEM TYPE	ENCHANTMENT
Hlaalu	Heavy Waist	Health
TRAIT	**SET NAME**	**QUALITY**
Training	—	Fine

Noteworthy Tasks

- Go to Balmora Valley
- Use Gilan's Memory Stone at Various Locations
- Observe Gilan's Memories
- Reunite the Leranos

Receive Gilan's Memory Stone and take it to a few sites around the Balmora area. At each location, use the stone to play one of Gilan's memories; watch the scene play out if desired, or immediately head to the next location. Begin at **Balmora Valley** just northeast of town and then head to **Caldera Crater** to the north. Beware of Nilthog the Unbroken, who resides in the area. Next, use the Memory Stone at **Balmora Overlook** right outside town, followed by a spot just north of the wall.

Observe Gilan's memories at various locations in and a round Balmora.

Back at Lerano's House, Gilan asks one last favor—for his children, Neria and Mils, to visit. Find Mils fishing on the east side of the **waterway** and Neria at the **stables**. If available, you can attempt to persuade one of the children. Enter Lerano's House and head upstairs to complete the quest.

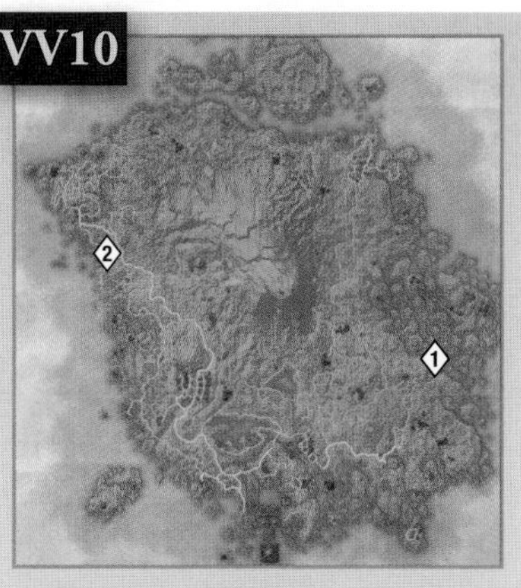

Ancestral Adversity

Quest Giver	Elfbetta the Shy
Prerequisite	None
Quest Giver Location	Outside the Dreloth Ancestral Tomb
Reward	Gold, Pauldrons of the Warrior-Poet, Experience

Pauldrons of the Warrior-Poet

STYLE	ITEM TYPE	ENCHANTMENT
Ancient Elf	Heavy Shoulders	Health
TRAIT	**SET NAME**	**QUALITY**
Reinforced	Warrior-Poet	Fine

Noteworthy Tasks

- Find Narsis Dren in the Dreloth Ancestral Tomb
- Investigate the Creature
- Find Narsis Dren in the Veloth Ancestral Tomb
- Place the Four Offerings
- Enter the Undertomb
- Solve the Floor Puzzle
- Enter the Tomb of the Matriarch
- Enter the Treasure Vault

Talk to Elfbetta the Shy and offer to find Narsis Dren, who's just inside the **Dreloth Ancestral Tomb**. Investigate the creature that Narsis mentions to find a tiny spider, before exploring deeper inside the tomb. Inside the **Ancestor Prayer Room**, the treasure vault Narsis seeks is missing. Follow him farther inside, where you run into the Grievous Twilight. Exit the tomb through the mob, or return the way you came, and check in with Elfbetta.

Follow Narsis Dren until you find a Grievous Twilight.

Travel to northwestern Vvardenfell and enter the **Veloth Ancestral Tomb**, west of the West Gash Wayshrine, where Narsis has locked himself inside the east room. Release and talk to the explorer to learn of a hidden passage inside the tomb. Proceed into the northwest chamber and examine the Honored Ancestors on the left or the Engraved Pedestal ahead to learn about the four Veloth ancestors.

Collect the four offerings that sit in the sand, and place them on the appropriate tombs:

Place the offerings upon the correct tombs.

Ancient Arrow	Tomb of Ondre Veloth
Ornate Goblet	Tomb of Valyne Veloth
Hand Mirror	Tomb of Llirala Veloth
Sack of Grain	Tomb of Elms Veloth

With the four offerings placed, play the harp, descend into the **Undertomb**, and talk to Narsis. As you explore deeper inside the tomb, watch out for Wraiths, raised panels in the flooring, and Bone Flayers that emerge from the sandpits. The panels trigger traps from the walls, which can be used against the mobs.

Inside the mausoleums, defeat the Skeletons and Hunger that emerge from the sand, then enter the **Mausoleums of the Elders** ahead. Explore further to find a five-by-five grid of unique floor switches. Use the series of seven tiles, presented on each side of the room, to decipher the correct order. Walk across the tiles in this order to open the exit, being careful not to reset the puzzle by making a misstep.

Step on the seven tiles in the correct order to complete the floor puzzle.

Talk to Narsis before entering the **Tomb of the Matriarch**. Fight through the Skeletons to find the Matriarch Rathila on the northern end. Defeat the elite mob before ascending the steps to the **Treasure Vault**. Talk to Narsis one last time before exiting the tomb. Talk to Elfbetta to complete the quest.

Defeat the Matriarch Rathila.

VV11

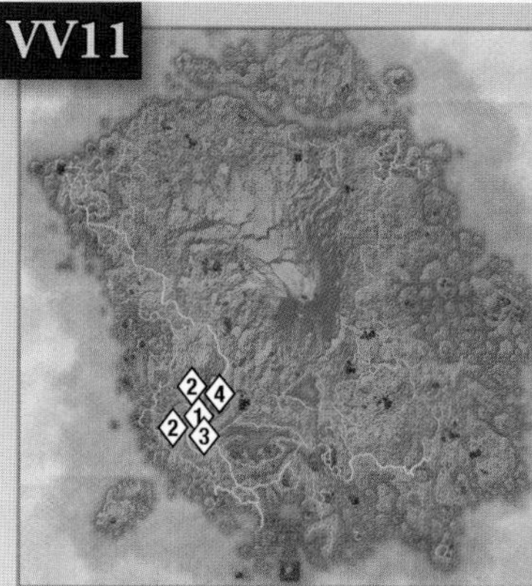

Like Blood from a Stone

Quest Giver	Malur Rethan
Prerequisite	None
Quest Giver Location	Outside Vassir-Didanat (South of Balmora)
Reward	Gold, Blackstone Hammer of the War Maiden, Diamond Necklace (Ornate), Diamond Ring (Ornate), Experience

Blackstone Hammer of the War Maiden

STYLE	ITEM TYPE	ENCHANTMENT
Hlaalu	Two-Handed Mace	Damage Shield
TRAIT	**SET NAME**	**QUALITY**
Defending	War Maiden	Fine

Noteworthy Tasks

- Obtain the Vassir-Didanat Mine Key
- Enter Vassir-Didanat Ebony Mine
- Find Gavros
- Defeat the Assassin at Rethan Manor
- Kill Malur Rethan
- Return to Councilman Rayveth

Steal the Vassir-Didanat Mine Key.

There are two ways to obtain the Vassir-Didanat Mine Key. Pick the simple lock and enter **Rethan Manor** southwest of Balmora. Sneak upstairs and grab the key from Benar Rethan's Desk. To receive the Foreman's key, pickpocket Foreman Nox, who stands near the well, just north of the Balmora stables. Use the key to enter **Vassir-Didanat Mine**. Iron Hound mobs patrol outside and inside the mine.

While exploring the mine, beware of the purple gas clouds that poison the player with Accelerated Transposition. Watch for Stonefiends that occupy the later portions of the mine. Fight your way to the south side of the mine and examine the Unfinished Letter (Lorebook) that sits on a table.

Grab the Daedric Formula from the laboratory.

On the west side of the mine, enter the **Daedric Laboratory** and examine the Test Results (Lorebook) on the table. Continue east to find Gavros, swipe the Daedric Formula off the nearby table, and use the nearby **Lift Room** to reach the mine entrance. Exit the Iron Hound camp and check in with Malur Rethan.

Return to **Rethan Manor** to find a Hired Assassin outside the house. Defeat the adversary and collect the Assassin's Orders (Lorebook) next to the fire, before talking to Councilman Rayveth inside the **Randy Netch Inn**.

Find Malur Rethan inside his house in Balmora.

Break into **Rethan's House** on the east side of Balmora, sneak down to the lower floor, and kill Malur Rethan. Take the Mysterious Formula that sits on the console table and return to Councilman Rayveth. Decide whether to hand over or destroy the scroll to complete the quest.

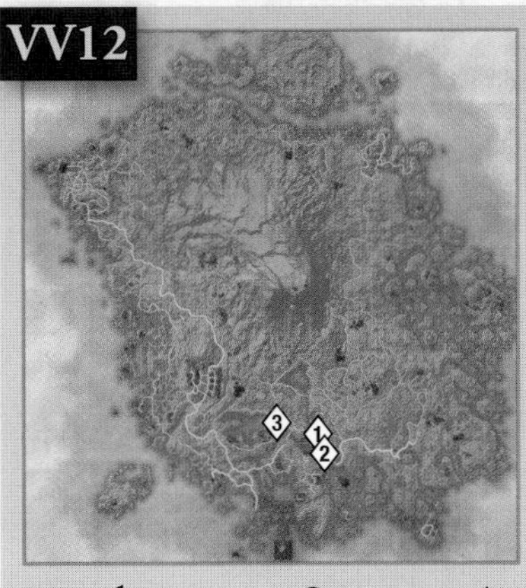

Nothing to Sneeze At

Quest Giver	Tilenra Sildreth
Prerequisite	None
Quest Giver Location	Suran
Reward	Gold, Stained Alchemy Smock, Sir Socks's Ball of Yarn Furnishing, Experience

Stained Alchemy Smock

STYLE	ITEM TYPE	ENCHANTMENT
Telvanni	Light Chest	Magicka
TRAIT	**SET NAME**	**QUALITY**
Impenetrable	—	Fine

Noteworthy Tasks

- Talk to Menaldinion at His Clinic
- Harvest Emperor Parasol Lichen
- Pour Tilenra's Potion on the Plants

After initially talking to Tilenra Sildreth, visit Menaldinion at **Menaldinion's Clinic** on the south side of Suran. Read Teas & Tisanes for Aches and Pain, received from Menaldinion, for a Lorebook credit. Tilenra asks you to harvest Emperor Parasol Lichen for her. Watch out for Iron Hound mobs northwest of Suran and pick the plant next to the lake.

Harvest Emperor Parasol Lichen for Tilenra.

After collecting the potion from Tilenra, use it on the two plants outside Menaldinion's Clinic. Bounce between the two NPCs to complete the quest.

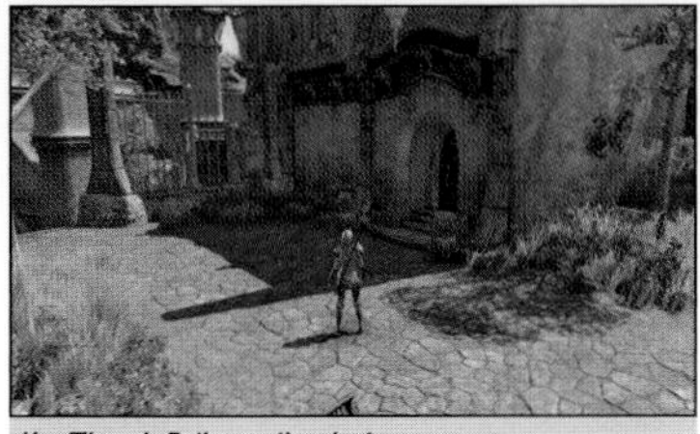

Use Tilenra's Potion on the plants.

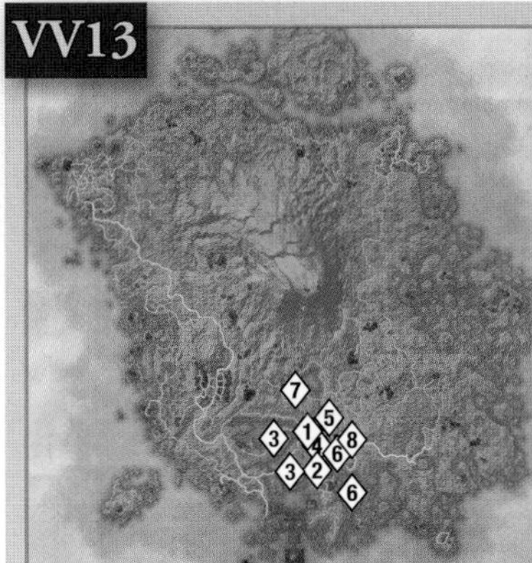

The Scarlet Judge

Quest Giver	The Scarlet Judge
Prerequisite	None
Quest Giver Location	Suran Wayshrine
Reward	Gold, the Scarlet Necklace, Experience, Regalia of the Scarlet Judge Costume

The Scarlet Necklace

STYLE	ITEM TYPE	ENCHANTMENT
—	Neck	Adds Physical Resistance
TRAIT	**SET NAME**	**QUALITY**
Healthy	—	Fine

Noteworthy Tasks

- Talk to a Prisoner
- Kill Overseer Torvayn
- Collect Testimony from Prisoners
- Meet Scarlet Judge at Ules Manor
- Go to the Iron Hound Camp
- Find a Way Into Suran Prison
- Collect the Scarlet Judge's Regalia
- Retrieve Stolen Evidence from Inanius Egg Mine
- Confront Marshal Hlaren
- Talk to Melar Sadus

The Scarlet Judge needs your assistance with his current investigation. Iron Hound mobs occupy much of the surrounding territory, so remain alert. Talk to one of the prisoners southwest of Suran, kill Overseer Torvayn, and then collect testimony from the three prisoners working the nearby land. They lead you to two manors west of town.

Investigate the manors.

Enter **Master Kharekh's Manor**, take out the mobs inside, and descend to the lower level, where a Letter to Kharekh gra-Bagrat (Lorebook) sits on a console table. Find **Mistress Dren's Manor** west of Suran on the lake. Fight your way into the house, climb to the third floor, and pick the lock to reach Mistress Dren's Residence. Collect the Letter to Marshal Hlaren (Lorebook) from the corner table.

After talking to the Scarlet Judge at **Ules Manor**, find the **Iron Hound camp** north of Suran. Smash four Supply Crates and burn three Weapon Caches around the ruins. Captain Cedus stands near one of the weapon racks. Either kill her or flee the area after burning the weapons. Return to Suran and talk to Constable Gretga to find out the judge has been jailed.

Intimidating Remas Belan is the optimal method to obtain the key.

Three people on the south side of town can assist you in obtaining a key to Suran Prison. At the **Keymaker's Tower**, Remas Belan can be intimidated to make you the key. Constable Kren and Dredyni Imayn are both at **Desele's House of Earthly Delights**. Dredyni mentions Mirel's key that lies next to his body on an island to the south. Constable Kren gives up the key, but at a cost.

Enter **Suran Prison** on the northeast side of town, sneak downstairs—using hiding spots to avoid being spotted by the Hireling Guards—and find Melar Sadus. Follow his lead and travel to **Warden Libo's Hunting Camp** north of Suran. Upon arrival, two tasks become available: **Collect Captain Lido's Chest Key** and **The Scarlet Judge's Regalia**.

Sneak through Suran Prison to find Melar Sadus.

An Iron Hound Tracker sits at the campfire, the chest is next to a nearby tree, and the Warden patrols between the two locations. It's possible to sneak to the chest and pick the simple lock to gain the disguise. Or take out Warden Libo to get his chest key.

Recover the Scarlet Judge's Regalia from Warden Libo.

Return to Gretga and then head east to the back entrance to **Inanius Egg Mine**. Explore the Kwama- and Iron Hound-infested mine while recovering the three pieces of evidence. The Slave Testimony counts as a Lorebook. Farther inside, confront and defeat Marshal Hlaren before handing the evidence over to Constable Gretga just outside the nearby exit. Visit Melar Sadus, who now sits outside the prison, to complete the quest.

Confront Marshal Hlaren inside Inanius Egg Mine.

VV14

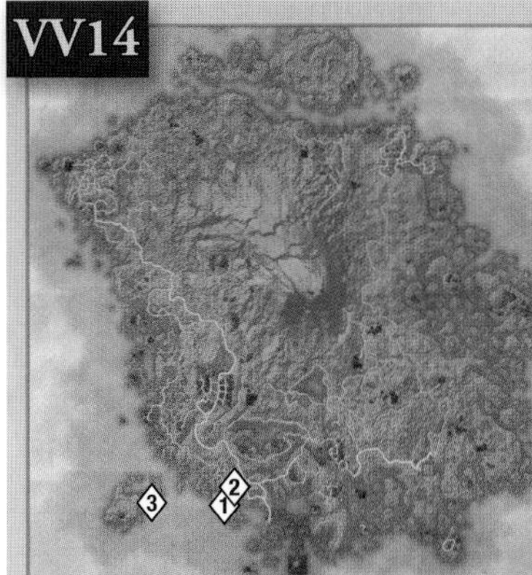

Breaking Through the Fog

Quest Giver	Deminah Salvi
Prerequisite	Travel to Vvardenfell (Skipping Tutorial)
Quest Giver Location	Seyda Neen
Reward	Gold, Governor's Ring of the War Maiden, Experience

Governor's Ring of the War Maiden

STYLE	ITEM TYPE	ENCHANTMENT
—	Ring	Adds Magicka Recovery
TRAIT	**SET NAME**	**QUALITY**
Arcane	War Maiden	Fine

Noteworthy Tasks

- Talk to Cherishes-Water
- Acquire Findun's Special Blend
- Ask Townsfolk About Almsivi
- Acquire Parchment from the Governor
- Search for Evidence on Firemoth Island

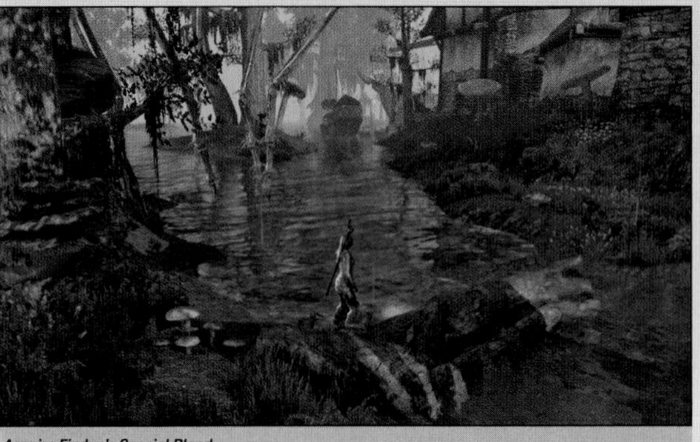

Acquire Findun's Special Blend.

Breaking Through the Fog is only available for players who have skipped the Morrowind tutorial, Broken Bonds, by traveling from another zone. Investigate the lighthouse mystery by talking to Sergeant Delms, who is currently at the top of the **Seyda Neen Lighthouse**. He leads you to Cherishes-Water; find her sitting in the water nearby. With the Intimidate perk, you can press her for a quicker answer. Otherwise, she wants you to acquire Findun's Special Blend for her. This can be purchased at **Findun's Goods** for 30 gold or gathered behind the Tavern by the Sea.

Return to Cherishes-Water and use the blend in the surrounding pool of water to refresh her memory. Search the nearby **Tree Hollow** for a clue. Numerous people around Seyda Neen may be questioned, but you can go straight to Findun's Goods. Tell Marise Rothrano that you have her reward, and find out how she got past the guards. Next, head to the docks and check in with Deminah Salvi, who asks you to acquire parchment from the governor.

One option is to steal the parchment from the Guard House.

The paper can be obtained by sneaking into the Guard House or ask Marise Rothrano to swipe the parchment. If you decide to do it yourself, enter the **Guard House** and use the basket to hide from the guard. Then move into the **Governor's Room** to collect the Blank Parchment Sheet and read the Unfinished Report.

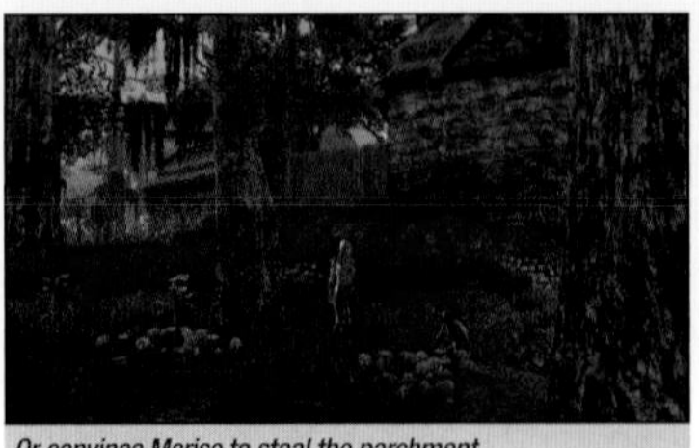

Or convince Marise to steal the parchment.

Or use the Persuade perk to convince Marise Rothrano, found inside Findun's Goods, to grab the paper. Talk to Sergeant Delms outside the Guard House to create a distraction, and then meet up with Marise.

Use the ship's wheel to reach **Firemoth Island** and grab the Captain's Note pinned to the boathouse. Use the boat to return to Seyda Neen and talk to Deminah Salvi inside the **Governor's Office** to complete the quest.

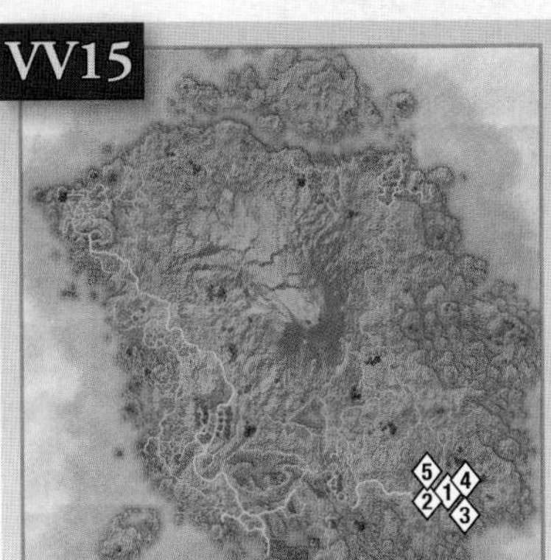

VV15

An Armiger's Duty

Quest Giver	Buoyant Armiger
Prerequisite	None
Quest Giver Location	Molag Mar Wayshrine
Reward	Gold, Holy Helm of the Warrior-Poet, Experience

Tribal Helm of the Defiler

STYLE	ITEM TYPE	ENCHANTMENT	TRAIT	SET NAME	QUALITY
Buoyant Armiger	Medium Head	Stamina	Sturdy	Infector	Fine

Noteworthy Tasks

- Search the Ashlander Camp for Evidence
- Search Three Pilgrim Campsites
- Explore the Helan Ancestral Tomb
- Search for the Ruddy Man
- Enter Dreudurai Glass Mine
- Kill the Change Ruddy Man Spawn to Ruddy Broodmother

Search the Ashlander Camp for evidence.

Lead Baren Maloren out of the Helan Ancestral Tomb.

Visit **Penitent Pilgrim Inn** at Molag Mar, where Captain Naros asks you to search for evidence at the nearby Ashlander Camp without killing any of the Ashlanders. The camp is restricted, so remain in stealth while searching the area. Baskets offer hiding spots if you're in jeopardy of being spotted, though you can also flee outside the trespassing zone. Collect the Torn Page (Lorebook) and Ritual of Appeasement (Lorebook) before examining the stone altar at the ritual site.

Defeat the Ruddy Broodmother inside the Dreudurai Glass Mine.

Ibaal sends you to three pilgrim camps to the north. Examine and collect proof at all three locations. Examine the Mutilated Remains, the Buoyant Armiger, and the Devotee Journal (Lorebook). Next, you're sent to the **Helan Ancestral Tomb**. Find Baren Maloren at the back of the tomb and lead him out without setting off the traps. Run up the side of the first corridor to avoid the blades, and then stick to the right corner to avoid a flame from above. If a trap is triggered, Baren returns to the starting location.

Lead Ibaal in a search for the Ruddy Man to the northwest. Once you find it, observe the monster, which leads you to the **Dreudurai Glass Mine**. After checking in with Captain Naros, collect a luring potion from Ibaal and enter the mine.

While exploring the mine, keep an eye out for mud cocoons and release the three captives from inside. Make a left at the first opportunity to find the first guy under a wooden deck. A pair of Dreugh guard the second in the northwest corner of the mine, while the third is just beyond the boss.

Find the disturbed earth near the center of the mine and use Wise-Womens' Potion to draw the Ruddy Broodmother out. The elite mob can be a tough fight if you're not paying attention. Watch for its Lightning Field skill and dodge roll out of the area to avoid big damage. Report to Captain Naros and Ibaal after defeating the monster.

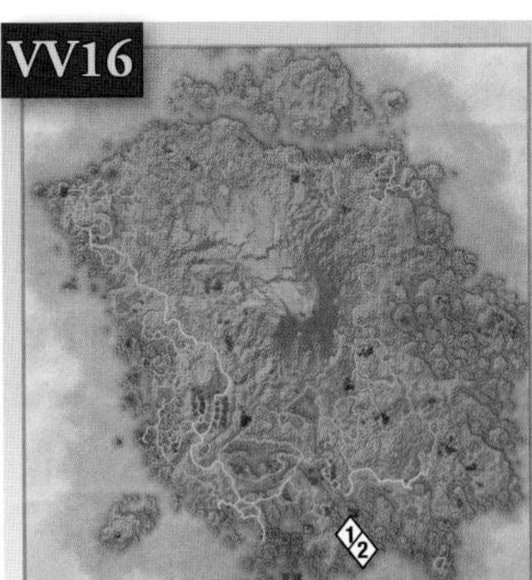

VV16

A Web of Troubles

Quest Giver	Lady Clarisse Laurent
Prerequisite	None
Quest Giver Location	Northwest of Bal Fell
Reward	Gold, Griskild's Tenderizer, Experience

Griskild's Tenderizer

STYLE	ITEM TYPE	ENCHANTMENT	TRAIT	SET NAME	QUALITY
Xivkyn	One-Handed Hammer	Berserker	Sharpened	—	Fine

Noteworthy Tasks

- Find the Missing Mages
- Capture a Mind Spider
- Follow Stibbons into Bal Fell
- Stop the Ritual

Follow Dralane to the Bal Fell entrance.

Defeat Mad Griskild to stop the ritual.

Lady Clarisse Laurent wants you to find missing mages at the nearby ruins. Talk to Mehdbeq, located on the south side of the ruin, before searching for Stibbons' trail. Examine the Spice Pouch, the ***Investigator Vale and the Temple of Stendarr*** book, and the Serving Bowl to find him to the west. After following Dralane Elarven to the **Bal Fell entrance**, return to Stibbons and use Lady Laurent's Signal Wand. Check in with Lady Laurent, who joins Stibbons and the Vestige.

Next, capture one of the Mind Spiders, found at the highest point of the ruins. At Lady Laurent's camp, release the spider and follow Stibbons into Bal Fell. Once inside, talk to Clarisse and stop the ritual inside the tomb by defeating Mad Griskild, at which point his spiders vanish. Return to the camp to receive the quest reward.

VECTOR QUESTS

Several quests are implemented to simply lead the player to another quest or location. Two of these tasks lead you to daily quests in Ald'ruhn and Vivec City. Check out the **Daily, Repeatable Quests** section of this chapter for a list of possible jobs.

V1

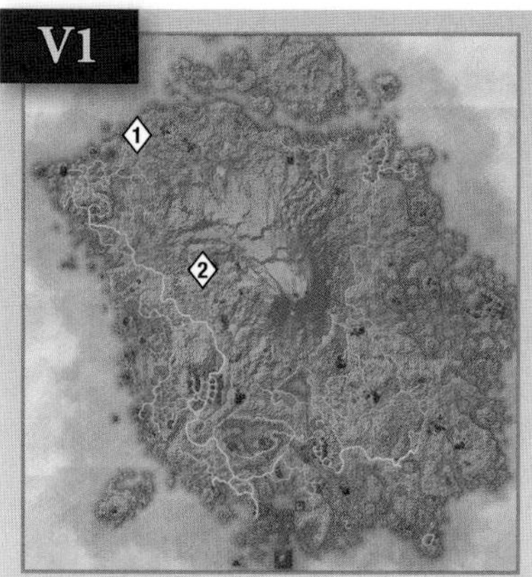

Ashlander Relations

Quest Giver	Udami
Prerequisite	Ancestral Ties
Quest Giver Location	EachUrshilaku Camp and Ald'ruhn
Reward	Gold, Experience

Noteworthy Tasks

- Talk to Zanammu in Ald'ruhn

Udami directs you to Zanammu, located in a hut near **Skar**, in Ald'ruhn. Talk to him to learn about two more daily quests. Numani-Rasi offers relic-preservation quests, requiring the player to collect a set number of relics from the given location and return them to her. Huntmaster Sorim-Nakar gives a daily beast hunt, which asks the player to take out a specific beast in Vvardenfell. Return to Numani-Rasi or Sorim-Nakar to receive your quest reward.

Visit Ald'ruhn every day to take on beast and relic hunts.

V2

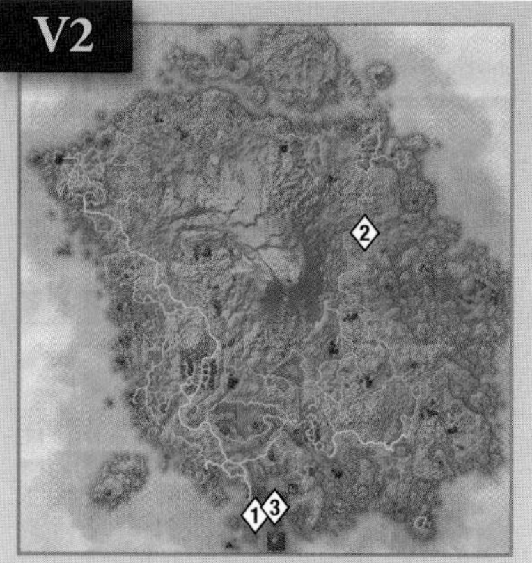

A Friend in Need

Quest Giver	Canthion (Housing Broker)
Prerequisite	None
Quest Giver Location	Vivec City (Next to Bank)
Reward	Gold, Vivec City Inn House, ***Anthology of Abodes Available for Acquisition*** Scroll, Experience

Noteworthy Tasks

- Talk to Szugogroth
- Talk to Bulag Idolus in Pulk Delve
- Craft or Purchase Furniture for Your Home
- Meet Canthion at the New House

Quest: A Friend in Need is available in Vivec City if it has not been completed elsewhere in Tamriel. Talk to Szugogroth inside the **Vivec Outlaws Refuge** and then check his bag for old paperwork, leading you to Pulk Delve. Inside the delve, take care of the bandits on your way to Bulag Idolus. Ask her for the deed and key. Decide whether she lives or dies before returning to Canthion.

He wants you to get furniture for your home. The easiest method is to visit a Home Goods Furnisher, such as the one in the Abbey of St. Delyn. If you possess a pattern and the required materials, you can craft one at the appropriate station. Talk to Canthion inside St. Delyn's Inn to receive the Vivec City Inn house.

Meet Canthion at your house with furniture.

V3

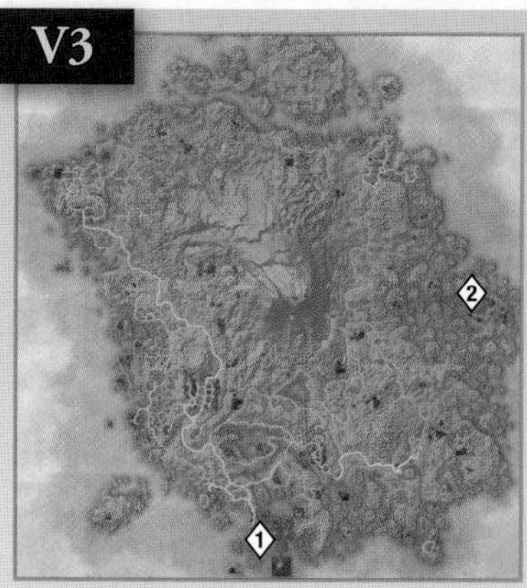

A Late Delivery

Quest Giver	Edryno Giryon
Prerequisite	None
Quest Giver Location	Vivec City (Near the Canton of St. Olms the Just)
Reward	Gold, Experience

Noteworthy Tasks

- Deliver Rare Mushrooms to Vaelin Oren

Edryno Giryon has a shipment of rare mushrooms to be delivered to Sadrith Mora on the east side of Vvardenfell. Boatswain Synda Imyam offers a ride to the city from the **Pilgrim's Approach** on the northwest side of town. Find Vaelin inside the Council House.

Synda Imyam takes you directly to Sadrith Mora.

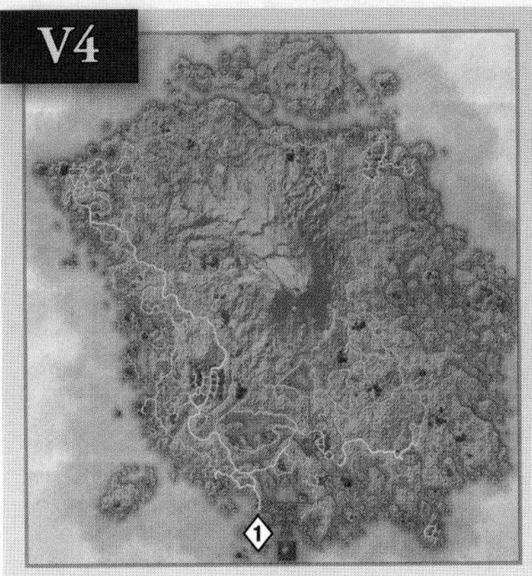

For Glory!

Quest Giver	"For Glory!" Flyer
Prerequisite	Level 10
Quest Giver Location	Vivec City and Outside Battlegrounds
Reward	Gold, Experience

Noteworthy Tasks

- Talk to Battlemaster Rivyn
- Complete a Battleground

Once you reach Level 10, talk to Battlemaster Rivyn for an introduction to the Battlegrounds and PvPvP. Complete a Battleground to complete the quest.

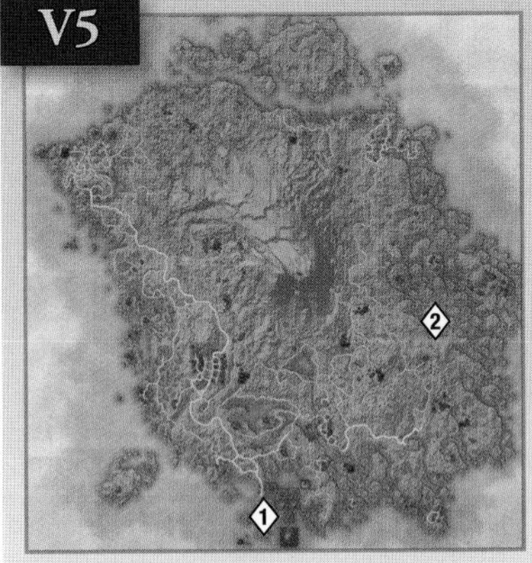

To Tel Fyr

Quest Giver	Daynillo Rethul
Prerequisite	Level 10
Quest Giver Location	Vivec City (East of the Gladiator's Quarters)
Reward	Gold, Experience

Noteworthy Tasks

- Talk to Daynea Rethul at the Halls of Fabrication

Daynillo Rethul directs you to the Halls of Fabrication Trial on the east side of Vvardenfell. A boat at the **Vivec City docks** can take you there, or you can stop there during your adventures. Talk to Daynea Rethul inside the Trial staging area.

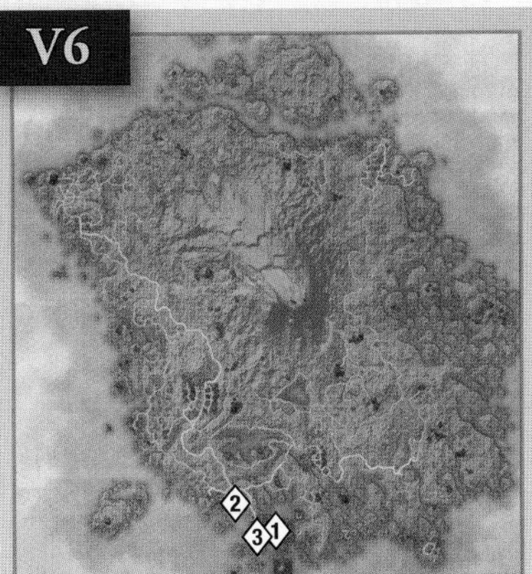

Crafting Consumables Certification

Quest Giver	Danel Telleno
Prerequisite	Level 6
Quest Giver Location	Vivec City (St. Delyn Guild Halls)
Reward	Gold, Reward Item, 1000 Alchemy/Enchanting/Provisioning Inspiration

Noteworthy Tasks

- Collect the Required Materials
- Craft the Item

CERTIFICATION	REQUIRED MATERIALS
Provisioning	Recipe: Roast Pig White Meat
Enchanting	Jora, Oko, Ta Runes
Alchemy	Natural Water Columbine, Mountain Flower (or Bugloss)
CRAFT A...	**REWARD ITEM**
Roast Pig	Cooking Supplies (Banana Surprise and Mazte Recipes)
Trifling Glyph of Health	Jejota Rune
Sip of Health	5x Natural Water

Danel Telleno is located at the Mages Guild in the major cities, including Vivec City. Find him at the **St. Delyn Guild Halls** and express interest in Provisioning, Enchanting, or Alchemy certification. Note that you can only work on one of the six certifications at a time.

First you must find the required materials. For Provisioning, Danel points you to the recipe inside a nearby trunk. Learn it, find white meat, and then go to the west side of town to find a Cooking Fire. For Enchanting and Alchemy, the runes, water, and plants are harvested outside of town at a location noted on your map.

Find the Roast Pig Recipe near Danel Telleno.

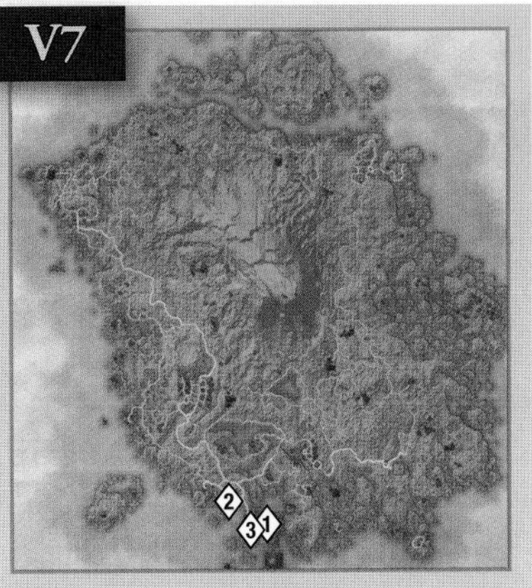

Crafting Equipment Certification

Quest Giver	Millenith
Prerequisite	Level 6
Quest Giver Location	Vivec City (St. Delyn Guild Halls)
Reward	Gold, Reward Item, 1000 Blacksmithing/Clothing/Woodworking Inspiration

Noteworthy Tasks

- Collect Material
- Craft a Weapon or Armor
- Deconstruct an Item

CERTIFICATION	REQUIRED MATERIALS
Blacksmith	Iron Ore (10)
Woodworker	Rough Maple (10)
Clothier	Raw Jute (10)
CRAFT A...	**REWARD ITEM**
Iron Dagger	Honing Stone
Maple Bow	Pitch Resin
Homespun Gloves	Hemming Tannin

Millenith can be found at the Fighters Guild in the major cities, including Vivec City. Find her at the **St. Delyn Guild Halls** and tell her you are interested in certification. She gives you three choices: Blacksmith, Woodworker, or Clothier certification. Select one at a time and complete the following tasks: gather the material, craft the item, and deconstruct the item. For these quests, the required resources spawn just outside of town, and are marked on your map.

Use the crafting stations to craft weapons and apparel.

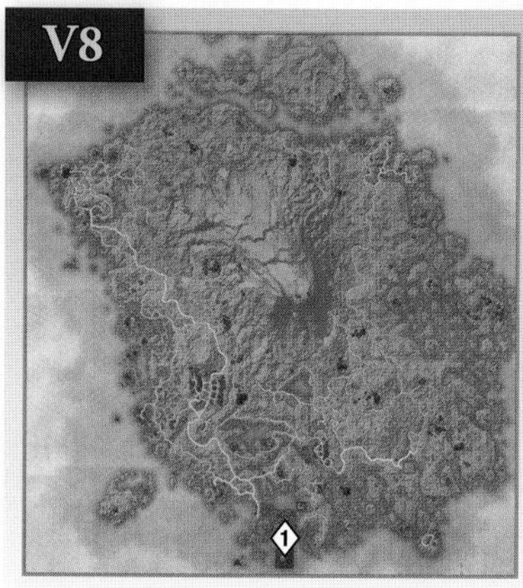

A Call for Aid

Quest Giver	"Adventurers Wanted!" Flyer
Prerequisite	Complete Divine Conundrum
Quest Giver Location	Vivec City (North Side of Temple Canton)
Reward	Gold, Experience

Noteworthy Tasks

- Talk to Unel Darano in the Justice Offices

Reading the "Adventures Wanted!" flyer that hangs just north of Temple Canton leads to the **Justice Office**, where Unel Darano introduces the player to the Vivec City daily quests. Beleru Omoril offers group dailies that require the player, preferably with a group, to defeat a challenging monster in Vvardenfell, along with a secondary job found in the boss's area. Traylan Omoril's jobs are requested from the Temple and take place at the six delves, requiring more subtlety to complete.

A contact for each job can be sought out in Vivec City. Talk to the NPC for more information about the tasks. Once the tasks have been completed, return to the same NPC to receive the reward.

DAILY QUESTS

R1 Ald'ruhn Daily Relic-Preservation Quests

Quest Giver	Numani-Rasi
Prerequisite	Ashlander Relations (Available Once Per Day)
Quest Giver Location	Ald'ruhn (East Hut)
Reward	Gold, Gift of Urshilaku Gratitude, Experience

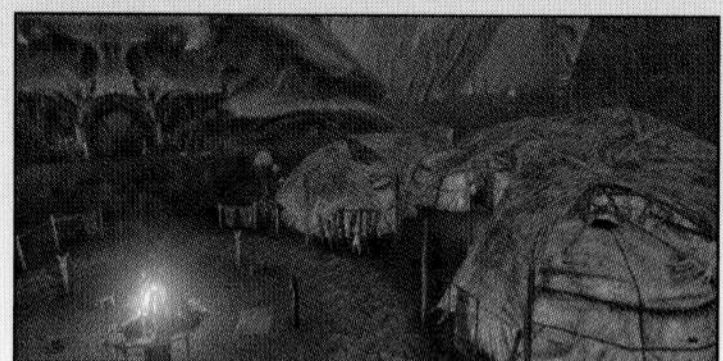

Relics of Ashalmawia

Job Location	Ashalmawia Shrine (Northwest of Ald'ruhn, Near the Coast)

Noteworthy Tasks

- Gather Eight Ashalmawia Relics

Relics of Ashurnabitashp

Job Location	Ashurnabitashpi Shrine (Northern Coast, West of the Forgotten Wastes)

Noteworthy Tasks

- Gather Eight Ashurnabitashpi Relics

Relics of Assarnatamat

Job Location	Assarnatamat Shrine (Between Ald'ruhn and Balmora)

Noteworthy Tasks

- Gather Eight Assarnatamat Relics

Relics of Dushariran

Job Location	Dushariran Shrine (Northwest of Ald'ruhn)

Noteworthy Tasks

- Gather Eight Dushariran Relics

Relics of Ebernanit

Job Location	Ebernanit Shrine (West of the Forgotten Wastes)

Noteworthy Tasks

- Gather Eight Ebernanit Relics

Relics of Maelkashishi

Job Location	Maelkashishi Shrine (East of West Gash)

Noteworthy Tasks

- Gather Eight Maelkashishi Relics

Relics of Yasammidan

Job Location	Yasammidan Ruins

Noteworthy Tasks

- Gather Eight Yasammidan Relics

R2 Ald'ruhn Daily Beast Hunt

Quest Giver	Huntmaster Sorim-Nakar
Prerequisite	Ashlander Relations (Available Once Per Day)
Quest Giver Location	Ald'ruhn (South Hut)
Reward	Gold, Huntmaster's Recognition, Experience

Ash-Eater Hunt

Job Location	West of Matus-Akin Egg Mine

Noteworthy Tasks

- Hunt Down Ash-Eater
- Optional Steps: Disturb Mounds to Attract Ash-Eater

Great Zexxin Hunt

Job Location	Southwest of the Halls of Fabrication

Noteworthy Tasks

- Hunt Down Great Zexxin
- Hints: Search for Great Zexxin's Trail

King Razor-Tusk Hunt

Job Location	South of Pulk Delve

Noteworthy Tasks

- Hunt Down King Razor-Tusk
- Optional Steps: Kill Kagouti to Lure King Razor-Tusk

Mother Jagged-Claw Hunt

Job Location	Far Southeast Vvardenfell

Noteworthy Tasks

- Hunt Down Mother Jagged-Claw
- Optional Steps: Disturb Mud Piles to Attract Mother Jagged-Claw

Old Stomper Hunt

Job Location	Southwest of Nchuleftingth Public Dungeon

Noteworthy Tasks

- Hunt Down Old Stomper
- Hints: Search for Old Stomper's Trail

Tarra-Suj Hunt

Job Location	East of Nchuleftingth Public Dungeon

Noteworthy Tasks

- Hunt Down Tarra-Suj
- Optional Steps: Kill Nix-Hounds to Attract Tarra-Suj

Writhing Sveeth Hunt

Job Location	West of the Nchuleftingth Wayshrine

Noteworthy Tasks

- Hunt Down Writhing Sveeth
- Optional Steps: Destroy Fetcherfly Nests to Lure Writhing Sveeth

R3 Consumables Crafting Writs

Quest Giver	Bulletin Board
Prerequisite	Crafting Consumables Certifications (Available Once Per Day)
Quest Giver Location	Vivec City (Near Foundation's Embrace)
Reward	Gold, Alchemist's Vessel/Enchanter's Coffer/Provisioner's Pack, Alchemy/Enchanting/Provisioning Inspiration

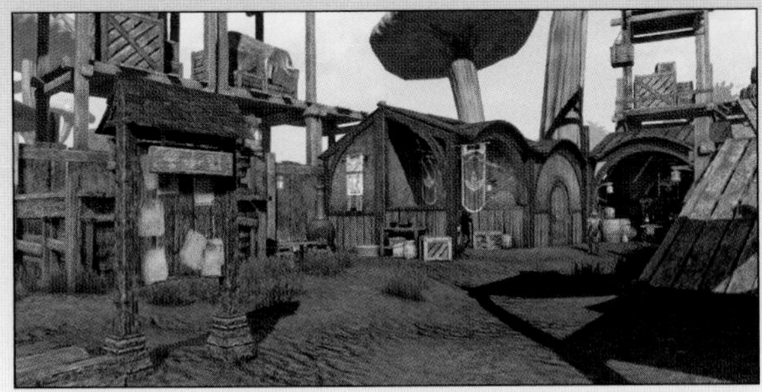

Completing consumable crafting certifications from Danel Telleno activates the corresponding writs at a bulletin board, located near **Foundation's Embrace** in Vivec City. Provisioning writs require a food-and-drink item to be crafted at a Cooking Fire. Enchanting writs ask for a glyph to be created at an Enchanting Table, as well as the gathering of a specific rune. For Alchemy, a writ asks for an appropriate-level potion, along with a specified reagent (x3) or solvent (x3). Note that crafting writs can be accepted from bulletin boards in all major cities. The goods are delivered to collection locations throughout Tamriel.

R4 Equipment Crafting Writs

Quest Giver	Bulletin Board
Prerequisite	Crafting Equipment Certifications (Available Once Per Day)
Quest Giver Location	Vivec City (Near Foundation's Bulwark)
Reward	Gold, Blacksmith's Crate/Clothier's Satchel/Woodworker's Case, Blacksmithing/Clothing/Woodworking Inspiration

After you complete at least one certification from Millenith, daily jobs become available within the crafting discipline(s) that you have been certified in. The Blacksmithing, Clothing, and Woodworking crafting writs are available each day at a bulletin board in Vivec City near **Foundation's Bulwark**. A writ requires you to craft a selection of weapons and/or apparel. As you upgrade the crafting discipline and the first Passive Ability, the equipment created increases in level. Note that crafting writs can be accepted from bulletin boards in all major cities. The goods are delivered to collection locations throughout Tamriel.

R5 Vivec City Group Boss Daily Quests

Quest Giver	Beleru Omoril
Prerequisite	Call to Aid (Available Once Per Day)
Quest Giver Location	Vivec City (Justice)
Reward	Gold, Hall of Justice Bounty Dispensation, Experience

The Anxious Apprentice

Contact	Nara Varam
Contact Location	St. Olms Square
Job Location	Dubdil Alar Tower

Noteworthy Tasks

- Stop Dubdil Alar's Experiment
- Retrieve Research Notes

A Creeping Hunger

Contact	Tirvina Avani
Contact Location	St. Olms Waistworks
Job Location	Sulipund Grange

Noteworthy Tasks

- Defeat Wuyuvus
- Gather Relic Bones
- Gather Relic Tablet
- Gather Relic Skull

Culling the Swarm

Contact	Dinor Salvi
Contact Location	St. Olms Waistworks
Job Location	West of the Halls of Fabrication

Noteworthy Tasks

- Defeat the Queen's Consort
- Kill Kwama Near Missir-Dadalit Egg Mine (8)

Oxen Free

Contact	Bravosi Felder
Contact Location	St. Olms Square
Job Location	North of Balmora

Noteworthy Tasks

- Defeat Nilthog the Unbroken
- Gather Caldera Mushrooms (6)

Salothan's Curse

Contact	Ivulen Andromo
Contact Location	St. Olms Waistworks
Job Location	Salothan's Council (East of Gnisis)

Noteworthy Tasks

- Defeat Orator Salothan
- Defeat Wraiths (4)

Siren's Song

Contact	Valga Celatus
Contact Location	St. Olms Waistworks
Job Location	Northwest of Tel Branora

Noteworthy Tasks

- Defeat Kimbrudhil the Songbird
- Recover Cargo (3)

R6 Vivec City Delve Daily Quests

Quest Giver	Traylan Omoril
Prerequisite	Call to Aid (Available Once Per Day)
Quest Giver Location	Vivec City (Justice Office)
Reward	Gold, Hall of Justice Explorer's Dispensation, Experience

Daedric Disruptions

Contact	Savile Alam
Contact Location	St. Delyn Plaza
Job Location	Ashalmawia Depths Delve

Noteworthy Tasks

- Disrupt the Dark Ritual (Ruins Outside Delve)
- Disrupt the Ritual of Knowledge (Inside Delve in Sunken Vaults)
- Disrupt the Dremora Worship Ritual (Inside Delve on Lower Level of Main Cavern)
- Disrupt the Clannfear Feast (Inside Delve in Sunken Vault)

Kwama Conundrum

Contact	Kylia Thando
Contact Location	St. Delyn Plaza
Job Location	Matus-Akin Egg Mine Delve

Noteworthy Tasks

- Plant Poisoned Feed (Just Inside Entrance, but Only Accessible from Central Cavern)
- Retrieve a Kwama Egg (On Barrel on North Side, Follow Right Path from Entrance)
- Acquire Breeding Research (Far Southwest Chamber)

Planting Misinformation

Contact	Evos Hledas
Contact Location	St. Delyn Plaza
Job Location	Zainsipilu Delve

Noteworthy Tasks

- Place Unintelligible Instructions Near the Crops (Center of Main Cavern)
- Place Incoherent Notes on the Research Table (West Chamber, Behind Zvvius the Hive Lord)

Tax Deduction

Contact	Alves Droth
Contact Location	St. Delyn Plaza
Job Location	Pulk Delve

Noteworthy Tasks

- Collect Vos Tax Records (Southwest Corner)
- Collect Sadrith Mora Tax Records (Lower Level)
- Collect Molag Mar Tax Records (Upper Level)
- Collect Stolen Taxes (Far East Side, Guarded by Bralsa Inlador)

Tribal Troubles

Contact	Dredase-Hlarar
Contact Location	St. Delyn Plaza
Job Location	Nchuleft Delve

Noteworthy Tasks

- Collect the Cog: Nchuleft Ruins
- Collect the Rod: Nchuleft Depths (East Side of Bottom Level)
- Collect the Gear: Nchuleft Depths (Northwest Corner of Third Level)
- Collect the Core: Nchuleft Depths (Defeat Nchuthand Far-Hurler at Bottom of Tower)

Unsettled Syndicate

Contact	Vorar Vendu
Contact Location	St. Delyn Plaza
Job Location	Khartag Point Delve

Noteworthy Tasks

- Search the Campsite for Slave Activity (Far Northern Delve)
- Kill Avrusa Duleri (Center of Delve)

VIVEC CITY MUSEUM

M1 The Ancestral Tombs

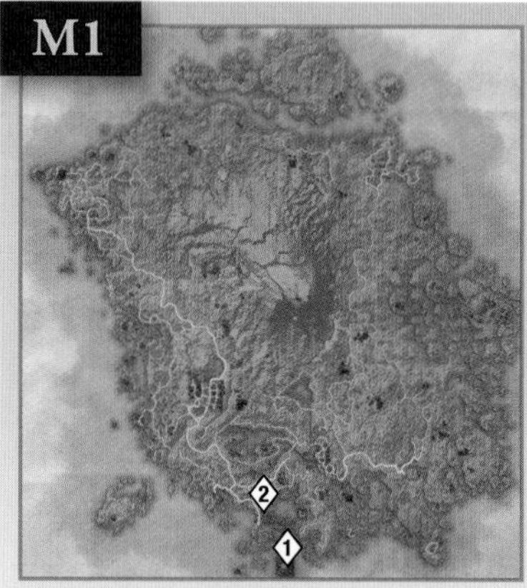

Quest Giver	Librarian Bradyn
Prerequisite	None
Quest Giver Location	Vivec City (Library of Vivec)
Reward	Gold, Explorer's Comfortable Shoes, Experience

Explorer's Comfortable Shoes

STYLE	ITEM TYPE	ENCHANTMENT	TRAIT	SET NAME	QUALITY
Breton	Light Feet	Adds Maximum Magicka	Well-Fitted	—	Fine

Noteworthy Tasks

- Take a Rubbing at the Othrelas Ancestral Tomb
- Return to Librarian Bradyn

Librarian Bradyn wishes you to collect rubbings from Ancestral Tombs around Vvardenfell. Each one adds to the model he builds inside the **Library of Vivec**. Check in with him after collecting the nearby Othrelas rubbing to receive the reward.

Visit 29 more Ancestral Tombs and return the rubbings to Librarian Bradyn. Refer to the atlas for all locations, with a full listing in the **Appendices**.

M2

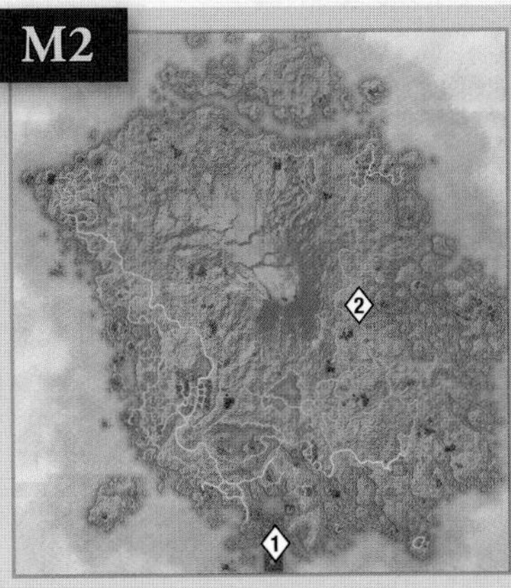

The Lost Library

Quest Giver	Librarian Bradyn
Prerequisite	Complete The Ancestral Tombs, Collect All 30 Ancestral Tomb Rubbings
Quest Giver Location	Vivec City (Library of Vivec)
Collectible	Vvardenfell Scale Model Bust—Complete Quest
Reward	Gold, Andule's Cuirass of the Defiler, Experience

Andule's Curiass of the Defiler

STYLE	ITEM TYPE	ENCHANTMENT	TRAIT	SET NAME	QUALITY
Redoran	Medium Chest	Stamina	Infused	Infector	Epic

Noteworthy Tasks

- Find the Lost Library
- Light the Brazier of Wisdom
- Light the Brazier of Knowledge
- Retrieve Indoril Genealogy
- Retrieve Redoran Genealogy
- Retrieve Hlaalu Genealogy
- Retrieve Dres Genealogy
- Retrieve Telvanni Genealogy

Once all 30 Ancestral Tomb rubbings are collected for Librarian Bradyn, he offers a second quest—to find the lost Library of Andule. Examine the missing piece of the model to discover its location, **east of the volcano and southeast of Falensarano Ruins**. Proceed inside.

Examine the statue to the left before moving to the floor puzzle. Examine the three Daedric Tiles before the doorway and memorize the symbols. In order to walk through the next room, you may only move between these symbols. Stray from them and you're reset to the beginning. Make your way to the two braziers, Wisdom in the southeast corner and Knowledge to the north, and light them to allow access to the Ancient Vaults.

Enter the Library of Andule.

Stick to the three given Daedric symbols to reach the braziers.

Four Lorebooks are available in the hallway ahead, one for each house: Indoril, Redoran, Hlaalu, and Dres. Reading them provides the answers needed to retrieve each Genealogy. Let's start with House Dres on the right. Talk to the Dres Ancestor Spirit and provide the following answers to gain access to the Dres Genealogy:

- **"House Dres holds slavery to be their sacred right and duty."**
- **"Because Dres feeds Morrowind with its agricultural might."**
- **"Dres believes Dunmer should keep to themselves and focus on improving Morrowind."**

House Indoril is the first room on the left. Answer the Indoril Ancestor Spirit's questions as follows to earn the Indoril Genealogy:

- **"Religion."**
- **"Be preserved at all costs."**
- **"Outsiders may visit, but they must always be watched carefully."**

House Hlaalu sits down the hall on the right. Speak to the Hlaalu Ancestor Spirit and answer as follows before collecting the Hlaalu Genealogy:

- **"Succeed at business and turn a tidy profit."**
- **"Compromise while always seeking to obtain the best possible deal."**
- **"Acknowledge Dunmer culture, but adapt as necessary to succeed."**

And last, talk to the Redoran Ancestor Spirit and answer his questions as listed below to retrieve the Redoran Genealogy:

- **"To fulfill your duty and maintain your honor."**
- **"We must accept and endure the harshness of life."**
- **"The way of the warrior."**

With the four Genealogies in hand, collect the Telvanni Genealogy at the end of the hall. Return to Librarian Bradyn.

Retrieve the Telvanni Genealogy before returning to the Librarian.

GUILD QUESTS

Just as in other major cities around Tamriel, four guilds may be joined in Vvardenfell: Fighters Guild, Mages Guild, Dark Brotherhood, and Thieves Guild. We explain how to get these quest lines started, though all four require travel outside Vvardenfell to complete.

Fighters Guild: Anchors from the Harbour

Quest Giver	Bera Moorsmith
Prerequisite	Join Fighters Guild by Talking to Hall Steward
Quest Giver Location	Fighters Guild in Balmora, Sadrith Mora, Vivec City, and Other Major Cities
Reward	Gold, Anchorstone Amulet, Experience

Noteworthy Tasks

- Talk to Sees-All-Colors in Vulkhel Guard
- Complete Quest Outside of Vvardenfell

Bera Moorsmith tracks you down at any Fighters Guild once you're a member.

By expressing interest in the Fighters Guild to the Hall Steward at the Fighters Guild in Vivec City, Balmora, or Sadrith Mora, the player is able to join the guild and gain access to the skill line. Once the main quest line is complete, Bera Moorsmith tracks you down anytime you're near a Fighters Guild. She asks that you talk to Sees-All-Colors in Vulkhel Guard.

Mages Guild: Long Lost Lore

Quest Giver	Valaste
Prerequisite	Join Mages Guild by Talking to Hall Steward
Quest Giver Location	Mages Guild in Vivec City and Other Major Cities
Reward	Gold, the Amulet of Eyevea, Experience

Noteworthy Tasks

- Talk to Valaste
- Complete Quest Outside of Vvardenfell

Talk to the Magister at the Mages Guild in Vivec City, Balmora, or Sadrith Mora to join the guild and gain access to the skill line. Once the main quest line is complete, talk to Valaste at the Mages Guild to begin the first quest, **Long Lost Lore**.

Dark Brotherhood: Voices in the Dark

Quest Giver	Amelie Crowe
Prerequisite	Own Dark Brotherhood DLC or ESO Plus Membership, Complete the Vvardenfell Story Quest Line
Quest Giver Location	Any Outlaws Refuge, Including Vivec City
Reward	Gold, Dark Brotherhood Reputation

Noteworthy Tasks

- Talk to Amelie Crowe
- Complete Quest in Anvil, Gold Coast

Talk to Amelie Crowe in Vivec Outlaws Refuge.

Talk to Amelie Crowe in Vivec Outlaws Refuge to begin the Dark Brotherhood quest line. The refuge is accessible from St. Delyn Square or through an entrance south of the bank. Amelie references the Dark Brotherhood, who are recruiting new members in Anvil, on the Gold Coast. Meet her there to continue the quest.

Thieves Guild: Partners In Crime

Quest Giver	Quen
Prerequisite	Own Thieves Guild DLC or ESO Plus Membership, Complete the Vvardenfell Story Quest Line
Quest Giver Location	Any Outlaws Refuge, Including Vivec City
Reward	Gold, Unidentified Bahraha's Curse Foot Armor, Thieves Guild Leathers

Noteworthy Tasks

- Talk to Quen
- Meet Quen at the Docks
- Complete Quest in Hew's Bane

Find Quen at the Vivec Outlaws Refuge to begin the Thieves Guild quest line. The refuge is accessible from St. Delyn Square or through an entrance south of the bank. Meet her at the Woodhearth Docks in Anvil, Gold Coast to continue **Quest: Partners in Crime**.

UNDAUNTED PLEDGES

Undaunted enclaves are located at the three cities: Balmora, Sadrith Mora, and Vivec City. Collect Undaunted daily quests and use any earned keys on their chests.

D1

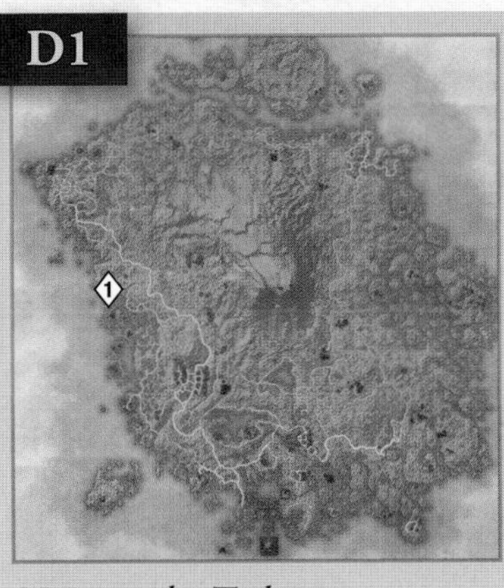

A Smuggler's Last Stand

Quest Giver	Nakhul
Prerequisite	None
Quest Giver Location	Outside Khartag Point Delve
Reward	Gold, Chain-Breaker Gauntlets, Experience

Chain-Breaker Gauntlets

STYLE	ITEM TYPE	ENCHANTMENT
Orc	Heavy Hands	Health
TRAIT	**SET NAME**	**QUALITY**
Well-Fitted	—	Fine

Noteworthy Tasks

- Find Khartag
- Find Mabkir
- Find Jaree-Eeto
- Find Wih-Waska

Read the Blood-Soaked Letter next to Mabkir.

Camonna Tong have attacked the people smugglers at **Khartag Point**, and Nakhul asks you to retrieve Khartag and the slaves. Note that they can be found in any order. Step inside the delve and bring up the map for their locations. The three slaves are scattered around the outer loop. Move cautiously, as Camonna Tong and Dreugh inhabit the entire cave. Follow the right corridor to find Mabkir's body next to a Blood-Soaked Letter (Lorebook).

Continue around the outside to the east side, but before continuing to the second slave, find the skyshard through the narrow opening on the left. Find a Dreugh named Old Rust-Eye in the northeast corner of the cave. Take it out, or sneak along the right wall to avoid the fight. Tucked inside a small cubbyhole on the right is Wih-Waska.

Rescue Wih-Waska on the northeast side of the cave.

Watch out for a River Troll as you follow the cave west and then south. Three cutthroats have trapped Jaree-Eeto on a ledge in the western chamber. Take out the Camonna Tong and talk to the slave.

Avrusa Duleri stands between you and Khartag.

Lastly, from the center of the delve, duck through the waterfall and follow the path south to find Khartag. Avrusa Duleri stands in the way, but she can be avoided by sneaking next to the wall. Once you've found all four, report back to Nakhul.

D2

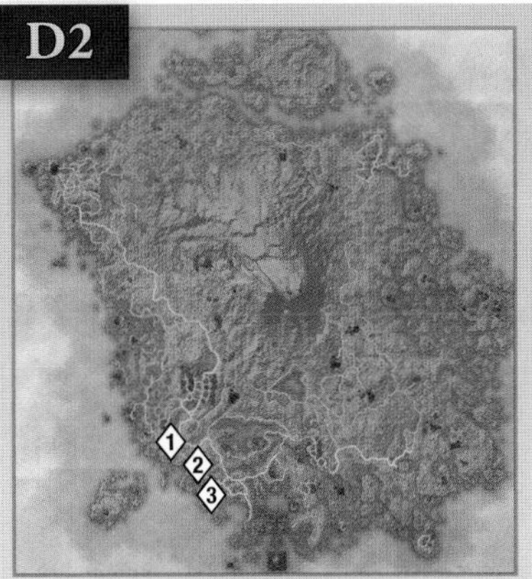

A Hidden Harvest

Quest Giver	Halinjirr
Prerequisite	None
Quest Giver Location	Next to Zainsipilu Delve
Reward	Gold, Sugar-Hemp Sash, Experience

Sugar-Hemp Sash

STYLE	ITEM TYPE	ENCHANTMENT
Khajiit	Light Waist	Magicka
TRAIT	**SET NAME**	**QUALITY**
Training	—	Fine

Noteworthy Tasks

- Obtain Halinjirr's Toxin
- Find Halinjirr's Notes
- Poison the Crop
- Decide Halinjirr's Fate

Enter **Zainsipilu Delve** and fight your way into the main cavern. Hidden by a waterfall, a narrow tunnel branches off to the northeast. A skyshard, protected by two Cliff Striders, is found at the end of the path.

Collect a skyshard in a small cavern on the northeast side of the delve.

Back at the main cavern, fight your way to the right and collect Halinjirr's Notes (Lorebook) off a busted crate just right of the lava against the northern wall. Next, head southwest across the wooden bridge. Packs of bandits are scattered throughout the delve, so be careful not to pull too many in at once.

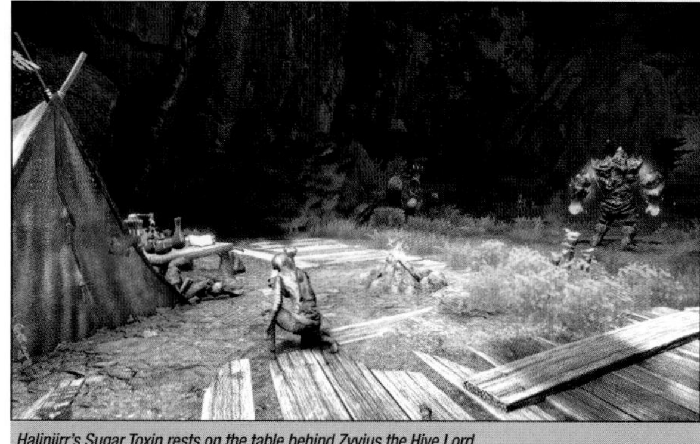
Halinjirr's Sugar Toxin rests on the table behind Zvvius the Hive Lord.

Poison the Underground Spring.

Wind your way into a smaller room to find Zvvius the Hive Lord, an elite Fetcherfly hive. He can be avoided by sneaking around the outside, but watch out for the Nix-Hounds and Fetcherfly hives that occupy the perimeter. Collect Halinjirr's Sugar Toxin off the table behind the boss before returning to the wooden bridge.

With the poison and notes in hand, find an **Underground Spring** at the base of the waterfall along the northwest edge of the chamber. Use the poison and then exit Zainsipilu.

Falura wants you to turn Halinjirr in to the authorities. Check in with Halinjirr and decide whether to report his actions. Visit Captain Bethes in **Seyda Neen** if you decided to rat him out.

D3

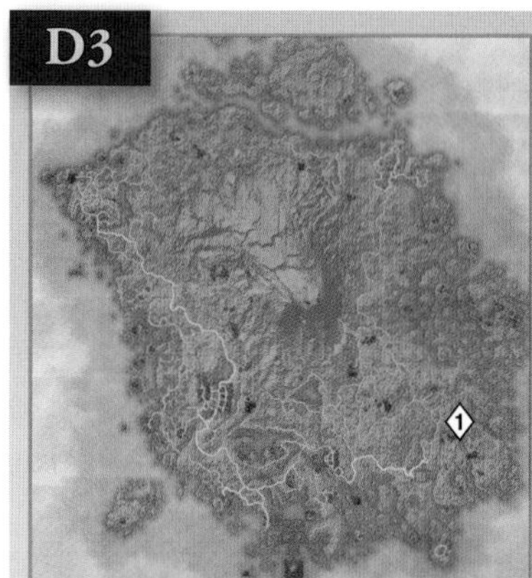

A Dangerous Breed

Quest Giver	Ridena Devani
Prerequisite	None
Quest Giver Location	Outside Matus-Akin Egg Mine
Reward	Gold, Kwama-Hide Cops, Experience

Kwama-Hide Cops

STYLE	ITEM TYPE	ENCHANTMENT	TRAIT	SET NAME	QUALITY
Hlaalu	Medium Shoulders	Stamina	Training	—	Fine

Noteworthy Tasks

- Wipe Out the Scribs-In-Waiting
- Destroy the Royal Egg
- Kill Drovos Nelvayn

Ridena has three tasks for you: destroy an egg, wipe out the Scribs-in-waiting, and deal with Drovos. Enter **Matus-Akin Egg Mine** and take a peek at the map to find their locations. The three tasks can be completed in any order, though two Lorebooks are available along the left path, while a third sits near Drovos. A skyshard can be collected on the lower level in the middle of the delve; watch out for the named Kwama warrior, Th'krak the Tunnel-King.

Watch out for the Rumblegarde and Kwama mobs as you navigate the walkways and corridors to the far west side of the delve. Then head south to find a smaller cavern, full of Kwama. Set the nest on fire before exiting the room and heading north.

The path leads you to a lower, wet area. Enter the tunnel ahead and destroy the royal egg at the other end. Return to the damp cavern, and spot the campsite to the left. There you find Drovos Nelvayn hanging out with a Rumblegarde rowdy and Battlemage, so defeat the trio. With all three tasks taken care of, exit the delve and talk to Ridena to complete the quest.

Collect the skyshard visible from the southern walkway.

Defeat Drovos Nelvayn and the Rumblegarde.

PUBLIC DUNGEON QUESTS

D4

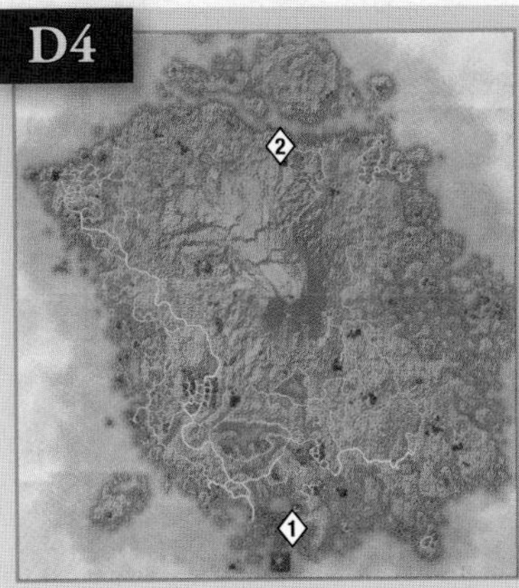

Echoes of a Fallen House

Quest Giver	Tythis Nirith
Prerequisite	None
Quest Giver Location	Forgotten Wastes Public Dungeon (Just Inside Entrance)
Collectibles	Dreamer's Chime Memento—Complete Quest Sixth House Robe Costume—Collect the seven fragments rarely dropped by foes in Forgotten Wastes to make Runebox and consume for costume
Reward	Gold, Nirith's Bulwark of the Defiler, Experience

Nirith's Bulwark of the Defiler

STYLE	ITEM TYPE	ENCHANTMENT	TRAIT	SET NAME	QUALITY
Daedric	Shield	Stamina	Reinforced	Infector	Fine

Noteworthy Tasks

- Enter Forgotten Wastes Public Dungeon
- Find Clues to Nevena's Whereabouts (4)
- Find a Way Inside the Wakener's Hall
- Defeat Wakener Maras

The Sixth House occupies much of the dungeon.

Touch base with Tythis , who has followed his sister to this dungeon, near the beginning of the Forgotten Wastes Public Dungeon before looking for Nevena. Start your search in the **Drinith Ancestral Tomb**, where groups of Sixth House mobs are difficult to handle for solo players. Join others as you explore the Forgotten Wastes. Keep an eye out for raised rocks in the floor, as they trigger Blade or Fire Traps. Use them to your advantage against incoming foes.

The first clue, the Diviner's Journal, is found in the first room on the right. Next, grab the Wakener's Sermon off the pedestal just before the main chamber. A pair of Hungers join the group of mobs inside, so be ready for a tough fight.

If not already collected, nab the skyshard.

The next hallway leads into the **Caverns of Kogoruhn**, where the final two clues are found. A skyshard is also available by following the right trail. Follow the walkway as it winds its way down into the cavern—fighting your way through the Sixth House camps, including an Iron Atronach. Plot your path carefully, as it's easy to be overwhelmed by the enemy.

Find the final clue next to the exit to the Forgotten Depths.

Before dropping to the lower level, read the Excavation Orders sitting amongst a pile of crates. Fight through another Iron Atronach and a cluster of Sixth House members to find the final clue, the Guardian's Decree, next to the exit to the Forgotten Depths. This leads you into the next area in search for a way inside the Wakener's Hall.

Use the bells in the correct order.

Fight your way to the southeast to find six bells sitting in front of an archway.

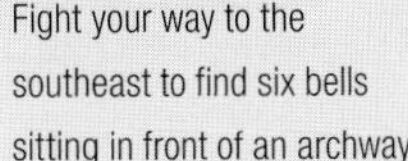

Take note of the six symbols that run along the bottom of the arch. These match the symbols that lie in front of the bells, though in a slightly different order. If the bells are numbered from left to right, use them in the following order: 1, 2, 4, 3, 6, 5. This unlocks the entrance to Wakener's Hall.

Enter **Wakener's Hall** and beat up on Wakener Maras until Nevena Nirith shows up. Defeat the pair and grab Nevena's Diary, which sits next to the fire. Return to Tythis and give him the news to complete the quest.

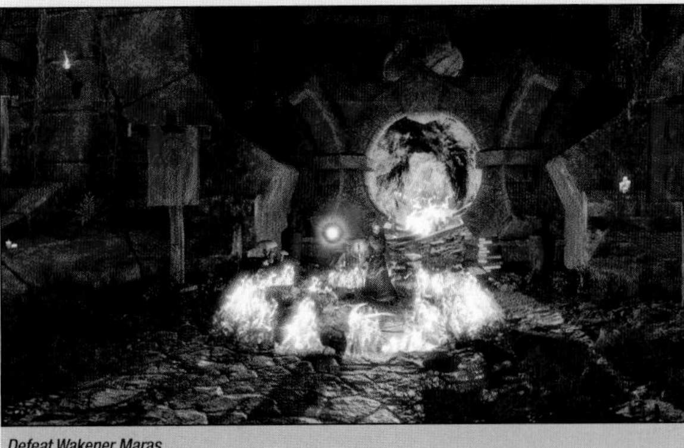
Defeat Wakener Maras.

D4 Forgotten Wastes Group Event

Location	Forgotten Wastes
Bosses	Stone-Boiler Omalas, Brander Releth, Mountain-Caller Hlaren
Boss Difficulty	Hard
Reward	Experience, 1 Skill Point
Stone-Boiler Omalas's Abilities	Heat Wave, Volcanic Debris, Empower Atronach
Brander Releth's Abilities	Fire Rune, Volcanic Debris, Empower Atronach
Mountain-Caller Hlaren's Abilities	Heat Wave, Fire Rune, Volcanic Debris, Empower Atronach
Iron Atronach Abilities	Iron Hand, Rock Stomp, Lava Wave, Blast Furnace, Subduction

Adds

	FLAME ATRONACHS	SIXTH HOUSE			
		CLARION SEERS	TORMENTORS	WATCHERS	ASH-WEAVERS
Intro	2	2	2	0	0
Omalas	2	0	2	0	0
Releth	2	0	0	2	0
Hlaren	2	0	0	0	2

The Forgotten Wastes group event takes place on the west side of the outdoor area, out front of the **Sixth House stronghold**. At the top of the steps, a ceremony begins with two Flame Atronachs, two Clarion Seers, and two Tormentors—as the three bosses continue the ritual from the balconies above. Clear out the mobs to get at the first boss, Stone-Boiler Omalas.

Stone-Boiler Omalas drops in after you clear out the initial mobs.

The three bosses appear one at a time, along with a crowd of trash mobs. Their abilities are very similar, including the ability to spawn and heal an Iron Atronach, along with one or two fire skills.

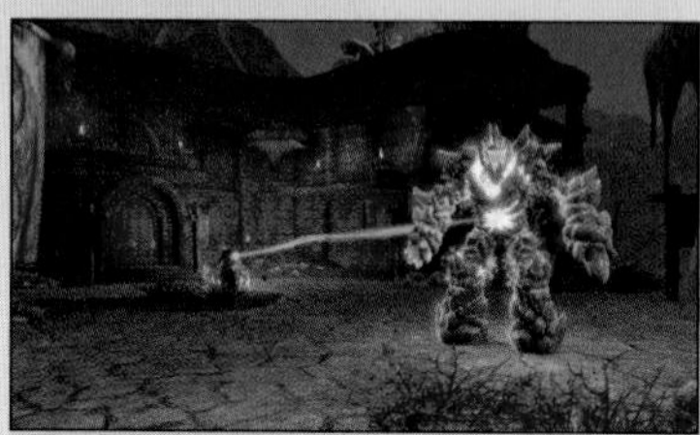

Interrupt the boss to keep the Iron Atronach out of the fight.

The first one possesses the Heat Wave skill, which sends a fire attack straight along the ground. The second boss, Brander Releth, has the Fire Rune ability, which launches two rings of fire onto the ground. The final boss, Mountain-Caller Hlaren, has the capability to use both of these skills and summon two Iron Atronachs, making her less predictable and tougher to deal with.

Have a player stay close to the boss while others deal with the lesser mobs, since the Iron Atronach summon, heal, and Heat Wave can all be interrupted. When the boss crosses his or her arms, an Iron Atronach is incoming.

Note that all mobs must be defeated before the next boss joins the fight. If the group is wiped out and revives at the spot, progress is not lost.

Don't forget the usual buffs to improve your odds of success, such as high-level food and an appropriate Mundus Stone. Stay on the move to avoid the Fire Rune attack, step to the side to avoid the Heat Wave, and do what you can to keep Iron Atronachs out of the fight. When the Iron Atronach dies, waves of lava are sent from its location, so remain aware.

Watch out for the rings of fire created with the Fire Rune skill.

D5

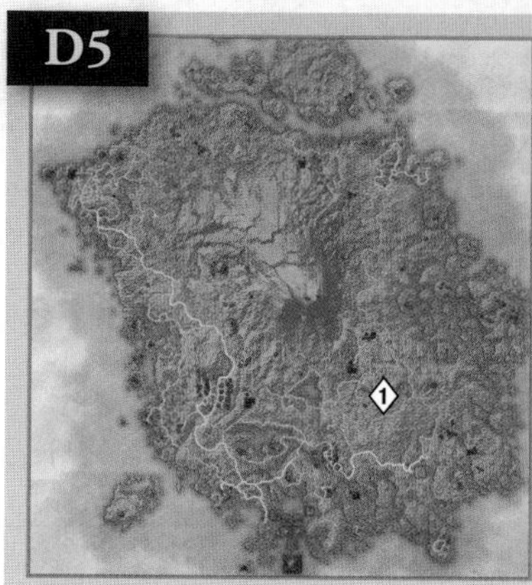

The Heart's Desire

Quest Giver	Neramo
Prerequisite	None
Quest Giver Location	Outside Nchuleftingth Public Dungeon
Collectibles	Neramo's Lightning Stick—Complete Quest Dwemer Theodolite Pet—Collect Fragments Rarely Dropped by Foes to Make Runebox and Consume for Pet
Reward	Gold, Artificer's Coat of the War Maiden, Experience

Artificer's Coat of the War Maiden

STYLE	ITEM TYPE	ENCHANTMENT
Dwemer	Light Chest	Magicka
TRAIT	**SET NAME**	**QUALITY**
Infused	War Maiden	Fine

Noteworthy Tasks

- Enter Nchuleftingth Public Dungeon
- Rescue Three Survivors
- Retrieve the Dwemer Control Rod
- Defeat Artisan Lenarmen

Enter **Nchuleftingth** and follow the path straight ahead to find Vimy Lacroix. She asks that you rescue three survivors—Kasouda, Thollidor, and Tyrnea—who are still missing in the dungeon while you search for the Dwemer Control Rod. The place is crawling with Bronzefist and Dwarven mobs, so be careful not to draw too many in at once. It is advised that you join other players when attempting to tackle this quest.

Return to the intersection and follow the walkways to the left to reach a lower level. Find the first survivor just ahead with the second group of Bronzefists. Take them down, set Thollidor free, and then follow the water out to a big open cavern. The second survivor is held captive on a platform to the right, surrounded by Dwarven automata. Destroy the automata before rescuing Tyrnea Stone.

Release Thollidor from the Bronzefists.

Enter **Nchuleftingth Bailey** and continue into the ruins to the right. Follow the left path to reach **Nchuleftingth Lavaworks**. Follow the walkway past more Dwarven and Bronzefists to find Kasouda. Continue around the perimeter of Lavaworks, following another ramp south to the Control Room.

Move inside and wait for Vimy to disable the trap before collecting the Broken Dwemer Control Rod from the control device. Back in the Lavaworks, run up the left walkway to the rock ledge. The skyshard is found right of the exit. Once you're ready to leave, talk to Neramo and then return to Nchuleftingth Ruins.

The skyshard is found just inside Nchuleftingth Lavaworks.

The left steps lead into **Nchuleftingth Cathedra**, where Neramo and Vimy join in on the fight against Artisan Lenarmen and his Dwarven robots. Adds are added to the fight as Lenarmen's health reaches certain thresholds. Wipe them out to avoid being overwhelmed. Once he's defeated, follow Neramo and Vimy through the left door and collect the Bthark Prism from the Dwarven Strongbox. Exit to Vvardenfell through the nearby door, and talk to Neramo at the camp to complete the quest.

Help Neramo and Vimy defeat Lenarmen.

D5 Nchuleftingth Group Event

Location	Nchuleftingth Core
Boss	Nchulaeon the Eternal
Boss Difficulty	Hard
Reward	Experience, 1 Skill Point
Nchulaeon's Abilities	Overcharge Expulsion, Momentum
Environmental Hazards	Searing Steam, Dwarven Charge-Wire (Charge-Wire Shock), Steam Piston (Spike Trap or Piston Thrust)

Adds

CHAMBER	DWARVEN SPIDERS	DWARVEN SPHERES	DWARVEN ARQUEBUS	DWARVEN CENTURIONS
West Rd. 1	8	0	0	0
West Rd. 2	4	2	0	0
East Rd. 1	0	2	2	0
East Rd. 2	0	2	2	0
South Rd. 1	0	1	1	1
South Rd. 2	4	1	1	0
Central	2*	1*	0	2†

** One of the following combinations spawns into the northern corners of the chamber: four Spiders, two Spiders and a Sphere, or two Spheres. Destroy the group and more roll in; the supply never ends.*

† Destroy the two Centurions and two more appear, though that's where the giants end.

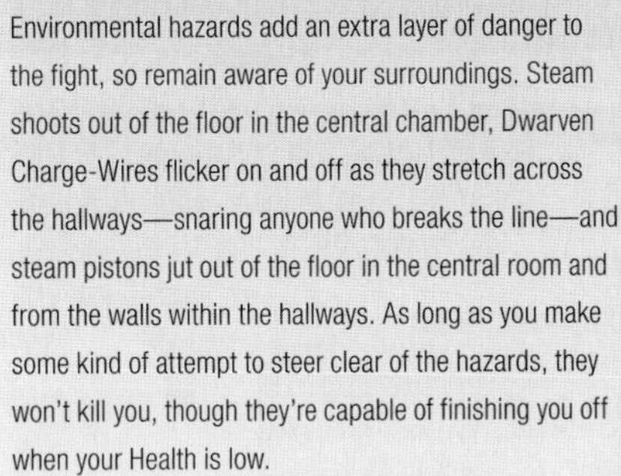

Find Nchulaeon in the center of **Nchuleftingth Core**, accessible from the Nchuleftingth Ruins. The large Dwarven automation begins by moving into the western room, where it parks itself in a charging station, while Dwarven Spiders spew out of the surrounding holes. Stay out of the boss's way as it moves, or risk being knocked down or taking unnecessary damage from its lightning skill. When sitting atop its stand, it cannot be attacked.

Nchulaeon rolls into the west chamber at the start of the event.

Environmental hazards add an extra layer of danger to the fight, so remain aware of your surroundings. Steam shoots out of the floor in the central chamber, Dwarven Charge-Wires flicker on and off as they stretch across the hallways—snaring anyone who breaks the line—and steam pistons jut out of the floor in the central room and from the walls within the hallways. As long as you make some kind of attempt to steer clear of the hazards, they won't kill you, though they're capable of finishing you off when your Health is low.

Be careful when retreating from the Automaton.

Nchulaeon does not possess many skills itself. Its Overcharge Expulsion launches a lightning bolt at its target as it follows a straight line, and a simple knockback attack has the potential to knock the player down but causes no damage. Look for the boss to flash before the lightning attack, and a gold flicker means it's about to clear out nearby targets.

Clear out Dwarven mobs in each chamber to keep Nchulaeon moving.

After you clear the Spiders out of the western room, a second round of robots appears. Destroy this group, and Nchulaeon dismounts from its perch and rolls into the eastern chamber, pausing for a brief moment at its original position. Dwarven Spheres and Arquebuses file into the second room. After two rounds of the spherical robots are defeated, the boss moves into the southern room, where a Centurion joins a variety of mobs. Defeat two more rounds to force the boss back into the center, where it remains for the duration of the fight—simply pivoting in order to target its enemies.

Manage the adds while fighting Nchulaeon the Eternal.

Two Centurions, along with a mix of Spiders and Spheres, join Nchulaeon the Eternal in the middle room. Destroy the two Centurions and another pair shows up, though that's it for the giants. The smaller droids continue to spawn after you eliminate the group. Keeping one Spider or Sphere around makes the battlefield much less crowded. With the adds under control, focus your attention on the boss.

Note that if the group is wiped out, the event must be restarted, with Nchulaeon in its original position.

FORGING THE FUTURE

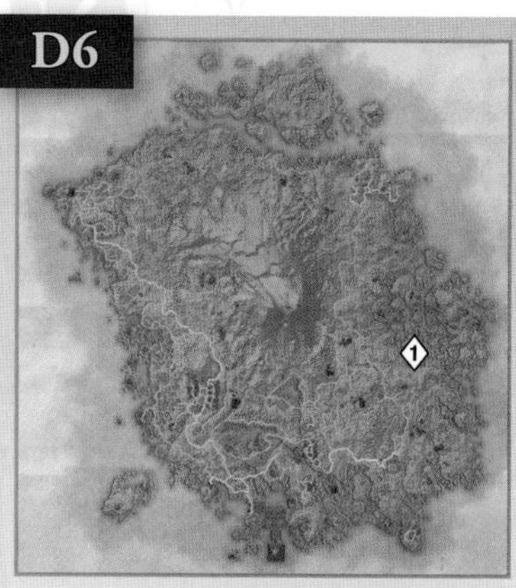

- QUEST GIVER: Divayth Fyr
- PREREQUISITE: None
- QUEST GIVER LOCATION: Tel Fyr
- COLLECTIBLE: Trophy: Assembly General Furnishing (Plaque)
  Collectible – Complete Quest
  Bust: Dwarven Colossus Furnishing (Bust)
  Collectible - Complete Quest on Veteran Hard Mode
- REWARD: Gold, Fabricant's Burnished Coffer
  (Undaunted Weekly Reward), Experience

Noteworthy Tasks:

- Shut Down the Halls of Fabrication

ACHIEVEMENT: SCHOLAR OF SEHT'S MYSTERIES

Four notes are hidden within the Halls of Fabrication. Collecting them all earns the Scholar of Seht's Mysteries Achievement.

Note/Artifact	Location
Telvanni Additional Specifications (Lorebook)	Tel Fyr - trial staging area
Telvanni Journal (Lorebook)	Abanabi Cave – center
Cogitation Log 1322331455212478 (Lorebook)	Reprocessing Yard – southeast corner atop garbage heap
Divayth Fyr's Notes (Lorebook)	Reprocessing Yard – south side of Refabrication Committee fight

Trials are setup for twelve players: two healers, two tanks, and the rest DPS—though you can create a group with any combination of characters that you wish. Join eleven players in Tel Fyr and collect the Forging the Future quest from Divayth Fyr in the staging area. Besides the Normal Trial, a Veteran version is also available for a more challenging experience.

Divayth Fyr needs help investigating the strange contraptions that have emerged beneath Tel Fyr and shutting down the source. Halls of Fabrication consists of five boss fights with Dwarven mobs scattered in between. Proceed into Abanabi Cave to begin the adventure.

Wind through the cave until you reach a gate, which opens once all of the fabricants have been defeated. Enter the small arena to find two Hunter-Killer Fabricants.

Destroy the fabricants to open the gate.

RETURN TO TEL FYR

A player can recall to the staging area outside Abanabi Cave at a cost, by selecting Halls of Fabrication on the map. Once ready to return, a portal returns the player to the previous location inside the Trial.

HUNTER-KILLER FABRICANTS

TWO VERMINOUS FABRICANTS FORM THE VANGUARD OF THE FORCES POURING THROUGH THE RIFT. THEY PROWL THE AREA LOOKING FOR POSSIBLE THREATS.

Locations	Abanabi Cave
Achievement	Kill Process

ABILITIES

Charged Gore: The Hunter Killer impales the target with its horn, causing a bleed.

CHARGED GORE ON VETERAN DIFFICULTY

On Veteran, players are also affected with Defile, which reduces healing received.

Shock Lash/Static Cascade: The Fabricant whips its tail around and launches small orbs of lightning.

Lightning Lunge/Predatory Programming: Fabricant lunges at a target a short distance away. This can be blocked to avoid Predatory Programming. Otherwise, The Fabricant pounces and begins eating his victim. This ability should be interrupted.

Rending Leap: Used on players that are out of melee range, doing damage and applying a snare.

Snap/Residual Static: Base attack that also has a chance to drop (50%) a lightning area effect (Residual Static) on the ground. Residual Static damage increases with prolonged exposure.

Proximity Static: As the Fabricants get close to each other, they form a visual bond. The longer they are close together, the more damage they do. This bonus damage slowly fades after they are separated. Players that intersect this visual bond take high damage. This bond is used to break the shields on the Refabricated Spheres so they can be damaged and Spheres take increased damage the longer they are intersected with the beam.

ADDITIONAL MONSTERS

Refabricated Spheres

Shield: Protected by a shield until it is broken via Proximity Static.

Venom Burst/Venom Injection: Ability, which does damage and puts a stacking Damage Over Time on players. Venom Injection can be removed via cleanse abilities.

Taking Aim: Interruptible high damage attack.

Super Charged: Spheres do bonus damage once one of the Hunter-Killers has been killed.

Shalk Fabricant

These are ordinary fabricant shalks that appear twice throughout the fight.

STRATEGY

Players need two tanks for this fight. Each tank taunts and keeps a Hunter-Killer Fabricant busy while DPS players attack them. As Refabricated Spheres spawn, the tanks need to bring the Hunter-Killers close enough to form a Proximity Static bond to break the shield. DPS should then focus on and kill the Spheres.

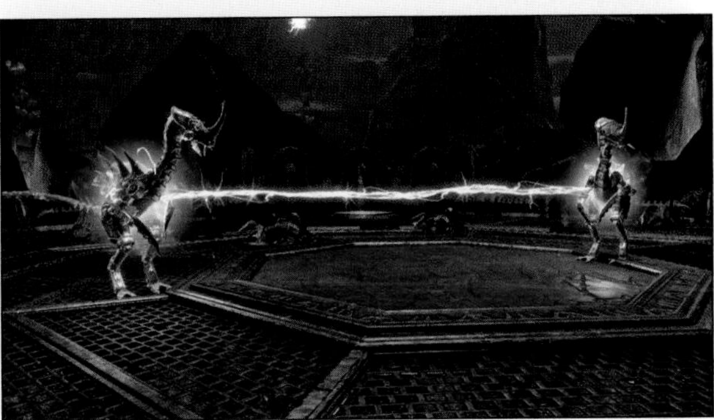

As the fight progresses, more and more Spheres appear, making this job all the more difficult. Once the shield is broken, the Tanks should separate the Hunter-Killers so as not to allow the Proximity Static buff to increase damage too much.

Once a Hunter-Killer is killed, players are no longer able to force Proximity Static, which means they no longer are able to break shields on the Spheres. In order to prevent becoming overwhelmed, both Hunter-Killers should be killed relatively close in time to one another.

Note that there is an achievement, Kill Process, which requires that one of the fabricants be killed, while the other still has at least half of its health remaining—making this fight even more challenging.

PINNACLE FACTOTUM

THE FIRST FACTOTUM PLAYERS ENCOUNTER. SENT FROM THE HALLS OF FABRICATION ONCE THE HUNTER-KILLERS ARE DISPATCHED TO ELIMINATE THE THREAT.

Locations	Abanabi Cave
Achievement	Power House

ABILITIES

Direct Current: Channeled lightning attack, which does damage and drains Magicka. This needs to be interrupted.

Targets a random player and affects multiple players in its cone of vision. The selected targets take ramping damage over time and if the channel is allowed to finish, Overcurrent hits them. This damaging projectile blast can't be dodged or reflected but can be blocked. A target not blocking is stunned and knocked down. A target that does block will suffer a staggering blow. In both cases, an AoE blast ignites on the target causing damage to other players. This damage is named Overcurrent Arcs.

Heavy Shock: A wave of energy is launched from the Pinnacle Factotum. The wave can be blocked or dodged. A target not blocking is knocked backwards and stunned. A target that blocks suffers a stagger.

Flux Burst/Static Diffusion: The Pinnacle Factotum teleports to a random player within the room and does damage. A Static Diffusion pool is then dropped on the ground, which does increased damage the longer a player remains inside.

Sharpened Conduit/Direct Current: A spear of pure shock impacts the area and stays. The spear then casts Direct Current on targets, causing damage and draining magicka. The spear must be killed in order to prevent this damage.

Shocking Smash: Blockable attack which hits everything in front of him and creates small lightning orbs that branch out in a star pattern.

Lightning Strike/Arcing Bolt/Proximity Jolt: Basic attack that aims for additional targets, hitting them with a small area of effect ability.

Palm Strike: The Pinnacle Factotum creates mirage clones of himself in a circle around the target. The clones activate one by one doing damage. If these are not blocked, it results in a Heavy Shock wave launching from the clone. The Target cannot move from within the small radius once the Mirages appear or they are killed instantly via Electrocution.

The damage must be blocked while facing into the direction that the Palm Strike is originating from in order to prevent the Heavy Shock wave.

PALM STRIKE ON VETERAN DIFFICULTY

A stacking bleed debuff called Pummeled is applied to the player if the Palm Strike is not blocked correctly. Once all four Palm Strikes finish, the bleed begins doing damage. The more stacks of the bleed, the more damage dealt with each tick. Damage from this bleed is called Aftershock. This bleed effect is immune to player removal abilities.

Standing too close to the outer edge of the room causes the targeted player to be knocked inward towards the center.

Terminal Vault: Pinnacle Factotum teleports to the center of the room and begins channeling a spell that wipes out all enemies. This is interrupted when all of the power switches are used at the top of the Liminal Transformer.

ADDITIONAL MONSTERS

Centurions

Open Wounds: A ticking bleed that causes damage called Rupture. This negative effect is immune to player removal abilities.

Hack: A basic attack that applies a single stack of the Open Wounds debuff. This is a bleed that ticks over 10 seconds. The damage from the bleed is called Rupture.

Hammer: High damage attack which should be blocked—applying a single stack of Open Wounds.

Spin Cycle/Spare Shrapnel: The Centurion spins following a target and launching small area effects in a radius around it. This ability only happens if the Centurion's current target is out of melee range. So it's important to have a tank within melee range as often as possible. Damage from Spin Cycle applies a single stack of Open Wounds.

Pressure Release: Rotating cone area effects of steam as the Centurion sits in place

PRESSURE RELEASE ON VETERAN DIFFICULTY

Players hit by Pressure Release also gain a stacking debuff called Scalded. Scalded decreases healing received by 10% per stack and lasts for 15 seconds. This debuff is immune to player removal abilities.

MECHANICS

Liminal Transformer

- This incredible generator of energy is what the Pinnacle Factotum uses to power the boss and disrupt the Planar Rift.
- While active, the Liminal Transformer funnels energy into the Pinnacle Factotum. This energy increases the damage done by the Pinnacle Factotum.

LIMINAL TRANSFORMER DIFFERENCES ON VETERAN DIFFICULTY

On Veteran, the energy pumped into the Pinnacle Factotum also provides it with a shield. This occurs with every individual volley of energy.

- The heart of the Liminal Transformer is on the upper platform and players must defeat the Refabricated Spheres that are actively disabling the power switches, which connect to the Liminal Transformer.
- While running around on the upper level, the Liminal Transformer spills over with energy. This ability is called Electric Overflow and connects to a random player via a beam from the Liminal Transformer. The longer this beam is connected, the more damage the target takes. And just like in the Hunter-Killer Fabricant encounter, this beam obliterates shields that it passes through. Electric Overflow also puts a debuff on the Refabricated Spheres causing them to take increased damage, and does a small amount of damage on its own. Any player that is targeted by Electric Overflow should make sure the beam crosses through the Refabricated Spheres.

- Also, the Electric Overflow never targets the same player twice in a row. So in order to get the most mileage out of Electric Overflow's potential, it's imperative to have multiple players engaging with the upper level mechanics.
- Once a Refabricated Sphere is defeated, the power switch that it was channeling becomes usable. In normal mode, once a switch has been pushed, the switch doesn't need to be hit again to trigger the shutdown.

LIMINAL TRANSFORMER SWITCHES ON VETERAN DIFFICULTY

All four switches must be hit at the same time in order to trigger the Liminal Transformer shutdown and stop the Pinnacle Factotum from overloading the Planar Rift. If the timing of the switch pressing is not right, the switches reset.

- When the Liminal Transformer is triggered to enter emergency shutdown, a large explosion is moments away. Any organic matter on the upper platform must clear the area and drop back down to the ground below.

Planar Rift

- This is the gateway into Clockwork City. Divayth Fyr works to stabilize the rift in order to use it to enter Clockwork City.
- The volatile nature of the rift manifests into a hazard for players when it spits out Unstable Energy projectiles. These projectiles target random players and should be avoided.
- If the Liminal Transformer is allowed to be active for too long, the Planar Rift will become far too unstable and the excess energy will blow out from the rift and kill everyone in the group.

Divayth Fyr's Slowfall spell

- Just as Divayth Fyr provided a way to reach the top, he provides a safe way back to the ground.
- This spell is placed on all four openings surrounding the platform. The same opening that players levitated through.
- Dropping through the opening grants players a temporary protection from fall damage.

Divayth Fyr's Teleportation spell

- If a player dies up top and the Liminal Transformer is not active, Divayth Fyr will teleport their corpse back down to the bottom.

LOWER LEVEL STRATEGY

This fight requires two tanks. When first engaging, one tank will keep the attention of the Pinnacle Factotum. The Factotum should be faced away from the rest of the trial group to avoid the damage from his Shock Smash. Players will need to be careful to avoid his Heavy Shock and Shockwave orbs. Shortly after the fight begins, a Refabricated Centurion will become active. This Centurion should be taunted by the second tank. DPS players should focus on the Centurion to remove its damage from the fight. Tanking the two monsters apart is wise to avoid splash damage from either monster spilling over onto the other tank.

Everyone should be sure to get out of any area of effect spells quickly. Watch for Unstable Energy from the Planar Rift as well when the Liminal Transformer is active. Interrupting the Direct Current ability is important and there will be constant pressure from the Pinnacle Factotum's Arcing Bolts and any Heavy Shock waves that generate from a failed block during Palm Strikes. So healers will need to stay vigilant and keep the group heathy.

When the Liminal Transformer is activated by the Pinnacle Factotum, players need to travel up to the top platform using Divayth Fyr's levitation spell. Those that remain will need to continue to avoid the mechanics and destroy centurions as they awaken. Also as the fight progresses and more mechanics are introduced, it will be the bottom group's task to keep up with the additional enemies such as the Sharpened Conduits and the Short Circuiting Centurions.

UPPER LIMINAL TRANSFORMER STRATEGY

At various intervals, the Liminal Transformer is activated by the Pinnacle Factotum, in an attempt to disrupt the Planar Rift and provide the Pinnacle Factotum with additional power. Players will need to use Divayth Fyr's levitation spell, located on four nearby platforms to reach the upper level. Once on the upper level, players need to shut down the Liminal Transformer. In order to do this, players must defeat the Refabricated Spheres engaged with the Liminal Transformers' power switches.

One player at the top randomly becomes tethered by Electric Overflow, which is a beam similar to the one in the Hunter-Killer Fabricant fight. If this beam passes over a Sphere, the shield (in veteran) is instantly broken and the Spheres take increased damage the longer they are intersected by the beam. Players however take damage as the beam is connected to them and anyone crossing the beam also takes damage. After all of the Spheres are destroyed, players must activate the switches, which trigger the emergency shutdown on the Liminal Transformer and cease the disruption of the Planar Rift. In Veteran, these switches must be activated within 2s of each other. Afterwards, Divayth Fyr will activate a slow fall spell, allowing players to return to the lower section, where the fight rages on against the Pinnacle Factotum.

UNIQUE MONSTERS

Not seen until the Transport Circuit, the following three types of factotums appear multiple times and are unique to the trial.

CALEFACTOR

LARGE FACTOTUM USING A TWO-HANDED SWORD

Locations	Transport Circuit, Reprocessing Yard, Halls of Fabrication
Achievement	Refabricant Slayer

Abilities

Scalding Shield: Flame shield, which reflects projectiles and damages nearby enemies.

Steam Breath: High damage frontal cone ability, which snares as well as doing damage. Targets hit also have their resistances reduced.

Powered Realignment: Blockable attack that sends sparks flying behind the target if it is not blocked.

Dessicate: Cleaving strike which hits all targets in front of the Calefactor. A Heavy Bleed also affects enemies hit. Subsequent hits increase the damage of the bleed.

CAPACITOR

LARGE FACTOTUM WITH CANNONS FOR ARMS

Locations	Reprocessing Yard, Halls of Fabrication
Achievement	Refabricant Slayer

Abilities

Conduit Strike/Draining Shock: The Capacitor attacks the location of the furthest target with a lightning strike from the sky. This strike branches into smaller jolts emerging from the site of impact. Enemies hit are affected by Draining Shock, which stuns, does damage, and drains magicka until the stun is broken.

Self-Induction: Enemies around the Capacitor take damage, lose a percentage of their Max Magicka, and are snared for two seconds.

Discharge: The Capacitor fires bolts of electricity at its enemies doing damage and reducing their resistance to shock attacks.

DISSECTOR

LARGE FACTOTUM USING DUAL BLADES

Locations	Transport Circuit, Reprocessing Yard, Halls of Fabrication
Achievement	Refabricant Slayer

Abilities

Invasive Cut: Blockable attack which stuns and knocks back when undefended. In addition, enemies who fail to block are also affected by Phlebotomize, which is a cleansable bleed that increases in damage each tick.

Hoist Subject: The Dissector launches a chain from its hand, which grabs and pulls an enemy close.

Dissection: Frontal cone attack that damages and affects those hit with Blood Loss. Subsequent hits increase the damage of Blood Loss.

Defeating Pinnacle Fabricant creates a Rift at the center of the arena, which sends each player to the Transport Circuit. Refabricated Spiders attack throughout the loop. Similar to those found in Clockwork City, Whirring Blade Traps also pose a danger as they glide along grooves in the walkway.

ARCHCUSTODIAN

THE TRANSIT CIRCUIT IS PATROLLED AND MAINTAINED BY THE ARCHCUSTODIAN. AS THREATS ARE REGISTERED, IT DEPLOYS COUNTER MEASURES AND CLEANS UP ANY INTRUDERS.

Locations	Transport Circuit
Achievement	Arc-Custodian

ABILITIES

Vaporization Protocol: As the Archocustodian traverses the Transit Circuit, it pulses fire underneath which does high damage.

Static Shield: Prevents all damage to the Archcustodian while active. In Veteran difficulty, it also increases the Damage of monsters that get within 15m.

Power Rail Discharge: Once engaged, if players retreat further than 50m from the Archcustodian, it repeatedly damages them until they either return to within 50m or die.

ADDITIONAL MONSTERS/HAZARDS

Whirring Blade Trap: Spinning Blade damages players and affects them with the Serrated Blade bleed effect. This is a stacking bleed which intensifies with more hits.

Shock Pylon: Shock Walls connect between the pylons which creates a line which damages, snares and drains magicka of players that touch it.

Dissector: Refer to entry above.

Calefactor: Refer to entry above.

STRATEGY

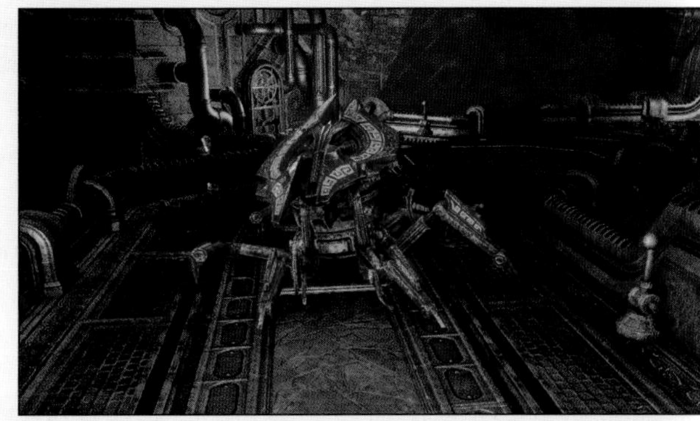

The Transit Circuit is populated by Refabricated Spiders as players emerge from the portal. Engaging these spiders causes the Halls of Fabrication defenses to engage. Shock Walls and Whirring Blade Traps become a persistent threat in the Circuit.

When players approach the Archcustodian it begins traversing the Circuit. The Archcustodian is shielded from damage and pulses a powerful fire ability around it. In addition, players that move too far away, after the Archcustodian is engaged, will take increased damage from Power Rail Discharge.

Players must use the switches near the inactive Shock Pylons located around the Transit Circuit as the Archcustodian gets near to break the shield and stun the Archcustodian. They then have a few seconds to damage the Archcustodian before it re-engages the shield and starts walking again. After a switch is pushed, two Factotums spawn and engage. These are a combination of Calefactors and/or Dissectors.

REFABRICATION COMMITTEE REACTOR, RECLAIMER, AND REDUCER

THREE FACTOTUMS ARE ACTIVATED IN THE REPROCESSING YARD IN A DESPERATE ATTEMPT TO KEEP INTRUDERS OUT OF THE ASSEMBLY CORE.

Locations	Processing Yard
Achievement	Planned Obsolescence

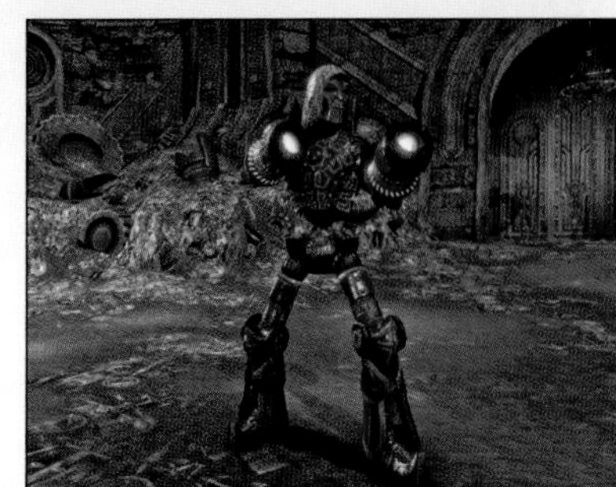

ABILITIES

Reactor Abilities

Clash: A blockable attack that deals high damage if not blocked.

ONE-SHOT ON VETERAN DIFFICULTY

On Veteran, this attack must be blocked by the tank or dodged, as it does enough damage to one-shot most characters.

Grasping Limbs: The Reactor plunges its sword into the ground and fires off bolts of shock that awaken scrapped machines. Mechanical limbs reach up in a 2.5m radius in multiple locations, stunning players caught inside and dealing damage that increases with every tick.

Overloading Aura (Veteran difficulty only): Every 30 seconds the Reactor begins firing shock projectiles at its current target. Each hit increases in damage and applies a stacking effect on the target. When the target reaches six stacks, the projectile instantly kills them.

Reducer Abilities

Clash: A blockable attack that deals high damage if not blocked.

ONE-SHOT ON VETERAN DIFFICULTY

On Veteran, this attack must be blocked by the tank or dodged, as it does enough damage to one-shot most characters.

Fulminate: The Reducer sends out three fiery line attacks that travel out in three directions. Targets hit by these traveling firestorms are affected by a high damage over time effect. If the line strikes a wall before it expires, it bounces off two new lines back out from the wall (this only occurs once). The line also explodes at the end of its path, dealing additional fire damage to anyone caught inside.

Overheating Aura (Veteran difficulty only): Every 30 seconds the Reducer begins firing flame projectiles at its current target. Each hit increases in damage and applies a stacking effect on the target. When the target reaches six stacks, the projectile instantly kills them.

Reclaimer Abilities

Shock: Light attack that targets random players and hits for light damage.

Conduit Strike: The Reclaimer targets three players farthest away and fires a bolt of lightning that stuns any affected player and drains their magicka. Creates multiple lines of shock that travel out from the target and have the same effect.

Reclaim the Ruined: The Reclaimer fires bolts of energy to random points across the scrapyard, causing Ruined Factotums to rise up. These Factotums slowly march toward the Reclaimer, who is surrounded by a field of energy. If the Factotum reaches the energy pool, they become charged with energy, running at a random player and exploding—dealing massive damage (Catastrophic Discharge).

SHARED MECHANICS

Overcharge: When the bosses get below fixed health thresholds (90%, 65%, 35%, and 15%), they begin to Overcharge. The first portion of this ability causes the overcharging boss to buff the other bosses if they are within 15 meters. The second portion of this ability triggers when a boss drops below a second set of thresholds (70%, 40%, and 20% health). At that point the boss becomes immune to all damage and begins dealing more damage over time. Once all three bosses are invulnerable, bringing them close together arcs the energy between them and breaks their shield. The bosses are briefly stunned before returning to the fight.

Perimeter Explosions: When any boss drops below 25% health, waves of Ruined Factotums begin spawning and exploding around the perimeter of the scrapyard. Every few waves will be larger and larger, slowly filling the space with exploding Factotums that can eventually overwhelm the players.

STRATEGY

Place a tank on the Reducer and Reactor, keeping the bosses a safe distance apart so as not to allow them to buff each other. Split group damage across all three in order to trigger the Overcharge ability at roughly the same time for each boss. When the bosses become immune, quickly bring them close together to stun them and clear their invulnerability.

With attacks continually emanating from the three bosses, the fight can get quite chaotic. Stay on the move, keeping an eye out for mechanical arms, Ruined Factotums, and incoming attacks.

OVERLOADING AURA STRATEGY

On Veteran difficulty only, watch out as the effect from Reducer's Overheating Aura and Reactor's Overloading Aura stacks on their targets. The two tanks must swap the Reactor and Reducer when this ability occurs to avoid death.

Once a boss's health goes below 25%, the Perimeter Explosions begin and the fight becomes a race to the finish. Remain as close to the center of the room as possible to avoid the explosions.

Fight through more Calefactors, Dissectors, and Capacitors and avoid the Whirring Blade Traps in the next hallway. Electrified water hampers your speed with Shock Wall. Continue into the Core Assembly, where a Clockwork Colossus sits dormant at the north end of the room. The disembodied voice that has been speaking with the players tells them that they cannot be permitted to interrupt fabrication any further.

ASSEMBLY GENERAL

A MECHANISM OF LIMITED INTELLIGENCE THAT ONCE SERVED SOTHA SIL. ITS PURPOSE WAS TO MONITOR THE HALLS OF FABRICATION AND ENSURE PRODUCTION CONTINUES. BOTH TIME AND THE CURRENT MALFUNCTION OF THE FACTORY HAVE TAKEN THEIR TOLL ON ITS PROGRAMMING. IT MUST PRODUCE AND ANY IMPEDIMENT BARRING IT FROM FULFILLING THAT PURPOSE MUST BE REMOVED WITH RUTHLESS PRECISION.

Locations	Core Assembly
Achievement	Halls of Fabrication Vanquisher, Environmentally Conscious, Terminal Terminator, Accept no Substitute, Stress Tested, Like Clockwork

ABILITIES

Enkindle (Left Arm): Spews fire out in long column.

Rotary Blade (Right Arm): The blade doesn't hit as far out or as hard, but it does apply a bleed.

Quake (Body): If a tank is not in range of the Assembly General's attacks, it jumps in the air—knocking down and damaging everyone in the area. If allowed to do this too much in a short duration everyone dies.

Stomp (Body): A blockable stomp attack that causes knockback and area damage.

Bombard (Body): Explosives are launched from its back affecting an area that is centered at a random player's feet (not the tank).

Disassembly Command (Body): Stomps with his right foot and sends out sparks to the middle of the room, where areas of clockwork arms attempt to attack and pull players to their knees.

ABILITIES AFTER PHASE 1.1, STRATEGIC UPDATE

Titanic Smash: After Phase 1.1, the colossus winds up and hits the tank, launching the player far away. This player is given a debuff, which causes the tank to take more damage from the boss's Stomp. If the tank is standing against a wall, the force of the impact outright kills the player.

Tactical Assessment: After Phase 1.1, a player, other than the tank, is "scanned." A factotum is created with one ability based on the weapon and class of the player scanned.

ENVIRONMENTAL HAZARDS

Blade Traps: Spinning blades hit any players caught in their paths.

Power Sinks: Electrified orbs on either side of the boss damage and drain magicka from any player they contact. These are easily avoided; just remain alert.

Toxic coolant: A green coolant vents into a defined area. Those standing in the area choke on the poison.

DESIRED ROLES

Keeping a tank on the boss's body in the trench, while also giving both arms a target, is vital to success.

Main Tank: Fights in the trenches, keeping the boss taunted and staying within range so he doesn't Quake.

Off Tank: If main tank is hit by uppercut, takes over that role and picks up adds.

DPS Kiter or Second Off Tank: Remain on platforms to keep the tank from getting hit by extra damage.

STRATEGY

The final boss fight follows a narrative as the group reduces its health to the following health levels:

100% Health (Phase 0): The group aggros the Assembly General and gas fills the space behind the boss. It begins with both arms intact and all of its regular abilities available. A tank should stick to the body and the remaining players need to split up on the platforms. Each arm targets players on the nearby platforms first, but if no players are available, they target the trench.

90% Health: The right (blade) arm explodes and falls off sending sparks to the right platform stunning and damaging any in the area.

87% Health: The left (cannon) arm explodes and falls off sending sparks to the right platform stunning and damaging any in the area.

85% Health (Phase 1.1, Strategic Update): The boss walks toward the center and the gas disappears. Once it arrives at the center spot, the colossus regenerates its arms and drops to a knee. At this point the blade traps spawn in and four terminals, located at the end of each trench, become active and attackable. This is signified by electricity shooting into the colossus. During this time all damage done to the boss is reflected back in the form of electric shock.

Players must concentrate damage on the terminals and shut them down. For each terminal that isn't shut down in 60 seconds the boss reactivates with lightning arcs striking each player for damage relative to the number of terminals still active. After this is complete, the colossus walks to the south, as poison gas is pumped in between the southern location and southern wall.

In addition to its basic attacks the boss now has access to Titanic Smash, & Tactical Assessment. When its uppercut is ready, the colossus winds up and knocks the main tank through the air and out of range—dropping threat on him. At this point, the off tank needs to pick up the body, as the main tank takes over on the blade arm. Then, the colossus performs Tactical Assessment and creates a factotum based on the scanned player.

70% Health: The right (blade) arm explodes and falls off.

67% Health: The left (cannon) arm explodes and falls off.

65% Health (Phase 1.1, Strategic Update): The boss walks to the center and again regenerates both arms before dropping to a knee. After taking care of the terminals, gas begins to fill the area between the eastern wall and eastern tanking location as the colossus walks to that location.

50% Health: The right (blade) arm explodes and falls off.

47% Health: The left (cannon) arm explodes and falls off.

45% Health (Phase 1.1, Strategic Update): Once again, the boss walks to the center, regenerates arms, and drops to a knee. Destroy the terminals and gas fills the area between the western wall and western tanking location as the colossus walks to that location.

30% Health: The right (blade) arm explodes and falls off.

27% Health: The left (cannon) arm explodes and falls off.

25% Health (Phase 2.0, Final Burn): The colossus's Bombard ability now launches heat-seeking projectiles that hit the two targets furthest from the boss. As time goes by, more projectiles are fired—4, 6, 8, 10, maxing out at 12. Each one hits a different player, but if there are not 12 targets, a player will get hit multiple times.

Simultaneously, poison is vented in at the end of each trench, blocking certain areas off. Eventually, players have nowhere to fight, but the very center. If the group takes too long in this phase, the boss vents steam that causes players to take more damage from the projectiles and Toxic Coolant.

With the General Assembly defeated, loot the boss and talk to Divayth Fyr to complete the quest. A couple chests and heavy sacks are available too, before entering the portal back to Tel Fyr.

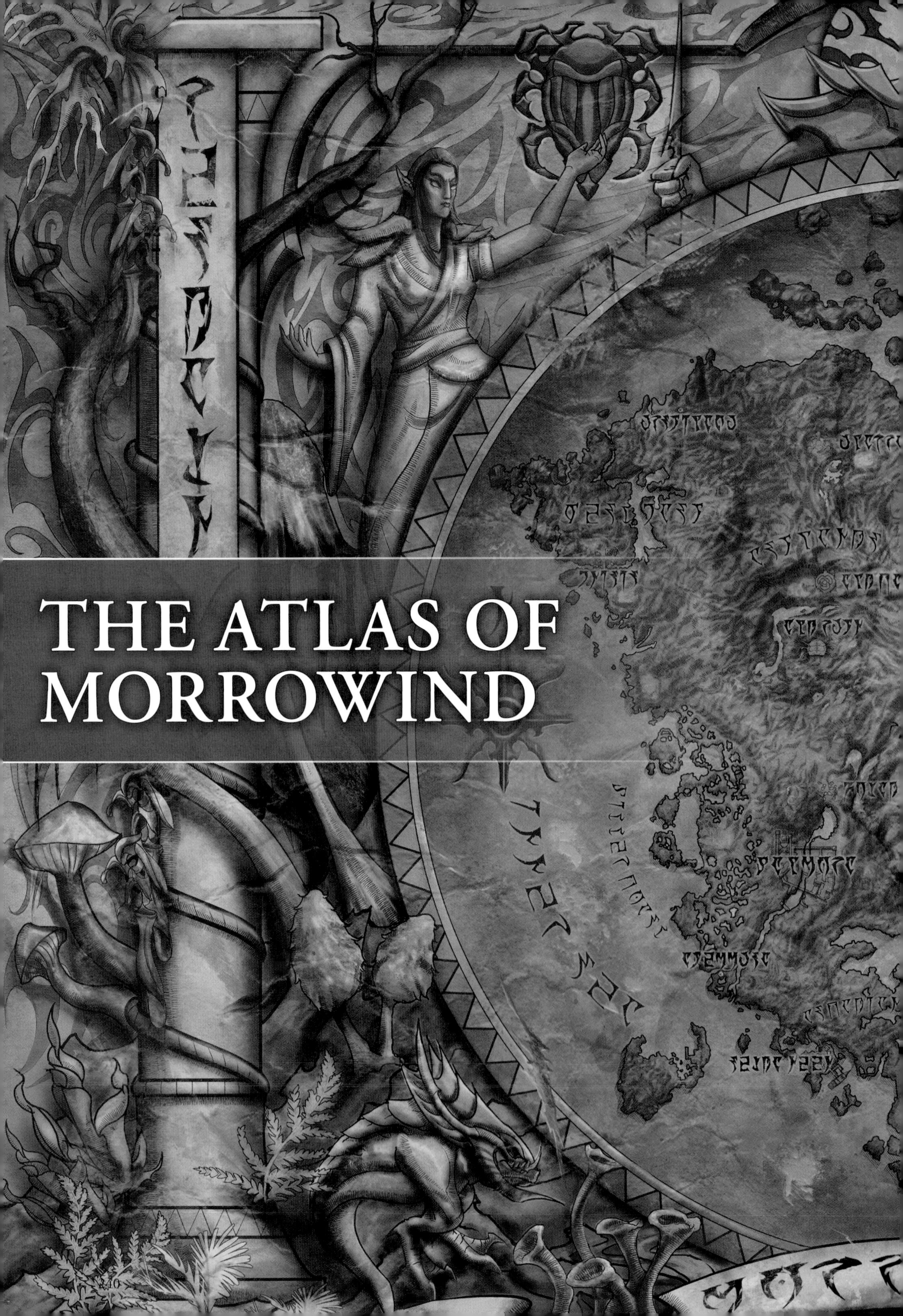
THE ATLAS OF
MORROWIND

AN OVERVIEW OF THE LAND OF VVARDENFELL

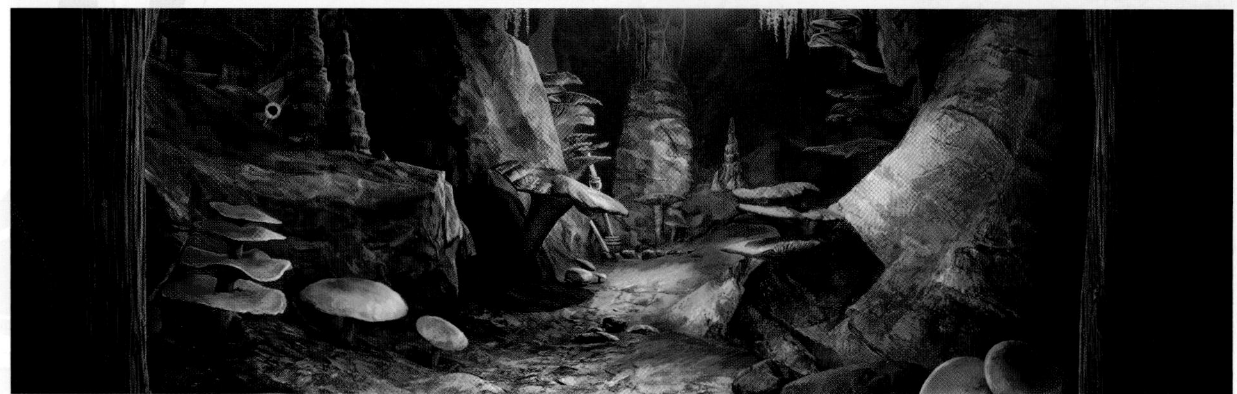

Welcome to a thorough guide to every location across the island of Vvardenfell. The ancient Dunmeri families have segmented this land into a number of separate regions, and current cartographers saw little reason to change this method of dividing the realm into manageable segments for your reference. Although regions aren't visible on your in-game maps, the borders between them have been drawn along roads, rivers, and steep mountains wherever possible, so you may visualize where you are more easily.

REGIONS & LEGEND

This Atlas is divided into seven sub-chapters; these are the accessible regions of Vvardenfell, starting with the one you visit first. The order is as follows:

- Bitter Coast (southwest)
- West Gash (west)
- Ascadian Isles (south)
- Ashlands (north)
- Grazelands (northeast)
- Molag Amur (central-east)
- Azura's Coast (east)

In each sub-chapter, locations are shown with the in-game icon that appears on your compass and maps, but a host of unmarked locations and other useful knowledge is also imparted. For larger dungeons and settlements, interior maps have been provided. These help you explore major locations and flag important items. The following icons are used to help you gain the greatest knowledge during your pursuit of treasure and fame across Vvardenfell.

LOCATIONS & TYPE

The following icons are associated with particular locations across Vvardenfell. They each have their own Atlas entry and detail.

PRIMARY LOCATION (KNOWN):

These are locations that appear on your in-game map, with a familiar icon and something you can use as an anchor point when navigating this realm. The number of the icon refers to the number in the sub-chapter, so simply cross-reference it.

SECONDARY LOCATION (UNKNOWN):

These are locations that do not appear on your in-game map. Some are as large, or larger than "known" locations, so it's important not to overlook them. Some are Dunmeri or Dwemer ruins, small camps, or large underground areas; they could be anything! Make sure you visit them at least once. These areas are also known as "unmarked" or "secondary" locations.

ANCESTRAL TOMB:

The resting place of one of the great ancient Dunmeri families. Note there are other tombs with different icons attached to them.

BATTLEGROUND:

Ferocious PvPvP battles and elite gear are available at this arena-like location.

CAMP:

A small location, usually with a gathering of tents and a fire.

CITY:

Usually the largest settlement in a region, complete with multiple interior buildings once you cross the city's threshold. Expect Merchants, quests, docks, Silt Striders, and other activities.

CRAFTING:

A special crafting table allowing specific sets of equipment to be created is found at this location.

DELVE DUNGEON:

A particularly tough subterranean adventure awaits you at this location. Expect multiple foes, bosses, and group battling.

GROUP BOSS:

A particularly tough entity lurks in this area. Slaying it requires multiple adventurers.

HOMESTEAD ESTATE:

A house you can purchase once specific costs (gold or crowns) are paid.

INTERESTING LOCATION:

These appear at locations that are of interest, and also appear on your in-game map.

MINE:

An underground location of winding, Dunmeri-made tunnels and caverns.

RAID DUNGEON:

If you wish to test your mettle to its very limits, feel free to journey to this particular dungeon entrance.

TOWN:

A large settlement with multiple buildings, interior locations such as inns and markets, and quests to start.

WAYSHRINE:

A marker you teleport to when maneuvering around the world, or after you die. Unlock these as you go.

WORLD MAP ICONS

These icons usually indicate tiny individual locations, such as Fishing Holes, promise of Merchant activity, areas where quests may begin, or spots where collectibles can be found. Many don't have Atlas entries, so you're encouraged to seek these out via the guide map.

ANCESTRAL TOMB RUBBINGS:

Dunmeri family tomb doors that must be accessed as part of Quest: (M2) **The Lost Library**.

HEAVY SACKS:

A large bag of goodies, which should be found and added to your inventory. Note that not all of these items are active in Vvardenfell at once, so not every location shown may give you a Sack.

MAGES GUILD BOOKS:

There are ten Mages Guild books to find, and multiple copies are scattered about Vvardenfell. The guide map provides a letter to show you which book is at a particular locale. Once you find one of these books, the others of the same type disappear, so only ten need to be secured. Here are all ten book names:

Mages Guild Books

MAP BOOK LETTER	NAME OF BOOK
A	The Living Gods
B	Kwama Mining
C	Sanctioned Murder (Morag Tong)
D	House of Troubles
E	Invocation of Azura
F	Vivec and Mephala
G	Kwama Eggs
H	The Great Houses
I	Faith of the Dark Elves
J	On Stepping Lightly by Narsis Dren

MERCHANTS:

Flags a particular location as having a Merchant. The exact type and number are detailed within the Atlas location entry. Consult your in-game map for specific Merchants (Fighters Guild, Enchanter, etc.).

PORT CITY (INTERIOR MAPS ONLY):

The docks at a coastal city or town indicate whether you can fast-travel to a settlement with the same-sized docks.

QUEST MARKERS:

Expect to begin a quest in the general vicinity of this area.

RARE FISHING:

The world map flags every single Fishing Hole, which is important, as there are 12 new rare fish to catch! Some can be randomly caught in any of the following four Fishing Holes, but some only appear in certain types of water.

Rare Fishing Holes

SALTWATER	**Very Rare:** Resdaynian Sailfin	**Rare:** Weeping Pygmy Shark	**Rare:** Ghost Octopus
FRESHWATER	**Very Rare:** Shalk-Brother Crayfish	**Rare:** Pity Bombil	**Rare:** Hoaga Oto
RIVER	**Very Rare:** Ash Blindfish	**Rare:** Netch-Hook Eel	**Rare:** Pilgrim Goby
FOUL	**Very Rare:** Oanna	**Rare:** Firemouth Guiyu	**Rare:** Sleeper Coffinfish

SHRINE OF THE SEVEN GRACES:

Visit each of these shrines to earn The Pilgrim's Path Achievement.

SKYSHARDS:

This helpful imbuing shaft of light is pinpointed. Note the lighter color refers to exterior skyshards you can easily access, while the darker color refers to skyshards within a location's interior, usually a dungeon.

SILT STRIDER (INTERIOR MAPS ONLY):

Indicates whether the town or city has a Silt Strider you can use to fast-travel to other settlements with this feature.

SURVEY REPORTS:

This is the general location for each crafting skill's survey report.

THIEVES TROVES:

A small box of equipment utilized by cutthroats. Gather these as a member of the Thieves Guild. Note that not all of these items are active in Vvardenfell at once, so not every location shown may give you a Trove.

TREASURE CHESTS:

Gain reasonable to valuable items by finding these. Note that only 160 chests are active in Vvardenfell at once, so not all locations shown on the map may give you a chest.

TREASURE MAP LOCATIONS:

If you find a treasure map, which has a Roman numeral and drawing associated with it, this is where the drawing leads you.

VIVEC SERMONS:

Gather the first 36 of these sermons in any order. They appear as glowing Lorebooks and are each individually numbered (so Sermon #23 will always be in the same place). Collect all 36, then the 37th, to earn the Tribunal Preacher Achievement.

LOCATION STATISTICS

Every location in Vvardenfell contains a list of pertinent information so you're better informed regarding what to expect within a settlement or dungeon. The following explains what all the listed data means.

❖ **Area of Interest—Crafting Stations:**
These range from the plentiful cooking fires to the rarer stations and tables used for your six crafting skills. If a location has one, it's marked here.

❖ **Area of Interest—Crafting Sets:**
You're able to craft sets of equipment here.

❖ **Area of Interest—Battleground:**
This location features PvPvP Battleground content.

❖ **Area of Interest—Delve:**
This is a Delve Dungeon.

❖ **Area of Interest—Homestead:**
This is a home you can purchase.

❖ **Area of Interest—Port City:**
This is a town or city on the coast, with a Navigator to find and a boat you can chart to another port city.

❖ **Area of Interest—Skyshard:**
This imbuement is available here.

❖ **Area of Interest—Silt Strider:**
You can fast-travel to another town or city from here with this area of interest.

❖ **Area of Interest—Trial:**
A fearsome Trial awaits you and your guild at this location.

❖ **Area of Interest—Wayshrine:**
This location has or is a Wayshrine, and you can teleport here, or return here after death.

❖ **Entities:**
Expected enemies and neutral entities are listed here. Note that the Bestiary contains information on how to defeat Morrowind-specific foes.

❖ **Entity (Boss):**
The location has a tough and usually named boss.

❖ **Item of Interest—Lorebook:**
There's a Lorebook here.

❖ **Item of Interest—Mages Guild Book:**
There's a Mages Guild book here, if you haven't gathered an identical version of it already.

❖ **Item of Interest—Stone:**
A special floating stone is available here, as part of Quest: (VV5) At Any Cost.

❖ **Item of Interest—Vivec Sermon:**
One of the 37 Vivec Sermons, as part of the Tribunal Preacher Achievement, is available here.

❖ **Merchant:**
This location has a Merchant, and his or her name and type is listed. This could be a Caravaner, Clothier, Innkeeper, Traveling Merchant, Mystic, Enchanter, Alchemist, Blacksmith, Elite Gear Vendor, Guild Trader, Stablemaster, Magister, Banker, Hall Steward, Navigator, or a simple Merchant.

❖ **Related Quest:**
If you're having trouble entering a remote area, or can't reach an interior chamber, it's usually because you don't have a related quest active. This lists any pertinent quest in such areas, as well as quests you can start in the general vicinity.

❖ **Warning—Restricted Area (Trespass):**
Enter this location and expect to pick a lock, then pick a fight, as entities are hostile to your snooping and sneaking. You will accrue a Bounty if you're spotted in such an area.

LOCATION SUMMATION

Due to the sheer size of Vvardenfell, and the random nature of what can sometimes appear, it's impossible to track everything with 100% accuracy. You should also look to the **Appendices** chapter for charts showing where the most important collectibles can be found.

BITTER COAST

The southwestern coast of Vvardenfell is known for its slightly fetid salt marshes, and the remains of smuggling operations both recent and long-forgotten. Hidden by an almost constant fog, the region hasn't experienced the worst of the rumbling from Red Mountain, but the many inland waterways and ponds still border on the putrid, making this the only region where foul-water fishing is possible. The region stretches from Arenim Manor at its northern extreme, to the town of Seyda Neen at its southernmost point. The slaver base of Firemoth Island, where you begin your adventure, is also located off the coast.

Locations

No.	Location
01	Arenim Manor
02	Mallapi Cave
03	Aleft
04	Addadshashanammu
05	Ashalmimilkala
06	Hlormaren Stronghold
07	Ashurnibibi
08	Ahemmusa Camp
09	Shulk Ore Mine
10	Rethan Manor
11	Fishing Hovel
12	Zainsipilu
13	Firemoth Island
14	Sarys Ancestral Tomb
15	Andrano Ancestral Tomb
16	Seyda Neen Wayshrine
17	Seyda Neen

01 ARENIM MANOR

Entities:	Redoran
Item of Interest:	Vivec Sermons
Warning:	Restricted Area (Trespassing)

This walled settlement with a drawbridge (usually raised) is owned by the Arenims, a minor noble family. Currently it is under Redoran governance.

The exterior grounds has an accessible Arenim Warehouse near a moored boat and sealed boathouse. The Warehouse interior has two levels, leading to the main floor of the manor. The manor is situated inside a walled garden, with plenty of Redorans guarding. Inside the manor, you have access to a large banquet hall and adjacent kitchen, with a trapdoor down to the basement, which links back to the Warehouse. Upstairs is a landing, and three doors—one to an exterior balcony, one sealed, and one to the Councilor's Quarters.

02 MALLAPI CAVE

Entities:	Dreugh, Fetcherflies, Spiders, Warclaws
Related Quest:	Of Faith and Family
Warning:	Restricted Area (Trespassing)

This minor cave complex is on the northern edge of the Bitter Coast marsh, close to the Telvayn Ancestral Tomb rubbing.

After a small entrance, a secondary door leads to the Back Tunnels. The northern part of the tunnels (with planks over the soft ground) is the domain of Warclaws, while Dreugh lurk in the south passage. Note the exit ladder on the eastern side of the interior, leading to a trapdoor exit in West Gash (Location: Mallapi Cave Back Tunnels).

03 ALEFT

This small Dwemer ruin, and place of reputed Daedric activity, sits on one of the many small marsh islands. It is currently inaccessible. Scour the swamp surrounding for a treasure chest and other collectibles to the east.

04 ADDADSHASHANAMMU

Entities:	Seducers, Winged Twilights

A reputed Shrine to Sheogorath, this Daedric structure houses Seducer foes as well as Winged Twilights. Currently, the entrance to any subterranean areas are sealed and inaccessible. Come for the sacrificial bodies strewn about. Stay for the Fishing Holes, Heavy Sack, and Thieves Trove in the vicinity.

05 ASHALMIMILKALA

Area of Interest:	Skyshard
Entities:	Dunmer

The Daedric shrines along the Bitter Coast continue at this island, an old and dilapidated sanctum of Mehrunes Dagon. Currently, this is a small Dunmer camp, close to the skyshard and a Heavy Sack situated by the shore.

BITTER COAST—OVERVIEW AND COLLECTIBLES

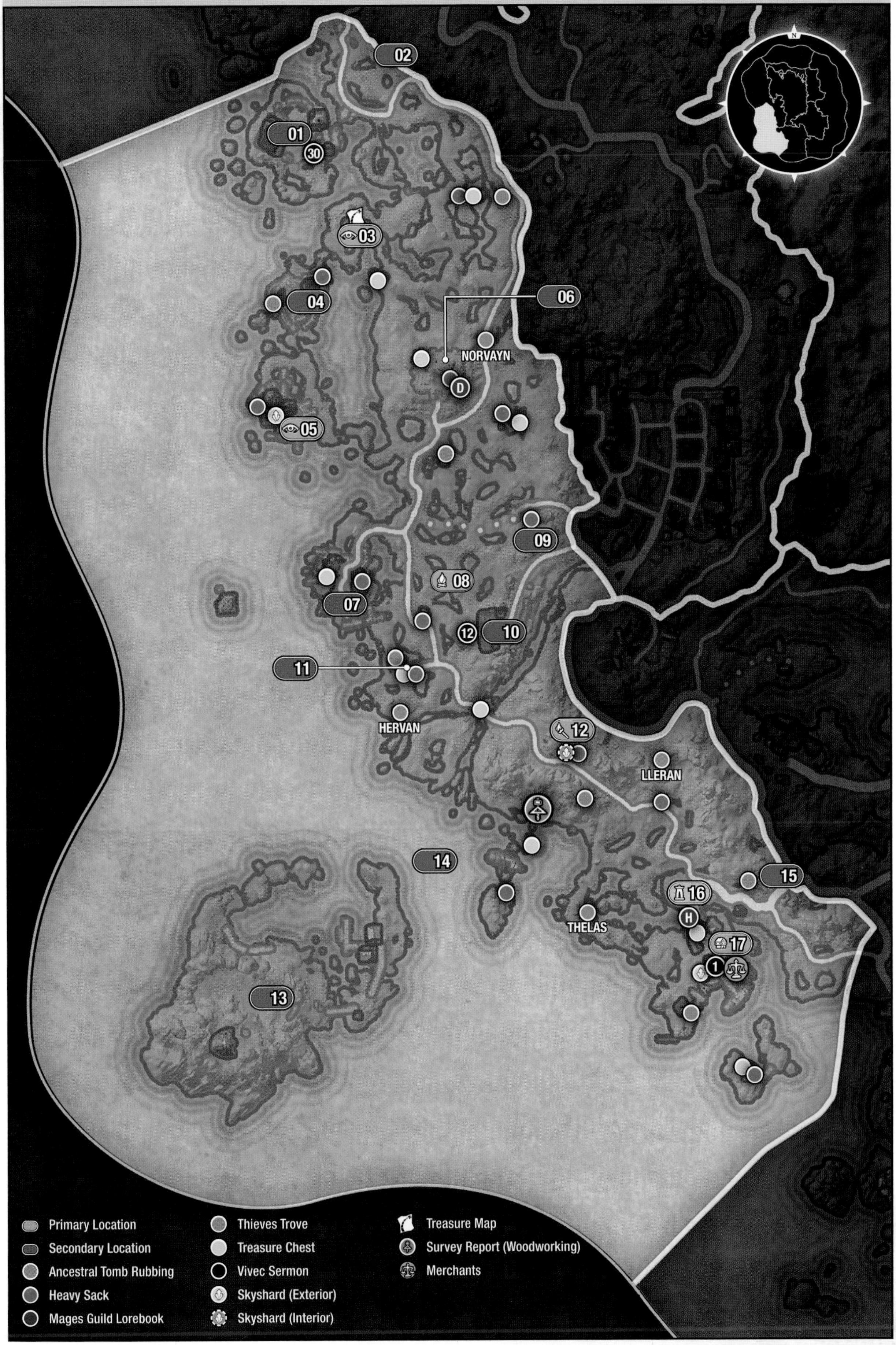

02
01
30
03
04
06
NORVAYN
D
05
09
08
07
12
10
11
HERVAN
12
LLERAN
14
15
16
THELAS
H
17
1
13

- Primary Location
- Secondary Location
- Ancestral Tomb Rubbing
- Heavy Sack
- Mages Guild Lorebook
- Thieves Trove
- Treasure Chest
- Vivec Sermon
- Skyshard (Exterior)
- Skyshard (Interior)
- Treasure Map
- Survey Report (Woodworking)
- Merchants

BITTER COAST—QUESTS

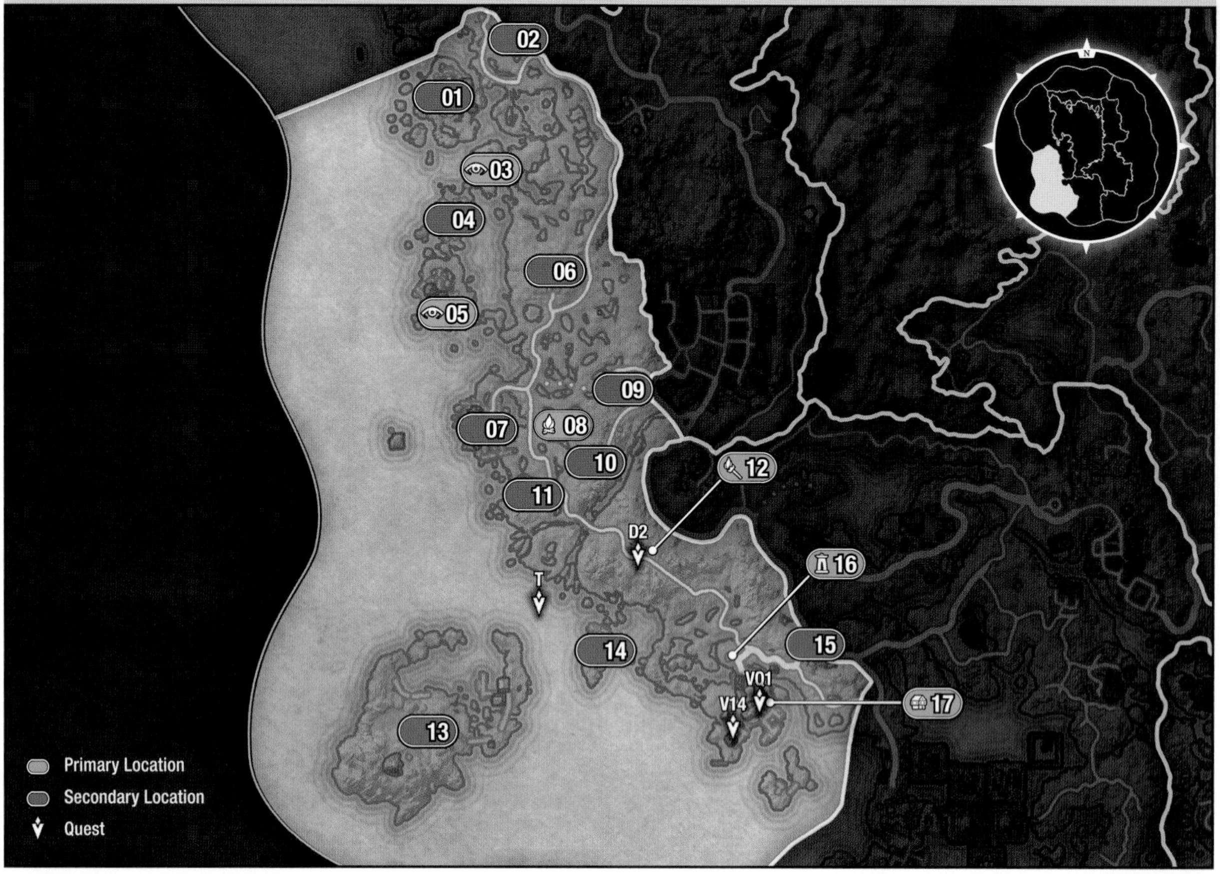

01
02
03
04
05
06
07
08
09
10
11
12
13
14
15
16
17
D2
T
V01
V14

Primary Location
Secondary Location
Quest

BITTER COAST—FISHING

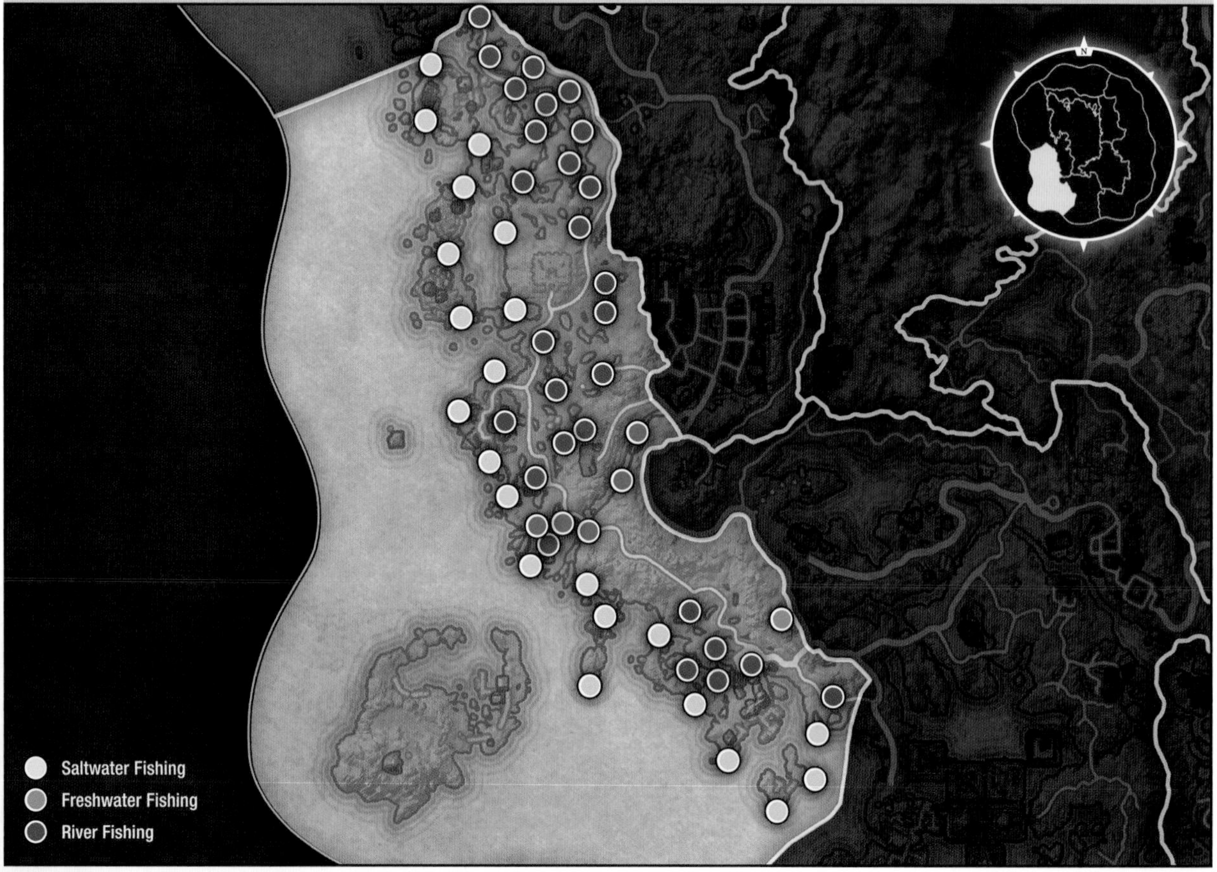

Saltwater Fishing
Freshwater Fishing
River Fishing

06 HLORMAREN STRONGHOLD

Entities:	Nycotics
Item of Interest:	Mages Guild Book (The House of Troubles)
Related Quest:	Family Reunion

Previously, when the Dunmer were a real force to be reckoned with, this stronghold served as a show of strength. Now this fortification is home to an unruly and vicious band of Dunmer, the Nycotic cult. Note the Mages Guild book on the upper crenellations, and the nearby tomb rubbing to the northeast. Enter here during **Quest: Family Reunion**, by obtaining the Hlormaren Stronghold Key from one of the cultists.

Interior: This single-level jail holds prisoners to free during the quest, a large torture chamber, and a roughly L-shaped outer corridor, with alcoves and minimal cultists to offer resistance.

07 ASHURNIBIBI

Entities:	Ogrims, Nixads, Malacath Guards
Related Quest:	Fleeing the Past

A sprawling shrine to the Daedric entity Malacath (god-king of the Orcs), its once-impenetrable high walls are now slowly sinking into the mire. Close to the entrance inside this complex, the Outer Chambers house guards still sworn to Malacath.

Interior: Inside the ruins is a rough set of chambers and an underground river, guarded by Malacath's Dunmer and some powerful Ogrims. Work your way counterclockwise to a statue of Malacath and into the Inner Chambers, then southward along a watery inlet and back to the Outer Chambers.

08 AHEMMUSA CAMP

Entities:	Dunmer

Used by one of the Ashlander tribes, a few Dunmer are camped here, as the swamp becomes wider and slightly more fetid.

09 SHULK ORE MINE

Entities:	Insects, Nycotics, River Troll
Item of Interest:	Lorebook (Miner's Warning)
Related Quest:	Divine Inquiries

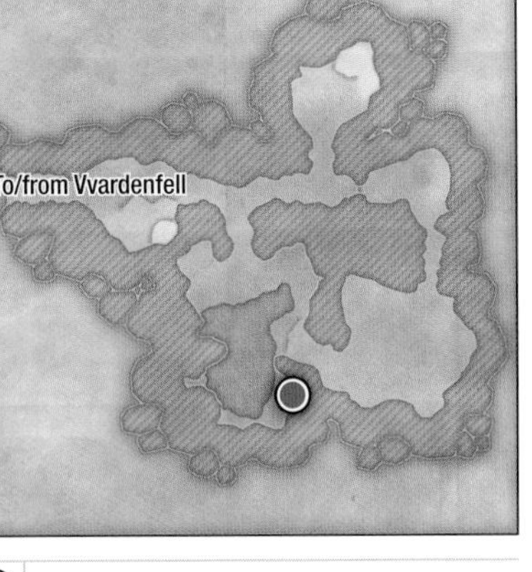

Miner's Warning

House Hlaalu has staked claim to this old mine, which has an entrance close to the regional border, on the outskirts of Balmora in the West Gash region. A rudimentary wooden planked path winds around the rock outcrop where the entrance is located.

Interior: Inside, the mine has been overrun by lunatic Dunmer from the Nycotic cult. South is a broken bridge over a small waterlogged lake with a River Troll, and an alcove where you can find the Miner's Warning. North is a Nycotics' camp and access to the Deep Mine Chambers, a sacrificial area to the southeast. Work your way around here in a clockwise direction.

10 RETHAN MANOR

Entities:	Rethan Guards
Item of Interest:	Vivec Sermons
Warning:	Restricted Area (Trespassing)

On a rocky promontory overlooking the swamps (and a Fishing Hole) of the Bitter Coast, southwest of Balmora, is the Hlaalu House stronghold known as Rethan Manor. You're free to wander the grounds, but unlocking the door to the interior (Simple difficulty) means you're trespassing.

Inside, expect Argonian workers and a few Rethan guards who don't take kindly to your infiltration. There's a ground and upper floor to pilfer from, as well as a small cellar. Outside, be sure to check the skeletal remains of a camper at the foot of the rock promontory for a Vivec tome **(#12)**.

11 FISHING HOVEL

Entities:	Dunmer

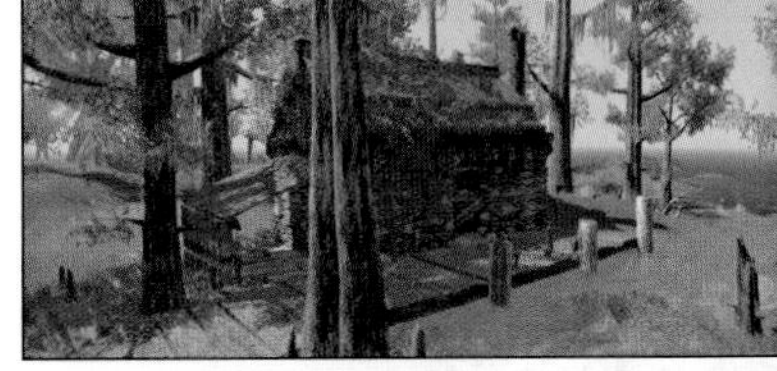

A couple of Dunmer fishermen can be found here, close to a Fishing Hole and small ramshackle stone hut, just north of the Heran Ancestral Tomb. Note the nearby collectibles (on the guide map).

12 ZAINSIPILU

Area of Interest:	Delve, Skyshard
Entities:	Bandits, Fetcherfly Hives, Insects, Kagouti, Nix-Hounds, Zvvius the Hive Lord
Related Quest:	A Hidden Harvest

On the idyllic path from Seyda Neen, close to the quest giver for **Quest: A Hidden Harvest**, is this bandit cave complex.

Interior: Inside, after a narrow and winding tunnel containing Nix-Hounds, the place opens up into a huge underground cavern. Bandits are on the wooden plank ledges around the edge, and a lava flow bisects the area running north to south. Note the skyshard in the northeast corner. Also beware of a terrifying beast called Zvvius the Hive Lord, a Fetcherfly Hive Golem, located in the dead-end cavern to the southwest.

 Skyshard

13 FIREMOTH ISLAND

Entities:	Slavers
Item of Interest:	Lorebook (Good Travels!)
Related Quest:	The Wailing Prison, Broken Bonds

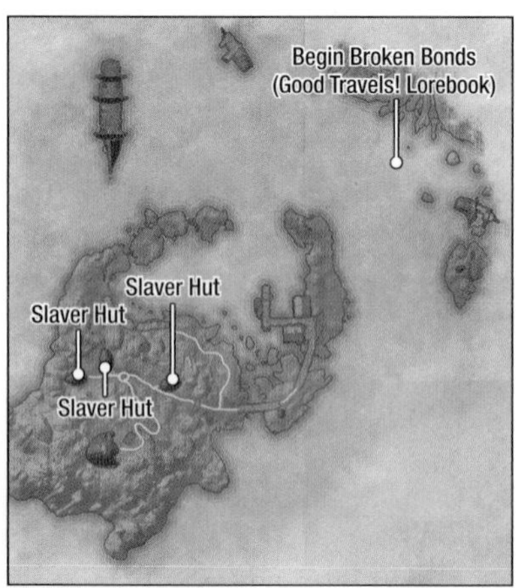

This fort sits on a cluster of volcanic islands southwest off the Bitter Coast. You begin your exploration of Vvardenfell at this location, during **Quest: Broken Bonds**. Note the location of the Lorebook Good Travels! and quest start is aboard a ship at the start of the Tutorial. Once you've fled the island, it becomes inaccessible.

14 SARYS ANCESTRAL TOMB

A small island (known locally as Aharunartus) and slaver hideaway between Fort Firemoth and the mainland holds little but a tomb door, a fishing hole, and the remains of the scuttled ship. Note the minor collectibles nearby. The tomb itself leads a small, waterlogged interior with some minor scenery to loot.

15 ANDRANO ANCESTRAL TOMB

Entities:	Skaafin
Related Quest:	Divine Conundrum

Off the main path from Seyda Neen around Lake Amaya in the Ascadian Isles region, near a clump of impressive fungi, is the entrance to this accessible ancestral tomb. One of the leading Redoran families rests their deceased here.

Inside, work your way counterclockwise around the tomb, which has been defiled by Skaafin. Enter the Hall of Remembrance heading south to access the initial entrance room from the Summoning Chamber.

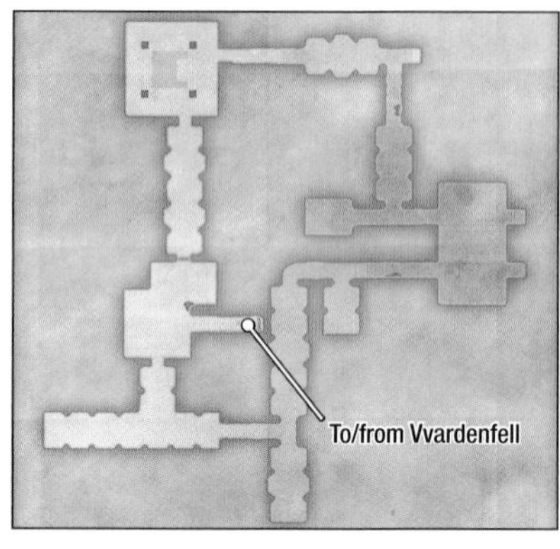

16 SEYDA NEEN WAYSHRINE

Area of Interest:	Wayshrine

A place of teleportation sits just north of the coastal town that bears its name. Note the tombs of Thelas (west), Lleran (north), and Othrelas (east) of this landmark.

17 SEYDA NEEN

Area of Interest:	Cooking Fire, Skyshard, Silt Strider
Entities:	House Guards
Items of Interest:	Lorebook (Understanding the Living Gods), Lorebook (Pact Pamphlet), Mages Guild Book (The Great Houses and Their Use)
Merchants:	Caravaner Medyn Hleran, Chef Chow-Chow, Grocer Snarzikha, Findun
Related Quest:	Divine Conundrum, (VV14) Breaking Through The Fog

Welcome to the Gateway to Morrowind! This port town borders the Ascadian Isles, and the much larger Vivec City, to the east, and is set up to process travelers as they arrive.

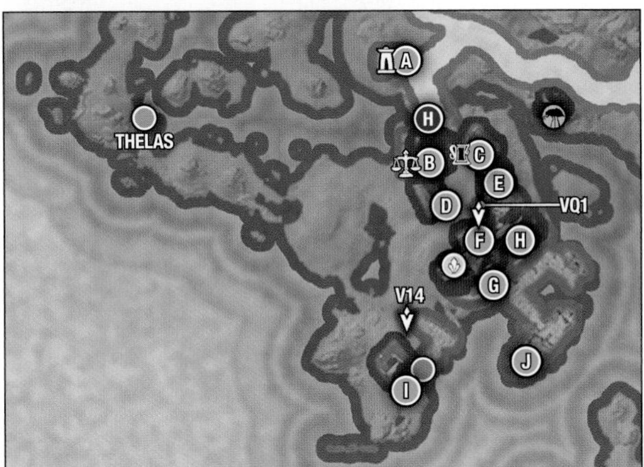

Quest	Skyshard
Ancestral Tomb Rubbing	Inn
Mage's Guild Lorebook	Vendor
Silt Strider	Wayshrine
Thieves Trove	

Ⓐ Seyda Neen Wayshrine

Venture northward out of the settlement to reach this point, as detailed previously. Check the Mages Guild book on the bridge just south of here, and the Silt Strider for traveling options; the beast is parked to the east.

Ⓑ Findun's Goods

Seek ye a Merchant? Findun can find you a number of choice items if you visit his shop.

Ⓒ Tavern by the Sea

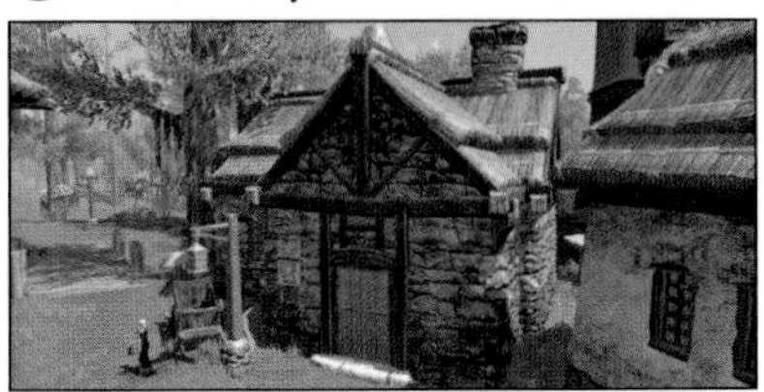

There's a Cooking Fire and a Chef here, if you're partial to Dunmeri cuisine, though the Chef is an Argonian.

Ⓓ Snarzikha's Grocery

Should you require your comestibles to be fresh, head to this Merchant. A Caravaner stops here from time to time, too.

Ⓔ Andrilo's House

Warning:	Restricted Area (Trespassing)

Entering this house requires a Lockpick (Simple difficulty). Feel free to annoy Andrilo and steal her sweetroll collection if the mood takes you.

Ⓕ Governor's Office

Sergeant Garil usually wanders around this formal office, which grants access to the adjoining buildings, as well as an exterior courtyard where you can find a skyshard.

Ⓖ Census and Excise Office

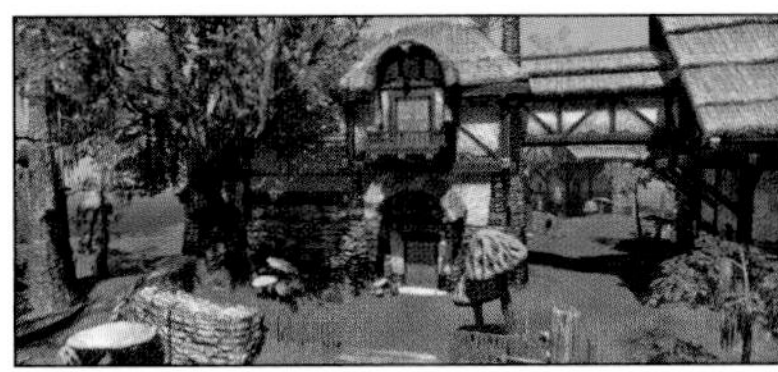

This links to the exterior courtyard, Governor's Office, and Guard Tower. Synedelius Ergalla checks in immigrants to these parts.

Ⓗ Guard House

Warning:	Restricted Area (Trespassing)

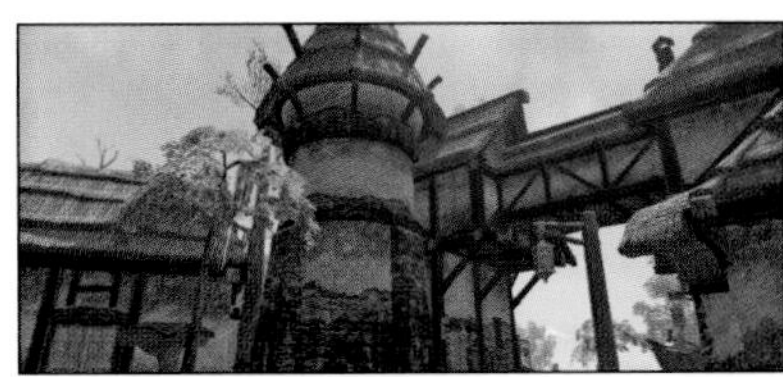

There's little need to break in here, as the house guard becomes vicious. The tower leads into the Census and Excise Office.

Ⓘ Seyda Neen Lighthouse

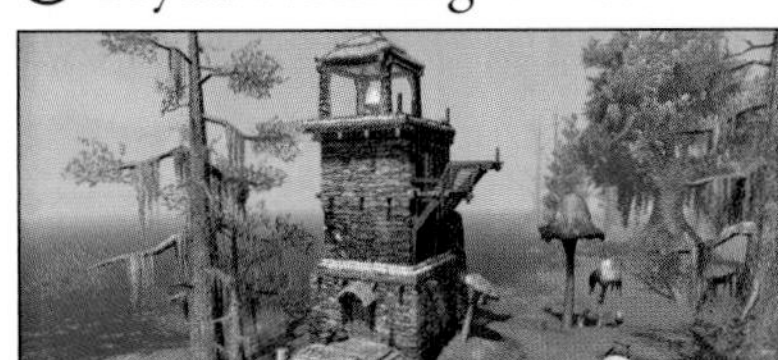

Feel free to enter the lighthouse and climb to the top. Note the Thieves Trove in the vicinity.

Ⓙ The Windstorm

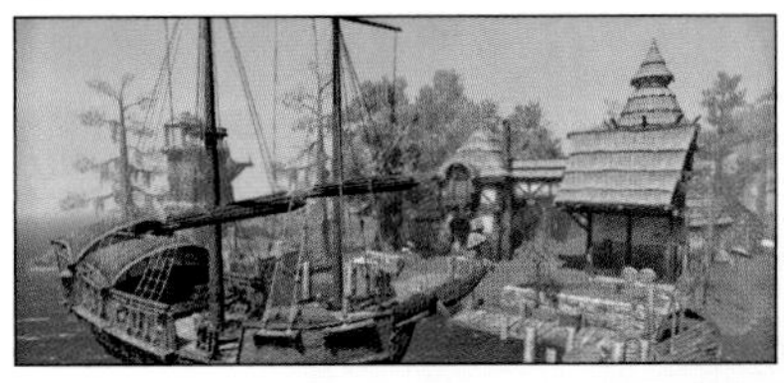

A fine sailing ship is moored in the harbor. Note the Lorebook on the dock cart.

WEST GASH

Running between the Bitter Coast and Red Mountain to the south, from the city of Balmora all the way northward to the Sea of Ghosts and the coastal town of Gnisis, West Gash is an area of grassy highlands that gets progressively rockier the farther north and east you travel. Storms of ash deposit choking clouds and unwanted beasts. House Redoran had a garrison here, but recent bandit gangs—notably the Red Exiles and Warclaws—have caused more than a simple annoyance, and caution should be used when exploring this area.

Locations

#	Location	#	Location
01	Yasammidan	18	Randas Ancestral Tomb
02	Arkngthunch-Sturdumz	19	Ularra
03	Ald Velothi Harbor House	20	Khartag Point
04	Ashalmawia	21	Red Exile Camp
05	Urshilaku Camp	22	Hleran Ancestral Tomb
06	Urshilaku Camp Wayshrine	23	Ald'ruhn Wayshrine
07	Mysterious Ruin (Bethamez)	24	Ald'ruhn
08	Maelkashishi	25	Mallapi Cave Back Tunnels
09	Drivam's House (Gnisis)	26	Ramimilk
10	Gnisis	27	Red Exile Tent
11	Gnisis Wayshrine	28	Kudanat Mine
12	Berandas	29	Redoran Garrison
13	Salothan's Council	30	Nilthog's Hollow
14	Dushariran	31	Assarnatamat
15	Veloth Ancestral Tomb	32	Boundary Bridge
16	Ashimanu Cave	33	Balmora
17	West Gash Wayshrine	34	Balmora Wayshrine

01 YASAMMIDAN

Entities:	Air Atronachs, Clannfear

On the far northwestern promontory, by the water's edge, is a large Shrine to Mehrunes Dagon. The structure is waterlogged but still impressive. Come for the collectibles, or if you're desperate for some Blessed Thistle.

02 ARKNGTHUNCH-STURDUMZ

Area of Interest:	Skyshard
Entities:	Insects, Dwarven Automatons, Spectrals
Related Quest:	Divine Intervention

On the northwestern edge of Gnisis, past the rope-bridge ravines, is a small Dwemer ruin with a domed tower and stone bridge. At the base of the bridge's span is a skyshard. Cross the bridge to enter this Graveyard of the Ghost Invaders. Check the ledge lip of the exterior dome for Heavy Sacks.

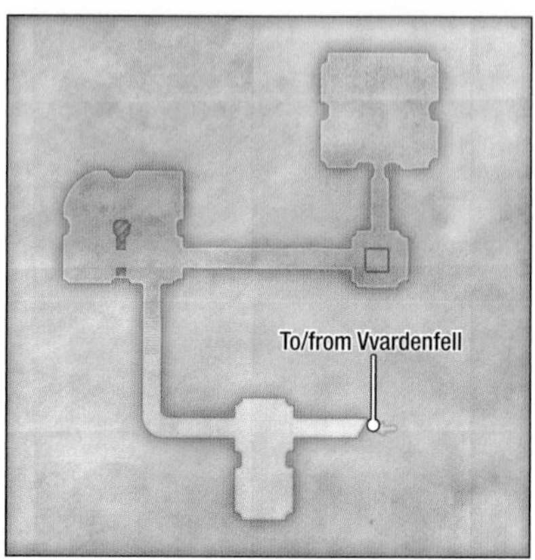

Interior: Inside are three main linked chambers, with increasingly fearsome foes along the way, including a platoon of Spectrals, as well as the expected Dwarven Automatons. The blasting lava of the final chamber usually houses a Centurion.

03 ALD VELOTHI HARBOR HOUSE

Area of Interest:	Homestead

Near a small set of docks along the northern coast is an imposing harbor house known as Ald Velothi. Once a military outpost, this dwelling can be yours for the right amount of crowns or gold! It features a small walled garden and two entrances, along with a multi-floor interior.

WEST GASH—OVERVIEW AND COLLECTIBLES

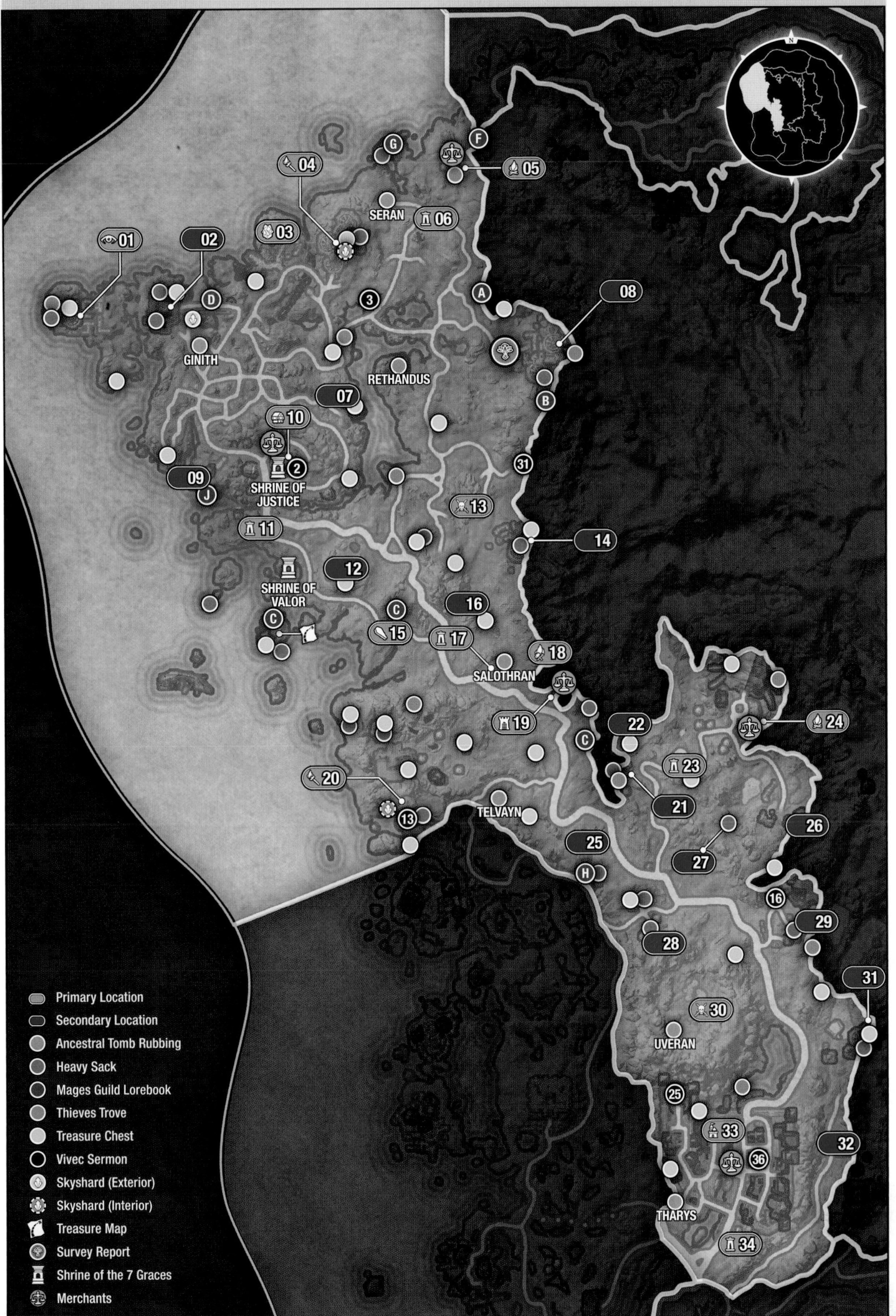

WEST GASH—QUESTS/FISHING

04 ASHALMAWIA

Areas of Interest:	Delve, Skyshard
Entities:	Clannfear, Daedroth, Insects, Ogrims, Scamps, Worm Cultists, Phobbiicus
Item of Interest:	Stone of Ashalmawia
Related Quest:	At Any Cost

If you plan to pray to Molag Bal, this is the place in West Gash to do it. The sprawling ruins hosts a number of Worm Cultists throughout the exterior, and a door to the main chambers below.

Interior Level 1 (Ashalmawia Shrine): An entrance passage leads to a junction, more Worm Cultists, and tomb vaults to the left (west), with steps down to the Sunken Vaults. To the right (east) is a mine corridor, with overgrown tunnels leading to a large altar and the Stone of Ashalmawia, and an entrance to Level 2 in the northwest area.

Interior Level 2 (Sunken Vaults): Enter via the upper vaults, and you reach the lower vaults and a skyshard to the south. The vaults lead to rough tunnels and out to the base of a large cavern, where a ferocious Phobbiicus, flanked by two Ogrims, is ready to taste your blood. Approach from the mine area, and you're atop the cavern and must descend via a series of shrines and rope-bridges, until the boss is faced.

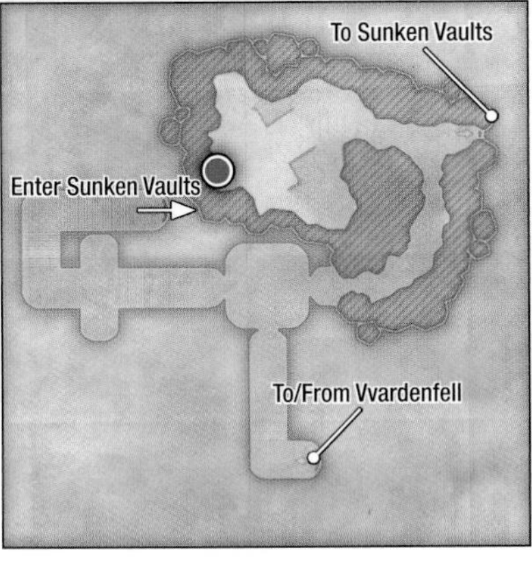

Ashalmawia: Interior Level 1

Stone of Ashalmawia

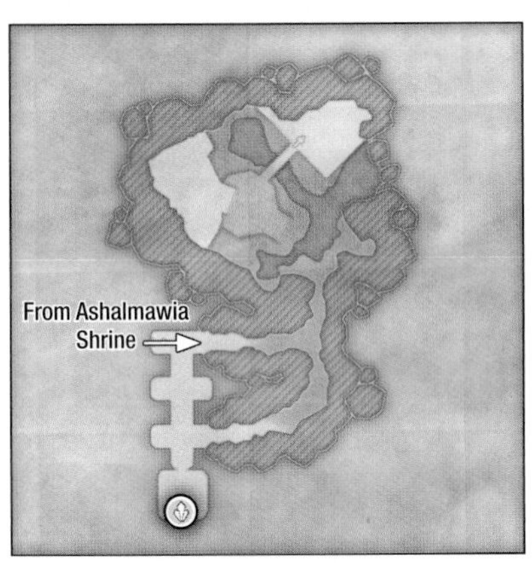

Ashalmawia: Interior Level 2 (Upper)

Skyshard

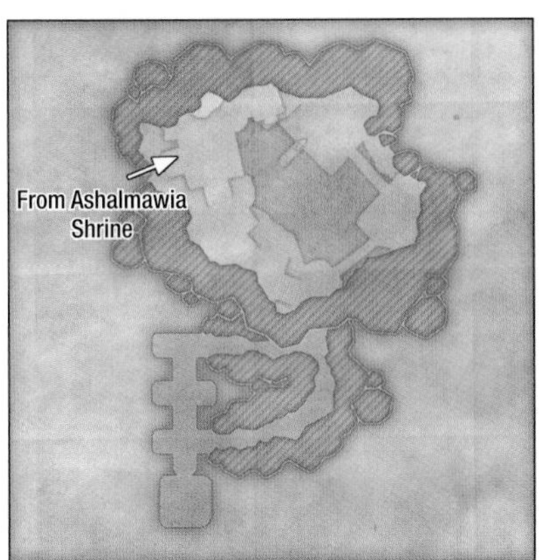

Ashalmawia: Interior Level 2 (Lower)

05 URSHILAKU CAMP

Entities:	Dunmer
Related Quest:	Haunted Grounds, Ashlander Relations

This small camp is named for one of the Ashlander tribes. It's the closest location in West Gash to the molten wasteland of the Ashland region. Come here for the Cooking Fire, a Thieves Trove, and a chat with one of the Dunmer to begin a quest.

06 URSHILAKU CAMP WAYSHRINE

Area of Interest:	Wayshrine

A few paces southwest of the camp, this Wayshrine offers easy access to the northern part of West Gash, and the nearby Seran Ancestral Tomb just west of here.

07 MYSTERIOUS RUIN (BETHAMEZ)

On the west side of the narrow lake, close to the rope-bridge ravines of Gnisis, is a strange Dwemer ruin, near a Fishing Hole and treasure chest. It is actually the exit from an ancient Dwemer location called Bethamez, accessed via the Gnisis Egg Mine, within the nearby town of the same name. Note you can't access the interior from this direction.

08 MAELKASHISHI

Entities:	Durzog, Kwama, Profane Bond Cultists
Items of Interest:	Mages Guild Book (The Living Gods), Mages Guild Book (Kwama Mining for Fun and Profit)

You can expect trouble if you visit this large Shrine to Sheogorath, set against the impenetrable volcanic wall of Vvardenfell. The place is overrun with Dunmer Cultists of the Profane Bond. The interior is inaccessible, so scout the area for a Heavy Sack, Thieves Trove, and two Mages Guild books. One (***The Living Gods***) is north at a skull-filled camping spot guarded by a Durzog, along the volcanic region border near a cave alcove containing a treasure chest. The other (***Kwama Mining for Fun and Profit***) is on the perimeter path just south of the shrine.

09 DRIVAM'S HOUSE (GNISIS)

Area of Interest:	Port City
Item of Interest:	Mages Guild Book (On Stepping Lightly)

The Boatmaster lives here, in a small house you can unlock and steal from if you wish. Otherwise, speak to Ranor Sadralo to set sail for Sadrith Mora, and usually another port city in Vvardenfell (Vivec City or Tel Mora). Or head up and into Gnisis, or check the small dock to the south for a Fishing Hole and Mages Guild book.

10 GNISIS

Area of Interest:	Cooking Fire, Silt Strider, Port City
Entities:	Ordinator Guards
Items of Interest:	Lorebook (Egg Mines and You!), Lorebook (The Truth in Sequence: Volume 5)
Merchant:	Caravener Amili Yahaz, Innkeeper Bolayn Andalor, Mystic Evylu Nethalen, Traveling Merchant Fanisea Saram (Balmora and Gnisis)
Related Quest:	(VV1) A Melodic Mistake, (VV2) Hatching a Plan, (VV3) Haunted Grounds

The largest settlement in northwest Vvardenfell, Gnisis is a town close to the coast, just south of a maze-like valley of rope-bridges and pathways, and atop a large egg mine. It's dominated by a temple structure. There are three scattered treasure chests in the vicinity, as well as a Mages Guild book over at Drivam's House, which is where it's listed.

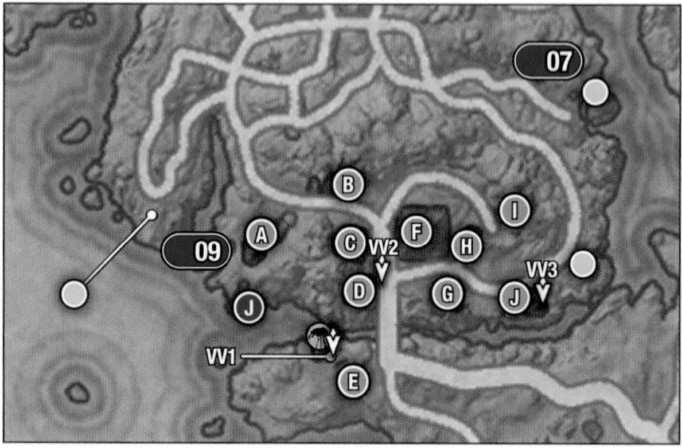

Secondary Location	Treasure Chest	Silt Strider
Quest	Mages Guild Lorebook	Location

Ⓐ Drivam's House

Find this location by the docks. It's covered in the previous entry of this Atlas.

Ⓑ Arvs-Drelen

This old Velothi tower stands close to the large rock arch on the threshold of the western entrance to Gnisis. The interior cannot be breached.

Ⓒ The Resting Kwama

The watering hole at Gnisis has an Innkeeper named Bolayn Andalor who can ply you with drink. There's also a Lorebook to snag, and Traldrisa Marys is here, playing the lute. Check downstairs for a wine cellar and a couple of bedrooms.

Ⓓ Romoren's House

Warning:	Restricted Area (Trespassing)

There's little need to barge into this family's home... but you can.

Ⓔ Gnisis Wayshrine

This marks the southern threshold and bridge into Gnisis, and is detailed elsewhere in this chapter. Note the Silt Strider nearby.

Ⓕ Gnisis Temple

The landmark temple houses the Mystic of Gnisis, Evylu Nethalen, along with her acolyte. The well-to-do Iidari Andavel is upstairs on the large circular library balcony.

Ⓖ Lathdar's House

Warning:	Restricted Area (Trespassing)

If you fancy yourself a bit of a thief, feel free to enter this small dwelling unannounced. You'll need to unlock the door (Intermediate difficulty) first, though.

Ⓗ Shandasi's House

Warning:	Restricted Area (Trespassing)

With its firm lock (Advanced difficulty), accessing this dwelling requires a Lockpick. Inside, Shulki Shandasi isn't pleased by your antics.

Ⓘ Gnisis Egg Mine

Entities:	Dwarven Automatons, Dwarven Centurions, Kwama, Scrib
Related Quest:	A Melodic Mistake, Hatching a Plan

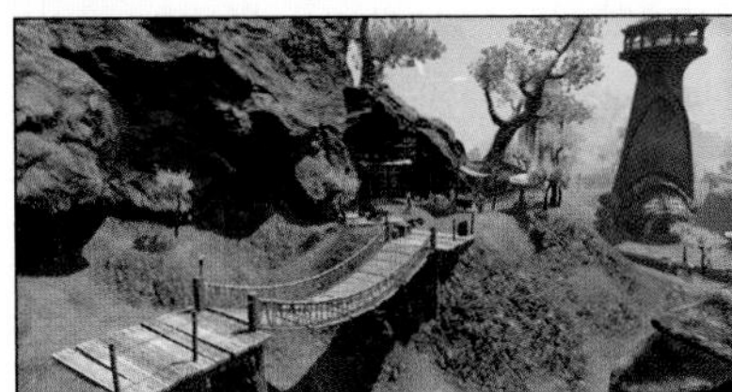

Seek out the quest before entering this mine, over a small rope-bridge on the northeast area of town.

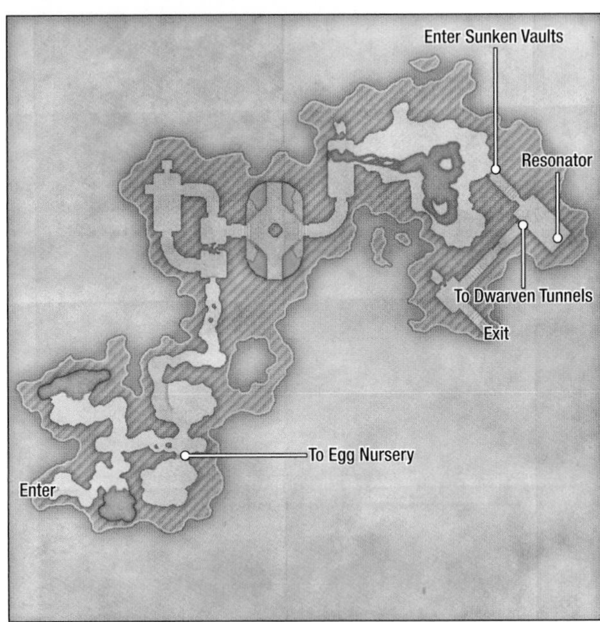

Interior (Gnisis Egg Mine): Kwama scuttle along this series of tunnel caverns and interlocking passages. Head northward into a glowing tunnel, and the atmosphere becomes a lot more clanking and Dwarven. You're able to maneuver into the lost ruins of Bethamez, a Dwemer area.

Interior (Egg Nursery): This chamber of eggs is accessed only during **Quest: Hatching a Plan**.

Interior (Bethamez): Expect Centurions and other Dwarven constructs to waylay your exploration along the northern part of this interior. The winding passage leads across a furnace chamber and into a huge cavern with a large tower-like structure—the sanctum.

Interior (Dwarven Sanctum and Tunnels): Pass through a resonator chamber and into exit tunnels that bring you out to the Mysterious Ruin (shown elsewhere in this chapter).

Ⓙ Egg Mine Barracks

Soldiers stationed here to guard the egg mine offer little more than passing comments. The real action is inside the mine.

11 GNISIS WAYSHRINE

Area of Interest:	Wayshrine

On the southern side of the river ravine, close to the Silt Strider and Gnisis itself, stands the city's Wayshrine.

12 BERANDAS

Entities:	Netch
Item of Interest:	Lorebook (The Vvardvark Experiment)

This Dunmer fortification is locked up tight, so the only items to pilfer are those from a treasure chest in the vicinity, as well as a Lorebook slowly fading on an exterior table. Also note the Mages Guild Book, and other collectible treasure, on the small islands offshore, to the southwest and west of here.

13 SALOTHAN'S COUNCIL

Entities:	Salothan's Troops, Spectral Hosts (Bosses)
Area of Interest:	Group Boss

Should you wish to challenge yourself against the Undead, visit this unholy circle, where the Council of Salothan used to meet. They still do, though their forms are more ferocious and ethereal.

14 DUSHARIRAN

Entities:	Quarra

Amid the gruesome evidence of past sacrifices, this Shrine to Malacath is now home to a small band of Quarra Cultists. Search the area for a possible Heavy Sack and treasure chest. The interior of this shrine is inaccessible.

15 VELOTH ANCESTRAL TOMB

Entities:	Bone Flayers, Hunger, Insects, Shrooms, Skeletons, Wraiths, Matriarch Rathila (Boss)
Item of Interest:	Mages Guild Book (The Great Houses and Their Use)
Related Quest:	(VV10) Ancestral Adversity

Nestled among the rocks, close to the side road and shoreline, is a tomb of the Velothi family. An adventurer with a cart can be spoken to before you enter the vaults. Also explore the upper rock outcrops for a Mages Guild book near a non-mobile skeleton.

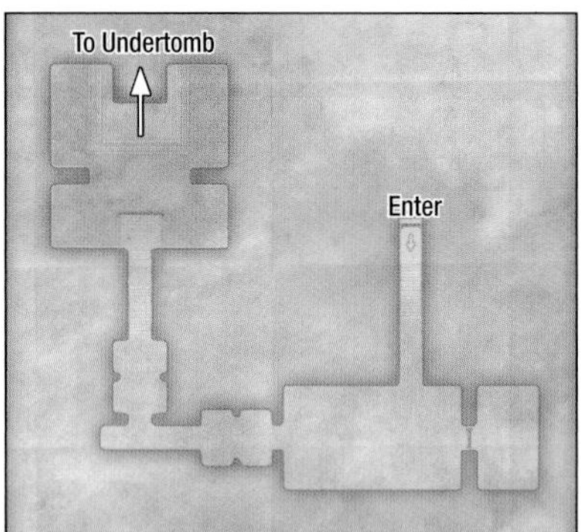

Velothi Ancestral Tomb Level 1 (Initial Chambers)

Interior Level 1 (Initial Chambers): This area is a dead end without Narsis Dren, whom you befriend during **Quest: Ancestral Adversity** over at the Dreloth Ancestral Tomb in Azura's Coast region. The locked door requires a wall panel to be pushed. Follow Narsis to the engraved pedestal in the prayer chamber (northwest) and complete the offering puzzle. Consult the quest for the answer.

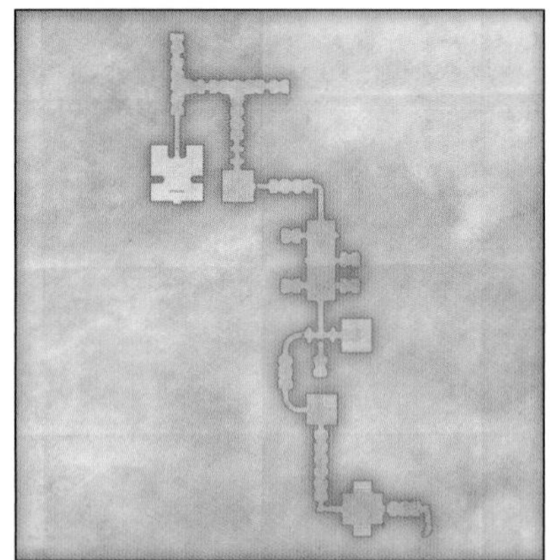

Velothi Ancestral Tomb Level 2 (Veloth Undertomb)

Interior Level 2 (Veloth Undertomb): This is only accessible during the quest. The initial chambers involve ridding the area of Wraiths and Bone Flayers. The second part of the level (Undertomb Mausoleums) features a room with traps, and a long burial chamber with an assortment of revolting foes. After you slay them, unlock Narsis at the room to the left (east). The third part of the level (Mausoleums of the Elders) contains more skeletal foes and Wraiths, a passage of traps, and a floor puzzle to unlock.

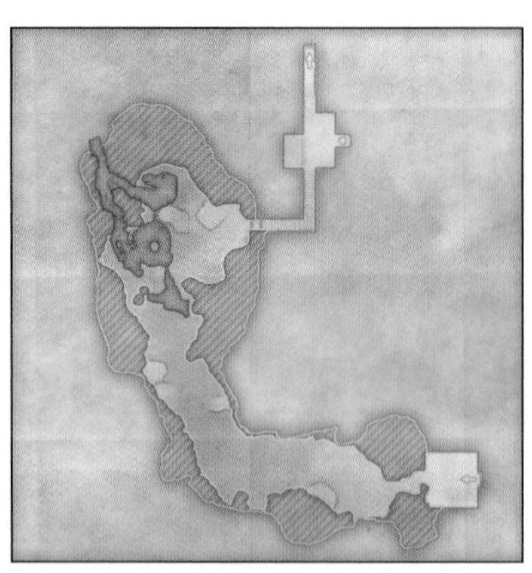

Velothi Ancestral Tomb Level 3 (Tomb of the Matriarch)

Interior Level 3 (Tomb of the Matriarch): The lowest level of the tomb features a rugged cave system with Skeletons and Shrooms. The second part of the level (Treasure Vault) features stairs to the vault, and an exit back to the upper level. Of course, before you get there, Matriarch Rathila, a gigantic skeletal beast, rises from the mire to slaughter you!

16 ASHIMANU CAVE

Entities:	Kwama, Kwama Queen
Related Quest:	Ancestral Ties

An unassuming mine shaft from the outside, this grotto is where Wild Kwama lurk, and the going gets increasingly slow as you intrude on the nests of the Kwama Queen in the northern interior passage end. Come here during the quest for a specific item.

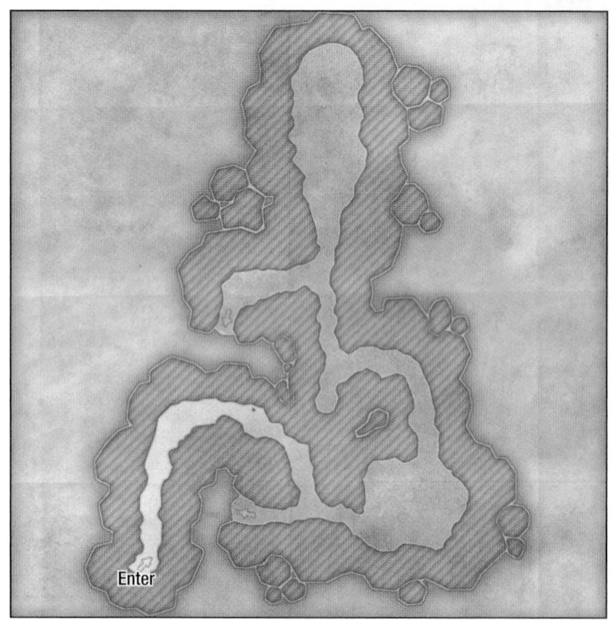

Ashimanu Cave (Upper)

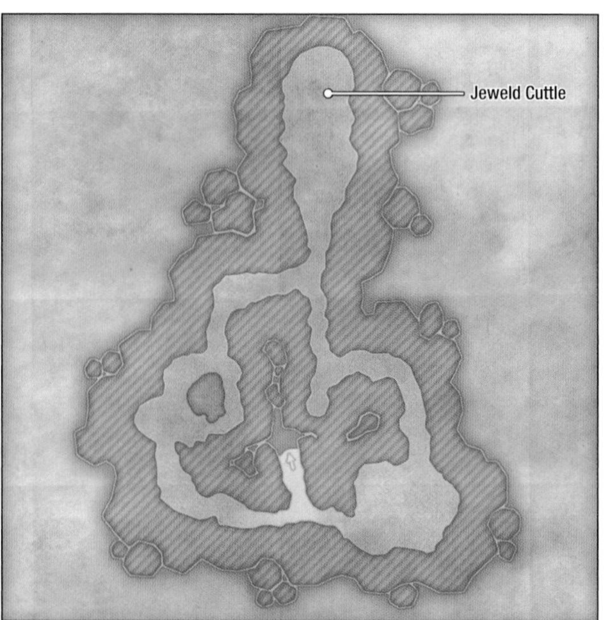

Ashimanu Cave (Lower)

17 WEST GASH WAYSHRINE

Area of Interest:	Wayshrine

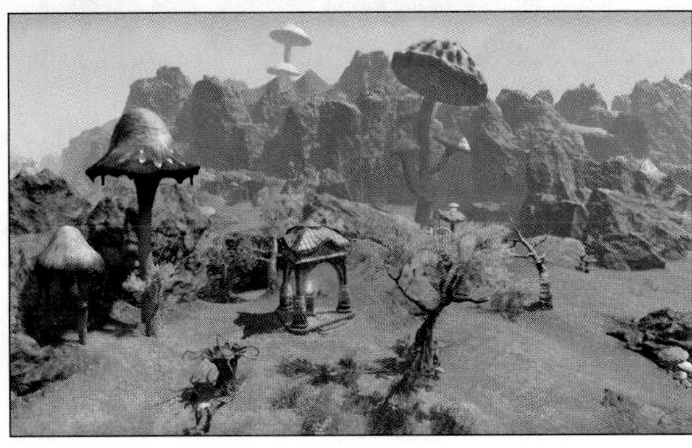

Head here to travel to the middle of West Gash, close to a number of primary locations as well as the Salothran Ancestral Tomb rubbing.

18 RANDAS ANCESTRAL TOMB

Crafting:	Crafting Stations (Sets)

If you wish to craft items and equipment of Daedric Trickery, head into this small ancestral tomb, which is devoid of entities except those seeking crafting perfection.

19 ULARRA

Area of Interest:	Battleground
Merchant:	Urbalash

Come here to try your skills at facing others in combat. There's an Orc Merchant outside, selling some pretty sweet equipment (Battlefield Elite).

20 KHARTAG POINT

Area of Interest:	Skyshard
Entities:	Camonna Tong, Dreugh, Netch, Red Exile, River Trolls
Item of Interest:	Vivec Sermons
Related Quest:	A Smuggler's Last Stand

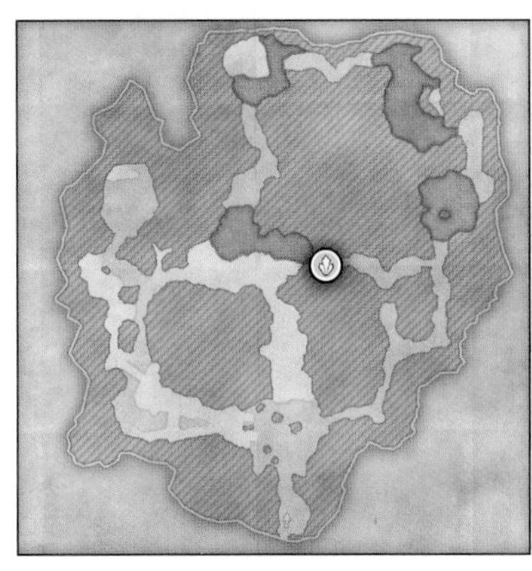

Skyshard

This Dunmer stronghold is currently under the command of a ragtag band of Red Exile ne'er-do-wells, though there's a second, more interesting side to this place—a smuggler's cave underneath the main stronghold, on the edge of the region boundary.

The topside area consists of half a dozen Red Exile tents, over a dozen foes, and further enemies around and atop the stone structure. The stronghold is inaccessible.

The smuggling cave features a small band of Dunmer assassins (the Camonna Tong), a Vivec Sermon **(#13)**, and an Orc named Nakhul to start the listed quest.

Interior: This is a collection of narrow and watery tunnels, many with Camonna Tong foes. Watch for River Trolls, Netch, and Dreugh farther into this cave system. Be on the lookout for a skyshard at the end of a narrow tunnel; you need to be on the western area near a pool to reach the passage that accesses it.

21 RED EXILE CAMP

Entities:	Red Exile

The far western edge of the large volcanic dip in this part of the region houses a group of tents, and a few Red Exile foes to meet and beat.
Check the area for a couple of collectibles.

22 HLERAN ANCESTRAL TOMB

Entities:	Hleran Guards (Specters)
Related Quest:	Ancestral Ties

Across the lava pool is an ancestral tomb that's difficult to both spot and reach. Inside, the ghosts of this Dunmer family are pondering the lava flows infiltrating their sanctum.

Interior: The interior features a couple of Spectral foes from the Hleran House in every chamber. Continue to explore until you reach the door to the second part of the tomb (Dranoth's Ancestral Tomb). Here you conclude the quest, providing it's active.

23 ALD'RUHN WAYSHRINE

Area of Interest:	Wayshrine
Related Quest:	(VV6) Ancestral Ties

On the path to Ald'Ruhn is a Wayshrine and a vantage point. There's a treasure chest and a quest to start, providing previous quests of this type have been completed.

24 ALD'RUHN

Crafting:	Cooking Fire
Entities:	Ashlander Guards, Guar, Red Exile, Gulakhan Yus-Zashten (Boss)
Item of Interest:	Lorebook (The Grave of Skar)
Merchant:	Vasamannu
Related Quest:	(VV6) Ancestral Ties, (R1) Daily Relic Preservation, (R2) Daily Beast Hunt

Amid the clouds of ash and rivers of lava is a collection of Redoran-esque structures hiding in the shadow of Red Mountain. The main structure owes its curious shape to the fact that it's the hollowed-out remains of a gargantuan land crab, Skar.

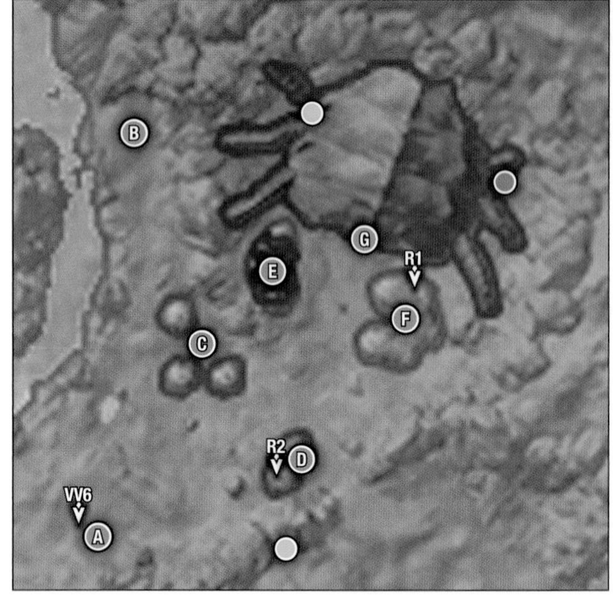

Quest		Treasure Chest	
Thieves Trove		Location	

A Ald-Ruhn Wayshrine

The outskirts of the settlement has a Wayshrine, detailed in an adjacent Atlas location.

B Small Shrine

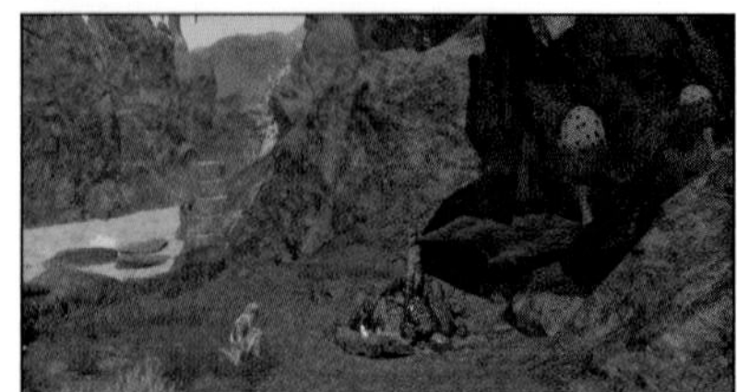

Ashlanders pray to this small grave shrine, where minor loot can be found.

C Guar Pens

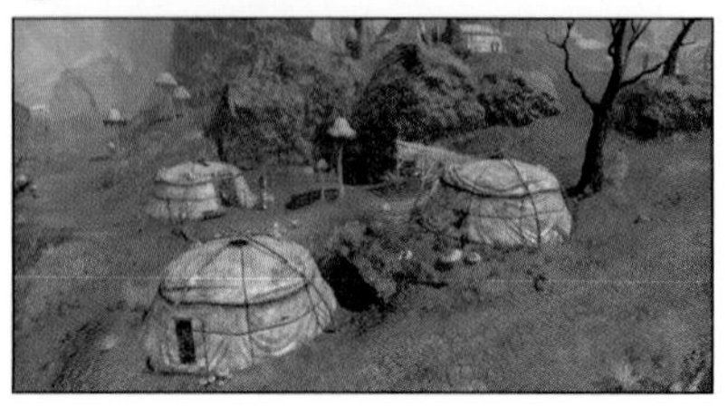

The Ashlanders are justly proud of their Guar-rearing, and the pens here are a testament to this.

Ⓓ Ashlander Outer Tents

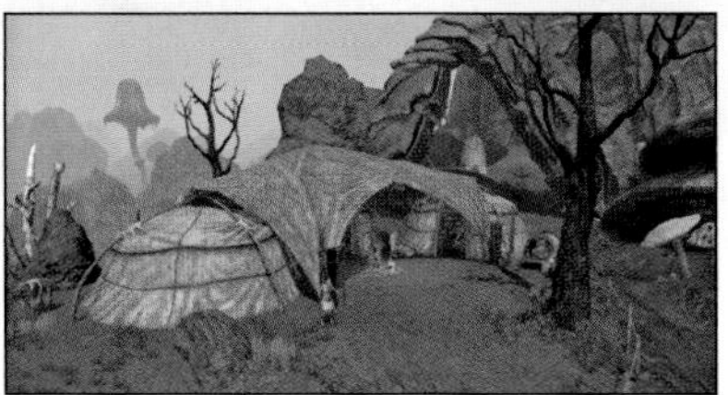

A group of Ashlanders stays here, in case of attack from the south. You can find a campfire and trader here.

Ⓔ Ashlander Prayer Circle (West)

A Lorebook is hidden inside one of the finely spun tents to the left (west) of the prayer circle.

Ⓕ Ashlander Wise Woman's Hut

The eastern side of the prayer circle has a number of tents dotted around, and one leads to Wise Woman Dovrosi's Hut. Seek her out during questing.

Ⓖ Skar

A large unders-Skar and main structure is not accessed until **Quest: Divine Delusions**, where an epic battle is fought. Note the interior map below.

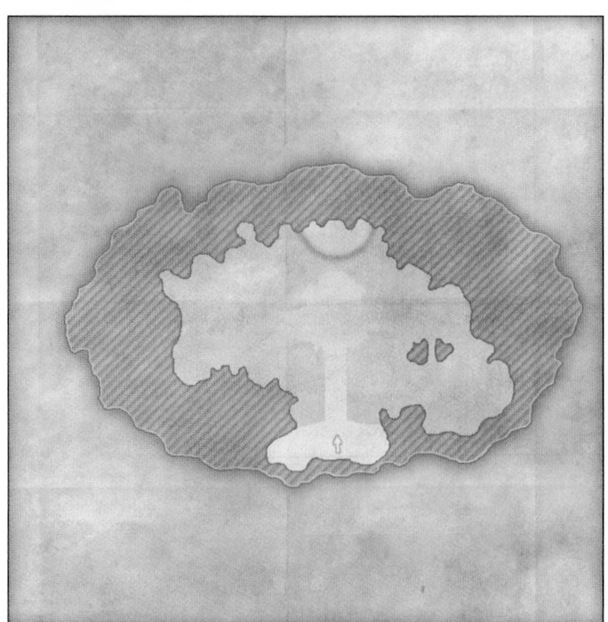

Ald'Ruhr: Skar

25 MALLAPI CAVE BACK TUNNELS

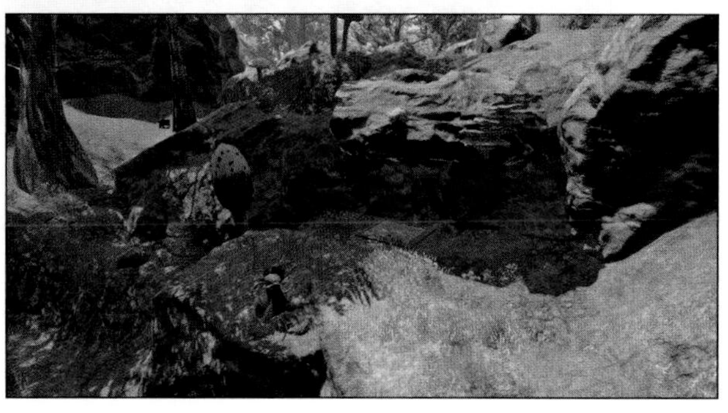

This trapdoor hidden under a rocky outcrop allows access to Mallapi Cave in the Bitter Coast region. Refer to that location for more details.

26 RAMIMILK

Entities:	Flame Atronachs
Item of Interest:	Stone of Ramimilk
Related Quest:	At Any Cost

Take the path from Ald'ruhn, or scramble here via other means, to view this Shrine to Molag Bal. Snuff the life from a couple of Flame Atronachs before investigating the interior of this Daedric temple.

Interior: As you'd expect, given the topography, a good amount of lava threatens the shrine. Also of interest is a large stone, and some Dunmer scholars in the vicinity, related to the quest.

27 RED EXILE TENT

Entities:	Red Exile

Guarding a hefty Heavy Sack, this motley Dunmer duo are of little threat. It's the larger congregation of Warclaws to the southwest you need worry about.

28 KUDANAT MINE

Entities:	Warclaws, Wormmouths
Item of Interest:	House Redoran Orders
Related Quest:	Of Faith and Family

A band of Warclaws is currently camped at this slaver hideaway and mine. Expect half a dozen tents both big and small, and a sizable band of furry foes to contend with. The mine requires a key, found in the tent closest to the entrance, during the quest.

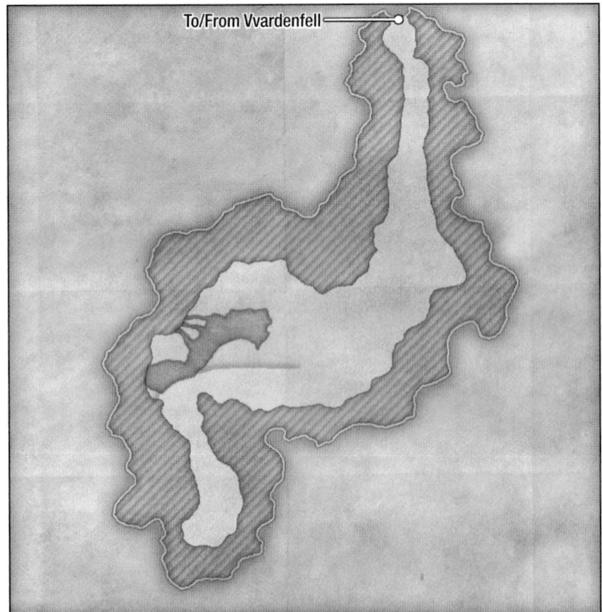

Interior: The mine tunnel descends and opens into a natural cavern, where quest objectives are met, as well as two beefy Warclaw foes.

29 REDORAN GARRISON

Entities:	Guars, Warclaws
Related Quest:	Family Reunion

This imposing fortification is now in the hands of the Warclaws. Enter via the outer wall, and via the steps to the upper door. It's worth exploring this during the quest.

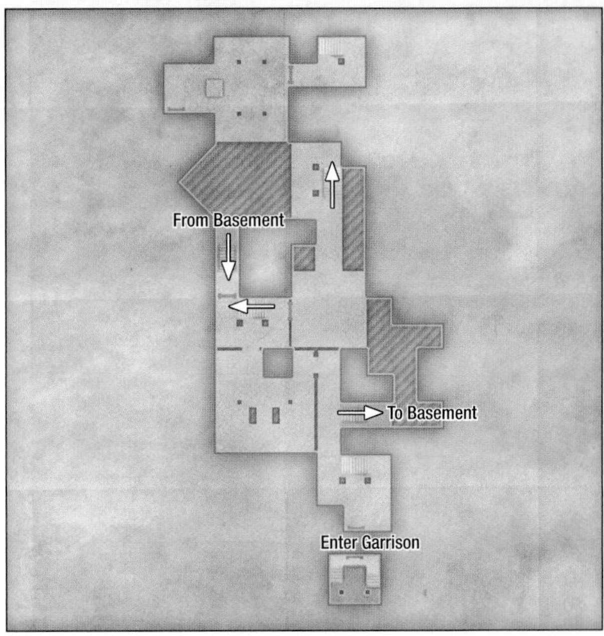

Redoran Garrison Interior 1 (First Floor)

Interior 1 (Redoran Garrison): Come through this entrance hallway to reach the Garrison Chambers.

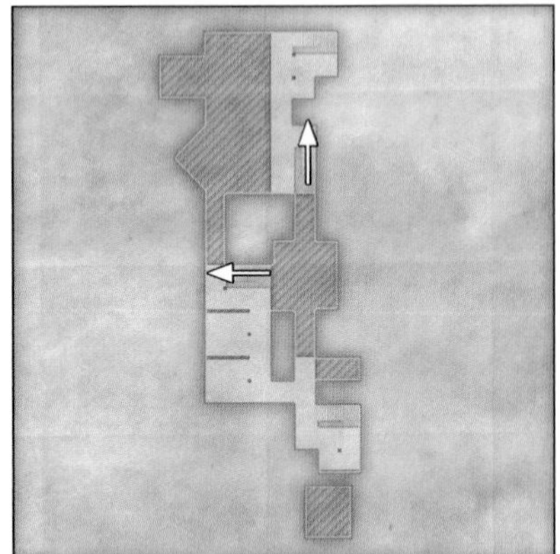

Redoran Garrison Interior 2 (Second Floor)

Interior 1 (Garrison Chambers and Kitchens): This is the main area, with stairs up at the north and south ends, and a large hallway with stairs to the cellar in the middle. A big kitchen area is to the northwest (the middle of the adjacent map), with doors at the foot of the north stairs to the Garrison Meeting Hall, and the exit door from the Cellar (approach from below).

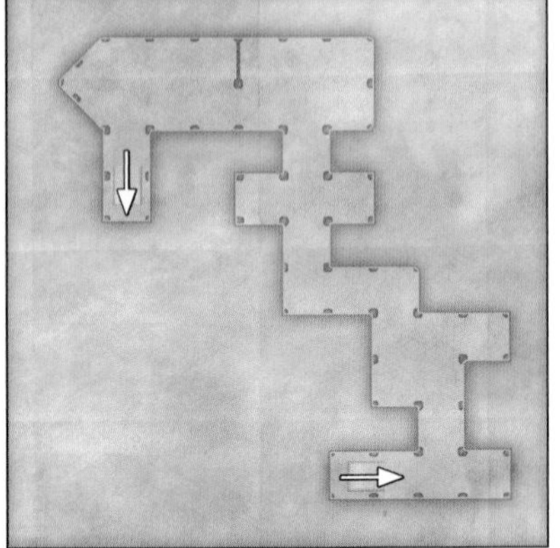

Redoran Garrison Interior 3 (Cellar Basement)

Interior 1 (Garrison Meeting Hall): Only accessible during the quest, expect a council meeting to degenerate into blind, ugly violence. Three hardened Warclaws are here. Head from the main chamber to a hallway with stairs leading up.

Interior 2 (Upstairs): Accessed via either set of steps from below, a large landing library and two impressive bedchambers can be explored.

Interior 1 and 2 (Garrison Meeting Hall): Access this area during the quest. The main hall is reached from upstairs, and a fight into the main meeting chamber is necessary.

Interior 3 (Cellar): Head here from the stairs down from the Garrison Chambers, and weave through a series of connecting storage rooms and Warclaw fights. Exit up to the Kitchens, or head out from the Inner Halls during the quest.

30 NILTHOG'S HOLLOW

Entities:	Nix-Hounds, Nilthog the Unbroken (Nix-Ox)
Area of Interest:	Group Boss

A beast both ferocious and disgusting lurks inside this natural arena. Bring friends to finish the Nix-Ox and its minions.

31 ASSARNATAMAT

Entities:	Brigands

Here's another shrine to a Daedric deity, this one to Mehrunes Dagon. A group of brigands makes their home here. Introduce them to the afterlife if you wish, but watch your step, as lava oozes everywhere. The interior of this location is inaccessible. Come here for the Heavy Sack and Thieves Trove.

32 BOUNDARY BRIDGE

Entities:	Brigands

To the east of Balmora, running along the southeastern edge of this region, is a long canyon crossed by an impressive bridge. The bridge leads from Balmora to the Dwemer ruin of Arkngthand (in the Ascadian Isles region). Both are inaccessible; use the canyon as an alternate north-south route.

33 BALMORA

Crafting:	Cooking Fire (2)
Area of Interest:	Silt Strider
Entities:	House Guards, Ordinator Guards, Redoran
Item of Interest:	Lorebook (The Truth in Sequence: Volume 2), Vivec Sermon
Merchant:	Traveling Merchant Fanisea Saram, Mystic Tends-All-Things, Innkeeper Carellon, Caravaner Nevos Sareloth, Hall Steward Delte Nethri, Stablemaster Nothas Vules, Guild Trader Ginette Malarelie, Guild Trader Mahrahdr, Guild Trader Narril, Magister Vilyn Veleth
Related Quest:	(VV9) The Memory Stone, (MT1) Fleeing the Past, (MT2) Of Faith and Family, (MT3) A Purposeful Writ, (MT4) Family Reunion

This imposing and grand city is the seat of House Hlaalu, and the second city to Vivec. Translated to "Forest of Stone" in Dunmeri, this fortress-like settlement is bisected by the River Odai, and is perhaps the best place for Merchants and quests outside of Vivec City.

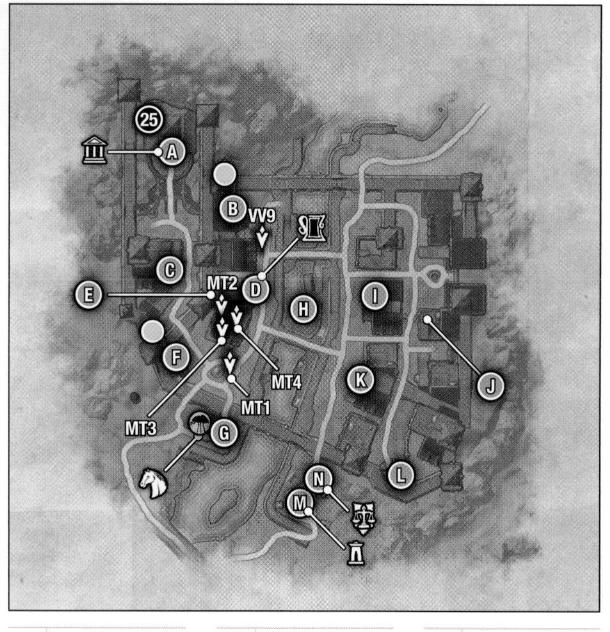

Quest		Stable		Location	
Treasure Chest		Museum		Vivic Sermon	
Silt Strider		Guild Kiosk			
Inn		Wayshrine			

(A) Balmora Tribunal Temple

This location is worth exploring if you wish to speak to the Mystic or obtain the Vivec Sermon tome **(#25)** on a table inside. There's a Lorebook on a bench here, too.

(B) Lerano's House

This is the home of the well-to-do Gilan Lerano. You visit here if you undertake his quest.

Ⓒ Redoran Kinhouse

Initially sealed, this dwelling only becomes accessible with questing.

Ⓓ The Randy Netch Inn

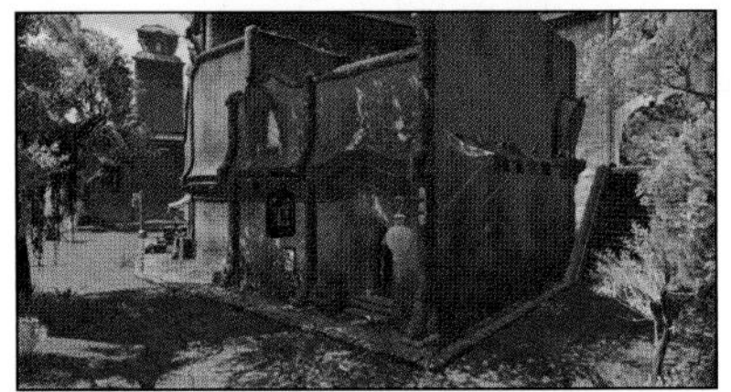

Visit this watering hole to speak and trade with the Innkeeper, and use the cooking stove. There's bound to be some rumor and scuttlebutt if you ask the right people.

Ⓔ Abandoned Cellar

In an alleyway behind the inn, there's a trapdoor down to a hidden cellar where assassins congregate, providing the appropriate quest is active.

Ⓕ Fighters Guild Merchant

If you need to trade or join this organization, visit the vendor at the tent here.

Ⓖ Balmora Stable Gate

Close to the Silt Strider and caravan tower, these stables house a number of Guar rather than horses. Speak to the Stablemaster if you wish.

Ⓗ River Odai

The center of town is bisected north to south by the River Odai. Note the two bridges, and perimeter walls keeping the inhabitants safe.

Ⓘ Retheran's House

Warning: | **Restricted Area (Trespass)**

This locked abode requires you to unlock the door (Advanced difficulty), and snooping around gets you in trouble. This is a large townhouse, with a Safebox in the bedroom.

Ⓙ Rethan's House

This abode is locked up tight and can't be entered unless a relevant quest is active.

Ⓚ Lod Drono's Townhouse

Warning: | **Restricted Area (Trespass)**

After unlocking (Simple difficulty), you can creep around this dwelling, incurring the wrath of the inhabitants, Redoran fighters.

Ⓛ Cooking Fire

This area contains an open-air kitchen, wine cellar, and alley with a small Cooking Fire.

Ⓜ Balmora Wayshrine

This Wayshrine is detailed elsewhere in this Atlas.

Ⓝ Balmora Market Gate

Stalls are erected, and there's plenty of merchandise on offer here, thanks to three Guild Traders. Magister Vilyn Veleth is also present.

34 BALMORA WAYSHRINE

Area of Interest: | **Wayshrine**

Should you wish to easily reach this city, utilize the Wayshrine at the south edge of the settlement, close to the Ascadian Isle region.

ASCADIAN ISLES

Perhaps the most picturesque, and certainly the most majestic region of Vvardenfell, the floodplain and irrigation make the area around Vivec City perfect for farming and other agricultural pursuits. Plantations and farmsteads are dotted through the landscape, many utilizing Argonian labor. Northwest is the town of Suran, famed for its market, but the main reason to visit the Ascadian Isles is to view the spectacular Vivec City, with a temple to a living god, and a place for pilgrimages to begin.

ASCADIAN ISLES—OVERVIEW AND COLLECTIBLES

ASCADIAN ISLES—QUESTS

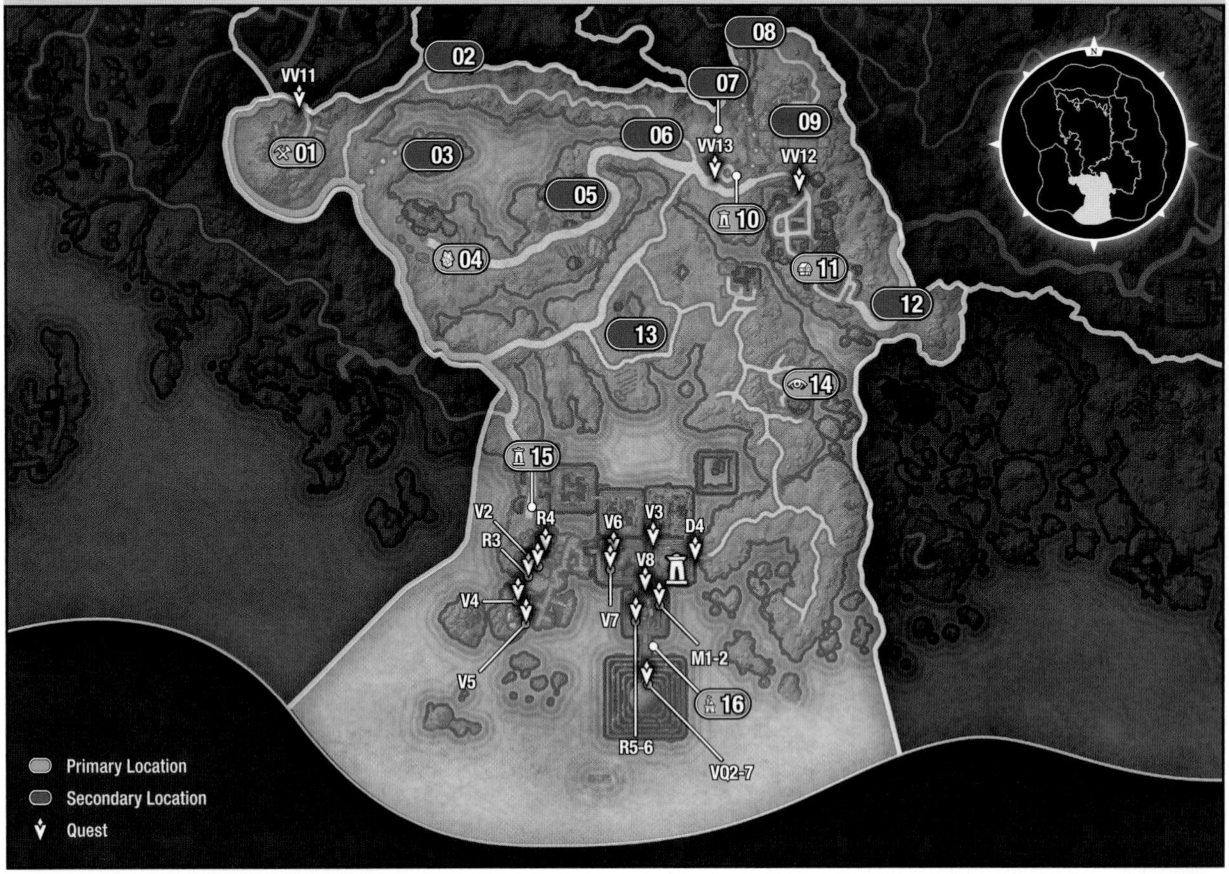

Primary Location
Secondary Location
Quest

ASCADIAN ISLES—FISHING

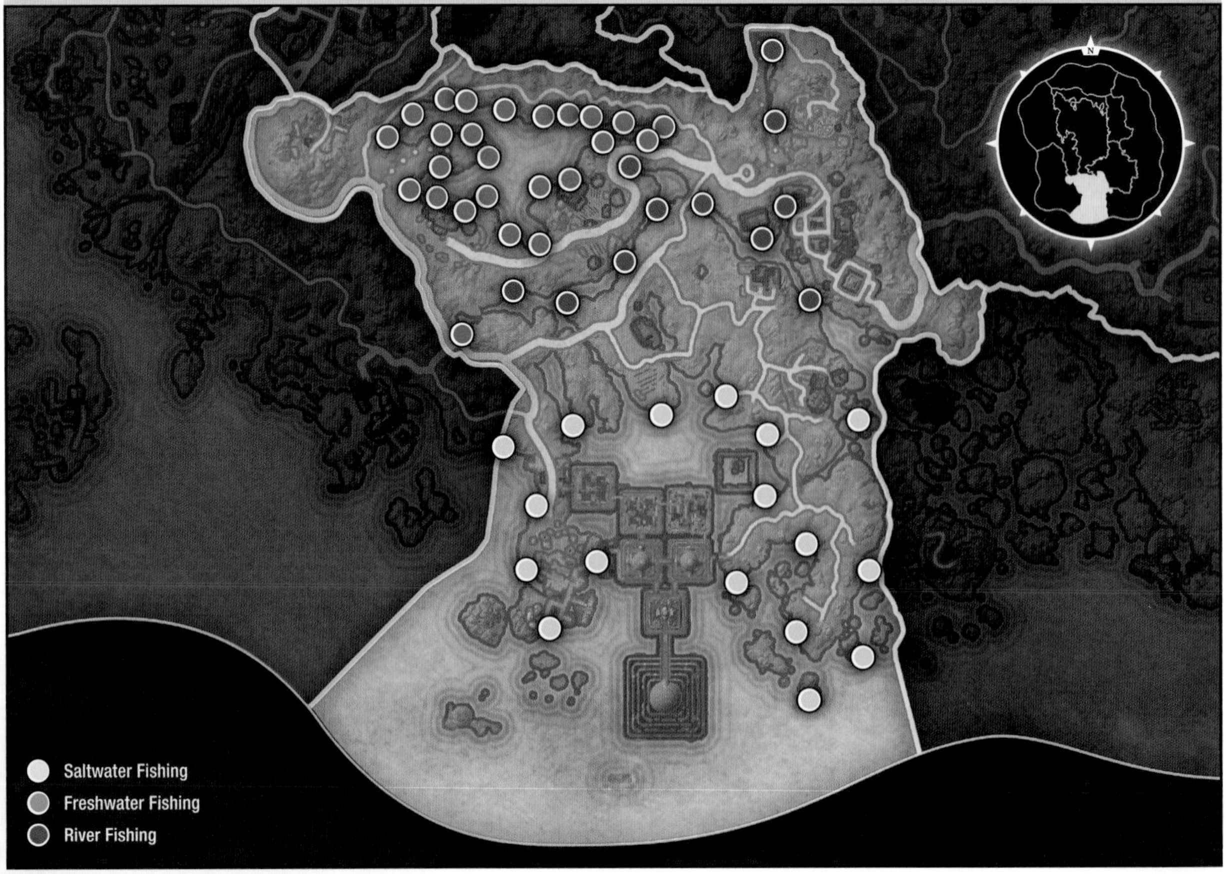

Saltwater Fishing
Freshwater Fishing
River Fishing

Locations

01	Vassir-Didanat Mine	07	Ruined Ancestral Tomb	13	Master Kharekh's Residence
02	Foyada Quarry (INACCESSIBLE) (Arkngthand)	08	Quarry Bridge and Dam	14	Ald Sotha
03	Fishing Lodge	09	Bal Ur	15	Vivec City Wayshrine
04	Amaya Lake Manor	10	Suran Wayshrine	16	Vivec City
05	Mistress Dren's Residence	11	Suran		
06	Amaya Lake Docks	12	Inanius Egg Mine		

01 VASSIR-DIDANAT MINE

Entities:	**Iron Hounds, Stonefiends**
Related Quest:	**Like Blood from a Stone**

Once the necessary keys have been acquired during the quest, you're free to explore this mine, now under the jurisdiction of the Iron Hound gang of Dunmer reprobates. The exterior has a number of wooden platforms, so expect archers. There's also access into West Gash, via the northern exit into the Boundary Bridge canyon.

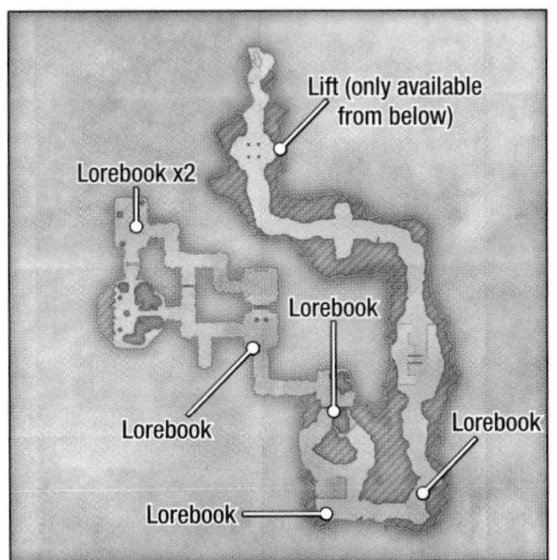

Vassir-Didanat Mine Interior 1 (Ebony Mine and Daedric Laboratory)

Interior 1 (Vassir-Didanat Ebony Mine): The mine tunnel is easy to follow, though the unpleasant gas leaks and Stonefiends become more of a problem the deeper you go. As you head deeper, a Daedric shrine is uncovered, along with further Stonefiends and gas. Pass the statue of Clavicus Vile, to the Daedric Laboratory.

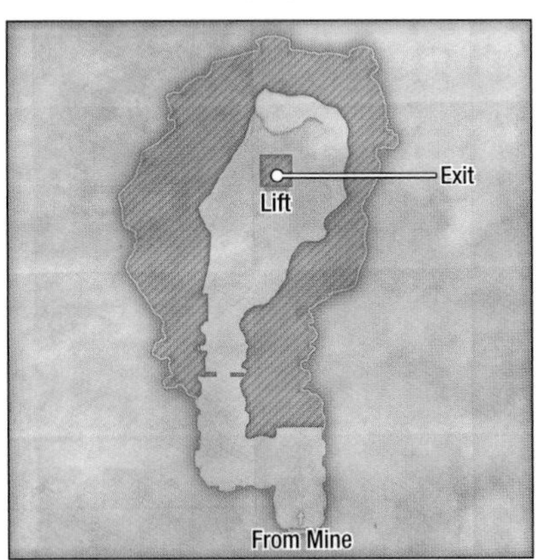

Vassir-Didanat Mine Interior 2 (Lift Room)

Interior 1 (Daedric Laboratory): The second part of this underground area is a gas-filled Daedric Laboratory, with access to the lift room.

Interior 2 (Lift Room): A rickety mine lift allows easy access to the mine exit.

02 FOYADA QUARRY (INACCESSIBLE) (ARKNGTHAND)

This wooden barricade wall sits at the foot of the old Dwemer ruins of Arkngthand, and is impassable. To access the nearby Foyada Quarry Battleground, head to the Molag Amur region.

03 FISHING LODGE

Item of Interest:	**Vivec Sermon**

Inside this small fishing hut, near a Fishing Hole off Lake Amaya, is a Cooking Fire, as well as a Vivec Sermon **(#21)**. Ooh, is that a sweetroll?

04 AMAYA LAKE MANOR

Area of Interest:	**Homestead**

Close to the idyllic lake of the same name, this impressive manor house with a large walled courtyard garden can be yours for the correct amount of crowns or gold! Think of the potential here! Plus, you're close to Vivec City for travel and goods.

05 MISTRESS DREN'S RESIDENCE

Entities:	Iron Hounds
Related Quest:	The Scarlet Judge

The Iron Hounds currently claim this manor and grounds as their own. Inside, most of the house belonging to the famed botanist and bamboo-grower is on the upper floor, with an exit to exterior stairs up to Mistress Dren's bed quarters, and an upper exit with splendid views of the lake and grounds. Search the area throughout for two Heavy Sacks and a Thieves Trove.

06 AMAYA LAKE DOCKS

The far western side of the lake is just south of the pathway that heads west to the Sarano Ancestral Tomb rubbing. This seemingly peaceful spot offers a Fishing Hole. Find the minor collectibles around here—a Heavy Sack and Thieves Trove.

07 RUINED ANCESTRAL TOMB

Entities:	Guar

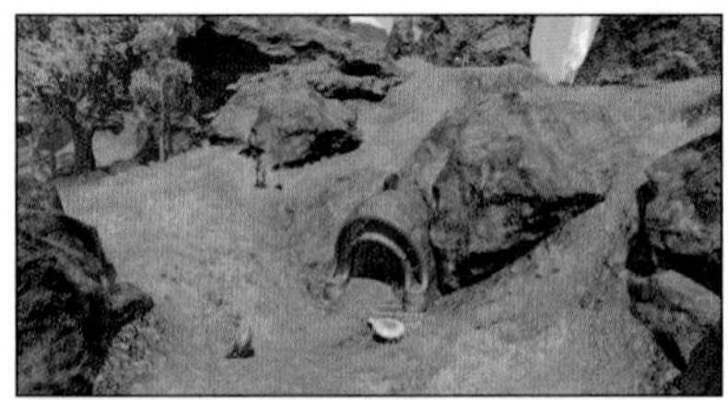

A rubble-strewn entrance to a long-forgotten tomb is cut into the hillside just north of the Suran Wayshrine. It's inaccessible.

08 QUARRY BRIDGE AND DAM

This small and shallow dam across the Nabia River, with winch equipment sitting on a wooden bridge, is manned by a couple of Dunmer. It's east of Marandas in Molag Amur, and is a good landmark to use as the boundary between regions.

09 BAL UR

Entities:	Clannfear, Iron Hounds, Scamps, Phylaraak
Items of Interest:	Mages Guild Book (Kwama Mining for Fun and Profit), Stone of Bal Ur
Related Quest:	The Scarlet Judge, At Any Cost

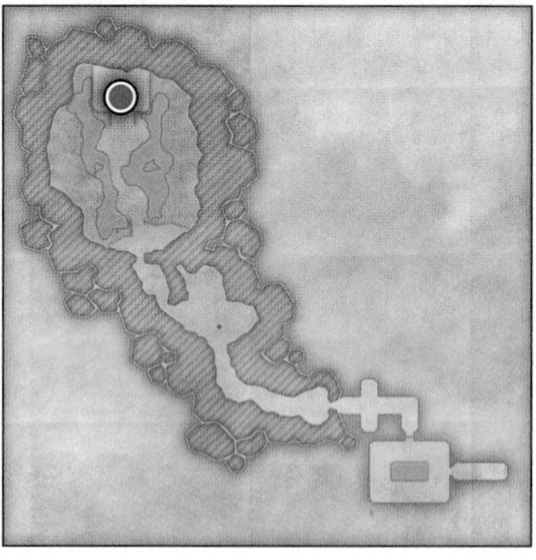

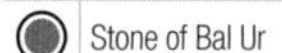 Stone of Bal Ur

The Iron Hounds have taken over this ancient Daedric Shrine to Molag Bal, on the edge of the Nabia River. There's a Mages Guild book, as well as a Thieves Trove and Heavy Sack. You burn and smash the Iron Hounds' equipment during **Quest: The Scarlet Judge**. Don't overlook the interior door on the eastern edge near the region boundary cliff wall.

Interior 1 (Bal Ur): Inside are steps to a sacrificial lava hall, where the Iron Hounds have a small barracks. Access the door to the north to reach the Underground.

Interior 1 (Bal Ur Underground): The Iron Hound foes give way to more Daedric opponents, and the shrine becomes a gigantic lava chamber with a fearsome central cliff path up to the fabled Stone of Bal Ur, and an encounter with the floating tendrils of Phylaraak.

10 SURAN WAYSHRINE

Area of Interest:	Wayshrine
Related Quest:	The Scarlet Judge

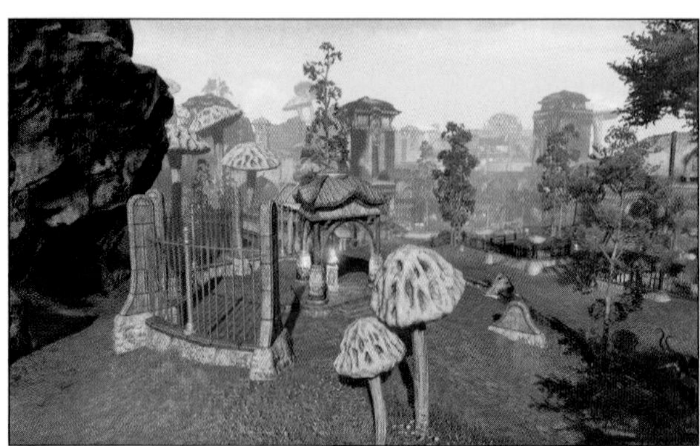

Should your travels need to be quickened, seek this Wayshrine on the western edge of Suran town. Note the nearby quest that commences after speaking to a Dunmer in need.

11 SURAN

Area of Interest:	Silt Strider
Crafting:	Cooking Fire
Entities:	House Guards, Iron Hounds, Nix-Oxen, Ordinator Guards
Item of Interest:	Lorebook (Blessed Almalexia's Fables for Morning), Lorebook (Brave Little Scrib Song), Lorebook (Drunken Aphorisms), Lorebook (The Truth in Sequence: Volume 3), Mages Guild Book (Invocation of Azura), Vivec Sermon (3)
Merchant:	Caravaner Faven Thendas, Mivanu Neleth, Alchemist Faldiniel, Innkeeper Dovyn Trandel

Suran is a market town and landmark settlement on the edge of the Ascadian Isles and Molag Amur regions. Hlaalu slavers are known to be active in these parts, and there's a sizable prison here as well as merriment at a local tavern for the locals. From here, pilgrims set off toward Mount Kand and the rough wilderness of Molag Amur.

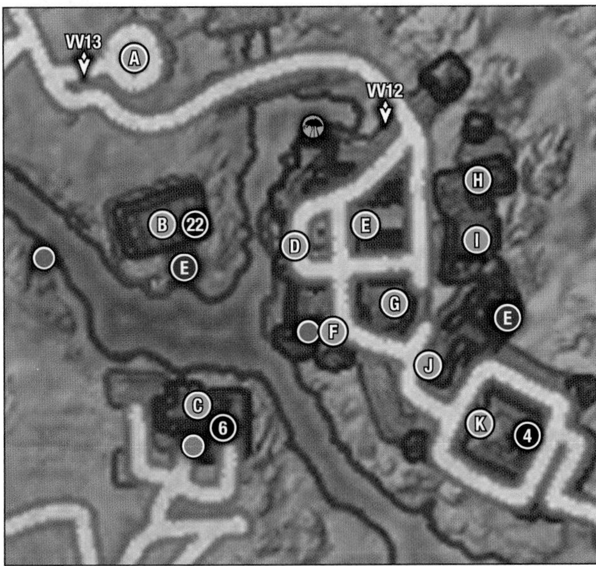

Quest	Thieves Trove
Silt Strider	Treasure Chest
Heavy Sack	Vivec Sermon
Mages Guild Lorebook	

(A) Suran Wayshrine

Find this Wayshrine on the northern outskirts of town. It's detailed in the previous Atlas entry.

(B) Ules Manor

This well-to-do manor house and farmland sits just west of the main town. Head inside to inspect the impressive splendor the local lord lives in. Obtain a Vivec Sermon from a side table inside, and a Mages Guild book outside on the dock area.

(C) Iron Hound Manor

The Iron Hound Clan are active at this manor, which is inaccessible, though there's a Vivec Sermon to be found in the exterior courtyard.

(D) Suran Market and Docks

The majority of the Merchants you find at this town ply their wares here. Come here for general merchandise and alchemy items.

(E) Farano's Boarding House

There's a Lorebook on a bench outside this large dwelling. Come in via either entrance, and gather a second Lorebook inside. This is a place for a rest and a bath.

(F) Keymaker's Tower

A set of vertical chambers inside this tower leads to Remas Belan's private quarters.

(G) Desele's House of Earthly Delights

A favored tavern in these parts, you can purchase from an Innkeeper, and grab a Lorebook in the kitchens.

(H) Suran Prison

Warning:	Restricted Area (Trespass)

Enter here at your discretion, as you'll be trespassing into a prison with a sizable jail dungeon. Hireling guards aren't pleased by your intrusion.

Ⓘ Ralaal's House

Warning:	Restricted Area (Trespass)

There are three entrances to this dwelling, and all are locked (Intermediate difficulty). Inside, the residents aren't too pleased by your intrusion.

Ⓙ Menaldinion's Clinic

Keeping the townsfolk safe from the pox, this clinic features Menaldinion himself, as well as a Cooking Fire.

Ⓚ Suran Temple

Guarded by Ordinators, this sacred place is worth exploring for the Lorebook and the Vivec Sermon, both on the ground floor.

012 INANIUS EGG MINE

Entities:	Iron Hounds, Kwama, Marshall Hlaren
Related Quest:	The Scarlet Judge

Close to the Velas and Releth Ancestral Tomb rubbings, on the backside of Suran, is an unassuming mine entrance. It's only accessible during the aforementioned quest.

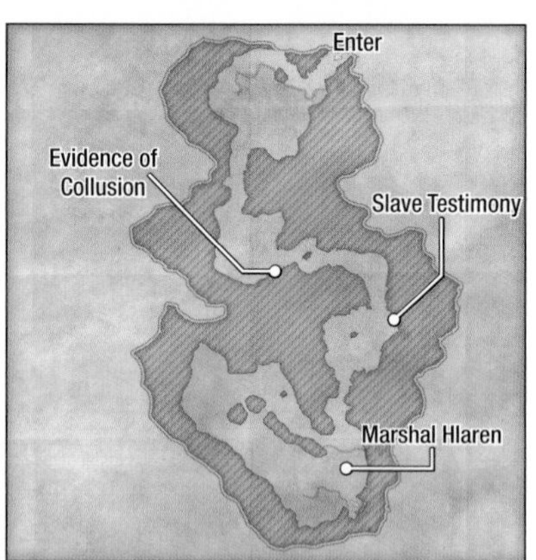

Interior: Inside, work your way down the rugged path of this immense mining cavern, slaughtering Kwama near their nests. There are Iron Hounds, and a significant quest-related individual to confront in the lowest part of this mine. The exit in the southeast wall brings you out to the entrance area.

13 MASTER KHAREKH'S RESIDENCE

Entities:	Iron Hounds
Related Quest:	The Scarlet Judge

A small farmstead just outside the town of Suran features a field of wheat and a residence by the river. Note the smattering of collectibles in and around the location, including a Vivec Sermon **(#11)** inside.

14 ALD SOTHA

Entities:	Clannfears, Fiendroths, Scamps, Hungers
Item of Interest:	Vivec Sermon

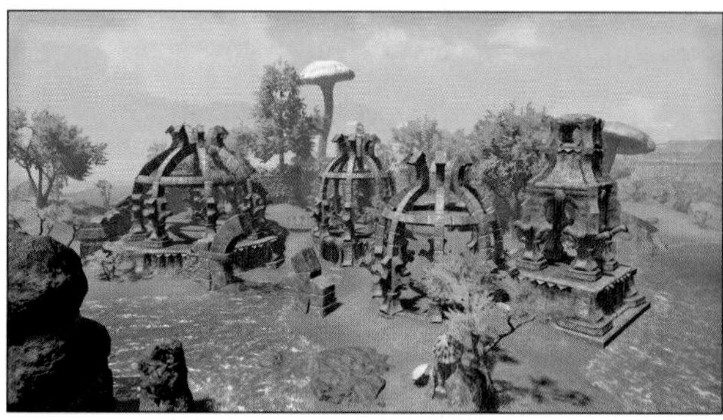

Set on a peninsula northeast of Vivec City, this sprawling Shrine to Mehrunes Dagon is among the biggest on Vvardenfell. Currently, it's home to a variety of Daedric minions. Though the interior cannot be accessed, there's a treasure chest and, more importantly, a Vivec Sermon **(#24)** on the western side of the rocky outcrop, just outside the ruins.

15 VIVEC CITY WAYSHRINE

Area of Interest:	Wayshrine

Adjacent to the Silt Strider, and close to the region border with the Bitter Coast, this Wayshrine is on the northwest edge of Vvardenfell's sprawling capital city.

16 VIVEC CITY

Area of Interest:	Homestead, Port City, Silt Strider
Entities:	Buoyant Armigers, Guar, House Guard, Kagouti
Items of Interest:	Lorebook (On Moving Ebonheart), Lorebook (Ordinators: A Comprehensive Guide), Lorebook (Testimonials on Baar Dau), Lorebook (The Truth in Sequence: Volume 1), Vivec Sermon (3)
Location:	Port City
Related Quest:	(D4) Echoes of a Fallen House, (M1) The Ancestral Tombs, (M2) The Lost Library, (R3) Consumable Crafting Writs, (R4) Equipment Crafting Writs, (R5) Group Boss Daily Quest, (R6) A Friend in Need, (V2) A Late Delivery, (V3) For Glory!, (V4) To Tel Fyr, (V5) Crafting Certifications, (V6) A Call for Aid, (V7) Delve Daily Quest, (V8) Divine Conundrum, (VQ2) Divine Inquiries, (VQ3) Divine Delusions, (VQ4) Divine Interventions, (VQ5) Divine Disaster, (VQ6) Divine Restoration, (VQ7) Divine Blessings

The largest city on Vvardenfell, Vivec City resides on the southern coast of the island and comprises a series of island "cantons"—pyramid-like structures that are specific districts. The largest of these cantons is the palace where the Living God Vivec is said to dwell.

Note that due to the large number of locations in this city, Merchants and crafting stations are flagged in the specific locations where they appear.

(A) Entrance: Pilgrim's Approach

Merchant:	Caravan Its[XXX], Stablemaster Drel Trandel, Boatswain Synda Imyam

Travelers reach Vivec City via the path from the Bitter Coast, Silt Strider, or by boat. You can do the same, or set off to other large settlements from this point.

(B) Vivec City Wayshrine (1 of 2)

This Wayshrine is detailed previously in the Atlas. It sits at the entrance to Pilgrim's Market.

(C) Pilgrim's Market

Merchant:	Guild Trader Atazha, Guild Trader Jena Calvus, Guild Trader Lorthodaer, Guild Trader Mauhoth, Guild Trader Rinami, Guild Trader Sebastian Brutya

This is the place for purchasing an impressive array of quality items, as it has the widest assortment of anywhere in Vvardenfell.

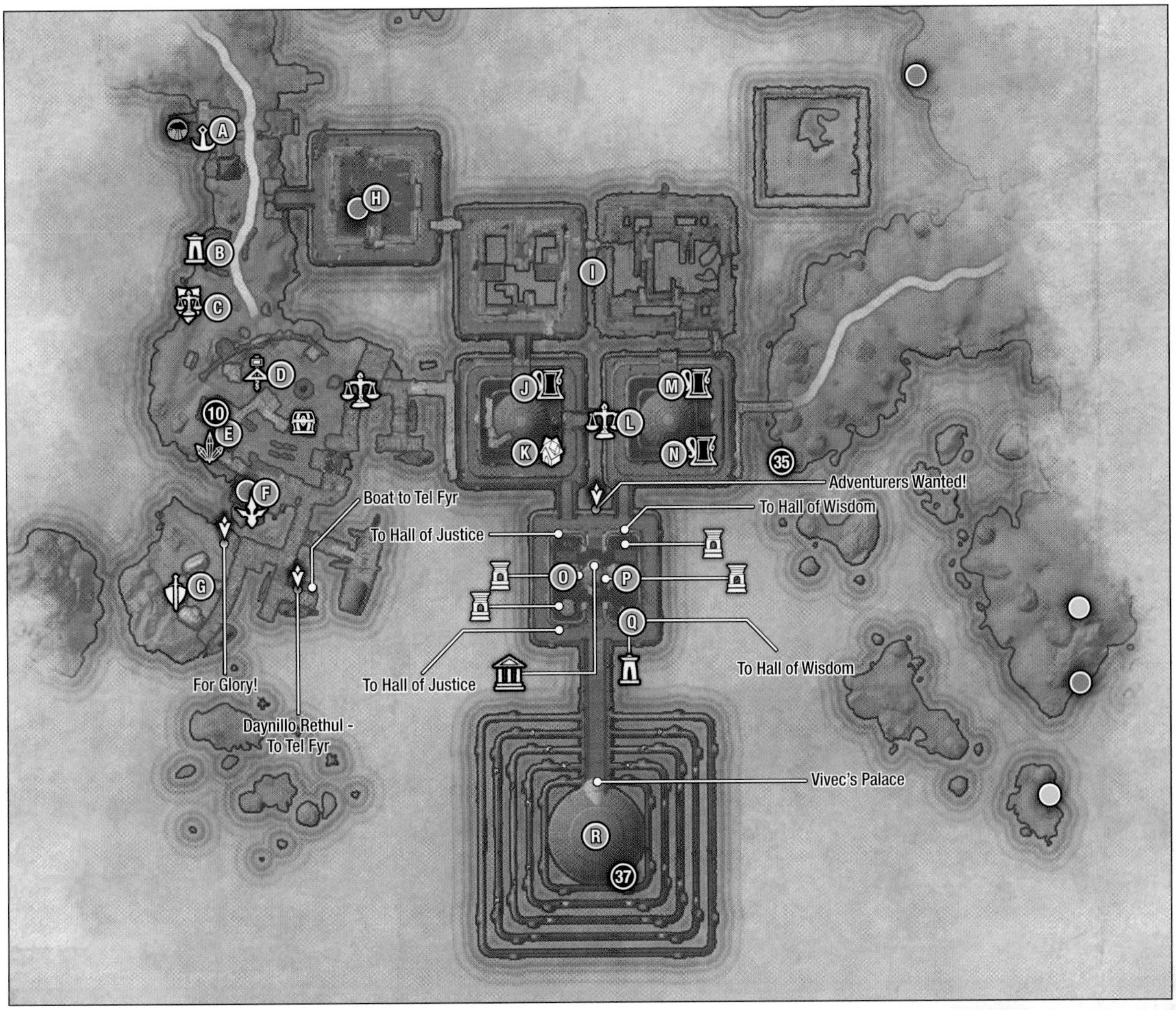

Adventurers Wanted!
To Hall of Wisdom
Boat to Tel Fyr
To Hall of Justice
To Hall of Justice
To Hall of Wisdom
For Glory!
Daynillo Rethul - To Tel Fyr
Vivec's Palace

Ⓓ Foundation's Bulwark, Rising, and Labor

Crafting:	Blacksmithing Station, Clothing Station, Woodworking Station
Merchant:	Banker Anral Selvilo, Banker Dayna Imayn, Blacksmith Stalkun, Carpenter Murgonak, Clothier Nurov Belvayn, General Goods Merchant Jeeba-Noo

Continue farther into the sprawling market to trade with a variety of specialized Merchants, and make use of the crafting stations that take your fancy. Note the Equipment Crafting Writs noticeboard.

Ⓔ Foundation's Embrace

Crafting:	Alchemy Station, Cooking Fire, Enchanting Table
Merchant:	Enchanter Cuilalme, Alchemist Lenasa Telvanni

The next part of the market is known as Foundation's Embrace, and features crafting and Merchants of a more magical nature. There's a Consumables Crafting Writ noticeboard here. Up by the dock winch, there's a Lorebook. A Vivec Sermon is to be found nearby, too.

Ⓕ Vivec City Outlaws Refuge

Crafting:	Cooking Fire
Merchant:	Fence Steps-in-Alleys, Fence Urshra, Guild Trader Relieves-Burdens, Quarith, Moneylender Obenion

Adjacent to Foundation's Embrace is a slightly seedier Outlaws Refuge, where the Merchants are less legitimate.

Ⓖ Gladiator's Quarters

Merchant:	Elite Gear Colotarion, Battlegrounds Merchant Alyze Metayer, Battlegrounds Furnisher Brelda Ofemalen, Battlegrounds Furnisher Llivas Driler

The southern part of the Merchant quarter is reserved for gladiators, and the Merchants who can sell you specialized wares.

Ⓗ Northeast Canton

This canton, allowing access to the harbor area, is under construction.

Ⓘ North Cantons (Looters)

The north cantons, which have been taking a bit of a battering from Red Mountain, are under construction. Expect some unpleasant looters roaming this maze of half-finished corridors.

Ⓙ Canton of St. Delyn the Wise (North)

Area of Interest:	Homestead
Merchant:	Magus Caydeire Dechery, Mystic Hasudel, Achievement Furnisher Drops-No-Glass, Home Goods Furnisher Heralda Garscroft, Prestige Furnisher Narwaawende, Magister Tolendir Gals, Home Goods Furnisher Uzipa

Visit the north side of the canton, and into St. Delyn Waistworks, and enjoy access to the Mages Guild, the south part of the canton, and a variety of Merchants.

Ⓚ Canton of St. Delyn the Wise (South)

Area of Interest:	Homestead
Merchant:	Armsman Erikar Five-Blades, General Goods Merchant Sosia Epinard, Armorer Svargret Goodsword, Hall Steward Riray Dalo, Fence Steps-in-Alleys, Fence Urshra

The southern side of the canton has an entrance into the same Saint Delyn Waistworks, but this side allows quicker access to the Fighters Guild, and a number of additional merchants.

Don't forget that if you complete the related quest (V2) A Friend in Need, you receive a free Vivec City Inn Room to use as a home.

Ⓛ St. Olms Plaza

Merchant:	General Goods Merchant Div Nervion

The western upper side of this canton has a door leading up to a General Goods Merchant.

Ⓜ Canton of St. Olms the Just (North)

Crafting:	Clothing Station, Cooking Fire
Merchant:	Leatherworker Atzurbesh, Chef Gilbara Morrard, Brewer Herdora, Pack Merchant Azazi

Enter from the north, and access the Farmers and Laborers Hall, as well as the Tailors and Dyers Hall.

Ⓝ Canton of St. Olms the Just (South)

Merchant:	Grocer Angedreth, Tailor Ivela Telvanni, Dye Station

Enter from the south, and you can reach the Brewers and Fishmongers Hall, as well as the Tanners and Miners Hall.

Ⓞ Temple Canton: Hall of Justice

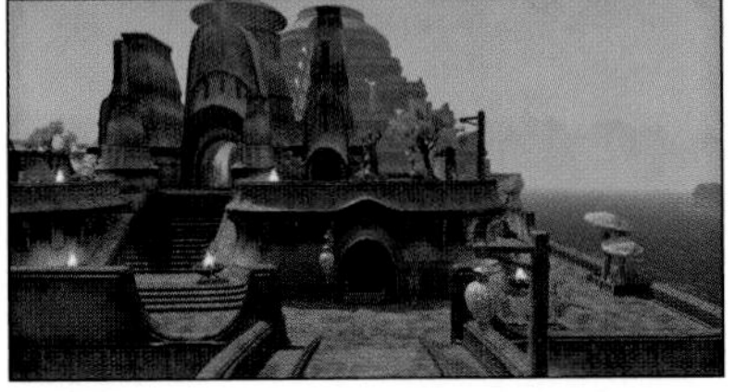

Check the exterior balcony for a Lorebook before entering the Hall of Justice, where you can speak to the Ordinators and gather a second Lorebook.

Ⓟ Temple Canton: Library of Vivec

Merchant	Curator Librarian Bradyn

If you seek knowledge, head to one of the finest book repositories in all of Tamriel. Quests are available here, as well as a curator.

Ⓠ Temple Canton: Exterior Wayshrine (2 of 2) and Shrines

Shrines:	Shrine of the Father of Mysteries, Shrine to Mara, Shrine of Mother Morrowind, Shrine of the Warrior-Poet

The upper exterior of this canton features three shrines, and a Wayshrine that allows easy access to and from the palace. The Archcanon's Office is also here, with a Lorebook for the taking.

Ⓡ Vivec's Palace

The great Vivec himself resides in the tallest canton of all, along with his trusted Archcanon Tarvus and a number of impressively armored Buoyant Armigers. Head here for some questing.

The Clockwork City

Entities:	Skaafin, Fabricants, Factotums, Jovval Mortal-Bane (Boss), Clockwork Cores (Bosses), Barbas (Boss)
Related Quest:	Divine Restoration

The hidden city of Clockwork Guardians and other oddities is accessible during the related quest, when you reach the Archcanon's Office in Vivec City. Enter the portal to be transported to this underground Dwemer kingdom, where you and Barilzar must battle through the catacombs.

The Clockwork City Interior 1: Seht's Vault

Interior 1 (Seht's Vault): A vast entrance bridge contains Daedric forces you must overcome before facing and defeating a Clockwork Guardian and opening the Clockwork City.

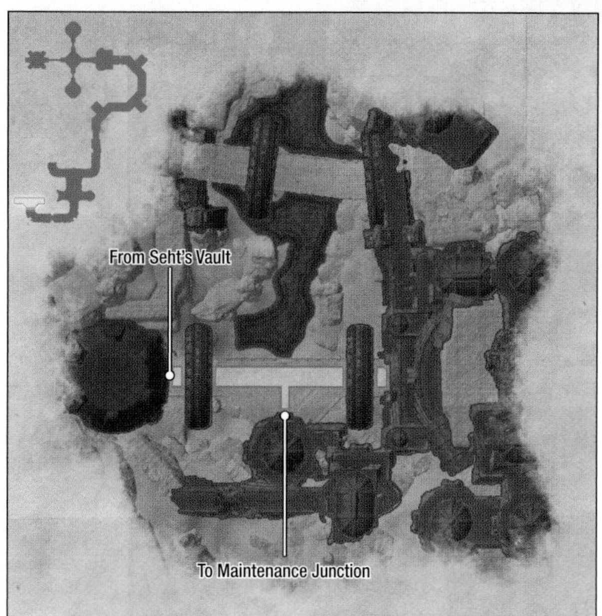

The Clockwork City Interior 2: Dockworks

Interior 2 (Dockworks): Step out of the portal from Seht's Vault, and start exploring. Your only option is to access Maintenance Junction.

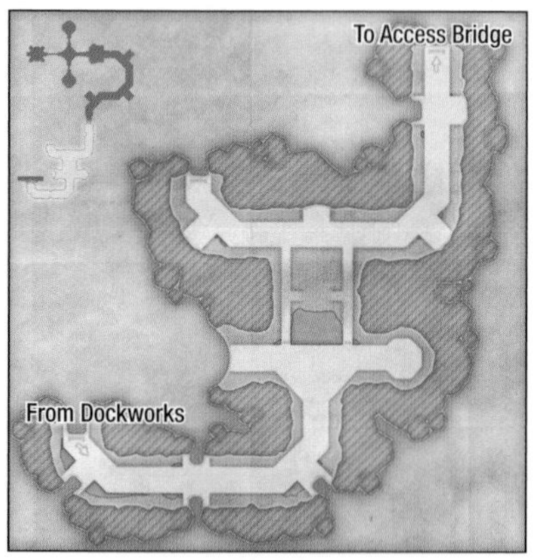

The Clockwork City Interior 3: Maintenance Junction

Interior 3 (Maintenance Junction): Head down the grated corridors to the trap-filled gate area, where Factotums must be fended off before the gate is unlocked. Northeast you can reach the Access Bridge. A boss named Jovval lurks on the northern platform corridor.

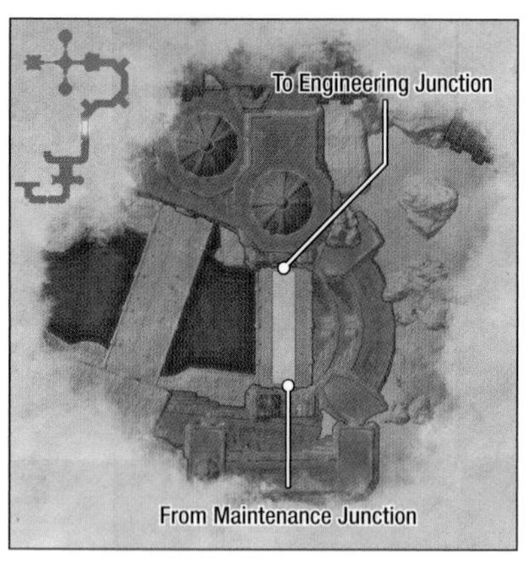

The Clockwork City Interior 4: Access Bridge

Interior 4 (Access Bridge): This is the only way forward and allows you to reach the Engineering Junction almost immediately.

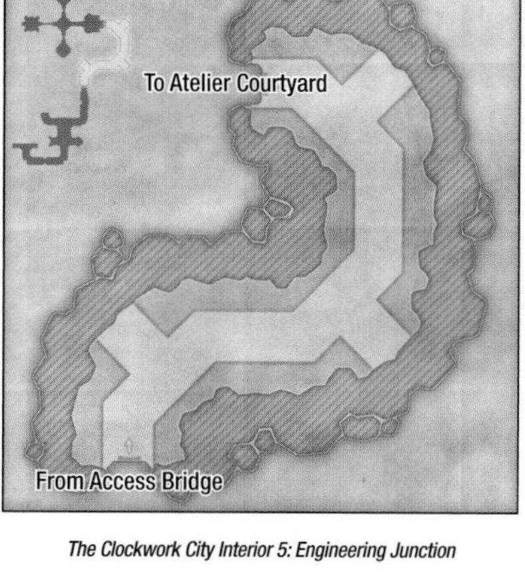

The Clockwork City Interior 5: Engineering Junction

Interior 5 (Engineering Junction): Expect Fabricants to attack as you wind through a large corridor area with traps and alcoves.

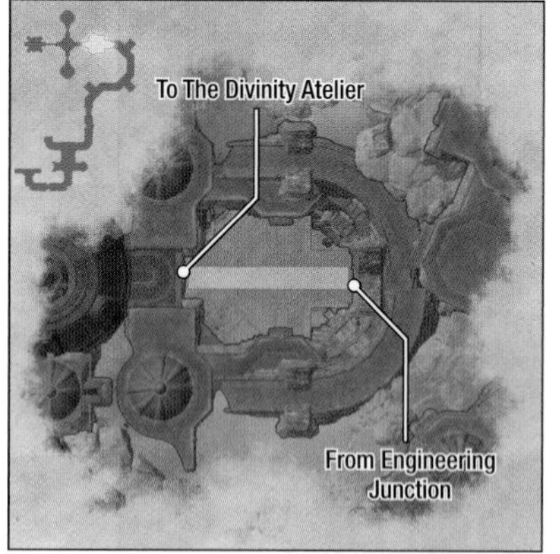

The Clockwork City Interior 6: Atelier Courtyard

Interior 6 (Atelier Courtyard): In this ornate courtyard, you have a chat with Barilzar before heading into the Divinity Atelier.

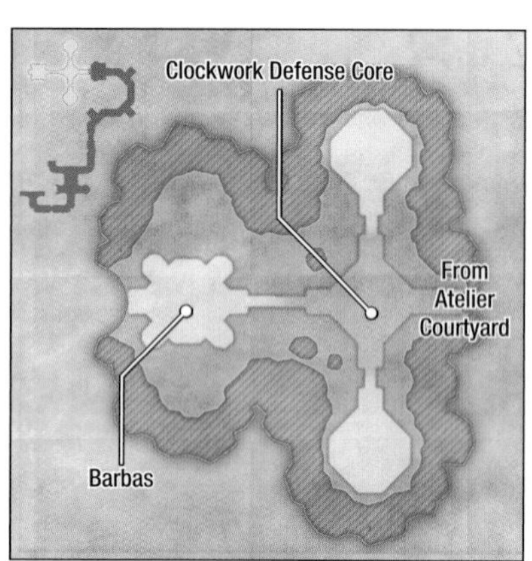

The Clockwork City Interior 7: Divinity Atelier

Interior 7 (Divinity Atelier): Barbas activates a fearsome Clockwork Defense Core in this platform area. Destroy it, remove the gate barriers, and destroy two more cores before facing Barbas.

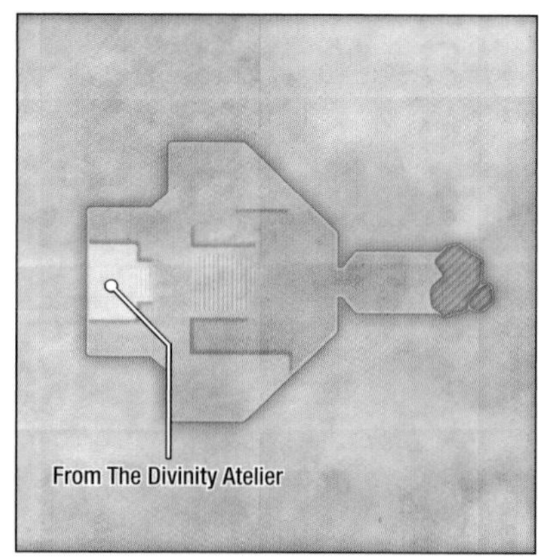

The Clockwork City Interior 8: Shrine to Clavicus Vile

Interior 8 (Shrine to Clavicus Vile): Your final destination is a small shrine room with a large daedric prince to talk to!

ASHLANDS

Bearing the brunt of the ash clouds and grim precipitation from the ominous Red Mountain to the south, this is a gray desert of ruined ancient structures and mires of choked flora and fauna now adapting to life under a rumbling volcano, constantly under threat of encroachment by pyroclastic flows. Even though Molag Amur shares some of this environmental blight, Ashlands is far less mountainous, with a boundary to the Sea of Ghosts (north), Grazelands (east), and West Gash (west). Expect Daedric and Dwemer ruins (and worse!) to loom up at you, through the gloom-filled clouds.

THE SLAUGHTERFISH OF SHEOGORAD

The wild region of islands along the northern coast of Vvardenfell is currently inaccessible. This is the region of Sheogorad, which is not for exploring, lest you wish a thrashing and violent death at the teeth of Slaughterfish, which will attack those foolish enough to swim northward from Ashlands. Heed this fair warning: you do not wish to add your soul to the Sea of Ghosts!

THE IMPENETRABLE RED MOUNTAIN

The Red Mountain—the gigantic volcano that Vvardenfell was formed by—is as inhospitable as it is inaccessible. Keep your travels to the Ashlands region when exploring to the north.

ASHLANDS—LOCATIONS/COLLECTIBLES/FISHING

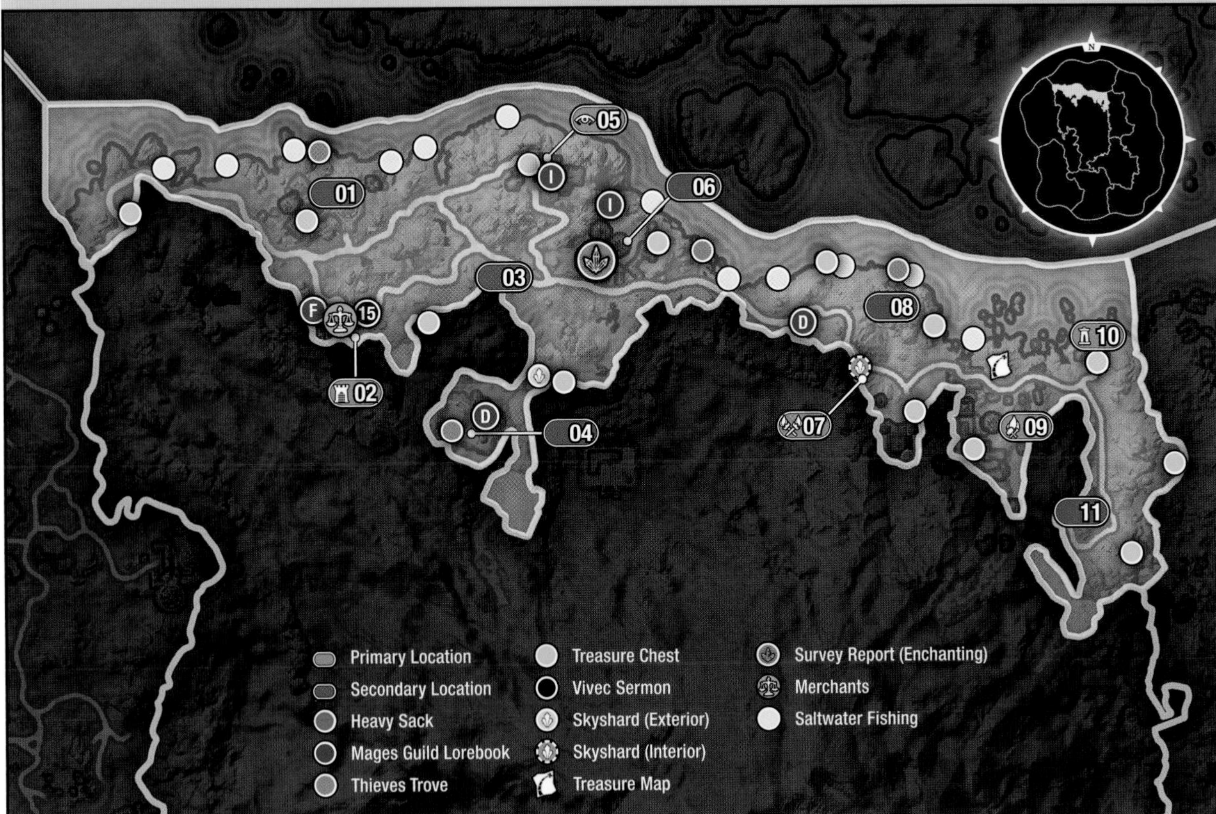

Locations

No.	Location
01	Ashurnabitashpi
02	Ald Carac
03	Llando Ancestral Tomb
04	Falasmaryon
05	Valenvaryon
06	Ebernanit
07	Forgotten Wastes
08	Indaren Ancestral Tomb
09	Zergonipal
10	Valley of the Wind Wayshrine
11	Cavern of the Incarnate

01 ASHURNABITASHPI

Entities:	Red Exile

Campfires are lit at this ancient monument to Mehrunes Dagon, though the Dunmer present aren't here to summon a Daedric Prince, but rather to slay those entering this sanctum. Check the area for a chest and Heavy Sack.

02 ALD CARAC

Area of Interest:	Battleground
Items of Interest:	Mages Guild Book (Vivec and Mephala), Vivec Sermon
Merchant:	Farthalem

One of the main reasons to venture this far north is to access the Ald Carac Battlegrounds. Check the Merchant selling some elite gear before the mayhem begins. Then check the outskirts for a couple of books—a Mages Guild tome in a small camp behind one of the tents, and the Vivec Sermon **(#15)** on Farthalem's cart.

03 LLANDO ANCESTRAL TOMB

Entities:	Nix-Hounds, Skavengers

The remains of an underground tomb; until recently firmly sealed and inaccessible. Now the door can be pried open, and the interior explored. Inside is a single entrance chamber with a runestone and minor loot.

04 FALASMARYON

Area of Interest:	Skyshard
Entities:	Fetcherfly Nests, Flame Atronachs
Item of Interest:	Mages Guild Book (The House of Troubles)

A Dunmeri stronghold, abandoned to the encroaching lava flows, houses little but danger. Enter via the lava river with the skyshard glowing on it, and under the rock arch. The structure has an inaccessible interior, but the ramparts can be checked for a Heavy Sack, Thieves Trove, and a Mages Guild book.

05 VALENVARYON

Entities:	Ghosts
Item of Interest:	Mages Guild Book (Varieties of Faith: The Dark Elves)

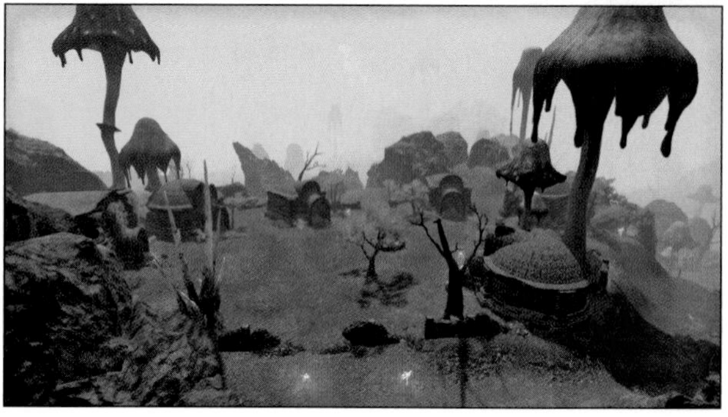

Back before the ash fell, this coastal hilltop settlement was erected by Dunmer stonemasons. Now it is literally a ghost town, by which we mean "full of ghosts." Slay the specters and seek out a chest and sack, as well as a Mages Guild book in the central gathering circle.

06 EBERNANIT

Entities:	Air Atronachs, Flame Atronachs, Nix-Hounds
Item of Interest:	Mages Guild Book (Varieties of Faith: The Dark Elves)

Back when the Daedric Princes were worshipped a little more fervently, this Shrine to Mehrunes Dagon was erected. The place has an inaccessible interior, and the outside is dangerous for those who cannot fight Atronachs. Note the scattering of collectibles here and slightly farther east along the coast: two Heavy Sacks, a chest, and a Thieves Trove. There's a Mages Guild book behind a tall toadstool just north of the ruins.

07 FORGOTTEN WASTES

Areas of Interest:	Public Dungeon, Skyshard
Entities:	Ambush Beetles, Cliff Striders, Fetcherfly Hives, Flame Atronach, Hive Golems, Hungers, Insects, Iron Atronach, Nix-Oxen, Shalk, Sixth House Cultists, Conflagrator Llaals (Boss: Dunmer), Mynar Igna (Boss: Iron Atronach), Voracity (Boss: Hunger), Confessor Dradas (Boss: Dunmer), Coaxer Veran (Boss: Dunmer), Castigator Athin (Boss: Dunmer), Wakener Maras (Boss: Dunmer), Nevena Nirith (Boss: Dumner)
Related Quest:	Echoes of a Fallen House

Is this the location of the sixth great Dunmer House? Though the outside mine door is unassuming, once you enter this place, you'll find a load of exploring to do.

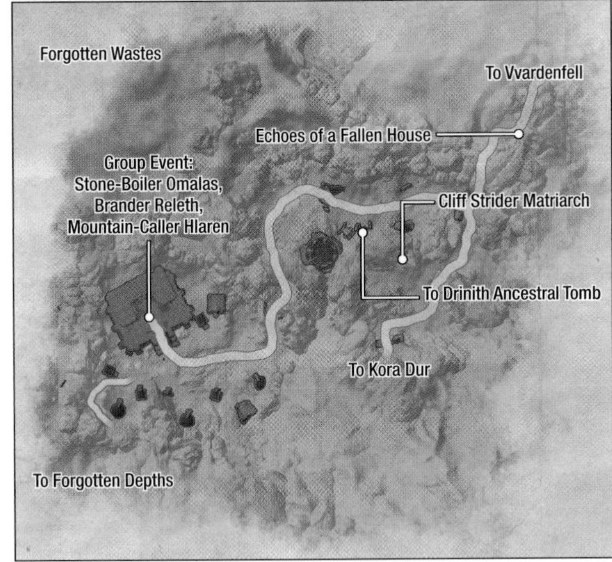

Interior 1: Forgotten Wastes

Interior 1 (Forgotten Wastes): Here you find a natural tunnel, a Dunmer named Tythis Nirith to chat to, and the beginning of the quest associated with this dungeon. Head south, battling a variety of beasts, to reach a door to Kora Dur, manned by Dunmer of an unknown house. Head west at the junction, encountering Shalk, and enter the Drinith Ancestral Tomb. Or keep going, winding through a path of beasts to reach a massive cavern where Sixth House Dunmer are defending their stronghold from encroaching lava. Expect a massive battle at this location: is that an Iron Atronach? Although the stronghold's interior isn't accessible, there's a wooden scaffold to the southwest that is, offering a route up and into a high tunnel that leads down to the Forgotten Depths.

Interior 2 (Kora Dur): Explore this set of caverns, where the Sixth House is hard at work excavating (and battling you, obviously). To the west, a lava flow pierces the cavern. Conflagrator Llaals, a powerful Dunmeri mage, is here, along with his summoned Iron Aronach Mynar Igna. Head north to face more Sixth House Cultists digging the walls, and gain access into the Caverns of Kogoruhn.

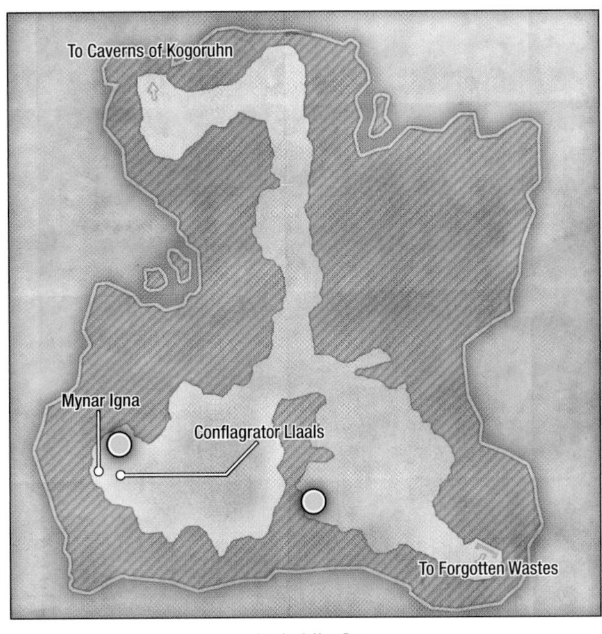

Interior 2: Kora Dur

◯	Treasure Chest

Interior 3 (Drinith Ancestral Tomb): Enter from the Forgotten Wastes to start at the top of this tomb. Enter via the Caverns of Kogoruhn, and you begin at a rough mine tunnel. This tomb is teeming with Sixth House foes, as well as a couple of vicious Hungers and a boss named Voracity. Seek clues to the quest throughout these narrow halls, and watch for traps.

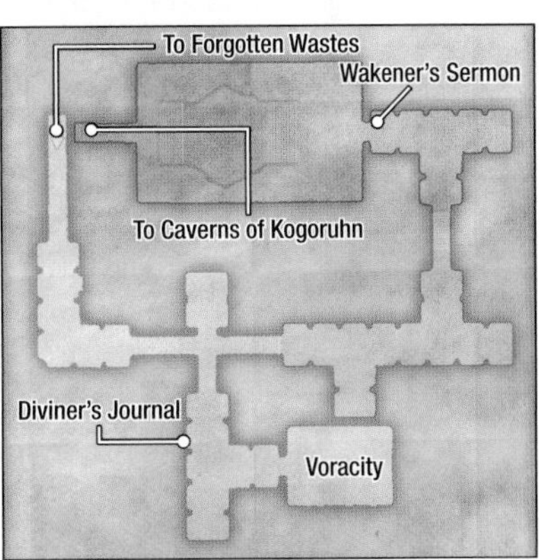

Interior 3: Drinith Ancestral Tomb

Interior 4 (Caverns of Kogoruhn): A large blue torch lights the entrance to a precarious set of ledges and down to a massive excavation area, where you battle more Dunmer. Walk the plank to reach a skyshard sitting on a mine cart. At the base of the ledges is a mining camp where Sixth House foes and Atronachs congregate. Push on past the giant lava flow to the south, and through the massive Daedric gate (southwest), to reach access to the Forgotten Depths. Or head northwest into a narrow mining tunnel to a secondary camp and a dead end. Don't forget two more quest clues along the way.

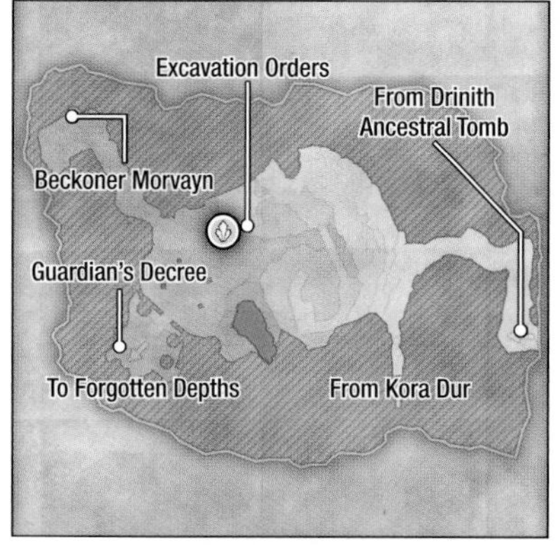

Interior 4: Caverns of Kogoruhn

Skyshard

Interior 5 (Forgotten Depths): This is a ceremonial bell chamber of the Sixth House, accessed either from the Caverns of Kogoruhn or the Forgotten Wastes. It's a short hack-and-slash into this main chamber, where Confessor Dradas, Coaxer Veran, and Castigator Athin are ready to repel intruders, along with other Dunmer from this cursed house.

Ring the bells in the proper order (1, 2, 4, 3, 6, 5—the runes on the gate in front of the bells show you the order) to reach the final chamber, the Wakener's Hall. Here you face Wakener Maras, a powerful Dunmeri mage.

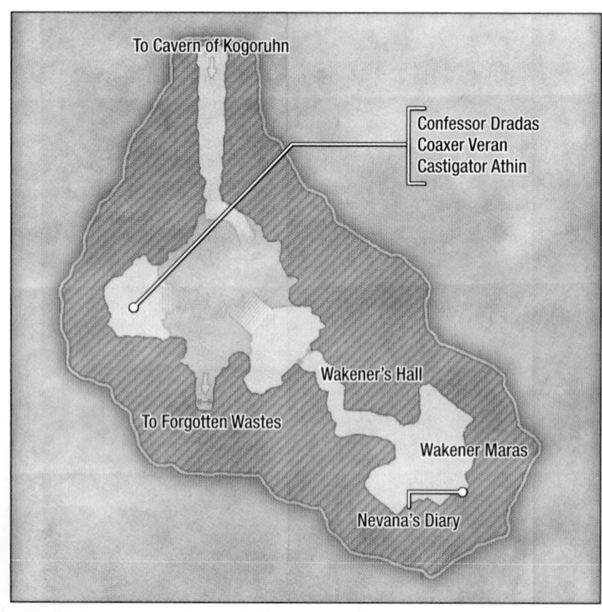

Interior 5: Forgotten Depths

08 INDAREN ANCESTRAL TOMB

Entities:	Fetcherfly Hives

Close to the Forgotten Wastes is a sealed tomb door, currently inaccessible. Check the shoreline nearby for a possible chest and Thieves Trove. This could be the tomb of the Indaren family, though it cannot be verified.

09 ZERGONIPAL

Area of Interest:	Crafting Stations
Entities:	Flame Atronachs

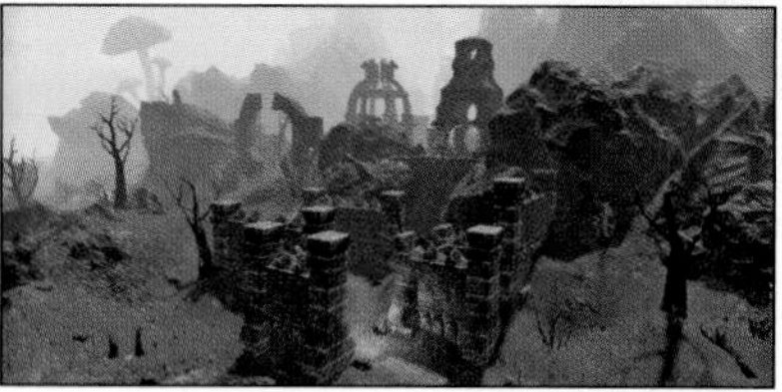

Here's another Daedric shrine, this one squeezed in between the sea and the lava. Once a sanctum to Malacath, this set of ruins offers a possible couple of chests and Heavy Sack, as well as the chance to accidentally fall into lava, or hot-foot it across a pyroclastic flow. Also try out some crafting at the stations here.

10 VALLEY OF THE WIND WAYSHRINE

Area of Interest:	Wayshrine

This Wayshrine is a good landmark to find when you're traveling between the Ashlands and Grazelands regions. It's also close to the Favel Ancestral Tomb rubbing.

11 CAVERN OF THE INCARNATE

Related Quest:	Divine Delusions

Head south from the Wayshrine, then follow the rough stone steps up to this suspiciously serene grotto, with flowing water and quest-related activities. This is a shimmering shrine dedicated to Azura.

During the Divine Delusions quest, visit Wise Woman Dovrosi at the cave and commune with the three spirits found inside.

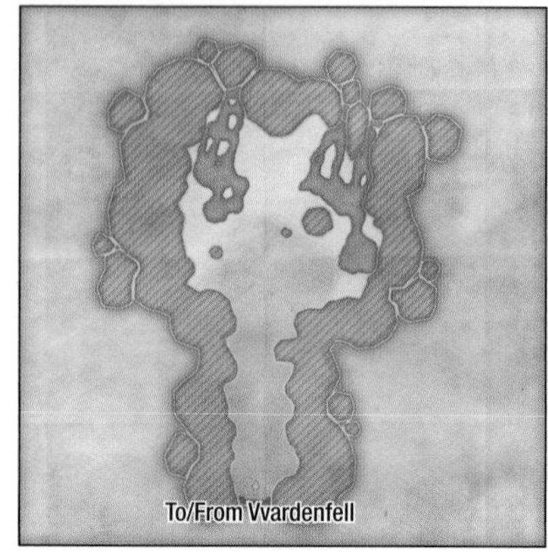

GRAZELANDS

This strip of mostly tranquil pasture and meadowlands wedged in the northeast corner of Vvardenfell suffers little from the effects of Red Mountain, unlike its neighboring regions to the west and south. As the stoneflower and wickwheat sway in the gentle breezes, one would be forgiven for assuming this area has little in the way of troubles. But there are usurpers stalking the farmlands, and once you leave the coastal town of Vos—twinned with Tel Mora on the adjacent island along Azura's Coast, which shares this region's eastern border—there are horrors awaiting those seeking adventure in remote hillsides.

GRAZELANDS—COLLECTIBLES/QUESTS/FISHING

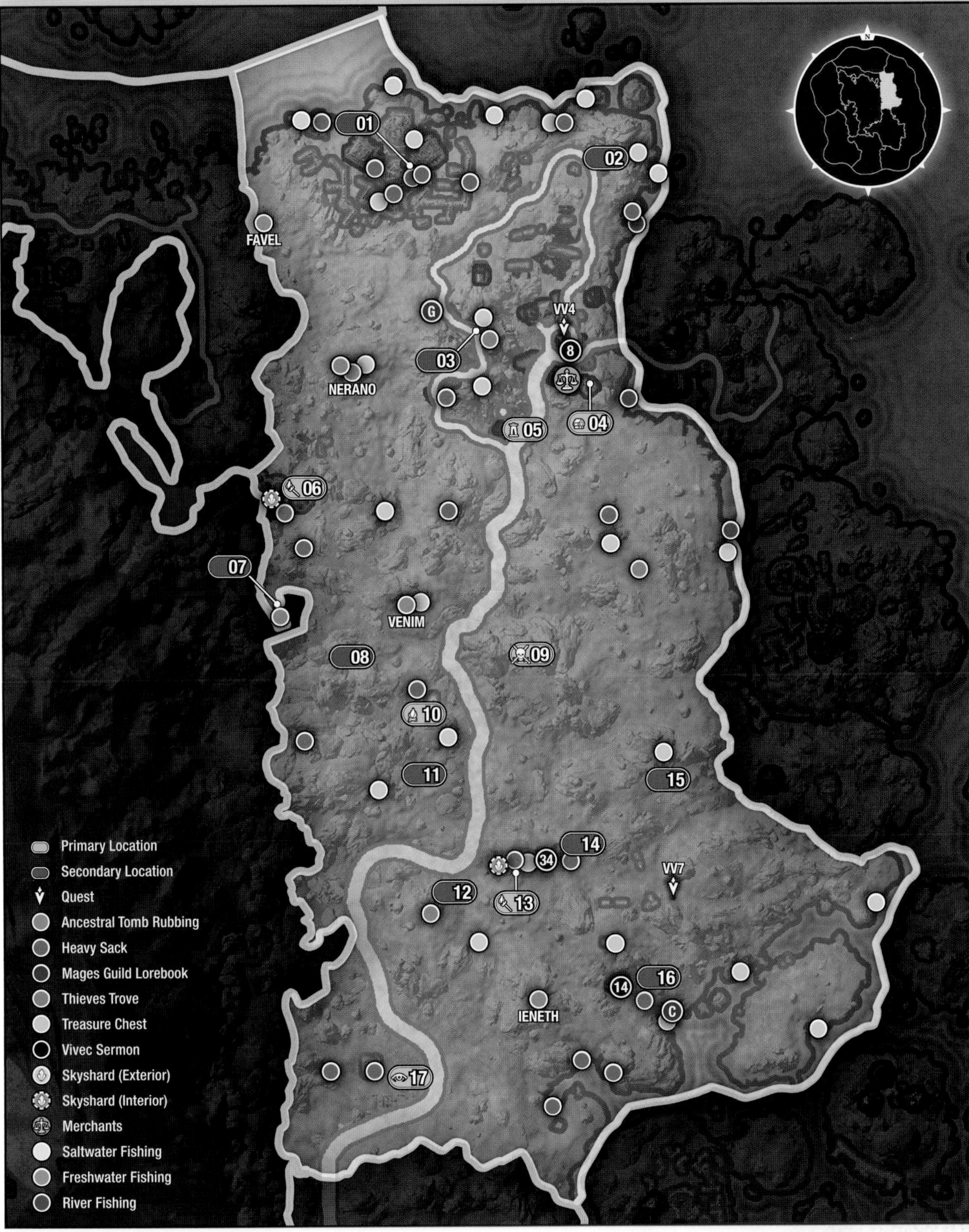

Locations

01	Kushtashpi	07	Scavenger's Ruin	13	Pulk
02	Northern Farmstead	08	Pyroclastic Flow (Zainab Camp)	14	An Unfortunate Experiment
03	Poacher's Treehouse	09	Dubdil Alar Tower	15	Rubble-Filled Door
04	Vos	10	Zainab Camp	16	The Shoreline Farmstead
05	Tel Mora Wayshrine	11	Sethan Ancestral Tomb	17	Falensarano Ruins
06	Nchuleft	12	Aralen Ancestral Tomb		

01 KUSHTASHPI

Entities:	**Flame Atronachs, Scamps**
Item of Interest:	**Stone of Kushtashpi**
Related Quest:	**At Any Cost**

Expect moderate otherworldly incursions as you explore this waterlogged coastal temple to the Daedric Prince Molag Bal. Be sure you thoroughly explore the place; there are a couple of Fishing Holes, up to three Heavy Sacks, and two treasure chests. Plus, the fabled Stone of Kushtashpi is floating inside one of the domed structures. There is no interior to explore, however.

02 NORTHERN FARMSTEAD

Entities:	**Guarx, Nix-Oxen**
Item of Interest:	**Lorebook (Dark Elves, Dark Hearts)**

North of Vos is a small farmstead with a couple of small waterlogged fields and grazing animals, as well as Argonian workers. Check the area for a Lorebook near the small farmhouse, as well as a couple of Heavy Sacks and a treasure chest. There's a second farm hut on the southwestern edge of the area, where a Dunmer named Sur Bail wanders and tends to his crops.

03 POACHER'S TREEHOUSE

Item of Interest:	**Mages Guild Book (The Art of Kwama Egg Cooking)**

Between a cluster of rocks atop a hill is a small poacher's camp. Near his hammock is an odd little treehouse with (thankfully inanimate) skeletons sitting and guarding the place. Note the Mages Guild book near a half-buried skeleton on the northwestern edge of this rocky outcrop, near the stairs carved into the hill. There's a possible treasure chest and Thieves Trove here, too.

04 VOS

Areas of Interest:	**Cooking Fire, Silt Strider**
Entities:	**Nix-Oxen, House Guards, Savarak's Guards**
Items of Interest:	**Lorebook (Blessed Almalexia's Fables for Evening), Vivec Sermon**
Merchants:	**Navigator Bolnora Romavel, Caravaner Adosi Delvi, Dridyn Ledd**
Related Quests:	**(VV4) Reclaiming Vos**

The Dunmer have been farming this area for centuries. Though it shares goods and services with Tel Mora, across the shore on Azura's Coast, it should be seen as a separate settlement, except when obtaining Merchant services.

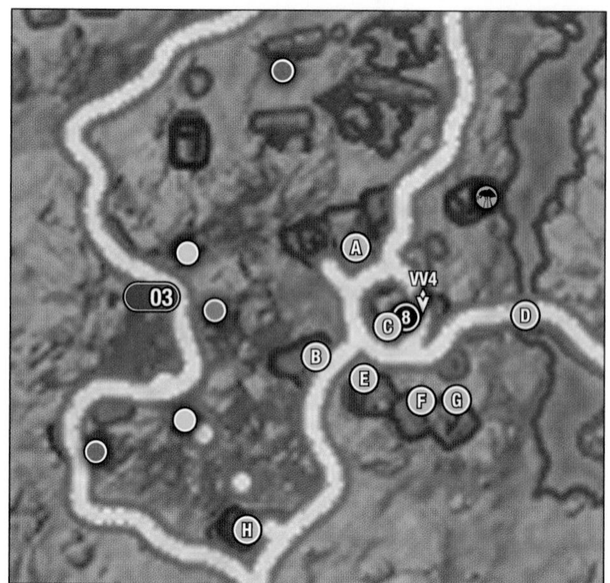

Quest		Treasure Chest	
Silt Strider		Heavy Sack	
Thieves Trove		Vivec Sermon	

Ⓐ Savarak's Manse

Warning:	Restricted Area (Trespassing)

Once you're through the unlocked door, you can trespass around inside, notably the wine cellar and bookshelves downstairs, though you'll be fighting a guard. Or check outside for a Lorebook on the veranda table.

Ⓑ Varo's House

This is a simple home with a lock (Simple difficulty) to pry open. You can venture inside, though the resident isn't too thrilled.

Ⓒ The Gathering House

This tavern is well worth stopping at, if only to obtain the Vivec Sermon **(#8)** on a wall table inside. Earyaorne plays the drums, and there's a Cooking Fire for some of your crafting needs.

Ⓓ Docks to Tel Mora

If you want to cross into Azura's Coast and explore the decidedly more fungal town of Tel Mora, do so via this bridge.

Ⓔ Selvayn's House

Bralen Selvayn lives here. Though his home security is lax (Simple difficulty), he's in quite a huff when you barge in.

Ⓕ Tradehouse

Visit the Merchant Dridyn Ledd for all your equipment-based needs. Love gold and rumors? You'll love this place. There's a Cooking Fire here, too.

Ⓖ Storehouse

The Tradehouse keeps its goods inside here, behind a locked door (Advanced difficulty). This isn't the good stuff; there's little to pilfer.

Ⓗ Tel Mora Wayshrine

The far south of Vos has the Wayshrine to the adjacent town of Tel Mora. Consult that Altas entry for more information.

05 TEL MORA WAYSHRINE

Area of Interest:	Wayshrine

This is the only Wayshrine on Vvardenfell that marks a settlement in a different region—the town of Tel Mora, which is across the cliff bridge to the east of Vos, in Azura's Coast. Check the general vicinity—the rocks to the north—for a possible chest and Heavy Sack.

06 NCHULEFT

Area of Interest:	Delve
Entities:	Ash Exiles, Ash Hoppers, Dwarven Centurions, Dwarven Automatons, Insects, Scavengers
Item of Interest:	Skyshard
Related Quest:	Divine Intervention

A large Dwemer ruin—some say once a heavy manufacturing facility—sits against the massive rock wall preventing access to Red Mountain. A small band of Ash Exile Dunmer guards the entrance door. This is a delve.

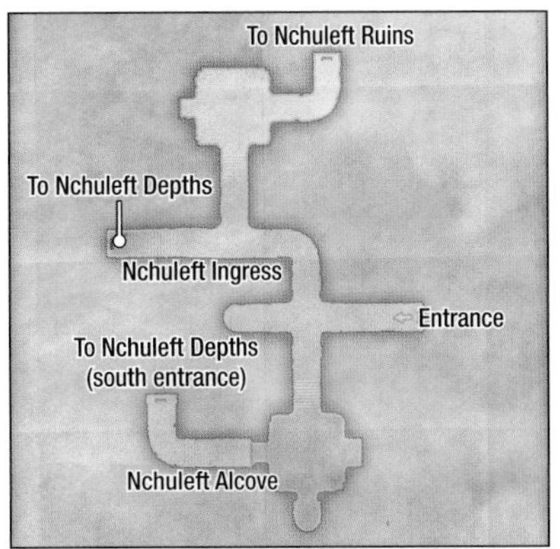

Interior 1: Nchuleft Ingress and Alcove

Interior 1 (Nchuleft Ingress and Alcove): Some Ash Exiles are thieving the Dwemer objects from the walls in this series of connecting passages. The south "alcove" area is usually best traveled when exiting, and returning from the Depths. The northern area features steps down to the Depths, as well as a chamber and exit into the Ruins.

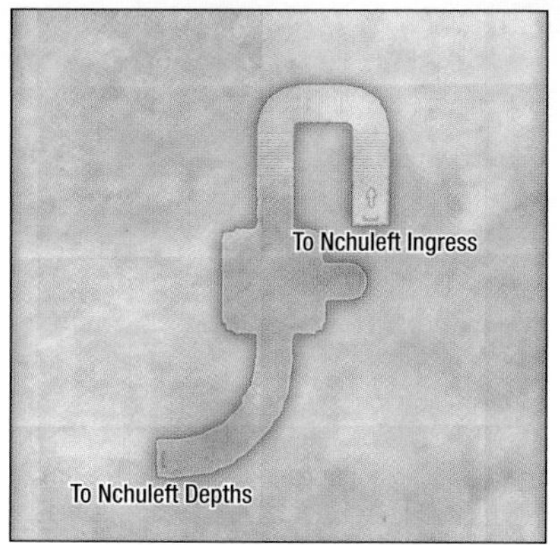

Interior 2: Nchuleft Ruins

Interior 2 (Nchuleft Ruins): This connecting corridor and chamber allow access down to the Depths. You meet a few Ash Exiles along the way. This brings you out into the Depths at the closest point to the skyshard.

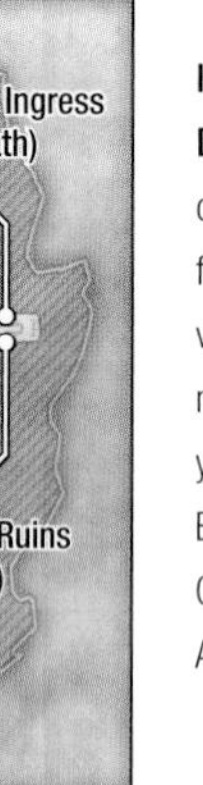

Interior 3: Nchuleft Depths

Skyshard

Interior 3 (Nchuleft Depths): This giant central column with three floors can be accessed via stairs and ramps no matter which route you take to get here. Expect to fight numerous Centurions and Arquebuses in this area.

07 SCAVENGER'S RUIN

Just south of Nchuleft is a gully to the west; avoid the bear trap here. Scale the rocky ground, turning south to reach the remains of a dwelling—a huntsman's cottage now without roof or most of its walls. A scavenger named Mevil Rendar resides here. There's a Thieves Trove, too.

08 PYROCLASTIC FLOW (ZAINAB CAMP)

The topography to the west of Zainab Camp is treacherous to say the least; a giant pyroclastic flow oozes down from Red Mountain, making the going slow. Explore the general area cautiously, attempting to find a Heavy Sack south of this marker.

09 DUBDIL ALAR TOWER

Entities:	Research Assistants, Skaafin, Dubdil Alar (Dunmeri Mage)
Area of Interest:	Group Boss

A powerful mage sacrifices his assistants and summons a number of Skaafin at this fungal high tower.

10 ZAINAB CAMP

Entities:	Ashlander Guards

It is, perhaps, heartening to meet Dunmer who don't immediately want to spill your blood. A small camp of them exist here, close to the main road stretching north to south through this region. Note the Heavy Sack and possible treasure chest in the vicinity.

11 SETHAN ANCESTRAL TOMB

Entities:	Kwama
Item of Interest:	Lorebook (The Vile Truth of Barbas)

Foraging Kwama are grazing this area (directly south of Zainab Camp), said to be the site of an old burial ground. Fortunately, the door isn't sealed as tight as you'd expect, and there's an interior to investigate: Grab a Lorebook, some armor and weaponry, and the contents of a coffer.

12 ARALEN ANCESTRAL TOMB

When the main road through Grazelands winds west, there's a sealed tomb door by the blue lantern marking the area. The tomb is inaccessible. It's just across from Pulk, which is to the east.

13 PULK

Area of Interest:	Delve
Entities:	Bandits, Insects, Nix-Hounds, Scavengers
Item of Interest:	Skyshard

A renowned hideout for bandits, Pulk has an unassuming exterior.

Interior: Once you're through the mine door, there's an impressive set of mine tunnels leading down into a huge natural cavern, where a multitude of bandits and other beasts lurk. The place is worth heading into, as there's a skyshard on the bottom floor. Exit the same way you came from.

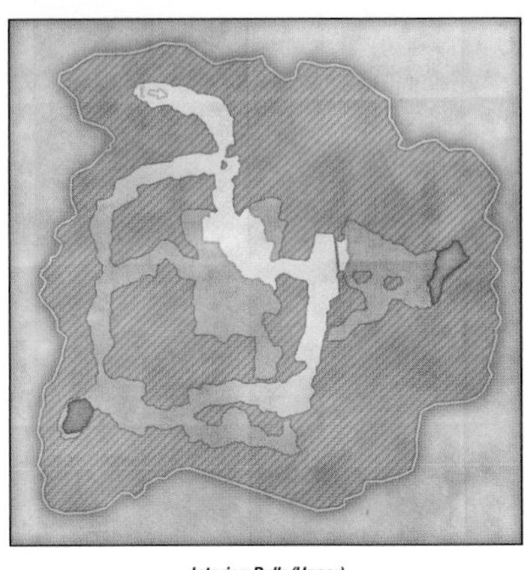

Interior: Pulk (Upper)

Interior: Pulk (Lower)

Skyshard

14 AN UNFORTUNATE EXPERIMENT

Entities:	Kagouti
Related Quest:	If the Spell Fits

On the edge of the grounds of Hanud Tower, which is across the boundary in the Azura's Coast region, are the remains of an explosion, close to a campsite and the remains of some walled gardens. Farther east is a frozen fellow named Stromgruf the Steady, who starts the listed quest. Also check the area for a Heavy Sack.

15 RUBBLE-FILLED DOOR

Entities:	Durzog

Close to Azura's Coast is a hillside with a tomb door carved into it. Alas, the rubble indicates the location is inaccessible. Check the area immediately north for a possible chest.

16 THE SHORELINE FARMSTEAD

Entities:	Netch Gougers
Item of Interest:	Mages Guild Book (Sanctioned Murder), Vivec Sermon

One of the few parts of the coastline that isn't encroached on by the Azura's Coast region, this small farmstead would be idyllic except for the incursion of Netch Gougers. Note the Fishing Hole, Mages Guild book under the giant toadstool by the shoreline Fishing Hole, and Vivec Sermon **(#14)** atop the small farmstead itself. Finally, note the Ieneth Ancestral Tomb rubbing due west of here.

17 FALENSARANO RUINS

Merchant:	Taluri Salen

This Dunmeri stronghold on the southern edge of the Grazelands houses a small band of adventurers attempting to dig out the stronghold entrances. Currently, the stone fortification's interior is inaccessible. However, there's a Merchant to trade with, and a couple of Heavy Sacks nearby.

MOLAG AMUR

Perhaps the most inhospitable of all the navigable regions of Vvardenfell, Molag Amur is either traversed through as quickly as possible, or languished in as part of a pilgrimage to the main topographical area of height and note, Mount Kand. However, farther north and closer to the ash storms and constant creeping death of the pyroclastic flows from Red Mountain, fewer adventurers dare tread, for this is an area of permanent bleakness and choking air. Daedra are active, there are numerous ruins to avoid (or explore!), and the only respite comes when visiting the decidedly more civilized Lake Nabia, and the southeastern town of Molag Mar.

MOLAG AMUR—COLLECTIBLES/QUESTS/FISHING

Locations

No.	Location	No.	Location	No.	Location
01	Library of Andule	11	Camp and Pyroclastic Flow	21	Lower Mountain Arches (Mount Kand)
02	Gimothran Ancestral Tomb	12	Sulipund Grange	22	Inanius Egg Mine Back Entrance
03	Zalkin-Sul	13	Foyada Quarry	23	Telasero
04	Mzanchend	14	Ashunartes	24	Red Exile Campsite
05	Dulo Ancestral Tomb	15	Marandus	25	Dreudurai Glass Mine
06	Galom Daeus	16	Vandus Ancestral Tomb	26	Helan Ancestral Tomb
07	Missir-Dadalit Egg Mine	17	Erabenimsun Camp	27	Molag Mar
08	Nchuleftingth Wayshrine	18	Mountain Pass Tent (Mount Kand)	28	Molag Mar Wayshrine
09	Nchuleftingth	19	Alas Ancestral Tomb (Mount Kand)		
10	Tusenend	20	Mountain Pass Ravine (Mount Kand)		

01 LIBRARY OF ANDULE

Entities:	**Fetcherfly Hive Golems, Ancestor Spirits**
Related Quest:	**The Lost Library**

Brazier of Knowledge
Indoril
Redoran
To Ancient Vaults
Enter
Dres
Hlaalu
Brazier of Wisdom

Easily overlooked, this unassuming entrance off the beaten path at the far north end of this region, just southeast of the Falensarano Ruins in Grazelands, leads to a library of yore.

Interior 1: There is genealogy of the four main families inside this strange crypt-like knowledge repository. Consult the quest to understand how to solve the puzzles and unlock the hidden areas (shown on the map) of this library.

02 GIMOTHRAN ANCESTRAL TOMB

Entities:	**Fetcherfly Nests**

This sealed tomb entrance has no interior, but the exterior is guarded well, and there's a Heavy Sack for your troubles.

03 ZALKIN-SUL

Entities:	**Dwarven Automatons, Insects, Kwama, Mzanchend Guardian (Centurion)**
Related Quest:	**The Magister Makes a Move**

Due west of Mzanchend, close to a massive lava flow, is the entrance to an egg mine. This links to the Dwemer ruin, so the following interior investigation applies to both this and the next location. It's worth having the quest active so you can fully explore these interiors. Before you enter, check the Serano Ancestral Tomb rubbing just south of here.

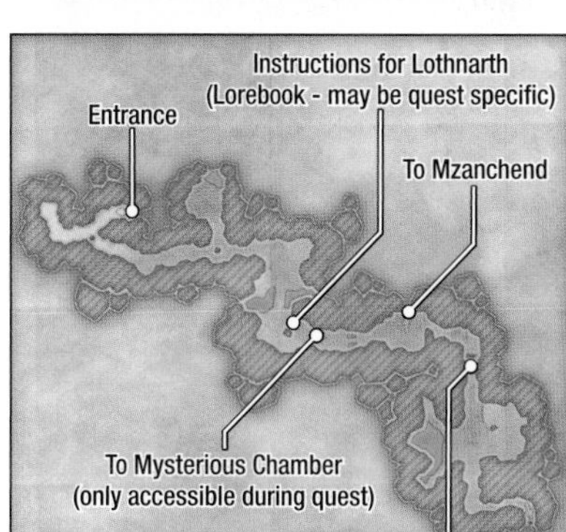

Zalkin-Sul Egg Mine and Mzanchend: Interior 1 (Egg Mine, Mysterious Chamber, East Mine)

Interior 1 (Zalkin-Sul Egg Mine): After you maneuver through some guards, this Kwama egg mine (and further guards) can be encountered. Halfway along this winding cavern tunnel, there's a door to a Mysterious Chamber, accessible during the quest.

Interior 1 (Mysterious Chamber): A strange Dwemer prism and mechanical contraption are rotating here. North is access to Mzanchend, while the cavern tunnel continues to the east mine.

Interior 1 (East Mine): The eastern (actually southeastern) part of the mine features a large cavern with Kwama nests, fleeing slaves, and an exit out into Vvardenfell, just north of the Nchuleftingth Wayshrine. Use this during your escape.

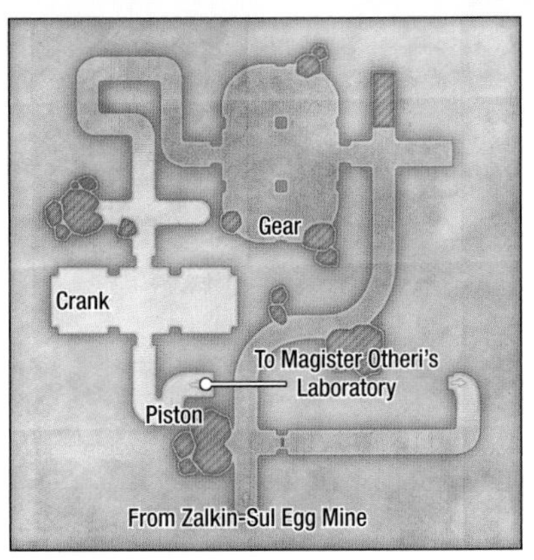

Zalkin-Sul Egg Mine and Mzanchend: Interior 2 (Mzanchend)

Interior 2 (Mzanchend): Only accessible during the quest, this giant workshop for creating Centurions features an easily navigable corridor to various large chambers, with Automatons along the way. Grab the mechanical parts as you go.

Zalkin-Sul Egg Mine and Mzanchend: Interior 2 (Mzanchend)

Interior 3 (Magister Otheri's Laboratory): This large chamber is dominated by a powerful Dwemer Centurion that activates when you encroach. The last of the quest items are here, along with an exit to the east, which brings you back to the southeast area of the Mzanchend interior.

04 MZANCHEND

Entities:	Dwarven Automatons
Items of Interest:	Skyshard, Mages Guild Book (Invocation of Azura)
Related Quest:	The Magister Makes a Move

This large Dwemer ruin sitting on a river of lava contains Dwarven mechanical sentries to worry about. You can also find a host of collectibles, including two possible chests, a Heavy Sack, and a Thieves Tome, as well as a Mages Guild book near some cogs. Don't forget to access the skyshard! Speaking of access, the interior of Mzanchend can be explored, but only if entered via the Zalkin-Sul Egg Mine to the west, with the quest active.

05 DULO ANCESTRAL TOMB

Entities:	Fetcherfly Nests, Nix-Hounds
Item of Interest:	Lorebook (The Wailing Door)

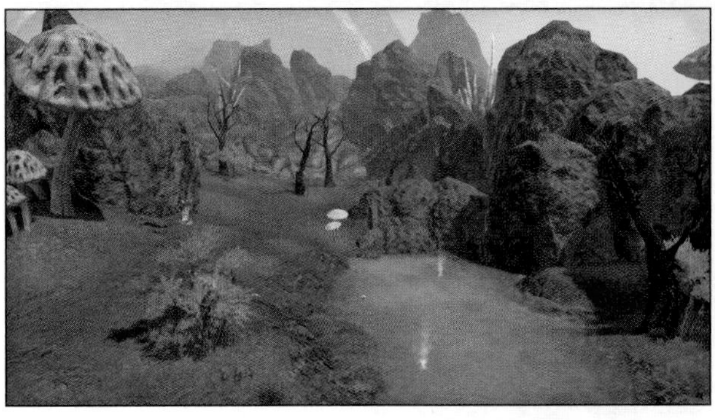

Pass Galom Daeus, and investigate a shallow bubbling pool to the west; said to be the close to the Dulo Ancestral tomb. There's a tomb door here, and it creaks open, leading to a mausoleum to ransack, though only the initial chamber is accessible. Grab the Lorebook, and some minor equipment before looting a coffer and leaving.

06 GALOM DAEUS

Entities:	Berne Clan, Dwarven Automatons, Dwarven Centurions, Insects
Related Quest:	Divine Intervention

This Dwemer ruin overlooks a river of lava, and is adjacent to the main path through this fiery region. There's a Heavy Sack within the exterior grounds, as well as a possible chest guarded by a Centurion near the lava's edge.

Interior (Galom Daeus): Inside, the Berne Clan of Dunmer skulk about, the smell of vampirism and blood in the metallic air. Venture farther into the Dwemer construct to face a Centurion and access a door into the Manufactory.

Interior (Galom Daeus Manufactory): The Berne Clan have made it all the way to this large chamber, with a strange chest bathed in writhing light. Seek the quest for the answers.

07 MISSIR-DADALIT EGG MINE

Area of Interest:	Group Boss
Entities:	Kwama
Entity:	The Queen's Consort (Kwama Warrior)

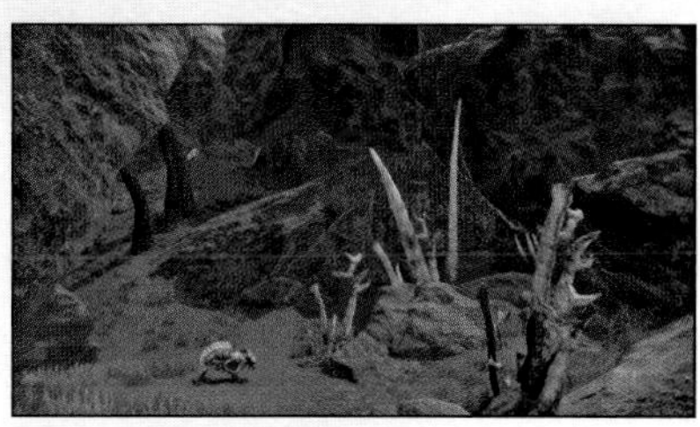

A powerful guardian of a giant Kwama nest resides here. Bring your best weapons and competency for this boss battle. Then check the Andas and Maren Ancestral Tomb rubbings to the east and south, respectively, afterward.

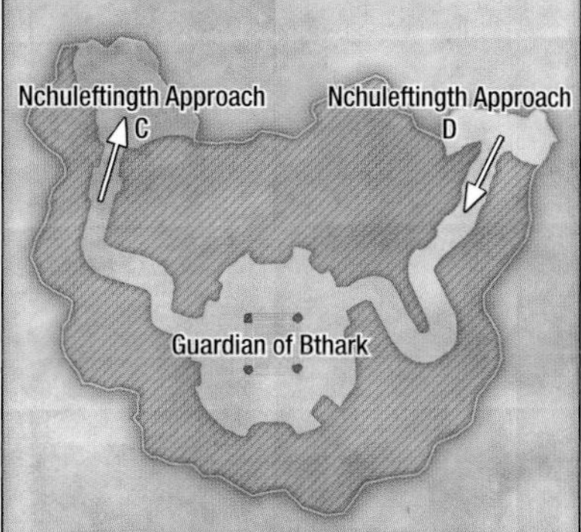

Nchuleftingth Interior 2: Lower Entrance

Interior 2 (Lower Entrance): Bronzefist foes are up to no good in this underground river. Follow the river and watch for kagouti and Dwarven Automaton foes.

08 NCHULEFTINGTH WAYSHRINE

Area of Interest:	Wayshrine
Item of Interest:	Vivec Sermon

The marking place for the Dwemer ruin of the same name is located at the junction of the major roads in this region. Just north is a mine exit, inaccessible unless you're escaping from Zalkin-Sul to the northwest. Check the abandoned cart for a Vivec Sermon **(#26)**.

Nchuleftingth Interior 3: Approach

Interior 3 (Approach): In this gigantic underground cavern, there's a number of Dwarven foes to worry about, including Centurions. Move toward the small towers, and access the Bailey area. Or continue in a clockwise manner around the edge, and head up to a fearsome fight with the Guardian of Bthark and access back to the initial chambers.

09 NCHULEFTINGTH

Areas of Interest:	Public Dungeon, Skyshard
Entities:	Insects, Bronzefist, Dwarven Automatons, Dwarven Centurions, Netch, Kagouti, Guardian of Bthark (Centurion Boss), Renduril the Hammer (Boss), Friar Hadelar (Boss), Nchulaeon the Eternal (Boss), Artisan Lenarmen (Boss)
Related Quest:	The Heart's Desire

Close to the middle of Molag Amur is the ancient Dwemer catacombs built late in the reign of the Deep-Elves. This is the Public Dungeon of Nchuleftingth. Expect seven separate interiors to explore, and a lengthy battle!

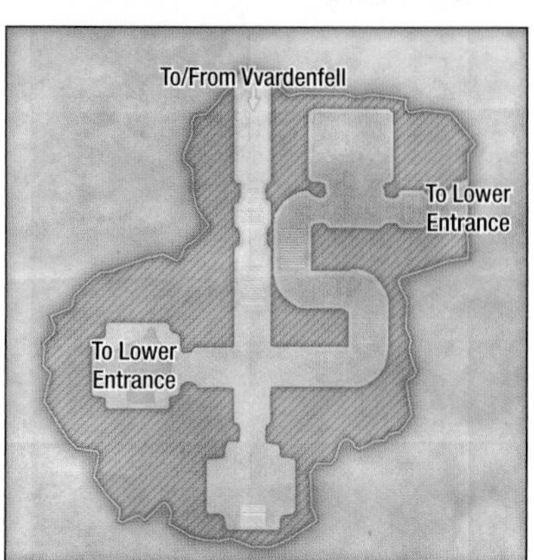

Nchuleftingth Interior 1: Entrance

Interior 1 (Entrance): This overgrown entrance area has a long central corridor and a junction with a large hole to the west, offering access farther into the area. Or turn east, wind your way down a corridor, and out toward the Approach.

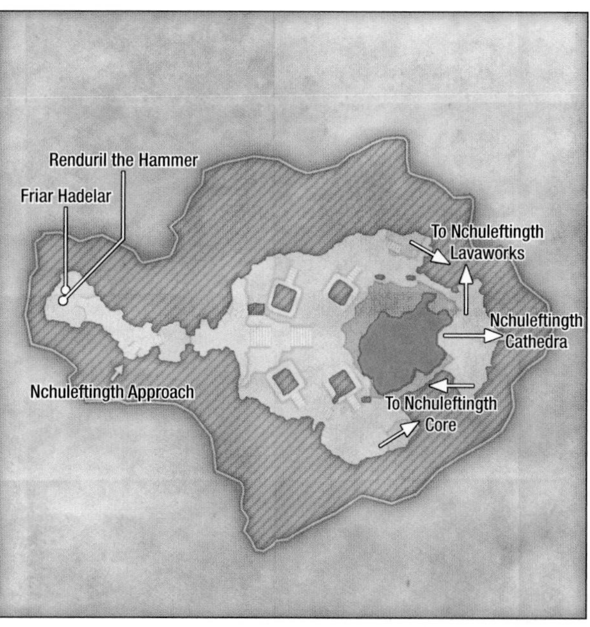

Nchuleftingth Interior 4: Bailey and Ruins

Interior 4 (Bailey and Ruins): Check the large ruined opening to the west to run into Renduril the Hammer and Friar Hadelar. Then head east, open the door to the Ruins, and engage a number of Bronzefist foes by a large lava pool. Carefully work your way around the lava lake to the north and access the Lavaworks (you can also reach a second entrance to the Lavaworks if you're in the vicinity of the Cathedra entrance), or head south and access the Core. Due west is the Cathedra.

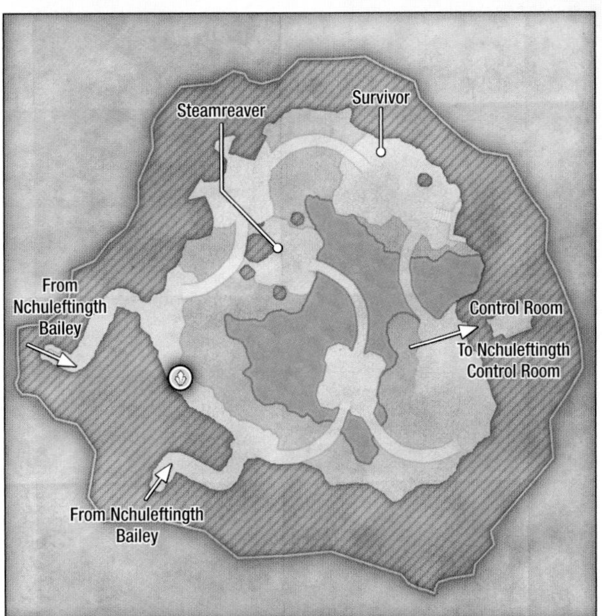

Nchuleftingth Interior 5: Lavaworks and Control Room

⊙	Skyshard

Interior 5 (Lavaworks and Control Room): As you'd expect from the name, this is a gigantic lake of lava, with precarious platforms and ledges to traverse along the way. Expect Dwarven foes, and an eventual descent to the small dead-end Control Room. Note the skyshard on a southwest ledge.

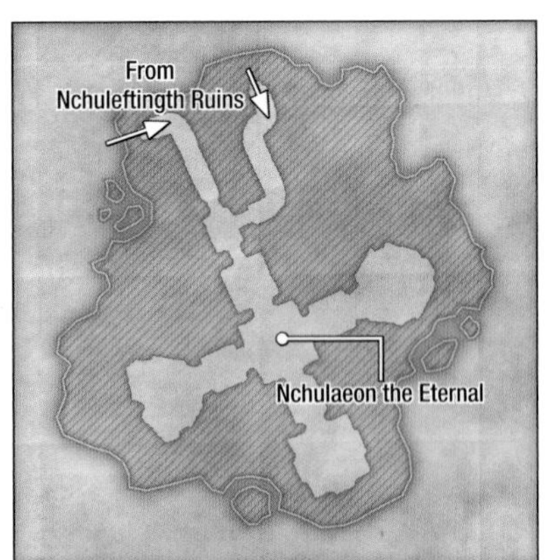

Nchuleftingth Interior 6: Core

Interior 6 (Core): This allows access back to the Ruins, which is handy if you don't want to face the colossal Nchulaeon the Eternal, a giant Dwarven construct.

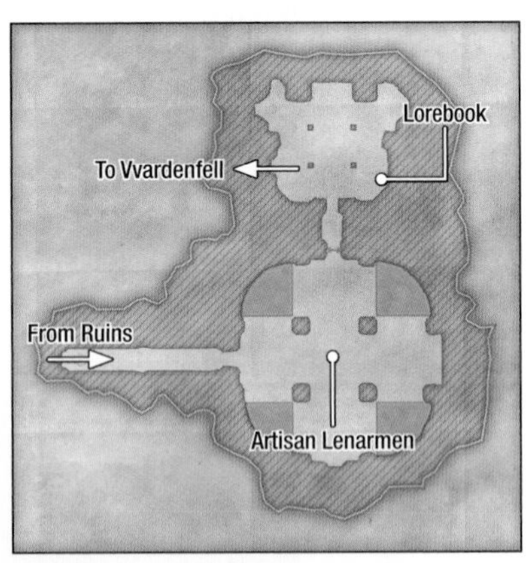

Nchuleftingth Interior 6: Core

Interior 7 (Cathedra): This is only accessible while you're completing the quest and have secured the Dwemer Control Rod. The Cathedra features two gigantic platform locations with connecting corridors. Here, you'll help Neramo and Vimy take on Artisan Lenarmen, retrieve the Bthark Prism, and escape.

10 TUSENEND

Entities:	**Daedroth, Flame Atronach, Profane Bond, Spiders, Kythiirix (Spider Boss)**
Item of Interest:	**Mages Guild Book (Vivec and Mephala)**
Related Quest:	**At Any Cost**

This Molag Bal Shrine, hidden in the volcanic foothills, has a Thieves Trove and a Heavy Sack to search for on the exterior, while you battle Daedric forces.

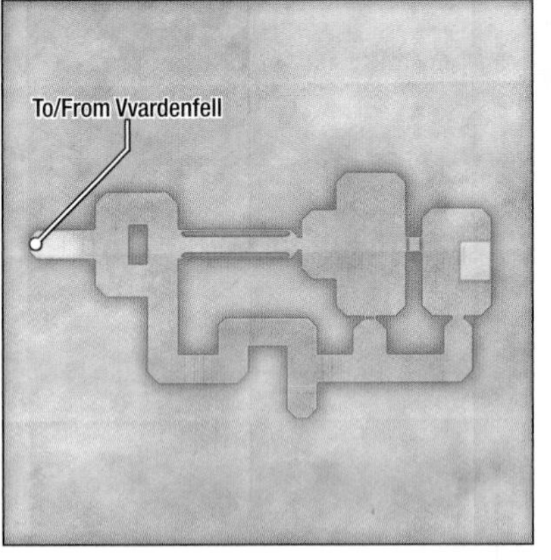

Farther to the northwest, after a short detour to Azura's Coast to reach the slopes of the mountain on the other side of this ruin, there are a couple of skeletons and a Mages Guild Book to obtain, if you fancy the hike.

Interior (Tusenend): Venture into the shrine, ideally during the quest, and battle the Profane Bond clan of shifty Dunmer. Exploring this book repository requires a circular route, and encounters with Spiders as well as some light reading.

11 CAMP AND PYROCLASTIC FLOW

Entities:	**Alit**

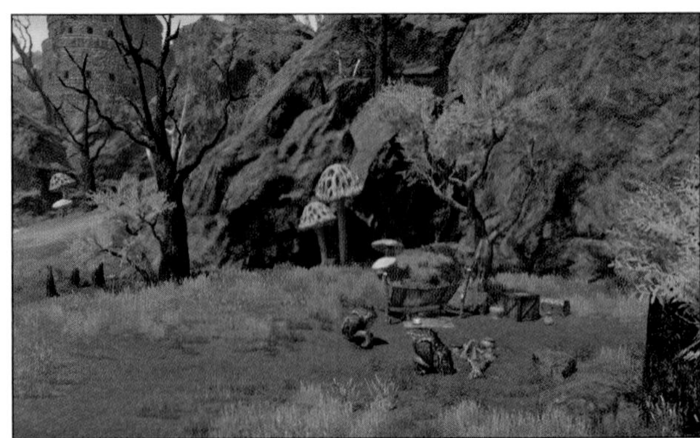

Over on the western side of the region, along the path around Lake Nabia, is a small camp holding a possible chest and Heavy Sack.

12 SULIPUND GRANGE

Area of Interest:	Group Boss
Entity:	Wuyuvus ([XXX])

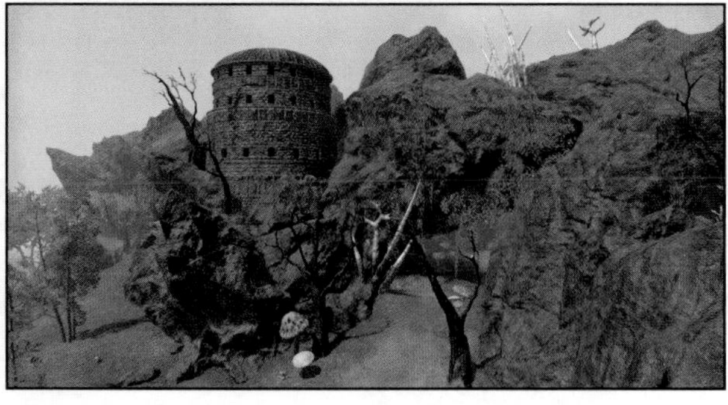

A vicious bloodsucker lurks inside the large cave by the side of this Velothi tower.

13 FOYADA QUARRY

Area of Interest:	Battlegrounds
Entities:	Guar
Items of Interest:	Mages Guild Book (On Stepping Lightly), Vivec Sermon
Merchant:	Keshlar (Elite)

Quarrying blocks in the mountains close to the old Dwemer ruin of Arkngthand has halted for the moment, allowing you to challenge others to battle. Seek the Merchant for some stellar gear, and search the area just east and west of him for a Mages Guild book and Vivec Sermon **(#23)**. The sermon is on a pile of wooden planks near the docks.

14 ASHURARTES

Entities:	Flame Atronachs

A compact Daedric Shrine to Malacath sits close to the battlegrounds and houses little of value, unless you gain spiritual betterment from battling Flame Atronachs and finding a Heavy Sack.

15 MARANDUS

Area of Interest:	Crafting Stations
Entities:	Nix-Oxen

A fortress stronghold constructed by Dunmeri hands, this is worth the visit simply due to the abundance of crafting stations available for your tinkering pleasure.

16 VANDUS ANCESTRAL TOMB

This ancestral tomb, topped with some fungi growing on the door, is inaccessible, and only useful as a route marker to distinguish the border between this region and Ascadian Isles, to the south.

17 ERABENIMSUN CAMP

Entities:	Dunmeri Adventurers

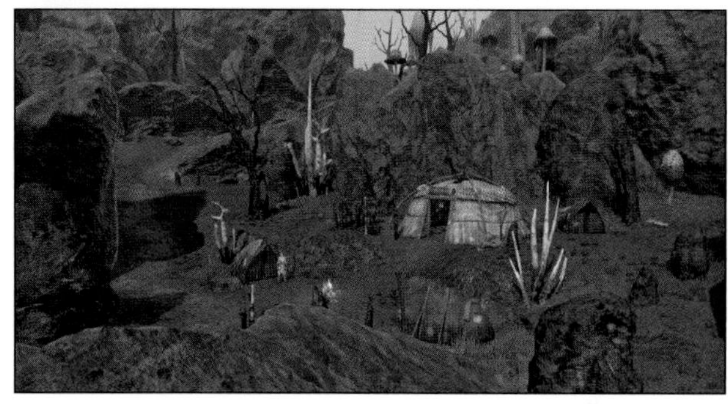

A small contingent of Dunmeri have set up camp here, at the northern foothills of Mount Kand. There's a Thieves Trove here.

18 MOUNTAIN PASS TENT (MOUNT KAND)

Entities:	Great Shalks

A tiny campsite on one of the unmarked paths around Mount Kand holds a possible treasure chest. The camper is gone, perhaps eaten by the Great Shalk in the vicinity.

19 ALAS ANCESTRAL TOMB (MOUNT KAND)

Entities:	Cliff Skippers
Item of Interest:	Skyshard

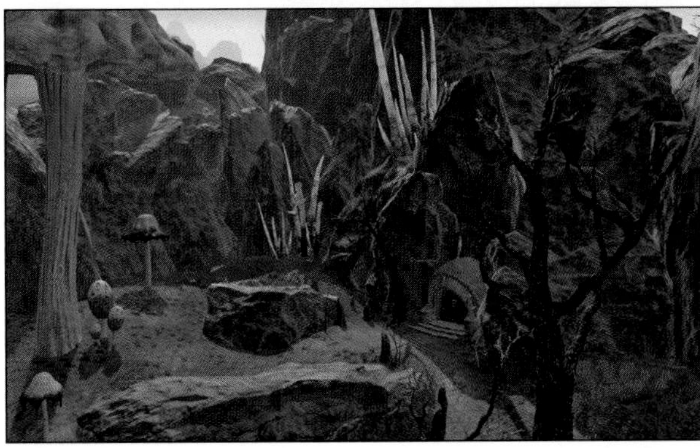

Use this inaccessible tomb door as a landmark while hiking the northeastern side of Mount Kand. Check the path to the east for a skyshard, and some nearby areas for a possible chest and Thieves Trove.

20 MOUNTAIN PASS RAVINE (MOUND KAND)

Entities:	Alits

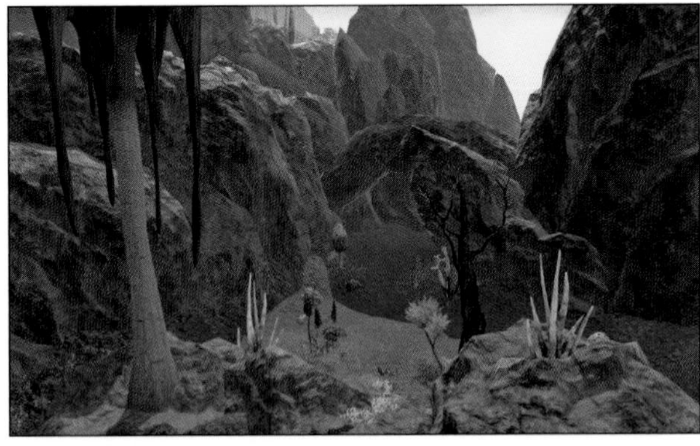

Why go the long way around Mount Kand when you can journey up through the unmarked ravine? Search the area between the two roads to begin your hike, and look for the natural arches.

21 LOWER MOUNTAIN ARCHES (MOUND KAND)

Entities:	Great Shalks
Item of Interest:	Mages Guild Book (On Stepping Lightly)

Just southeast of Erabenimsun Camp is another ravine path, allowing quicker access north and south than following the road around Mount Kand. Check the area above and behind the spikes near the first natural arch close to the camp for a skeleton near a Mages Guild book.

22 INANIUS EGG MINE BACK ENTRANCE

Entities:	Netch
Related Quest:	(VV13) The Scarlet Judge

This is the rear exit of the Inanius Egg Mine, and isn't accessible unless you're exiting from the mine itself. Details of the mine exploration can be found in the Ascadian Isles region, and the corresponding part of the Atlas.

23 TELASERO

Entities:	Netch

Due west of Molag Mar, and just east of Suran in the Ascadian Isles region, this Dunmer fortification has been left to slowly sink into the soft and sandy ground. The area's interior is inaccessible. Note the Thieves Trove here, as well as a Heavy Sack and the Velas Ancestral Tomb rubbing to the south.

24 RED EXILE CAMPSITE

Entities:	Red Exiles

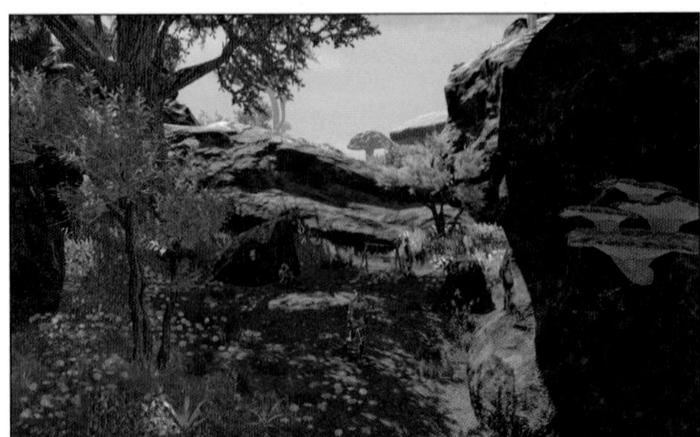

Just southeast of the Raviro Ancestral Tomb rubbing is a cluster of large rocks and a small Dunmeri camp between them.

25 DREUDURAI GLASS MINE

Entities:	Dreugh, Shalk
Related Quest:	An Armiger's Duty

An old mine still filled with an abundance of glass harder than metal is accessible close to the Silt Strider for Molag Mar. Enter during **Quest: The Buoyant Armiger**; the quest giver is nearby, by the Raviro Ancestral Tomb.

To/From Vvardenfell

Interior: The initial mining tunnel opens up to a huge cavern, with a lava flow bisecting it from west to east. Various ledges and precarious paths allow access around this cavern, and to a large U-shaped tunnel structure to the north.

26 HELAN ANCESTRAL TOMB

Item of Interest:	Vivec Sermon
Related Quest:	(VV15) An Armiger's Duty

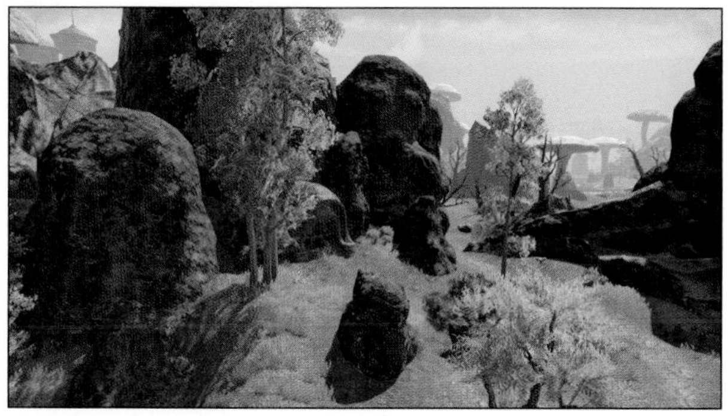

This accessible tomb is on the border between Molag Amur and Azura's Coast, close to the Wayshrine. The interior (not mapped) is small, suspiciously quiet, and the Vivec Sermon **(#28)** is found at the far end of the tomb.

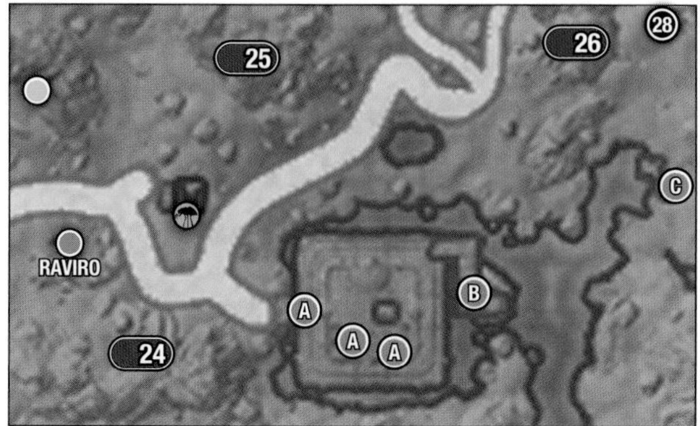

Skyshard	Ancestral Tomb Rubbing
Treasure Chest	Vivec Sermon

27 MOLAG MAR

Area of Interest:	Silt Strider
Crafting:	Cooking Fire
Entities:	House Guards
Item of Interest:	Lorebook (Buoyant Armigers: Swords of Vivec)
Merchant:	Caravaner Narisa Androm, Innkeeper Servus Alor
Related Quest:	An Armiger's Duty

Constructed in the style of a single canton seen throughout Vivec City, Molag Mar is a base camp for those taking the pilgrimage to the nearby mountains. Armigers hang out here, and recent repairs to the settlement mean the only interior location is the tavern. Be on the lookout for Narisa Androm; this Caravaner has choice items to barter for.

(A) The Penitent Pilgrim Inn

Accessed at three points inside the settlement, this three-floor inn features a Cooking Fire, as well as an Innkeeper more than happy to sell you some goods. Check the Lorebook on a nearby table, too.

(B) Molag Mar Docks

Cargo vessels are moored here, but this doesn't offer you travel to other port cities. Instead, amuse yourself at the Fishing Hole.

(C) Molag Mar Wayshrine

This Wayshrine is just across the border in the Azura's Coast region, and is detailed in the corresponding part of the Atlas.

28 MOLAG MAR WAYSHRINE

Area of Interest:	Wayshrine

The Wayshrine for Molag Mar is technically on the shore of Azura's Coast, but close enough to be included in this region. There are a couple of fishing spots, and easy access to the aforementioned city, as well as the southeast coast.

AZURA'S COAST

Although it is technically the largest of all the regions of Vvardenfell, Azura's Coast is the most sparsely populated. It's the primary territory of House Telvanni, who lay claim to the main settlements here, from the northern coastal tower of Tel Mora to the main island city of Sadrith Mora, and down to the southwestern tip of the coast and the mushroom-tangled wonder of Tel Branora. If you seek saltwater fishing, tombs, coves, and caves to explore, and the particularly brutal Halls of Fabrication to really test your mettle, journey eastward.

Locations

01	Black Snail Smugglers' Isle	22	Nchardumz (North)
02	Tel Mora	23	Nchardumz (Southeast)
03	Esutanamus	24	Almurbalarammi
04	Pinsun	25	Barilzar's Tower
05	Hanud Tower	26	Red Exile Rock Camp
06	Vassamsi Grotto and Mine	27	Grave Marker
07	Hlervi Ancestral Tomb	28	Shrine of Azura
08	Yansirramus	29	Mzahnch
09	Tel Aruhn	30	Lady Laurent's Camp
10	Sadrith Mora	31	Bal Fell
11	Sadrith Mora Wayshrine	32	Red Exile Toadstool Camp
12	Sadrith Mora Dock and Slave Field	33	Zaintiraris
13	Anudnabia	34	Hlaalu Ancestral Tomb
14	Halls of Fabrication (Tel Fyr)	35	Mawia
15	Dreloth Ancestral Tomb	36	Abebaal Egg Mine (Abandoned)
16	Kaushtarari	37	Marvani Ancestral Tomb
17	Tel Galen	38	Shipwreck Cove
18	Andalen Ancestral Tomb	39	Tel Branora Wayshrine
19	Matus-Akin Egg Mine	40	Tel Branora
20	Holamayan Monastery	41	Beran Ancestral Tomb
21	Shashpilamat		

01 BLACK SNAIL SMUGGLERS' ISLE

Entities:	Black Snails (Gang)
Item of Interest:	Mages Guild Book (The Living Gods)

With the strange fungal tower of Tel Mora to the west, this medium-sized island is home to a band of Black Snail smugglers, and some valuables to loot—a possible treasure chest, Heavy Sack, Thieves Trove, and a Mages Guild book near a half-sunk rowing boat on the north side of the island. There's some fishing to do here, too.

02 TEL MORA

Location:	Port Settlement
Entities:	Tel Mora Protectors
Items of Interest:	Lorebook (Skin Blights By Any Other Name), Vivec Sermon
Merchant:	Navigator Bolnora Romavel, Caravaner Adosi Delvi, Alchemist Menwendel
Related Quest:	(VV4) Reclaiming Vos, (VV5) At Any Cost

A large island off the coast of the Grazelands region, twinned with the town of Vos to the east, Tel Mora is dominated by a huge tower of fungal growths, from which the coastal settlement takes its name. Though it shares goods and services with Vos across the shore in Grazelands, it should be seen as a separate settlement, except when obtaining Merchant services. The Silt Strider and a trader are up the cliff at Vos.

Note the the location "Black Snail Smugglers' Isle" is shown on this town map. For the items and area (including the Mages Guild book), consult that Atlas reference.

Quest	Thieves Trove
Heavy Sack	Treasure Chest
Mages Guild Lorebook	Vivec Sermon

AZURA'S COAST (NORTH)—OVERVIEW/COLLECTIBLES/QUESTS/FISHING

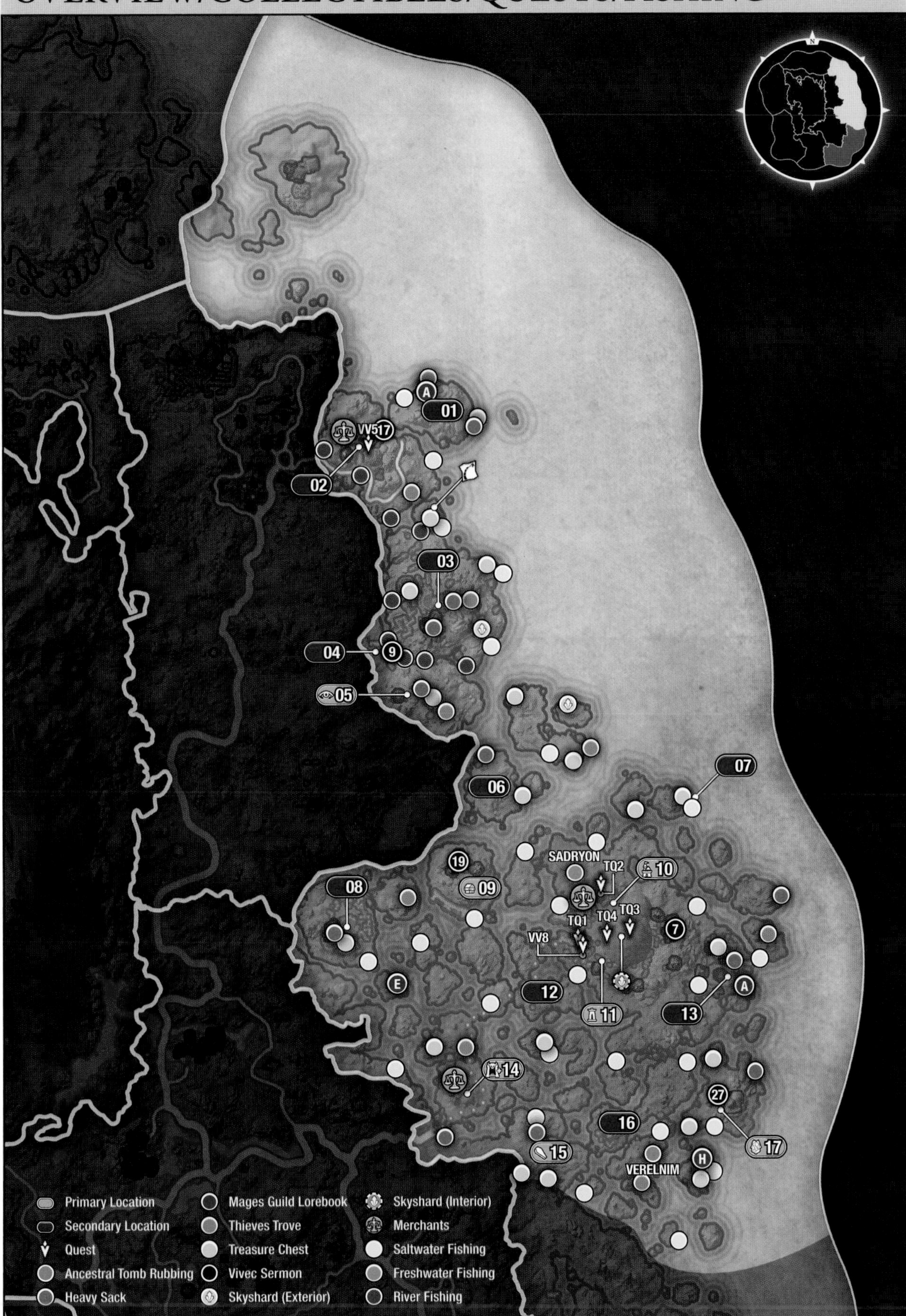

AZURA'S COAST (SOUTH)—OVERVIEW/COLLECTIBLES/QUESTS/FISHING

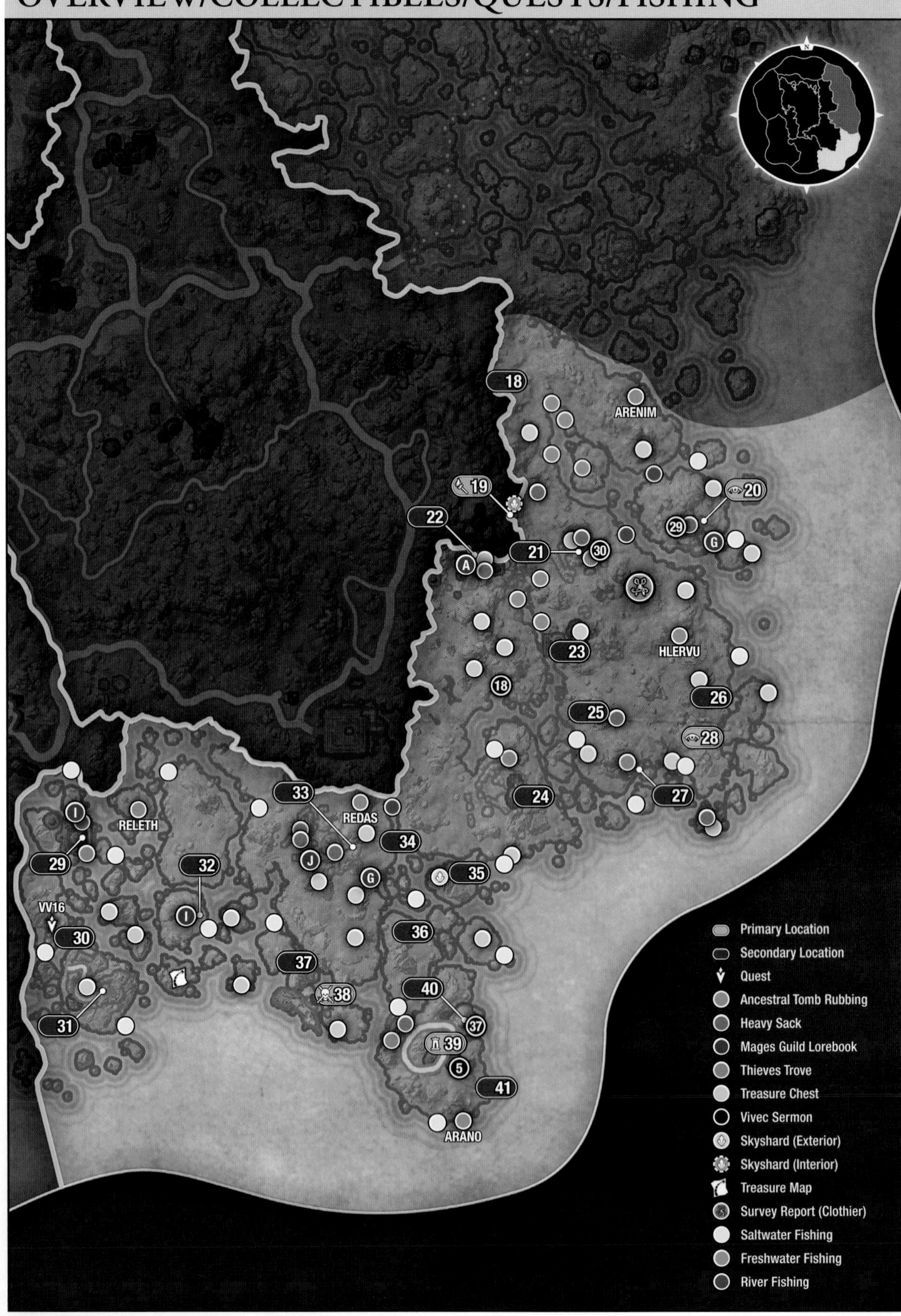

Ⓐ Docks to Vos

Traverse between the docks and the Grazelands town of Vos when seeking Merchants or access to the mainland.

Ⓑ Tel Mora Docks

A couple of boats and a Navigator named Bolnora Romavel allow you to travel to any other port settlement.

Ⓒ Tobor's House

Warning:	Restricted Area (Trespass)

Pry open the locked door (Intermediate difficulty) to trespass into this dwelling. As the folks in here use spells, expect combat.

Ⓓ Athram's House

Warning:	Restricted Area (Trespass)

It's worth trespassing into this rock dwelling with a locked door (Simple difficulty) for the Vivec Sermon (#17), upstairs on a table.

Ⓔ Tel Mora (Tower)

The main tower of Tel Mora features a po-faced steward named Seden, whom you can speak to about the owner of the tower, Mistress Dratha. Use a portal to reach her upstairs chambers.

Ⓕ Menwendel's Nursery

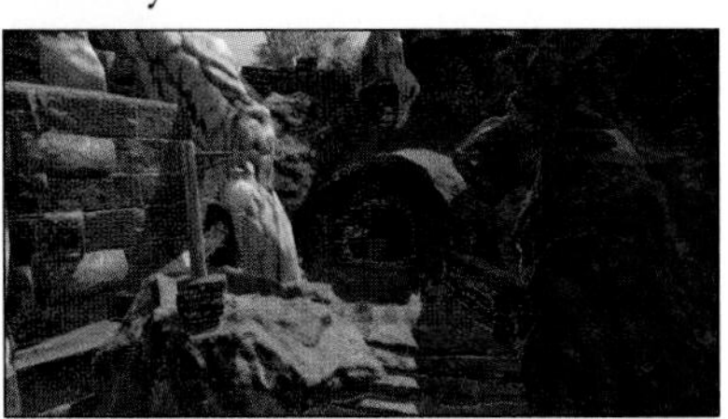

Don't leave Tel Mora without visiting this Alchemist's paradise. There are more mushrooms than you can comfortably stuff into a knapsack, and the cellar has a Lorebook all about skin blights.

03 ESUTANAMUS

Entities:	Clannfear, Daedroth, Winged Twilights
Item of Interest:	Skyshard
Related Quest:	(VV5) At Any Cost

This large island dedicated to the Daedric Prince Molag Bal is sprawling, with plenty of Daedric foes to worry about. Scattered across the island are two possible treasure chests, two Heavy Sacks, and a Thieves Trove. On the eastern shore of the island, there are fewer foes, more Fishing Holes, and a skyshard.

04 PINSUN

Entities:	Black Snails (Gang)
Item of Interest:	Vivec Sermon
Related Quest:	(VV4) Reclaiming Vos

Smugglers hold their ill-gotten gains at this small dock and mine, a time-honored practice that continues to this day. Black Snail Dunmer rove the area; check their docked boat for a Vivec Sermon **(#9)**.

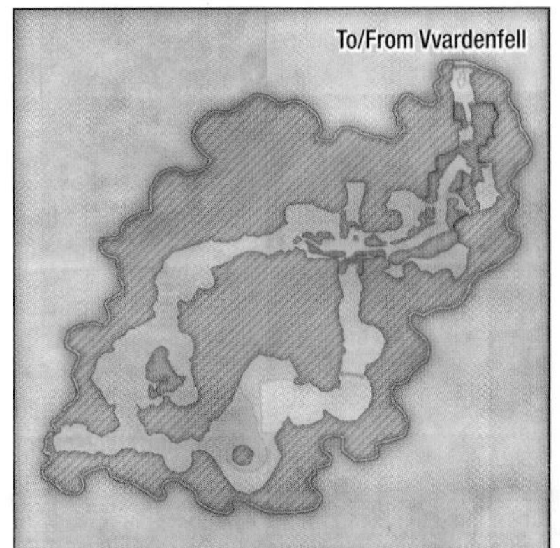

Interior (Pinsun): Inside is a rough-hewn mine tunnel, some glowing fungi, and a whole lot more Black Snail foes. Work your way clockwise around this roughly circular interior, as there's a door along the main south tunnel that's only accessible heading south to north.

05 HANUD TOWER

Entities:	Kagouti

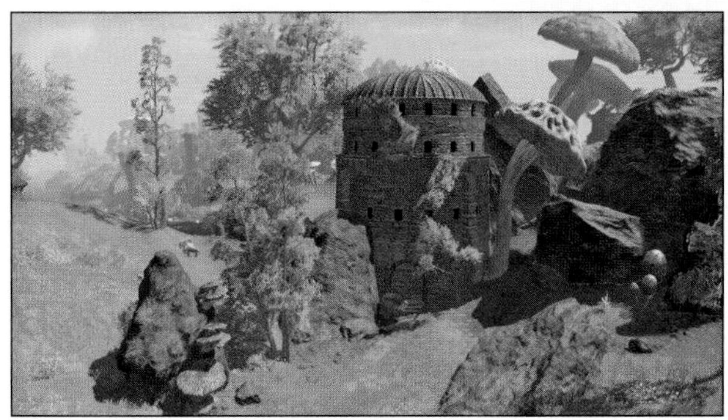

Though this Velothi tower is situated on an area of mainland close to the Grazelands region, it is nevertheless part of Azura's Coast, much like the nearby Pinsun mine. The place is walled up and inaccessible, so use it as a landmark. Check the general area, mainly to the east, for a Heavy Sack, possible chest, and a Thieves Trove.

06 VASSAMSI GROTTO AND MINE

Entities:	Argonian Slaves, Vassamsi Guards, Slavemaster Arenim (Dunmeri Boss)
Item of Interest:	Skyshard
Related Quest:	The Heart of a Telvanni

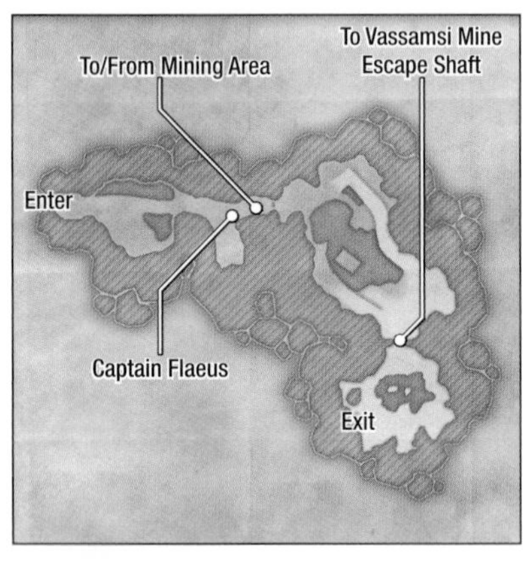

A pair of islands off the coast of Grazelands contains an interesting interior grotto to explore. Before heading inside, check the island northeast of this one; there's a skyshard, two possible treasure chests, and a Thieves Trove. Vassamsi Island itself has a possible chest and a Heavy Sack. Enter via the grotto or mine entrance.

Interior (Grotto and Mining Area): There are three distinct chambers, each segmented by a wooden door. South (Escape Shaft) is a green arena where you face Slavemaster Arenim. The northeast (Mining) area is a waterlogged chamber, and the western mine corridor has a small wooden stilt cage. Expect Argonian slaves and Vassamsi guards.

07 HLERVI ANCESTRAL TOMB

Entities:	Netch
Item of Interest:	Lorebook (Vvardenfell Flora and Fauna)

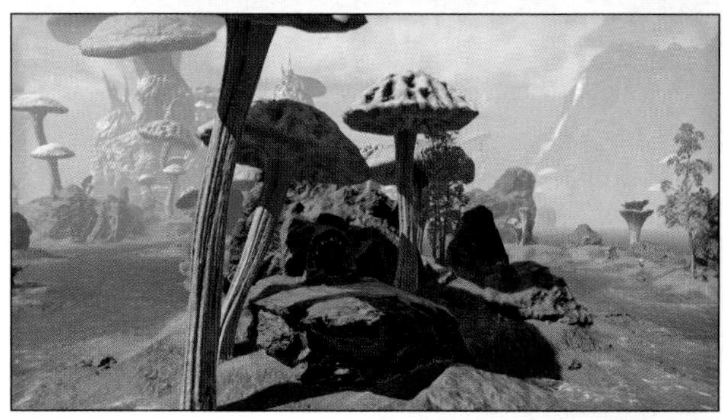

A small island north of Sadrith Mora, still may house the remains of the Hlervi Family, and though the tomb was once sealed off and impenetrable, it is worth exploring the interior of. Inside, is a small waterlogged chamber with a lorebook, some pure water, and minor chests to loot. Also come here for the views and the possible two exterior treasure chests.

08 YANSIRRAMUS

Entities:	Dremora, Brakuum (Ogrim)
Item of Interest:	Mages Guild Book (Invocation of Azura)
Related Quest:	(VV5) At Any Cost

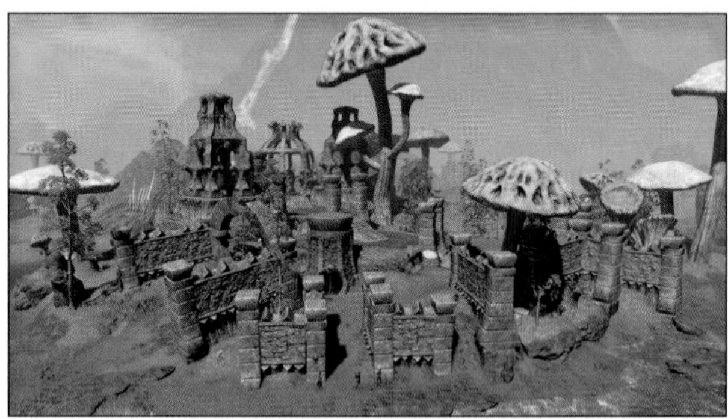

In this shrine complex to Molag Bal, Daedric forces are present on the surface of the ruins, along with a lumbering bag of pustules known as Brakuum. A Heavy Sack and chest are your possible rewards, along with the thrill of spilling Daedric blood. The interior is currently inaccessible. Check the small island just southeast of here for a missing Mages Guild book.

09 TEL ARUHN

Entities:	House Guards
Item of Interest:	Vivec Sermon
Related Quests:	(TQ3) Objections and Obstacles, (TQ5) The Heart of Telvanni

Magister Gothren, who's not too keen on outlanders, resides in the fungal tower of this small island town. Though the structures are impressive, the adjacent city of Sadrith Mora to the southeast has taken a little of the shine away from this place of slavers. Remember that the easiest way to access this town is via the entrance door up from the docks.

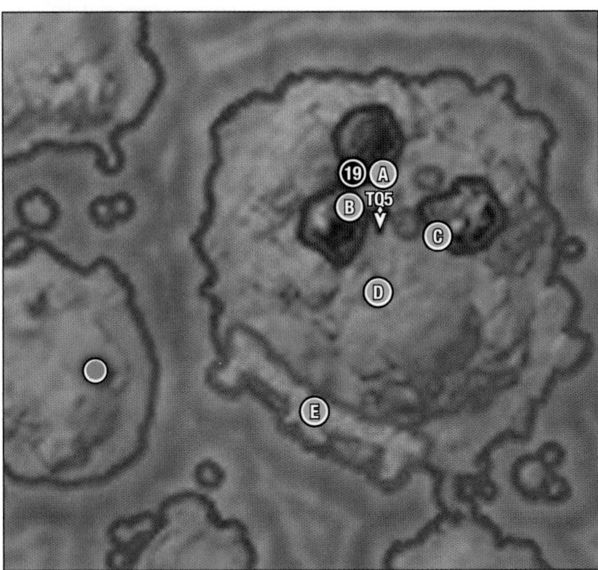

	Quest
	Thieves Trove
	Vivec Sermon

Ⓐ Vedran's House

Warning:	Restricted Area (Trespass)

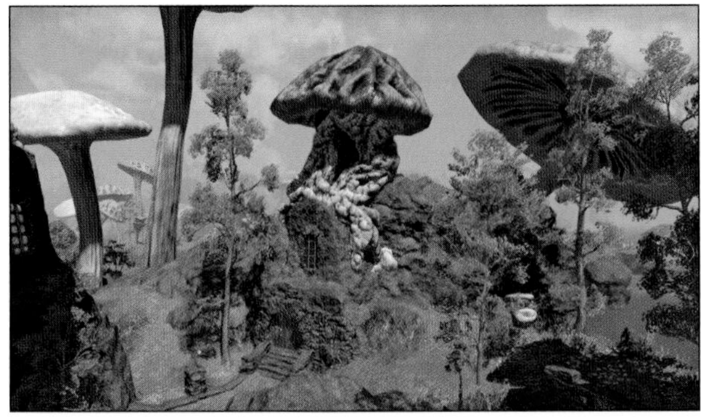

This is locked (Intermediate difficulty), and snoopers venturing inside are not welcome. But it's worth trespassing to snag the Vivec Sermon **(#19)** on the bench just inside the front door. There's a Safebox upstairs too, if you're really intent on stealing.

Ⓑ Slavemaster's House

Warning:	Restricted Area (Trespass)

After accessing the locked door (Advanced difficulty), you can sneak around the dwelling of Cooks-Fine-Things, a Khajiit and Argonian owner.

Ⓒ Selaro's Tower

Warning:	Restricted Area (Trespass)

Though not quite as impressive a structure as the main tower, this locked locale (Advanced difficulty) has a small Guar stables in the cellar downstairs, and a Safebox to loot.

Ⓓ Tel Aruhn Tower

The tower is inaccessible unless a quest is active, and there's a portal inside to the private chambers of Magister Gothren.

Ⓔ Tel Aruhn Docks

A couple of moored ships, a light guard presence, and a grumbling dock worker are to be found here. Check the door in the rock outcrop north of the dock to enter Tel Aruhn.

10 SADRITH MORA

Areas of Interest:	Wayshrine, Skyshard
Crafting:	Alchemy Station, Cooking Fire (3), Enchanting Table,
Entities:	House Guards, Sentries
Items of Interest:	Lorebook (Testimonials on Mushroom Towers), Lorebook (The Worth of Glass), Vivec Sermon
Location:	Port City
Merchants:	Alchemist Telare Relenim, Boatswain Rinori Mathendis, Enchanter Vaden Inlador, General Goods Merchant Makes-No-Ripples, Guild Trader Felayn Uvaram, Guild Trader Runik, Guild Trader Ruxultav, Hall Steward Vedelea Tenim, Magister Bertis Benethran, Mystic Ervyna Duleri
Related Quests:	(TQ1) A Hireling of House Telvanni, (TQ2) Rising to Retainer, (TQ3) Objections and Obstacles, (TQ4) The Magister Makes a Move, (TQ5) The Heart of a Telvanni, (VV8) Bound by Love

Known in the Dunmeri tongue as "Forest of Mushrooms," this island city requires access via a wade through the islands of the Zafirbel Bay, by Wayshrine, or by boat. This toadstool citadel is the seat of power of House Telvanni.

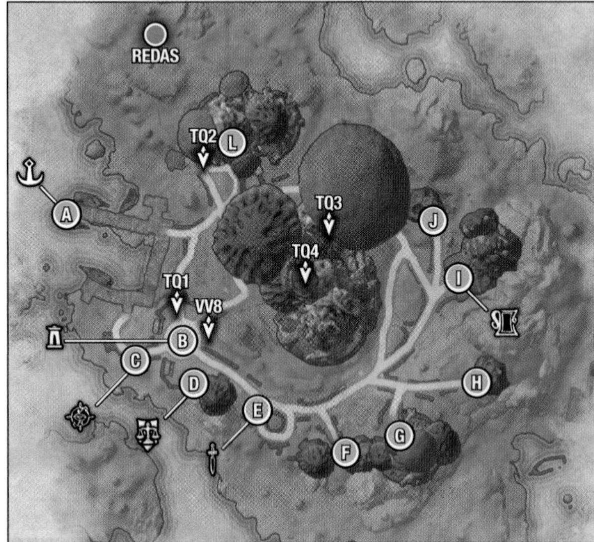

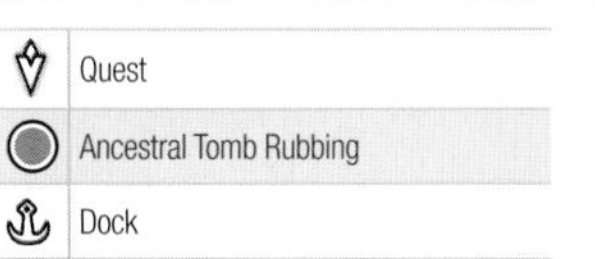

Quest	Mages Guild
Ancestral Tomb Rubbing	Guild Kiosk
Dock	Fighters Guild
Wayshrine	Inn

(A) Sadrith Mora Docks

Merchant:	Boatswain Rinori Mathendis

An accomplished Navigator is here to take you to or from any other port city on Vvardenfell.

(B) Sadrith Mora Wayshrine

This Wayshrine, close to the market area, is discussed in an adjacent Atlas entry. Check it for further information.

(C) Mages Guild Encampment

Crafting:	Cooking Fire
Merchant:	Magister Bertis Benethran

Visit the Magister by the tent near the shore, and sign up to be a student of the Mages Guild.

(D) Sadrith Mora Market (Guild Traders)

Merchants:	Guild Trader Felayn Uvaram, Guild Trader Runik, Guild Trader Ruxultav

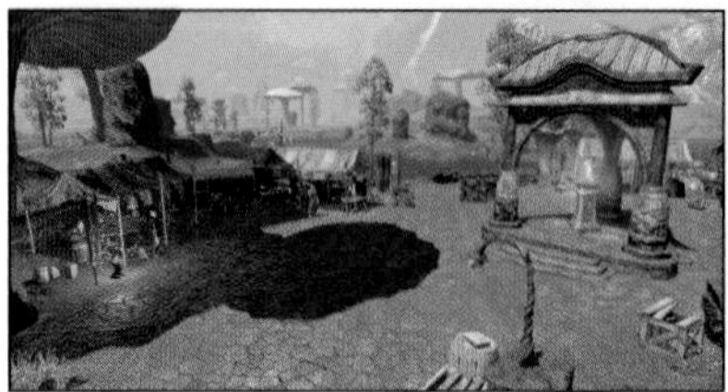

The main part of the market square consists of three veteran Guild Traders, able to sell a guild's wares for the very best prices.

(E) Fighters Guild Encampment

Crafting:	Cooking Fire
Merchant:	Hall Steward Vedelea Tenim

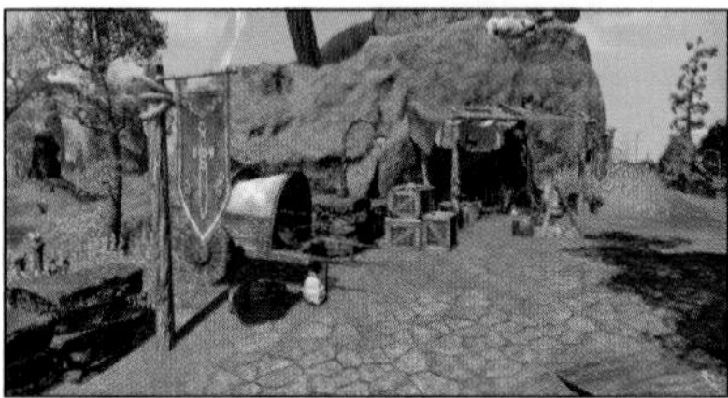

Speak with the Hall Steward if you're interested in joining the Fighters Guild, or wish to purchase wares here.

(F) Nilvon's House

Warning:	Restricted Area (Trespass)

After unlocking the lock (Simple difficulty), investigate this cozy hovel with a cellar and a perturbed stranger questioning why you're here.

(G) Givyn Tower

Warning:	Restricted Area (Trespass)

Access the door (Simple difficulty) and sneak around in here, using the hiding spots if you wish. Beware of sentries attacking you. Inside is a trapdoor leading to a basement. The basement leads to an earthen cavern, more sentries, and a cubbyhole of books.

Ⓗ Sun-in-Shadow's House

This abode is firmly locked and only available for venturing into during a relevant quest.

Ⓘ Gateway Inn

Crafting:	Cooking Fire
Merchant:	General Goods Merchant Makes-No-Ripples

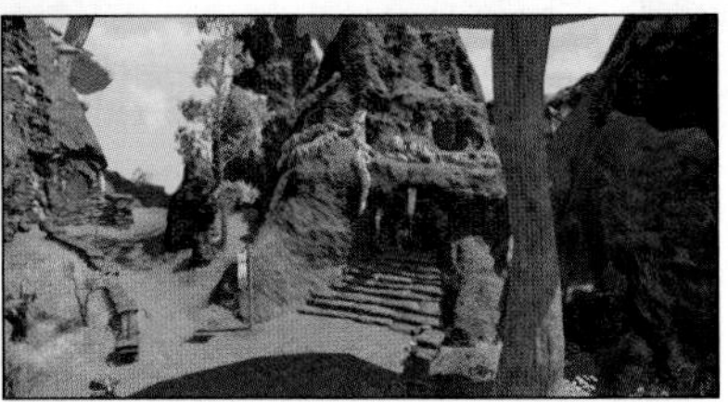

This tavern offers the finest food and drink, and a couple of choice Lorebooks; one of them is the Vivec Sermon tome you seek **(#7)**, upstairs on the landing table.

Ⓙ Bandas' House

Warning:	Restricted Area (Trespass)

Another lock (Simple difficulty), and another Dunmeri family rudely interrupted. Expect the guards to be summoned.

Ⓚ Reram's House

Warning:	Restricted Area (Trespass)

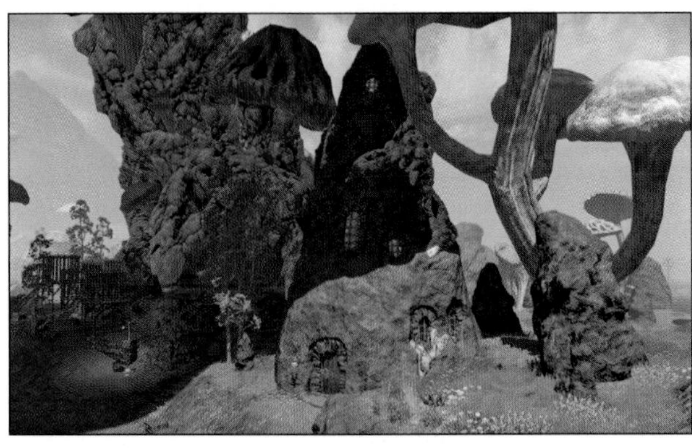

After a trickier lock (Advanced difficulty), this dwelling, which is under the canopy of a giant mushroom, offers a grumpy resident decidedly nonplussed by your hijinks.

Ⓛ Council House

Warning:	Restricted Area (Trespass)

The main Telvanni Council meets in this imposing structure, with Argonian slave cages situated outside. Inside the structure is a central portal, allowing access to the Council Audience Chamber. Around the edge of the entrance hall are three further doors—to the Tel Branora Mouth Chambers, the Wizard's Study, and the Council Hall.

Interior (Council Audience Chamber): You may view political wranglings of the Telvanni Council from the seating provided here.

Interior (Tel Branora Mouth Chambers): Rulings from the southern settlement are heard here, in a circular chamber with a fancy seat.

Interior (Wizard's Study): The head wizard resides in this circular room.

Interior (Council Hall): An imposing grand hall leads to the Mouth Chamber, which you'll need to trespass to enter.

Ⓜ Tel Naga

Area of Interest:	Skyshard
Crafting:	Alchemy Station, Enchanting Table
Merchants:	Alchemist Telare Relenim, Enchanter Vaden Inlador, Mystic Ervyna Duleri
Warning:	Restricted Area (Trespass)

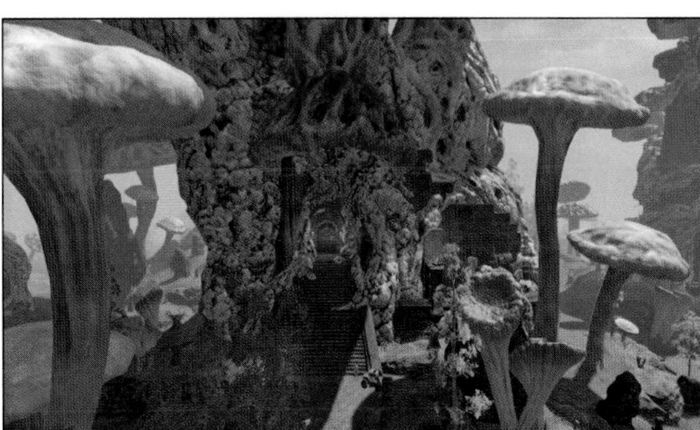

The primary mushroom structure of this city, the main circular chamber features a noticeboard you can check for quests, as well as stores and workstations for Alchemy and Enchanting. There's a door to the Adepts' Hall, and a central portal to the Magister's Retreat.

Adepts' Hall: You must trespass to enter here, so beware of starting a fight with these magicians.

Magister's Retreat: These are the inner chambers of the ruler of the city. Don't forget to access the skyshard before leaving Sadrith Mora.

11 SADRITH MORA WAYSHRINE

Area of Interest:	Wayshrine

The Wayshrine of the city of Sadrith Mora is in the center of the marketplace, near the main docks. Notable quests are listed in the Sadrith Mora portion of this Atlas.

12 SADRITH MORA DOCK AND SLAVE FIELD

Entities:	Argonians

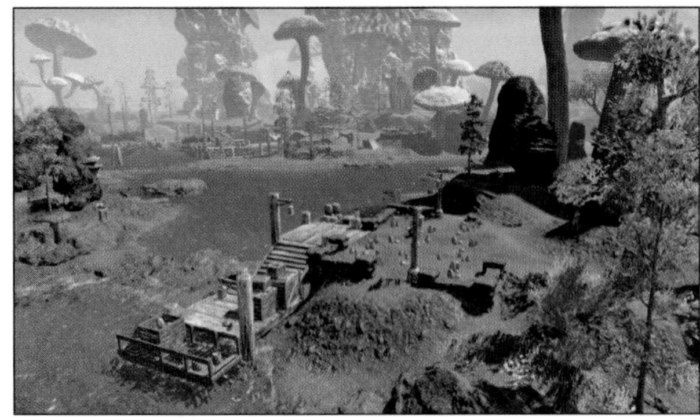

Indentured Argonian workers harvest crops on the island southwest of Sadrith Mora, near a dock where cargo vessels unload their crates.

13 ANUDNABIA

Entities:	Dremora, Hungers, Kagouti
Item of Interest:	Mages Guild Book (The Living Gods)

On the island of Sadrith Mora, the western edge of the city houses a great Daedric shrine, with a contingent of Daedra to slaughter when you arrive. Check the area, and the two small islands to the north, for two Heavy Sacks, a possible chest, a Thieves Trove, and a Mages Guild book on the southeastern water's edge, below a sagging stone ruin section sliding into the sea.

14 HALLS OF FABRICATION (TEL FYR)

Area of Interest:	Trial
Crafting:	Alchemy Station, Blacksmithing Station, Clothing Station, Enchanting Table, Woodworking Station,
Entities:	Capacitors, Calefactors, Dissectors, Dwarven Automatons (Fabricants), Guar (Fabricants), Kagouti (Fabricants), Nix-Hounds (Fabricants), Ruptured Centurions, Shalks (Fabricants), Spiders (Fabricants), Hunter-Killer Fabricants (Bosses), Pinnacle Factotum (Boss), Archcustodian (Boss), Reactor (Boss), Reclaimer (Boss), Reducer (Boss), Assembly General (Boss)
Item of Interest:	Lorebook (Telvanni Memo)
Related Quest:	Forging the Future

A Velothi tower smothered in writhing fungal growths is the entrance to a series of exceptionally tough Trials created by Sotha Sil. Head into these parts unknown only if you have the mettle necessary to survive!

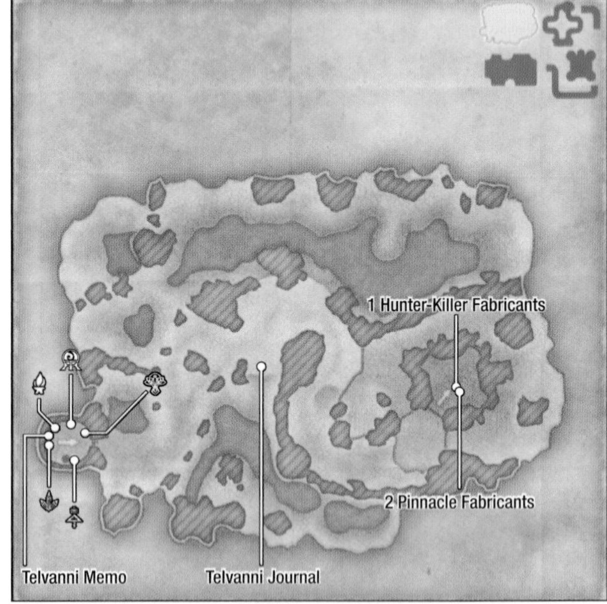

Halls of Fabrication Interior 1: Abanabi Cave

Interior 1 (Abanabi Cave): After potentially stopping to craft at the entrance, head into this gigantic cave of terror, where Fabricants of foes you may have faced are ready to battle. Head to the arena, where two reptilian Hunter-Killer Fabricants must be defeated. Your reward is a chest, more foes, then a battle with the Pinnacle Factotum. Enter the Rift, and into the next part of the Trial.

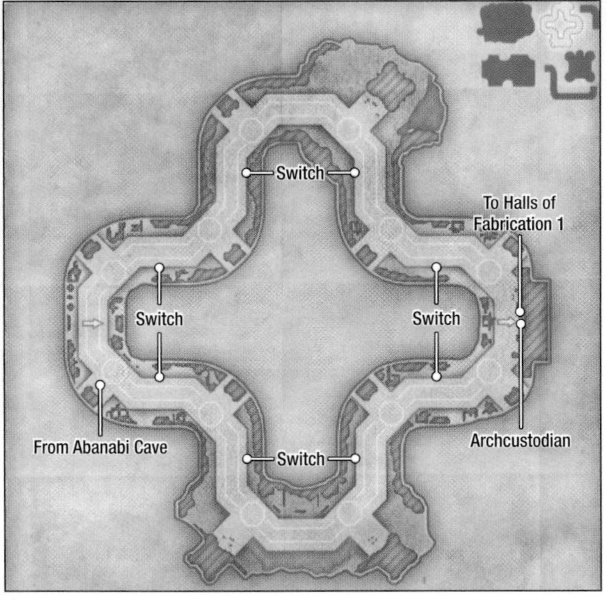

Halls of Fabrication Interior 2: Transport Circuit

Interior 2 (Transport Circuit): You deal with Spiders in this roughly circular corridor. Continue in either direction until you reach and fight the giant arachnid Archcustodian. You can then enter the Reprocessing Yard via the Halls of Fabrication.

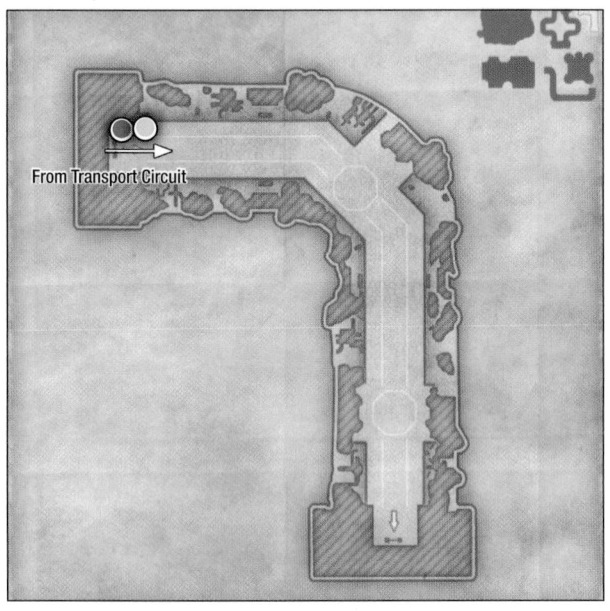

Halls of Fabrication Interior 3: Halls of Fabrication 1

Heavy Sack | Treasure Chest

Interior 3 (Halls of Fabrication 1): An L-shaped corridor contains numerous traps and Calefactors. Defeat three foes: the roughly human-sized Capacitor, Calefactor, and Dissector. Battle three more of them to open the door into the Reprocessing Yard.

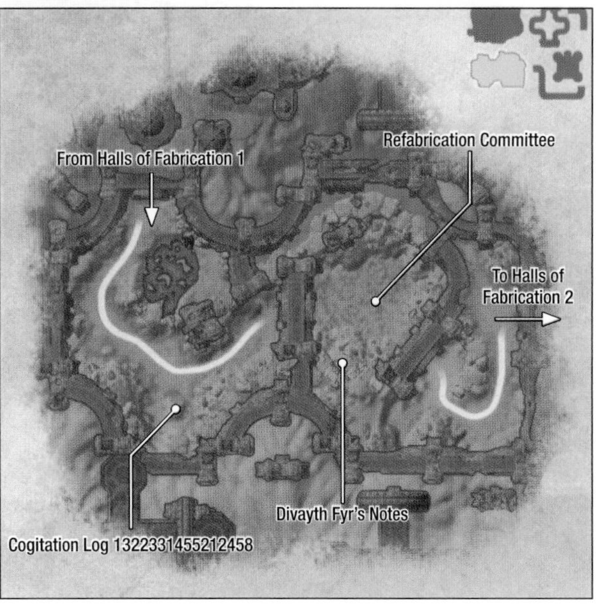

Halls of Fabrication Interior 4: Reprocessing Yard

Interior 4 (Reprocessing Yard): This seems like a sandy exterior area, until you look up and see you're in a giant dome structure. Battle the Ruptured Centurions, a contingent of Arquebuses, and some previously fought foes to open the central gate. After a chat with Divayth Fyr, you face three new bothersome foes: the Reactor, Reclaimer, and Reducer. A second gate opens, allowing you up a slope and into a second Halls of Fabrication corridor.

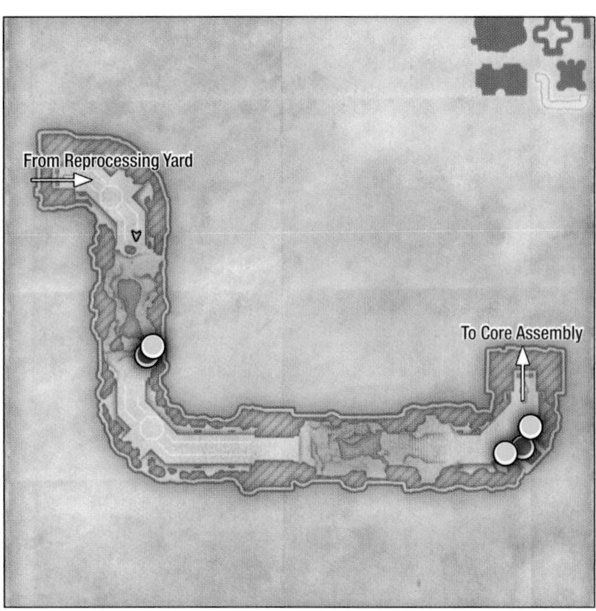

Halls of Fabrication Interior 5: Halls of Fabrication 2

Heavy Sack | Treasure Chest

Interior 5 (Halls of Fabrication 2): Previously encountered enemies must be slain to open a gate through into a sunken grotto. Then head up the other side to a final entrance into Core Assembly. Check the chests and Heavy Sack before leaving.

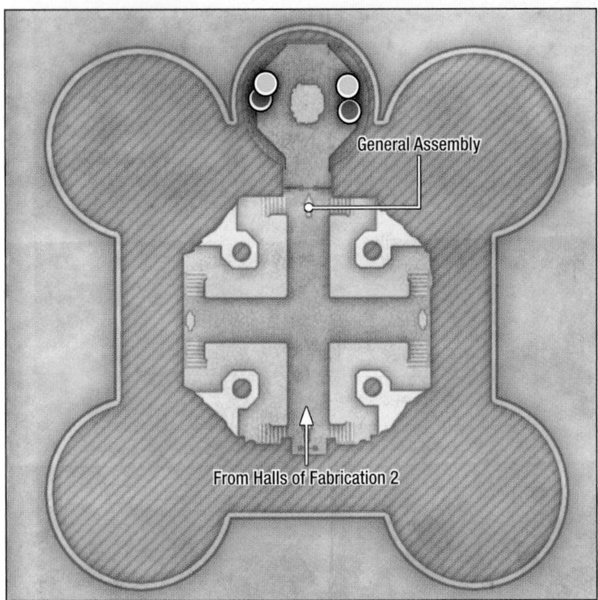

Halls of Fabrication Interior 6: Core Assembly

 Heavy Sack 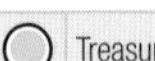 Treasure Chest

Interior 6 (Core Assembly): The Assembly General, a Centurion-like construct like nothing you've ever seen before, roars into life. This is your final Trial challenge.

15 DRELOTH ANCESTRAL TOMB

Entities:	Daedrats, Grievous Twilight
Related Quest:	Ancestral Adversity

Explore this tomb on the shores of Azura's Coast. Check the general outside area for a Heavy Sack and two possible chests (to the south) before heading inside. Enter here to speak to Narsis Dren during the quest.

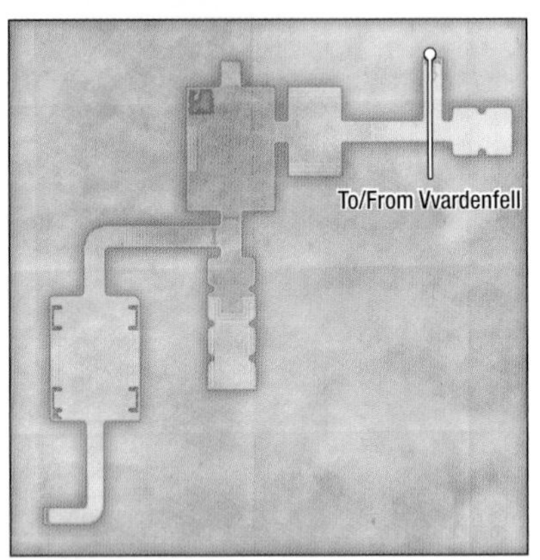

Interior Level 1: A frightening arachnid shadow looms over this area, but the main threats are lowly Daedrats.

Interior Level 1 (Prayer Room): In this long chamber, Narsis uncovers a secret door to the remaining chambers of this place.

Interior Level 1 (Dreloth Ancestral Tomb): A looming Grievous Twilight awaits you in a chamber after a flight of stairs, before a final corridor to the outside and a high exit door.

16 KAUSHTARARI

Entities:	Skaafin, Chodala (Boss)
Related Quest:	(VQ4) Divine Intervention

This is a rather diminutive Shrine to Malacath, given the size of the island it sits on, but one with an interior to explore. Note the Verelnim Ancestral Tomb rubbing on the island just southeast of here, along with a Thieves Trove.

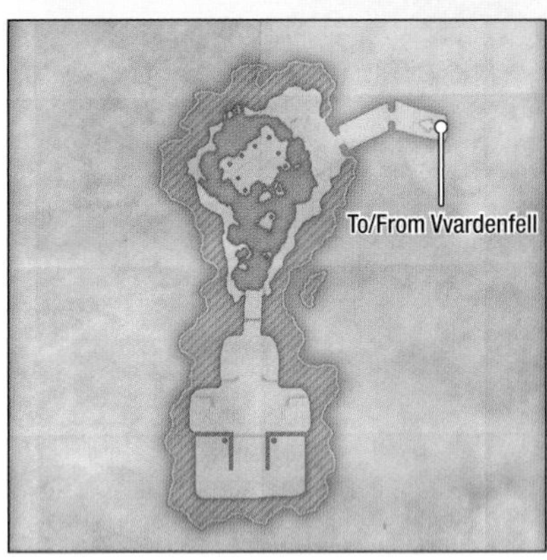

Interior: This is only accessible during the quest. A waterlogged chamber containing Skaafin is the only way into the inner shrine.

Interior (Malacath's Shrine): A giant statue of Malacath watches over the powerful mage Chodala, who must be defeated, along with his Skaafin minions.

17 TEL GALEN

Area of Interest:	Homestead
Item of Interest:	Mages Guild Book (The Great Houses and Their Use), Vivec Sermon

On the outer eastern edge of the region is your very own island paradise! Purchase it from the Crown Store for a reasonable sum to enjoy fungal growths and the looming Daedric presence in the vicinity. There's a Vivec Sermon **(#27)**, two possible chests on the shore, and a Heavy Sack. Also check the small island immediately south for a Mages Guild book near an old log.

18 ANDALEN ANCESTRAL TOMB

This tomb is shut up tight and can't be entered. Also note the Arenim Ancestral Tomb rubbing directly east from here, on the coastal peninsula.

19 MATUS-AKIN EGG MINE

Area of Interest:	Delve
Entities:	Ash Hoppers, Fetcherfly Hives, Kwama, Rumblegardes, Scribs, Th'krak the Tunnel-King (Kwama Warrior)
Item of Interest:	Skyshard
Related Quest:	(D3) A Dangerous Breed

This Kwama egg mine is easily spotted on the boundary mountain separating the regions. Note the Heavy Sack nearby.

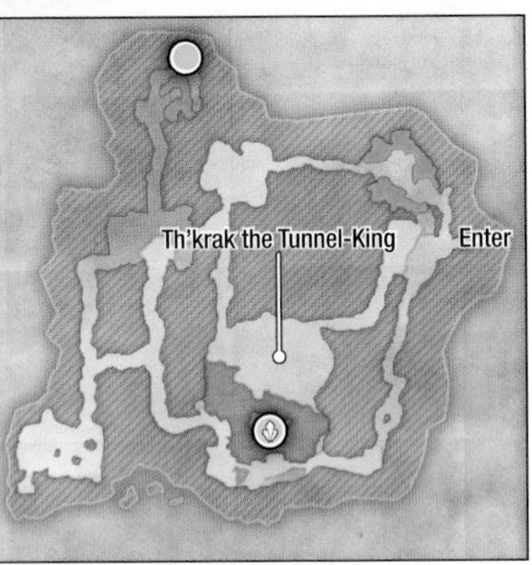

Treasure Chest

Skyshard

Interior: Inside, this is a somewhat labyrinthine layout of interconnected passages and caverns. The Rumblegarde clan rule the roost here, until you reach the main central cavern where a huge Kwama prowls about. Note the skyshard in this giant southerly chamber, on an island.

20 HOLAMAYAN MONASTERY

Entities:	Dunmer, Scavengers
Items of Interest:	Mages Guild Book (The Art of Kwama Egg Cooking), Vivec Sermon

The monastery tower is currently sealed. The island and surrounding area offer a few chests, but the more impressive collectibles are a Heavy Sack, a Vivec Sermon **(#29)** on the barrels near the tower, and a Mages Guild book at the small dock area.

21 SHASHPILAMAT

Entities:	Bandits
Item of Interest:	Vivec Sermons

Here's another Daedric Shrine to Malacath, this one taken over by a few hapless bandits. Scour the exterior for a possible chest, a Heavy Sack, a Thieves Trove, and a Vivec Sermons **(#20)** near a corpse and a cart.

22 NCHARDUMZ (NORTH)

23 NCHARDUMZ (SOUTHEAST)

Entities:	Dwarven Automatons
Item of Interest:	Mages Guild Book (The Living Gods)

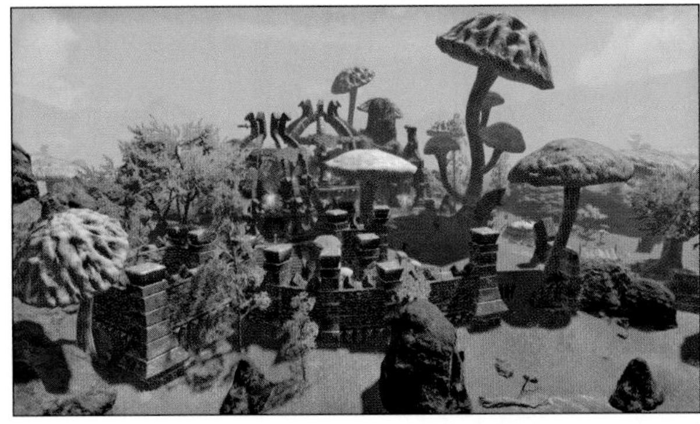

A vast and sprawling Dwemer under-dwelling, this place is so large it has two rusting protrusions to investigate. Though neither has an interior, there are treasure chests to possibly find in both locales, and the northern exterior also has a Heavy Sack and a Mages Guild book.

24 ALMURBALARAMMI

Entities:	Ashlanders
Items of Interest:	Ritual of Appeasement, Torn Page
Related Quest:	(VV15) An Armiger's Duty
Warning:	Restricted Area (Trespassing)

This Shrine to the Daedric Prince Sheogorath sits on a southern peninsula, southeast of Molag Mar. A group of Ashlanders make their home here, and you'll need to trespass in order to uncover some clues for the related quest. Check the northern part of the ruins for a Thieves Trove.

25 BARILZAR'S TOWER

Entities:	Skaafin, Hunger
Related Quests:	(VQ2) Divine Inquiries, (VQ4) Divine Intervention

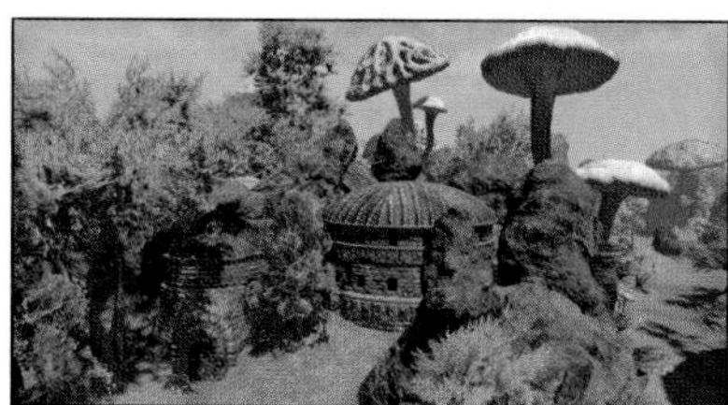

Also known colloquially as Odirniran, this Velothi tower is the current residence of the Dunmeri mage Barilzar, and features some interesting Dwemer mechanical elements once you explore inside during the quest. Check the outside for a Heavy Sack before entering.

Inner Sanctum
Tower Understructure
Laboratory
To/From Vvardenfell

Interior 1 (Tower Entryway): This L-shaped corridor from the outside is ideally accessible during the quest.

Interior 1 (Barilzar's Laboratory): This single circular chamber contains Dwemer machinery cranking away.

Interior 1 (Tower Understructure): Stairs lead down to a storage room and strange Dwemer furnace. Expect enemy resistance here.

Interior 1 (Barilzar's Inner Sanctum): The Dunmer named for this location resides here in a stone-walled bedchamber, until freed during the quest. Don't forget the trapdoor exit.

26 RED EXILE ROCK CAMP

Entities:	Red Exiles

A small campsite features a few of these miscreants guarding a possible treasure chest

27 GRAVE MARKER

Entities:	Kwama

Atop a hillock guarded by a rocky outcrop is the grave of Ke'Val. Note the Thieves Trove and scattered chests on this part of the peninsula.

28 SHRINE OF AZURA

Entities:	Alits

A large statue of the Daedric deity herself looks out over the seas at the edge of this peninsula. Note the Heavy Sack on the tiny island due south of this immense statue.

29 MZAHNCH

Item of Interest:	Mages Guild Book (Varieties of Faith: The Dark Elves)

East of Ald Sotha is a large Dwemer ruin covering almost the entirety of the island it sits on. Though the interior isn't accessible, there's a book, Heavy Sack, and Thieves Trove dotted about the island that you can retrieve.

30 LADY LAURENT'S CAMP

Item of Interest:	Lorebook (Investigator Vale in Vvardenfell)
Related Quest:	A Web of Troubles

Lady Clarisse Laurent is at this location. A slightly haughty Breton (aren't they all?) requires your assistance.

31 BAL FELL

Entities:	Infernal Performers, Mind Spiders, River Trolls, Spiders, Mad Griskild (Boss)

Something strange is going on at the ruins of Bal Fell, an old Daedric Shrine to Sheogorath just south of Lady Laurent's camp. Begin the quest at the nearby camp, which allows you access inside this place, to stop some unholy cavorting.

32 RED EXILE TOADSTOOL CAMP

Entities:	Red Exile (Gang), Netch
Item of Interest:	Mages Guild Book (Varieties of Faith: The Dark Elves)

A small island with giant fungus offers a shady spot for some clandestine adventuring, courtesy of a small band of Red Exile members. Check the tiny islands surrounding this one for a possible treasure chest (there are four that may be available).

33 ZAINTIRARIS

Entities:	Fetcherfly Hive Golems, Fiendroths, Hungers, Scamps, Seducers, Warclaws, Izhavi the Petty (Boss: Watcher)
Items of Interest:	Mages Guild Book (On Stepping Lightly), Mages Guild Book (The Art of Kwama Egg Cooking)
Related Quest:	A Hireling of House Telvanni

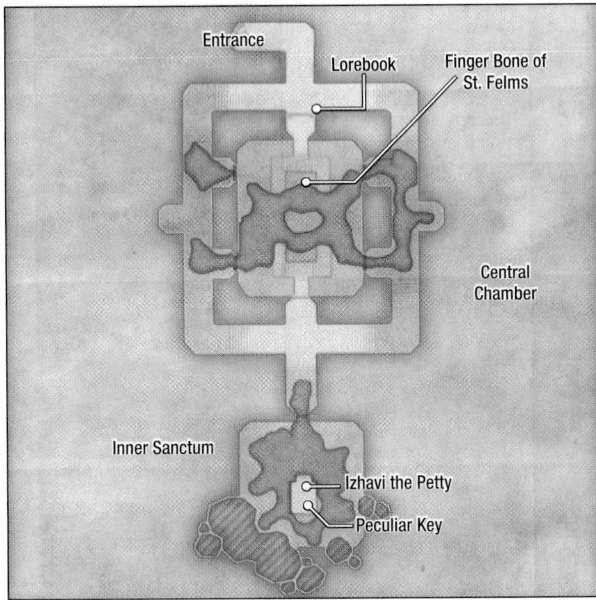

The southern peninsula stretches out from Molag Mal, in the Molag Amur region, to the seas. Here you can explore a particularly impressive Daedric ruin, constructed to honor Sheogorath, as well as a scattering of up to four chests on the peninsula itself. The immediate vicinity of these ruins is home to a band of Warclaws. Check the area for two Heavy Sacks, a Thieves Trove, the Redas Ancestral Tomb rubbing, and two Mages Guild books. And that's before you even step inside the place!

One book is outside the southern exterior wall, behind a rock. The other is to the east, just south of the Hlaalu Ancestral Tomb, under a giant toadstool.

Access this structure during the quest by lighting the appropriate braziers above the door. Check the quest in this guide for the solution; it involves matching the braziers with skulls around them after you read the Lorebook in the center.

Interior: Run down the L-shaped corridor to a Lorebook. Then check the exterior corridors, fighting Seducers and Hungers.

Interior (Inner Sanctum): Accessed before the central area, the massive floating eye of Izhavi the Petty must be destroyed before you continue. Take the peculiar key, which opens the Central Chamber.

Interior (Central Chamber): Scamps and a statue of Molag Bal are positioned near a large chest with a quest item to gather before escaping.

34 HLAALU ANCESTRAL TOMB

Entities:	Red Exile (Gang)

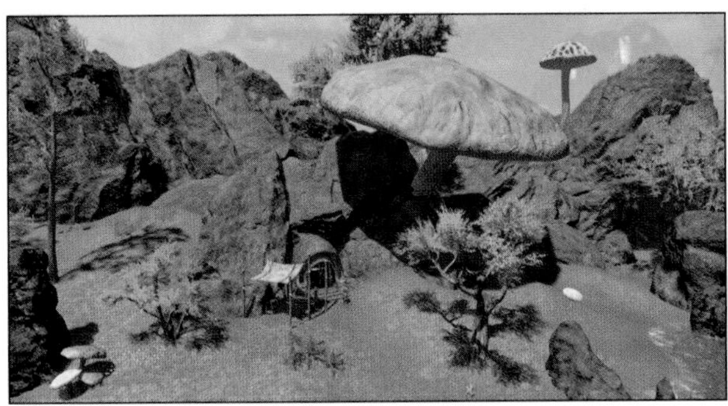

A firmly sealed family tomb, irrelevant to your adventuring, has acquired the curiosity of some Dunmeri tomb raiders. Hinder their progress if you wish.

35 MAWIA

Item of Interest:	Skyshard

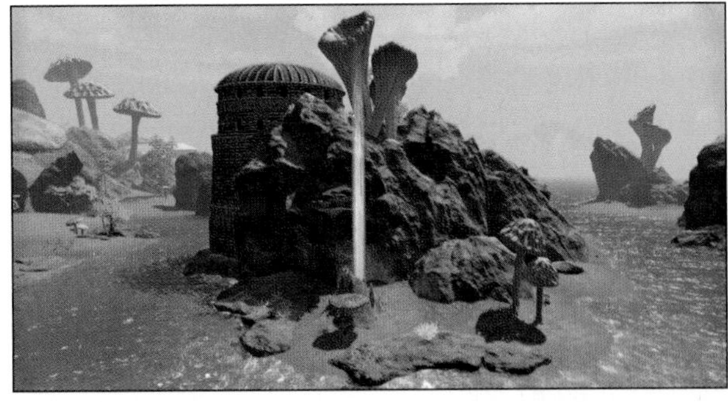

Come to this small island with its sealed Velothi tower to secure the skyshard's power.

36 ABEBAAL EGG MINE (ABANDONED)

Entities:	Alits, Fetcherfly Hive Golems

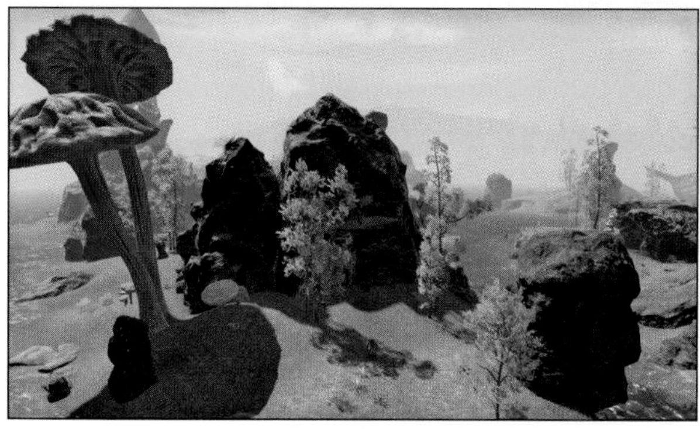

This Kwama egg mine is completely abandoned, such that the entrance is firmly sealed and can't be currently accessed. Instead, check the area nearby for a Fishing Hole. There's a possible chest on the smaller island to the east.

37 MARVANI ANCESTRAL TOMB

This sealed tomb entrance can't be penetrated. Mooch around here if you want to find a couple of chests on the small islands just west and northwest of here, or you're about to engage the enemies at the Group Boss location to the southeast.

38 SHIPWRECK COVE

Entity:	Kimbrudhil the Songbird
Area of Interest:	Group Boss
Item of Interest:	Lorebook (Faith in the Shadow of Red Mountain)

The unruly pirate gang known as the Songbirds is ready to repel all intruders. Note the old—and inaccessible—tomb door to the Arys Ancestral Tomb within this shoreline arena. Check the south shore for a possible chest.

39 TEL BRANORA WAYSHRINE

Area of Interest:	Wayshrine

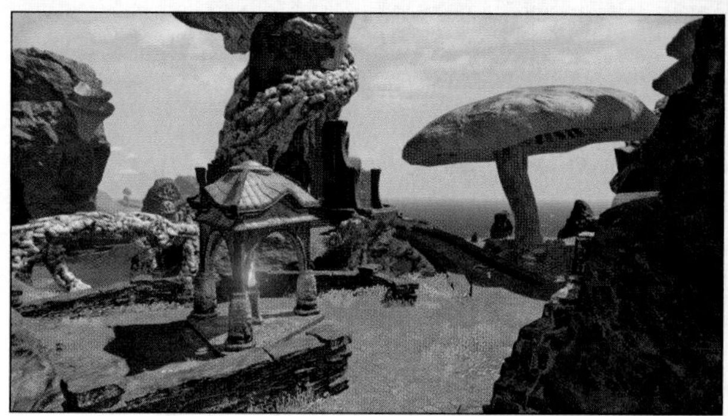

The coastal settlement of Tel Branora has its own Wayshrine, adjacent to the strange fungal growths on the towers of the place itself. Check the next location (Tel Branora) for information on collectibles and other areas of interest.

40 TEL BRANORA

Entities:	House Guards
Items of Interest:	Lorebook (The Flames of the Fetcherfly), Vivec Sermon (2)

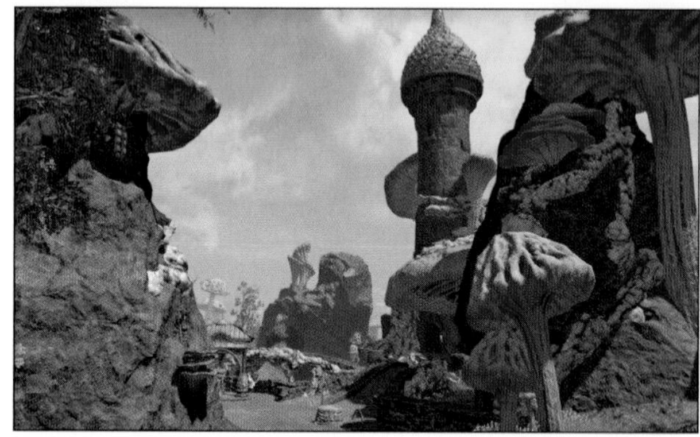

A settlement at the extreme southeast corner of Vvardenfell, on one of the many small islands of this region, Tel Branora is dominated by a large, fungi-clad mage's tower.

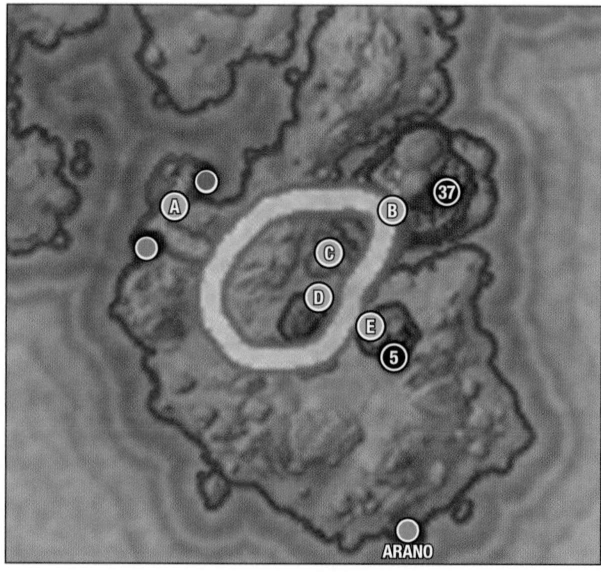

Legend	
Ancestral Tomb Rubbing	Thieves Trove
Heavy Sack	Vivec Sermon

Ⓐ Tel Branora Pier

On this small wooden construct, uncover a moored vessel, a Heavy Sack, and a hidden Thieves Trove.

Ⓑ Tel Branora (Tower)

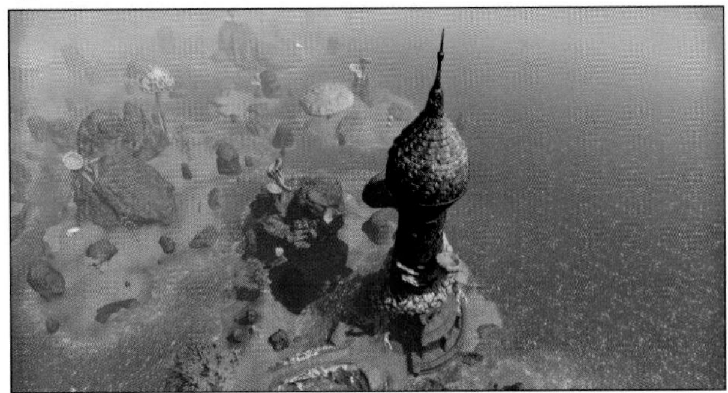

The most imposing structure on this island, and arguably in the vicinity, is this mage's tower. The 37th Vivec Sermon is kept inside the entrance hall at this location, assuming all previous Vivec Sermons have been collected. The tower belongs to Magister Therana, an exceedingly private individual. Talk to Adept Glistel to start up a chat.

In the center of the tower is a strange portal that transports you to Therana's Chambers. It's optimal to do so when questing.

Ⓒ Tel Branora Wayshrine

This Wayshrine is detailed in the previous Altas entry.

Ⓓ Tistar's House

Warning:	Restricted Area (Trespassing)

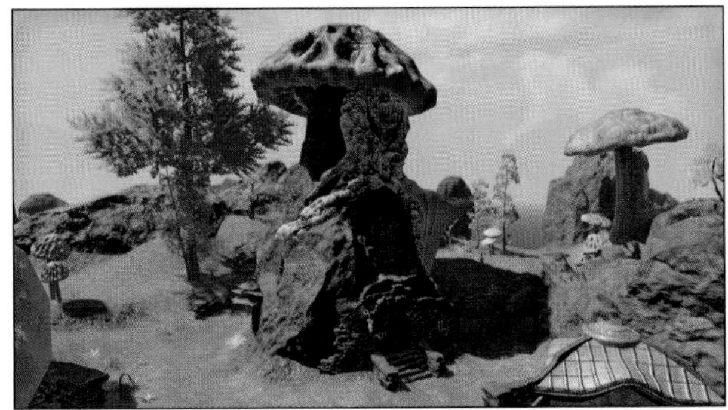

Tistar's house is locked (Intermediate difficulty) and won't get you cornered by enemies, but the two Dunmer who live here aren't happy to see you. Check upstairs for a Safebox, if you're the pilfering sort.

Ⓔ Dalen's House

Warning:	Restricted Area (Trespassing)

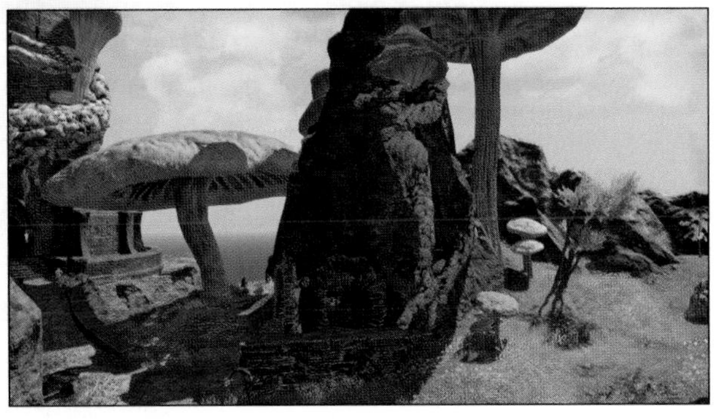

It's worth attempting a trespass into this dwelling, as there's a Vivec Sermon downstairs in the cellar.

41 BERAN ANCESTRAL TOMB

Item of Interest:	Lorebook (Faith in the Shadow of Red Mountain)

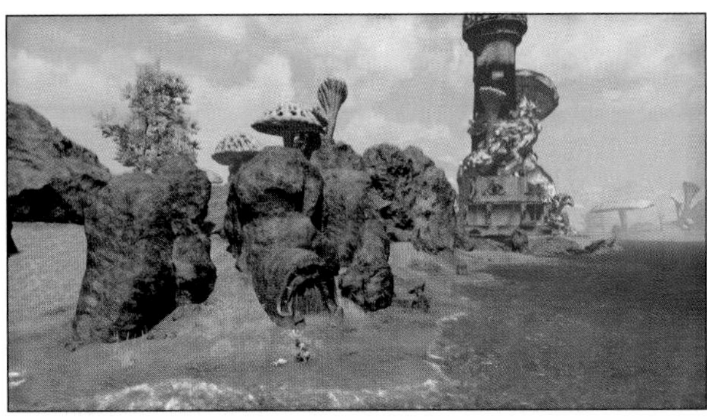

A small tomb on the southeast shore of the island that Tel Branora sits on. Enter the tomb to find a small subterranean chamber with a lorebook, and a coffer to pillage.

MORROWIND BESTIARY

Enemies and bosses introduced in *Elder Scrolls Online: Morrowind* are examined in this chapter. We list where each enemy is found, associated quests and Achievements, as well as details regarding their most prominent abilities.

NEW BASE MOBS

Seven new enemies are introduced to the Tamriel wildlands in Vvardenfell.

Cliff Strider

LOCATION	QUEST	ACHIEVEMENT
WILDERNESS	N/A	CLIFF-STRIDERS' BANE

Abilities

Feast: Sends nearby Cliff Striders into a frenzy, causing them to use basic attacks more often.		
Damage: N/A	**Purpose:** Social Buff	**Status Effects:** N/A
Strategy: Start moving/use defensive abilities.		
Retch: Vomits up its last meal, dealing damage in a cone and leaving an area of effect on the ground.		
Damage: Low Cone AoE, Circle AoE over time	**Purpose:** Area Denial	**Status Effects:** N/A
Strategy: Avoid.		
Dive: Swoops over the battlefield, raking targets with its claws.		
Damage: Moderate Circle AoE	**Purpose:** Gap Closer	**Status Effects:** Knockback
Strategy: Avoid.		

Dwarven Arquebus

LOCATION	QUEST	ACHIEVEMENT
DWARVEN RUINS	N/A	N/A

Abilities

Polarizing Field: Charges the air with electricity, damaging whatever damages nearby Dwarven Automata.		
Damage: Low upon damaging nearby Dwarven Automata	**Purpose:** Social Buff	**Status Effects:** N/A
Strategy: Interrupt or kill the Arquebus. Distance Automata from the Arquebus.		
Impulse Mine: Throws a small Dwarven device that explodes when enemies approach it. Damages players far away from the device slightly when it goes off.		
Damage: Moderate Shock Circle AoE, Low Shock Circle AoE	**Purpose:** Area Denial	**Status Effects:** N/A
Strategy: Avoid.		
Siege Ballista: Hurls a shock projectile at its target, which throws a shock projectile to either side in turn.		
Damage: Low Shock Circle AoE over time	**Purpose:** Area Denial	**Status Effects:** N/A
Strategy: Avoid. Move toward or away from the Arquebus—do not strafe.		
Shock Barrage: Channels a stream of projectiles on a single target.		
Damage: Over time	**Purpose:** Ranged Heavy Attack	**Status Effects:** N/A
Strategy: Interrupt or break line of sight with the Arquebus.		

Fetcherfly Hive Golem

LOCATION	QUEST	ACHIEVEMENT
WILDERNESS	N/A	N/A

Abilities

Colonize: Summons a Fetcherfly colony that grows into a Fetcherfly nest.		
Damage: Nests fight like Fetcherfly nests	**Purpose:** Area Denial	**Status Effects:** N/A
Strategy: Hive Golem takes more damage with active nests. Use AoEs or destroy the Fetcherfly Hive Golem to destroy its nests.		
Fetcherfly Storm: Sends swarms of biting flies careening across the battlefield.		
Damage: Moderate Moving Circle AoE over time	**Purpose:** Area Denial	**Status Effects:** Silence
Strategy: Avoid.		
Focused Swarm: Throws a swarm of exploding flies to detonate on a distant location.		
Damage: Moderate Circle AoE	**Purpose:** Area Denial	**Status Effects:** N/A
Strategy: Avoid.		

Fetcherfly Nest

LOCATION	QUEST	ACHIEVEMENT
WILDERNESS	N/A	N/A

Abilities

Summon Swarm: Summons a swarm of molten flies to harry its opponent.		
Damage: Swarms attack by damaging targets around them	**Purpose:** Area Denial	**Status Effects:** N/A
Strategy: Use AoEs or destroy the nest to destroy its swarms.		
Heat Vents: Ignites the air around the nest.		
Damage: Low Circle AoE over time	**Purpose:** Area Denial	**Status Effects:** N/A
Strategy: Interrupt or avoid.		
Bombard: Throws a swarm of exploding flies to detonate on a distant location.		
Damage: Moderate Circle AoE	**Purpose:** Area Denial	**Status Effects:** N/A
Strategy: Avoid.		

Hunger

LOCATION	QUEST	ACHIEVEMENT
ANCESTOR TOMBS AND DAEDRIC SHRINES	N/A	N/A

Abilities

Spring: Rapidly closes on its prey.		
Damage: Low Circle AoE at destination	**Purpose:** Gap Closer	**Status Effects:** Stagger
Strategy: Avoid.		
Torpor: Sprays targets with hallucinogenic gas, causing them to see enemies that aren't there.		
Damage: Low Cone AoE	**Purpose:** Disorient	**Status Effects:** Stun, Hallucination
Strategy: Avoid.		
Hollow: Vanishes into an Oblivion pocket, then appears suddenly, knocking targets to the ground.		
Damage: Moderate Circle AoE	**Purpose:** Offensive Teleport	**Status Effects:** Knockback
Strategy: Avoid.		
Devour: Pulls its prey into an embrace, draining Health and healing itself.		
Damage: Over time	**Purpose:** Heal/Stun	**Status Effects:** Stun
Strategy: Block, break free, or get an ally to interrupt the Hunger. Defile the Hunger to significantly reduce healing taken.		

Iron Atronach

LOCATION	QUEST	ACHIEVEMENT
FORGOTTEN WASTES	N/A	N/A

Abilities

Blast Furnace: Bombards the battlefield with fireballs.		
Damage: Multiple Low Circle AoEs over time	**Purpose:** Area Denial	**Status Effects:** N/A
Strategy: Avoid.		
Rock Stomp: Explodes the ground beneath the Atronach, then distant foes.		
Damage: Multiple Moderate Circle AoEs	**Purpose:** Heavy Attack	**Status Effects:** N/A
Strategy: Avoid.		
Lavawave: Sends a slow-moving wall of erupting lava toward its enemies.		
Damage: Multiple Moving Low Circle AoEs in a Cone over time	**Purpose:** Area Denial	**Status Effects:** N/A
Strategy: Avoid.		
Subduction: When the Atronach dies, it sends waves of lava toward its foes.		
Damage: Low Moving Circle AoE over time	**Purpose:** Post-Death Area Denial	**Status Effects:** N/A
Strategy: Avoid.		

Nix-Ox

LOCATION	QUEST	ACHIEVEMENT
WILDERNESS	N/A	N/A

Abilities

Winnow: Leaps upon a distant target.		
Damage: Moderate Circle AoE	**Purpose:** Gap Closer	**Status Effects:** Knockback
Strategy: Avoid.		
Nix-Call: Rallies nearby Nix-Oxen and Nix-Hounds, making them immune to debilitating effects and increasing their damage by 10%. Nix-Hounds gain access to a short-range projectile.		
Damage: N/A	**Purpose:** Social Buff	**Status Effects:** N/A
Strategy: Use AoEs or burn the Nix-Ox down.		
Acid Spray: Sprays acid around itself, leaving pools upon the ground.		
Damage: Low Cone AoE, Circle AoE over time.	**Purpose:** Area Denial	**Status Effects:** N/A
Strategy: Avoid.		
Shriek: Channeled sonic shockwave.		
Damage: 2x Low Cone AoE	**Purpose:** Heavy Attack	**Status Effects:** Stagger
Strategy: Avoid.		

DAEDRIC SHRINE SPECIAL ENEMIES

Seven of the daedric shrines possess an elite enemy, most of which are seen during the At Any Cost quest. The last task of the quest has you fight Xykenaz at a new location.

Brakuum

MONSTER	LOCATION	QUEST	ACHIEVEMENT
OGRIM	YANSIRRAMUS	AT ANY COST	N/A

Abilities

Body Slam: Charges across the battlefield, trampling anything in its way.		
Damage: High Rectangle AoE over time	**Purpose:** Heavy Attack	**Status Effects:** Stun
Strategy: Avoid or block.		
Regeneration: Bellows fiercely, closing its wounds.		
Damage: N/A	**Purpose:** Self-Heal	**Status Effects:** N/A
Strategy: Interrupt. Wounds heal faster over time.		
Stomp: Stomps down hard, causing a small earthquake.		
Damage: Moderate Circle AoE	**Purpose:** Heavy Attack	**Status Effects:** Snare
Strategy: Avoid.		
Boulder Toss: Hurls a boulder at a distant foe.		
Damage: Moderate Circle AoE	**Purpose:** Ranged Heavy Attack	**Status Effects:** Stun
Strategy: Avoid.		

Daragaz

MONSTER	LOCATION	QUEST	ACHIEVEMENT
DAEDROTH	KUSHTASHPI	AT ANY COST	N/A

Abilities

Ground Tremor: Strikes the ground, sending shockwaves across the battlefield.		
Damage: Low Moving Circle AoE over time	**Purpose:** Area Denial	**Status Effects:** Stagger, Snare
Strategy: Avoid or interrupt.		
Fiery Breath: Breathes fire upon its foes.		
Damage: Low Cone AoE over time	**Purpose:** Area Denial	**Status Effects:** N/A
Strategy: Avoid.		
Burst of Embers: Spits a fireball at a distant foe. Sets the ground aflame where it lands.		
Damage: Moderate Circle AoE, Low Circle AoE over time	**Purpose:** Ranged Heavy Attack	**Status Effects:** Knockback
Strategy: Avoid or block.		

Izhavi the Petty

MONSTER	LOCATION	QUEST	ACHIEVEMENT
WATCHER	ZAINTIRARIS	A HIRELING OF HOUSE TELVANNI	N/A

Abilities

Doom Truth's Gaze (A): Rakes the ground in front of it with five beams.		
Damage: 50% current Health in Moving Circles over time	**Purpose:** Area Denial	**Status Effects:** Stun
Strategy: Avoid.		
Doom Truth's Gaze (B): Rakes the ground with two horizontal beams that close on a point in front of the watcher.		
Damage: Moderate Damage in Moving Circles over time	**Purpose:** Area Denial	**Status Effects:** Stun
Strategy: Avoid.		
Shockwave: Flails its tentacles, damaging everything nearby.		
Damage: Low Circle AoE	**Purpose:** Slow nearby players	**Status Effects:** Snare
Strategy: Avoid or block.		

Kythiirix

MONSTER	LOCATION	QUEST	ACHIEVEMENT
SPIDER DAEDRA	TUSENEND	AT ANY COST	N/A

Abilities

Storm: Summons a lightning storm over a debilitated target.		
Damage: High Circle AoE	**Purpose:** Heavy Attack	**Status Effects:** N/A
Strategy: Avoid.		
Lightning Onslaught: Rakes the ground with slow-moving shock pillars.		
Damage: Multiple Moving Moderate Circle AoEs	**Purpose:** Area Denial	**Status Effects:** N/A
Strategy: Avoid.		
Summon Spiderling: Summons a Spiderling to fight alongside.		
Damage: Spiderlings attack and snare targets	**Purpose:** Harass and Crowd Control, trigger Storm	**Status Effects:** Spiderlings snare targets
Strategy: Spider Daedra takes more damage while its Spiderling is up. Killing the Spider Daedra kills its Spiderling.		

Phylaraak

MONSTER	LOCATION	QUEST	ACHIEVEMENT
WATCHER	BAL UR	AT ANY COST	N/A

Abilities

Doom Truth's Gaze (A): Rakes the ground in front of it with five beams.		
Damage: Moderate Damage in Moving Circles over time	**Purpose:** Area Denial	**Status Effects:** Stun
Strategy: Avoid.		
Doom Truth's Gaze (B): Rakes the ground with two horizontal beams that close on a point in front of the watcher.		
Damage: 50% Maximum Health in Moving Circles over time	**Purpose:** Area Denial	**Status Effects:** Stun
Strategy: Avoid.		
Shockwave: Flails its tentacles, damaging everything nearby.		
Damage: Low Circle AoE	**Purpose:** Slow nearby players	**Status Effects:** Snare
Strategy: Avoid or block.		

Xykenaz

MONSTER	LOCATION	QUEST	ACHIEVEMENT
N/A	PRISON OF XYKENAZ	AT ANY COST	N/A

Abilities

Shock Aura: Fills the air around the caster with electricity.		
Damage: Moderate Circle AoE	**Purpose:** Heavy Attack	**Status Effects:** Knockback
Strategy: Avoid or Interrupt.		
Lightning Form: Infuses herself with lightning, damaging nearby targets and increasing physical and spell resistance for the duration.		
Damage: Low Circle AoE	**Purpose:** Defensive, Area Denial	**Status Effects:** N/A
Strategy: Stay away while the effect is active.		
Uppercut: Strikes from below, knocking the opponent into the air.		
Damage: High	**Purpose:** Heavy Attack	**Status Effects:** Knockback
Strategy: Block or distance.		

Zylara

MONSTER	LOCATION	QUEST	ACHIEVEMENT
N/A	ASHALMAWIA	AT ANY COST	N/A

Abilities

Negate Magic: Creates a bubble of antimagic around the targeted location.		
Damage: N/A	**Purpose:** Area Denial	**Status Effects:** Silence, Dispels summons and AoEs in the radius
Strategy: Avoid.		
Ice Cage: Creates a circle of frozen ground around the target.		
Damage: Low Donut AoE over time	**Purpose:** Area Denial	**Status Effects:** Snare
Strategy: Avoid or stay put.		
Uppercut: Strikes from below, knocking the opponent into the air.		
Damage: High	**Purpose:** Heavy Attack	**Status Effects:** Knockback
Strategy: Block or distance.		

VVARDENFELL QUESTS

Bosses and named mobs are a part of most quests, and every one of them is listed here with all pertinent information.

Barbas

MONSTER	LOCATION	QUEST	ACHIEVEMENT
N/A	CLOCKWORK CITY VAULT	DIVINE RESTORATION	HAND OF A LIVING GOD

Abilities

Lunge: Rushes the target, swinging his blades when he arrives. Prefers to lunge at rooted targets.		
Damage: Moderate Cone AoE	**Purpose:** Gap Closer	**Status Effects:** Knockback
Strategy: Avoid. Stay close to Barbas and he won't lunge.		
Spinning Blades: Leaps into the air, slicing nearby targets with both blades.		
Damage: High Circle AoE	**Purpose:** Heavy Attack	**Status Effects:** Knockback
Strategy: Avoid.		
Divine Hijack: Channels Vivec's stolen energy to create a pattern of divine destruction.		
Damage: Many Moderate Circle AoEs	**Purpose:** Area Denial	**Status Effects:** Knockback
Strategy: Avoid.		
Barbs: Hurls a bolt of flame at a distant target, rooting that target in place.		
Damage: Moderate	**Purpose:** Crowd Control, triggers Lunge	**Status Effects:** Root
Strategy: Dodge roll. Stay close to Barbas and he won't use Barbs.		

Captain Cedus

MONSTER	LOCATION	QUEST	ACHIEVEMENT
N/A	SURAN	THE SCARLET JUDGE	SCARLET JUDGE

Abilities

Lightning Onslaught: Sends two shock pillars careening across the battlefield.

Damage: High Moving Circle AoE over time	**Purpose:** Heavy Attack	**Status Effects:** N/A

Strategy: Avoid.

Ice Cage: Creates a circle of frozen ground around the target.

Damage: Low Donut AoE over time	**Purpose:** Area Denial	**Status Effects:** Snare

Strategy: Avoid or stay put.

Captain Flaeus

MONSTER	LOCATION	QUEST	ACHIEVEMENT
N/A	VASSAMSI MINE	THE HEART OF A TELVANNI	RISING SUN

Abilities

Uppercut: Strikes from below, knocking his opponent into the air.

Damage: High	**Purpose:** Heavy Attack	**Status Effects:** Knockback

Strategy: Block or distance.

Cleave: A wide horizontal swing.

Damage: Moderate Cone AoE	**Purpose:** Heavy Attack	**Status Effects:** N/A

Strategy: Avoid.

Chodala

MONSTER	LOCATION	QUEST	ACHIEVEMENT
N/A	KAUSHTARARI	DIVINE INTERVENTION	BEARER OF THE BLESSED STAFF

Abilities

Sunder's Echo: Strikes the ground, causing molten slag to erupt from the ground.

Damage: Low Circle AoE over time	**Purpose:** Area Denial	**Status Effects:** N/A

Strategy: Avoid. Pillars deal the most damage when they appear and when they end.

Empowered Strike: Teleports to a distant target, striking the ground at the target's location.

Damage: Moderate Circle AoE	**Purpose:** Gap Closer	**Status Effects:** Stun

Strategy: Avoid or block.

Cleave: A wide horizontal swing.

Damage: Moderate Cone AoE	**Purpose:** Heavy Attack	**Status Effects:** N/A

Strategy: Avoid.

Clockwork Assembly Core

MONSTER	LOCATION	QUEST	ACHIEVEMENT
DWARVEN SENTRY	CLOCKWORK CITY—DIVINITY ATELIER	DIVINE RESTORATION	HAND OF A LIVING GOD

Abilities

Shock Lasso: Pulls a distant target to the Assembly Core.

Damage: N/A	**Purpose:** Gap Closer, triggers Pulse	**Status Effects:** Stun/Snare

Strategy: Block or stay near the Assembly Core.

Pulse: Electrifies the ground near the Assembly Core, which explodes in a burst of shock.

Damage: Moderate Circle AoE	**Purpose:** Heavy Attack	**Status Effects:** N/A

Strategy: Avoid.

Thunderbolt: Sends a wave of shock careening toward its target.

Damage: Moderate Moving Circle AoE	**Purpose:** Heavy Attack	**Status Effects:** N/A

Strategy: Avoid.

Fabricate Beetle: Summons a Fabricant Beetle to fight at its side. Up to three Beetles can be active at a time.

Damage: Beetles damage players	**Purpose:** Harass	**Status Effects:** N/A

Strategy: Beetles have very little Health and can be dispatched easily.

Clockwork Defense Core

MONSTER	LOCATION	QUEST	ACHIEVEMENT
DWARVEN SENTRY	CLOCKWORK CITY—DIVINITY ATELIER	DIVINE RESTORATION	HAND OF A LIVING GOD

Abilities

Shock Lasso: Pulls a distant target to the Defense Core.		
Damage: N/A	**Purpose:** Gap Closer, triggers Pulse	**Status Effects:** Stun/Snare
Strategy: Block or stay near the Defense Core.		
Pulse: Electrifies the ground near the Defense Core, which explodes in a burst of shock.		
Damage: Moderate Circle AoE	**Purpose:** Heavy Attack	**Status Effects:** N/A
Strategy: Avoid.		
Thunderbolt: Sends a wave of shock careening toward its target.		
Damage: Moderate Moving Circle AoE	**Purpose:** Heavy Attack	**Status Effects:** N/A
Strategy: Avoid.		
Defensive Flare: Throws a shock projectile at one target.		
Damage: Moderate	**Purpose:** Ranged Attack	**Status Effects:** N/A
Strategy: Standing near the Defense Core will stop it from using this attack.		

Clockwork Guardian

MONSTER	LOCATION	QUEST	ACHIEVEMENT
N/A	CLOCKWORK CITY	DIVINE RESTORATION	HAND OF A LIVING GOD

Abilities

Oily Smoke: Breathes a gout of black smoke and sparks upon enemies in front of the Guardian.		
Damage: Low Cone AoE over time	**Purpose:** Area Denial	**Status Effects:** N/A
Strategy: Avoid.		
Lava Whip: Whips its target with a fiery lariat.		
Damage: High	**Purpose:** Heavy Attack	**Status Effects:** Off-Balance
Strategy: Block or distance yourself from the Guardian.		

Clockwork Mediator Core

MONSTER	LOCATION	QUEST	ACHIEVEMENT
DWARVEN SENTRY	CLOCKWORK CITY—DIVINITY ATELIER	DIVINE RESTORATION	HAND OF A LIVING GOD

Abilities

Thunderbolt: Sends a wave of shock careening toward its target.		
Damage: Moderate Moving Circle AoE	**Purpose:** Heavy Attack	**Status Effects:** N/A
Strategy: Avoid.		
Sparks: Orders unoccupied sentries to fire shock projectiles at its target.		
Damage: Low	**Purpose:** Harry	**Status Effects:** N/A
Strategy: Destroy the circling sentries.		
Pulse: Orders unoccupied sentries to electrify the ground around themselves.		
Damage: Moderate Circle AoE	**Purpose:** Area Denial	**Status Effects:** N/A
Strategy: Destroy the circling sentries.		
Repair: Orders unoccupied sentries to heal the Mediator Core.		
Damage: N/A	**Purpose:** Self-Heal	**Status Effects:** N/A
Strategy: Interrupt or destroy the circling sentries.		
Defensive Flare: Throws a shock projectile at one target.		
Damage: Moderate	**Purpose:** Ranged Attack	**Status Effects:** N/A
Strategy: Standing near the Mediator Core will stop it from using this attack.		

Curate Erydno

MONSTER	LOCATION	QUEST	ACHIEVEMENT
N/A	SHULK ORE MINE	DIVINE INQUIRIES	N/A

Abilities

Summon Skaafin: Summons a Skaafin Witchling to her side.

Damage: Skaafin Witchlings damage players	**Purpose:** Harass	**Status Effects:** N/A

Strategy: Curate takes more damage with an active Skaafin. Killing the Curate will kill the Skaafin.

Heat Wave: Sends a surge of flame toward her adversary.

Damage: Heavy Moving Circle AoE over time	**Purpose:** Area Denial	**Status Effects:** N/A

Strategy: Avoid.

Fire Runes: Hurls a fireball at her foe and a nearby location.

Damage: Low Circle AoE over time	**Purpose:** Area Denial	**Status Effects:** N/A

Strategy: Avoid.

Curate Skaliz

MONSTER	LOCATION	QUEST	ACHIEVEMENT
N/A	HLORMAREN STRONGHOLD	FAMILY REUNION	NARYU'S CONFIDANT

Abilities

Summon Skaafin: Summons a Skaafin Witchling to his side.

Damage: Skaafin Witchlings damage players	**Purpose:** Harass	**Status Effects:** N/A

Strategy: Curate takes more damage with an active Skaafin. Killing the Curate will kill the Skaafin.

Whirlwind: Leaps into the air, slicing nearby targets with both blades.

Damage: High Circle AoE	**Purpose:** Heavy Attack	**Status Effects:** N/A

Strategy: Avoid.

Assassinate: Stabs his target in the back.

Damage: Moderate	**Purpose:** Heavy Attack	**Status Effects:** N/A

Strategy: Don't let the Curate behind you.

Dagger-Beak

MONSTER	LOCATION	QUEST	ACHIEVEMENT
CLIFF STRIDER	GNISIS	HATCHING A PLAN	KWAMA MINER

Abilities

Feast: Sends nearby Cliff Striders into a frenzy, causing them to use basic attacks more often. No adds in fight, so this ability is only used if another Cliff Strider is pulled over to Dagger-Beak or vice versa.

Damage: N/A	**Purpose:** Social Buff	**Status Effects:** N/A

Strategy: Start moving/use defensive abilities.

Retch: Vomits up its last meal, dealing damage in a cone and leaving an area of effect on the ground.

Damage: Low Cone AoE, Circle AoE over time	**Purpose:** Area Denial	**Status Effects:** N/A

Strategy: Avoid.

Dive: Swoops over the battlefield, raking targets with its claws.

Damage: Moderate Circle AoE	**Purpose:** Gap Closer	**Status Effects:** Knockback

Strategy: Avoid.

Dwarven Centurion Alpha

MONSTER	LOCATION	QUEST	ACHIEVEMENT
DWARVEN CENTURION	GNISIS EGG MINE	A MELODIC MISTAKE	N/A

Abilities

Powered Up: While the Centurion is near its Dwemer Power Crystal, it deals 20% more damage.

Damage: No damage	**Purpose:** Area Denial	**Status Effects:** N/A

Strategy: Keep the Centurion away from the Dwemer Power Crystal.

Sweeping Spin: The Centurion winds itself up and spins, damaging nearby targets with its hammer and blade arms.

Damage: Moderate Circle AoE	**Purpose:** Heavy Attack	**Status Effects:** N/A

Strategy: Avoid.

Steam Breath: Vents steam upon its adversaries.

Damage: Low Cone AoE over time	**Purpose:** Heavy Attack	**Status Effects:** N/A

Strategy: Avoid.

Galgalah

MONSTER	LOCATION	QUEST	ACHIEVEMENT
LICH	VALENVARYON	HAUNTED GROUNDS	N/A

Abilities

Defiled Ground: Desecrates a patch of earth with necromantic energies.

Damage: Low Circle AoE over time	**Purpose:** Area Denial	**Status Effects:** Snare

Strategy: Avoid.

Soul Cage: Summons magic crystals to bathe the battlefield in freezing light and explode in a hail of ice.

Damage: Low Circle AoE over time, Moderate Circle AoE	**Purpose:** Area Denial	**Status Effects:** Stun (end only)

Strategy: Avoid.

Gulakhan Yus-Zashten

MONSTER	LOCATION	QUEST	ACHIEVEMENT
N/A	ALD'RUHN—SKAR	DIVINE DELUSIONS	VOICE OF THE FAILED INCARNATES

Abilities

Ash Storm: Ground beneath her target erupts.

Damage: Low Circle AoE over time	**Purpose:** Area Denial	**Status Effects:** N/A

Strategy: Avoid or interrupt.

Fiery Breath: Breathes a gout of fire upon enemies in front of Gulakhan.

Damage: High Cone AoE	**Purpose:** Heavy Attack	**Status Effects:** N/A

Strategy: Avoid.

Lava Whip: Whips its target with a fiery lariat.

Damage: High	**Purpose:** Heavy Attack	**Status Effects:** Off-Balance

Strategy: Block or distance yourself from Gulakhan.

Hazbur

MONSTER	LOCATION	QUEST	ACHIEVEMENT
N/A	WEST OF TEL ARUHN	THE HEART OF A TELVANNI	RISING SUN

Abilities

Bombard: Fires explosive arrows that rain upon the battlefield.

Damage: Low Circle AoE	**Purpose:** Area Denial	**Status Effects:** N/A

Strategy: Avoid.

Chilled Ground: Freezes a large section of ground that suppresses movement through it.

Damage: Circle AoE, no damage	**Purpose:** Area Denial	**Status Effects:** Snare

Strategy: Avoid. This attack is only used at range.

Quake Shot: Fires at the ground, ending shockwaves out in a cone.

Damage: Moderate Cone AoE, Moderate Moving Circle AoE over time	**Purpose:** Heavy Attack	**Status Effects:** Stagger

Strategy: Avoid. This attack is only used up close.

Hired Assassin

MONSTER	LOCATION	QUEST	ACHIEVEMENT
N/A	RETHAN MANOR—SOUTH OF BALMORA	LIKE BLOOD FROM A STONE	EBONY ENFORCER

Abilities

Teleport Strike: Steps through the shadows and arrives in front of her target.

Damage: Moderate	**Purpose:** Gap Closer	**Status Effects:** Stun

Strategy: Block.

Shadow Cloak/Veiled Strike: Vanishes into the shadows to deliver a sneak attack.

Damage: High	**Purpose:** Heavy Attack	**Status Effects:** Stun

Strategy: Block. Use Reveal effects to detect the assassin.

Jovval Mortal-Bane

MONSTER	LOCATION	QUEST	ACHIEVEMENT
SKAAFIN	CLOCKWORK CITY—MAINTENANCE JUNCTION	DIVINE RESTORATION	N/A

Abilities

Skaafin Flare: Hurls a ball of flame at its target.

Damage: Moderate	**Purpose:** Ranged Attack	**Status Effects:** N/A

Strategy: Roll Dodge.

Devastating Leap: Leaps into air and lands devastating blow on the target.

Damage: Moderate	**Purpose:** Heavy Attack	**Status Effects:** N/A

Strategy: Block or Avoid. Does not use at distance.

Lagdabash

MONSTER	LOCATION	QUEST	ACHIEVEMENT
N/A	WEST OF TEL ARUHN	THE HEART OF A TELVANNI	RISING SUN

Abilities

Whirlwind: Leaps into the air slicing nearby targets with both blades.

Damage: High Circle AoE	**Purpose:** Heavy Attack	**Status Effects:** N/A

Strategy: Avoid

Assassinate: Stabs her target in the back.

Damage: Moderate	**Purpose:** Heavy Attack	**Status Effects:** N/A

Strategy: Don't let the her behind you.

Mad Griskild

MONSTER	LOCATION	QUEST	ACHIEVEMENT
N/A	BAL FELL	A WEB OF TROUBLES	N/A

Abilities

Summon Spider: Summons two ranged Spiders to attack his opponents.

Damage: Spiders damage players	**Purpose:** Harass	**Status Effects:** N/A

Strategy: Defeat the first two Spiders before Mad Griskild's Health drops to 40% or below, or you'll have to fight four Spiders at once.

Summon Exploder: Summons two Spiders that chase a target and explode.

Damage: Moderate Circle AoE	**Purpose:** Area Denial	**Status Effects:** Snare

Strategy: Avoid or kill Spiders before they explode.

Teleport Strike: Steps through the shadows and arrives in front of his target.

Damage: Moderate	**Purpose:** Gap Closer	**Status Effects:** Stun

Strategy: Block.

Siphoning Strikes: Surrounds his weapons in shadow magic, reducing damage dealt but causing him to heal 1% of his Maximum Health for every hit.

Damage: No damage	**Purpose:** Self-Heal	**Status Effects:** N/A

Strategy: Don't let him hit you. Deal continuous damage or afflict Mad Griskild with Defile to reduce the healing he receives.

Terror: Throws a shadowy skull projectile to frighten his adversary.

Damage: Low	**Purpose:** Crowd Control	**Status Effects:** Fear

Strategy: Interrupt.

Malur Rethan

MONSTER	LOCATION	QUEST	ACHIEVEMENT
N/A	BALMORA	LIKE BLOOD FROM A STONE	EBONY ENFORCER

Abilities

Throw Dagger: Readies a dagger, then throws it at his opponent. Being struck by the dagger causes the target to bleed.

Damage: Heavy, then over time	**Purpose:** Heavy Ranged Attack	**Status Effects:** Snare

Strategy: Interrupt or keep close to Malur Rethan; he won't use this ability while you're close to him. Block to avoid the damage over time and Snare effect.

Heavy Attack: Heavy melee attack.

Damage: Heavy	**Purpose:** Heavy Attack	**Status Effects:** N/A

Strategy: Block or outrange the attack.

Marshal Hlaren

MONSTER	LOCATION	QUEST	ACHIEVEMENT
N/A	INANIUS EGG MINE	THE SCARLET JUDGE	SCARLET JUDGE

Abilities

Dark Talons: Grabs up to six targets with molten talons.

Damage: Moderate Circle AoE	**Purpose:** Crowd Control	**Status Effects:** Root

Strategy: Dodge roll.

Brace: Shields himself, reducing incoming damage and rendering it immune to debilitating effects. Attacking Marshal Hlaran while he's bracing will stagger the player.

Damage: N/A	**Purpose:** Defensive, interfaces with Power Bash	**Status Effects:** Stagger, Stun, Off-Balance

Strategy: Don't use heavy attacks. If his target is staggered by Brace, Marshal Hlaran will use Power Bash on that target.

Power Bash: Delivers a heavy melee attack.

Damage: Heavy	**Purpose:** Heavy Attack	**Status Effects:** Stagger into Disorient

Strategy: Block or outrange the attack.

Dragonknight Standard: Summons a standard that lands on the battlefield, damaging nearby enemies and reducing the healing they take.

Damage: Low Circle AoE over time	**Purpose:** Area Denial	**Status Effects:** Major Defile (-30% Healing Taken)

Strategy: Avoid.

Matriarch Rathila

MONSTER	LOCATION	QUEST	ACHIEVEMENT
BONE COLOSSUS	VELOTH ANCESTRAL TOMB	ANCESTRAL ADVERSITY	N/A

Abilities

Wake the Dead: Summons three Bone Flayers to attack its enemies, then explode.

Damage: Bone Flayers damage targets, then explode in a Heavy Circle AoE	**Purpose:** Harass	**Status Effects:** N/A

Strategy: Distance yourself from Bone Flayers before they explode.

Bone Saw: Stomps the ground, damaging everything in front of it.

Damage: Moderate Cone AoE	**Purpose:** Heavy Attack	**Status Effects:** Stagger

Strategy: Avoid.

Necrotic Wave: Stomps the ground, which erupts in a shockwave of necrotic energy.

Damage: Moderate Circle AoE	**Purpose:** Heavy Attack	**Status Effects:** Knockback

Strategy: Avoid.

Mertis Othren

MONSTER	LOCATION	QUEST	ACHIEVEMENT

Abilities

Teleport Strike: Steps through the shadows and arrives in front of his target.

Damage: Moderate	**Purpose:** Gap Closer	**Status Effects:** Stun

Strategy: Block.

Shadow Cloak/Veiled Strike: Vanishes into the shadows to deliver a sneak attack.

Damage: High	**Purpose:** Heavy Attack	**Status Effects:** Stun

Strategy: Block. Use Reveal effects to detect Mertis.

Nerandas

MONSTER	LOCATION	QUEST	ACHIEVEMENT
N/A	PINSUN	RECLAIMING VOS	HAND OF THE MISTRESS

Abilities

Aura of Protection: Summons a totem to reduce damage taken by nearby allies.

Damage: No damage	**Purpose:** Defensive	**Status Effects:** N/A

Strategy: Destroy the totem or pull Nerandas out of its aura. Destroying the totem stuns Nerandas and sets him off-balance.

Olfrig

MONSTER	LOCATION	QUEST	ACHIEVEMENT
N/A	ASHURNIBIBI	FLEEING THE PAST	N/A

Abilities

Fiery Grip: Throws a fiery chain at his target, drawing it close.		
Damage: Low	**Purpose:** Gap Closer	**Status Effects:** Stun
Strategy: Block.		
Dark Talons: Grabs up to six targets with molten talons.		
Damage: Moderate Circle AoE	**Purpose:** Crowd Control	**Status Effects:** Root
Strategy: Dodge roll.		
Uppercut: Strikes from below, knocking his opponent into the air.		
Damage: High	**Purpose:** Heavy Attack	**Status Effects:** Knockback
Strategy: Block or outrange the attack.		

Othloth Salavel

MONSTER	LOCATION	QUEST	ACHIEVEMENT
N/A	BALMORA	FLEEING THE PAST	N/A

Abilities

Brace: Shields himself, reducing incoming damage and rendering it immune to debilitating effects. Attacking Othloth Salavel while he's bracing will stagger the player.		
Damage: N/A	**Purpose:** Defensive, interfaces with Power Bash	**Status Effects:** Stagger, Stun, Off-Balance
Strategy: Don't use heavy attacks. If his target is staggered by Brace, Othloth will use Power Bash on that target.		
Power Bash: Delivers a heavy melee attack.		
Damage: Heavy	**Purpose:** Heavy Attack	**Status Effects:** Stagger into Disorient
Strategy: Block or outrange the attack.		

Overseer Torvayn

MONSTER	LOCATION	QUEST	ACHIEVEMENT
N/A	SURAN	THE SCARLET JUDGE	SCARLET JUDGE

Abilities

Heavy Strike: Heavy sword blow.		
Damage: Moderate	**Purpose:** Heavy Attack	**Status Effects:** N/A
Strategy: Block or outrange the attack.		
Retaliation: Blocks briefly, then goes in for the kill.		
Damage: Moderate	**Purpose:** Heavy Attack	**Status Effects:** Stagger, Stun, Off-Balance
Strategy: Don't use heavy attacks while he's blocking, or you won't be able to avoid the attack. Wait for him to finish blocking, then block yourself or outrange the attack.		
Javelin: Hurls a javelin at a distant foe.		
Damage: Moderate	**Purpose:** Heavy Ranged Attack	**Status Effects:** Stagger
Strategy: Interrupt or stay close to Overseer Torvayn—he only uses this attack from a distance.		

Ralasa Delvi

MONSTER	LOCATION	QUEST	ACHIEVEMENT
N/A	SADRITH MORA	OBJECTIONS AND OBSTACLES	N/A

Abilities

Winter's Reach: Creates a frozen vortex that moves across the battlefield.		
Damage: Heavy Moving Circle AoE over time	**Purpose:** Area Denial	**Status Effects:** Snare
Strategy: Avoid or interrupt.		
Ice Barrier: Creates a wall of ice between Ralasa and her target that intercepts projectile attacks directed at her.		
Damage: No damage	**Purpose:** Defensive	**Status Effects:** N/A
Strategy: Move behind or to either side of the wall, destroy the wall, or use melee attacks.		
Void: Summons shadow energy that careens across the battlefield.		
Damage: High Moving Circle AoE over time	**Purpose:** Area Denial	**Status Effects:** N/A
Strategy: Avoid.		

Ruddy Broodmother

MONSTER	LOCATION	QUEST	ACHIEVEMENT
DREUGH WARRIOR	DREUDURAI GLASS MINE	AN ARMIGER'S DUTY	PILGRIM PROTECTOR

Abilities

Brace: Shields itself, reducing incoming damage and rendering it immune to debilitating effects. Attacking the Dreugh while it's bracing will stagger the player.		
Damage: N/A	**Purpose:** Defensive	**Status Effects:** Stagger, Stun, Off-Balance
Strategy: Don't use heavy attacks.		
Shocking Rake: Electrifies the ground in front of it.		
Damage: Low Cone AoE over time	**Purpose:** Area Denial	**Status Effects:** N/A
Strategy: Avoid.		
Lightning Tow: Pulls a target to him.		
Damage: Moderate	**Purpose:** Gap Closer, interfaces with Lightning Field	**Status Effects:** Stun
Strategy: Block.		
Lightning Field: Blasts nearby targets with a shock pulse.		
Damage: Heavy Circle AoE	**Purpose:** Heavy Attack	**Status Effects:** N/A
Strategy: Avoid.		

Ruinfang the Wicked

MONSTER	LOCATION	QUEST	ACHIEVEMENT
N/A	SOUTHWEST OF HANUD	IF THE SPELL FITS	N/A

Abilities

Raise the Earth: Summons a bear to attack his adversaries.		
Damage: Bear damages opponents	**Purpose:** Harass	**Status Effects:** N/A
Strategy: Caster takes more damage with an active bear. Killing the caster kills the bear.		
Gore: Hurls a Spectral Haj Mota across the battlefield.		
Damage: Heavy Moving Circle AoE over time	**Purpose:** Heavy Attack	**Status Effects:** Knockback
Strategy: Avoid.		
Dive: Calls a Spectral Cliff Strider to explode at the target's location.		
Damage: Moderate Circle AoE	**Purpose:** Area Denial	**Status Effects:** N/A
Strategy: Avoid.		

Savarak Fels

MONSTER	LOCATION	QUEST	ACHIEVEMENT
N/A	EAST OF TEL MORA	RECLAIMING VOS	HAND OF THE MISTRESS

Abilities

Winter's Reach: Creates a frozen vortex that moves across the battlefield.		
Damage: Heavy Moving Circle AoE over time	**Purpose:** Area Denial	**Status Effects:** Snare
Strategy: Avoid or interrupt.		
Ice Barrier: Creates a wall of ice between the Savarak and his target that intercepts projectile attacks directed at him.		
Damage: No damage	**Purpose:** Defensive	**Status Effects:** N/A
Strategy: Move behind or to either side of the wall, destroy the wall, or use melee attacks.		
Void: Summons shadow energy that careens across the battlefield.		
Damage: High Moving Circle AoE over time	**Purpose:** Area Denial	**Status Effects:** N/A
Strategy: Avoid.		

Slavemaster Arenim

MONSTER	LOCATION	QUEST	ACHIEVEMENT
N/A	VASSAMSI MINE	THE HEART OF A TELVANNI	RISING SUN

Abilities

The Slavemaster's Chains: Binds an adversary with magical chains.		
Damage: Circle AoE, no damage	**Purpose:** Crowd Control	**Status Effects:** Stun
Strategy: Stand farther than 30m from the Slavemaster.		
Raise the Earth: Summons a bear to attack his adversaries.		
Damage: Bear damages opponents	**Purpose:** Harass	**Status Effects:** N/A
Strategy: Caster takes more damage with an active bear. Killing the caster kills the bear.		
Dive: Calls a Spectral Cliff Strider to explode at the target's location.		
Damage: Moderate Circle AoE	**Purpose:** Area Denial	**Status Effects:** N/A
Strategy: Avoid.		
Dark Reach: Pulls the target in with magical chains.		
Damage: Low	**Purpose:** Gap Closer	**Status Effects:** Stun
Strategy: Block.		
Brand's Cleave: Strikes at nearby enemies, knocking them to the ground.		
Damage: Moderate Circle AoE	**Purpose:** Heavy Attack	**Status Effects:** Stun
Strategy: Avoid or block. Slavemaster only uses this attack up close, so stay away from him to avoid this attack.		

Veya Releth

MONSTER	LOCATION	QUEST	ACHIEVEMENT
N/A	REDORAN GARRISON MEETING HALL	FAMILY REUNION	NARYU'S CONFIDANT

Abilities

Teleport Strike: Steps through the shadows and arrives in front of her target.		
Damage: Moderate	**Purpose:** Gap Closer	**Status Effects:** Stun
Strategy: Block.		
Soul Tether: Strikes at the souls of nearby enemies. The original target of the attack is bound to Veya, supplying her with a steady stream of Health.		
Damage: Moderate Circle AoE, Low over time	**Purpose:** Heavy Attack and Light Heal	**Status Effects:** Stun
Strategy: Avoid or block.		
Whirlwind: Leaps into the air, slicing nearby targets with both blades.		
Damage: High Circle AoE	**Purpose:** Heavy Attack	**Status Effects:** N/A
Strategy: Avoid.		
Shadow Cloak/Veiled Strike: Vanishes into the shadows to deliver a sneak attack.		
Damage: High	**Purpose:** Heavy Attack	**Status Effects:** Stun
Strategy: Block. Use Reveal effects to detect Veya.		

Warclaw Banobani

MONSTER	LOCATION	QUEST	ACHIEVEMENT
N/A	KUDANAT MINE	OF FAITH AND FAMILY	N/A

Abilities

Uppercut: Strikes from below, knocking her opponent into the air.		
Damage: High	**Purpose:** Heavy Attack	**Status Effects:** Knockback
Strategy: Block or outrange the attack.		
Shock Aura: Fills the air around the caster with electricity.		
Damage: Moderate Circle AoE	**Purpose:** Heavy Attack	**Status Effects:** Knockback
Strategy: Avoid or interrupt.		
Lightning Form: Infuses herself with lightning, damaging nearby targets and increasing Physical and Spell Resistance for the duration.		
Damage: Low Circle AoE	**Purpose:** Defensive, Area Denial	**Status Effects:** N/A
Strategy: Stay away from the Warclaw while the effect is active.		

Warclaw Ferhara

MONSTER	LOCATION	QUEST	ACHIEVEMENT
N/A	REDORAN GARRISON BASEMENT	FAMILY REUNION	NARYU'S CONFIDANT

Abilities

Lunge: Rushes the target, swinging both weapons upon arrival. If the target is far away, the attack does not occur. Prefers to lunge at rooted targets.		
Damage: Moderate Cone AoE	**Purpose:** Gap Closer	**Status Effects:** Knockback
Strategy: Avoid. Strafing is best.		
Pin: Fires a crossbow bolt that pins its target to the ground.		
Damage: Low	**Purpose:** Crowd Control, triggers Lunge	**Status Effects:** Root
Strategy: Dodge roll.		
Basilisk Powder: Throws a bag of silencing powder at a distant target, or spreads that bag into the air in front of it, according to range.		
Damage: Moderate Single or Low Cone AoE according to range	**Purpose:** Harass	**Status Effects:** Silence
Strategy: Interrupt.		

Warclaw Zabaseh

MONSTER	LOCATION	QUEST	ACHIEVEMENT
N/A	KUDANAT MINE	OF FAITH AND FAMILY	N/A

Abilities

Charge: Charges a distant target, damaging anything in his way.		
Damage: Moderate	**Purpose:** Gap Closer	**Status Effects:** Stagger
Strategy: Stay close to the Cavalier and he won't use this attack. Step out of path to avoid, stunning him.		

Warden Libo

MONSTER	LOCATION	QUEST	ACHIEVEMENT
N/A	MARANDAS	THE SCARLET JUDGE	SCARLET JUDGE

Abilities

Negate Magic: Creates a bubble of antimagic around the targeted location.		
Damage: N/A	**Purpose:** Area Denial	**Status Effects:** Silence, Dispels summons and AoEs in the radius
Strategy: Avoid.		
Ice Cage: Creates a circle of frozen ground around the target.		
Damage: Low Donut AoE over time	**Purpose:** Area Denial	**Status Effects:** Snare
Strategy: Avoid or stay put.		
Uppercut: Strikes from below, knocking his opponent into the air.		
Damage: High	**Purpose:** Heavy Attack	**Status Effects:** Knockback
Strategy: Block or distance.		

DELVE QUEST BOSSES

For two of the delve quests, a boss stands in the way of your objective, though Avrusa Duleri in Khartag Point can be avoided by sneaking along the wall.

Avrusa Duleri

MONSTER	LOCATION	QUEST	ACHIEVEMENT
N/A	KHARTAG POINT	A SMUGGLER'S LAST STAND	N/A

Abilities

Agonizing Fury: Slams the ground, sending shock bolts out from the impact site.		
Damage: Low Moving Circle AoE over time	**Purpose:** Area Denial	**Status Effects:** Snare
Strategy: Avoid.		
Shock Aura: Fills the air around the caster with electricity.		
Damage: Moderate Circle AoE	**Purpose:** Heavy Attack	**Status Effects:** Knockback
Strategy: Avoid or interrupt.		
Thunder Hammer: Strikes the ground, sending a wave of electricity out in a cone.		
Damage: Moderate Cone AoE	**Purpose:** Heavy Attack	**Status Effects:** N/A
Strategy: Avoid.		

Drovos Nelvayn

MONSTER	LOCATION	QUEST	ACHIEVEMENT
N/A	MATUS-AKIN EGG MINE	A DANGEROUS BREED	N/A

Abilities

Raise the Earth: Summons a bear to attack his adversaries.		
Damage: Bear damages opponents	**Purpose:** Harass	**Status Effects:** N/A
Strategy: Caster takes more damage with an active bear. Killing the caster kills the bear.		
Gore: Hurls a Spectral Haj Mota across the battlefield.		
Damage: Heavy Moving Circle AoE over time	**Purpose:** Heavy Attack	**Status Effects:** Knockback
Strategy: Avoid.		
Dive: Calls a Spectral Cliff Strider to explode at the target's location.		
Damage: Moderate Circle AoE	**Purpose:** Area Denial	**Status Effects:** N/A
Strategy: Avoid.		

PUBLIC DUNGEON QUESTS

Each public dungeon has an associated quest that sends players deep into the dungeon. Take on Artisan Lenarmen at the end of Nchuleftingth. Wakener Maras and Nevena Nirith team up against players in the Forgotten Wastes.

Artisan Lenarmen

MONSTER	LOCATION	QUEST	ACHIEVEMENT
N/A	NCHULEFTINGTH CATHEDRA	THE HEART'S DESIRE	N/A

Abilities

Auditory Command: Summons allies to the Artisan's side at 85%, 65%, 45%, and 35% Health thresholds.		
Damage: Allies damage players	**Purpose:** Harass	**Status Effects:** N/A
Strategy: Defeat the Artisan's allies when they spawn to avoid being overwhelmed.		
Agonizing Fury: Slams the ground, sending shock bolts out from the impact site.		
Damage: Low Moving Circle AoE over time	**Purpose:** Area Denial	**Status Effects:** Snare
Strategy: Avoid.		
Shock Aura: Fills the air around the caster with electricity.		
Damage: Moderate Circle AoE	**Purpose:** Heavy Attack	**Status Effects:** Knockback
Strategy: Avoid or interrupt.		
Thunder Thrall: Teleports in front of his adversary, calling lightning to strike the site.		
Damage: Heavy Circle AoE	**Purpose:** Gap Closer	**Status Effects:** N/A
Strategy: Avoid.		

Nevena Nirith

MONSTER	LOCATION	QUEST	ACHIEVEMENT
N/A	FORGOTTEN WASTES	ECHOES OF A FALLEN HOUSE	N/A

Abilities

Blink Strike: Leaps into the air, then teleports to her target's location, slamming into the ground with destructive force.		
Damage: Moderate Circle AoE	**Purpose:** Gap Closer	**Status Effects:** Stun
Strategy: Avoid or block.		
Dark Talons: Grabs up to six targets with molten talons.		
Damage: Moderate Circle AoE	**Purpose:** Crowd Control	**Status Effects:** Root
Strategy: Dodge roll.		
Dragonknight Standard: Summons a standard that lands on the battlefield, damaging nearby enemies and reducing the healing they take.		
Damage: Low Circle AoE over time	**Purpose:** Area Denial	**Status Effects:** Major Defile (-30% Healing Taken)
Strategy: Avoid.		

Wakener Maras

MONSTER	LOCATION	QUEST	ACHIEVEMENT
N/A	FORGOTTEN WASTES	ECHOES OF A FALLEN HOUSE	N/A

Abilities

Fire Runes: Hurls a fireball at his foe and a nearby location.		
Damage: Low Circle AoE over time	**Purpose:** Area Denial	**Status Effects:** N/A
Strategy: Avoid.		
Void: Summons shadow energy that careens across the battlefield.		
Damage: High Moving Circle AoE over time	**Purpose:** Area Denial	**Status Effects:** N/A
Strategy: Avoid.		
Radiant Magelight: Summons a light, revealing players from stealth and reducing incoming damage from sneak attacks by 50% for himself and nearby allies.		
Damage: Circle AoE, no damage	**Purpose:** Stealth Reveal	**Status Effects:** Reveal
Strategy: When using stealth in combat, stay far from Wakener Maras.		
Succubus Touch: Calls his target toward him and into danger.		
Damage: No damage	**Purpose:** Crowd Control	**Status Effects:** Fear
Strategy: Interrupt.		

ALD'RUHN DAILY BEAST HUNTS

Once **Quest: Ashlander Relations** has been completed, Huntmaster Sorim-Nakar in Ald'ruhn offers a daily quest that requires the player to defeat a specific creature in Vvardenfell.

Ash-Eater

MONSTER	LOCATION	QUEST	ACHIEVEMENT	HINT
ASSASSIN BEETLE	WEST OF ATUS-MAKIN EGG MINE	ASH EATER HUNT	N/A	DISTURB MOUNDS TO ATTRACT ASH-EATER

Abilities

Acid Blood: When killed, has a 50% chance to leave a pool of acid on the ground.

Damage: Circle AoE over time	**Purpose:** Area Denial	**Status Effects:** N/A

Strategy: Avoid. Be careful looting the corpse.

Collywobbles: Assassin Beetle infects the target with a disease, lowering damage done and applying a light Snare effect.

Damage: No damage	**Purpose:** Social Buff	**Status Effects:** Snare, reduces damage done by 15%

Strategy: Interrupt or outrange the attack.

Feast: Flies into a frenzy, quickly attacking four times.

Damage: Low, four hits	**Purpose:** Area Denial	**Status Effects:** N/A

Strategy: Outrange the attack.

Shadow Step: Teleports behind its target, where it deals 20% extra damage.

Damage: No damage	**Purpose:** Gap Closer	**Status Effects:** N/A

Strategy: Don't let the Assassin Beetle stay behind you.

Great Zexxin

MONSTER	LOCATION	QUEST	ACHIEVEMENT	HINT
NIX-OX	SOUTHWEST OF TEL FYR	GREAT ZEXXIN HUNT	N/A	SEARCH FOR GREAT ZEXXIN'S TRAIL

Abilities

Winnow: Leaps upon a distant target.

Damage: Moderate Circle AoE	**Purpose:** Gap Closer	**Status Effects:** Knockback

Strategy: Avoid.

Nix-Call: Rallies nearby Nix-Oxen and Nix-Hounds, making them immune to debilitating effects and increasing their damage by 10%. Nix-Hounds gain access to a short-range projectile.

Damage: N/A	**Purpose:** Social Buff	**Status Effects:** N/A

Strategy: Use AoEs or burn the Nix-Ox down.

Acid Spray: Sprays acid around itself, leaving pools upon the ground.

Damage: Low Cone AoE, Circle AoE over time	**Purpose:** Area Denial	**Status Effects:** N/A

Strategy: Avoid.

Shriek: Channeled sonic shockwave.

Damage: 2x Low Cone AoE	**Purpose:** Heavy Attack	**Status Effects:** Stagger

Strategy: Avoid.

King Razor-Tusk

MONSTER	LOCATION	QUEST	ACHIEVEMENT	HINT
BULL KAGOUTI	SOUTH OF PULK DELVE	KING RAZOR-TUSK HUNT	N/A	KILL KAGOUTI TO LURE KING RAZOR-TUSK

Abilities

Brace: Shields itself, reducing incoming damage and rendering it immune to debilitating effects. Attacking King Razor-Tusk while it's bracing will stagger the player.

Damage: N/A	**Purpose:** Defensive	**Status Effects:** Stagger, Stun, Off-Balance

Strategy: Don't use heavy attacks.

Toss: Gores its opponent with its tusks.

Damage: Moderate Cone AoE	**Purpose:** Heavy Attack	**Status Effects:** Knockback

Strategy: Avoid.

Chomp: Bites its opponent.

Damage: Moderate	**Purpose:** Heavy Attack	**Status Effects:** Stagger

Strategy: Block or outrange the attack.

Mother Jagged-Claw

MONSTER	LOCATION	QUEST	ACHIEVEMENT	HINT
MUDCRAB	FAR SOUTHEAST VVARDENFELL	MOTHER JAGGED-CLAW HUNT	N/A	DISTURB MUD PILES TO ATTRACT MOTHER JAGGED-CLAW

Abilities

Unforgiving Claws: Mother Jagged-Claw delivers a merciless pinch.

Damage	Purpose	Status Effects
Damage: Moderate	**Purpose:** Heavy Attack	**Status Effects:** N/A

Strategy: Block or outrange the attack.

Old Stomper

MONSTER	LOCATION	QUEST	ACHIEVEMENT	HINT
CLIFF STRIDER	SOUTHWEST OF NCHULEFTINGTH ENTRANCE	OLD STOMPER HUNT	N/A	SEARCH FOR OLD STOMPER'S TRAIL

Abilities

Feast: Sends nearby Cliff Striders into a frenzy, causing them to use basic attacks more often. No adds in fight, so this ability is only used if another Cliff Strider is pulled over to Old Stomper or vice versa.

Damage	Purpose	Status Effects
Damage: N/A	**Purpose:** Social Buff	**Status Effects:** N/A

Strategy: Start moving/use defensive abilities.

Retch: Vomits up its last meal, dealing damage in a cone and leaving an area of effect on the ground.

Damage	Purpose	Status Effects
Damage: Low Cone AoE, Circle AoE over time	**Purpose:** Area Denial	**Status Effects:** N/A

Strategy: Avoid.

Dive: Swoops over the battlefield, raking targets with its claws.

Damage	Purpose	Status Effects
Damage: Moderate Circle AoE	**Purpose:** Gap Closer	**Status Effects:** Knockback

Strategy: Avoid.

Tarra-Suj

MONSTER	LOCATION	QUEST	ACHIEVEMENT	HINT
NIX-HOUND PROWLER	EAST OF NCHULEFTINGTH ENTRANCE	TARRA-SUJ HUNT	N/A	KILL NIX-HOUNDS TO ATTRACT TARRA-SUJ

Abilities

Dampworm: Sprays the target with noxious gas.

Damage	Purpose	Status Effects
Damage: Moderate Cone AoE	**Purpose:** Heavy Attack	**Status Effects:** Snare

Strategy: Don't let Tarra-Suj get behind you.

Shadowstep: Tarra-Suj vanishes into the shadows, appearing behind its prey.

Damage	Purpose	Status Effects
Damage: No damage	**Purpose:** Positioning for Dampworm	**Status Effects:** N/A

Strategy: When Tarra-Suj casts Shadowstep, turn around.

Writhing Sveeth

MONSTER	LOCATION	QUEST	ACHIEVEMENT	HINT
FETCHERFLY HIVE GOLEM	WEST OF NCHULEFTINGTH WAYSHRINE	WRITHING SVEETH HUNT	N/A	DESTROY FETCHERFLY NESTS TO LURE WRITHING SVEETH

Abilities

Colonize: Summons a Fetcherfly colony that grows into a Fetcherfly nest.

Damage	Purpose	Status Effects
Damage: Nests fight like Fetcherfly nests	**Purpose:** Area Denial	**Status Effects:** N/A

Strategy: Hive Golem takes more damage with active nests. Use AoEs or destroy the Fetcherfly Hive Golem to destroy its nests.

Fetcherfly Storm: Sends swarms of biting flies careening across the battlefield.

Damage	Purpose	Status Effects
Damage: Moderate Moving Circle AoE over time	**Purpose:** Area Denial	**Status Effects:** Silence

Strategy: Avoid.

Focused Swarm: Throws a swarm of exploding flies to detonate on a distant location.

Damage	Purpose	Status Effects
Damage: Moderate Circle AoE	**Purpose:** Area Denial	**Status Effects:** N/A

Strategy: Avoid.

DELVE BOSSES

To complete the delves and earn the corresponding Achievements, you must defeat the bosses within—one per delve.

Bralsa Inlador

MONSTER	LOCATION	QUEST	ACHIEVEMENT
N/A	PULK	N/A	PULK EXPLORER

Abilities

Bombard: Fires explosive arrows that rain upon the battlefield.

Damage: Low Circle AoE	**Purpose:** Area Denial	**Status Effects:** N/A

Strategy: Avoid.

Chilled Ground: Freezes a large section of ground that suppresses movement through it.

Damage: Circle AoE, no damage	**Purpose:** Area Denial	**Status Effects:** Snare

Strategy: Avoid. This attack is only used at range.

Quake Shot: Fires at the ground, sending shockwaves out in a cone.

Damage: Moderate Cone AoE, Moderate Moving Circle AoE over time	**Purpose:** Heavy Attack	**Status Effects:** Stagger

Strategy: Avoid. This attack is only used up close.

Nchuthand Far-Hurler

MONSTER	LOCATION	QUEST	ACHIEVEMENT
DWARVEN ARQUEBUS	NCHULEFT	N/A	NCHULEFT EXPLORER

Abilities

Polarizing Field: Charges the air with electricity, damaging whatever damages nearby Dwarven Automata.

Damage: Low upon damaging nearby Dwarven Automata	**Purpose:** Social Buff	**Status Effects:** N/A

Strategy: Interrupt or kill the Arquebus. Distance Automata from the Arquebus.

Impulse Mine: Throws a small Dwarven device that explodes when enemies approach it. Damages players far away from the device slightly when it goes off.

Damage: Moderate Shock Circle AoE, Low Shock Circle AoE	**Purpose:** Area Denial	**Status Effects:** N/A

Strategy: Avoid.

Siege Ballista: Hurls a shock projectile at its target, which throws a shock projectile to either side in turn.

Damage: Low Shock Circle AoE over time	**Purpose:** Area Denial	**Status Effects:** N/A

Strategy: Avoid. Move toward or away from the Arquebus—do not strafe.

Shock Barrage: Channels a stream of projectiles on a single target.

Damage: Over time	**Purpose:** Ranged Heavy Attack	**Status Effects:** N/A

Strategy: Interrupt or break line of sight with the Arquebus.

Old Rust-Eye

MONSTER	LOCATION	QUEST	ACHIEVEMENT
DREUGH WARRIOR	KHARTAG POINT	N/A	KHARTAG POINT EXPLORER

Abilities

Brace: Shields itself, reducing incoming damage and rendering it immune to debilitating effects. Attacking the Dreugh while it's bracing will stagger the player.

Damage: N/A	**Purpose:** Defensive	**Status Effects:** Stagger, Stun, Off-Balance

Strategy: Don't use heavy attacks.

Shocking Touch: Blasts the target with Shock Damage.

Damage: High	**Purpose:** Heavy Attack	**Status Effects:** Stagger

Strategy: Block or move out of range.

Shocking Rake: Electrifies the ground in front of it.

Damage: Low Cone AoE over time	**Purpose:** Area Denial	**Status Effects:** N/A

Strategy: Avoid.

Phobbiicus

MONSTER	LOCATION	QUEST	ACHIEVEMENT
TITAN	ASHALMAWIA	N/A	ASHALMAWIA EXPLORER

Abilities

Soul Flame: Belches a wave of fire toward its opponent, leaving fire where it strikes.

Damage: High Moving Circle AoE, Low Circle AoE	**Purpose:** Ranged Heavy Attack	**Status Effects:** Stun, Snare

Strategy: Interrupt.

Wing Gust: Buffets the area beneath it with its wings.

Damage: Circle AoE, no damage	**Purpose:** Crowd Control	**Status Effects:** Knockback, Snare

Strategy: Avoid or block.

Th'krak the Tunnel-King

MONSTER	LOCATION	QUEST	ACHIEVEMENT
KWAMA WARRIOR	MATUS-AKIN EGG MINE	N/A	MATUS-AKIN EGG MINE EXPLORER

Abilities

Awaken the Colony: Summons Kwama workers to his side, reducing outgoing damage by 15%.		
Damage: Kwama Workers damage their targets	**Purpose:** Harass	**Status Effects:** N/A
Strategy: Use AoEs or avoid Kwama workers. Killing the boss kills its workers.		
Excavation: Hurls a boulder on the ground, summoning Kwama Scribs to his side.		
Damage: High Cone AoE, Kwama Scribs damage their targets	**Purpose:** Heavy Attack, Harass	**Status Effects:** N/A
Strategy: Use AoEs or avoid Kwama Scribs.		

Zvvius the Hive Lord

MONSTER	LOCATION	QUEST	ACHIEVEMENT
FETCHERFLY HIVE GOLEM	ZAINSIPILU	N/A	ZAINSIPILU EXPLORER

Abilities

Colonize: Summons a Fetcherfly colony that grows into a Fetcherfly nest.		
Damage: Nests fight like Fetcherfly nests	**Purpose:** Area Denial	**Status Effects:** N/A
Strategy: Hive Golem takes more damage with active nests. Use AoEs or destroy the Fetcherfly Hive Golem to destroy its nests.		
Fetcherfly Storm: Sends swarms of biting flies careening across the battlefield.		
Damage: Moderate Moving Circle AoE over time	**Purpose:** Area Denial	**Status Effects:** Silence
Strategy: Avoid.		
Focused Swarm: Throws a swarm of exploding flies to detonate on a distant location.		
Damage: Moderate Circle AoE	**Purpose:** Area Denial	**Status Effects:** N/A
Strategy: Avoid.		

FORGOTTEN WASTES PUBLIC DUNGEON CHAMPIONS

There are five encounters with Champions inside the Forgotten Wastes Public Dungeon, each balanced for two players. Within the Forgotten Depths, Coaxer Veran, Castigator Athin, and Confessor Dradas are grouped into one fight.

Beckoner Morvayn

MONSTER	LOCATION	QUEST	ACHIEVEMENT
N/A	FORGOTTEN WASTES—CAVERNS OF KOGORUHN	N/A	FORGOTTEN WASTES CONQUEROR, FORGOTTEN WASTES VANQUISHER

Defeating the Sixth House Ash-Weaver, Tormentor, and Watcher inside the northwest chamber of the Caverns of Kogoruhn causes Beckoner Morvayn to drop to your level.

Abilities

Teleport Strike: Steps through the shadows and arrives in front of his target.		
Damage: Moderate	**Purpose:** Gap Closer	**Status Effects:** Stun
Strategy: Block.		
Siphoning Strikes: Surrounds his weapons in shadow magic, reducing damage dealt but causing him to heal 1% of his Maximum Health for every hit.		
Damage: No damage	**Purpose:** Self-Heal	**Status Effects:** N/A
Strategy: Don't let him hit you. Deal continuous damage or afflict him with Defile to reduce the healing he receives.		
Terror: Throws a shadowy skull projectile to frighten his adversary.		
Damage: Low	**Purpose:** Crowd Control	**Status Effects:** Fear
Strategy: Interrupt.		

Castigator Athin

MONSTER	LOCATION	QUEST	ACHIEVEMENT
N/A	FORGOTTEN WASTES—FORGOTTEN DEPTHS	N/A	FORGOTTEN WASTES CONQUEROR, FORGOTTEN WASTES VANQUISHER

Abilities

Teleport Strike: Steps through the shadows and arrives in front of her target.

Damage: Moderate	**Purpose:** Gap Closer	**Status Effects:** Stun

Strategy: Block.

Siphoning Strikes: Surrounds her weapons in shadow magic, reducing damage dealt but causing her to heal 1% of her Maximum Health for every hit.

Damage: No damage	**Purpose:** Self-Heal	**Status Effects:** N/A

Strategy: Don't let her hit you. Deal continuous damage or afflict her with Defile to reduce the healing she receives.

Terror: Throws a shadowy skull projectile to frighten her adversary.

Damage: Low	**Purpose:** Crowd Control	**Status Effects:** Fear

Strategy: Interrupt.

Cliff Strider Matriarch

MONSTER	LOCATION	QUEST	ACHIEVEMENT
N/A	FORGOTTEN WASTES	N/A	FORGOTTEN WASTES CONQUEROR, FORGOTTEN WASTES VANQUISHER

Abilities

Feast: Sends nearby Cliff Striders into a frenzy, causing them to use basic attacks more often.

Damage: N/A	**Purpose:** Social Buff	**Status Effects:** N/A

Strategy: Start moving/use defensive abilities.

Retch: Vomits up its last meal, dealing damage in a cone and leaving an area of effect on the ground.

Damage: Low Cone AoE, Circle AoE over time	**Purpose:** Area Denial	**Status Effects:** N/A

Strategy: Avoid.

Dive: Swoops over the battlefield, raking targets with its claws.

Damage: Moderate Circle AoE	**Purpose:** Gap Closer	**Status Effects:** Knockback

Strategy: Avoid.

Coaxer Veran

MONSTER	LOCATION	QUEST	ACHIEVEMENT
N/A	FORGOTTEN WASTES—FORGOTTEN DEPTHS	N/A	FORGOTTEN WASTES CONQUEROR, FORGOTTEN WASTES VANQUISHER

Abilities

Rite of Passage: Heals the caster and shields nearby allies from 80% damage taken for the duration.

Damage: Circle AoE, no damage	**Purpose:** Defensive, Self-Heal	**Status Effects:** N/A

Strategy: Interrupt or pull allies out of the radius.

Burdening Eye: Summons a magic orb that pursues its target and explodes. Leaves a magic snare field where it explodes.

Damage: Moderate Circle AoE	**Purpose:** Area Denial	**Status Effects:** Snare

Strategy: Destroy the eye before it explodes.

Focused Healing: Channels Health into the targeted ally.

Damage: No damage	**Purpose:** Heal Self/Other	**Status Effects:** N/A

Strategy: Interrupt or kill the caster.

Spell Absorption: Channels a protective barrier around the targeted ally, preventing 90% of damage done for the duration.

Damage: No damage	**Purpose:** Defensive	**Status Effects:** N/A

Strategy: Interrupt or kill the caster.

Confessor Dradas

MONSTER	LOCATION	QUEST	ACHIEVEMENT
N/A	FORGOTTEN WASTES—FORGOTTEN DEPTHS	N/A	FORGOTTEN WASTES CONQUEROR, FORGOTTEN WASTES VANQUISHER

Abilities

Bombard: Fires explosive arrows that rain upon the battlefield.

Damage: Low Circle AoE	**Purpose:** Area Denial	**Status Effects:** N/A

Strategy: Avoid.

Chilled Ground: Freezes a large section of ground that suppresses movement through it.

Damage: Circle AoE, no damage	**Purpose:** Area Denial	**Status Effects:** Snare

Strategy: Avoid. This attack is only used at range.

Quake Shot: Fires at the ground, sending shockwaves out in a cone.

Damage: Moderate Cone AoE, Moderate Moving Circle AoE over time	**Purpose:** Heavy Attack	**Status Effects:** Stagger

Strategy: Avoid. This attack is only used up close.

Conflagrator Llaals

MONSTER	LOCATION	QUEST	ACHIEVEMENT
N/A	FORGOTTEN WASTES—KORA DUR	N/A	FORGOTTEN WASTES CONQUEROR, FORGOTTEN WASTES VANQUISHER

Abilities

Heat Wave: Sends a surge of flame toward his adversary.

Damage: Heavy Moving Circle AoE over time	**Purpose:** Area Denial	**Status Effects:** N/A

Strategy: Avoid.

Volcanic Debris: Summons a Flame Atronach from the sky, slamming into the ground to fight at his side.

Damage: Moderate Circle AoE, Flame Atronach attacks players	**Purpose:** Harass	**Status Effects:** Knockback

Strategy: Interrupt or kill Llaals to destroy the Atronach.

Empower Atronach: Channels a beam of healing energy on a Flame Atronach, restoring its Health.

Damage: No damage	**Purpose:** Heal Ally	**Status Effects:** N/A

Strategy: Interrupt or use this time to kill Conflagrator Llaals while he isn't attacking you.

Mynar Igna

MONSTER	LOCATION	QUEST	ACHIEVEMENT
IRON ATRONACH	FORGOTTEN WASTES—KORA DUR	N/A	FORGOTTEN WASTES CONQUEROR, FORGOTTEN WASTES VANQUISHER

Abilities

Blast Furnace: Bombards the battlefield with fireballs.

Damage: Multiple Low Circle AoEs over time	**Purpose:** Area Denial	**Status Effects:** N/A

Strategy: Avoid.

Rock Stomp: Explodes the ground beneath the Atronach, then distant foes.

Damage: Multiple Moderate Circle AoEs	**Purpose:** Heavy Attack	**Status Effects:** N/A

Strategy: Avoid.

Lavawave: Sends a slow-moving wall of erupting lava toward its enemies.

Damage: Multiple Moving Low Circle AoEs in a Cone over time	**Purpose:** Area Denial	**Status Effects:** N/A

Strategy: Avoid.

Subduction: When the Atronach dies, it sends waves of lava toward its foes.

Damage: Low Moving Circle AoE over time	**Purpose:** Post-Death Area Denial	**Status Effects:** N/A

Strategy: Avoid.

Voracity

MONSTER	LOCATION	QUEST	ACHIEVEMENT
HUNGER	FORGOTTEN WASTES—DRINITH ANCESTRAL TOMB	N/A	FORGOTTEN WASTES CONQUEROR, FORGOTTEN WASTES VANQUISHER

Abilities

Spring: Rapidly closes on its prey.

Damage: Low Circle AoE at destination	**Purpose:** Gap Closer	**Status Effects:** Stagger

Strategy: Avoid.

Torpor: Sprays targets with hallucinogenic gas, causing them to see enemies that aren't there.

Damage: Low Cone AoE	**Purpose:** Disorient	**Status Effects:** Stun, Hallucination

Strategy: Avoid.

Hollow: Vanishes into an Oblivion pocket, and then appears suddenly, knocking its targets to the ground.

Damage: Moderate Circle AoE	**Purpose:** Offensive Teleport	**Status Effects:** Knockback

Strategy: Avoid

Devour: Pulls its prey into an embrace, draining Health and healing itself.

Damage: Over time	**Purpose:** Heal/Stun	**Status Effects:** Stun

Strategy: Block or CC break.

NCHULEFTINGTH PUBLIC DUNGEON CHAMPIONS

You can find five encounters with Champions inside the Nchuleftingth Public Dungeon. Each of these fights is balanced for two players. At Nchuleftingth Bailey, Friar Hadelar and Renduril the Hammer team up against the players.

Friar Hadelar

MONSTER	LOCATION	QUEST	ACHIEVEMENT
N/A	NCHULEFTINGTH BAILEY	N/A	NCHULEFTINGTH CONQUEROR, NCHULEFTINGTH VANQUISHER

Abilities

Fire Runes: Hurls a fireball at his foe and a nearby location.

Damage: Low Circle AoE over time	**Purpose:** Area Denial	**Status Effects:** N/A

Strategy: Avoid.

Focused Healing: Channels Health into the targeted ally.

Damage: No damage	**Purpose:** Heal Self/Other	**Status Effects:** N/A

Strategy: Interrupt or kill the caster.

Guardian of Bthark

MONSTER	LOCATION	QUEST	ACHIEVEMENT
DWARVEN CENTURION	NCHULEFTINGTH UPPER APPROACH	N/A	NCHULEFTINGTH CONQUEROR, NCHULEFTINGTH VANQUISHER

Abilities

Whirlwind Function: The Centurion starts spinning its blade and hammer arms about itself as it moves, damaging everything in its path.

Damage: Low Circle AoE over time	**Purpose:** Area Denial	**Status Effects:** N/A

Strategy: The Guardian is slow while it channels its attack, so keep your distance and take it through hazards while avoiding the hazards yourself.

Smash: Cranks back with its hammer arm and strikes, damaging anyone in front of the Centurion.

Damage: Heavy Cone AoE	**Purpose:** Heavy Attack	**Status Effects:** Knockback

Strategy: Avoid or outrange the attack.

Sweeping Spin: The Centurion winds itself up and spins, damaging nearby targets with its hammer and blade arms.

Damage: Moderate Circle AoE	**Purpose:** Heavy Attack	**Status Effects:** N/A

Strategy: Avoid.

Steam Breath: Vents steam upon its adversaries.

Damage: Low Cone AoE over time	**Purpose:** Heavy Attack	**Status Effects:** N/A

Strategy: Avoid.

Mud-Tusk

MONSTER	LOCATION	QUEST	ACHIEVEMENT
TROLL	NCHULEFTINGTH	N/A	NCHULEFTINGTH CONQUEROR, NCHULEFTINGTH VANQUISHER

Abilities

Close Wounds: Mud-Tusk concentrates and his wounds begin to close.

Damage: No damage	**Purpose:** Self-Heal	**Status Effects:** N/A

Strategy: Interrupt.

Boulder Toss: Hurls a boulder at a distant target. If this lands near a buried Dwarven construct, the construct joins the fray.

Damage: Moderate Circle AoE	**Purpose:** Ranged Heavy Attack, Harass	**Status Effects:** Stun

Strategy: Avoid. Stand away from buried Dwarven constructs.

Lope: Charges a nearby target to attack when he arrives at their location.

Damage: Moderate Cone AoE	**Purpose:** Gap Closer	**Status Effects:** Stagger, Snare

Strategy: Avoid. Stay near Mud-Tusk and he won't use this attack.

Tremor: Pounds the ground, damaging nearby enemies. Buried Dwarven constructs struck by this attack join the fray.

Damage: Low Circle AoE over time	**Purpose:** Area Denial, Harass	**Status Effects:** N/A

Strategy: Avoid. Stand away from buried Dwarven constructs.

Swinging Cleave: Rears back and sweeps in front of him with two strikes.

Damage: Low Cone AoE, twice	**Purpose:** Heavy Attack	**Status Effects:** N/A

Strategy: Avoid.

Nilarion the Cavalier

MONSTER	LOCATION	QUEST	ACHIEVEMENT
N/A	NCHULEFTINGTH RUINS	N/A	NCHULEFTINGTH CONQUEROR, NCHULEFTINGTH VANQUISHER

Abilities

Shard Shield: Summons a shield of stone shards around an ally that absorbs 75% incoming damage before mitigation. Amount of the shield is 25% the Cavalier's Maximum Health + 17% ally Maximum Health. Damaging the shield damages the attacker for 25% of the amount shielded and stuns the attacker. This can occur as frequently as every second.

Damage: 25% of amount of incoming damage, when activated	**Purpose:** Defensive	**Status Effects:** Stun

Strategy: Kill the Cavalier first, or use abilities that prevent crowd-control effects (Immovable, Break Free) to take down the shield. Channeled, over-time, and non-damaging effects do not trigger the shield.

Shield Charge: Charges a distant target, damaging anything in his way.

Damage: Moderate	**Purpose:** Gap Closer	**Status Effects:** Stagger

Strategy: Stay close to the Cavalier and he won't use this attack.

Power Bash: Delivers a heavy melee attack.

Damage: Heavy	**Purpose:** Heavy Attack	**Status Effects:** Stagger into Disorient

Strategy: Block or outrange the attack.

Lava Whip: Whips its target with a fiery lariat.

Damage: High	**Purpose:** Heavy Attack	**Status Effects:** Off-Balance

Strategy: Block or distance yourself from the Cavalier.

Fiery Breath: Breathes fire upon nearby opponents.

Damage: High Cone AoE	**Purpose:** Heavy Attack	**Status Effects:** N/A

Strategy: Avoid.

Dutiful Fury: Damaging an ally of the Cavalier causes him to deal up to 5% stacking or up to 25% more damage with his next hit. When he causes damage, the stack count is reset.

Damage: N/A	**Purpose:** Social Buff	**Status Effects:** N/A

Strategy: Don't damage the Cavalier's allies.

Renduril the Hammer

MONSTER	LOCATION	QUEST	ACHIEVEMENT
N/A	NCHULEFTINGTH BAILEY	N/A	NCHULEFTINGTH CONQUEROR, NCHULEFTINGTH VANQUISHER

Abilities

'Til Death: Binds the targeted ally to her with a beam of life energy. If Renduril is alive when that ally dies, she switches places with her ally and heals that ally to 50% Maximum Health. Renduril's Health is set to 30% Maximum Health when this happens. If Renduril's Health was below 30%, she dies.

Damage: No damage	**Purpose:** Defensive	**Status Effects:** N/A

Strategy: Kill the ally first.

Shard Shield: Summons a shield of stone shards around an ally that absorbs 75% incoming damage before mitigation. Amount of the shield is 25% Renduril's Maximum Health + 17% ally Maximum Health. Damaging the shield damages the attacker for 25% of the amount shielded and stuns the attacker. This can occur as frequently as every second.

Damage: 25% of amount of incoming damage, when activated	**Purpose:** Defensive	**Status Effects:** Stun

Strategy: Kill Renduril first, or use abilities that prevent crowd-control effects (Immovable, Break Free) to take down the shield. Channeled, over-time, and non-damaging effects do not trigger the shield.

Shield Charge: Charges a distant target, damaging anything in his way.

Damage: Moderate	**Purpose:** Gap Closer	**Status Effects:** Stagger

Strategy: Stay close to Renduril and she won't use this attack.

Power Bash: Delivers a heavy melee attack.

Damage: Heavy	**Purpose:** Heavy Attack	**Status Effects:** Stagger into Disorient

Strategy: Block or outrange the attack.

Steamreaver

MONSTER	LOCATION	QUEST	ACHIEVEMENT
DWARVEN SPIDER	NCHULEFTINGTH LAVAWORKS	N/A	NCHULEFTINGTH CONQUEROR, NCHULEFTINGTH VANQUISHER

Abilities

Auditory Signal: Summons up to eight Dwarven Spiders to join the fray.

Damage: Dwarven Spiders damage players	**Purpose:** Harass	**Status Effects:** N/A

Strategy: Steamreaver only summons Spiders if he has fewer than two active on the field. Keep at least two Spiders alive to prevent him from summoning more.

PUBLIC DUNGEON GROUP EVENTS

In the outdoor area of the Forgotten Wastes, a group event leads you through three bosses, each of which can summon their own Iron Atronach or two. In Nchuleftingth Core, a powerful Dwarven Sentry named Nchulaeon the Eternal summons several clusters of Automata that challenge your group's crowd-control abilities.

Brander Releth

MONSTER	LOCATION	QUEST	ACHIEVEMENT
N/A	FORGOTTEN WASTES	N/A	FORGOTTEN WASTES GROUP EVENT

Brander Releth shows up after Stone-Boiler Omalas has been defeated.

Abilities

Volcanic Debris: Summons an Iron Atronach from the sky, slamming into the ground to fight at his side.		
Damage: Moderate Circle AoE, Iron Atronach attacks players	**Purpose:** Harass	**Status Effects:** Knockback
Strategy: Interrupt or kill Releth to destroy the Atronach.		
Empower Atronach: Channels a beam of healing energy on an Iron Atronach, restoring its Health.		
Damage: No damage	**Purpose:** Heal Ally	**Status Effects:** N/A
Strategy: Interrupt the spell.		
Fire Runes: Hurls a fireball at his foe and a nearby location.		
Damage: Low Circle AoE over time	**Purpose:** Area Denial	**Status Effects:** N/A
Strategy: Avoid.		

Mountain-Caller Hlaren

MONSTER	LOCATION	QUEST	ACHIEVEMENT
N/A	FORGOTTEN WASTES	N/A	FORGOTTEN WASTES GROUP EVENT

Mountain-Caller Hlaren shows up after Brander Releth has been defeated.

Abilities

Volcanic Debris: Summons an Iron Atronach from the sky, slamming into the ground to fight at her side. Hlaren can have two Iron Atronachs up at a time.		
Damage: Moderate Circle AoE, Iron Atronach attacks players	**Purpose:** Harass	**Status Effects:** Knockback
Strategy: Interrupt or kill Hlaren to destroy the Atronach.		
Empower Atronach: Channels a beam of healing energy on an Iron Atronach, restoring its Health.		
Damage: No damage	**Purpose:** Heal Ally	**Status Effects:** N/A
Strategy: Interrupt the spell.		
Heat Wave: Sends a surge of flame toward her adversary.		
Damage: Heavy Moving Circle AoE over time	**Purpose:** Area Denial	**Status Effects:** N/A
Strategy: Avoid.		
Fire Runes: Hurls a fireball at her foe and a nearby location.		
Damage: Low Circle AoE over time	**Purpose:** Area Denial	**Status Effects:** N/A
Strategy: Avoid.		

Nchulaeon the Eternal

MONSTER	LOCATION	QUEST	ACHIEVEMENT
DWARVEN SENTRY	NCHULEFTINGTH CORE	N/A	NCHULEFTINGTH GROUP EVENT

Nchulaeon moves into three adjacent rooms during the event, where groups of Dwarven Automata emerge from the walls. These mobs must be defeated to keep the fight progressing.

Abilities

Momentum: While outside its dock, Nchulaeon periodically creates a sonic pulse, knocking nearby enemies away from it and into hazards.		
Damage: Circle AoE, no damage	**Purpose:** Knock players into hazards	**Status Effects:** Knockback
Strategy: Don't stand near Nchulaeon if it isn't docked.		
Overcharge Expulsion: Sends a shock pillar careening toward its target.		
Damage: Moderate Moving Circle AoE over time	**Purpose:** Heavy Attack	**Status Effects:** N/A
Strategy: Dodge roll.		

Stone-Boiler Omalas

MONSTER	LOCATION	QUEST	ACHIEVEMENT
N/A	FORGOTTEN WASTES	N/A	FORGOTTEN WASTES GROUP EVENT

Defeat the Sixth House Clarion Seers and Tormentors, who begin the event, to force Stone-Boiler Omalas off his balcony.

Abilities

Volcanic Debris: Summons an Iron Atronach from the sky, slamming into the ground to fight at his side.		
Damage: Moderate Circle AoE, Iron Atronach attacks players	**Purpose:** Harass	**Status Effects:** Knockback
Strategy: Interrupt or kill Omalas to destroy the Atronach.		
Empower Atronach: Channels a beam of healing energy on an Iron Atronach, restoring its Health.		
Damage: No damage	**Purpose:** Heal Ally	**Status Effects:** N/A
Strategy: Interrupt the spell.		
Heat Wave: Sends a surge of flame toward his adversary.		
Damage: Heavy Moving Circle AoE over time	**Purpose:** Area Denial	**Status Effects:** N/A
Strategy: Avoid.		

GROUP BOSSES

At six locations around Vvardenfell, a group boss offers a challenge for groups of players. These experiences have been balanced for around four players. An Achievement is earned for defeating each one, and Beleru Omoril at the Justice Office offers a daily quest, requiring the player to defeat one of these bosses. Note that Orator Salothan, Councilor Reynis, General Tanasa, and Regent Beleth compose one group boss at Salothan's Council.

Councilor Reynis

MONSTER	LOCATION	QUEST	ACHIEVEMENT
N/A	SALOTHAN'S COUNCIL	SALOTHAN'S CURSE	SALOTHAN CURSEBREAKER

Abilities

Vengeance for Salothan: If Salothan is dead, transforms into a red ghostly skeleton. Damage done is increased by 20% and damage taken reduced by 15%.		
Damage: No damage	**Purpose:** Social Buff	**Status Effects:** N/A
Strategy: Don't kill Salothan first.		
Focused Healing: Channels Health into the targeted ally.		
Damage: No damage	**Purpose:** Heal Self/Other	**Status Effects:** N/A
Strategy: Interrupt or kill the caster.		
Rite of Passage: Heals the caster and shields nearby allies from 80% damage taken for the duration.		
Damage: Circle AoE, no damage	**Purpose:** Defensive, Self-Heal	**Status Effects:** N/A
Strategy: Interrupt or pull allies out of the radius.		
Winter's Reach: Creates a frozen vortex that moves across the battlefield.		
Damage: Heavy Moving Circle AoE over time	**Purpose:** Area Denial	**Status Effects:** Snare
Strategy: Avoid or interrupt.		
Ice Barrier: Creates a wall of ice between Councilor Reynis and her target that intercepts projectile attacks directed at her.		
Damage: No damage	**Purpose:** Defensive	**Status Effects:** N/A
Strategy: Move behind or to either side of the wall, destroy the wall, or use melee attacks.		
Negate Magic: Creates a bubble of antimagic around the targeted location.		
Damage: N/A	**Purpose:** Area Denial	**Status Effects:** Silence, Dispels summons and AoEs in the radius
Strategy: Avoid.		

General Tanasa

MONSTER	LOCATION	QUEST	ACHIEVEMENT
N/A	SALOTHAN'S COUNCIL	SALOTHAN'S CURSE	SALOTHAN CURSEBREAKER

Abilities

Vengeance for Salothan: If Salothan is dead, transforms into a red ghostly skeleton. Damage done is increased by 20% and damage taken reduced by 15%.		
Damage: No damage	**Purpose:** Social Buff	**Status Effects:** N/A
Strategy: Don't kill Salothan first.		
'Til Death: Binds the targeted ally to her with a beam of life energy. If General Tanasa is alive when that ally dies, she switches places with her ally and heals that ally to 50% Maximum Health. Tanasa's Health is set to 30% Maximum Health when this happens. If Tanasa's Health was below 30%, she dies.		
Damage: No damage	**Purpose:** Defensive	**Status Effects:** N/A
Strategy: Kill the ally first.		
Shard Shield: Summons a shield of stone shards around an ally that absorbs 75% incoming damage before mitigation. Amount of the shield is 25% Tanasa's Maximum Health + 17% ally Maximum Health. Damaging the shield damages the attacker for 25% of the amount shielded and stuns the attacker. This can occur as frequently as every second.		
Damage: 25% of amount of incoming damage, when activated	**Purpose:** Defensive	**Status Effects:** Stun
Strategy: Kill General Tanasa first, or use abilities that prevent crowd-control effects (Immovable, Break Free) to take down the shield. Channeled, over-time, and non-damaging effects do not trigger the shield.		

Lava Whip: Whips her target with a fiery lariat.			**Fiery Breath:** Breathes fire upon nearby opponents.		
Damage: High	**Purpose:** Heavy Attack	**Status Effects:** Off-Balance	**Damage:** High Cone AoE	**Purpose:** Heavy Attack	**Status Effects:** N/A
Strategy: Block or distance yourself.			**Strategy:** Avoid.		

Dark Talons: Grabs up to six targets with molten talons.		
Damage: Moderate Circle AoE	**Purpose:** Crowd Control	**Status Effects:** Root
Strategy: Dodge roll.		

Kimbrudhil the Songbird

MONSTER	LOCATION	QUEST	ACHIEVEMENT
NEREID	SHIPWRECK COVE	SIREN'S SONG	SONGBIRD SILENCER

You must defeat the Songbird's initial raiders, brutes, and cutthroats before Kimbrudhil exits her perch. More trash mobs join in during the fight.

Abilities

Songbird's Embrace: Lifts up to six players into the air, encapsulating them in bubbles that deal increasing damage over time. Affected players can burst their bubbles by using a Synergy that damages anything near them. Monsters (except Kimbrudhil) take 75% the players max health in damage. Kimbrudhil takes 150% the player's max health in damage.		
Damage: Increasing, over time	**Purpose:** Crowd Control	**Status Effects:** Stun
Strategy: If you can spare the Health, wait for an opportune moment to burst your bubble, as it can deal quite a lot of damage.		
Hurricane: Raises her hands, summoning a cyclone to damage players in a ring around her.		
Damage: Low Donut AoE over time	**Purpose:** Area Denial	**Status Effects:** Snare
Strategy: Stand near Kimbrudhil or avoid the attack.		
Waterspout: Summons a waterspout to careen across the battlefield.		
Damage: Moderate Moving Circle AoE over time	**Purpose:** Area Denial	**Status Effects:** Knockback
Strategy: Avoid.		
Shielding Spray: Geysers burst from the sea beneath her enemies.		
Damage: Multiple Moderate Circle AoEs	**Purpose:** Area Denial	**Status Effects:** N/A
Strategy: Avoid.		

Nilthog the Unbroken

MONSTER	LOCATION	QUEST	ACHIEVEMENT
NIX-OX	NILTHOG'S HOLLOW	OXEN FREE	BREAKER OF THE UNBROKEN

Abilities

Winnow: Leaps upon a distant target.		
Damage: Moderate Circle AoE	**Purpose:** Gap Closer	**Status Effects:** Knockback
Strategy: Avoid.		
Nix-Call: Rallies nearby Nix-Oxen and Nix-Hounds, making them immune to debilitating effects and increasing their damage by 10%. Nix-Hounds gain access to a short-range projectile.		
Damage: N/A	**Purpose:** Social Buff	**Status Effects:** N/A
Strategy: Use AoEs or burn the Nix-Ox down.		
Acid Spray: Sprays acid around itself, leaving pools upon the ground.		
Damage: Low Cone AoE, Circle AoE over time	**Purpose:** Area Denial	**Status Effects:** N/A
Strategy: Avoid.		
Shriek: Channeled sonic shockwave.		
Damage: 2x Low Cone AoE	**Purpose:** Heavy Attack	**Status Effects:** Stagger
Strategy: Avoid.		

Orator Salothan

MONSTER	LOCATION	QUEST	ACHIEVEMENT
N/A	SALOTHAN'S COUNCIL	SALOTHAN'S CURSE	SALOTHAN CURSEBREAKER

Orator Salothan is joined by his council: Councilor Reynis, General Tanasa, and Regent Beleth. A small group of Salothan's defenders and scouts are also present at Salothan's Council, with more joining in as the fight progresses. Loyalists may also spawn into the area.

Abilities

Salothan's Eternity: Used if Salothan's Health drops below 30%. Absorbs Health from an ally to heal himself. Damages every living councilor by 15% Salothan's current Health and heals him for 8% of his Maximum Health for every councilor struck.

Damage: No damage	**Purpose:** Self-Heal	**Status Effects:** N/A

Strategy: Kill Salothan's councilors before attempting to kill him.

Revenge: Used when a councilor is killed. Knocks nearby players back.

Damage: Circle AoE, no damage	**Purpose:** Social Buff	**Status Effects:** Knockback

Strategy: Stay away from Salothan when one of his councilors dies.

Uppercut: Strikes from below, knocking his opponent into the air.

Damage: High	**Purpose:** Heavy Attack	**Status Effects:** Knockback

Strategy: Block or outrange the attack.

Shock Aura: Used when Health is between 45% and 85%. Fills the air around the caster with electricity.

Damage: Moderate Circle AoE	**Purpose:** Heavy Attack	**Status Effects:** Knockback

Strategy: Avoid or interrupt.

Agonizing Bolts: Used when Health is between 45% and 85%. Sends pulses of shock across the battlefield, changing direction as they spread.

Damage: Multiple Moderate Circle AoEs	**Purpose:** Area Denial	**Status Effects:** Snare

Strategy: Avoid.

Lightning Form: Used when Health is between 45% and 85%. Infuses himself with lightning, damaging nearby targets and increasing Physical and Spell Resistance for the duration.

Damage: Low Circle AoE	**Purpose:** Defensive, Area Denial	**Status Effects:** N/A

Strategy: Stay away from Salothan while the effect is active.

The Queen's Consort

MONSTER	LOCATION	QUEST	ACHIEVEMENT
KWAMA WARRIOR	MISSIR-DADALIT EGG MINE	CULLING THE SWARM	CONSORT KILLER

Abilities

Kwama Rush: Charges a player, damaging that player when it arrives.

Damage: Low	**Purpose:** Gap Closer	**Status Effects:** Knockback

Strategy: Avoid or block.

Hardened/Unstable Chitin: Reduces damage taken by the Queen's Consort by 30%. Eggs drop from the ceiling. Eggs that survive to hatch source Kwama that fight players.

Damage: Kwama damage players	**Purpose:** Defensive, Harass	**Status Effects:** N/A

Strategy: Destroy the eggs before they hatch.

Noxious Bile: Sprays the battlefield with acid.

Damage: Low Cone AoE over time	**Purpose:** Heavy Attack	**Status Effects:** N/A

Strategy: Avoid.

Engorged Pustule: Punches the ground, causing pustules to erupt around the fight space. Pustules that survive to explode create hazards on the field.

Damage: Moderate Circle AoE over time	**Purpose:** Area Denial	**Status Effects:** N/A

Strategy: Destroy the pustules before they pop.

Call of the Consort: Used 30 seconds after Hardened or Unstable Chitin activates. Pounds the ground and shrieks, rallying nearby workers. Consumes Hardened Chitin/Unstable Chitin.

Damage: No damage	**Purpose:** Social Buff	**Status Effects:** N/A

Strategy: Destroy the eggs before they hatch.

Quill Barrage: Fires spikes out of its hands at targeted players throughout the battlefield. Spikes explode when they strike their targets.

Damage: 25% target Maximum Health Circle AoE	**Purpose:** Area Denial	**Status Effects:** N/A

Strategy: Avoid.

Crackling Quills: Used when Health is low. Fires spikes out of its hands at targeted players throughout the battlefield. Spikes explode when they strike their targets.

Damage: 30% target Maximum Health Circle AoE	**Purpose:** Area Denial	**Status Effects:** N/A

Strategy: Avoid.

Voltaic Purge: Used when Health is low. Sprays the battlefield with shock energy.

Damage: Moderate Cone AoE over time	**Purpose:** Heavy Attack	**Status Effects:** N/A

Strategy: Avoid.

Regent Beleth

MONSTER	LOCATION	QUEST	ACHIEVEMENT
N/A	SALOTHAN'S COUNCIL	SALOTHAN'S CURSE	SALOTHAN CURSEBREAKER

Abilities

Vengeance for Salothan: If Salothan is dead, transforms into a red ghostly skeleton. Damage done is increased by 20% and damage taken reduced by 15%.		
Damage: No damage	**Purpose:** Social Buff	**Status Effects:** N/A
Strategy: Don't kill Salothan first.		
Teleport Strike: Steps through the shadows and arrives in front of his target.		
Damage: Moderate	**Purpose:** Gap Closer	**Status Effects:** Stun
Strategy: Block.		
Soul Tether: Strikes at the souls of nearby enemies. The original target of the attack is bound to Regent Beleth, supplying him with a steady stream of Health.		
Damage: Moderate Circle AoE, Low over time	**Purpose:** Heavy Attack and Light Heal	**Status Effects:** Stun
Strategy: Avoid or block.		
Whirlwind: Leaps into the air, slicing nearby targets with both blades.		
Damage: High Circle AoE	**Purpose:** Heavy Attack	**Status Effects:** N/A
Strategy: Avoid.		
Shadow Cloak/Veiled Strike: Vanishes into the shadows to deliver a sneak attack.		
Damage: High	**Purpose:** Heavy Attack	**Status Effects:** Stun
Strategy: Block. Use Reveal effects to detect Regent Beleth.		

Skaafin Mehz the Cozener

MONSTER	LOCATION	QUEST	ACHIEVEMENT
N/A	DUBDIL ALAR TOWER	THE ANXIOUS APPRENTICE	CHEATER DEFEATER, LOOP ERADICATOR

At the start of Dubdil Alar's experiment, his assistants are transformed into Skaafin Witchlings, Bloodcleavers, trackers, masquers, tyrants, and miscreants. Eliminate these Scary-difficulty mobs before the boss appears.

To earn the Loop Eradicator Achievement, you must complete the final phase of the fight in less than 30 seconds.

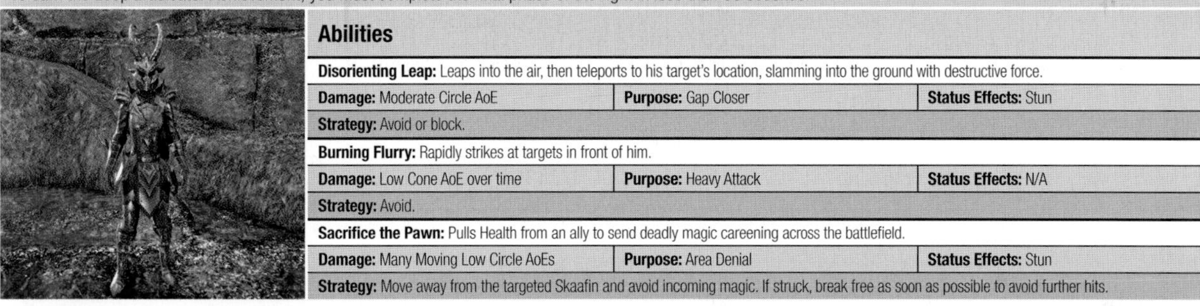

Abilities

Disorienting Leap: Leaps into the air, then teleports to his target's location, slamming into the ground with destructive force.		
Damage: Moderate Circle AoE	**Purpose:** Gap Closer	**Status Effects:** Stun
Strategy: Avoid or block.		
Burning Flurry: Rapidly strikes at targets in front of him.		
Damage: Low Cone AoE over time	**Purpose:** Heavy Attack	**Status Effects:** N/A
Strategy: Avoid.		
Sacrifice the Pawn: Pulls Health from an ally to send deadly magic careening across the battlefield.		
Damage: Many Moving Low Circle AoEs	**Purpose:** Area Denial	**Status Effects:** Stun
Strategy: Move away from the targeted Skaafin and avoid incoming magic. If struck, break free as soon as possible to avoid further hits.		

Wuyuvus

MONSTER	LOCATION	QUEST	ACHIEVEMENT
HUNGER	SULIPUND GRANGE	A CREEPING HUNGER	WUYUVUS SLAYER

Abilities

Spring: Rapidly closes on its prey.		
Damage: Low Circle AoE at destination	**Purpose:** Gap Closer	**Status Effects:** Stagger
Strategy: Avoid.		
Torpor: Sprays the entire battlefield with hallucinogenic gas, then vanishes from sight. Hungers are summoned to the fray.		
Damage: Low to all players over time, Hungers damage players	**Purpose:** Phase	**Status Effects:** Stun, Hallucination
Strategy: Defeating a Hunger damages Wuyuvus, so kill as many as you can before it returns.		
Hollow: Vanishes into an Oblivion pocket, and then appears suddenly, knocking targets to the ground.		
Damage: Moderate Circle AoE	**Purpose:** Offensive Teleport	**Status Effects:** Knockback
Strategy: Avoid.		
Devour: Pulls its prey in and onto the ground, draining Health and healing itself.		
Damage: Over time	**Purpose:** Heal/Stun	**Status Effects:** Stun
Strategy: Allies can interrupt Devour to free its target, but the target cannot break free.		

APPENDICES

The Appendices provide full lists of locations and items found throughout Vvardenfell, many of which are required for Achievements detailed in the next chapter.

INVENTORY

COLLECTIONS

Complete the following quests to receive the corresponding collectible.

TYPE	COLLECTIBLE	COMPLETE QUEST	LOCATION
Memento	Neramo's Lightning Stick	The Heart's Desire	Nchuleftingth
Memento	Dreamer's Chime	Echoes of a Fallen House	Forgotten Wastes
Furnishing	Vvardenfell Scale Model	The Lost Library	Vivec City Library
Memento	Replica Tonal Inverter	Divine Intervention	Vivec City
Head Marking	Bouyant Armiger Face Tattoo	Divine Blessings (Main story quest line)	Vivec City
Body Marking	Buoyant Armiger Body Tattoos	Divine Blessings (Main story quest line)	Vivec City
Head Marking	Morag Tong Face Tattoo	Family Reunion (Morag Tong quest line)	Balmora
Body Marking	Morag Tong Body Tattoo	Family Reunion (Morag Tong quest line)	Balmora
Personality	Telvanni Magister	The Heart of a Telvanni (Telvanni Quest line)	Sadrith Mora
Costume	Regalia of the Scarlet Judge	The Scarlet Judge	Suran
Furnishing (Trophy)	Trophy: Assembly General	Halls of Fabrication Trial (Any difficulty)	Halls of Fabrication
Furnishing (Bust)	Bust: Assembly General	Halls of Fabrication Trial (Veteran difficulty)	Halls of Fabrication
Skin	Fabrication Sheath	Trial Completion (Veteran) (Achievement)	Halls of Fabrication

Pre-order *Elder Scrolls Online: Morrowind* or purchase the Collector's Edition to unlock the following:

TYPE	COLLECTIBLE	HOW TO UNLOCK
Costume	Austere Warden Costume	Pre-order any version of The Elder Scrolls Online: Morrowind
Non-Combat Pet	Dwarven Spider Pet	Purchase The Elder Scrolls Online: Morrowind Collector's Edition
Non-Combat Pet	Dwarven War Dog	Pre-order any version of The Elder Scrolls Online: Morrowind
Mount	Armored War Horse	Pre-order any version of The Elder Scrolls Online: Morrowind
Upgrade	Morag Tong Conversion	Purchase The Elder Scrolls Online: Morrowind Collector's Edition

DWARVEN THEODOLITE PET

Find seven fragments (Dwemer Theodolite Eye, for example) in the Nchuleftingth Public Dungeon. These parts are rare drops from any foes in the dungeon. Combine the seven parts to create a Runebox. Consume this item to gain the Dwarven Theodolite Pet. The Runebox can also be sold or traded to another player.

SIXTH HOUSE ROBE COSTUME

Find seven fragments (Sixth House Incense of Toolwork, for example) in the Forgotten Wastes Public Dungeon. These parts are rare drops from any foes in the dungeon. Combine the seven parts to create a Runebox. Consume this item to gain the Sixth House Robe Costume. The Runebox can also be sold or traded to another player.

CRAFTING MOTIFS

Morrowind includes four new crafting Motifs. How to obtain the chapters and style items are revealed as follows.

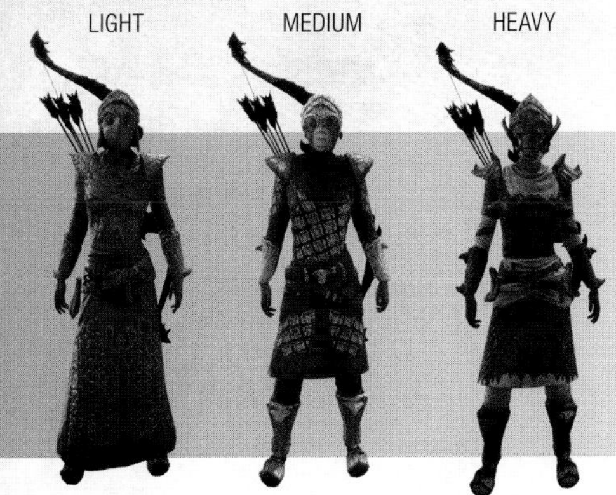

ASHLANDER

Crafting Motif 48: Ashlander Style

Complete the relic and hunting daily quests in Ald'ruhn in Vvardenfell to find Ashlander Motif chapters.

The style item, Ash Canvas, comes from those same activities, more commonly than chapters.

BUOYANT ARMIGER

Crafting Motif 47: Buoyant Armiger Style

Find Buoyant Armiger Motif chapters by opening treasure chests. While exceptionally rare, they appear more often for players who have completed Vvardenfell's main quest line and restored Vivec's power, or for players who have completed the museum quest. Completing both results in the best possible chance of finding these Motif chapters. Even so, they are quite the rare find indeed.

The style item's raw component, Viridian Dust, can be found by harvesting cloth, metal, and wood throughout Vvardenfell. The more chapters of the Buoyant Armiger style you know, the likelier you are to find it, but even if you don't know anything about how to craft Buoyant Armiger, you still have a chance to find some. Once you've found 10 of the raw material, refine it at any equipment-crafting station to craft Volcanic Viridian, which can then be used to craft in the Buoyant Armiger style. Requires Rank 10 of any of the Metalworking, Tailoring, or Woodworking passives.

MILITANT ORDINATOR

Crafting Motif 49: Militant Ordinator Style

Colotarion, the Battleground Elite Merchant in the Vivec City Battlegrounds camp, sells Militant Ordinator chapters exclusively. The chapters cost a significant amount of Alliance Points (AP), earned through PvP combat in Cyrodiil, the Imperial City, or Battlegrounds. The chapters cost as much as 500,000 AP.

The style item is sold by the same Merchant in its raw form, Dull Sphalerite, for 5,000 AP apiece. You must obtain ten of these, refine them into Lustrous Sphalerite at an equipment-crafting bench, and then use that to craft an item in this style. Requires Rank 8 of any of the Metalworking, Tailoring, or Woodworking passives.

MORAG TONG

Crafting Motif 30: Morag Tong Style

Morag Tong chapters are found by completing the world boss and delve boss daily quests in Vvardenfell. They drop rarely, so they're not a guarantee.

The style item, Boiled Carapace, is found the same way, but more commonly.

CRAFTING SETS

ASSASSIN'S GUILE

Region	Molag Amur
Location	Marandas (Northwest of Suran)

Look for the stone foundation east of Foyada Quarry. All three stations are found at the top of the steps.

Assassin's Guile Set

(2 items)	Adds X Spell Critical
(3 items)	Adds X Weapon Critical
(4 items)	Adds X Spell Damage, Adds X Weapon Damage
(5 items)	Increases the duration of your alchemical poisons by four seconds

DAEDRIC TRICKERY

Region	West Gash
Location	Randas Ancestral Tomb (Northwest of West Gash Wayshrine)

Enter the Randas Ancestral Tomb to find the three crafting stations.

Daedric Trickery Set

(2 items)	Adds X Maximum Health
(3 items)	Adds X Maximum Stamina
(4 items)	Adds X Maximum Magicka
(5 items)	While in combat you gain one of five random Major Buffs for 10 seconds every 20 seconds; eligible buffs are Expedition, Protection, Mending, Heroism, and Vitality

SHACKLEBREAKER

Region	Ashlands
Location	Zergonipal (Southwest of the Valley of the Wind Wayshrine)

Woodworking and Clothing Stations sit up on their own platforms, while the Blacksmithing Station is found near the lava river, behind the stone wall.

Shacklebreaker Set

(2 items)	Adds X Weapon Damage
(3 items)	Adds X Spell Damage
(4 items)	Adds X Magicka Recovery
	Adds X Stamina Recovery
(5 items)	Adds X Maximum Magicka
	Adds X Maximum Stamina

EQUIPMENT SETS

There are eleven available sets in *Morrowind*, beyond the three mentioned previously in the Crafting Sets section. Three are available as drops in the overland, four come from the Battlegrounds, and four more are available from the Halls of Fabrication Trial. Purchase "Unknown Containers" from the Battleground Merchant for a weapon from one of the Battleground sets.

OVERLAND SETS

NAME	WEIGHT	TYPICAL STYLE	EFFECT
Infector	Medium	Hlaalu	(2 items) Adds X Weapon Damage, (3 items) Adds X Weapon Critical, (4 items) Adds X Weapon Critical, (5 items) When you deal Critical Damage, you have a chance to summon a Hunger that spews poison on all enemies in front of it, dealing Poison Damage and stunning them; this effect can occur once every X seconds
War Maiden	Light	Telvanni	(2 items) Adds X Maximum Health, (3 items) Adds X Maximum Magicka, (4 items) Adds X Spell Damage, (5 items) Adds 400 Spell Damage to your Magic Damage abilities
Warrior-Poet	Heavy	Redoran	(2 items) Adds X Maximum Health, (3 items) Adds X Spell Resistance, (4 items) Adds X Physical Resistance, (5 items) Gain Major Toughness at all times, increasing your Maximum Health by 10%

BATTLEGROUND SETS

NAME	WEIGHT	EFFECT
Coward's Gear	Medium	(2 items) Adds X Maximum Health, (3 items) Adds X Stamina Recovery, (4 items) Adds X Stamina Recovery, (5 items) While sprinting, gain Major Expedition and Major Protection, increasing your movement speed and reducing your damage taken by 30%
Impregnable	Any	(2 items) Adds X Maximum Health, (3 items) Adds X Maximum Stamina, (4 items) Adds X Maximum Magicka, (5 items) Adds X Critical Resistance
Knight Slayer	Light	(2 items) Adds X Maximum Magicka, (3 items) Adds X Spell Damage, (4 items) Adds X Maximum Health, (5 items) Fully charged heavy attacks against players deal an additional 10% of their Maximum Health as Oblivion Damage
Vanguard's Challenge	Heavy	(2 items) Adds X Maximum Health, (3 items) Adds X Maximum Health, (4 items) Adds a percentage of healing taken, (5 items) When you taunt an enemy player, they deal 50% less damage to all other players, but 100% more damage to you for 15 seconds
Wizard's Riposte	Light	(2 items) Adds X Maximum Health, (3 items) Adds X Spell Damage, (4 items) Adds X Magicka Recovery, (5 items) When you take Critical Damage, you apply Minor Maim to the enemy for 15 seconds, reducing their damage done by 15%

TRIAL SETS

NAME	WEIGHT	EFFECT
Automated Defense	Heavy	(2 items) Adds X Maximum Health, (3 items) Gain Minor Aegis at all times, reducing your damage taken from dungeon and Trial monsters, (4 items) Adds a percentage of healing taken, (5 items) When you use an Ultimate Ability, you and the closest allies gain Major Aegis
Inventor's Guard	Light	(2 items) Adds X Magicka Recovery, (3 items) Gain Minor Aegis at all times, reducing your damage taken from dungeon and Trial monsters, (4 items) Adds a percentage of healing done, (5 items) When you use an Ultimate Ability, you and the closest allies gain Major Aegis, reducing damage taken from dungeon and Trial monsters
Master Architect	Light	(2 items) Adds X Maximum Magicka, (3 items) Gain Minor Slayer at all times, increasing damage done to dungeon and Trial monsters, (4 items) Adds X Spell Damage, (5 items) When you use an Ultimate Ability, you and the closest allies gain Major Slayer, increasing your damage done to dungeon and Trial monsters
War Machine	Medium	(2 items) Adds X Maximum Stamina, (3 items) Gain Minor Slayer at all times, increasing damage done to dungeon and Trial monsters, (4 items) Adds X Weapon Damage, (5 items) When you use an Ultimate Ability, you and the closest allies gain Major Slayer, increasing your damage done to dungeon and Trial monsters

FURNISHING PLANS

Furnishing plans new to *Morrowind* are listed as follows, sorted by the type of plan. The type dictates where the item can be created. Three requirements must be met in order to make the furnishing: own and learn the plan, possess the listed ingredients, and reach the Passive Ability levels as indicated.

FURNISHING BLUEPRINTS

CRAFTING STATION > WOODWORKING STATION

FURNISHING	CATEGORY	QUALITY	BEHAVIOR(S)	INGREDIENTS	REQUIRED SKILLS
Ashlander Cup, Empty	Hearth	Superior	—	Heartwood (8), Decorative Wax (5), Ash Canvas (0), Turpen (6)	Recipe Improvement (2), Woodworking (5)
Ashlander Cup, Mazte	Hearth	Superior	—	Heartwood (8), Decorative Wax (5), Ash Canvas (0), Turpen (6)	Recipe Improvement (2), Woodworking (5)
Dres Divider, Chains	Suite	Epic	—	Heartwood (12), Regulus (6), Bash (8), Decorative Wax (6), Obsidian (16), Mastic (3)	Metalworking (2), Tailoring (4), Recipe Improvement (2), Woodworking (8)
Dres Divider, Honeycomb	Suite	Epic	—	Heartwood (12), Regulus (6), Bash (8), Decorative Wax (6), Obsidian (16), Mastic (3)	Metalworking (2), Tailoring (4), Recipe Improvement (2), Woodworking (8)
Dres Divider, Screen	Suite	Epic	—	Heartwood (12), Regulus (8), Bash (6), Decorative Wax (6), Obsidian (16), Mastic (3)	Metalworking (2), Tailoring (4), Recipe Improvement (2), Woodworking (8)
Dres Shelf, Block	Library	Fine	—	Heartwood (5), Obsidian (6), Pitch (9)	Woodworking (3)
Dres Sideboard, Display	Hearth	Superior	—	Heartwood (7), Mundane Rune (5), Obsidian (8), Turpen (6)	Potency Improvement (2), Woodworking (4)
Dres Table, Kitchen	Dining	Superior	—	Heartwood (9), Mundane Rune (5), Alchemical Resin (5), Obsidian (12), Turpen (6)	Potency Improvement (2), Solvent Proficiency (2), Woodworking (6)
Dres Trestle, Corridor	Dining	Superior	—	Heartwood (8), Alchemical Resin (5), Obsidian (10), Turpen (6)	Solvent Proficiency (2), Woodworking (5)
Hlaalu Armchair, Mossy Cushion	Dining	Epic	Sittable	Heartwood (12), Bash (8), Mundane Rune (6), Alchemical Resin (6), Obsidian (16), Mastic (3)	Tailoring (4), Potency Improvement (2), Solvent Proficiency (2), Woodworking (8)
Hlaalu Armchair, Polished	Dining	Epic	Sittable	Heartwood (11), Alchemical Resin (7), Decorative Wax (8), Obsidian (14), Mastic (3)	Solvent Proficiency (3), Recipe Improvement (4), Woodworking (7)
Hlaalu Armchair, Polished	Dining	Superior	Sittable	Heartwood (8), Decorative Wax (6), Obsidian (10), Turpen (6)	Recipe Improvement (3), Woodworking (5)
Hlaalu Bench, Polished	Dining	Superior	Sittable	Heartwood (9), Mundane Rune (5), Alchemical Resin (5), Decorative Wax (5), Obsidian (12), Turpen (6)	Potency Improvement (2), Solvent Proficiency (2), Recipe Improvement (2), Woodworking (6)
Hlaalu Bookcase, Empty	Library	Superior	—	Heartwood (9), Decorative Wax (6), Obsidian (12), Turpen (6)	Recipe Improvement (3), Woodworking (6)
Hlaalu Bookcase, Orderly	Library	Epic	—	Heartwood (12), Regulus (6), Alchemical Resin (6), Decorative Wax (8), Obsidian (16), Mastic (3)	Metalworking (2), Solvent Proficiency (2), Recipe Improvement (4), Woodworking (8)
Hlaalu Box, Trinket	Parlor	Epic	—	Heartwood (12), Regulus (8), Mundane Rune (8), Obsidian (16), Mastic (3)	Metalworking (4), Potency Improvement (4), Woodworking (8)
Hlaalu Cabinet of Drawers, Clerk	Hearth	Epic	—	Heartwood (11), Regulus (8), Decorative Wax (7), Obsidian (14), Mastic (3)	Metalworking (4), Recipe Improvement (3), Woodworking (7)
Hlaalu Cabinet, Clerk	Hearth	Epic	—	Heartwood (11), Regulus (7), Alchemical Resin (5), Decorative Wax (7), Obsidian (14), Mastic (3)	Metalworking (3), Solvent Proficiency (1), Recipe Improvement (3), Woodworking (7)
Hlaalu Cabinet, Open	Hearth	Superior	—	Heartwood (9), Regulus (5), Decorative Wax (5), Obsidian (12), Turpen (6)	Metalworking (2), Recipe Improvement (2), Woodworking (6)
Hlaalu Chest, Secure	Suite	Epic	—	Heartwood (12), Regulus (8), Mundane Rune (8), Obsidian (16), Mastic (3)	Metalworking (4), Potency Improvement (4), Woodworking (8)
Hlaalu Cupboard, Formal	Hearth	Epic	—	Heartwood (12), Regulus (8), Decorative Wax (8), Obsidian (16), Mastic (3)	Metalworking (4), Recipe Improvement (4), Woodworking (8)
Hlaalu Cupboard, Open	Hearth	Superior	—	Heartwood (9), Regulus (4), Decorative Wax (5), Obsidian (12), Turpen (6)	Metalworking (1), Recipe Improvement (2 Woodworking (6)
Hlaalu Desk, Scholar's	Library	Epic	—	Heartwood (12), Alchemical Resin (8), Decorative Wax (8), Obsidian (16), Mastic (3)	Solvent Proficiency (4), Recipe Improvement (4), Woodworking (8)
Hlaalu Dresser, Open	Suite	Superior	—	Heartwood (9), Regulus (5), Decorative Wax (5), Obsidian (12), Turpen (6)	Metalworking (2), Recipe Improvement (2), Woodworking (6)
Hlaalu Dresser, Scroll Drawers	Suite	Superior	—	Heartwood (8), Regulus (4), Decorative Wax (5), Obsidian (10), Turpen (6)	Metalworking (1), Recipe Improvement (2), Woodworking (5)
Hlaalu Dresser, Scroll Rack	Suite	Superior	—	Heartwood (8), Regulus (4), Decorative Wax (5), Obsidian (10), Turpen (6)	Metalworking (1), Recipe Improvement (2), Woodworking (5)
Hlaalu End Table, Formal Scales	Parlor	Epic	—	Heartwood (12), Mundane Rune (8), Decorative Wax (8), Obsidian (16), Mastic (3)	Potency Improvement (4), Recipe Improvement (4), Woodworking (8)
Hlaalu End Table, Formal Turtle	Parlor	Epic	—	Heartwood (12), Mundane Rune (7), Decorative Wax (9), Obsidian (16), Mastic (3)	Potency Improvement (3), Recipe Improvement (5), Woodworking (8)
Hlaalu Footlocker, Secure	Suite	Epic	—	Heartwood (11), Regulus (7), Mundane Rune (8), Obsidian (14), Mastic (3)	Metalworking (3), Potency Improvement (4), Woodworking (7)
Hlaalu Hanger, Mounted	Miscellaneous	Fine	—	Heartwood (5), Obsidian (6), Pitch (9)	Woodworking (3)
Hlaalu Jar, Sealed Malachite	Hearth	Epic	—	Heartwood (12), Mundane Rune (8), Alchemical Resin (8), Obsidian (16), Mastic (3)	Potency Improvement (4), Solvent Proficiency (4), Woodworking (8)

FURNISHING	CATEGORY	QUALITY	BEHAVIOR(S)	INGREDIENTS	REQUIRED SKILLS
Hlaalu Nightstand, Formal	Suite	Epic	—	Heartwood (11), Regulus (7), Decorative Wax (8), Obsidian (14), Mastic (3)	Metalworking (3), Recipe Improvement (4), Woodworking (7)
Hlaalu Nightstand, Scholar's	Suite	Epic	—	Heartwood (11), Regulus (5), Alchemical Resin (7), Decorative Wax (7), Obsidian (14), Mastic (3)	Metalworking (1), Solvent Proficiency (3), Recipe Improvement (3), Woodworking (7)
Hlaalu Rack, Barrel	Hearth	Fine	—	Heartwood (5), Obsidian (6), Pitch (9)	Woodworking (3)
Hlaalu Settee, Polished	Parlor	Superior	Sittable	Heartwood (9), Mundane Rune (5), Alchemical Resin (7), Obsidian (12), Turpen (6)	Potency Improvement (2), Solvent Proficiency (4), Woodworking (6)
Hlaalu Shelf, Long	Library	Superior	—	Heartwood (8), Regulus (4), Decorative Wax (5), Obsidian (10), Turpen (6)	Metalworking (1), Recipe Improvement (2), Woodworking (5)
Hlaalu Sideboard, Low Cabinet	Hearth	Epic	—	Heartwood (11), Regulus (7), Decorative Wax (8), Obsidian (14), Mastic (3)	Metalworking (3), Recipe Improvement (4), Woodworking (7)
Hlaalu Sideboard, Scholar's	Hearth	Epic	—	Heartwood (11), Regulus (7), Decorative Wax (8), Obsidian (14), Mastic (3)	Metalworking (3), Recipe Improvement (4), Woodworking (7)
Hlaalu Sideboard, Scribe's	Hearth	Epic	—	Heartwood (11), Regulus (7), Alchemical Resin (6), Decorative Wax (6), Obsidian (14), Mastic (3)	Metalworking (3), Solvent Proficiency (2), Recipe Improvement (2), Woodworking (7)
Hlaalu Stool, Polished	Workshop	Fine	Sittable	Heartwood (6), Obsidian (8), Pitch (9)	Woodworking (4)
Hlaalu Table, Formal Floral	Dining	Epic	—	Heartwood (12), Mundane Rune (10), Decorative Wax (6), Obsidian (16), Mastic (3)	Potency Improvement (6), Recipe Improvement (2), Woodworking (8)
Hlaalu Table, Formal Turtle	Dining	Epic	—	Heartwood (12), Mundane Rune (10), Decorative Wax (6), Obsidian (16), Mastic (3)	Potency Improvement (6), Recipe Improvement (2), Woodworking (8)
Hlaalu Wardrobe, Formal	Suite	Epic	—	Heartwood (12), Regulus (7), Alchemical Resin (6), Decorative Wax (7), Obsidian (16), Mastic (3)	Metalworking (3), Solvent Proficiency (2), Recipe Improvement (3), Woodworking (8)
Indoril End Table, Rounded	Suite	Superior	—	Heartwood (9), Decorative Wax (6), Obsidian (12), Turpen (6)	Recipe Improvement (3), Woodworking (6)
Indoril Shelf, Long	Library	Superior	—	Heartwood (8), Regulus (4), Decorative Wax (5), Obsidian (10), Turpen (6)	Metalworking (1), Recipe Improvement (2), Woodworking (5)
Redoran Armchair, Sanded	Dining	Epic	Sittable	Heartwood (12), Alchemical Resin (8), Decorative Wax (8), Obsidian (16), Mastic (3)	Solvent Proficiency (4), Recipe Improvement (4), Woodworking (8)
Redoran Bench, Sanded	Dining	Superior	Sittable	Heartwood (8), Alchemical Resin (5), Obsidian (10), Turpen (6)	Solvent Proficiency (3), Woodworking (5)
Redoran Chair, Sanded	Dining	Superior	Sittable	Heartwood (8), Decorative Wax (6), Obsidian (10), Turpen (6)	Recipe Improvement (3), Woodworking (5)
Redoran End Table, sanded	Suite	Superior	—	Heartwood (8), Decorative Wax (5), Obsidian (10), Turpen (6)	Recipe Improvement (2), Woodworking (5)
Redoran Fork, Wooden	Hearth	Superior	—	Heartwood (8), Decorative Wax (5), Obsidian (10), Turpen (6)	Recipe Improvement (2), Woodworking (5)
Redoran Incense Holder, Curved	Undercroft	Fine	—	Heartwood (5), Obsidian (6), Pitch (9)	Woodworking (3)
Redoran Knife, Wooden	Hearth	Superior	—	Heartwood (8), Decorative Wax (5), Obsidian (10), Turpen (6)	Recipe Improvement (2), Woodworking (5)
Redoran Settee, Sanded	Parlor	Superior	Sittable	Heartwood (8), Alchemical Resin (6), Obsidian (10), Turpen (6)	Solvent Proficiency (3), Woodworking (5)
Redoran Sideboard, Display	Hearth	Superior	—	Heartwood (8), Decorative Wax (5), Obsidian (10), Turpen (6)	Recipe Improvement (2), Woodworking (5)
Redoran Spoon, Wooden	Hearth	Superior	—	Heartwood (8), Decorative Wax (5), Obsidian (10), Turpen (6)	Recipe Improvement (2), Woodworking (5)
Redoran Stool, Sanded	Workshop	Fine	Sittable	Heartwood (6), Obsidian (8), Pitch (9)	Woodworking (4)
Redoran Table, Formal Floral	Dining	Epic	—	Heartwood (12), Mundane Rune (8), Decorative Wax (8), Obsidian (16), Mastic (3)	Potency Improvement (4), Recipe Improvement (4), Woodworking (8)
Redoran Table, Formal Turtle	Dining	Epic	—	Heartwood (12), Mundane Rune (8), Decorative Wax (8), Obsidian (16), Mastic (3)	Potency Improvement (4), Recipe Improvement (4), Woodworking (8)
Redoran Table, Kitchen	Dining	Superior	—	Heartwood (9), Decorative Wax (6), Obsidian (12), Turpen (6)	Recipe Improvement (3), Woodworking (6)
Redoran Trestle, Corridor	Dining	Superior	—	Heartwood (9), Decorative Wax (6), Obsidian (12), Turpen (6)	Recipe Improvement (3), Woodworking (6)

FURNISHING DESIGNS

CRAFTING STATION > COOKING FIRE

FURNISHING	CATEGORY	QUALITY	BEHAVIOR(S)	INGREDIENTS	REQUIRED SKILLS
Ashlander Platter, Bread and Cheese	Hearth	Superior	—	Mundane Rune (5), Decorative Wax (9), Heartwood (4), Ash Canvas (1), Bervez Juice (6)	Potency Improvement (2), Recipe Improvement (6), Woodworking (1)
Ashlander Platter, Ceramic	Hearth	Superior	—	Heartwood (4), Mundane Rune (5), Decorative Wax (9), Ash Canvas (1), Bervez Juice (6)	Potency Improvement (2), Recipe Improvement (6), Woodworking (1)
Daedric Candles, Group	Lighting	Epic	Light, Interactable	Decorative Wax (10), Mundane Rune (6), Alchemical Resin (8), Daedra Heart (12), Frost Mirriam (3)	Potency Improvement (2), Solvent Proficiency (4), Recipe Improvement (6)
Daedric Candles, Ritual Set	Lighting	Epic	Light, Interactable	Decorative Wax (10), Mundane Rune (8), Alchemical Resin (6), Daedra Heart (12), Frost Mirriam (3)	Potency Improvement (4), Solvent Proficiency (2), Recipe Improvement (6)
Dres Bowl, Dinner	Hearth	Fine	—	Decorative Wax (5), Heartwood (3), Obsidian (6), Flour (20)	Recipe Improvement (3), Woodworking (1)
Dres Bowl, Empty	Hearth	Superior	—	Decorative Wax (7), Heartwood (5), Obsidian (8), Bervez Juice (6)	Recipe Improvement (4), Woodworking (2)
Dres Bowl, Saltrice Mash	Hearth	Superior	—	Decorative Wax (8), Heartwood (6), Obsidian (10), Bervez Juice (6)	Recipe Improvement (5), Woodworking (3)
Dres Bowl, Serving	Hearth	Fine	—	Decorative Wax (5), Heartwood (3), Obsidian (6), Flour (20)	Recipe Improvement (3), Woodworking (1)
Dres Candles, Meditation	Lighting	Superior	Light, Interactable	Decorative Wax (7), Alchemical Resin (5), Obsidian (8), Bervez Juice (6)	Solvent Proficiency (2), Recipe Improvement (4)
Dres Cup, Empty (Greef—no greef in game)	Hearth	Superior	—	Decorative Wax (8), Mundane Rune (5), Obsidian (10), Bervez Juice (6)	Potency Improvement (2), Recipe Improvement (5)
Dres Cup, Empty (Mazte—no Mazte in game)	Hearth	Fine	—	Decorative Wax (5), Obsidian (6), Flour (20)	Recipe Improvement (3)
Dres Cup, Empty (Sujamma—no Sujamma in game)	Hearth	Epic	—	Decorative Wax (10), Mundane Rune (9), Heartwood (6), Obsidian (14), Frost Mirriam (3)	Potency Improvement (5), Recipe Improvement (6), Woodworking (2)
Dres Cup, Filled (Mazte)	Hearth	Fine	—	Decorative Wax (5), Obsidian (6), Flour (20)	Recipe Improvement (3)

FURNISHING	CATEGORY	QUALITY	BEHAVIOR(S)	INGREDIENTS	REQUIRED SKILLS
Dres Cup, Mazte (Greef)	Hearth	Superior	—	Decorative Wax (9), Mundane Rune (6), Obsidian (12), Bervez Juice (6)	Potency Improvement (3), Recipe Improvement (6)
Dres Cup, Mazte (was Sujamma)	Hearth	Epic	—	Decorative Wax (10), Mundane Rune (9), Heartwood (7), Obsidian (16), Frost Mirriam (3)	Potency Improvement (5), Recipe Improvement (6), Woodworking (3)
Dwarven Candles, Cup	Lighting	Superior	Light, Interactable	Decorative Wax (9), Regulus (5), Dwemer Frame (12), Bervez Juice (6)	Metalworking (2), Recipe Improvement (6)
Dwarven Candles, Plate	Lighting	Superior	Light, Interactable	Decorative Wax (5), Regulus (9), Alchemical Resin (5), Dwemer Frame (12), Bervez Juice (6)	Metalworking (6), Solvent Proficiency (2), Recipe Improvement (2)
Dwarven Candlestick, Laboratory	Lighting	Epic	Light, Interactable	Decorative Wax (10), Regulus (7), Mundane Rune (7), Alchemical Resin (6), Dwemer Frame (12), Frost Mirriam (3)	Metalworking (3), Potency Improvement (3), Solvent Proficiency (2), Recipe Improvement (6)
Dwarven Candlestick, Orrery	Lighting	Epic	Light, Interactable	Decorative Wax (10), Regulus (6), Mundane Rune (8), Alchemical Resin (6), Dwemer Frame (12), Frost Mirriam (3)	Metalworking (2), Potency Improvement (4), Solvent Proficiency (2), Recipe Improvement (6)
Indoril Candelabra, Chamber Shrine	Lighting	Epic	Light, Interactable	Decorative Wax (10), Regulus (8), Mundane Rune (6), Obsidian (12), Frost Mirriam (3)	Metalworking (4), Potency Improvement (2), Recipe Improvement (6)
Indoril Candelabra, Temple	Lighting	Epic	Light, Interactable	Decorative Wax (10), Regulus (8), Alchemical Resin (6), Obsidian (12), Frost Mirriam (3)	Metalworking (4), Solvent Proficiency (2), Recipe Improvement (6)
Indoril Candelabra, Temple	Lighting	Epic	Light, Interactable	Decorative Wax (10), Regulus (8), Alchemical Resin (6), Obsidian (12), Frost Mirriam (3)	Metalworking (4), Solvent Proficiency (2), Recipe Improvement (6)
Indoril Candle, Temple	Lighting	Epic	Light, Interactable	Decorative Wax (10), Regulus (7), Alchemical Resin (7), Obsidian (12), Frost Mirriam (3)	Metalworking (3), Solvent Proficiency (3), Recipe Improvement (6)
Redoran Bowl, Empty	Hearth	Superior	—	Decorative Wax (7), Heartwood (5), Obsidian (8), Bervez Juice (6)	Recipe Improvement (4), Woodworking (2)
Redoran Bowl, Saltrice Mash	Hearth	Superior	—	Decorative Wax (8), Heartwood (6), Obsidian (10), Bervez Juice (6)	Recipe Improvement (5), Woodworking (3)
Redoran Cup, Empty	Hearth	Epic	—	Decorative Wax (10), Mundane Rune (10), Heartwood (5), 0-14), Frost Mirriam (3)	Potency Improvement (6), Recipe Improvement (6), Woodworking (1)
Redoran Cup, Mazte	Hearth	Epic	—	Decorative Wax (10), Mundane Rune (10), Heartwood (6), Obsidian (16), Frost Mirriam (3)	Potency Improvement (6), Recipe Improvement (6), Woodworking (2)

FURNISHING DIAGRAMS

CRAFTING STATION > BLACKSMITHING STATION

FURNISHING	CATEGORY	QUALITY	BEHAVIOR(S)	INGREDIENTS	REQUIRED SKILLS
Daedric Bench, Ashen	Dining	Superior	Sittable	Regulus (9), Bash (6), Heartwood (6), Daedra Heart (12), Dwarven Oil (6)	Metalworking (6), Tailoring (3), Woodworking (3)
Daedric Pedestal, Ritual	Dining	Superior	—	Regulus (9), Mundane Rune (7), Alchemical Resin (5), Daedra Heart (12), Dwarven Oil (6)	Metalworking (6), Potency Improvement (4), Solvent Proficiency (2)
Dres Cannister, Portable	Hearth	Fine	—	Regulus (5), Obsidian (6), Honing Stone (9)	Metalworking (3)
Dres Cauldron, Floral Banded	Hearth	Superior	—	Regulus (9), Mundane Rune (6), Obsidian (12), Dwarven Oil (6)	Metalworking (6), Potency Improvement (3)
Dres Pot, Sauce	Hearth	Fine	—	Regulus (6), Obsidian (8), Honing Stone (9)	Metalworking (4)
Dwarven Bench, Forged	Dining	Superior	—	Regulus (8), Mundane Rune (6), Dwemer Frame (10), Dwarven Oil (6)	Metalworking (5), Potency Improvement (3)
Dwarven Boiler, Central	Structures	Epic	—	Regulus (13), Mundane Rune (11), Alchemical Resin (6), Dwemer Frame (18), Grain Solvent (3)	Metalworking (9), Potency Improvement (7), Solvent Proficiency (2)
Dwarven Bowl, Forged	Hearth	Superior	—	Regulus (9), Decorative Wax (7), Dwemer Frame (12), Dwarven Oil (6)	Metalworking (6), Recipe Improvement (4)
Dwarven Bowl, Forged Serving	Undercroft	Superior	—	Regulus (9), Alchemical Resin (5), Decorative Wax (5), Dwemer Frame (12), Dwarven Oil (6)	Metalworking (6), Solvent Proficiency (2), Recipe Improvement (2)
Dwarven Cannister, Sealed	Hearth	Fine	—	Regulus (5), Dwemer Frame (6), Honing Stone (9)	Metalworking (3)
Dwarven Chandelier, Barred	Lighting	Epic	Light, Interactable	Alchemical Resin (8), Regulus (11), Mundane Rune (7), Dwemer Frame (14), Grain Solvent (3)	Metalworking (7), Potency Improvement (3), Solvent Proficiency (4)
Dwarven Chandelier, Braced	Lighting	Epic	Light, Interactable	Alchemical Resin (7), Regulus (11), Mundane Rune (8), Dwemer Frame (14), Grain Solvent (3)	Metalworking (7), Potency Improvement (4), Solvent Proficiency (3)
Dwarven Chandelier, Caged	Lighting	Epic	Light, Interactable	Alchemical Resin (9), Regulus (11), Mundane Rune (6), Dwemer Frame (14), Grain Solvent (3)	Metalworking (7), Potency Improvement (2), Solvent Proficiency (5)
Dwarven Chandelier, Framework	Lighting	Superior	Light, Interactable	Alchemical Resin (5), Regulus (8), Mundane Rune (5), Dwemer Frame (10), Dwarven Oil (6)	Metalworking (5), Potency Improvement (2), Solvent Proficiency (2)
Dwarven Engine, Boiler	Workshop	Superior	—	Regulus (9), Mundane Rune (7), Alchemical Resin (5), Dwemer Frame (12), Dwarven Oil (6)	Metalworking (6), Potency Improvement (4), Solvent Proficiency (2)
Dwarven Engine, Fan	Workshop	Epic	—	Regulus (12), Mundane Rune (10), Alchemical Resin (6), Dwemer Frame (16), Grain Solvent (3)	Metalworking (8), Potency Improvement (6), Solvent Proficiency (2)
Dwarven Engine, Switch	Workshop	Epic	—	Regulus (13), Mundane Rune (11), Alchemical Resin (6), Dwemer Frame (18), Grain Solvent (3)	Metalworking (9), Potency Improvement (7), Solvent Proficiency (2)
Dwarven Engine, Turbine	Workshop	Epic	—	Regulus (13), Mundane Rune (11), Alchemical Resin (6), Dwemer Frame (18), Grain Solvent (3)	Metalworking (9), Potency Improvement (7), Solvent Proficiency (2)
Dwarven Goblet, Forged	Workshop	Superior	—	Regulus (8), Mundane Rune (5), Dwemer Frame (10), Dwarven Oil (6)	Metalworking (5), Potency Improvement (2)
Dwarven Jar, Sealed	Hearth	Superior	—	Regulus (9), Alchemical Resin (5), Decorative Wax (5), Dwemer Frame (12), Dwarven Oil (6)	Metalworking (6), Solvent Proficiency (2), Recipe Improvement (2)
Dwarven Jug, Sealed	Hearth	Superior	—	Regulus (9), Alchemical Resin (5), Decorative Wax (5), Dwemer Frame (12), Dwarven Oil (6)	Metalworking (6), Potency Improvement (2), Recipe Improvement (2)
Dwarven Pew, Refined	Parlor	Epic	—	Regulus (12), Mundane Rune (10), Alchemical Resin (6), Dwemer Frame (16), Grain Solvent (3)	Metalworking (8), Potency Improvement (6), Solvent Proficiency (2)
Dwarven Pipe Cap, Bolted	Workshop	Fine	—	Regulus (6), Mundane Rune (4), Dwemer Frame (8), Honing Stone (9)	Metalworking (4), Potency Improvement (2)
Dwarven Pipe, Corner	Workshop	Superior	—	Regulus (9), Mundane Rune (7), Dwemer Frame (12), Dwarven Oil (6)	Metalworking (6), Potency Improvement (4)

FURNISHING	CATEGORY	QUALITY	BEHAVIOR(S)	INGREDIENTS	REQUIRED SKILLS
Dwarven Pipe, Elbow	Workshop	Superior	—	Regulus (8), Mundane Rune (6), Dwemer Frame (10), Dwarven Oil (6)	Metalworking (5), Potency Improvement (3)
Dwarven Pipe, Full Column	Workshop	Superior	—	Regulus (9), Mundane Rune (7), Dwemer Frame (12), Dwarven Oil (6)	Metalworking (6), Potency Improvement (4)
Dwarven Pipe, Half Column	Workshop	Superior	—	Regulus (8), Mundane Rune (6), Dwemer Frame (10), Dwarven Oil (6)	Metalworking (5), Potency Improvement (3)
Dwarven Pipe, Quarter Column	Workshop	Superior	—	Regulus (8), Mundane Rune (5), Dwemer Frame (10), Dwarven Oil (6)	Metalworking (5), Potency Improvement (2)
Dwarven Pipeline Cap, Sealed	Workshop	Fine	—	Regulus (5), Mundane Rune (3), Dwemer Frame (6), Honing Stone (9)	Metalworking (3), Potency Improvement (1)
Dwarven Pipeline Cap, Sealed	Workshop	Fine	—	Regulus (5), Mundane Rune (3), Dwemer Frame (6), Honing Stone (9)	Metalworking (3), Potency Improvement (1)
Dwarven Pipeline, Column	Workshop	Superior	—	Regulus (9), Mundane Rune (7), Dwemer Frame (12), Dwarven Oil (6)	Metalworking (6), Potency Improvement (4)
Dwarven Pipeline, Elbow	Workshop	Superior	—	Regulus (8), Mundane Rune (5), Alchemical Resin (4), Dwemer Frame (10), Dwarven Oil (6)	Metalworking (5), Potency Improvement (2), Solvent Proficiency (1)
Dwarven Pipeline, Full Column	Workshop	Epic	—	Regulus (11), Mundane Rune (9), Alchemical Resin (6), Dwemer Frame (14), Grain Solvent (3)	Metalworking (7), Potency Improvement (5), Solvent Proficiency (2)
Dwarven Pipeline, Junction	Workshop	Superior	—	Regulus (9), Mundane Rune (6), Alchemical Resin (5), Dwemer Frame (12), Dwarven Oil (6)	Metalworking (6), Potency Improvement (3), Solvent Proficiency (2)
Dwarven Plate, Forged	Hearth	Superior	—	Regulus (9), Mundane Rune (5), Decorative Wax (5), Dwemer Frame (12), Dwarven Oil (6)	Metalworking (6), Potency Improvement (2), Recipe Improvement (2)
Dwarven Pot, Sealed	Hearth	Fine	—	Regulus (5), Dwemer Frame (6), Honing Stone (9)	Metalworking (3)
Dwarven Table, Workbench	Dining	Superior	—	Regulus (9), Mundane Rune (7), Dwemer Frame (12), Dwarven Oil (6)	Metalworking (6), Potency Improvement (4)
Dwarven Urn, Sealed	Undercroft	Fine	—	Regulus (5), Dwemer Frame (6), Honing Stone (9)	Metalworking (3)
Dwarven Valve, Disconnected	Structures	Superior	—	Regulus (8), Mundane Rune (5), Dwemer Frame (10), Dwarven Oil (6)	Metalworking (5), Potency Improvement (2)
Dwarven Vase, Forged	Parlor	Superior	—	Regulus (8), Decorative Wax (5), Dwemer Frame (10), Dwarven Oil (6)	Metalworking (5), Recipe Improvement (2)
Dwarven Vessel, Sealed	Hearth	Superior	—	Regulus (9), Decorative Wax (7), Dwemer Frame (12), Dwarven Oil (6)	Metalworking (6), Recipe Improvement (4)
Hlaalu Boxes, Compact	Parlor	Superior	—	Regulus (9), Alchemical Resin (5), Heartwood (4), Obsidian (12), Dwarven Oil (6)	Metalworking (6), Solvent Proficiency (2), Woodworking (1)
Hlaalu Cannister, Trinket	Parlor	Epic	—	Regulus (11), Mundane Rune (7), Alchemical Resin (8), Obsidian (14), Grain Solvent (3)	Metalworking (7), Potency Improvement (3), Solvent Proficiency (4)
Hlaalu Sconce, Vellum	Lighting	Epic	Light, Interactable	Regulus (11), Clean Pelt (6), Alchemical Resin (7), Heartwood (6), Obsidian (14), Grain Solvent (3)	Metalworking (7), Tailoring (2), Solvent Proficiency (3), Woodworking (2)
Indoril Bellows, Practical	Miscellaneous	Superior	—	Regulus (9), Clean Pelt (5), Heartwood (5), Obsidian (12), Dwarven Oil (6)	Metalworking (6), Tailoring (2), Woodworking (2)
Indoril Box, Trinket	Parlor	Epic	—	Regulus (12), Mundane Rune (8), Heartwood (8), Obsidian (16), Grain Solvent (3)	Metalworking (8), Potency Improvement (4), Woodworking (4)
Indoril Brazier, Cauldron	Lighting	Epic	Light, Interactable	Regulus (12), Mundane Rune (8), Decorative Wax (8), Obsidian (16), Grain Solvent (3)	Metalworking (8), Potency Improvement (4), Recipe Improvement (4)
Indoril Brazier, Kettle	Lighting	Epic	Light, Interactable	Regulus (11), Mundane Rune (7), Decorative Wax (8), Obsidian (14), Grain Solvent (3)	Metalworking (7), Potency Improvement (3), Recipe Improvement (4)
Indoril Brazier, Knotwork	Lighting	Epic	Light, Interactable	Regulus (9), Mundane Rune (6), Obsidian (12), Dwarven Oil (6)	Metalworking (6), Potency Improvement (3)
Indoril Brazier, Pedestal	Lighting	Epic	Light, Interactable	Regulus (11), Mundane Rune (8), Decorative Wax (7), Obsidian (14), Grain Solvent (3)	Metalworking (7), Potency Improvement (4), Recipe Improvement (3)
Indoril Cannister, Trinket	Parlor	Epic	—	Regulus (12), Mundane Rune (8), Alchemical Resin (8), Obsidian (16), Grain Solvent (3)	Metalworking (8), Potency Improvement (4), Solvent Proficiency (4)
Indoril Cassone, Sealed	Parlor	Epic	—	Regulus (11), Mundane Rune (8), Alchemical Resin (7), Obsidian (14), Grain Solvent (3)	Metalworking (7), Potency Improvement (4), Solvent Proficiency (3)
Indoril Chandelier, Knotwork	Lighting	Superior	Light, Interactable	Alchemical Resin (6), Regulus (8), Obsidian (10), Dwarven Oil (6)	Metalworking (5), Solvent Proficiency (3)
Indoril Chest, Fortified	Suite	Superior	—	Regulus (9), Mundane Rune (6), Obsidian (12), Dwarven Oil (6)	Metalworking (6), Potency Improvement (3)
Indoril Footlocker, Fortified	Suite	Superior	—	Regulus (8), Mundane Rune (5), Obsidian (10), Dwarven Oil (6)	Metalworking (5), Potency Improvement (2)
Indoril Platter, Floral	Hearth	Epic	—	Regulus (11), Mundane Rune (8), Decorative Wax (7), Obsidian (14), Grain Solvent (3)	Metalworking (7), Potency Improvement (4), Recipe Improvement (3)
Indoril Vault, Sealed	Suite	Epic	—	Regulus (12), Mundane Rune (9), Alchemical Resin (7), Obsidian (16), Grain Solvent (3)	Metalworking (8), Potency Improvement (5), Solvent Proficiency (3)
Redoran Incense Holder, Mesh	Undercroft	Epic	—	Regulus (7), Mundane Rune (7), Alchemical Resin (5), Heartwood (11), Obsidian (14), Grain Solvent (3)	Metalworking (3), Potency Improvement (3), Solvent Proficiency (1), Woodworking (7)
Redoran Incense Pot, Beastly	Hearth	Epic	—	Regulus (11), Mundane Rune (6), Alchemical Resin (7), Decorative Wax (6), Obsidian (14), Grain Solvent (3)	Metalworking (7), Potency Improvement (2), Solvent Proficiency (3), Recipe Improvement (2)
Redoran Plate, Floral	Hearth	Epic	—	Regulus (11), Mundane Rune (8), Alchemical Resin (7), Obsidian (14), Grain Solvent (3)	Metalworking (7), Potency Improvement (4), Solvent Proficiency (3)
Redoran Plate, Meal	Hearth	Epic	—	Regulus (12), Mundane Rune (8), Decorative Wax (8), Obsidian (16), Grain Solvent (3)	Metalworking (8), Potency Improvement (4), Recipe Improvement (4)
Redoran Steamer, Iron	Hearth	Epic	—	Regulus (12), Mundane Rune (8), Alchemical Resin (8), Obsidian (16), Grain Solvent (3)	Metalworking (8), Potency Improvement (4), Solvent Proficiency (4)
Redoran Tray, Floral	Hearth	Epic	—	Regulus (12), Mundane Rune (8), Alchemical Resin (8), Obsidian (16), Grain Solvent (3)	Metalworking (8), Potency Improvement (4), Solvent Proficiency (4)
Velothi Brazier, Temple	Lighting	Epic	Light, Interactable	Regulus (12), Mundane Rune (8), Decorative Wax (8), Obsidian (16), Grain Solvent (3)	Metalworking (8), Potency Improvement (4), Recipe Improvement (4)

FURNISHING FORMULAS

CRAFTING STATION > ALCHEMY STATION					
FURNISHING	**CATEGORY**	**QUALITY**	**BEHAVIOR(S)**	**INGREDIENTS**	**REQUIRED SKILLS**
Daedric Brazier, Standing	Lighting	Epic	Light, Interactable	Alchemical Resin (12), Regulus (7), Mundane Rune (9), Daedra Heart (16)	Metalworking (3), Potency Improvement (5), Solvent Proficiency (8)
Daedric Brazier, Table	Lighting	Epic	Light, Interactable	Alchemical Resin (11), Regulus (8), Mundane Rune (7), Daedra Heart (14)	Metalworking (4), Potency Improvement (3), Solvent Proficiency (7)
Daedric Chandelier, Ritual	Lighting	Epic	Light, Interactable	Alchemical Resin (9), Regulus (12), Mundane Rune (7), Daedra Heart (16), Grain Solvent (3)	Metalworking (8), Potency Improvement (3), Solvent Proficiency (5)
Dres Censer, Chains	Undercroft	Superior	Light	Alchemical Resin (9), Regulus (5), Mundane Rune (5), Obsidian (12)	Metalworking (2), Potency Improvement (2), Solvent Proficiency (6)
Dres Incense Stand, Chains	Undercroft	Epic	—	Alchemical Resin (11), Regulus (8), Mundane Rune (7), Daedra Heart (14)	Metalworking (4), Potency Improvement (3), Solvent Proficiency (7)
Dwarven Lamppost, Powered	Lighting	Epic	Light, Interactable	Alchemical Resin (12), Regulus (8), Mundane Rune (7), Decorative Wax (5), Dwemer Frame (16)	Metalworking (4), Potency Improvement (3), Solvent Proficiency (8), Recipe Improvement (1)
Dwarven Lantern, Oil	Lighting	Epic	Light, Interactable	Alchemical Resin (11), Regulus (7), Mundane Rune (6), Decorative Wax (6), Dwemer Frame (14)	Metalworking (3), Potency Improvement (2), Solvent Proficiency (7), Recipe Improvement (2)
Dwarven Sconce, Barred	Lighting	Epic	Light, Interactable	Alchemical Resin (11), Regulus (8), Mundane Rune (7), Dwemer Frame (14)	Metalworking (4), Potency Improvement (3), Solvent Proficiency (7)
Dwarven Sconce, Framework	Lighting	Superior	Light, Interactable	Alchemical Resin (8), Regulus (6), Dwemer Frame (10)	Metalworking (3), Solvent Proficiency (5)
Dwarven Sconce, Powered	Lighting	Epic	Light, Interactable	Alchemical Resin (11), Regulus (8), Mundane Rune (6), Decorative Wax (5), Dwemer Frame (14)	Metalworking (4), Potency Improvement (2), Solvent Proficiency (7), Recipe Improvement (1)
Hlaalu Lamp, Portable	Lighting	Fine	Light, Interactable	Alchemical Resin (6), Regulus (3), Obsidian (8)	Metalworking (1), Solvent Proficiency (4)
Hlaalu Lantern, Classic Vellum	Lighting	Epic	Light, Interactable	Alchemical Resin (11), Regulus (8), Clean Pelt (7), Obsidian (14)	Metalworking (4), Tailoring (3), Solvent Proficiency (7)
Hlaalu Lantern, Modest Vellum	Lighting	Epic	Light, Interactable	Alchemical Resin (11), Regulus (7), Clean Pelt (6), Decorative Wax (6), Obsidian (14)	Metalworking (3), Tailoring (2), Solvent Proficiency (7), Recipe Improvement (2)
Hlaalu Lantern, Oversized Vellum	Lighting	Epic	Light, Interactable	Alchemical Resin (11), Regulus (7), Clean Pelt (8), Obsidian (14)	Metalworking (3), Tailoring (4), Solvent Proficiency (7)
Hlaalu Lantern, Stationary	Lighting	Fine	Light, Interactable	Alchemical Resin (5), Regulus (3), Obsidian (6)	Metalworking (1), Solvent Proficiency (3)
Hlaalu Mirror, Standing	Suite	Epic	—	Alchemical Resin (11), Regulus (7), Mundane Rune (7), Heartwood (5), Obsidian (14)	Metalworking (3), Potency Improvement (3), Solvent Proficiency (7), Woodworking (1)
Hlaalu Streetlight, Vellum	Lighting	Epic	Light, Interactable	Alchemical Resin (11), Regulus (6), Clean Pelt (6), Heartwood (7), Obsidian (14)	Metalworking (2), Tailoring (2), wp 7), Woodworking (3)
Indoril Candelabra, Shrine	Lighting	Superior	Light, Interactable	Alchemical Resin (8), Regulus (6), Obsidian (10)	Metalworking (3), Solvent Proficiency (5)
Indoril Incense Cup, Silver	Hearth	Superior	—	Alchemical Resin (9), Regulus (7), Obsidian (12)	Metalworking (4), Solvent Proficiency (6)
Indoril Lantern, Hanging	Lighting	Superior	Light, Interactable	Alchemical Resin (8), Decorative Wax (5), Obsidian (10)	Solvent Proficiency (5), Recipe Improvement (2)
Indoril Lightpost, Stone	Lighting	Fine	Light, Interactable	Alchemical Resin (5), Mundane Rune (3), Obsidian (6)	Potency Improvement (1), Solvent Proficiency (3)
Indoril Sconce, Shrine	Lighting	Epic	Light, Interactable	Alchemical Resin (12), Regulus (8), Decorative Wax (8), Obsidian (16)	Metalworking (4), Solvent Proficiency (8), Recipe Improvement (4)
Indoril Sconce, Temple	Lighting	Epic	Light, Interactable	Alchemical Resin (11), Regulus (8), Decorative Wax (7), Obsidian (14)	Metalworking (4), Solvent Proficiency (7), Recipe Improvement (3)
Indoril Shelf, Block	Library	Fine	—	Alchemical Resin (5), Heartwood (3), Obsidian (6)	Solvent Proficiency (3), Woodworking (1)
Indoril Streetlight, Brick	Lighting	Superior	Light, Interactable	Alchemical Resin (8), Mundane Rune (6), Obsidian (10)	Potency Improvement (3), Solvent Proficiency (5)
Indoril Streetlight, Full Stone	Lighting	Fine	Light, Interactable	Alchemical Resin (6), Mundane Rune (4), Obsidian (8)	Potency Improvement (2), Solvent Proficiency (4)
Indoril Streetlight, Stone	Lighting	Fine	Light, Interactable	Alchemical Resin (5), Mundane Rune (3), Obsidian (6)	Potency Improvement (1), Solvent Proficiency (3)

FURNISHING PATTERNS

CRAFTING STATION > CLOTHING STATION					
FURNISHING	**CATEGORY**	**QUALITY**	**BEHAVIOR(S)**	**INGREDIENTS**	**REQUIRED SKILLS**
Dres Carpet, Chains	Parlor	Fine	—	Bash (6), Obsidian (8), Hemming (9)	Tailoring (4)
Dres Carpet, Fertile Peat	Parlor	Superior	—	Bash (9), Alchemical Resin (5), Decorative Wax (5), Obsidian (12), Embroidery (6)	Tailoring (6), Solvent Proficiency (2), Recipe Improvement (2)
Dres Rug, Chains	Parlor	Epic	—	Bash (12), Mundane Rune (7), Alchemical Resin (9), Obsidian (16), Elegant Lining (3)	Tailoring (8), Potency Improvement (3), Solvent Proficiency (5)
Dres Runner, Chains	Parlor	Epic	—	Bash (11), Mundane Rune (6), Alchemical Resin (9), Obsidian (14), Elegant Lining (3)	Tailoring (7), Potency Improvement (2), Solvent Proficiency (5)
Dres Tapestry, Thorns	Parlor	Superior	—	Bash (9), Alchemical Resin (6), Obsidian (12), Embroidery (6)	Tailoring (6), Solvent Proficiency (3)
Hlaalu Banner, Floral	Parlor	Superior	—	Bash (8), Alchemical Resin (5), Obsidian (10), Embroidery (6)	Tailoring (5), Solvent Proficiency (2)
Hlaalu Bed, Canopy	Suite	Epic	—	Bash (12), Alchemical Resin (6), Heartwood (10), Obsidian (16), Elegant Lining (3)	Tailoring (8), Solvent Proficiency (2), Woodworking (6)
Hlaalu Bed, Double Pillow	Suite	Superior	—	Bash (9), Heartwood (6), Obsidian (12), Embroidery (6)	Tailoring (6), Woodworking (3)
Hlaalu Bed, Single	Suite	Fine	—	Bash (6), Heartwood (3), Obsidian (8), Hemming (9)	Tailoring (4), Woodworking (1)
Hlaalu Bed, Single Pillow	Suite	Superior	—	Bash (8), Heartwood (5), Obsidian (10), Embroidery (6)	Tailoring (5), Woodworking (2)
Hlaalu Bench, Mossy Cushion	Dining	Epic	—	Bash (12), Mundane Rune (6), Alchemical Resin (6), Heartwood (8), Obsidian (16), Elegant Lining (3)	Tailoring (8), Potency Improvement (2), Solvent Proficiency (2), Woodworking (4)
Hlaalu Carpet, Garden Moss	Parlor	Superior	—	Bash (9), Decorative Wax (6), Obsidian (12), Embroidery (6)	Tailoring (6), Recipe Improvement (3)
Hlaalu Mat, Welcoming	Parlor	Fine	—	Bash (6), Obsidian (8), Hemming (9)	Tailoring (4)
Hlaalu Settee, Mossy Cushion	Parlor	Epic	Sittable	Bash (12), Mundane Rune (6), Alchemical Resin (6), Heartwood (8), Obsidian (16), Elegant Lining (3)	Tailoring (8), Potency Improvement (2), Solvent Proficiency (2), Woodworking (4)
Hlaalu Stool, Mossy Cushion	Workshop	Epic	Sittable	Bash (11), Alchemical Resin (5), Decorative Wax (6), Heartwood (8), Obsidian (14), Elegant Lining (3)	Tailoring (7), Solvent Proficiency (1), Recipe Improvement (2), Woodworking (4)

FURNISHING	CATEGORY	QUALITY	BEHAVIOR(S)	INGREDIENTS	REQUIRED SKILLS
Hlaalu Tapestry, Floral	Parlor	Superior	—	Bash (9), Alchemical Resin (6), Obsidian (12), Embroidery (6)	Tailoring (6), Solvent Proficiency (3)
Hlaalu Towels, Folded	Miscellaneous	Superior	—	Bash (8), Alchemical Resin (5), Obsidian (10), Embroidery (6)	Tailoring (5), Solvent Proficiency (2)
Indoril Banner, Almalexia	Parlor	Epic	—	Bash (12), Mundane Rune (7), Decorative Wax (6), Alchemical Resin (7), Obsidian (16), Elegant Lining (3)	Tailoring (8), Potency Improvement (3), Solvent Proficiency (3), Recipe Improvement (2)
Indoril Banner, Sotha Sil	Parlor	Epic	—	Bash (12), Mundane Rune (8), Alchemical Resin (8), Obsidian (16), Elegant Lining (3)	Tailoring (8), Potency Improvement (3), Solvent Proficiency (3), Recipe Improvement (2)
Indoril Banner, Vivec	Parlor	Epic	—	Bash (12), Mundane Rune (7), Decorative Wax (7), Alchemical Resin (6), Obsidian (16), Elegant Lining (3)	Tailoring (8), Potency Improvement (3), Solvent Proficiency (2), Recipe Improvement (3)
Indoril Carpet, Almalexia	Parlor	Epic	—	Bash (12), Mundane Rune (6), Alchemical Resin (10), Obsidian (16), Elegant Lining (3)	Tailoring (8), Potency Improvement (2), Solvent Proficiency (6)
Indoril Carpet, Grand Almalexia	Parlor	Epic	—	Bash (13), Mundane Rune (7), Alchemical Resin (10), Obsidian (18), Elegant Lining (3)	Tailoring (9), Potency Improvement (3), Solvent Proficiency (6)
Indoril Carpet, Grand Sotha Sil	Parlor	Epic	—	Bash (13), Mundane Rune (8), Decorative Wax (6), Alchemical Resin (7), Obsidian (18), Elegant Lining (3)	Tailoring (9), Potency Improvement (4), Solvent Proficiency (3), Recipe Improvement (2)
Indoril Carpet, Grand Vivec	Parlor	Epic	—	Bash (13), Mundane Rune (9), Decorative Wax (8), Obsidian (18), Elegant Lining (3)	Tailoring (9), Potency Improvement (5), Recipe Improvement (4)
Indoril Carpet, Sotha Sil	Parlor	Epic	—	Bash (12), Mundane Rune (7), Decorative Wax (6), Alchemical Resin (7), Obsidian (16), Elegant Lining (3)	Tailoring (8), Potency Improvement (3), Solvent Proficiency (3), Recipe Improvement (2)
Indoril Carpet, Vivec	Parlor	Epic	—	Bash (12), Mundane Rune (8), Decorative Wax (8), Obsidian (16), Elegant Lining (3)	Tailoring (8), Potency Improvement (4), Recipe Improvement (4)
Indoril Rug, Almalexia	Parlor	Epic	—	Bash (12), Mundane Rune (7), Alchemical Resin (9), Obsidian (16), Elegant Lining (3)	Tailoring (8), Potency Improvement (3), Solvent Proficiency (5)
Indoril Rug, Sotha Sil	Parlor	Epic	—	Bash (12), Mundane Rune (8), Decorative Wax (6), Alchemical Resin (6), Obsidian (16), Elegant Lining (3)	Tailoring (8), Potency Improvement (4), Solvent Proficiency (2), Recipe Improvement (2)
Indoril Rug, Vivec	Parlor	Epic	—	Bash (12), Mundane Rune (8), Decorative Wax (8), Obsidian (16), Elegant Lining (3)	Tailoring (8), Potency Improvement (4), Recipe Improvement (4)
Indoril Runner, Almalexia	Parlor	Epic	—	Bash (11), Mundane Rune (6), Alchemical Resin (9), Obsidian (14), Elegant Lining (3)	Tailoring (7), Potency Improvement (2), Solvent Proficiency (5)
Indoril Runner, Sotha Sil	Parlor	Epic	—	Bash (11), Mundane Rune (7), Alchemical Resin (6), Decorative Wax (6), Obsidian (14), Elegant Lining (3)	Tailoring (7), Potency Improvement (3), Solvent Proficiency (2), Recipe Improvement (2)
Indoril Runner, Vivec	Parlor	Epic	—	Bash (11), Mundane Rune (8), Decorative Wax (7), Obsidian (14), Elegant Lining (3)	Tailoring (7), Potency Improvement (4), Recipe Improvement (3)
Indoril Tapestry, Almalexia	Parlor	Epic	—	Bash (12), Mundane Rune (7), Alchemical Resin (7), Obsidian (16), Elegant Lining (3)	Tailoring (8), Potency Improvement (3), Solvent Proficiency (3), Recipe Improvement (2)
Indoril Tapestry, Sotha Sil	Parlor	Epic	—	Bash (12), Mundane Rune (8), Alchemical Resin (8), Obsidian (16), Elegant Lining (3)	Tailoring (8), Potency Improvement (4), Solvent Proficiency (4)
Indoril Tapestry, Vivec	Parlor	Epic	—	Bash (12), Mundane Rune (7), Alchemical Resin (6), Obsidian (16), Elegant Lining (3)	Tailoring (8), Potency Improvement (3), Solvent Proficiency (2), Recipe Improvement (3)
Redoran Armchair, Fungal Cushion	Dining	Epic	Sittable	Bash (12), Decorative Wax (7), Heartwood (9), Obsidian (16), Elegant Lining (3)	Tailoring (8), Recipe Improvement (3), Woodworking (5)
Redoran Bed, Canopy	Suite	Epic	—	Bash (12), Alchemical Resin (6), Decorative Wax (6), Heartwood (8), Obsidian (16), Elegant Lining (3)	Tailoring (8), Solvent Proficiency (2), Recipe Improvement (2), Woodworking (4)
Redoran Bed, Double Pillow	Suite	Superior	—	Bash (8), Heartwood (5), Obsidian (10), Embroidery (6)	Tailoring (5), Woodworking (2)
Redoran Bed, Single	Suite	Fine	—	Bash (6), Heartwood (3), Obsidian (8), Hemming (9)	Tailoring (4), Woodworking (1)
Redoran Bed, Single Pillow	Suite	Superior	—	Bash (9), Heartwood (6), Obsidian (12), Embroidery (6)	Tailoring (6), Woodworking (3)
Redoran Bench, Fungal Cushion	Dining	Epic	—	Bash (11), Alchemical Resin (6), Heartwood (9), Obsidian (14), Elegant Lining (3)	Tailoring (7), Solvent Proficiency (2), Woodworking (5)
Redoran Carpet, Volcanic Ash	Parlor	Superior	—	Bash (9), Alchemical Resin (6), Obsidian (12), Embroidery (6)	Tailoring (6), Solvent Proficiency (3)
Redoran Carpet, Volcanic Sands	Parlor	Fine	—	Bash (6), Obsidian (8), Hemming (9)	Tailoring (4)
Redoran Mantle Cloth, Crimson Cover	Miscellaneous	Epic	—	Bash (11), Mundane Rune (7), Alchemical Resin (8), Obsidian (14), Elegant Lining (3)	Tailoring (7), Potency Improvement (3), Solvent Proficiency (4)
Redoran Mantle Cloth, Crimson Coverlet	Miscellaneous	Superior	—	Bash (8), Mundane Rune (6), Obsidian (10), Embroidery (6)	Tailoring (5), Potency Improvement (3)
Redoran Settee, Fungal Cushion	Parlor	Epic	Sittable	Bash (11), Alchemical Resin (6), Heartwood (9), Obsidian (14), Elegant Lining (3)	Tailoring (7), Solvent Proficiency (2), Woodworking (5)
Redoran Stool, Fungal Cushion	Workshop	Epic	Sittable	Bash (11), Decorative Wax (7), Heartwood (8), Obsidian (14), Elegant Lining (3)	Tailoring (7), Recipe Improvement (3), Woodworking (4)
Redoran Table Runner, Gilded Ochre	Parlor	Epic	—	Bash (12), Mundane Rune (8), Alchemical Resin (8), Obsidian (16), Elegant Lining (3)	Tailoring (8), Potency Improvement (4), Solvent Proficiency (4)

FURNISHING PRAXES

CRAFTING STATION > ENCHANTING TABLE

FURNISHING	CATEGORY	QUALITY	BEHAVIOR(S)	INGREDIENTS	REQUIRED SKILLS
Daedric Base, Ashen	Structures	Epic	—	Mundane Rune (12), Regulus (8), Alchemical Resin (8), Daedra Heart (16), Rekuta (3)	Metalworking (4), Potency Improvement (8), Solvent Proficiency (4)
Daedric Platform, Ashen	Structures	Epic	—	Mundane Rune (12), Regulus (8), Alchemical Resin (8), Daedra Heart (16), Rekuta (3)	Metalworking (4), Potency Improvement (8), Solvent Proficiency (4)
Daedric Urn, Ashen	Undercroft	Epic	—	Mundane Rune (11), Regulus (8), Alchemical Resin (7), Daedra Heart (14), Rekuta (3)	Metalworking (4), Potency Improvement (7), Solvent Proficiency (3)
Dres Jar, Stoneflower	Hearth	Superior	—	Mundane Rune (9), Alchemical Resin (6), Obsidian (12), Denata (6)	Potency Improvement (6), Solvent Proficiency (3)
Dres Teapot, Ceramic	Hearth	Superior	—	Mundane Rune (9), Regulus (5), Decorative Wax (5), Obsidian (12), Denata (6)	Metalworking (2), Potency Improvement (6), Recipe Improvement (2)
Dwarven Altar, Stairs	Structures	Epic	—	Mundane Rune (11), Regulus (9), Alchemical Resin (6), Dwemer Frame (14), Rekuta (3)	Metalworking (5), Potency Improvement (7), Solvent Proficiency (2)

FURNISHING	CATEGORY	QUALITY	BEHAVIOR(S)	INGREDIENTS	REQUIRED SKILLS
Dwarven Amphora, Sealed	Hearth	Superior	—	Mundane Rune (9), Regulus (5), Alchemical Resin (5), Dwemer Frame (12), Denata (6)	Metalworking (2), Potency Improvement (6), Solvent Proficiency (2)
Dwarven Basin, Forged	Undercroft	Superior	—	Mundane Rune (8), Regulus (5), Dwemer Frame (10), Denata (6)	Metalworking (2), Potency Improvement (5)
Dwarven Bookcase, Full	Library	Epic	—	Mundane Rune (11), Regulus (9), Alchemical Resin (6), Dwemer Frame (14), Rekuta (3)	Metalworking (5), Potency Improvement (7), Solvent Proficiency (2)
Dwarven Platform, Steps	Structures	Epic	—	Mundane Rune (11), Regulus (9), Alchemical Resin (6), Dwemer Frame (14), Rekuta (3)	Metalworking (5), Potency Improvement (7), Solvent Proficiency (2)
Dwarven Table, Assembly	Dining	Epic	—	Mundane Rune (11), Regulus (9), Alchemical Resin (6), Dwemer Frame (14), Rekuta (3)	Metalworking (5), Potency Improvement (7), Solvent Proficiency (2)
Dwarven Table, Refined	Dining	Epic	—	Mundane Rune (12), Regulus (10), Alchemical Resin (6), Dwemer Frame (16), Rekuta (3)	Metalworking (6), Potency Improvement (8), Solvent Proficiency (2)
Hlaalu Amphora, Sealed Orichalcum	Hearth	Epic	—	Mundane Rune (12), Regulus (8), Heartwood (8), Obsidian (16), Rekuta (3)	Metalworking (4), I 8), Woodworking (4)
Hlaalu Cannister, Sealed Azurite	Hearth	Epic	—	Mundane Rune (12), Regulus (9), Alchemical Resin (7), Obsidian (16), Rekuta (3)	Metalworking (5), Potency Improvement (8), Solvent Proficiency (3)
Hlaalu Censer, Mesh	Undercroft	Epic	—	Mundane Rune (11), Regulus (8), Alchemical Resin (7), Obsidian (14), Rekuta (3)	Metalworking (4), Potency Improvement (7), Solvent Proficiency (3)
Hlaalu Jar, Garden Moss	Hearth	Superior	—	Mundane Rune (8), Decorative Wax (5), Obsidian (10), Denata (6)	Potency Improvement (5), Recipe Improvement (2)
Hlaalu Vase, Gilded	Parlor	Epic	—	Mundane Rune (11), Alchemical Resin (7), Decorative Wax (8), Obsidian (14), Rekuta (3)	Potency Improvement (7), Solvent Proficiency (3), Recipe Improvement (4)
Redoran Amphora, Sealed Marble	Hearth	Epic	—	Mundane Rune (12), Regulus (9), Decorative Wax (7), Obsidian (16), Rekuta (3)	Metalworking (5), Potency Improvement (8), Recipe Improvement (3)
Redoran Incense Holder, Ceramic Pan	Undercroft	Superior	—	Mundane Rune (9), Alchemical Resin (7), Obsidian (12), Denata (6)	Potency Improvement (6), Solvent Proficiency (4)
Redoran Jar, Jazbay	Hearth	Superior	—	Mundane Rune (9), Decorative Wax (6), Obsidian (12), Denata (6)	Potency Improvement (6), Recipe Improvement (3)
Redoran Urn, Dusky Marble	Undercroft	Epic	—	Mundane Rune (12), Regulus (8), Alchemical Resin (8), Obsidian (16), Rekuta (3)	Metalworking (4), Potency Improvement (8), Solvent Proficiency (4)
Redoran Urn, Imprinted Clay	Undercroft	Fine	—	Mundane Rune (5), Obsidian (6), Jejota (9)	Potency Improvement (3)
Redoran Urn, Pale Marble	Undercroft	Epic	—	Mundane Rune (11), Regulus (9), Decorative Wax (6), Obsidian (14), Rekuta (3)	Metalworking (5), Potency Improvement (7), Recipe Improvement (2)
Telvanni Arched Light, Organic Azure	Lighting	Epic	Light, Interactable	Mundane Rune (12), Regulus (8), Alchemical Resin (8), Stinkhorn (16), Rekuta (3)	Metalworking (4), Potency Improvement (8), Solvent Proficiency (4)
Telvanni Armchair, Organic	Dining	Epic	Sittable	Mundane Rune (12), Bash (6), Alchemical Resin (8), Decorative Wax (6), Stinkhorn (16), Rekuta (3)	Tailoring (2), Potency Improvement (8), Solvent Proficiency (4), Recipe Improvement (2)
Telvanni Bed, Organic	Suite	Epic	—	Mundane Rune (12), Bash (8), Decorative Wax (8), Stinkhorn (16), Rekuta (3)	Tailoring (4), Potency Improvement (8), Recipe Improvement (4)
Telvanni Bookcase, Organic	Library	Epic	—	Mundane Rune (12), Alchemical Resin (8), Heartwood (8), Stinkhorn (16), Rekuta (3)	Potency Improvement (8), Solvent Proficiency (4), Woodworking (4)
Telvanni Candelabra, Organic	Lighting	Epic	Light, Interactable	Mundane Rune (11), Regulus (6), Alchemical Resin (7), Decorative Wax (6), Stinkhorn (14), Rekuta (3)	Metalworking (2), Potency Improvement (7), Solvent Proficiency (3), Recipe Improvement (2)
Telvanni Chair, Organic	Dining	Epic	Sittable	Mundane Rune (11), Alchemical Resin (8), Decorative Wax (7), Stinkhorn (14), Rekuta (3)	Potency Improvement (7), Solvent Proficiency (4), Recipe Improvement (3)
Telvanni Desk, Organic	Library	Epic	—	Mundane Rune (12), Alchemical Resin (7), Decorative Wax (6), Heartwood (7), Stinkhorn (16), Rekuta (3)	Potency Improvement (8), Solvent Proficiency (3), Recipe Improvement (2), Woodworking (3)
Telvanni End Table, Organic	Parlor	Epic	—	Mundane Rune (11), Alchemical Resin (7), Decorative Wax (6), Heartwood (6), Stinkhorn (14), Rekuta (3)	Potency Improvement (7), Solvent Proficiency (3), Recipe Improvement (2), Woodworking (2)
Telvanni Lamp, Organic Azure	Lighting	Epic	Light, Interactable	Mundane Rune (12), Alchemical Resin (8), Decorative Wax (8), Stinkhorn (16), Rekuta (3)	Potency Improvement (8), Solvent Proficiency (4), Recipe Improvement (4)
Telvanni Lantern, Organic Azure	Lighting	Epic	Light, Interactable	Mundane Rune (11), Regulus (6), Alchemical Resin (8), Decorative Wax (5), Stinkhorn (14), Rekuta (3)	Metalworking (2), Potency Improvement (7), Solvent Proficiency (4), Recipe Improvement (1)
Telvanni Nightstand, Organic	Suite	Epic	—	Mundane Rune (12), Alchemical Resin (8), Decorative Wax (6), Heartwood (6), Stinkhorn (16), Rekuta (3)	Potency Improvement (8), Solvent Proficiency (4), Recipe Improvement (2), Woodworking (2)
Telvanni Sconce, Organic Azure	Lighting	Epic	Light, Interactable	Mundane Rune (11), Regulus (7), Alchemical Resin (6), Decorative Wax (6), Stinkhorn (14), Rekuta (3)	Metalworking (3), Potency Improvement (7), Solvent Proficiency (2), Recipe Improvement (2)
Telvanni Shelves, Organic	Library	Epic	—	Mundane Rune (11), Alchemical Resin (8), Heartwood (7), Stinkhorn (14), Rekuta (3)	Potency Improvement (7), Solvent Proficiency (4), Woodworking (3)
Telvanni Sofa, Organic	Parlor	Epic	—	Mundane Rune (12), Bash (7), Alchemical Resin (7), Decorative Wax (6), Stinkhorn (16), Rekuta (3)	Tailoring (3), Potency Improvement (8), Solvent Proficiency (3), Recipe Improvement (2)
Telvanni Stool, Organic	Workshop	Epic	Sittable	Mundane Rune (11), Alchemical Resin (7), Decorative Wax (6), Heartwood (6), Stinkhorn (14), Rekuta (3)	Potency Improvement (7), Solvent Proficiency (3), Recipe Improvement (2), Woodworking (2)
Telvanni Table Runner, Bordered Azure	Parlor	Epic	—	Mundane Rune (12), Bash (8), Alchemical Resin (8), Stinkhorn (16), Rekuta (3)	Tailoring (4), Potency Improvement (8), Solvent Proficiency (4)
Telvanni Table Runner, Gilded Azure	Parlor	Epic	—	Mundane Rune (11), Bash (8), Alchemical Resin (7), Stinkhorn (14), Rekuta (3)	Tailoring (4), Potency Improvement (7), Solvent Proficiency (3)
Telvanni Table, Organic Game	Dining	Epic	—	Mundane Rune (11), Alchemical Resin (8), Heartwood (7), Stinkhorn (14), Rekuta (3)	Potency Improvement (7), Solvent Proficiency (4), Woodworking (3)
Telvanni Table, Organic Grand	Dining	Epic	—	Mundane Rune (12), Alchemical Resin (8), Heartwood (8), Stinkhorn (16), Rekuta (3)	Potency Improvement (8), Solvent Proficiency (4), Woodworking (4)
Telvanni Throne, Organic	Gallery	Epic	Sittable	Mundane Rune (12), Bash (6), Alchemical Resin (7), Decorative Wax (7), Stinkhorn (16), Rekuta (3)	Tailoring (2), Potency Improvement (8), Solvent Proficiency (3), Recipe Improvement (3)
Tribunal Tablet of Almalexia	Gallery	Epic	—	Mundane Rune (12), Regulus (8), Alchemical Resin (6), Decorative Wax (6), Obsidian (16), Rekuta (3)	Metalworking (4), Potency Improvement (8), Solvent Proficiency (2), Recipe Improvement (2)

QUEST REWARDS

All quest rewards have been consolidated into the following table.

QUEST	REWARD	STYLE	ITEM TYPE	ENCHANTMENT	TRAIT	SET NAME	QUALITY
Divine Conundrum	Canon's Staff of the Tribunal	Buoyant Armiger	Frost Staff	Damage Health	Powered	—	Fine
Divine Inquiries	Buoyant Armiger's Brogans	Buoyant Armiger	Heavy Feet	Health	Sturdy	—	Fine
Divine Delusions	Greaves of the Warrior-Poet	Ashlander	Heavy Legs	Health	Divines	Warrior-Poet	Superior
Divine Intervention	Great Axe of the Defiler	Ashlander	Two-Handed Axe	Absorb Health	Powered	Infector	Superior
Divine Disaster	Buoyant Armiger's Chapeau	Buoyant Armiger	Light Head	Magicka	Infused	—	Fine
Divine Disaster	Buoyant Armiger's Cummerbund	Buoyant Armiger	Medium Waist	Stamina	Infused	—	Fine
Divine Restoration	Blade of the Warrior-Poet	Buoyant Armiger	One-Handed Sword	Absorb Stamina	Decisive	Warrior-Poet	Superior
Divine Blessings	Breastplate of the Warrior-Poet	Buoyant Armiger	Heavy Chest	Health	Infused	Warrior-Poet	Epic
Fleeing the Past	Redoran Honor Gauntlets	Redoran	Medium Hands	Stamina	Reinforced	—	Fine
Of Faith and Family	Warclaws Battle Bow	Khajiit	Bow	Berserker	Decisive	—	Fine
A Purposeful Writ	Executioner's Helm	Morag Tong	Medium Head	Stamina	Well-Fitted	—	Fine
Family Reunion	Veya's Axe of the Defiler	Morag Tong	One-Handed Axe	Poison	Infused	Infector	Superior
A Hireling of House Telvanni	Robe of Ambition	Telvanni	Light Chest	Magicka	Infused	—	Fine
Rising to Retainer	Telvanni Retainer's Ring	—	Ring	Magic Damage +	Magicka	—	Fine
Objections and Obstacles	Magister's Elegant Boots	Telvanni	Medium Feet	Stamina	Prosperous	—	Fine
The Magister Makes a Move	Magister's Exquisite Gloves	Telvanni	Light Hands	Magicka	Prosperous	—	Fine
The Heart of a Telvanni	Tear-Stained Staff of the War Maiden	Telvanni	Healing Staff	Frost	Defending	War Maiden	Superior
A Melodic Mistake	Kwama-Cutter	Redoran	Two-Handed Sword	Reduce Armor	Sharpened	—	Fine
Hatching a Plan	Revus's Spare Staff of the War Maiden	Redoran	Lightning Staff	Reduce Armor	Precise	War Maiden	Fine
Haunted Grounds	Spirit-Walker Leggings	Hlaalu	Medium Legs	Stamina	Divines	—	Fine
Reclaiming Vos	Dratha's Epaulettes of the War Maiden	Telvanni	Light Shoulders	Magicka	Infused	War Maiden	Fine
At Any Cost	Dark Staff of the War Maiden	Daedric	Fire Staff	Absorb Magicka	Infused	War Maiden	Superior
Ancestral Ties	Seal of Hleran	—	Neck	Bash & Block Cost -	Robust – Max Stamina +	Infector	Fine
If the Spell Fits	Stromgruf's Ensorcelled Pants	Nord	Light Legs	Magicka	Divines	—	Fine
Enslaved by Love	Star-Shell Dagger	Telvanni	Dagger	Damage Shield	Infused	—	Fine
The Memory Stone	Belt of Notched Memories	Hlaalu	Heavy Waist	Health	Training	—	Fine
Ancestral Adversity	Pauldrons of the Warrior-Poet	Ancient Elf	Heavy Shoulders	Health	Reinforced	Warrior-Poet	Fine
Like Blood from a Stone	Blackstone Hammer of the War Maiden	Hlaalu	Two-Handed Mace	Damage Shield	Defending	War Maiden	Fine
Nothing to Sneeze At	Stained Alchemy Smock	Telvanni	Light Chest	Magicka	Impenetrable	—	Fine
The Scarlet Judge	The Scarlet Necklace	—	Neck	Adds Physical Resistance	Healthy	—	Fine
Breaking Through the Fog	Governor's Ring of the War Maiden	—	Ring	Adds Magicka Recovery	Arcane	War Maiden	Fine
An Armiger's Duty	Holy Helm of the Warrior-Poet	Buoyant Armiger	Heavy Head	Health	Sturdy	Warrior-Poet	Fine
A Web of Troubles	Griskold's Tenderizer	Xivkyn	One-Handed Hammer	Berserker	Sharpened	—	Fine
The Ancestral Tombs	Explorer's Comfortable Shoes	Breton	Light Feet	Adds Maximum Magicka	Well-Fitted	—	Fine
The Lost Library	Andule's Curiass of the Defiler	Redoran	Medium Chest	Stamina	Infused	Infector	Epic
A Smuggler's Last Stand	Chain-Breaker Gauntlets	Orc	Heavy Hands	Health	Well-Fitted	—	Fine
A Hidden Harvest	Sugar-Hemp Sash	Khajiit	Light Waist	Magicka	Training	—	Fine
A Dangerous Breed	Kwama-Hide Cops	Hlaalu	Medium Shoulders	Stamina	Training	—	Fine
Echoes of a Fallen House	Nirith's Bulwark of the Defiler	Daedric	Shield	Stamina	Reinforced	Infector	Fine
The Heart's Desire	Artificer's Coat of the War Maiden	Dwemer	Light Chest	Magicka	Infused	War Maiden	Fine

RARE FISH

Morrowind includes 12 new rare fish. These can be found all over the zone, but some fish—the Ash Blindfish or Oanna, for example—may be much harder for the master angler to hook simply due to Vvardenfell's pelagic location.

Saltwater (sea) fishing spots are available all around the coasts of Vvardenfell, including within Azura's Coast islands and Ascadian Isles.

Freshwater (lakes) fishing spots exist at several locations around Vvardenfell. The two big lakes, north of Vivec City, offer the most opportunities. More spots are found around Molag Mar, north of Balmora, north of Gnisis, as well as a few sites in the northeast region.

Rivers run near many of the towns in Vvardenfell. Find fishing spots near Balmora, Gnisis, Molag Mar, Suran, and Vos. Find more locations around the Ashalmawia and Esutanamus Daedric ruins.

Foul-water fishing spots dot the Bitter Coast. Find these sites near Seyda Neen, west of Balmora, and near the Daedric ruins within the region.

Rare Fish

TYPE OF WATER	FISH	RARITY
Saltwater	Resdaynian Sailfin	Very Rare
Saltwater	Ghost Octopus	Rare
Saltwater	Weeping Pygmy Shark	Rare
Freshwater	Shalk-Brother Crayfish	Very Rare
Freshwater	Hoaga Oto	Rare
Freshwater	Pity Bombil	Rare

TYPE OF WATER	FISH	RARITY
River	Ash Blindfish	Very Rare
River	Netch-Hook Eel	Rare
River	Pilgrim Goby	Rare
Foul Water	Oanna	Very Rare
Foul Water	Firemouth Guiyu	Rare
Foul Water	Sleeper Coffinfish	Rare

SURVEY REPORTS

Survey reports are a random reward from completed writs. They're similar to treasure maps, but instead of a drawing of the spot, a map leads you directly to the bounty. A group of materials is ready for you, and only you, to collect. Collecting the resources consumes the survey report.

ALCHEMIST SURVEY: VVARDENFELL

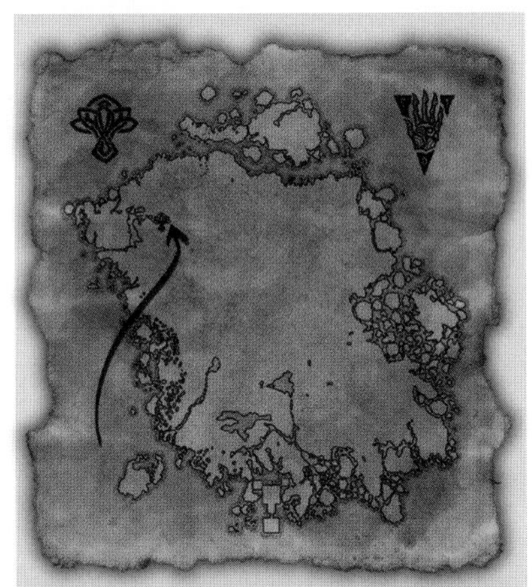

Region	West Gash
Location	West of Maelkashishi Ruins

CLOTHIER SURVEY: VVARDENFELL

Region	Azura's Coast
Location	Southeast of Shashpilamat Ruins

WOODWORKER SURVEY: VVARDENFELL

Region	Bitter Coast
Location	Southwest of Zainsipilu Delve, on Coast

BLACKSMITH SURVEY: VVARDENFELL

Region	Molag Amur
Location	East of Nchuleftingth Public Dungeon

ENCHANTER SURVEY: VVARDENFELL

Region	Ashlands
Location	Ebernanit Ruins

TREASURE MAPS

By using a treasure maps, a drawing of a specific location in Tamriel is shown. Find this location and interact with the small mound of dirt to find the treasure. This consumes the map. The treasure map locations are detailed in the Atlas chapter of this guide.

VVARDENFELL TREASURE MAP I

Region	Azura's Coast
Location	Island East of Bal Fell Ruins

VVARDENFELL TREASURE MAP II

Region	Azura's Coast
Location	Island North of Esutanamus Ruins

VVARDENFELL TREASURE MAP III

Region	West Gash
Location	Island South of Gnisis and West of Veloth Ancestral Tomb

VVARDENFELL TREASURE MAP IV

Region	Ascadian Isles
Location	North of Amaya Lake Manor, on Opposite Side of Lake

VVARDENFELL TREASURE MAP V

Region	Ashlands
Location	West of Valley of the Wind Wayshrine, North of Zergonipal

VVARDENFELL TREASURE MAP VI

Region	Molag Amur
Location	South of Erabenimsun Camp, Follow Narrow Path South

VVARDENFELL CE TREASURE MAP I

Region	Molag Amur
Location	South of Falensarano Ruins and North of Dwemer Structures, East of Road

VVARDENFELL CE TREASURE MAP II

Region	Molag Amur
Location	West of Erabenimsun Camp, Where Three Paths Converge

VVARDENFELL CE TREASURE MAP III

Region	Bitter Coast
Location	Aleft Ruins, Northeast Side

LOCATIONS

ANCESTRAL TOMBS

There are 30 ancestral tombs around Vvardenfell. Return rubbings of all 30 to Librarian Bradyn in Vivec City to unlock the lost Library of Andule and earn the Ancestral Tombs Hunter Achievement.

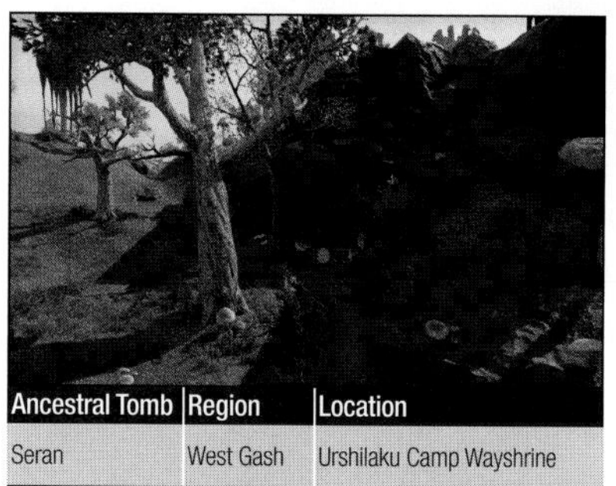

Ancestral Tomb	Region	Location
Seran	West Gash	Urshilaku Camp Wayshrine

Ancestral Tomb	Region	Location
Ginith	West Gash	East of Yasammadin

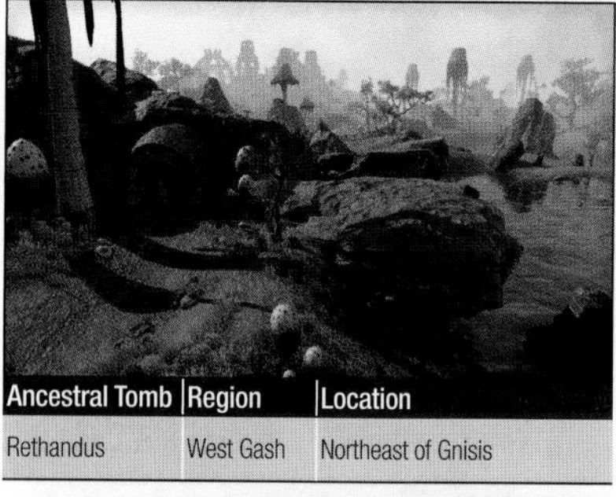

Ancestral Tomb	Region	Location
Rethandus	West Gash	Northeast of Gnisis

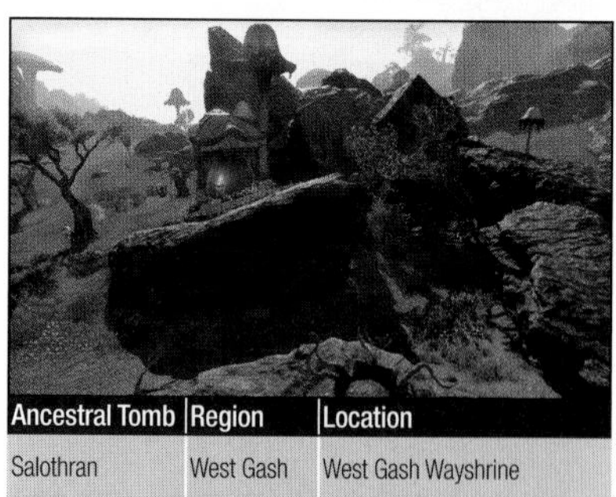

Ancestral Tomb	Region	Location
Salothran	West Gash	West Gash Wayshrine

Ancestral Tomb	Region	Location
Telvayn	West Gash	East of Khartag Point Delve

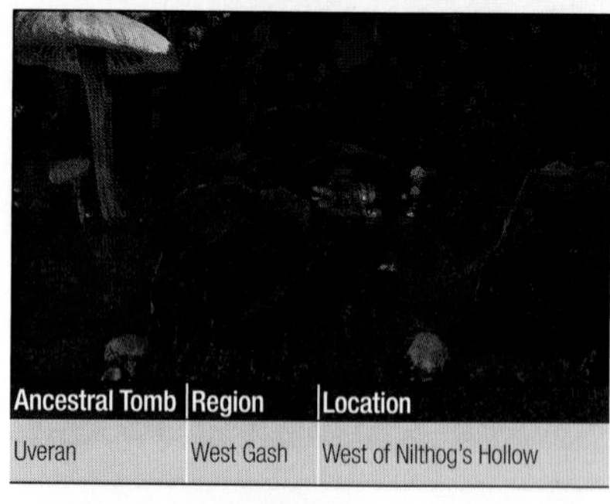

Ancestral Tomb	Region	Location
Uveran	West Gash	West of Nilthog's Hollow

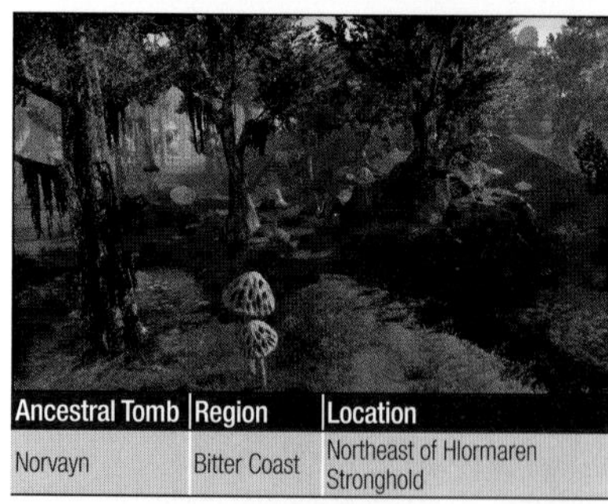

Ancestral Tomb	Region	Location
Norvayn	Bitter Coast	Northeast of Hlormaren Stronghold

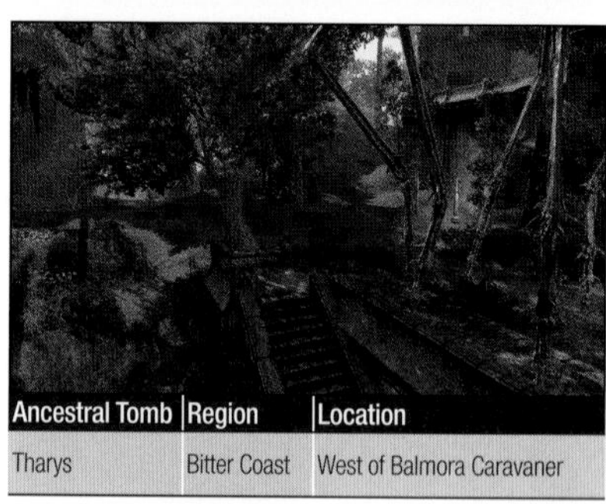

Ancestral Tomb	Region	Location
Tharys	Bitter Coast	West of Balmora Caravaner

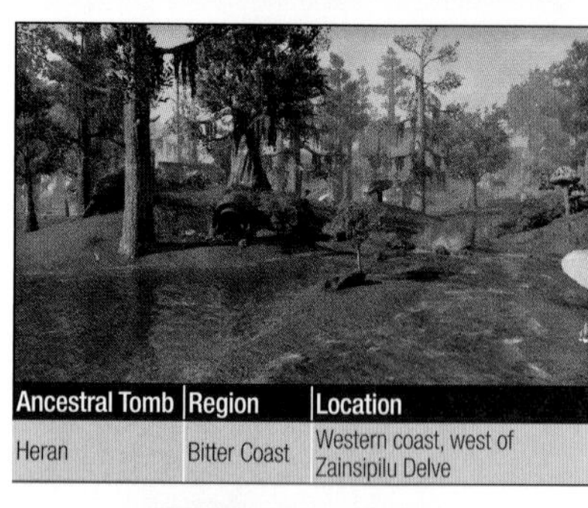

Ancestral Tomb	Region	Location
Heran	Bitter Coast	Western coast, west of Zainsipilu Delve

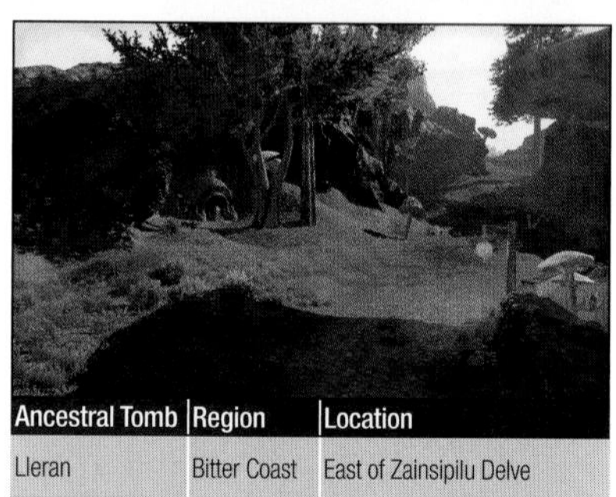

Ancestral Tomb	Region	Location
Lleran	Bitter Coast	East of Zainsipilu Delve

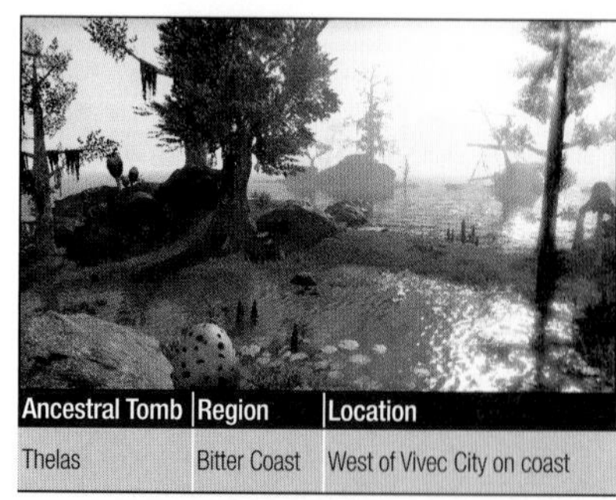

Ancestral Tomb	Region	Location
Thelas	Bitter Coast	West of Vivec City on coast

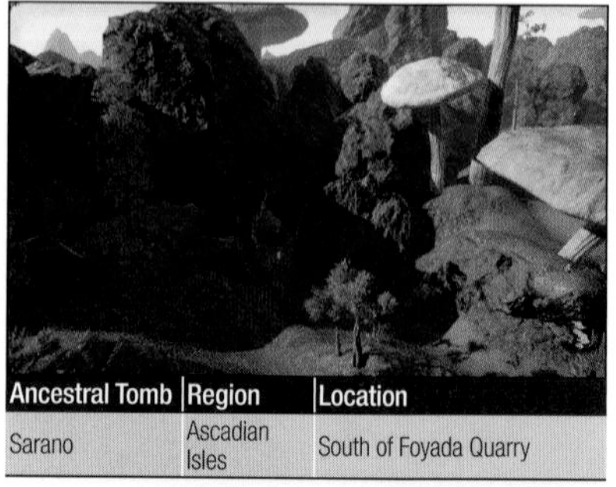

Ancestral Tomb	Region	Location
Sarano	Ascadian Isles	South of Foyada Quarry

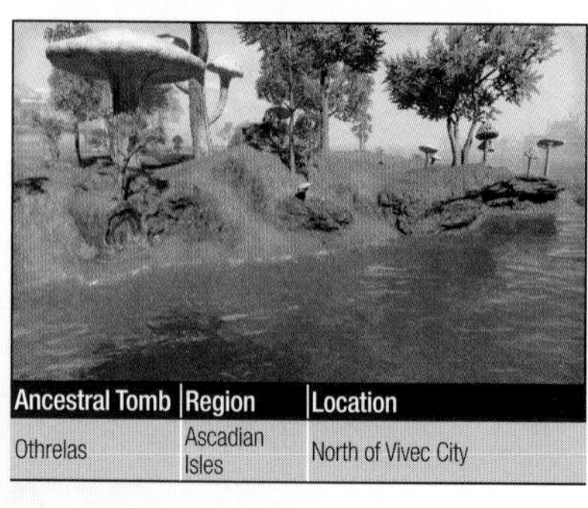

Ancestral Tomb	Region	Location
Othrelas	Ascadian Isles	North of Vivec City

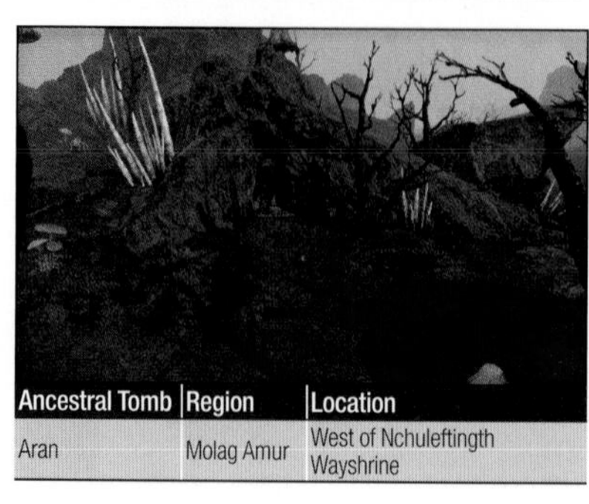

Ancestral Tomb	Region	Location
Aran	Molag Amur	West of Nchuleftingth Wayshrine

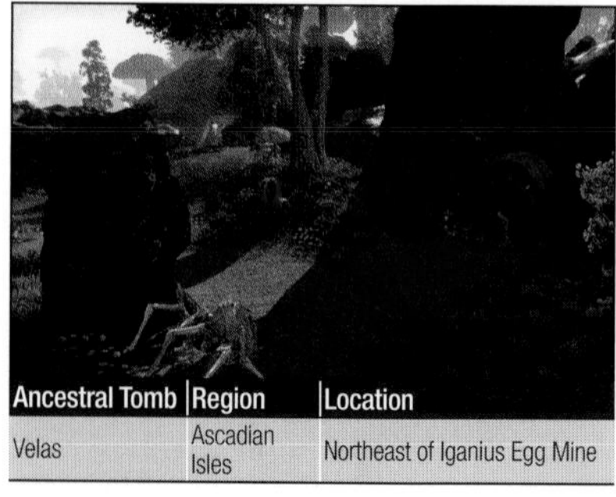

Ancestral Tomb	Region	Location
Velas	Ascadian Isles	Northeast of Iganius Egg Mine

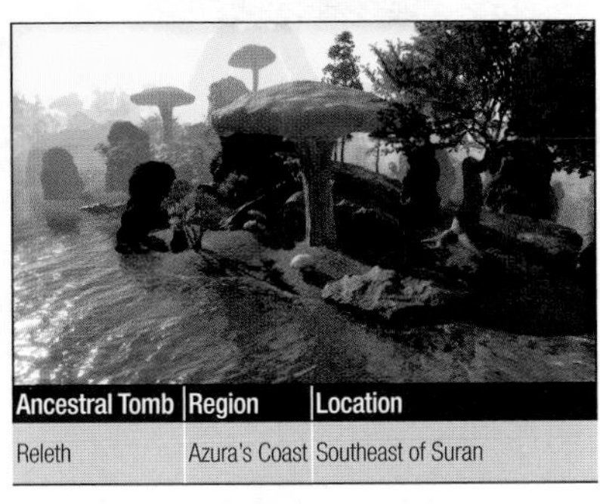

Ancestral Tomb	Region	Location
Releth	Azura's Coast	Southeast of Suran

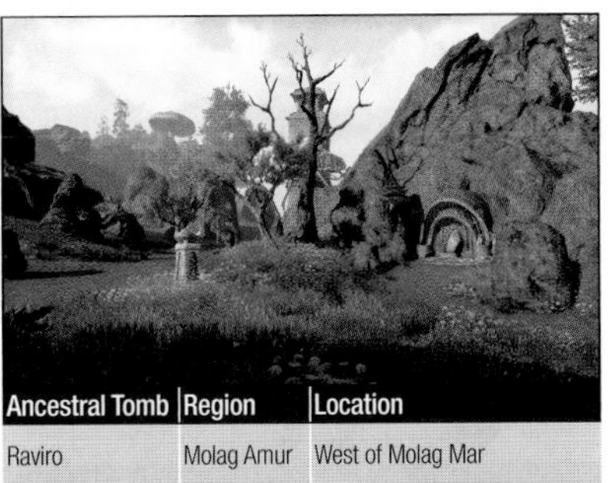

Ancestral Tomb	Region	Location
Raviro	Molag Amur	West of Molag Mar

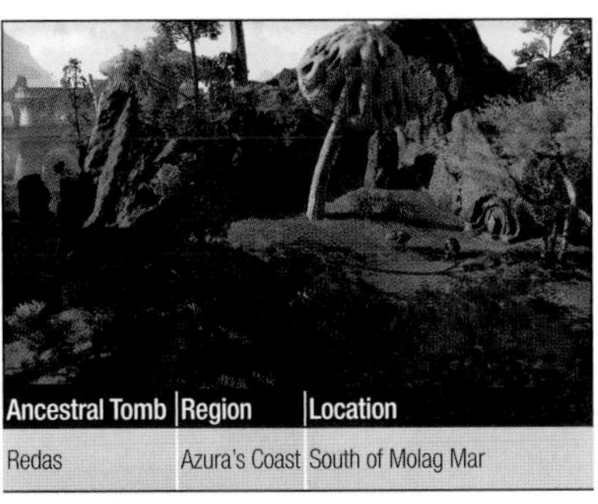

Ancestral Tomb	Region	Location
Redas	Azura's Coast	South of Molag Mar

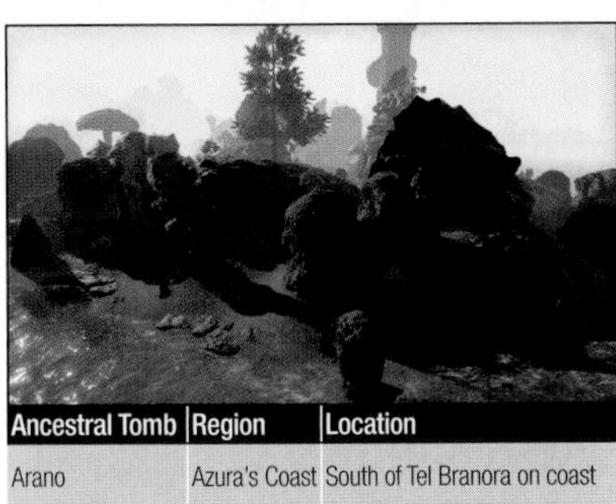

Ancestral Tomb	Region	Location
Arano	Azura's Coast	South of Tel Branora on coast

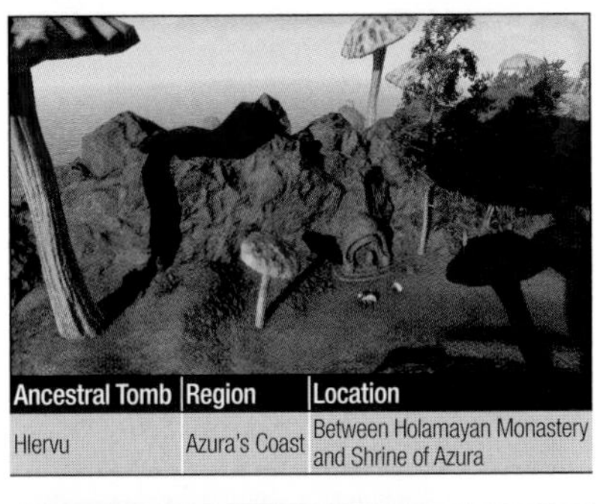

Ancestral Tomb	Region	Location
Hlervu	Azura's Coast	Between Holamayan Monastery and Shrine of Azura

Ancestral Tomb	Region	Location
Maren	Molag Amur	East of Nchuleftingth Wayshrine

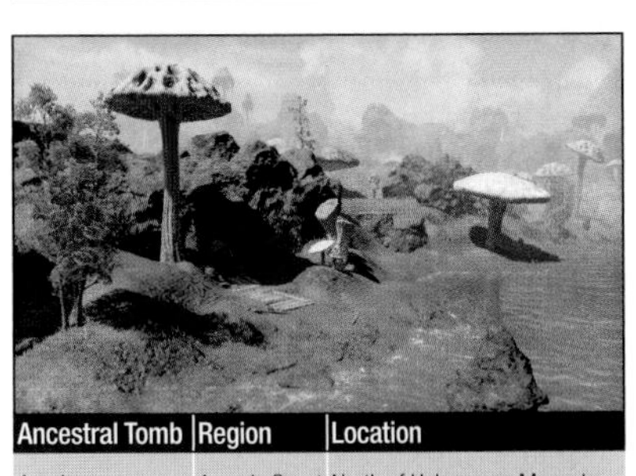

Ancestral Tomb	Region	Location
Arenim	Azura's Coast	North of Holamayan Monastery

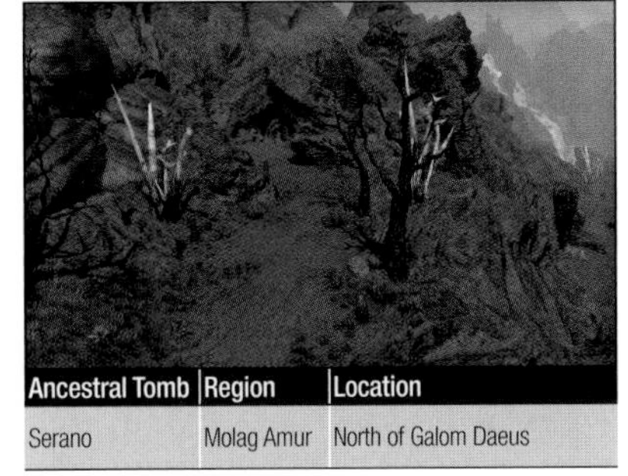

Ancestral Tomb	Region	Location
Serano	Molag Amur	North of Galom Daeus

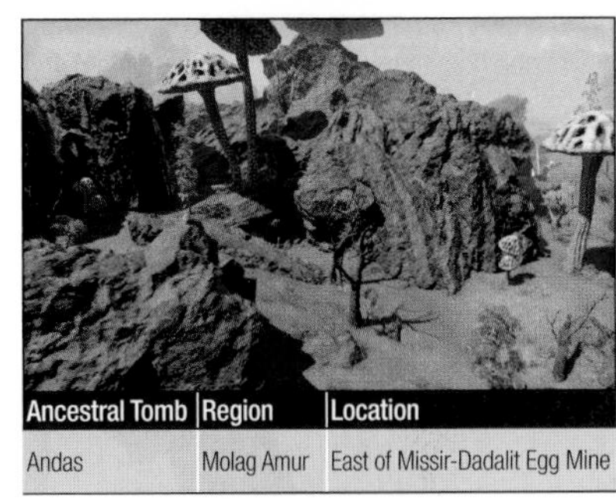

Ancestral Tomb	Region	Location
Andas	Molag Amur	East of Missir-Dadalit Egg Mine

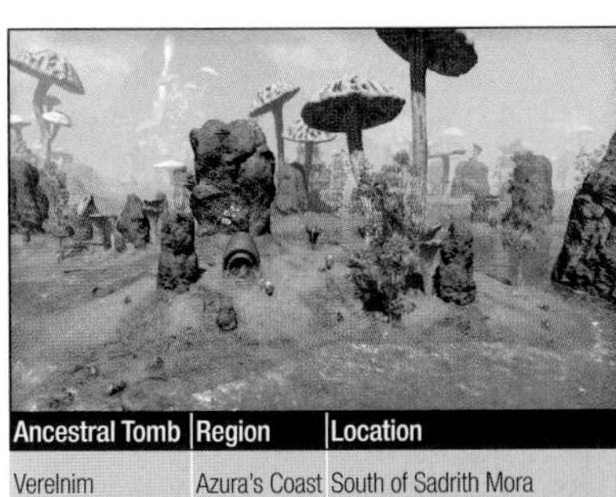

Ancestral Tomb	Region	Location
Verelnim	Azura's Coast	South of Sadrith Mora

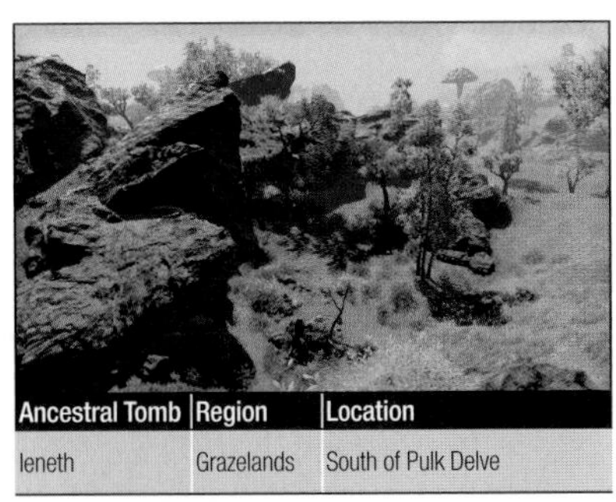

Ancestral Tomb	Region	Location
Ieneth	Grazelands	South of Pulk Delve

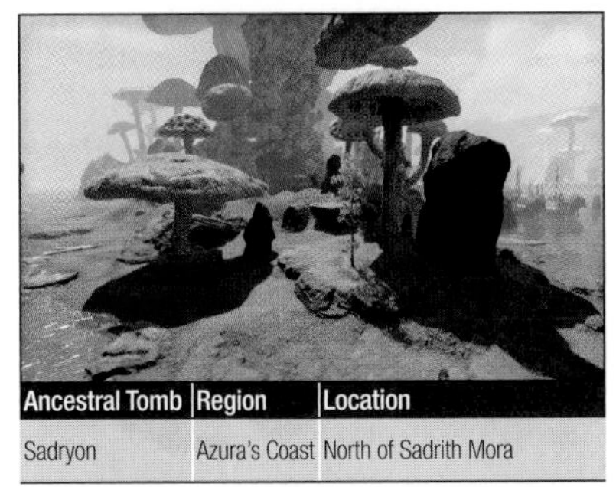

Ancestral Tomb	Region	Location
Sadryon	Azura's Coast	North of Sadrith Mora

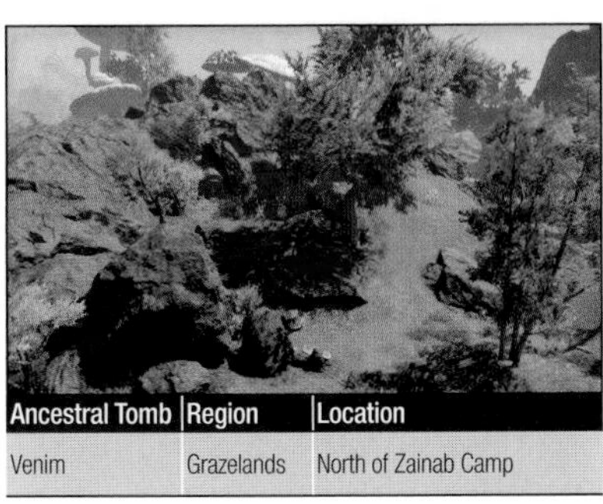

Ancestral Tomb	Region	Location
Venim	Grazelands	North of Zainab Camp

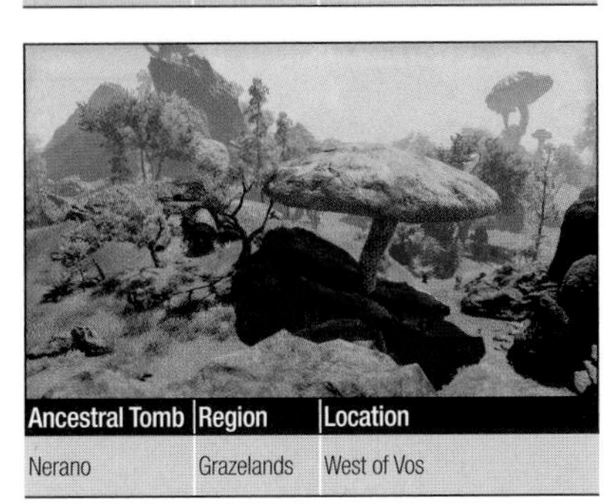

Ancestral Tomb	Region	Location
Nerano	Grazelands	West of Vos

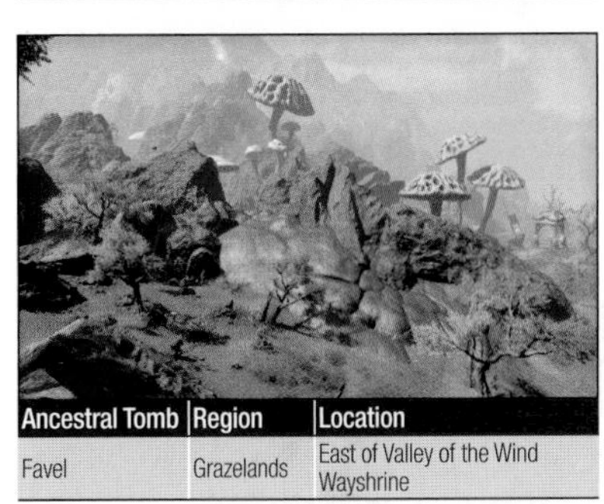

Ancestral Tomb	Region	Location
Favel	Grazelands	East of Valley of the Wind Wayshrine

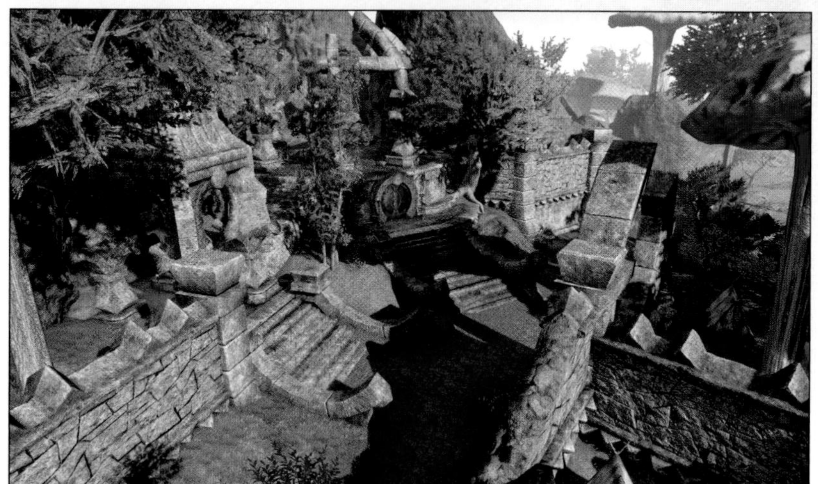

DAEDRIC RUINS

Look out for Daedric ruins as you explore Vvardenfell. Visit all 25 for the Daedric Explorer Achievement.

DAEDRIC RUIN	REGION	LOCATION
Kushtashpi	Grazelands	Northwest of Vos
Esutanamus	Azura's Coast	North of Hanud Tower
Yansirramus	Azura's Coast	West of Tel Aruhn
Anudnabia	Azura's Coast	East of Sadrith Mora
Kaushtarari	Azura's Coast	East of Halls of Fabrication Trial
Tusenend	Molag Amur	South of Halls of Fabrication Trial
Shashpilamat	Azura's Coast	Southeast of Matus-Akin Egg Mine Delve
Almurbalarammi	Azura's Coast	Southeast of Molag Mar
Zaintiraris	Azura's Coast	South of Molag Mar
Bal Fell	Azura's Coast	East of Vivec City
Ald Sotha	Ascadian Isles	South of Suran
Bal Ur	Ascadian Isles	North of Suran
Ashurnibibi	Bitter Coast	West of Ahemmusa Camp

DAEDRIC RUIN	REGION	LOCATION
Ashalmimilkala	Bitter Coast	West of Balmora on coast
Addadshashanammu	Bitter Coast	Northwest of Balmora on coast
Dushariran	West Gash	East of Salothan's Council
Yasammidan	West Gash	Northwest corner of Vvardenfell
Zergonipal	Ashlands	Southwest of Valley of the Wind Wayshrine
Ashalmawia	West Gash	Outside Ashalmawia Delve
Ashurnabitashpi	Ashlands	West of Valenvaryon
Assarnatamat	West Gash	Northeast of Balmora
Maelkashishi	West Gash	Northeast of Gnisis
Ebernanit	Ashlands	Southeast of Valenvaryon
Ashunartes	Molag Amur	East of Balmora, near Marandas
Ramimilk	West Gash	South of Ald'ruhn

HOUSING

Morrowind features three new homes, including a new inn room that's awarded after completing **Quest: A Friend in Need**, the housing intro quest in *Morrowind*. The other two are available for purchase with gold or crowns. An Achievement is required to purchase each home with gold.

ST. DELYN PENTHOUSE

Requirement	Awarded for Completing the Housing Quest, A Friend in Need
Price	Free
Location	St. Delyn's Inn, Vivec City
Style of House	Inn Room

ALD VELOTHI HARBOR HOUSE

Requirement for Gold Purchase	Champion of Vivec Achievement
Price (Gold/Crowns)	322,000/4,000
Furnished Price (Crowns)	5,000
Location	West of Ashalmawia Delve
Style of House	Redoran Estate

AMAYA LAKE LODGE

Requirement for Gold Purchase	Savior of Morrowind Achievement
Price (Gold/Crowns)	1,300,000/7,000
Furnished Price (Crowns)	8,800
Location	Southwest side of Lake Amaya
Style of House	Hlaalu Estate

MERCHANTS AND CRAFTING STATIONS

ALD CARAC BATTLEGROUND GATE

Elite Gear Merchant	Farthalem
Traveling Merchant	Breynshad Alasien (Between Urshilaku Camp, Ald Carac, and Valley of the Wind Wayshrine)

ALD'RUHN

Cooking Fire	
Merchant	Vasamannu

BALMORA

Cooking Fire	
Traveling Merchant	Fanisea Saram (Between Balmora and Gnisis)
BALMORA TRIBUNAL TEMPLE	
Mystic	Tends-All-Things
THE RANDY NETCH INN	
Cooking Fire	
Innkeeper	Carellon
STABLE GATE	
Caravaner	Nevos Sareloth
Hall Steward	Delte Nethri
Stablemaster	Nothas Vules
MARKET GATE	
Guild Trader	Ginette Malarelie
Guild Trader	Mahrahdr
Guild Trader	Narril
Magister	Vilyn Veleth

FOYADA QUARRY BATTLEGROUND GATE

Elite Gear Merchant	Keshlar
Traveling Merchant	Gordol Teddalennu (Between Halls of Fabrication and Foyada Quarry)

GNISIS

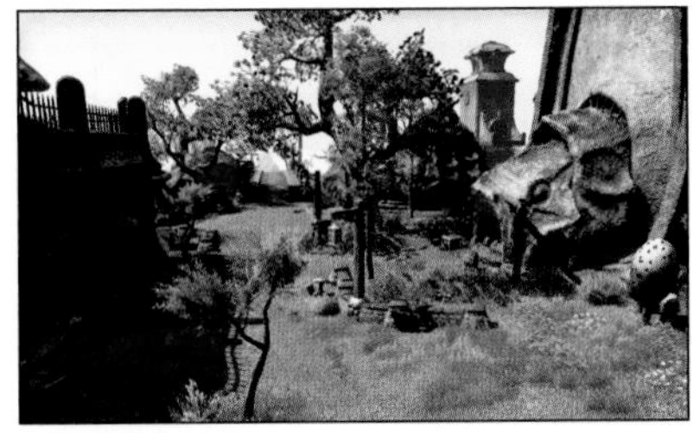

Caravaner	Amili Yahaz
Traveling Merchant	Fanisea Saram (Between Balmora and Gnisis)
THE RESTING KWAMA	
Cooking Fire	
Innkeeper	Bolayn Andalor
Gnisis Temple	
Mystic	Evylu Nethalen

HALLS OF FABRICATION TRIAL

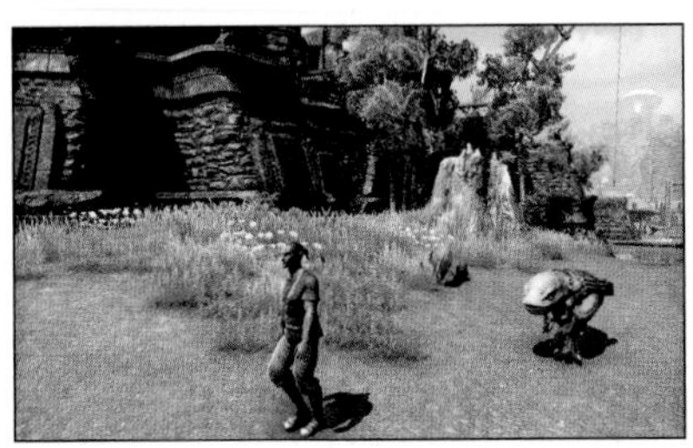

Traveling Merchant	Gordol Teddalennu (Between Halls of Fabrication and Foyada Quarry)
TEL FYR	
Alchemy Station	
Blacksmithing Station	
Cooking Fire	
Enchanting Table	
Woodworking Station	
Mystic	Velanda

MOLAG MAR

Caravaner	Narisa Androm

THE PENITENT PILGRIM INN

Innkeeper	Sevus Alor

SADRITH MORA

SADRITH MORA DOCKS	
Boatswain	Rinori Mathendis
TEL NAGA	
Alchemy Station	
Enchantment Table	
Mystic	Ervyna Duleri
Alchemist	Telare Relenim
Enchanter	Vaden Inlador
GATEWAY INN	
Cooking Fire	
General Goods Merchant	Makes-No-Ripples
MAGES GUILD ENCAMPMENT	
Cooking Fire	
Magister	Bertis Benethran
SADRITH MORA MARKET	

Guild Trader	Felayn Uvaram
Guild Trader	Runik
Guild Trader	Ruxultav
FIGHTERS GUILD ENCAMPMENT	
Cooking Fire	
Hall Steward	Vedelea Tenim

SEYDA NEEN

FINDUN'S GOODS	
Merchant	Findun
TAVERN BY THE SEA	
Cooking Fire	
Chef	Chow-Chow
SNARZIKHA'S GROCERY	
Grocer	Snarzikha
Caravaner	Medyn Hleran

SURAN

Caravaner	Faven Thendas
Merchant	Mivanu Neleth
Alchemist	Faldiniel
DESELE'S HOUSE OF EARTHLY DELIGHTS	
Cooking Fire	
Innkeeper	Dovyn Trandel

SEULARRA BATTLEGROUND GATE

Elite Gear Merchant	Urbalash

URSHILAKU CAMP

Cooking Fire	
Traveling Merchant	Breynshad Alasien (Between Urshilaku Camp, Ald Carac, and Valley of the Wind Wayshrine)

VIVEC CITY

PILGRIM'S APPROACH	
Caravan	Its
Stablemaster	Drel Trandel
Boatswain	Synda Imyam
PILGRIM'S MARKET	
Guild Trader	Atazha
Guild Trader	Jena Calvus
Guild Trader	Lorthodaer
Guild Trader	Mauhoth
Guild Trader	Rinami
Guild Trader	Sebastian Brutya
FOUNDATION'S BULWARK	
Blacksmithing Station	
Clothing Station	
Woodworking Station	
Carpenter	Murgonak
Clothier	Nurov Belvayn
Blacksmith	Stalkun
FOUNDATION'S EMBRACE	
Alchemy Station	
Cooking Fire	
Enchanting Table	
Enchanter	Cuilalme
Alchemist	Lenasa Telvanni
FOUNDATION'S RISING	
Banker	Anral Selvilo
Banker	Dayna Imayn
FOUNDATION'S LABOR	
General Goods Merchant	Jeeba-Noo
VIVEC OUTLAW REFUGE	
Cooking Fire	
Fence	Steps-in-Alleys
Fence	Urshra
Guild Trader	Relieves-Burdens
Merchant	Quarith
Moneylender	Obenion
GLADIATOR'S QUARTERS	
Elite Gear	Colotarion
Battlegrounds Merchant	Alyze Metayer
Battlegrounds Furnisher	Brelda Ofemalen
Battlegrounds Furnisher	Llivas Driler
CANTON OF ST. DELYN THE WISE (NORTH)	
Magus	Caydeire Dechery
Mystic	Hasudel

Achievement Furnisher	Drops-No-Glass
Home Goods Furnisher	Heralda Garscroft
Prestige Furnisher	Narwaawende
Magister	Tolendir Gals
Home Goods Furnisher	Uzipa
CANTON OF ST. DELYN THE WISE (SOUTH)	
Armsman	Erikar Five-Blades
General Goods Merchant	Sosia Epinard
Armorer	Svargret Goodsword
Hall Steward	Riray Dalo
Fence	Steps-in-Alleys
Fence	Urshra
ST. OLMS PLAZA	
General Goods Merchant	Div Nervion
CANTON OF ST. OLMS THE JUST (NORTH)	
Clothing Station	
Cooking Fire	
Leatherworker	Atzurbesh
Chef	Gilbara Morrard
Brewer	Herdora
Pack Merchant	Azazi
CANTON OF ST. OLMS THE JUST (SOUTH)	
Dye Station	
Grocer	Angedreth
Tailor	Ivela Telvanni
TEMPLE CANTON	
Curator	Librarian Bradyn
Shrine of Father of Mysteries	
Shrine to Mara	Shrine of Mother Morrowind
Shrine of Warrior-Poet	

VOS / TEL MORA

Navigator	Bolnora Romavel
Caravaner	Adosi Delvi
Navigator	Bolnora Romavel
TRADEHOUSE	
Merchant	Dridyn Ledd

MENWENDEL'S NURSERY

Alchemist	Menwendel

SERMONS

Read 36 sermons hidden around Vvardenfell to unlock a 37th in Vivec's Palace. The Tribunal Preacher Achievement is earned for reading them all.

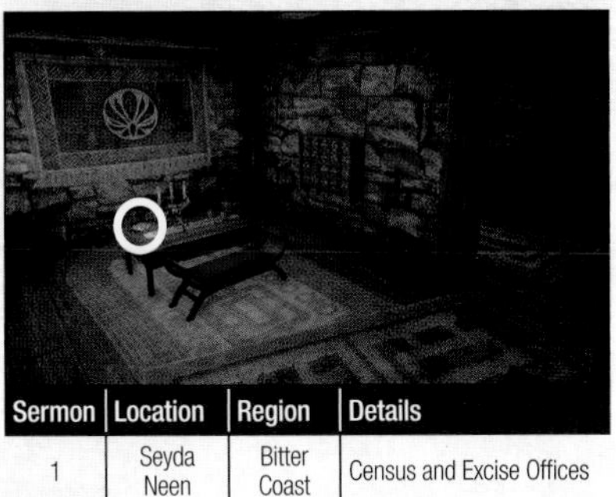

Sermon	Location	Region	Details
1	Seyda Neen	Bitter Coast	Census and Excise Offices

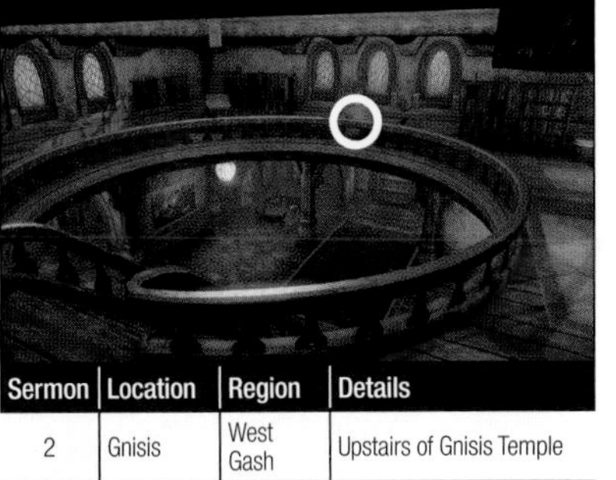

Sermon	Location	Region	Details
2	Gnisis	West Gash	Upstairs of Gnisis Temple

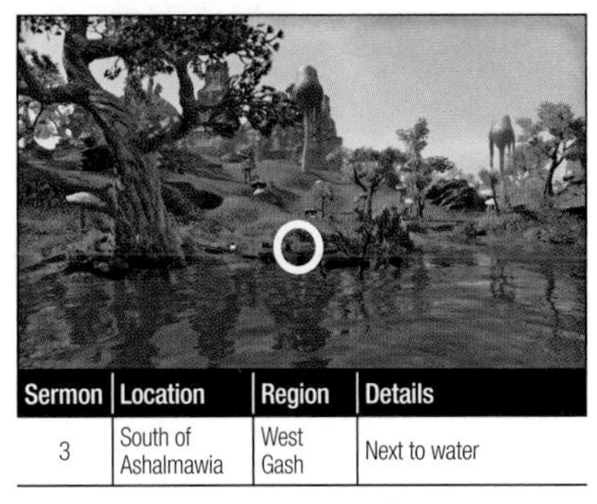

Sermon	Location	Region	Details
3	South of Ashalmawia	West Gash	Next to water

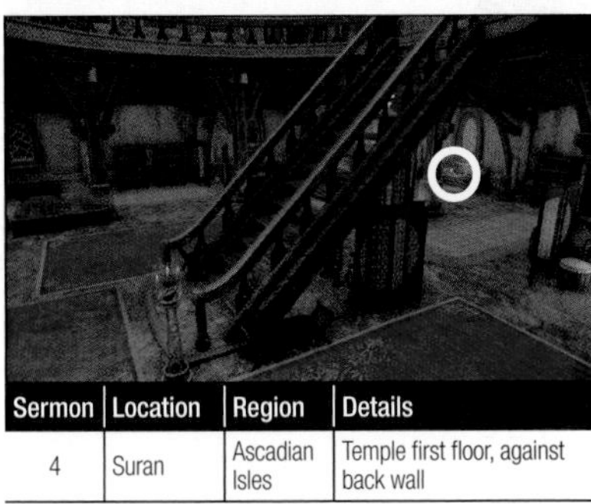

Sermon	Location	Region	Details
4	Suran	Ascadian Isles	Temple first floor, against back wall

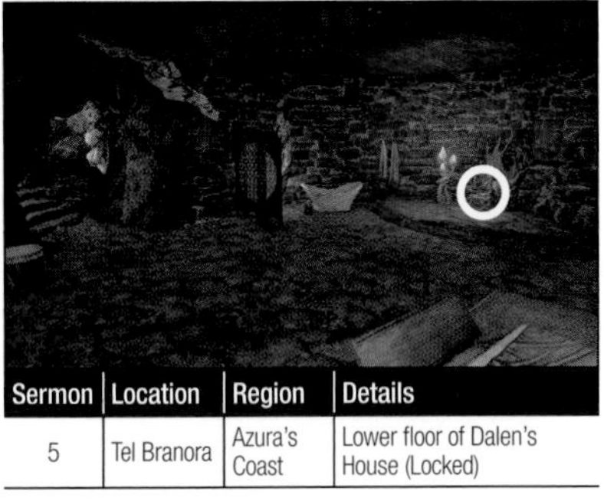

Sermon	Location	Region	Details
5	Tel Branora	Azura's Coast	Lower floor of Dalen's House (Locked)

Sermon	Location	Region	Details
6	Suran	Ascadian Isles	Manor southwest of Suran in courtyard

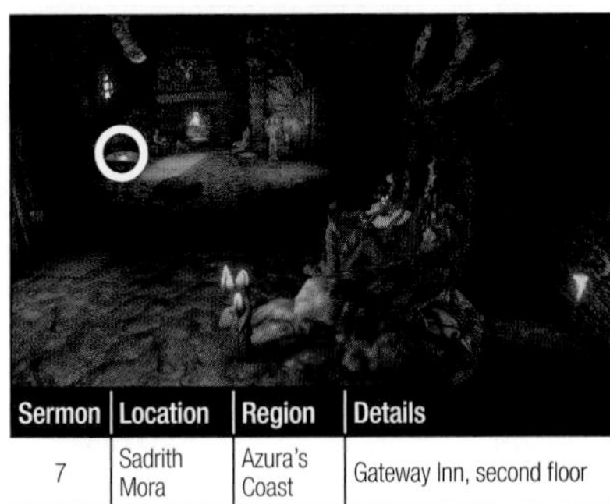

Sermon	Location	Region	Details
7	Sadrith Mora	Azura's Coast	Gateway Inn, second floor

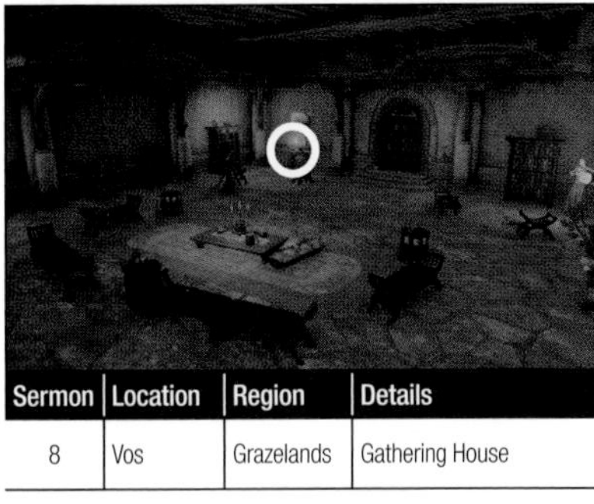

Sermon	Location	Region	Details
8	Vos	Grazelands	Gathering House

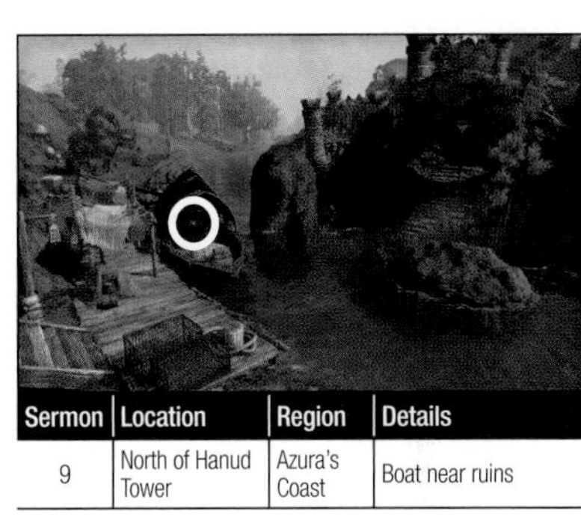

Sermon	Location	Region	Details
9	North of Hanud Tower	Azura's Coast	Boat near ruins

Sermon	Location	Region	Details
10	Vivec City	Ascadian Isles	Wooden scaffolding above Alchemy Station

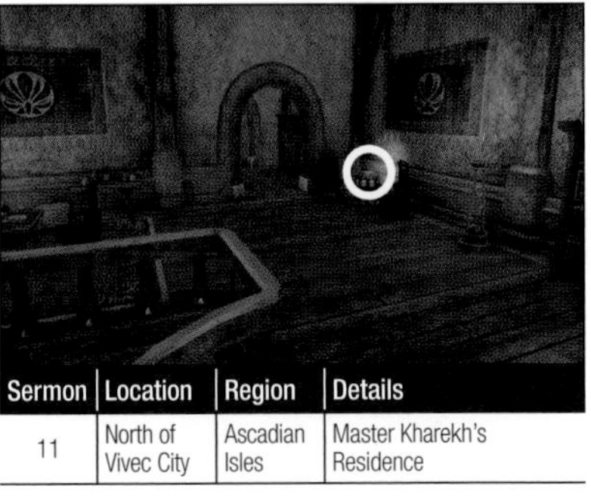

Sermon	Location	Region	Details
11	North of Vivec City	Ascadian Isles	Master Kharekh's Residence

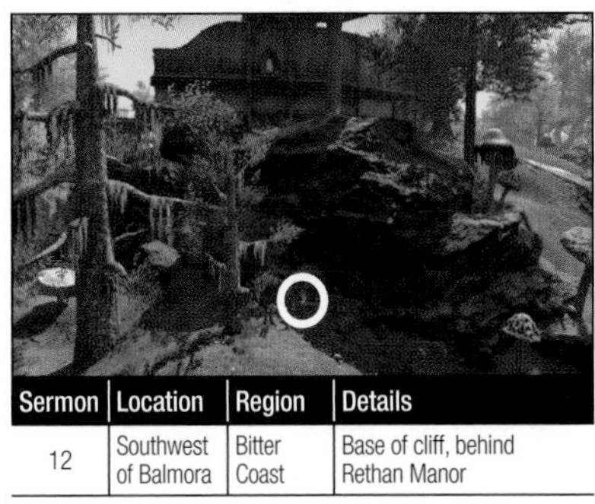

Sermon	Location	Region	Details
12	Southwest of Balmora	Bitter Coast	Base of cliff, behind Rethan Manor

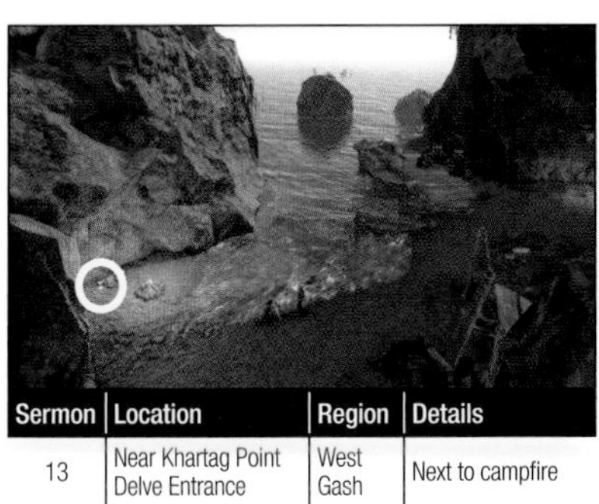

Sermon	Location	Region	Details
13	Near Khartag Point Delve Entrance	West Gash	Next to campfire

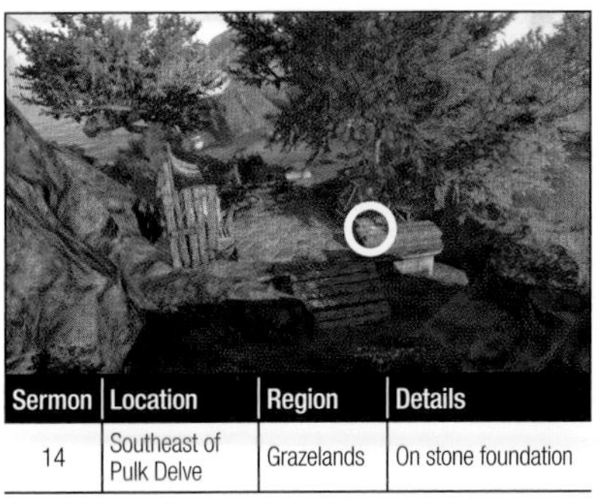

Sermon	Location	Region	Details
14	Southeast of Pulk Delve	Grazelands	On stone foundation

Sermon	Location	Region	Details
15	Ald Carac	Ashlands	Sitting on loaded cart

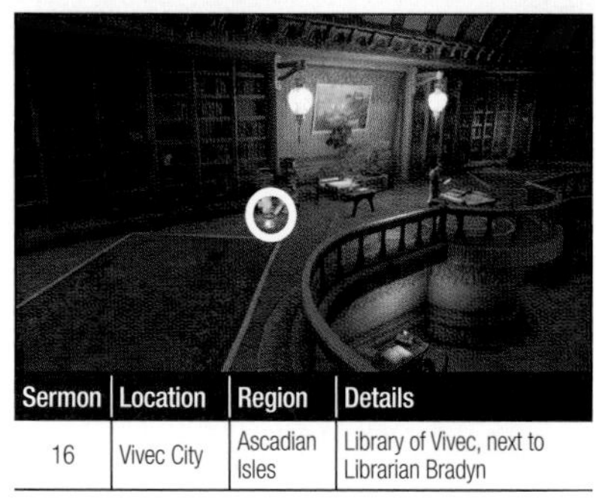

Sermon	Location	Region	Details
16	Vivec City	Ascadian Isles	Library of Vivec, next to Librarian Bradyn

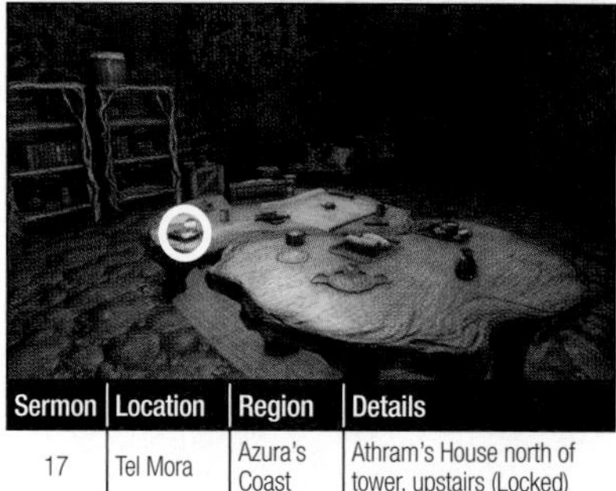

Sermon	Location	Region	Details
17	Tel Mora	Azura's Coast	Athram's House north of tower, upstairs (Locked)

Sermon	Location	Region	Details
18	East of Molag Mar	Azura's Coast	Northeast shore of lake, next to rowboat

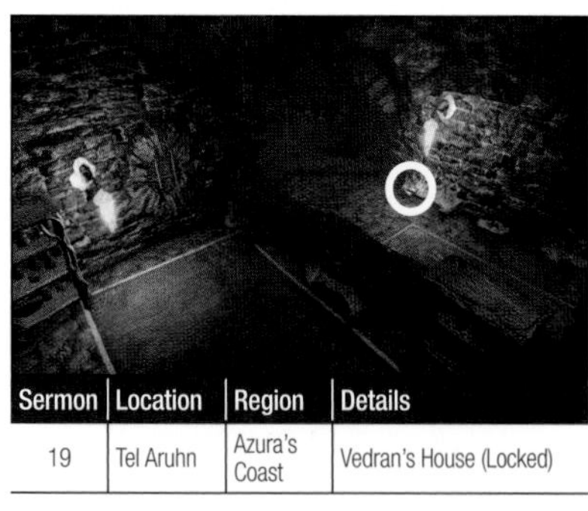

Sermon	Location	Region	Details
19	Tel Aruhn	Azura's Coast	Vedran's House (Locked)

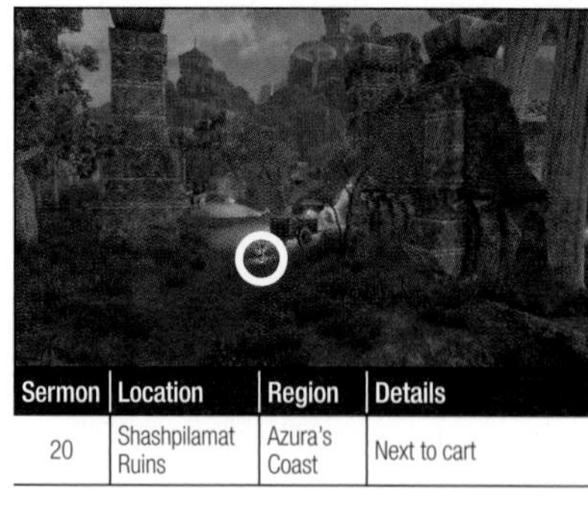

Sermon	Location	Region	Details
20	Shashpilamat Ruins	Azura's Coast	Next to cart

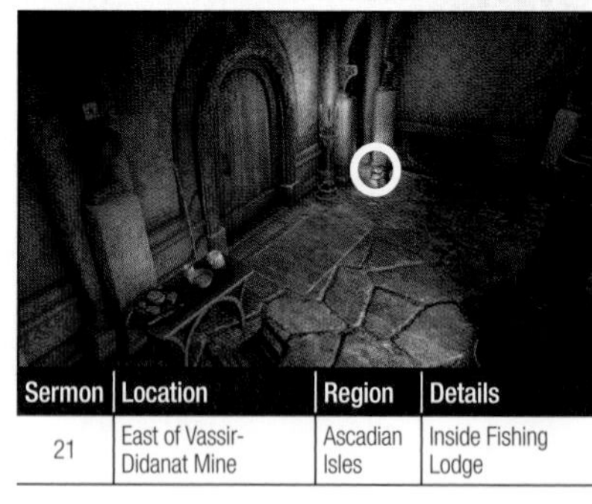

Sermon	Location	Region	Details
21	East of Vassir-Didanat Mine	Ascadian Isles	Inside Fishing Lodge

Sermon	Location	Region	Details
22	Suran	Ascadian Isles	Ules Manor, lower floor

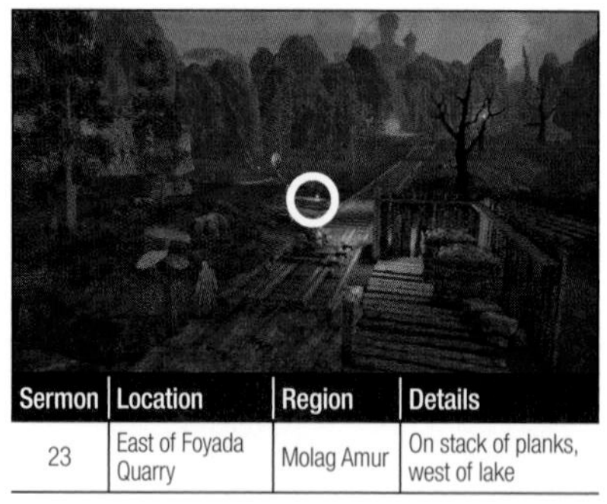

Sermon	Location	Region	Details
23	East of Foyada Quarry	Molag Amur	On stack of planks, west of lake

Sermon	Location	Region	Details
24	Southwest of Ald Sotha	Ascadian Isles	Base of rock and tree

Sermon	Location	Region	Details
25	Balmora	West Gash	Balmora Tribunal Temple, left side of first floor

Sermon	Location	Region	Details
26	Nchuleftingth Wayshrine	Molag Amur	In broken cart

Sermon	Location	Region	Details
27	Tel Galen House	Azura's Coast	Next to front gate

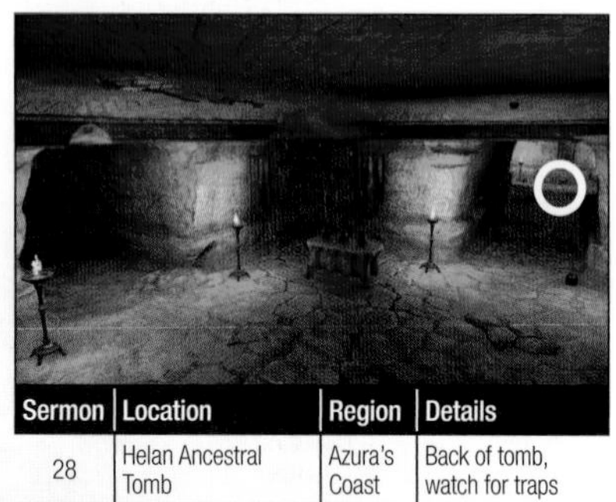

Sermon	Location	Region	Details
28	Helan Ancestral Tomb	Azura's Coast	Back of tomb, watch for traps

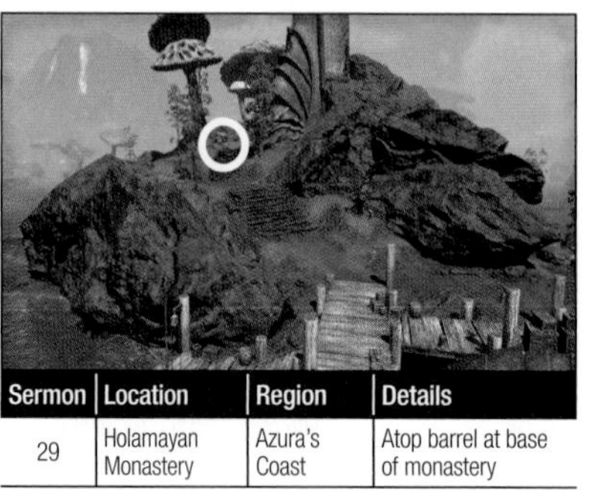

Sermon	Location	Region	Details
29	Holamayan Monastery	Azura's Coast	Atop barrel at base of monastery

Sermon	Location	Region	Details
30	Arenim Manor	Bitter Coast	Entryway in property wall, restricted area

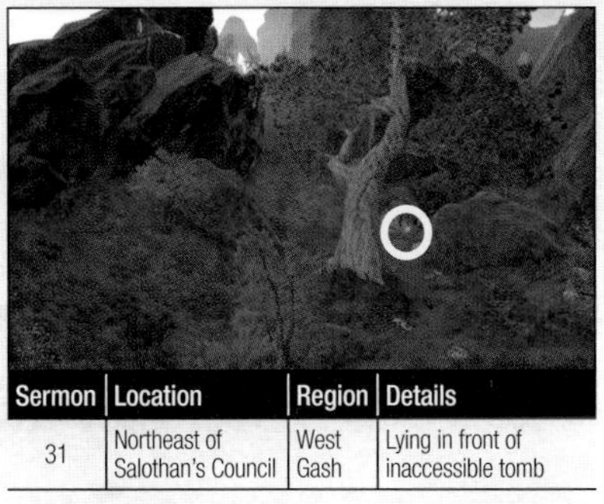

Sermon	Location	Region	Details
31	Northeast of Salothan's Council	West Gash	Lying in front of inaccessible tomb

Sermon	Location	Region	Details
32	West of Suran	Ascadian Isles	Behind Mistress Dren's residence, southeast side of Amaya Lake

Sermon	Location	Region	Details
33	Vassir-Didanat Mine	Ascadian Isles	On barrel, west of mine entrance

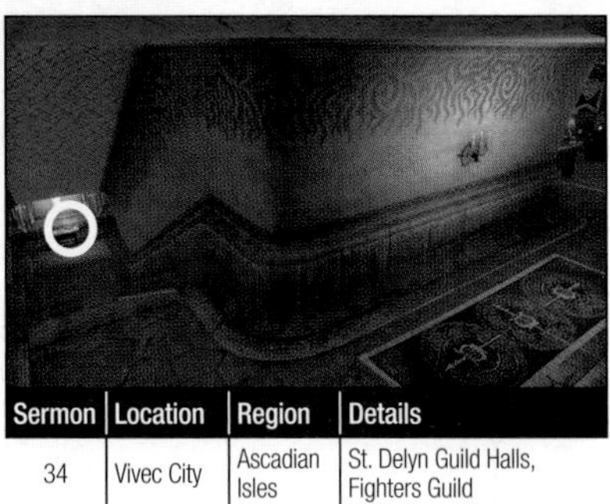

Sermon	Location	Region	Details
34	Vivec City	Ascadian Isles	St. Delyn Guild Halls, Fighters Guild

Sermon	Location	Region	Details
35	Vivec City	Ascadian Isles	St. Olms Guild Halls, Farmers and Laborers Hall

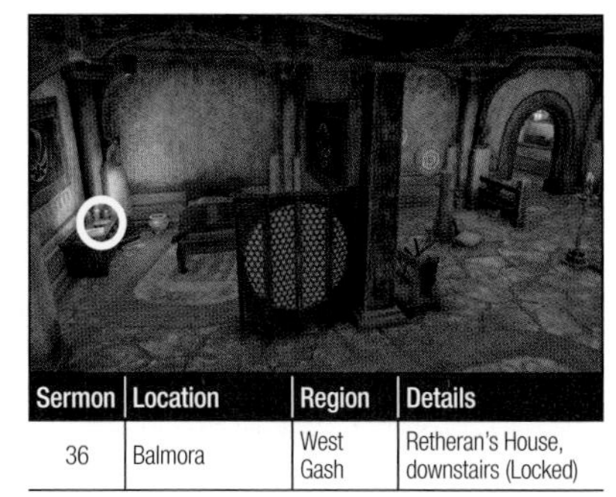

Sermon	Location	Region	Details
36	Balmora	West Gash	Retheran's House, downstairs (Locked)

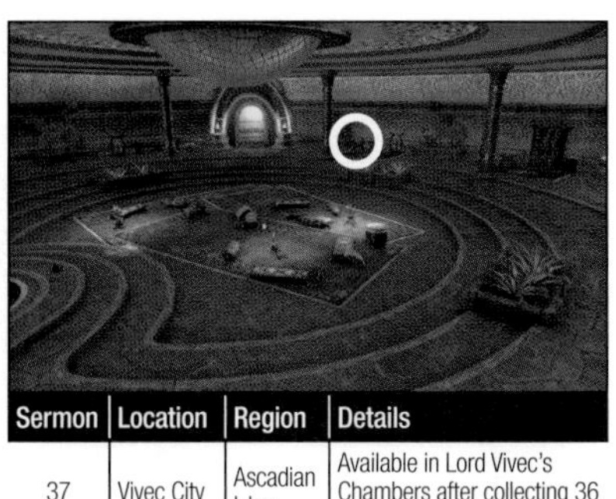

Sermon	Location	Region	Details
37	Vivec City	Ascadian Isles	Available in Lord Vivec's Chambers after collecting 36 sermons

SHRINES OF THE SEVEN GRACES

Read the inscription at the seven shrines to earn the Pilgrim's Path Achievement.

Shrine	Region	Location	Details
Shrine of Humility	Molag Amur	South of Foyada Quarry	North side of Lake Amaya, next to path

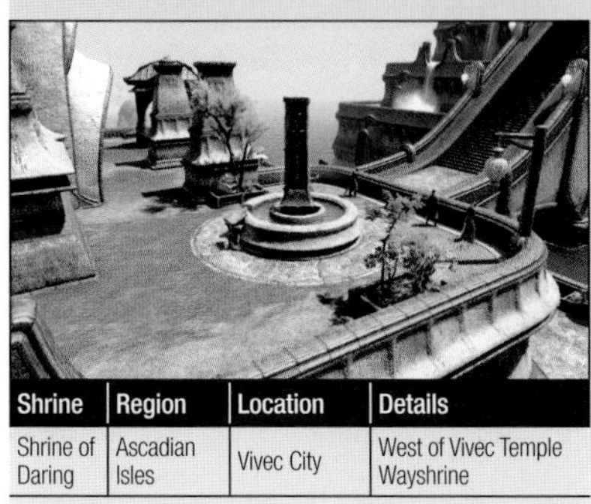

Shrine	Region	Location	Details
Shrine of Daring	Ascadian Isles	Vivec City	West of Vivec Temple Wayshrine

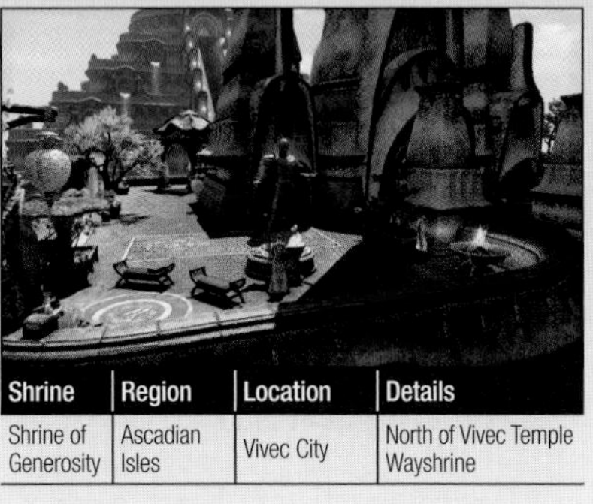

Shrine	Region	Location	Details
Shrine of Generosity	Ascadian Isles	Vivec City	North of Vivec Temple Wayshrine

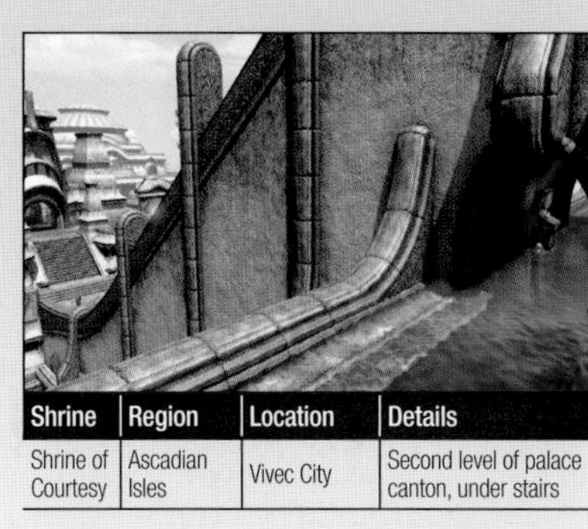

Shrine	Region	Location	Details
Shrine of Courtesy	Ascadian Isles	Vivec City	Second level of palace canton, under stairs

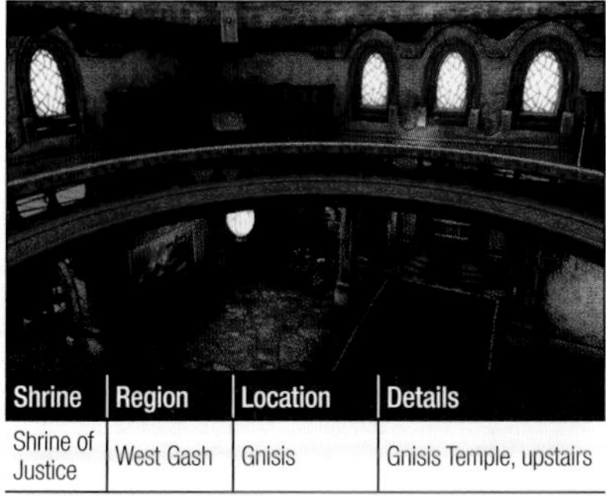

Shrine	Region	Location	Details
Shrine of Justice	West Gash	Gnisis	Gnisis Temple, upstairs

Shrine	Region	Location	Details
Shrine of Valor	West Gash	South of Gnisis	On coast, near rock arch

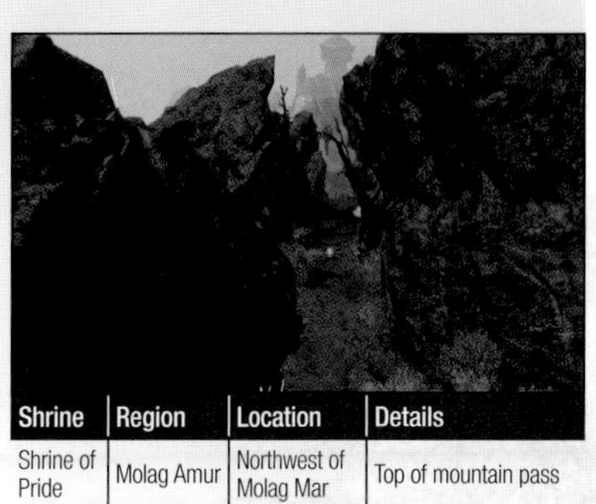

Shrine	Region	Location	Details
Shrine of Pride	Molag Amur	Northwest of Molag Mar	Top of mountain pass

SKYSHARDS

Earn a Skill Point for every three skyshards collected, for a total of six Skill Points hidden around Vvardenfell. For a list of only the in-game hints, refer to the **Achievements** section.

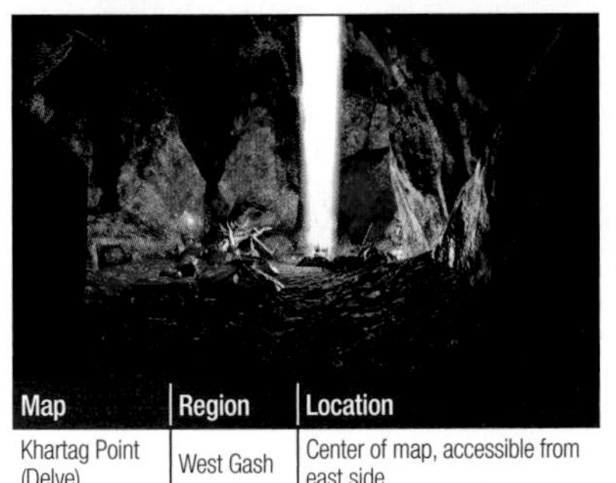

Map	Region	Location
Khartag Point (Delve)	West Gash	Center of map, accessible from east side

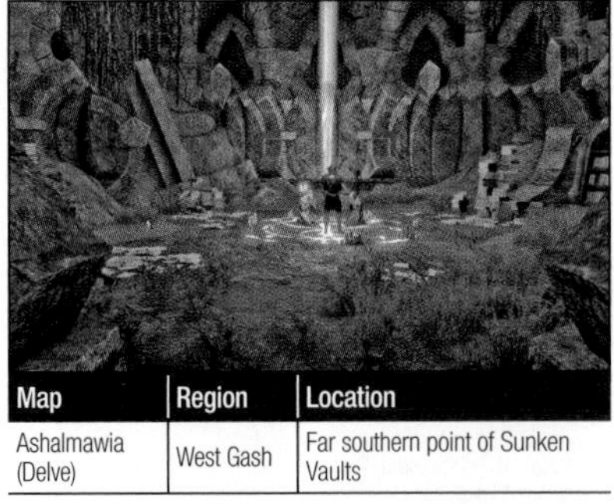

Map	Region	Location
Ashalmawia (Delve)	West Gash	Far southern point of Sunken Vaults

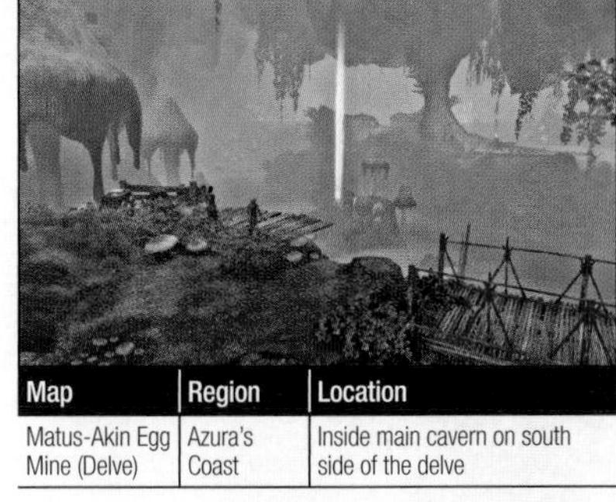

Map	Region	Location
Matus-Akin Egg Mine (Delve)	Azura's Coast	Inside main cavern on south side of the delve

Map	Region	Location
Zainsipilu (Delve)	Bitter Coast	Northeast cavern, accessible through narrow tunnel at waterfall

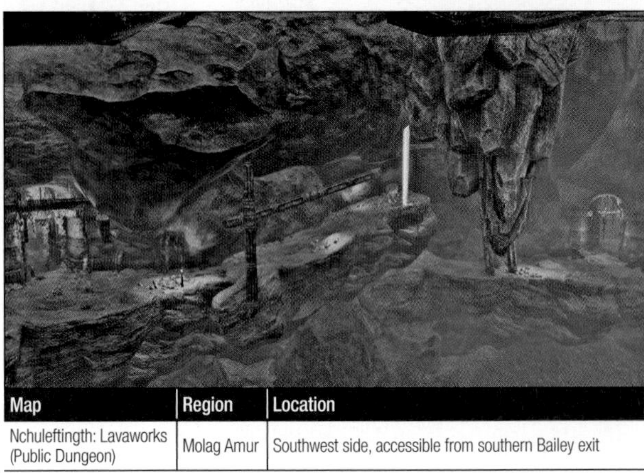

Map	Region	Location
Nchuleftingth: Lavaworks (Public Dungeon)	Molag Amur	Southwest side, accessible from southern Bailey exit

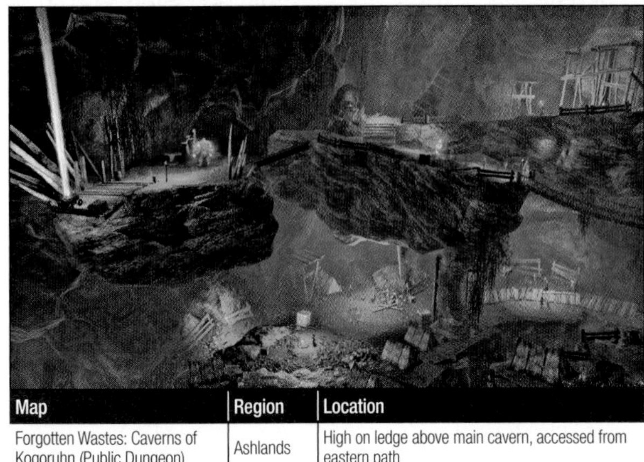

Map	Region	Location
Forgotten Wastes: Caverns of Kogoruhn (Public Dungeon)	Ashlands	High on ledge above main cavern, accessed from eastern path

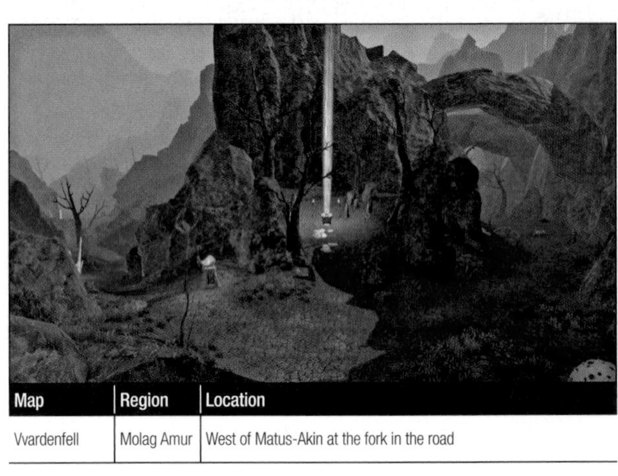

Map	Region	Location
Vvardenfell	Molag Amur	West of Matus-Akin at the fork in the road

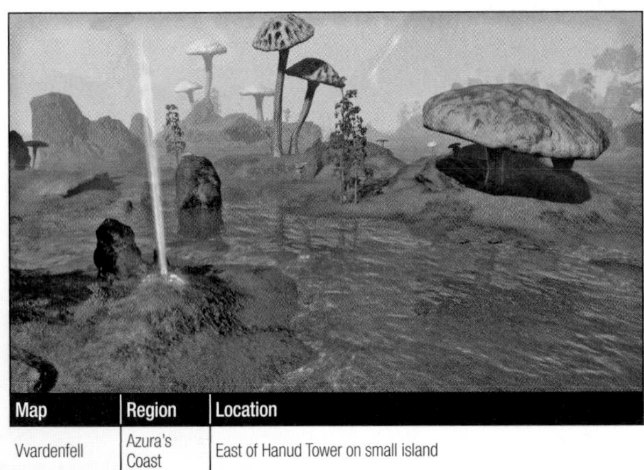

Map	Region	Location
Vvardenfell	Azura's Coast	East of Hanud Tower on small island

Map	Region	Location
Vvardenfell	Molag Amur	South of Falensarano Ruins on top of a Dwemer structure

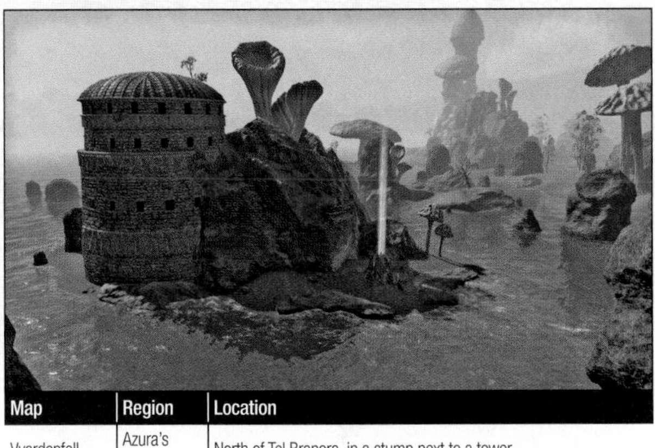

Map	Region	Location
Vvardenfell	Azura's Coast	North of Tel Branora, in a stump next to a tower

Map	Region	Location
Vvardenfell	Bitter Coast	Seyda Neen, courtyard of Census and Excise Offices

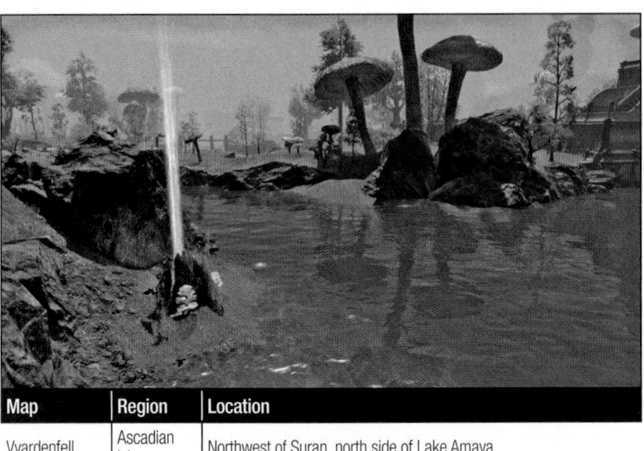

Map	Region	Location
Vvardenfell	Ascadian Isles	Northwest of Suran, north side of Lake Amaya

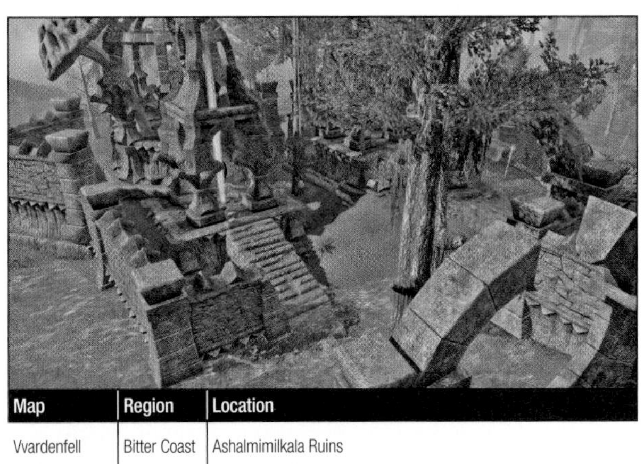

Map	Region	Location
Vvardenfell	Bitter Coast	Ashalmimilkala Ruins

Map	Region	Location
Vvardenfell	Ashlands	South of Valenvaryon Ruins, on a rock in a river of lava

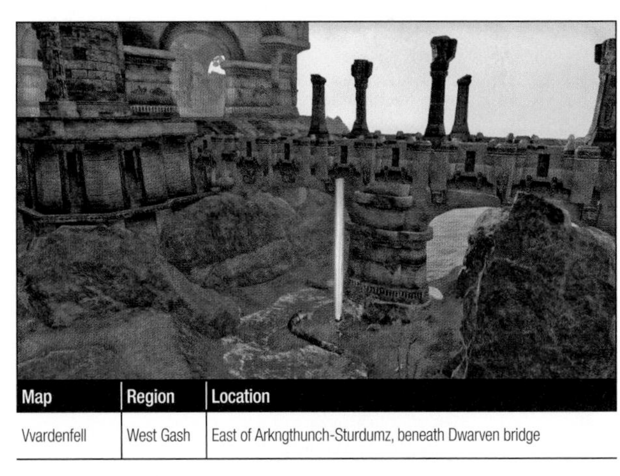

Map	Region	Location
Vvardenfell	West Gash	East of Arkngthunch-Sturdumz, beneath Dwarven bridge

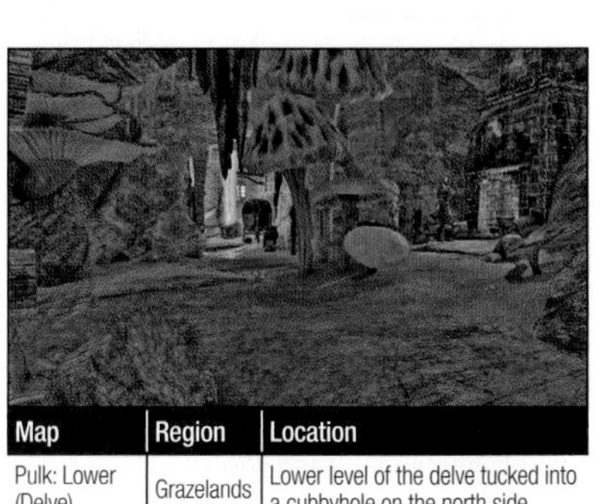

Map	Region	Location
Pulk: Lower (Delve)	Grazelands	Lower level of the delve tucked into a cubbyhole on the north side

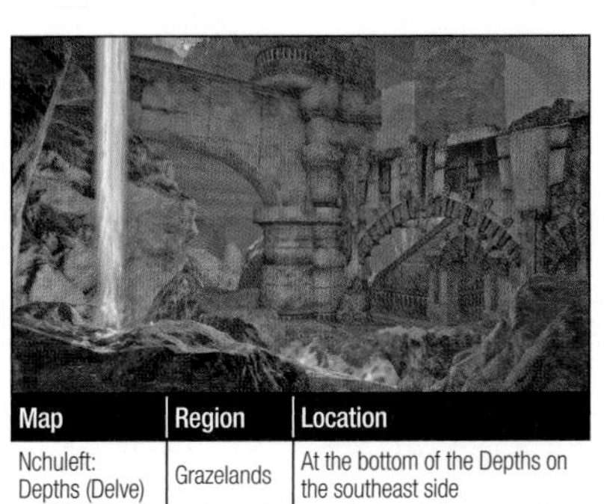

Map	Region	Location
Nchuleft: Depths (Delve)	Grazelands	At the bottom of the Depths on the southeast side

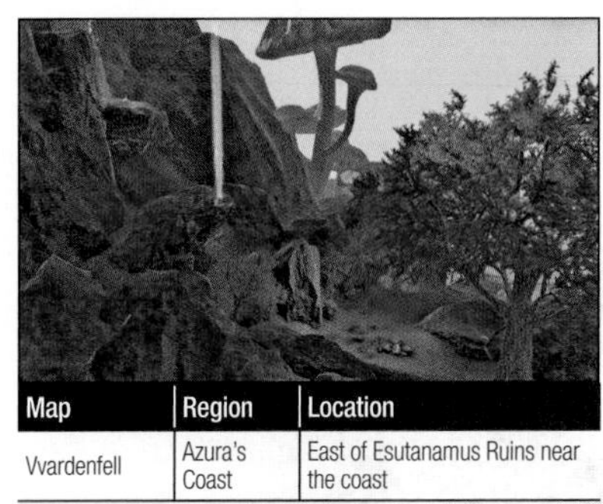

Map	Region	Location
Vvardenfell	Azura's Coast	East of Esutanamus Ruins near the coast

MORROWIND ACHIEVEMENTS

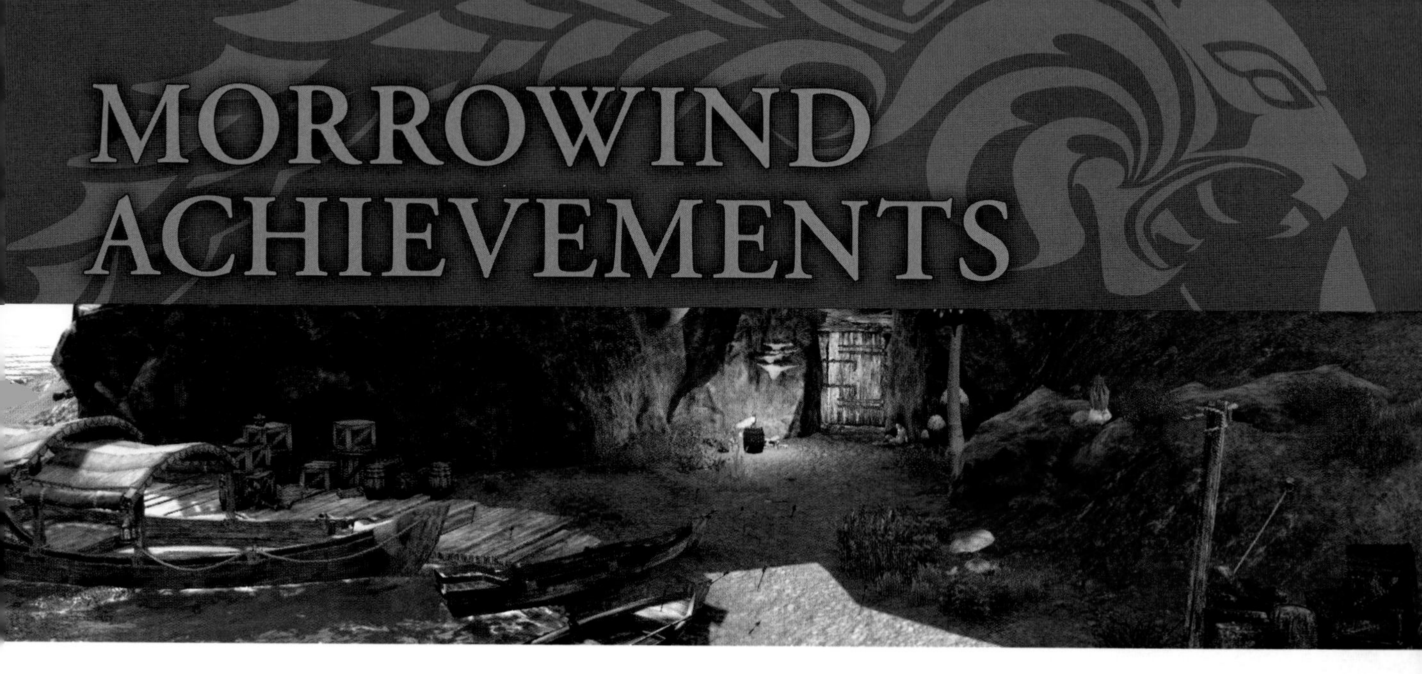

IN-GAME ACHIEVEMENTS

Morrowind offers numerous Achievements throughout the various facets of gameplay. Play through the Halls of Fabrication Trial, defeat group bosses, explore the four corners of Vvardenfell, complete quests, clear dungeons, and partake in Battlegrounds. Check Achievement status by selecting the Achievements tab within your Journal.

Titles, dyes, and a skin are unlocked with specific Achievements. These are noted in the description for that given Achievement.

MAIN STORY QUESTS

Restore Lord Vivec's lost power by completing the main story line.

NAME	DESCRIPTION	COMPLETE QUEST	POINTS
Voice of the Failed Incarnates	Disprove the dangerous claims of the Ashlander Chodala.	Divine Delusions	10
Bearer of the Blessed Staff	Recover the Blessed Staff, Sunna'rah, from the Ashlander Chodala, and determine the true nature of the threat to Lord Vivec.	Divine Intervention	10
Hand of a Living God	Follow a grave threat into Clockwork City, and recover Lord Vivec's stolen power.	Divine Restoration	10
Champion of Vivec	Restore Lord Vivec's lost power, save Vivec City, and be named Champion of Vivec. **Title:** Champion of Vivec **Dye:** Vehk's Mystic Blue	Divine Blessings	15

VVARDENFELL QUESTS

Complete Vvardenfell quests to earn the following Achievements.

NAME	DESCRIPTION	COMPLETE QUEST	POINTS
Naryu's Confidant	Help Naryu Virian and the Morag Tong in and around Balmora.	Family Reunion	10
Rising Sun	Help the Argonian slave, Sun-in-Shadow, gain her freedom.	The Heart of a Telvanni	10
Scarlet Judge	Help the Scarlet Judge foil Marshal Hlaren's plot in Suran.	The Scarlet Judge	10
Kwama Miner	Save the people of Gnisis from economic ruin by restoring the future of their Kwama mine.	Hatching a Plan	10
Hand of the Mistress	Foil a usurper's plot, and assist Mistress Dratha with plans to prolong her life.	Reclaiming Vos	10
Pilgrim Protector	End the threat to the pilgrims at Molag Mar.	An Armiger's Duty	10
Narsis' Apprentice	Help Narsis Dren discover the secret of the Veloth Ancestral Tomb.	Among the Ancient Ancestors	10
Ald'ruhn Annalist	Discover the secret of the Hleran Ancestral Tomb.	Ancestral Ties	10
Ebony Enforcer	Discover the truth behind the sudden spike in production at Vassir-Didanat Ebony Mine.	Like Blood from a Stone	5

ALD'RUHN DAILY QUESTS

By completing Quest: **Ashlander Relations**, daily beast hunts and relic-preservation quests become available in Ald'ruhn.

NAME	DESCRIPTION	POINTS
Ashlander Associate	Complete your first daily quest for Huntmaster Sorim-Nakar or Numani-Rasi.	5
Ashwalker	Complete 10 daily quests for Huntmaster Sorim-Nakar or Numani-Rasi.	10
Ashlands Relic Preserver	Complete all seven relic-preservation daily quests given by Numani-Rasi.	5
Ashlands Stalker	Complete all seven daily hunts for Huntmaster Sorim-Nakar.	5
Clanfriend	Complete 30 daily quests for Huntmaster Sorim-Nakar or Numani-Rasi. **Title:** Clanfriend	15

EXPLORE VVARDENFELL

Explore the six delves and nine Interesting Locations, as well as completing Vvardenfell quests.

NAME	DESCRIPTION	POINTS
Ashalmawia Explorer	Explore and clear Ashalmawia Delve.	5
Khartag Point Explorer	Explore and clear Khartag Point.	5
Matus-Akin Egg Mine Explorer	Explore and clear Matus-Akin Egg Mine.	5
Nchuleft Explorer	Explore and clear Nchuleft.	5
Pulk Explorer	Explore and clear Pulk.	5
Zainsipilu Explorer	Explore and clear Zainsipilu.	5
Morrowind Cave Delver	Explore and clear all six explorable caves in Vvardenfell, including Khartag Point, Ashalmawia, Zainsipilu, Matus-Akin Egg Mine, Pulk, and Nchuleft. Refer to our Vvardenfell map for the location of all six delves.	15
Morrowind Pathfinder	Discover all the striking locales in Vvardenfell. Refer to our Vvardenfell map for all nine Interesting Locations. Yasammadin Ashalmimilkala Shrine of Azura Holamayan Monastery Ald Sotha Hanud Tower Aleft Falensarano Ruins Valenvaryon	10
Morrowind Master Explorer	Discover and clear all explorable caves and striking locales in Vvardenfell. Earn the Morrowind Cave Delver and Morrowind Pathfinder Achievements.	15
Morrowind Grand Adventurer	Complete 32 quests in Vvardenfell.	50

PUBLIC DUNGEONS

Defeat the group events and champions in the Nchuleftingth and Forgotten Wastes Public Dungeons.

NAME	DESCRIPTION	POINTS
Forgotten Wastes Group Event	Defeat Stone-Boiler Omalas, Brander Releth, and Mountain-Caller Hlaren in the Forgotten Wastes.	50
Forgotten Wastes Vanquisher	Defeat three of the champions in the Forgotten Wastes. Refer to our maps for locations of all champions. Voracity Mynar Igna Beckoner Morvayn Coaxer Veran, Castigator Athin, and Confessor Dradas Cliff Strider Matriarch	10
Forgotten Wastes Conqueror	Defeat all of the champions in the Forgotten Wastes. See list above.	50
Nchuleftingth Group Event	Defeat Nchulaeon the Eternal in Nchuleftingth.	50
Nchuleftingth Vanquisher	Defeat three of the champions in Nchuleftingth. Refer to our maps for locations of all champions. Renduril the Hammer, and Friar Hadelar Guardian of Bthark Mud-Tusk Nilarion the Cavalier Steamreaver	10
Nchuleftingth Conqueror	Defeat all of the champions in Nchuleftingth. See list above.	50

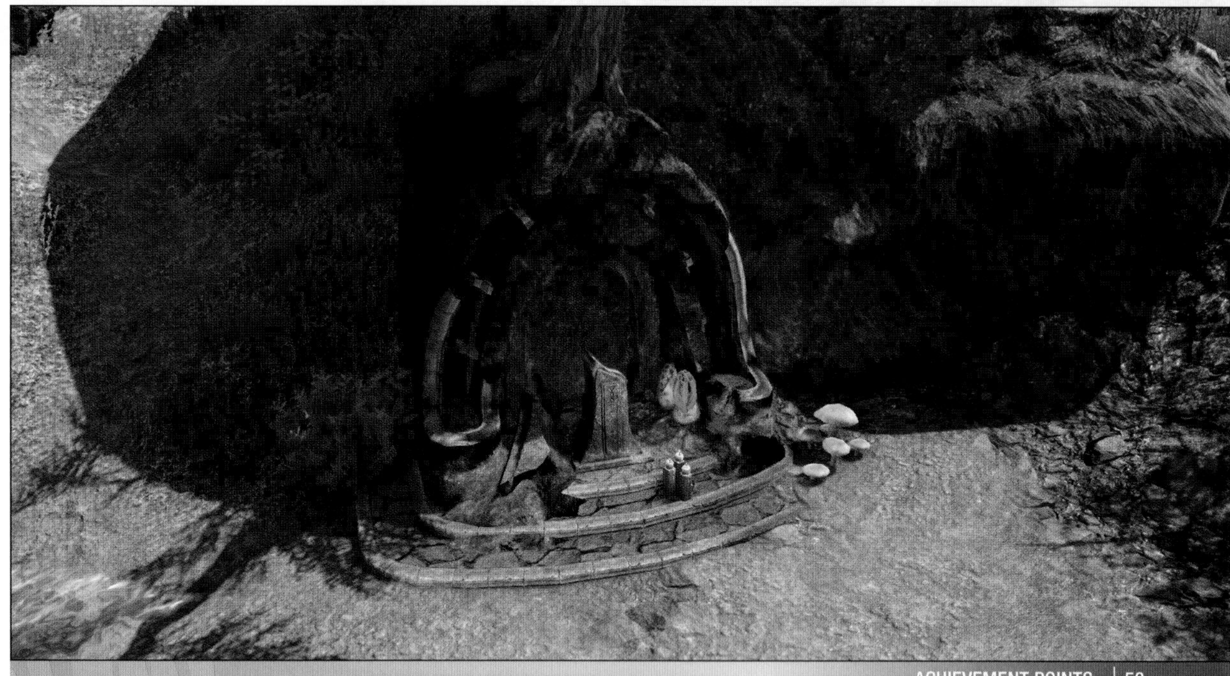

ANCESTRAL TOMBS HUNTER

ACHIEVEMENT POINTS	50
TITLE	LIBRARIAN

Find all 30 ancestral tombs in Vvardenfell, make a rubbing of the information they contain, and deliver these rubbings to Librarian Bradyn in Vivec City to discover the location of the lost Library of Andule. Othrelas is returned to the Librarian as part of **Quest: The Ancestral Tombs.** Deliver the remaining 29 rubbings to Bradyn to unlock his second quest, **The Lost Library**. Refer to the maps for all 30 locations, or to the **Appendices** for a full listing.

TRIBUNAL PREACHER

ACHIEVEMENT POINTS | 5

Read all 36 Vivec Sermons scattered across Vardenfell. Refer to our maps for all 36 locations, or to the **Appendices** for the full list.

MORROWIND MASTER ANGLER

ACHIEVEMENT POINTS | 5

Catch all 12 rare fish in Vvardenfell. Refer to the Rare Fish entry in the Appendices for a full list of available rare fish and where to find each one.

MORROWIND SKYSHARD HUNTER

ACHIEVEMENT POINTS | 10

Discover all 18 skyshards in Vvardenfell. Refer to our maps for exact locations of all 18 skyshards, with a full list in the **Appendices**. The hints given in the game are as follows:

At a small shrine where the road forks.
On an isle facing the Sea of Ghosts.
On a Dwemer overhang, above a river of lava.
On an outcropping overlooking a grisly scene.
In a hollow stump on the wetlands.
Withheld at customs and stored in the yard.
In a stump on the northern shore of Lake Amaya.
In the heart of crumbling Daedric ruins.
On a stranded rock in a river of lava.
Beneath the Dwarven bridge.
On a treacherous path overlooking a sea of fire.
Heaped onto a cart of stone left on a precarious perch.
Nestled with glittering treasures where the red crystals glow.
Hidden deep within a Shrine to the Prince of Corruption.
Where Cliff Striders bask under golden rays in their den.
On an islet in the subterranean lake.
In a cozy bandit's den.
In the deepest depths of a subterranean Dwemer ruin.

MORROWIND CRAFTING STYLES

For each of the four new styles in Morrowind, there are 14 chapters to collect, including the following: Axes, Belts, Boots, Bows, Chests, Daggers, Gloves, Helmets, Legs, Maces, Shields, Shoulders, Staves, and Swords. The following three are found around Vvardenfell or as Daily quest rewards. The fourth style is purchased from Battlegrounds merchants and listed with the PvP achievements later in this section.

ACHIEVEMENT	DESCRIPTION	ACHIEVEMENT POINTS
Ashlander Style Master	Learn every chapter in the Ashlander style book, occasionally found as rewards for completing daily quests for Huntmaster Sorim-Nakar and Numani-Rasi in Ald'ruhn. Note that you must complete Quest: Ashlander Relations to unlock these jobs.	50
Buoyant Armiger Style Master	Learn every chapter in the Bouyant Armiger style book, occasionally found in treasure chests across Vvardenfell.	50
Morag Tong Style Master	Learn every chapter in the Morag Tong style book, occasionally found in Bounty and Explorer's Dispensations from the Hall of Justice. Complete group boss and delve daily jobs from Beleru and Traylan Omoril to receive the rewards.	50

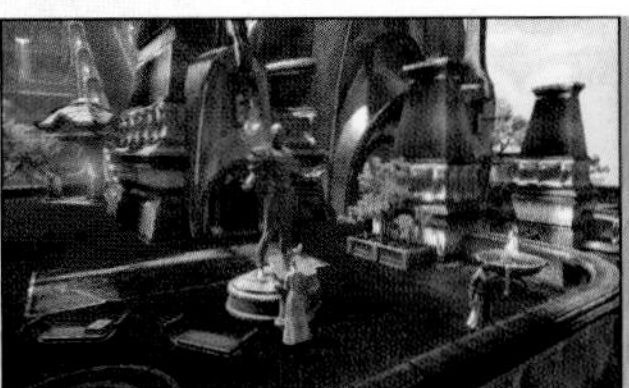

ACHIEVEMENT POINTS | 5

THE PILGRIM'S PATH

Visit the Shrines of the Seven Graces and read the inscriptions on each shrine. Refer to the **Maps** chapter for locations and the **Appendices** for a full list of the shrines.

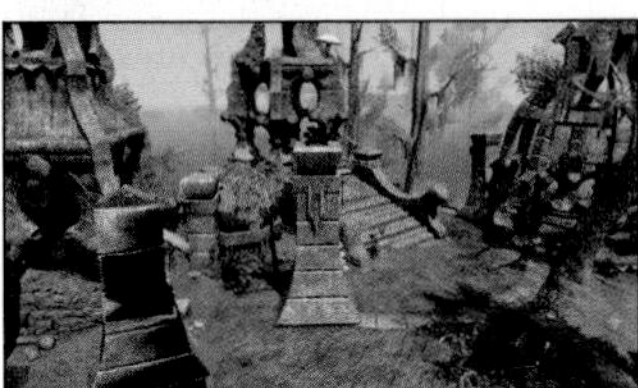

ACHIEVEMENT POINTS | 10

DAEDRIC EXPLORER

Visit all of the Daedric ruins in Vvardenfell. Refer to the **Maps** chapter for locations and the **Appendices** for a full list of all 25 ruins.

ACHIEVEMENT POINTS | 5

STRIDER CARAVANER

Visit the Silt Strider Caravaner at each of the stations in Vvardenfell. Visit the Caravaner at the following towns and use the Silt Strider to fast-travel around the zone.

TOWN	LOCATION	CARAVANER	DESTINATIONS
Balmora	Stable Gate	Nevos Sareloth	Gnisis, Vivec City
Gnisis	Gnisis Wayshrine	Amili Yahaz	Balmora, Vivec City
Molag Mar	West of town	Narisa Androm	Tel Mora, Suran
Seyda Neen	Northeast side of town	Medyn Hleran	Gnisis, Suran
Suran	North side of town	Faven Thendas	Seyda Neen, Vivec City, Molag Mar
Tel Mora	Northeast side of town	Adosi Delvi	Vivec City, Molag Mar
Vivec City	Pilgrim's Approach	Helseth Sadalvel	Suran, Balmora, Gnisis, Tel Mora

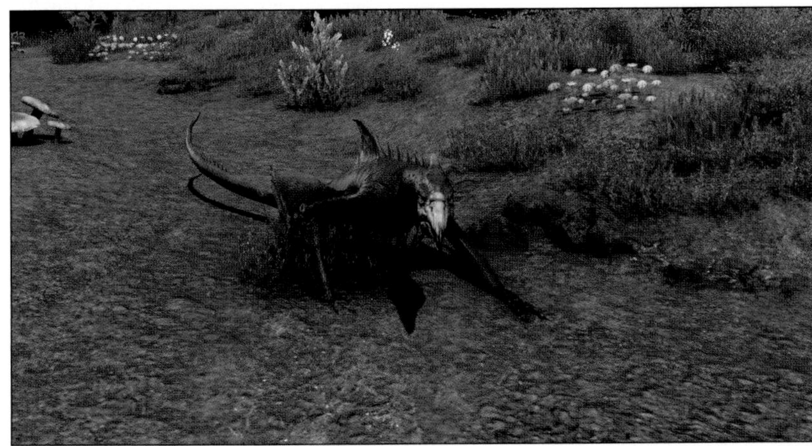

ACHIEVEMENT POINTS | 5

CLIFF STRIDERS' BANE

Do your part to eliminate the Cliff Strider menace by killing 100 Cliff Striders or Cliff Skippers in Vvardenfell. These pests can be found throughout the zone, but they're prevalent in the far northwest, north of Gnisis.

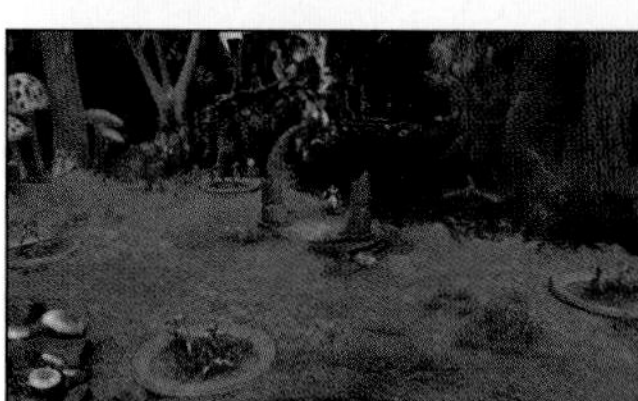

GROUP BOSSES

Gather a group of players and take on the six world bosses of Vvardenfell.

NAME	DESCRIPTION	POINTS
Consort Killer	Defeat the Queen's Consort at Missir-Dadalit Egg Mine.	10
Wuyuvus Slayer	Defeat Wuyuvus the Hunger at Sulipund Grange.	10
Salothan Cursebreaker	Defeat Orator Salothan, Regent Beleth, General Tanasa, and Councilor Reynis at Solathan's Council.	10
Breaker of the Unbroken	Defeat the Nix-Ox Nilthog the Unbroken at Nilthog's Hollow.	10
Cheater Defeater	Defeat the Skaafin, Mehz the Cozener, at Dubdil Alar Tower and seal the rift to Oblivion.	10
Loop Eradicator	Save Dubdil Alar from the consequences of his temporal experiments. Finish the final phase of the Skaafin, Mehz the Cozener, fight within 30 seconds to save Dubdil Alar.	5
Songbird Silencer	Defeat the Nereid Kimbrudhil the Songbird at Shipwreck Cove.	10
Defender of Morrowind	Defeat all six world bosses in Vvardenfell.	15

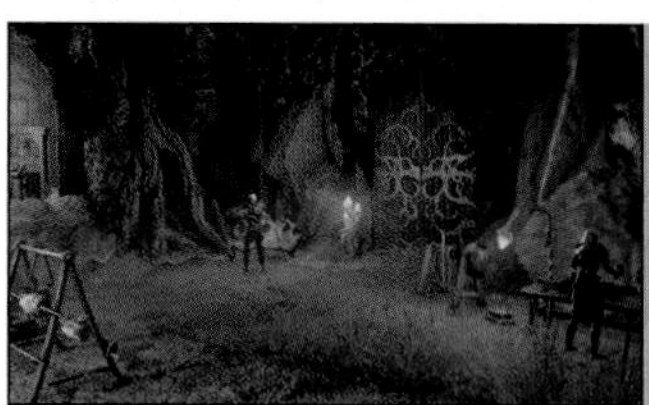

HALLS OF FABRICATION

Join 11 players at Tel Fyr and run the Halls of Fabrication Trial. In order to earn all 17 Achievements, the Trial must be completed within the specified criteria, such as a time limit, no group deaths, and more. Several Achievements are only earned on Veteran difficulty. Locations of the four notes can be found on the Halls of Fabrication maps.

NAME	DESCRIPTION	POINTS
Scholar of Seht's Mysteries	Discover all the notes scattered throughout the Halls of Fabrication. Refer to the Halls of Fabrication maps for locations. Telvanni Additional Specifications Telvanni Journal Cogitation Log 1322331455212478 Divayth Fyr's Notes	10
Refabricant Slayer	Defeat 100 Calefactors, Capacitors, or Dissectors in the Halls of Fabrication.	10
Kill Process	Defeat one Hunter-Killer Fabricant while the other still has at least half of its health remaining, before defeating the remaining Fabricant in Veteran Halls of Fabrication.	10
Power House	Defeat the Pinnacle Factotum without ever using energy from the generator to break a Refabricated Sentry's shield, in Veteran Halls of Fabrication.	15
Arc-Custodian	In Veteran Halls of Fabrication, defeat the Archcustodian using six or fewer Shock Pylons without ever missing an opportunity to disable it with one.	10
Planned Obsolescence	Defeat the Refabrication Committee in Veteran Halls of Fabrication without ever allowing the Reclaimer to overcharge a Ruined Factotum.	15
Halls of Fabrication Completed	Defeat the Assembly General and assist Divayth Fyr in stopping the flood of Animunculi coming from the Halls of Fabrication. **Title:** Clockwork Confounder **Dye:** Colossus Brass	15
Halls of Fabrication Conqueror	Defeat the Assembly General in Veteran Halls of Fabrication. **Title:** Divayth Fyr's Coadjuctor **Skin:** Fabrication Sheath	50
Environmentally Conscious	Defeat the Assembly General in Veteran Halls of Fabrication without any group member dying in traps and hazards.	15
Terminal Terminator	Defeat the Assembly General in Veteran Halls of Fabrication without letting any Terminals complete their activation sequence.	15
Time Trial: Halls of Fabrication	Complete Veteran Halls of Fabrication within a time limit of 40 minutes. Your Trial begins when you enter Abanabi Cave beneath Tel Fyr.	50
Well-Oiled Machine	Complete Veteran Halls of Fabrication without suffering a group member death.	50
Halls of Fabrication Vanquisher	Defeat the Assembly General after empowering it by resetting the circuit breaker in Veteran Halls of Fabrication.	50
Stress Tested	Complete Veteran Halls of Fabrication after resetting the circuit breaker and empowering the Assembly General, all without suffering a group member death. **Title:** Disassembly General	50
Like Clockwork	Complete Veteran Halls of Fabrication after resetting the circuit breaker and empowering the Assembly General, all within 40 minutes of entering Abanabi Cave and without suffering a group member death. **Title:** The Tick-Tock Tormentor	50
Accept No Substitute	Defeat five of each of the Tactical Facsimiles that the Assembly General creates, on any difficulty. Dragonknight Tactical Facsimile Nightblade Tactical Facsimile Sorcerer Tactical Facsimile Templar Tactical Facsimile Warden Tactical Facsimile	10
Dynamo	Complete each of the following Achievements related to defeating the Assembly General: Halls of Fabrication Completed Halls of Fabrication Conqueror Halls of Fabrication Vanquisher Time Trial: Halls of Fabrication Well-Oiled Machine Power House Terminal Terminator **Title:** The Dynamo	15

ACHIEVEMENT POINTS	50
TITLE	SAVIOR OF MORROWIND

SAVIOR OF MORROWIND

Complete quests, defeat bosses, and explore delves to become the Savior of Morrowind. Earn the following Achievements for the title of Savior of Morrowind:

Champion of Vivec: Restore Lord Vivec's lost power, save Vivec City, and be named Champion of Vivec by completing **Quest: Divine Blessings**.

Ancestral Tombs Hunter: Find all 30 ancestral tombs in Vvardenfell, make a rubbing of the information they contain, and deliver these rubbings to Librarian Bradyn in Vivec City.

Morrowind Grand Adventurer: Complete 32 quests in Vvardenfell.

Defender of Morrowind: Defeat all six group bosses in Vvardenfell.

Morrowind Master Explorer: Discover and clear all delves and striking locales in Vvardenfell.

Forgotten Wastes Group Event: Defeat Stone-Boiler Omalas, Brander Releth, and Mountain-Caller Hlaren in the Forgotten Wastes.

Nchuleftingth Group Event: Defeat Nchulaeon the Eternal in Nchuleftingth.

BATTLEGROUNDS

Compete in Battlegrounds, win medals, complete objectives, and spend your Alliance Points on Militant Ordinator Motif chapters to earn the following Achievements.

NAME	DESCRIPTION	POINTS
Pit Bully	Defeat 10 opponents in Battlegrounds.	5
Pit Fighter	Defeat 250 opponents in Battlegrounds.	10
Pit Hero	Defeat 1,000 opponents in Battlegrounds. **Title:** Bloodletter **Dye:** Firedrake's Flame	10
Newblood Relic Hunter	Seize your first relic in Battlegrounds.	5
Veteran Relic Hunter	Seize 20 relics in Battlegrounds.	10
Grand Relic Hunter	Seize 100 relics in Battlegrounds. **Title:** Relic Hunter **Dye:** Pit Daemon's Poison	15
Newblood Relic Guardian	Defeat a relic carrier for the first time in Battlegrounds.	5
Veteran Relic Guardian	Defeat 20 relic carriers in Battlegrounds.	10
Grand Relic Guardian	Defeat 100 relic carriers in Battlegrounds. **Title:** Relic Guardian	15
Newblood Standard-Bearer	Seize your first Capture Point in Battlegrounds.	5
Veteran Standard-Bearer	Seize 50 Capture Points in Battlegrounds.	10
Grand Standard-Bearer	Seize 250 Capture Points in Battlegrounds. **Title:** Standard-Bearer **Dye:** Stormlord's Lightning	15
Newblood Standard-Guardian	Earn 10 Defensive Execution Medals by defeating opponents attacking one of your Capture Points.	5
Veteran Standard-Guardian	Earn 100 Defensive Execution Medals by defeating opponents attacking one of your Capture Points.	10
Grand Standard-Guardian	Earn 500 Defensive Execution Medals by defeating opponents attacking one of your Capture Points. **Title:** Standard-Guardian	15
Victor	Win a Battleground match for the first time.	5
Crowd Favorite	Win 10 Battleground matches.	10
Conquering Hero	Win 50 Battleground matches. **Title:** Conquering Hero	15
Gladiator	Earn a lifetime score of 5,000 points in Battlegrounds.	10
Champion	Earn a lifetime score of 50,000 points in Battlegrounds.	15
Grand Champion	Earn a lifetime score of 250,000 points in Battlegrounds. **Title:** Grand Champion	50
Battleground Dominator	Control all four Capture Points simultaneously in a Domination match.	10
Battleground Butcher	Win a Team Deathmatch before any other team reaches 200 points. **Title:** Battleground Butcher	15
Tactician	Help your team capture both enemy relics within 10 seconds of each other. **Title:** Tactician	15
Claim-Staker	Seize at least four Capture Points without dying.	10
Paragon	Finish a Team Deathmatch battle with at least eight more kills than deaths. **Title:** Paragon	15
Triple Threat	Earn a Triple Threat Medal by capturing three enemy relics in a single Battleground match. **Title:** Relic Runner	15
Most Valuable Combatant	Earn a score of at least 3,000 points in a single Battleground match.	10
Quadruple Kill	Earn your first Quadruple Kill Medal by defeating four opponents in a Battleground match, each within ten seconds of the next. **Title:** The Merciless	15
Charging Champion	Earn your first Charging Champion Medal by dealing at least 500,000 points of damage in a single Battleground match.	10
Fearless Physician	Earn your first Fearless Physician Medal by healing at least 500,000 points of damage in a single Battleground match.	10
Steady Centurion	Earn your first Steady Centurion Medal by taking at least 250,000 damage while carrying relics or defending Capture Points in a single Battleground match.	10
Divine Protection	Earn your first Divine Protection Medal by healing at least 500,000 points of damage for relic carriers and Capture Point defenders in a single Battleground match.	10
Ultimate Strike	Earn your first Ultimate Strike Medal by defeating at least 20 opponents in a single Battleground match.	10
Dauntless Defense	Earn your first Dauntless Defense Medal by earning 1,000 points while defending a Capture Point.	10
Militant Ordinator Style Master	Learn every chapter in the Militant Ordinator style book, sold in exchange for Alliance Points by Battleground Supplies Merchants. This includes 14 chapters for each piece of armor and type of weapon.	50
Warden Slayer	Kill 10 enemy Wardens. Players who do not own Morrowind can earn this Achievement. This can be accomplished during any PVP activity.	10
Grand Warden Slayer	Kill 100 enemy Wardens. Players who do not own Morrowind can earn this Achievement. This can be accomplished during any PVP activity. **Dye:** Warden's Moss Green	15

ACHIEVEMENT FURNISHINGS

By completing certain Achievements, furnishings become available for purchase from the Achievement Furnishings vendor in Vivec City.

FURNISHING	CATEGORY	ACHIEVEMENT REQUIRED	COST (GOLD)
Ashlander Altar, Anticipations	Undercroft	Clanfriend	50,000
Ashlander Fence, Totems	Undercroft	Ashlands Relic Preserver	10,000
Ashlander Throne	Gallery	Voice of the Failed Incarnate	100,000
Ashlander Yurt, Netch-Hide	Structure	Ashlands Stalker	75,000
Banner of House Dres	Parlor	Morrowind Grand Adventurer	10,000
Banner of House Hlaalu	Parlor	Morrowind Grand Adventurer	10,000
Banner of House Indoril	Parlor	Morrowind Grand Adventurer	10,000
Banner of House Redoran	Parlor	Morrowind Grand Adventurer	10,000
Banner of House Telvanni	Parlor	Morrowind Grand Adventurer	10,000
Banner, Morag Tong	Parlor	Naryu's Confidant	25,000
Blessing Stone	Lighting	Bearer of the Blessed Staff	10,000
Blessing Stone Device	Workshop	Bearer of the Blessed Staff	20,000
Dwarven Brazier, Eternal	Lighting	Nchuleftingth Conqueror	50,000
Glass Crystal, Plume	Miscellaneous	Pilgrim Protector	15,000
Glass Crystal, Radiance	Miscellaneous	Pilgrim Protector	10,000
Glass Crystals, Bed	Miscellaneous	Pilgrim Protector	20,000
Kwama Queen Egg	Undercroft	Scarlet Judge	15,000
Replica Stone of Ashalmawia	Lighting	Hand of the Mistress	75,000
Sacred Guar Skull	Undercroft	Ald'ruhn Annalist	15,000
Silt Strider Shell, Hollow	Undercroft	Strider Caravaner	10,000
Statue, Cowering Ebony	Courtyard	Ebony Enforcer	50,000
Statue, Terrified Ebony	Courtyard	Ebony Enforcer	50,000
Statuette of Clavicus Vile, Masked	Gallery	Hand of a Living God	100,000
Tapestry, Morag Tong	Parlor	Naryu's Confidant	35,000
Tapestry, St. Veloth	Undercroft	Narsis' Apprentice	20,000
Telvanni Device, Static	Workshop	Rising Sun	50,000
Temple Doctrine: The 36 Lessons	Library	Tribunal Preacher	130,000
The 36 Lessons: Sermon 37	Library	Tribunal Preacher and Champion of Vivec	50,000
Totem of the Sixth House	Undercroft (Interactable, Animated, Audible)	Forgotten Wastes Vanquisher	100,000
Tribunal Shrine in Fountain	Courtyard	Savior of Morrowind	50,000
Triptych of the Triune	Undercroft	The Pilgrim's Path	50,000

BATTLEGROUNDS ACHIEVEMENT FURNISHINGS

Find two vendors in the Gladiator's Quarters of Vivec City who sell Battlegrounds Achievements Furnishings.

BRAZIER OF THE PIT DAEMONS	LIGHTING	GRAND CHAMPION	50,000
Chained Skull of the Firedrake	Undercroft	Grand Champion	100,000
Crown of the Firedrakes	Gallery	Grand Relic Guardian	100,000
Skull of the Pit Daemon	Gallery	Grand Relic Guardian	150,000
Skull of the Stormlords	Gallery	Grand Relic Guardian	125,000
Weathervane of the Stormlords	Lighting	Grand Champion	75,000

XBOX ONE ACHIEVEMENTS AND PLAYSTATION 4 TROPHIES

Earn six Achievements/Trophies on the Xbox One and PlayStation 4 consoles, respectively.

NAME	DESCRIPTION	XBOX ONE GAMERSCORE	PS4 TROPHY
Ancestral Tombs Hunter	Find all 30 ancestral tombs in Vvardenfell, and uncover the location of the lost Library of Andule.	20	Bronze
Champion of Vivec	Restore Lord Vivec's lost power, save Vivec City, and be named Champion of Vivec by completing Quest: Divine Blessings.	30	Silver
Halls of Fabrication Completed	Assist Divayth Fyr in stopping the flood of Animunculi coming from the Halls of Fabrication.	30	Silver
Triple Threat	Capture three enemy relics in a single Battleground match.	20	Bronze
Most Valuable Combatant	Earn a score of at least 3,000 points in a single Battleground match.	20	Bronze
Savior of Morrowind	Complete quests, defeat bosses, and explore delves to become the Savior of Morrowind.	100	Gold

XBOX ONE CHALLENGES

TIMELY SAVIOR OF MORROWIND

Earn the title of Savior of Morrowind within 30 days of the *Morrowind* update. This challenge is only available for a limited time—between June 6, 2017 and July 6, 2017. This requires completing the following:

- **Champion of Vivec:** Restore Lord Vivec's lost power, save Vivec City, and be named Champion of Vivec by completing **Quest: Divine Blessings**.
- **Ancestral Tombs Hunter:** Find all 30 ancestral tombs in Vvardenfell, make a rubbing of the information they contain, and deliver these rubbings to Librarian Bradyn in Vivec City.
- **Morrowind Grand Adventurer:** Complete 32 quests in Vvardenfell.
- **Defender of Morrowind:** Defeat all six group bosses in Vvardenfell.
- **Morrowind Master Explorer:** Discover and clear all delves and striking locales in Vvardenfell.
- **Forgotten Wastes Group Event:** Defeat Stone-Boiler Omalas, Brander Releth, and Mountain-Caller Hlaren in the Forgotten Wastes.
- **Nchuleftingth Group Event:** Defeat Nchulaeon the Eternal in Nchuleftingth.

MONTH OF BATTLE

Win 30 Battlegrounds in 30 days. This challenge runs from July 6, 2017 to August 6, 2017.

CONCEPT ART

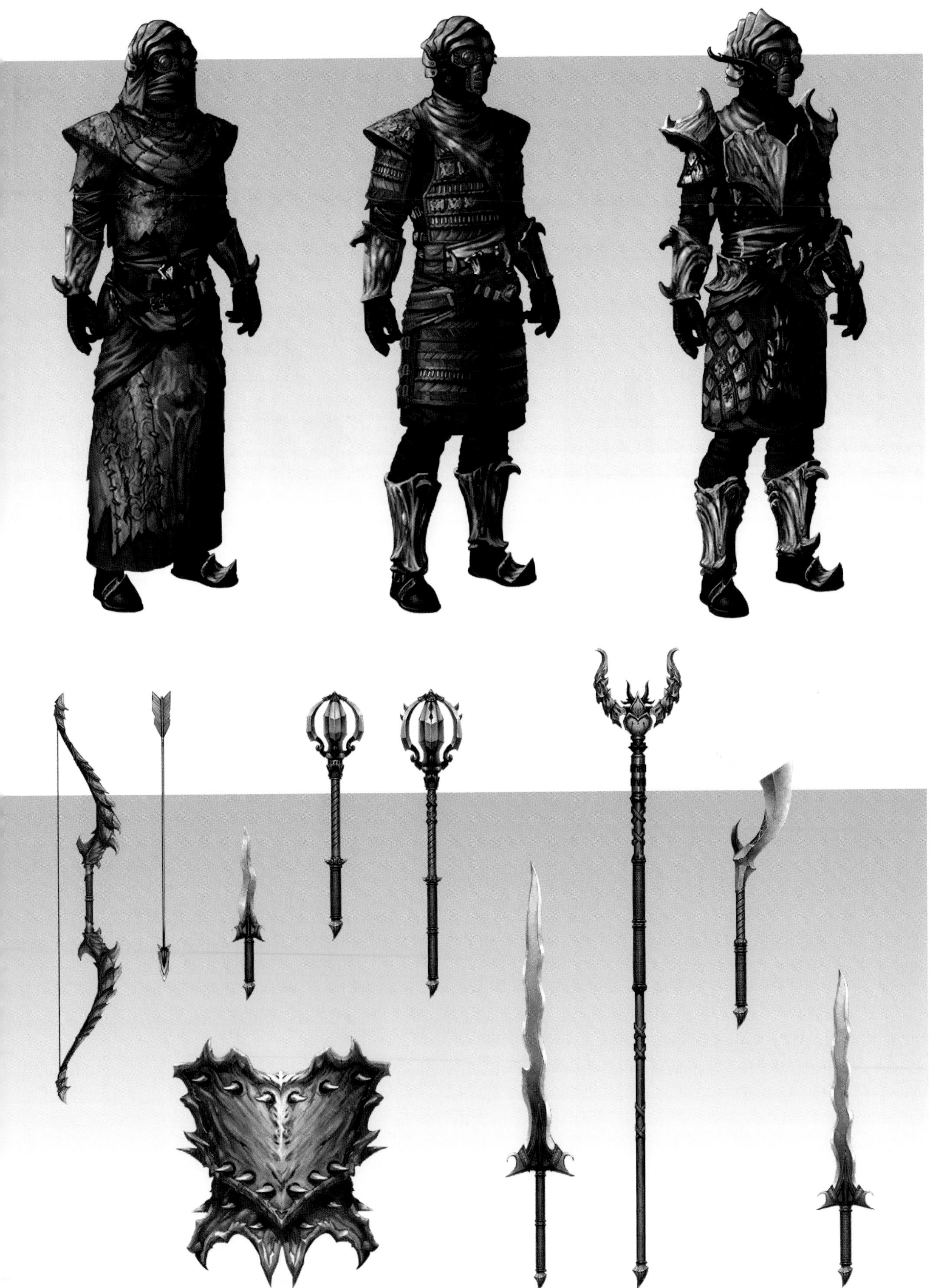

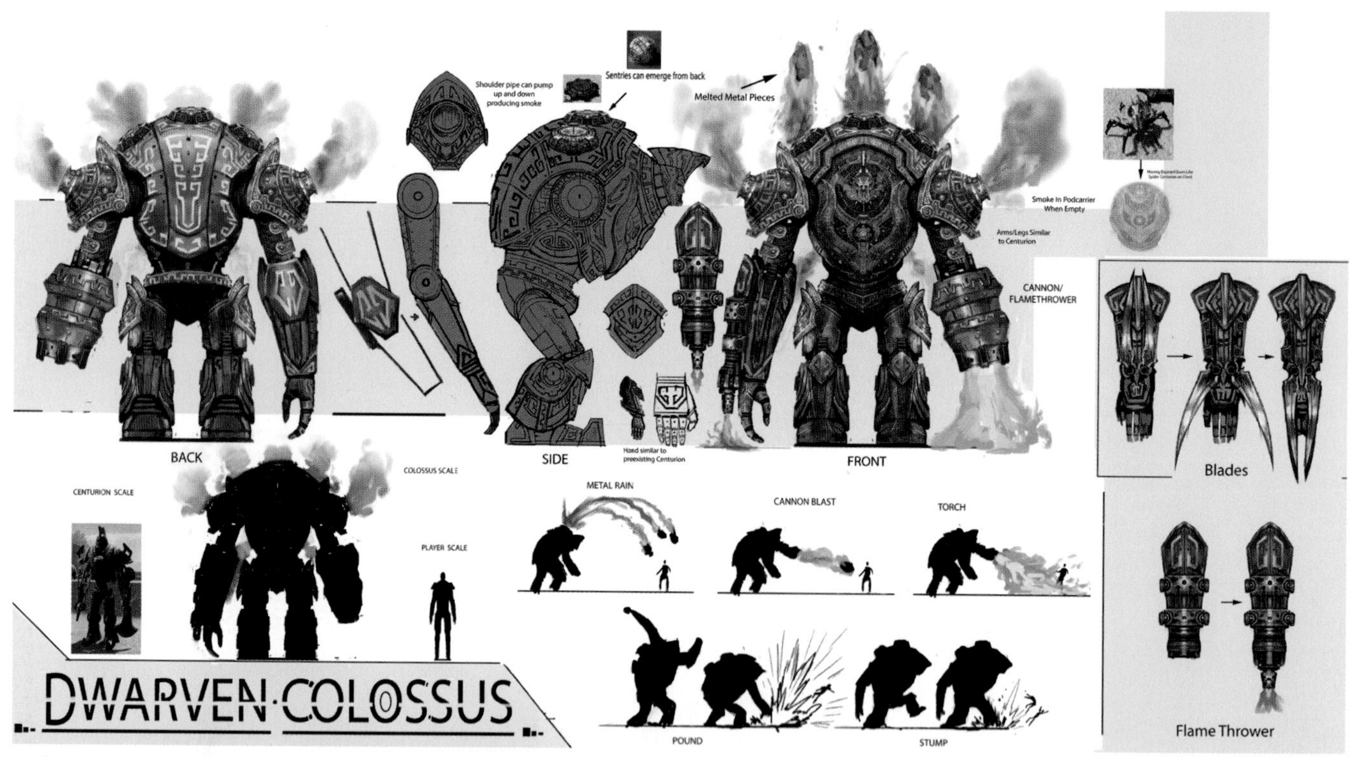
Shoulder pipe can pump up and down producing smoke
Sentries can emerge from back
Melted Metal Pieces
Smoke In Podcarrier When Empty
Arms/Legs Similar to Centurion
CANNON/ FLAMETHROWER
BACK
SIDE
Hand similar to preexisting Centurion
FRONT
Blades
CENTURION SCALE
COLOSSUS SCALE
PLAYER SCALE
METAL RAIN
CANNON BLAST
TORCH
DWARVEN·COLOSSUS
POUND
STUMP
Flame Thrower

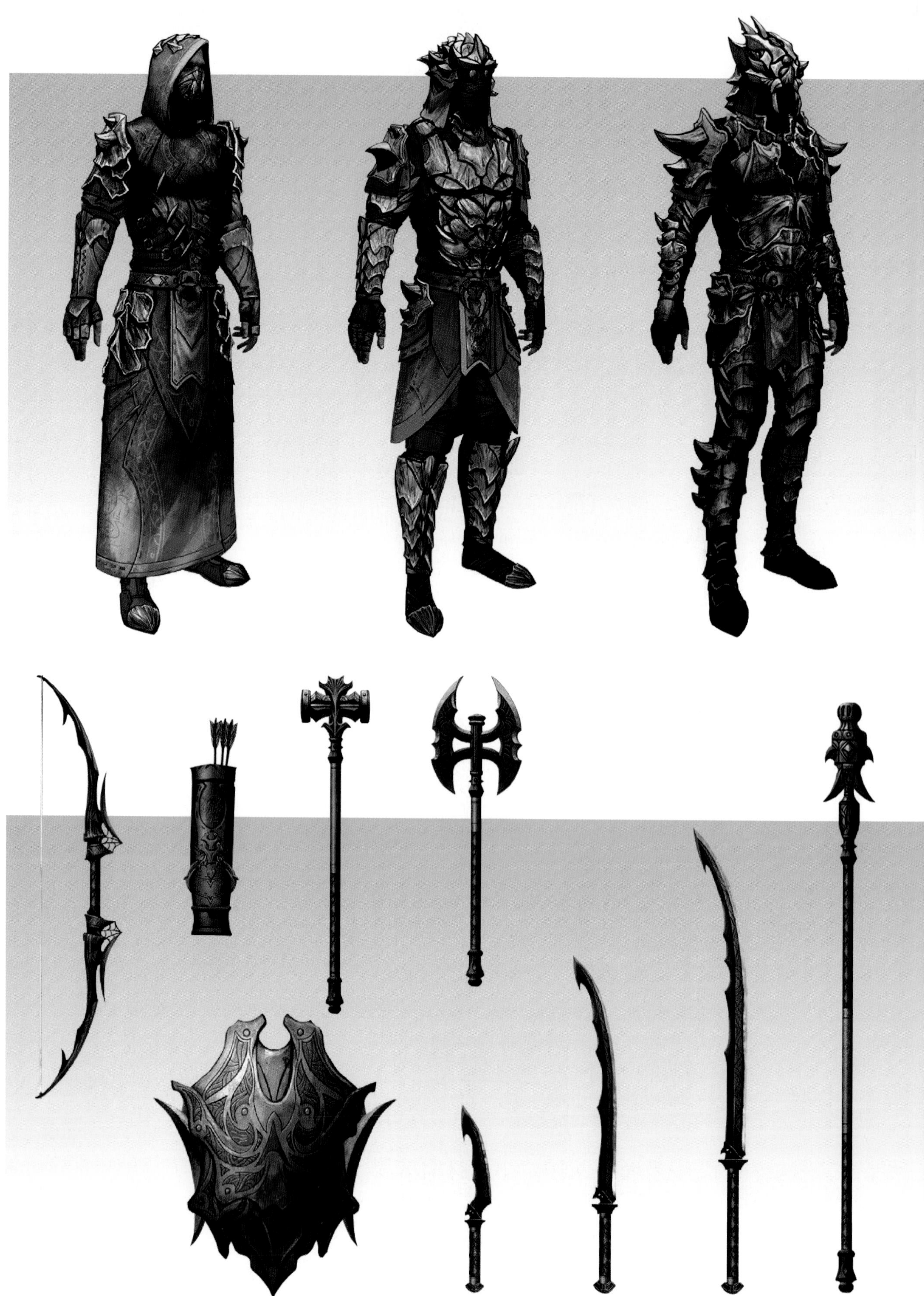

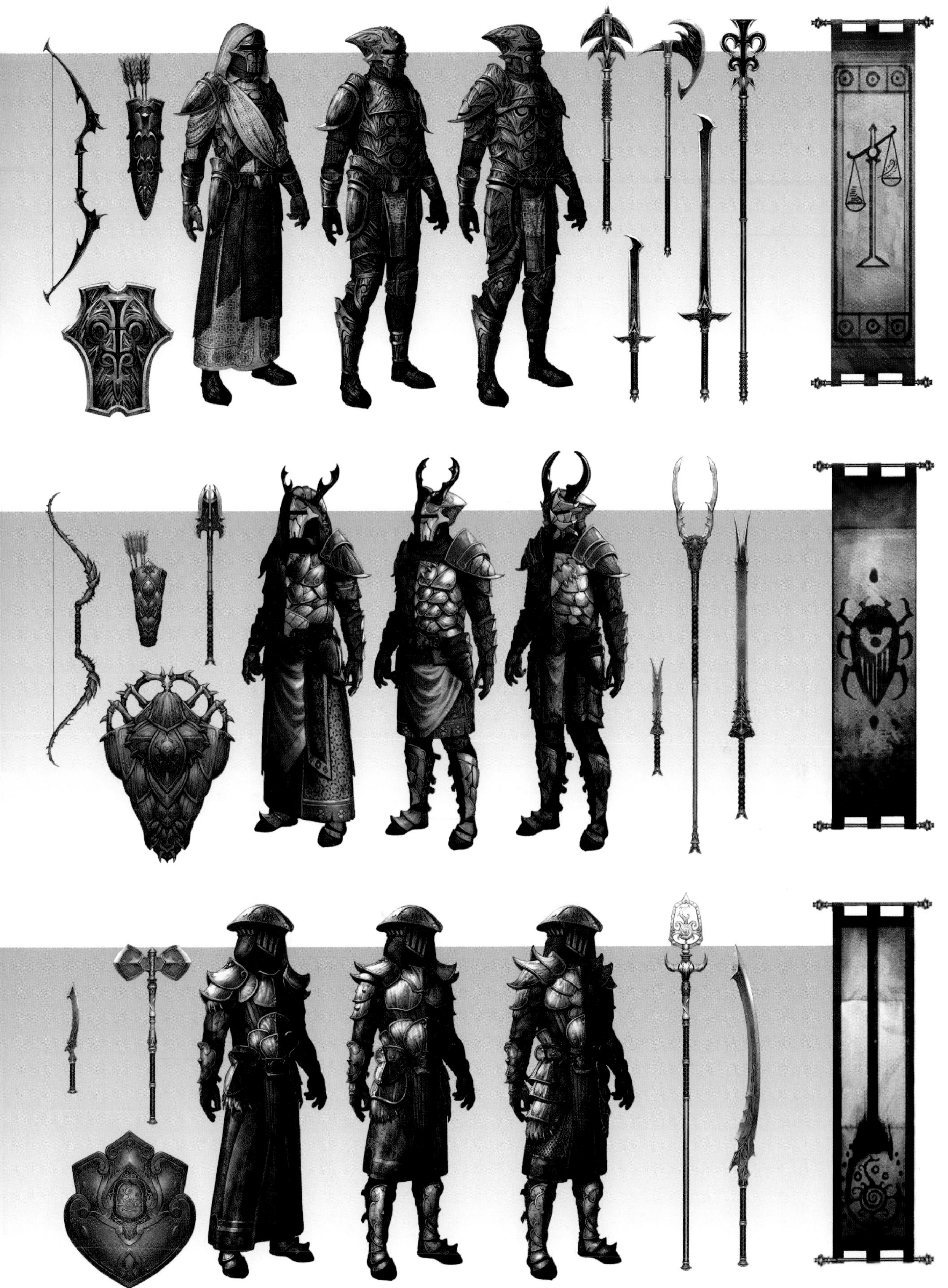

The Elder Scrolls
ONLINE
MORROWIND

Written by David S. J. Hodgson, Michael Owen, and Nick von Esmarch

DK/Prima Games, a division of Penguin Random House LLC
6081 East 82nd Street, Suite #400
Indianapolis, IN 46250

ISBN: Collector's Edition 978-0-7440-1825-7

Printing Code: The rightmost double-digit number is the year of the book's printing; the rightmost single-digit number is the number of the book's printing. For example, 17-1 shows that the first printing of the book occurred in 2017.

20 19 18 17 4 3 2 1

001-307914-May/2017

Printed in the USA.

CREDITS

Title Manager
Chris Hausermann

Development Editor
Serena Stokes

Book Designers
Dan Caparo
Tim Amrhein
Brent Gann

Production Designer
Justin Lucas
Wil Cruz

Production
Beth Guzman

PRIMA GAMES STAFF

VP & Publisher
Mike Degler

Editorial Manager
Tim Fitzpatrick

Design and Layout Manager
Tracy Wehmeyer

Licensing
Paul Giacomotto

Digital Publishing
Julie Asbury
Tim Cox
Shaida Boroumand

Operations Manager
Stacey Ginther

ACKNOWLEDGEMENTS

DAVID S. J. HODGSON

Sincere thanks to everyone at Bethesda for your hard work in the creation of this tome. Cheers to Chris, all at Prima, and to Nick and Michael for their exceptional diligence and creativity while working on this book. Thank you to my loving wife Melanie; Mum, Dad, and Ian; Loki; Cameron and Louie; Big ups to the South Coast Cactus and Succulent Society; The Moon Wiring Club, the Benningtons, Flaccus Terentius; and R, which is for R'lyeh, whose buildings fit together in a non-euclidean fashion, it's a wondrous sight, inspiring both awe and fright, and no end of murderous passion.

MICHAEL OWEN

The amazing assistance provided by Jessica Williams, John Chaffee, Mike Kochis, Rich Lambert, Zeb Cook, Mike Finnigan and everyone else at ZeniMax Online Studios and Bethesda Softworks was greatly appreciated. Special thanks are extended to the staff of Prima Games—Chris Hausermann, Dan Caparo, Serena Stokes, Tim Fitzpatrick, Jennifer Sims, and Tim Amrhein—for providing this opportunity and making my content look great on the page. A huge thanks goes out to Nick von Esmarch and David Hodgson for their utmost professionalism. Most of all, I would like to thank my loving wife, Michelle, for everything she does and putting up with my absence.

NICK VON ESMARCH

Thanks to everyone at Bethesda Softworks and ZeniMax Online Studios for some outstanding support. Special thanks to CJ, AJ, and Mike for helping us make the most of our time on site. Huge thanks to Jess and John for coming through time and again; you guys saved the day more times than I can count. And thanks to Adam, Shook, Zeb, Mike, and Rich for providing the answers to some of our biggest questions. Your time and expertise was very much appreciated.

Thanks to all at Prima—especially Chris, Serena, Daniel, Tim, and Tim for all of the hard work. And big thanks to David and Michael for ranking among the best authors one could hope to know.

Of course, I need to thank all of my family and friends for their patience and understanding during some very long hours. On that front, special thanks to Kurt and Damien for some much-needed laughs along the way, and to my beautiful Joy for everything she does/is.

Prima Games would like to thank the following individuals at Bethesda and ZeniMax Online for their effort, help, and support on this project:

Michael Kochis
Jessica Williams
Jeff Albertson
Yvonne Becker
Luke Blaize
Jo Burba
Jared Carr
John Chaffee
Zeb Cook
Bryan Dalzell
Carrie Day
Ala Diaz
Jacqueline Evans
Mike Finnigan
Matt Firor
Emerson Huang
Marc Hudgins
Rich Lambert
Michael Larrabee
AJ LaSaracina
Cullen Lee
Marcia Mitnick
Yvette Nash
Kyle Nowak
James Owen Lowe
Dan Montoya
Mandi Parker
Michael Phillips
Mike Rea
Michael Schroeder
Jeremy Sera
Lawrence Schick
Hilary Shapiro
Bill Slavicsek
Gary Steinman
Ryan Taljonick
Brandon Van Haren
Nate VanWyngarden
Samantha Weeks
Brian Wheeler
Sean Wicks
Eric Wrobel